A HISTORY OF
POLITICAL THOUGHT
IN THE
SIXTEENTH CENTURY

A History
of Political Thought
in the Sixteenth
Century

J. W. ALLEN

with a revised bibliography by
M. M. GOLDSMITH

LONDON

METHUEN & CO LTD

ROWMAN AND LITTLEFIELD

TOTOWA: NEW JERSEY

First published 1928
This edition reprinted 1977 by
Methuen & Co Ltd
11 New Fetter Lane London EC4P 4EE

ISBN 0 416 70620 7

and
Rowman and Littlefield
81 Adams Drive
Totowa New Jersey 07511

ISBN 0 87471 885 6

Printed in Great Britain by
Whitstable Litho Ltd Whitstable Kent

TO

DULCIE L. SMITH

JOHN WILLIAM ALLEN

J. W. Allen was born in London in 1865 and educated at Marlborough and at Balliol College, Oxford where he was an exhibitioner, taking First Class Honours in Modern History in 1887 (B.A. 1888, M.A. 1891). He was appointed lecturer in History at Bedford College in 1891 and to the chair of History there in 1910. Among his earlier works are editions of Shakespeare's *Coriolanus* and *Richard II* and a book with Thomas Seccombe entitled the *Age of Shakespeare*. At the beginning of the 1914–18 war he wrote *Germany and Europe* in which he justified England's going to war and denounced the militaristic theories put forward by some German thinkers (not Nietzsche) and the German government; he also distinguished between those views and the views which seemed widely held by the German people, advocating a generous peace on general principles rather than a punitive one.

J. W. Allen's most important books were published after his retirement in 1926: first came *A History of Political Thought in the Sixteenth Century* (1928) and then *English Political Thought 1603–1644* (1938) the first volume of a projected work which would have covered the period up to 1660, unfinished when he died in 1944.

He was remembered in Bedford College as an exciting teacher who encouraged a questioning attitude in his students, a charming conversationalist and a penetrating debater.

M. M. G.

CONTENTS

Part IV
Italy

INTRODUCTION

THE sixteenth century was a period of relatively rapid and of formally revolutionary change. It may be compared in that respect with two other great periods of European history and with them only : the twelfth century and the nineteenth. It is mere truism to say that the great changes that took place were results of a long process. As in other such cases, their suddenness and their revolutionary quality were in part illusory. Essential psychological change preceded the formal revolution.

So long ago as the commencement of the fourteenth century it had been pointed out that the Empire of Christendom was a useless fiction. It had been declared that the Church and the Papacy constituted the main obstacle to the development of efficient secular government. It had been asserted that the clergy as such had no right to speak in the name of the Church. On these texts the thinkers of the fourteenth century had enlarged considerably. All through the fourteenth and fifteenth centuries, the clergy and the Pope had been suffering loss of prestige and of moral authority. The actual constitution of the Church Catholic was increasingly undermined by heresy, by scepticism and by covetous jealousy of its property and its jurisdictions. It was increasingly menaced by the growth of nationalist sentiment and organization, at least in France and in England. A crash became inevitable, and in the sixteenth century the Church was torn to pieces. What we call the Reformation was, in one aspect, the definitive triumph of secular authority in a struggle with the Church already centuries old. In one country after another, the secular government established its local control of the Church, absorbing in the process much, at least, of its property and jurisdiction. In city after city, from Stralsund to Geneva, the Reformation appears as the last act of an age-long conflict between city and Bishop. Even in Catholic countries the same thing happened in some degree. When Francis I secured from the Pope in 1516 the right to appoint his own bishops and by the ordinance of Villers Coterêts in 1537, curtailed ecclesiastical jurisdiction, he was doing, so far as he could, what Henry VIII did in England. Ferdinand of Austria, like the Protestant Princes of North Germany, dissolved monasteries and appropriated the property. In Spain the Inquisition set up by the King in defiance of the Pope, was, among other things, a royal instrument for the control of the clergy. The Reformation was part of the process by which Europe was resolved into a series of independent, secular, sovereign States.

Along with the efforts of Princes and Magistrates to master and to dispossess the Church, went, part cause and part consequence, a great religious revival. It is, perhaps, a little unfortunate that the term ' Reformation ' has come to be so completely associated with Protestantism, that the Catholic revival is spoken of as Counter-Reformation. The religious revival of the century was Catholic as well as, and no less than, Protestant. A great effort was made by the Catholic Church to reform its discipline and administration and to define its doctrinal position. The intensity of the religiousness developed in Spain was at the least as great as appears in any Protestant country. Everywhere to the struggle over property and jurisdiction were added efforts to establish or maintain or propagate ' true religion '. Governments, however reluctantly, were compelled to take share and side in them. Confusion was confounded by the development of the Calvinistic ideal of a Church-State ; a development peculiarly embarrassing to Protestant governments.

Enormous in extent and intensity was the resulting friction. The Reformation involved huge transferences of property and jurisdiction. It involved war, and, above all, civil war. It necessitated efforts on the part of governments to organize their conquests and to make of the reformed church an instrument of their purposes. It involved what is called religious persecution. And it involved, of course, a vast and many-sided literary controversy.

It is an error to suppose that the sixteenth century saw the development of much that was strikingly new in political philosophy. Controversy was, of course, mainly concerned with questions men were forced, by what was happening, to consider. Many old questions were, therefore, stated in new terms. But all through the century, except at least in Italy, political thought remained essentially medieval in character. All through the century the main divisions of late medieval opinion were reproduced. This was a necessary consequence of the fact that the basic assumptions made in the sixteenth century were the same that had been made by medieval thinkers. All sides assumed that the Scriptures were the very Word of God and all assumed the existence of a ' natural ' moral law, recognized by all men alike and binding absolutely, world without end. Every one, too, saw or felt that, just as goodness in action is conformity with the Eternal Law, that is with God's purpose in creation, so a ' right ' is something which cannot be denied without defiance of God. Every conceivable ' right ' expresses Divine Will. Real authority, whether in a king or in the father of a family, is a right to demand obedience as a duty to God. On the basis of these propositions, usually assumed as axiomatic, the political thought of the century as a whole may fairly be said to have proceeded. But the dominant tendency and the general character of such thought differed widely, with widely differing conditions, in every country in Europe. Little that we can say will be even approximately true of all of them.

At the beginning of the century England and France alike may be said to have but just reconstituted central government after long anarchy. In both countries the establishment of order and security absolutely depended upon the effectiveness of the new monarchy. In both, therefore, there arose not only strong monarchical sentiment, but a tendency towards formation of theories of unlimited sovereignty in the monarch. But in both cases that tendency was thwarted, more or less completely. The lines on which political thought proceeded in the two countries rapidly diverged.

The effort of the monarchy effectively to centralize government in France broke down over almost innumerable obstacles. The French monarchy in the fifteenth century had had to reconquer a large part of France, not merely from the English. The driving out of the English was a relatively easy matter. There remained a number of provinces and of towns, organized for self-government and accustomed to an almost complete freedom from outside interference. The resistance of provincial and municipal tradition was increased by the lawlessness of the mass of the nobles and by the ambitions of *grands seigneurs*. Protestantism, allying itself with provincial and municipal feeling, of which, indeed, it was largely an expression, complicated the position indefinitely. Under these conditions the centralizing effort of the monarchy resulted in civil war. The claims made for the monarch were countered, first, by constitutional theories and, later, by the development of theories of popular sovereignty and a sacred right of rebellion. Once such assertions were made there was no escape from the discussion of fundamental questions. Yet, in the long run, as the result of terrible and disillusioning experience, all such theories became, in France, more and more discredited. Before the end of the century a theory of absolutism in the King, conceived as deriving authority directly from God, was becoming dominant. By the end of the century effective centralization of government had, at last, become possible.

But England was not afflicted with the accentuated and organized provincial divisions of France. Nowhere in English towns or counties was there any real tradition of self-governing independence. Largely, I think, for that very reason, England escaped the worst forms of religious division. On the other hand, England was possessed of a

Parliamentary tradition which France lacked. Weak and inchoate as this was at the beginning of the sixteenth century, the action of Henry VIII's government confirmed and defined it. Fortescue's conception of a *dominium politicum* was actually far more true of England under Elizabeth than it had been at the time he wrote. Though, therefore, England accepted fully, and far more fully than for a long time did France, the doctrine that active resistance to the supreme authority is never justified, it did not, like France, develop a belief in the absolute sovereignty of the monarch. There is really hardly a trace of such belief in English writings of the sixteenth century. While in France controversy turned more and more on fundamental questions concerning the nature and derivation of political authority and political obligation, in England controversy turned mainly on the import and implications of royal supremacy in ecclesiastical causes.

In the political chaos that was called the Empire nothing at first was distinct. For Germany the Reformation was the main factor in an almost complete disintegration. For the Princes and cities at least of northern Germany, it became a means of consolidating their local sovereignties and establishing a practical independence of Emperor and Diet. The ancient and deep division, the old antagonism, between northern and southern Germany, which had above all else, wrecked the medieval monarchy, now again expressed itself in the history of the German Reformation. Despite the amount of strictly religious controversy in Germany, nowhere else did the struggle turn so completely upon property and jurisdiction. As a consequence political thought in Germany was in the main strictly religious or simply juristic.

Italy, again, stood almost completely apart : and this was partly due to the peculiarity of the political conditions there existing. Republican sentiment remained strong in some at least of the cities ; yet almost everywhere republican government had broken down and been superseded. In the fifteenth century the cities had for the most part come definitively under princely government. But the Princes, adventurers and party leaders, condottieri or dominating capitalists, had behind them little or no vital tradition and little or no moral authority. Machiavelli could regard princely government in Italy as a necessary evil, a desperate remedy for a moral corruption that rendered a people incapable of governing itself. It would, indeed, have been difficult, in the early years of the sixteenth century, to think of the Italian prince as a viceroy of God. It was not very much less difficult at the close of the century.

It seems plain enough on the face of the facts that generalizations concerning the course or the character of political thought in western Europe as a whole, during the sixteenth century, can be but very roughly accurate. It will be best to defer any furthur attempt at such generalization till the concluding chapter. Enough has been said already to suggest that such attempt is but doubtfully worth making.

It might be said that political thought, in the sense at least in which the term is used here, is concerned with questions independent of mere circumstance and of circumstantial change. The question how far I am bound to obey the political sovereign and in what sense and for what reasons, is a question of political thought ; the question whether it be desirable to set up a new pump in the parish or introduce a system of State insurance, is not. Yet any attempt at definition on these lines is evidently futile. What is it that does not change ?

There are, it may be said, things that change so slowly that, for practical purposes, they do not change at all. Even so the fact remains that there has been very little, if any, political thinking really independent of quite rapidly changing circumstances. Men are constantly engaged in an on the whole highly successful effort to adjust their ideas to circumstance and, also, in an effort, very much less successful, to adjust circumstance to their ideas. They are constantly engaged in justifying the actual and in protesting and revolting against it. Their thought about the State and about all the many questions that connect with it, is an adjustment the character of which is determined by desire. At any one moment there exists an immense tangle of multiform circumstance and of multitudinous desires, diverse and conflicting. Out of all that, issues thought about society and government, its authority, its functions and organization.

Explanation of the genesis of this thought, begotten by desire on circumstance, is strictly impossible : we can do little more than note suggestive correlations. But conditions change only slowly and partially and men more slowly and partially still. The continuity of political thought is rooted in, and is in fact but an expression of, circumstantial continuity. What differentiates the political thought of one period of European history from that of another is mainly, the differences between the questions that are asked and between the assumptions that are made in answering. Fundamental questions tend to be asked at all times, but at any one time there are always questions with which thought is above all occupied. They differ from age to age. It is perhaps its assumptions that most profoundly distinguish the thought of one age from that of another. But, whatever may be the dominant assumptions and the dominant questions at any one time, the fundamental questions of political thought remain always the same and always, strictly speaking, unanswered.

The study of the history of political thought seems to me to exhibit still some of the characteristics of extreme youthfulness ; its crudity, its haste, its readiness to jump to conclusions. A good deal of current generalization would seem to represent guess-work or impressions derived one knows not how. Such generalizations may be useful as working hypotheses, so long as the student remembers that he is in danger of reading his hypothesis into his texts. Yet this danger is not perhaps very great. It is quite probable that, if he reads his texts faithfully, his hypothesis will quickly be forgotten.

The easy fluency with which, sometimes, we generalize concerning the thought of whole centuries or even concerning something vague and vast called the Middle Ages, suggests that we have hardly as yet realized the enormous difficulty of generalizing on this subject. We even speak, sometimes, of ' medieval thought ' as though that were a simple thing or a single system. It is useless to be content with half truths and injurious to state them as though they were more. Our frequent fluency in ambiguous suggestion and phrase, suggests that we do not realize that, in dealing with ideas, the utmost possible precision must be sought at all costs always. However difficult it may be to attain precision and definition, we have got nothing worth having till it is attained. We must for ever be asking not only what it was that our author meant, but what it is that we mean. Let us remember that guessing, after all, amounts to nothing, even though the guess by chance be correct.

There is, evidently, but one road to an understanding of the thought of any period ; and it is by way of a close, analytic and comparative study of texts. Fragments of political thought, suggestions of current opinion and current assumptions, may be gathered from all manner of sources, but so far as the political thought of a period finds definite expression, it is expressed in definite texts. It will be quite futile to lighten our labours by picking out a few writers or a few books that for some reason have become outstanding. If we adopt that method of approach, it is probable that we shall barely get into touch. The political thought of a period is to be found rather in the writings of obscure or anonymous persons than in the work of writers whose real distinction and originality makes them untypical.

The student who aspires to write of the political thought of any period requires a thorough knowledge of the conditions, social, political and economic, under which that thought was developed. Such knowledge can hardly be too thorough ; it is perhaps impossible that it should be thorough enough. But indeed when I come to consider the powers, qualities and qualifications that are needed by that ambitious student, I am painfully reminded of those sixteenth-century books which set forth the necessary virtues of the good Prince. Knowledge of texts, however exhaustive, patience, even indomitable, are not enough. He must possess power of accurate analysis, he must miss no subtlety of argument or distinction or connection. To be an historian is not enough ; he must be something, also, of a philosopher. He must sympathize with all points of view. He must, I think, love ideas for their own sake. His questioning must be ceaseless, his scepticism untiring, whatever his private faith. He needs above all that pure desire to understand which is the only defence against bewildering bias. He must never forget that his own opinion on questions discussed are completely irrelevant to his subject. Thinking of these things he may well be aghast at his own temerity.

Much of the work that has been done on the history of political thought seems to me to have been, to some extent, vitiated by an endeavour to exhibit ideas of the past in relation to something vaguely called ' modern thought '. Preoccupation with this something may amount to a distorting obsession. In some cases it might even seem that the thing called ' modern thought ' is in truth simply the writer's own. The temptation to dub one's own thought ' modern ', though one that should, surely, be easy to resist, is not, it seems, always resisted. In any case my thought and your thought and his thought which, however flatly contradictory, yet, taken together, actually make up modern thought, are all alike irrelevant to an understanding of the thought of a past century. It is, of course, true that the thought system of any thinker needs to be seen alongside other systems to be understood. Always for understanding we need comparisons. But the most illuminating comparisons are those between the thought of men concerned under similar conditions with the same problems and working on similar assumptions. The more time and change separate two thinkers the more difficult comparison and the more superficial and misleading it is likely to be. Only when the question discussed is detached completely from place and changing circumstance, can comparison between distant thinkers be of value.

I remember reading, once, a book on a certain thinker of old time, the writer of which seemed to regard his hero as having most meritoriously succeeded in anticipating certain of his own nineteenth-century conclusions. Such an attitude is, surely, not merely presumptuous. How is it possible rationally to believe that a thinker is meritorious or important because one happens to agree with him ? It would be pleasant to entertain that comforting conviction ; but I can see no ground for it. One cannot even, on that ground, claim that one's predecessor was ' advanced ', except in a sense that refers merely to time. If I have written this book as I should have written it, no one will be able to say what my own opinion is on any of the questions discussed or whether I have one. I have only the right to point out incoherencies and make comparisons. All that can be demanded of any system of thought is coherency and faithfulness to demonstrated fact.

One frequently meets statements to the effect that So-and-so made a valuable contribution to political thought. It is usually uncertain what is meant. The expression of any coherent system of ideas, unless it be simply a reproduction, is of course a contribution to thought. Possibly the reference is to this fact. Or it may be that all that is meant is, that So-and-so made a suggestion which was found, later on, to be practically useful in some way and in some sense. If this be all, the language used is not only ambiguous, but too pompous for the occasion. But, sometimes, there seems to be an implication that there exists a slowly accumulating body of ascertained truth concerning the problems involved in the existence of the State. It was to this body of truth that So-and-so made his contribution ; he did not merely enrich imagination with yet another unverifiable conception. Now I am not concerned either to confirm or deny this very bold proposition. It attracts by its audacity and repels by its seeming improbability. But it is clear that no one has a right to imply such an assertion and then proceed to take its validity for granted. Anyone who makes or implies it, is bound to tell us clearly of what system of ideas he is thinking. And before the value of So-and-so's contribution towards it can be taken for granted, the validity of that system requires demonstration. I have an uneasy suspicion that the mere attempt to state it, would make tolerably obvious the impossibility of that demonstration.

No valid reason exists for writing about political thought in the sixteenth century except that there actually are people who desire to know how men thought in those days. But there are quite good reasons for that desire. The thought of the men of those days was ultimately concerned with questions no more satisfactorily answered now than they were then ; and with questions that are, or may become, as practically important to us as to them. It may be that the assumptions with which their thought started are so unlike the assumptions we make, as to disable us from seeing their arguments and conceptions as other than fallacious and mistaken. So much the worse for us, I am inclined to say, if that be so. But even though their reasoning do not help us to solve their problems for ourselves, yet it is surely true that we can learn something from it of use to ourselves. We may learn, perhaps, to realize the extent to which conclusions depend upon assumption. We may learn to realize how many irreconcilable views may rationally be taken on the same question. We may perhaps learn, if we need to do so, to doubt our own possibly too glib assurances. If the old thinkers raise doubts in our minds on fundamental questions, that is all to the good. If they help us to see how much is involved in our own assumptions, that is all to the good. It is good for us, too, to have questions that puzzle us stated in terms to us unfamiliar. We may even learn to see the thought of our own passing moment as a thing as ephemeral as theirs. But unless we study their thought without any sort of prejudgement, we shall be unlikely ever to understand them. And if we come to it with an assumption of superiority, or a notion that the problems that perplexed them have by us been solved, then we are likely to get no good of it at all.

Yet it is not true that our thought is merely ephemeral and it is not true that theirs was so. For thought abides and is independent of time and circumstance. The questions it deals with are always with us. It may be that no one in the twentieth century will believe in the truth of the answer that was given in the sixteenth ; and it may be that in the twenty-fourth century no one will believe in the answers given to the same question now. The fact is irrelevant to the question of validity. A man's thought is not dead because he is dead and I am alive and think differently. In that sense, at least, my thought will soon be dead also. But the question will remain. It matters nothing when the answer was given or who believed it to be right. The question remains.

I am like other people ; I have left undone things I ought to have done and have done things I ought not to have done. There exists much relevant literature, especially of the period of the civil wars in France, which I have not read ; and more, almost certainly, than I even know of. I have sometimes referred to and even quoted from French pamphlets or treatises without having verified my references or quotations. I believe that in these cases my authority is fully sufficient : but this is a thing that ought not to be done. Concerning the Anabaptists I have expressed a view and an impression that I am conscious is founded on insufficient knowledge. This is a thing which should not, at least, be done without confession. Worse still, perhaps, I have altogether ignored the principles and implications of the theory of international law that was being developed in the sixteenth century from Victoria to Gentili. Fondly I have imagined that I should like best to deal with them in connection with the following century. In truth the thought of the sixteenth century is so rich and various and its literature so extensive, that perhaps it is wrong as yet for anyone to deal with it as a whole. To work out fully the political thought of France alone would require a book the size of this one. Work of this kind is, in the long run, of use or account only so far as it is thorough. All the evidence must be examined and collated, all the texts must be studied. Perhaps the right title for this book would be simply : ' Some of the Political Thought of the Sixteenth Century.' But nothing in the world is much more futile than apology. It were best, in concluding any book, to say simply, with the author of the Book of the Maccabees : ' If I have done well and as is fitting the story, it is that which I desired ; but if slenderly and meanly, it is that which I could attain unto.'

June 1928   J. W. A.

A HISTORY OF
POLITICAL THOUGHT
IN THE
SIXTEENTH CENTURY

A HISTORY OF POLITICAL THOUGHT IN THE SIXTEENTH CENTURY

PART I

LUTHERANISM AND CALVINISM

CHAPTER I

INTRODUCTORY

AMBIGUOUS as are the words standing at the head of this section, they are far less ambiguous than the word Protestantism. Loose talk about something called 'Protestantism' is one of the more serious difficulties that students of the sixteenth century must contend with. It is a word used in many different senses and sometimes, it seems, with no precise sense at all. It is even possible to use it in two senses within the same paragraph, and that once done no sense remains. The word is often used to signify rejection by Christians of the claims of the Papacy. That is a use alluring in its apparent simplicity. But, in that sense, Anglo-Catholics, old and new, are Protestants for all their protests and the Eastern churches are equally Protestant. Also the question might well be asked : ' What claims of what Papacy ? ' Rejection may be partial ; and the line between complete and incomplete rejection may be very fine. Cardinal Bellarmine certainly rejected the extreme claims put forth on behalf of Pope Sixtus V and he was rewarded with a place on the Index. The French Gallicans of the later years of the century went much further still in rejection ; and it is not so easy to distinguish between the official view of King Henry VIII of England and the views of Louis Servin, 'Catholic' minister of Henry IV.[1] Even for the sixteenth century alone, and putting aside the ambiguity already attached to the word ' Christian ', this use of the term ' Protestant ' leads into difficulties.

Less superficially the word ' Protestantism ' has been used to

[1] For Servin, see Pt. III, Chap. VII, p. 374.

signify a rejection not merely of Papal claims but of the conception of the Church as an institution of divine ordainment, organization and inspiration, furnished with an apostolic succession of priests and bishops endowed by ordination with mysterious, sacramental powers. This use of the term attempts, at least, to go deeper than the other ; but anyone who tries to make consistent use of it in this sense in reference to the sixteenth century, will find himself involved in hopeless difficulties. Was Luther himself in this sense a Protestant ?

It has been suggested that the essential feature of Protestantism was its denial of the doctrine of transubstantiation. But, apart from the evident inconvenience of a definition of Protestantism by reference to a mere negative, the line between transubstantiation and consubstantiation is surely a fine one. If we say that what Protestantism as such denied was that any substantial or objective change took place in the sacramental elements after consecration, we are in little better case. We shall then be compelled to say that Luther, for instance, was not a Protestant. It will follow also that it was possible utterly to deny the validity of Papal claims and yet be a Catholic. It is surely evident that no dividing line can accurately or reasonably be drawn here.

Intellectually, perhaps, the deepest difference between Lutherans or Calvinists on one side and Romanists on the other was on the question of free will. It was Luther's *De Servo Arbitrio* that made it for ever impossible for Erasmus to enter the Lutheran camp, whether or not other considerations would have restrained him. But to define Protestantism by reference to a particular doctrine of predestination would be to say that Hans Denck and Castellion and Coornhert were not Protestants. Also, and of course, very few people concerned themselves with this fundamental question or even understood what the question was.

What may be called the Protestant tradition, in this and in other countries, has been and is a serious stumbling-block in the way of understanding. There has even existed a tendency to use the word Protestantism as though, in the sixteenth century, all, or almost all, profound religiousness was Protestant. This illusion, just comprehensible in Calvin and Beza, has long been bereft of excuse. Protestantism has been represented as an effort to establish some kind of direct and personal relation between the individual soul and God. But within the Roman Church that effort was continuously being made ; and of intense consciousness of God I do not think there was more to be found among Lutherans or Calvinists than among Romanists. The religion of St. Teresa was far nearer to Hans Denck's than his was to Calvin's. That Luther, as he professed, learned much from Tauler, merely illustrates the fact that one of the roots of early Protestantism was Catholic mysticism. It seems that in the deeps of religious consciousness there is little room for distinction and for disputation none.

That denunciation of abuses more or less notorious, or revolt against the actual condition of the Church in one respect or another, did not, in the early sixteenth century, make a ' Protestant ', should hardly be worth saying. Indeed it seems a pity that the word Reformers, with a capital R, should habitually be used exclusively of Protestants. If all who denounced abuses and strove for reform in any sense were Protestants, then must we reckon as Protestants Erasmus and Contarini, Ignatius Loyola and Pope Paul IV.

It has been said that the essence of Protestantism consisted in an assertion of the right of the individual as such to think things out for himself and to reach conclusions without deference to any sort of authority. This notion appears in various and in different forms. A Protestant, it is said, is a person who abides faithfully by the reason or unreason that is in him, in defiance of thrones, principalities and powers that be. A Protestant is a person who claims a right to speak of things as he sees them, and in particular to work out his religion for himself and worship in his own way. Consequently, it is asserted, Protestantism was essentially a claim to freedom for the individual, a claim that no man should be coerced into saying he believes what he does not believe or into refraining from expression of his beliefs.

But little comment, I think, is needed. Who was it, in the sixteenth century, who made these claims or these assertions ? There would seem to be confusion. To claim that I am right in my conclusions is not to claim a right for other people to differ from me. To assert that someone or something claiming authority is entirely and wickedly mistaken is not a claim on behalf of the individual as such. A claim to worship in your own way is not a claim that every one has a right to do so. As to thinking for yourself, every one must do that who thinks at all. It is impossible to accept the authority of the Roman Church without first coming to the conclusion that it ought to be accepted. That conclusion may, of course, be reached without any systematic reasoning : but so equally may a conclusion to the contrary effect.

We are faced with awkward consequences. If the essence of Protestantism is a claim to liberty for the individual to reach his own conclusions about religion in his own way and express them freely without interference, who, in the sixteenth century, was a Protestant ? I am not denying that there were a few : there were more than seems to be generally supposed. But certainly Calvin was not a Protestant, nor Beza nor Knox nor Whitgift. Luther had leanings to Protestantism, but finally went over to the other side. Even Hooker stopped just short of Protestantism. To say that the development of Protestant Churches and systems of belief actually led to the establishment of religious toleration is, even so far as it is true, not in the least relevant. If the early Reformers had had their way, it would have led to no such thing. All things, in fact, worked together for that result; and that consummation was a complete defeat of Protestantism as Calvin understood it.

The absurdity of all this unhistorical generalization seems to me to be glaring. It appears that it was not Protestants who stood for liberty : it was the spirit of Protestantism. The implied divorce of spirit from body is not easily comprehended. Where is this spirit to be found ? If we look at the mere facts we shall find many spirits at work. Or will it be said that the inmost essence of Protestantism was scepticism or denial of the validity of Christian beliefs ? That Protestantism did, to a great extent, issue in such scepticism is certainly true ; but that, for it, was defeat, not victory. Nothing in the sixteenth century was so profoundly antagonistic to official Protestantism or to Protestant religious systems, as the scepticism and the pseudo-paganism that developed with the Renaissance.

It is of the first importance to a student that he should realize to the full the ambiguities involved in the term ' Protestantism '.[1] So he may hope to escape the bewildering effects of loose talk and audacious, and empty, generalization and himself be freed from these besetting sins. But the ambiguity remains and is radically inescapable. Certainly no attempt will be made here to define the term, for in dealing with actualities no definition defines. And the thing to be defined is, in this case, so complex and multiform, so compounded of incongruities, so much a matter of thoughts, sentiments and desires completely distinct even though to some extent converging, that any definition must needs be even unusually inadequate.

It is with the actualities of the sixteenth century that we have here to deal ; and these, if they escape definition, can at least be examined and described to a point. We know who those were who in that century were called Protestant ; we can see the formation of Protestant churches and of Protestant creeds ; we know who were in communion with Rome and who were not. There may be little in common between these things and people ; but that fact need not disturb us. We can use the term Protestantism of what we know, in a strictly historical sense. People, it is true, became Protestant for every conceivable reason. The desire to annex Church property and jurisdiction made very stout Protestants. A man bent on realizing some conception of national sovereignty might well become a Protestant, even though he had no religious convictions whatever. We must accept the consequences : the absurdity, if any, is in the facts themselves. We can always, when necessary, distinguish

---

[1] This is the excuse for an exordium that might, otherwise, be justly regarded as irrelevant.

between the Protestantism that was definitely religious and that which was not.

What I propose to examine in this section is the political thought that was intimately, and indeed necessarily associated with Protestant systems of religious belief and the organization of Protestant Churches. If we are to understand that thought and see it in its actual relations, we must begin, I fear, by ridding our minds of all unifying concepts concerning Protestantism and certainly of all that can only be expressed by reference to its spirit. Such concepts are completely unhistorical and breed nothing but confusion. As I have said already, there are very many spirits concerned. The first questions that we must ask seem to be these following : How far was any kind of political thought or any political ideal absolutely involved in any of the forms taken by early Protestantism ? What questions were directly and necessarily raised by the assertions made by the early Reformers ? What answers were given to these questions from points of view at once religious and Protestant ?

Certain partial answers to these questions may here at once be given in general terms. As early as 1520, in his three great treatises of that year, Luther utterly rejected all the claims of the Papacy. He asserted broadly that no coercive power whatever belonged properly to clergy, bishops or Pope, that clergy were subjects of the secular magistrate like other people and that the whole body of canon law was without validity. From these negative declarations positive consequences followed. Of the two sets of magistrates, civil and ecclesiastical, theoretically governing a united Christendom, the latter was, in the view of the early Reformers, simply abolished : the former survived as the sole recognized authority. At a blow Christendom was resolved, or dissolved, into a group, if not of ' states ', at least of independent, secular, territorial magistracies, governing persons and governing bodies. The sacerdotium was abolished and the regnum stood alone. Henceforth the civil magistrate was to be the only guardian of law and order and the only authority that could undertake a legal reform of the Church.

Before any conception of the State as a body independent of any external authority could be logically developed, the validity of the claims of the Roman Church had, of course, to be denied. But no kind of religious Protestantism was needed for that denial : the denial indeed could be made more simply from a completely unreligious point of view. That no coercive power belongs rightly to the Church had been asserted in the *Defensor Pacis* nearly two hundred years earlier.[1] The work of John of Jandun and Marsilio of Padua was more or less known to the early Reformers, and Luther himself appears to have read it. He may even have borrowed some weapons from

[1] The book was completed in 1324.

the scriptural armoury of the second Part of the book; but whether or no he had read the first Part, he never showed a sign of having understood it. Its thought was beyond him, and had he understood, he would assuredly have been profoundly shocked. For all that, the assertion that no civil magistrate was, in any sense or degree, bound to obey the Pope or recognize canon law as valid, was, for the early sixteenth century, both revolutionary and highly suggestive. This assertion was made by all the early Reformers, and it was one they could' hardly have avoided making. It was not for them to appeal, as Kings had done earlier, from the Pope to a General Council. The only General Council that could conceivably have helped them would have been a Council in which Protestant Churches were at least represented. But in 1520, there were no Protestant Churches. Their only possible allies were the secular Governments. The assertion that coercive authority rests solely with them simply had to be made. But there was really in their minds little more than a negative. Their positive assertion was that the claims of Pope and clergy were based on nothing but impo,ture and superstition. Later on, of course, the claims of the sacerdotium were revived, in an altered form, by Calvinism. The earlier reformers simply denied them.

It is difficult, or impossible, to estimate with any exactness the importance of the fact that Protestantism must have more or less abruptly released many minds from a conception of the commonwealth as necessarily subordinate in some degree to an ecclesiastical body. But in all very general historical statements lurks the demon exaggeration. The early Protestants were clear that the civil power was in no degree rightly subject to Papal control : they were not clear that it should not be in some sense subject to the Church.

'This power,' Luther wrote in 1520, 'the Church certainly has : that she can distinguish the Word of God from the words of men. . . . The mind pronounces with infallible assurance that three and seven are ten and yet can give no reason why this should be so, while it cannot deny that it is. . . . Even such a perception is there in the Church, by illumination of the Spirit, in judging and approving of doctrines.' [1]

There was in the minds of the early Protestants no idea of a State independent of any form of religion. Such a conception would have seemed to them a denial of God. Their difficulty was to say what or where is the Church.

Already, by means of a few sweeping negatives, what a harvest of awkward questions has been raised ! Round about them, controversial battle was to rage indecisively through the rest of the century. What is this Church which pronounces with infallible assurance, since it is not the Church of Rome ? Many of the earliest

[1] *An den Christlichen Adel,* 1520.

Reformers thought, indeed, that it might, in a sense, be the Church of Rome ; that it might, at least, be the old Church that they knew, renewed and transfigured. But the effort to reform the Church as a whole had never the remotest chance of succeeding, whatever Luther and others might hope for a while. It was bound to fail, and not merely because of the strength of the entrenched camps of its enemies. No sooner did religious Protestantism attempt to formulate its positive beliefs than disintegration began. Long before Luther's death the divisions of opinion among Protestants had become numerous and insurmountable. And as soon as the failure was clear and the hope had vanished, where was the Church of Protestantism to be found, among so many Protestant Churches ? The question was answered in various ways : we can only note here that it had to be answered.

But other questions also, equally troublesome and insistent, arose immediately. What should be the relation between the reformed Church and the secular magistrate ? How does the State stand in relation to God and the revelation in the Scriptures ? Whatever new forms it might take, this was the old question that had agitated so many medieval thinkers, Popes and Kings. Protestantism provided no escape from it ; or rather Protestantism raised it afresh in forms practically more acute than it had assumed for a long time. Never in the Middle Ages had this question been the subject of so much controversy as it was in the sixteenth century, for never before had it had so much practical bearing upon the lives of men.

All rightful coercive authority belongs to the secular magistrate : what, then, is his duty towards a Church unreformed ? The people loosely called Anabaptists, or many of them, denied that he could do anything but harm : but the Reformers in credit with the educated and the powerful, asserted that it was his duty to reform the Church in his dominions. It was his duty to establish and maintain true religion. That did not mean that it was his duty to establish any religion he might think ' true ' Far from it : he was to establish true religion and have no choice about it. What true religion is can be deduced from the Scriptures.[1] One sees that it will be needful either to assert, with Luther, that the deduction is easy or, with Calvin, that the true religion has been demonstrated. However preposterous such assertions may seem to the unregenerate, they will have to be made. But, however that may be, another question arises. What is to be the attitude of the magistrate towards misbelief ? Is he to maintain true religion by using his sword to destroy all other ? That question aroused much controversy. It can only here be noted

---

[1] Or, perhaps, can be decided by that Reformed Church that is to be. But until Reformed Churches were actually in existence there was evidently a difficulty. Later on, that initial difficulty was forgotten.

that there was nothing in Protestantism as such that forbade an affirmative answer, and that from a very early stage in its development and in fact as soon as it had seriously to face the question, the affirmative answer was that which it tended to give.

None of these questions received from the Reformers any precise and coherent answers until Calvin gave them. With the partial exception of Melanchthon, none of them seem to have felt concerned to consider seriously the nature or derivation of secular authority. But they were very much concerned with actual principalities and powers and their possible or probable modes of behaviour. There was just one question of practical politics which imperatively demanded immediate answer. It concerned their own duty in a perilous position. ' We,' they may be said to have put it, ' who have the truth, who desire to live and to worship according to God's Word and to order the Church in accordance with the Scriptures, are regarded as heretics and treated as criminals. What is our duty in relation to the civil magistrates, who persecute us and contemn the Word of God ? '

No sort of answer, however evasive, could of course be given to this question that did not involve some sort of theory of civil authority. The remarkable fact is that almost all the early reformers gave the same answer, even though it had not, for Luther and Tyndale and a quietist Anabaptist, quite the same meaning. Almost with one accord they proclaimed an all but unqualified duty of obedience to any and every duly constituted authority. You must of course obey God rather that man : no one in the sixteenth century so much as suggests anything else. But though you are bound to refuse to obey commands clean contrary to the law of God, you can never be justified in seeking to save yourself from punishment by any kind of forcible resistance. At most you will be justified in flight. For armed rebellion there is no justification in any case whatever. On this point Luther and Melanchthon, Tyndale and Calvin are all in a tale.

Almost all the Protestant reformers assumed from the first that it was necessary to establish formal and visible ' Churches ', with an official ministry, an official creed or ' confession ' and a defined system of government. They desired to destroy, more or less completely, the actual organization and the doctrinal system of the papal Church ; but for all that, the idea of the Church dominated their minds. It existed for them always as a fact, visible or invisible. They seem to have associated religion absolutely with the idea of a visible Church and earthly authority. Discovering that it was not possible to set up a renovated Church for all Christendom, they desired at least to organize local Churches. There were of course dissenters among them. ' I love any man whom I can help,' wrote Sebastian Franck in 1539, ' and I call him brother whether he be Jew or Samaritan.

. . . I cannot belong to any particular sect.'[1] Caspar Schwenckfeld denied that it was possible, in the circumstances, to establish any true visible Church. He hoped only for the spread of the invisible Church, constituted by those who had received the baptism of the Spirit and become new men. But the mass even of the Anabaptists endeavoured to establish a formal and visible Church. To do so without the co-operation of the civil power was, however, except on the minutest scale, practically impossible.

The idea that obedience to the civil magistrate is a religious duty, a duty, that is, to God and that forcible resistance to him is in no case justified, was as old, at least, as Christianity. It is not difficult to see why the early Protestants should have held and emphasized it. Even here there were, of course, dissidents : zealots who dreamed of reforming all things by the sword of the elect. None were more hated and feared by the orthodox Reformers than were these disturbing people. The leading Reformers declared that they found their doctrine of non-resistance in the Scriptures : later on other Protestants found there other doctrines very different. But on the one hand was the consciousness of the perilous pass into which they were come and of the peril of their cause ; on the other was the hope of support from those constituted authorities they could not but fear. The one thing, they felt, that they could not afford to do was to antagonize the secular magistrate, as such traitors to the cause as M ,zer and his allies were doing. Everywhere they saw in the civil power at once a possible ally and the only possible instrument for the reformation they desired. To Luther every German Prince was a possible ally, and so, at first, was even the Emperor himself. To Calvin Francis I was a possible ally even so late as 1535. The Reformers followed the line of least resistance at the moment. I am not suggesting the least conscious insincerity. In the Scriptures there was much to justify their attitude and in their own minds nothing that forbade. But that fear and hope were the main factors in determining this attitude there can be little, if any, doubt. The subsequent history of Protestantism in the sixteenth century seems to prove that everywhere and always the attitude of Protestants towards civil authority was determined by their particular circumstances.

There are, it may be said, three stages in the development of political thought specifically Protestant and religious during the sixteenth century. A general acceptance of a religious doctrine of non-resistance to constituted authority characterized the first stage. But it is important to note that along with this went the first crude attempt to construct a Protestant theocratic theory of what the State should be. These attempts were made by people called Anabaptists. ' Anabaptist ' thought is interesting and significant in various ways ;

[1] *The Book of the Seven Seals*, 1539.

but in none more than in this, that it illustrated the tendency of Protestantism in its earliest stage towards a theocratic theory of the State. But it was Calvin who first formulated such a theory in a coherent and superficially practicable form. The appearance of the Genevan political ideal marks the second phase in the evolution. Calvin started from much the same point as Pope Gelasius I and reached much the same conclusion as Pope Boniface VIII.[1] His conclusions are plainly expressed in the final version of the Institute and with still greater precision in the constitution of Geneva after 1555. He might well have taken as his text the declaration of John of Salisbury : ' Inutilis est constitutio principis, si non est ecclesiasticae disciplinae conformis.' [2]

But Calvin separated absolutely the conception of what the State ought to be from the conception of the duty of subject to ruler. What he saw as God's command was to him too explicit to be paltered with. God would have all men recognize Him as their true sovereign and His Word as their law. But if men found themselves actually living under a very different sovereignty, they must make no effort, however impious or idolatrous their ruler, to set up the kingdom of Heaven by force. According to Calvin the ' servants of God ' had a right to preach the Word and to worship in their own fashion and yet had no right forcibly to defend themselves against unjust punishment for so doing. It was a hard saying, and absurd, not logically, but practically ; since only those would believe it, for whom successful resistance was not possible. So long as Calvinists could hope to capture and make use of the secular magistrate, or so long as they had not with them sufficient force for effective rebellion, they adhered to the master's doctrine. But their acceptance of such a view could not outlast those conditions. As shrewd old Benjamin Franklin remarked : ' So convenient a thing it is to be a reasonable creature, since it enables one to find or to make a reason for everything one has a mind to do.' [3]

The making of reasons to justify armed resistance seems to have begun at Magdeburg in 1550.[4] But the third phase was not reached much before 1560 and its greatest prophet was John Knox. By that time the position of Protestantism had become very different from what it had been even so late as 1540. ' Calvinism', in particular, had fairly established itself in the Swiss region and was moderately strong in southern Germany. For twenty years it had been spreading and organizing itself in southern France and was now allying itself with provincial particularism and with the ambitions and jealousies of great nobles. In Scotland it was gathering strength in alliance

---

[1] For Calvin, see Chap. IV.   [2] *Policraticus*, ed. Webb, IV, 523ᵃ.
[3] In his Autobiography.   [4] See Chap. VI.

with the anti-French feeling aroused by the presence of French troops and agents. Alike in France and Scotland it was becoming an organized political party, strong enough to assert itself by armed rebellion. As soon as that point was reached Calvin's doctrine of the wickedness of rebellion began to be repudiated in Scotland and in France.

Where, as in England and northern Germany, the Protestants succeeded in securing the support of the secular sovereign, they continued loyally and consistently to preach their doctrine of non-resistance. In England, indeed, they did not get all they wanted ; and a tendency to seditious reasoning developed. But the difference between Cartwright and Knox is the difference between a Calvinism that may reasonably hope to become dominant and a Calvinism that knows itself helpless. Where, as finally in France, the secular authority becomes uncompromisingly hostile, they preach non-resistance only till the time comes when, by alliance with other forces, they are in a position to resist effectively. Once that day comes the teaching of Luther and of Calvin is ignored and replaced by theories very different.

I have spoken of political thought intimately or necessarily associated with Protestant systems of religious belief. The use of such a formula is, I think, fully justified by the facts ; but, nevertheless, it is apt to mislead. There might appear to be involved an implication that a main division of political opinion in the sixteenth century is coincident with the line between Catholic and Protestant. That, it seems to me, is quite clearly not the case.

The line of main division between those in the sixteenth century who thought of the State in terms of religion, was between those who identified or tended to identify Church and Commonwealth and those who practically separated the two. Almost all those who conceived of the Church as a body governing itself by its own organs apart from the State, held that the Church should have a controlling direction of all secular policy. On the other hand, those who regarded Church and Commonwealth as but two aspects of one thing, necessarily placed control of the Church in the hands of the civil magistrate. The controversy between the exponents of these two views is the sixteenth-century form of the medieval controversy as to the relation between Pope and Emperor. All through the century the main division of opinion in the Middle Ages was reproduced. That division corresponded in no way to the division between Catholic and Protestant. Calvin and Knox were as much champions of the view that set the Church apart from and above the State as was Pope Sixtus V. They were far more thoroughgoing with it than was Bellarmine. It was above all the Calvinists and the political papalists who, in the sixteenth century, reproduced the substance of what may conveniently, if somewhat inaccurately, be called the Hildebrandine theory of the relation of Church and State. But there were Catholic Imperialists as well as Protestant Hildebrandines. Those who tended to identify Church and State were the Protestant nationalists of England and the Catholic nationalists of France, along with the northern ' Lutherans ' and along with the irreligious everywhere. In France it was the Leaguers rather than the Huguenots who claimed supremacy for the Church ; while the views of the Gallican Catholics of France came to be barely distinguishable from those officially adopted in England under Henry VIII.

It has frequently been said that medieval political controversy was out of all relation to actual facts. It turned, it is supposed, on the relation between two powers assumed to be governing Christendom, while actually neither was governing nor could possibly do so. It is true that the unreality alike of the Empire and the regnum and even of the Papacy, even of Christendom itself, the actual disorder and localization of government, forced the great medieval thinkers into pure abstraction. They were engaged on the task of laying ideal foundations in a chaotic world. It was on the ideal foundations they supplied that the sixteenth century built its actualities. What the great controversy of the later Middle Ages really turned upon, was the question as to what is to be conceived as the end and purpose of government. The question of the relation between Pope and Emperor was merely the form in which a fundamental question was commonly argued.

If the purpose of life for every man be salvation in some sense and if this can be realized fully only in some other world, or heaven, there can hardly be any human activity so trivial as to be unrelated to that end. Quite certainly there can be no governmental action so unrelated. Governmental action that is not determined by reference to man's salvation in another world, cannot be conceived as rational. It was claimed, further, that the Church is a divinely established organization for the assistance and direction of man in the way of salvation. It was concluded that the Church, whether through its Pope or its General Councils, must control and direct all secular rulers.

On the other side it was asserted that, whatever may happen in the next world, government exists merely to assist in realizing what men desire in this. By all means let the clergy assist by pointing out the way of salvation, discourage sin, teach the revealed truths one must believe to be saved, and administer the necessary sacraments. But the clergy have no right to interfere in any way with the action of secular rulers, they have no coercive authority and no authority at all in relation to anything that has its origin and being in time.

It would evidently be absurd to say that the opposed views thus summarily presented had no practical bearing. In one form or another they are reproduced all through the sixteenth century. It is, I think, roughly true that the most profoundly religious minds of that period tended to take either the Hildebrandine view of things, or a view that ignored the State altogether. Those to whom the next world was more important than this one, those to whom understanding of the Scriptures was the first necessity of life, those who believed that they would go to Hell for misbelieving or for pretending to misbelieve, all these tended, if not to claim supremacy for the Church, at least to reject any kind of civil supremacy in relation to religion.

But it would, of course, be merely absurd to say that all the profoundly religious people of the century were either Papalists or Calvinists or mystics. In the sixteenth century the national State is becoming, or has become, distinct. New solutions of the old problem seem possible. It was possible to see a Church in the national State and to see the secular State as a theocracy. The conception of Church and Commonwealth as aspects of one thing made it possible to hold that the secular Prince was Head of the Church and yet that the end of social organization was the salvation of souls. The Prince was to take over the functions of the Pope and direct his subjects on the road to Heaven. To do this he must maintain true religion, extinguish heresy, punish the evildoer and reward him that did well. So would the old antagonism of spiritual and temporal power be reconciled and the State would be the Church and the Church the State.

Such an ideal might well appeal to the most religious of men. Yet the presumed possibility of realizing it depended on the assumptions of a general religiousness in the community and of general agreement as to the essentials of religion. Both these assumptions were false. It was not, in the main, the religious who supported the claim of the civil sovereign to control the Church. All those were ready to do so who cared more for this world than for a possible next, all those who did not wish to think, and normally did not think, of any other world than this, all those for whom the purpose of life was determined by desires referring to their immediate environment, all those who half believed or merely deceived themselves into thinking they believed, the religion they professed ; and all those who did not believe at all. And because all these together made up a vast majority, what was actually established was simply a State Church. The actual government that took over control of the Church and claimed, as it had to claim, to define true religion, cared little or nothing about other worlds than this or about a shadowy purpose in life. It had enough, and more than enough, to do in dealing with the pressing demands of this world. It tended to make of its Church a mere instrument of government for strictly secular ends and to make of religious formularies and beliefs a test of loyalty. Such a construction could, in the long run, satisfy no religious consciousness. The disillusionment was gradual and became complete only in the seventeenth century. When it is complete we have a State that refers, frankly, only to immediate needs and that ' tolerates ' religions.

CHAPTER II

LUTHER AND MELANCHTHON

§ 1. LUTHER

DESPITE the great amount of study that has been devoted in our times to the career and to the writings of Luther, it seems to me that the character of his political conceptions has often been gravely misunderstood and that his influence upon political thought has been both misrepresented and very grossly exaggerated. Luther has been spoken of as a great political thinker : I cannot myself find that he was in any strict sense, a political thinker at all. He has been described as a protagonist of something vaguely referred to as ' the theory of the divine right of kings '. He has even been styled a forerunner of the ' religion of the State '. To that phrase Luther himself would, I think, have been unable to attach any meaning whatever.

Evidently the best evidence we have of the character of his thought consists in his writings. They, it will hardly be disputed, prove at least that he was not in any sense, on any subject, a systematic thinker. He had too much passion and far too little patience. He improvised as naturally as Calvin systematized.[1] ' I have the thing but not the word,' said he ; and was not quite just to himself in saying so. At times he found great words. But passion and impatience mastered him and so strongly did he believe what, at the moment, he was saying, and so important did it seem to him, that he habitually exaggerated his phrasing. He said more than he meant and so slipped frequently into self-contradiction. He felt more than he considered and on the whole knew better what he did not believe than what he believed. All his books are *livres de circonstance* and items in an angry controversy. It is not easy to find any way among his clashing utterances. But he was a great soul and fundamentally honest. If we look only at his action in affairs, we may doubt his honesty ; but no one, I think, will do so who reads his writings. No humbug would have been so inconsistent as was Luther.

It has often been pointed out that Luther was profoundly influenced

---

[1] He spoke himself of the facility of his pen and the way his thoughts flowed from it unchecked. *Briefwechsel*, ed. Enders, II, p. 320.

by the writings of the later medieval mystics, by Suso and Ruysbroeck and Gerald de Groete and above all by Tauler and the *Theologia Germanica*. Impossible as it is to separate Luther's religion from his politics, this is a fact of importance. ' Neither in Latin nor in German,' he wrote of Tauler in 1516, ' have I ever found sounder or more wholesome doctrine, nor any that so fully accords with the Gospel.' [1] He found time, in spite of the multitudinous calls upon him, to prepare two editions of the *Theologia Germanica* and declared, in a preface, that he had learned from that work ' more of what God and Christ and man and all things are ' than from any other writings save those of St. Augustine [2] and the Bible.

It was just the element in his thought derived from, or at one, with that of the mystics that separated Luther most completely alike from Melanchthon and from Calvin. The world, I think, presented itself to him in two very different aspects. He never succeeded in reconciling his perceptions and wavered continually between two points of view. His deepest convictions were those he shared with the mystics. But his deepest convictions clashed continuously with his practical sense of what was immediately needed to secure the establishment of reformed Churches. Gradually the tares of the world partially choked the wheat. They never choked it altogether ; yet it may be said that in the long run, he sacrificed the deepest that was in him to mere practical politics. ' Luther,' said Caspar Schwenckfeld, quite wittily, ' has brought us up out of the land of Egypt and left us to perish in the wilderness.' But at least he did not himself see that he was doing that. His incoherence arose from the fact that he honestly held views he could not reconcile.

A great deal has been made by some writers of a supposed change in Luther's views after 1525. I do not think that any profound or important change occurred except upon two points ; and even there it was not complete. He was teaching the duty of obedience to constituted authorities as clearly and emphatically before the disaster of the Peasants' Revolt as he was after it. There appears later only a more exclusive insistence upon that very practical doctrine. There was, after 1525, more stress on the rights of Christian rulers, less on Christian liberty and the need of resistance ; more on the need of order and less on the priesthood of man. That this change was due to his desire to strengthen the hands and to allay the fears of friendly princes there can be no doubt. But it was a change of stress and not a change of view. Such a change of stress, it seemed to him, the times urgently required. On one very important and indeed fundamental matter his views do seem to have altered. He started his

---

[1] Letter to Spalatin.

[2] He came early under the influence of Augustine, a new edition of whose works was published in 1489 and another, at Basle, in 1509.

career as a reformer with a conception of ' faith ' that he may have derived from Catholic mysticism.　By the faith that justifies he seems, at first, to have meant an intimate sense of the presence and love of God, bringing with it assurance of redemption and safety.　It is difficult to be sure what in those early years he meant by the Word of God.　If it was not quite ' das innere Wort ' of Hans Denck, at least he did not identify it with the text of Scripture.[1]　' No one,' he wrote, in 1521, ' can understand God or God's Word unless it be revealed to him by the Holy Spirit ; but no one can receive anything of the Holy Spirit, unless he himself experience it.　In experience the Holy Spirit teaches as in his own school and outside that nothing of value can be learned.'[2]　But later, and after 1530 perhaps ordinarily, he seems to have used the word ' faith ' to signify mere conviction of the validity of dogma ; while the actual text of Scripture tended to become for him the only Word of God.　This change was never quite definite or clear to himself, but, so far as it went, it was radically important.　It affected of necessity both his theology and his politics.　It was, partly at least, his later conception of faith that made it possible for him to accept, as satisfactory structures, the churches set up in his name.　It must have helped also to bring about the other great change in his views, on the practical question of toleration.

From the first Luther had taught that the clergy were entitled to no special privilege.　They were mere subjects like other men. The temporal power was to do its office of protecting the good and punishing the wicked ' throughout the whole Christian body, without respect of persons, whether it has to deal with popes, bishops, priests, monks, nuns or whomsoever '.[3]　He contended from the first that it is the duty of the secular magistrate to undertake reform of the Church.　He went on definitely to claim for the Prince a right to appoint to benefice and to confiscate Church property.　It would have been difficult to escape such a conclusion.　With his vivid sense of actuality, Luther came to see more and more clearly that the Princes alone were in a position to do the work he wanted done. That they would not really do it in his sense he did not see so clearly. He used the means that came to hand and, like the ' practical ' man he was, he lost much to gain little.　But whatever the exact extent of the change in his views, it is important to notice that Luther's personal influence waned even as his views altered.　It was during the critical and formative years from 1520 to about 1530 that his influence was greatest.　Later the real direction of the Reformation in northern Germany was passing into the hands of the Princes, while, in the south, Luther's influence was fading.　Before he died,

---

[1] See his Preface to the Pauline Epistles.
[2] Preface to the Magnificat, 1521.　　[3] *An den Christlichen Adel*, 1520.

he was fast becoming isolated. On the one hand were State-ridden churches, on the other the ideals of Geneva.

Among the early Protestant reformers, Luther stood alone in power and alone in suggestiveness. The sweeping negatives with which religious Protestantism started its political career were all his. Having made them he was faced with questions, to which, for the most part, he could give only partial or confused or inconsistent answers. He dealt hardly at all with any problem of politics except as far as circumstances forced him to do so. He never thought at all in terms of the State. In the State as such he took no interest. He even made of its insignificance a reason for not offering resistance to its action. Just or unjust, he declared, it is not worth while to give one-self the trouble to resist it, since it can do no real harm.[1] He assumed the need of establishing reformed and visible churches and regarded it as the duty of the secular magistrate to see to it. But he did not con-cern himself with any question of the nature or derivation of authority.

Luther's answer to the question about the duty of subject to ruler was merely that which was given by all Protestants, save a relatively small number of 'Anabaptists', down to the time of the Magdeburg treatises of 1550. From 1520 onwards his language was less emphatic than Tyndale's and less lucidly explicit than Calvin's ; but it was clear and emphatic enough. He was, in his way, a patriotic German. In 1520 he was hoping for the establish-ment of a national German Church, freed from the Pope, and united under the Emperor and the Bible. But, from 1521 onwards, the attitude of Charles V and of Ferdinand made it quite evident that no such construction was possible. Thenceforward Luther could see in Germany only a chaos of conflicting claims and jurisdictions. His theoretic elimination of the claims of bishops and monasteries, cathedral chapters and clergy generally, greatly simplified that con-fusion. There remained a multitude of ' magistrates ' of various degrees, in more or less indefinite relations to each other and to the Emperor. So far as he thought politically at all, Luther thought only of Germany. In questions of the legal relation of magistrates of the Empire one to another, he either spoke with great caution or refused to speak at all. It may perhaps be held, he told the Elector of Saxony in 1530, that Princes of the Empire have, in certain cases, a right to resist the Emperor by force ; but all that he is certain of is, that no true Christian can set himself so to oppose his ruler, be he good or evil, but will rather suffer all manner of injustice. The Scriptures speak quite plainly. God has commanded obedience to magistrates in all things lawful by the law of God and has forbidden active resistance in any case and for any cause. The inferior magistrate must obey his superior ; the duty of the common man is simply to

[1] Sermon : *Von den guten Werken*, 1520.

obey the magistrate. ' God Almighty has made our Princes mad ' ; but he has ordered us to obey them and whoso shall resist them shall receive damnation. It is not a question of how magistrates came to be. Luther insists simply that God has commanded obedience to all such magistrates as actually there are. Simply because this is so, and for no other reason whatever, we must regard our magistrates, good or bad, as set over us by God. ' I will side always,' he declared in 1520, ' with him, however unjust, who endures rebellion and against him who rebels, however justly.' [1] To plead rights in the face of God's plain command is impious as well as illogical. ' Leiden, leiden, Kreuz, Kreuz, ist der Christen Recht, das und kein anderes ! ' [2] That cry came from the depth of Luther's being.

The command of God is all sufficient ; but Luther saw two good reasons for the command. He had a vivid sense that the whole social order, and so every one's security, would be endangered by the assertion of a right forcibly to resist constituted authority. If it should once be admitted, he wrote to the Elector of Saxony, that men have a right to resist rulers when rulers do wrong, ' there would remain neither authority nor obedience anywhere in the world ' [3] Herr Omnes cannot rightly distinguish between right and wrong and is given to passionate and random action. But, after all, Luther's deepest conviction on the matter was that force and violence can never be a real remedy for anything. He expressed himself in that sense again and again. Rebellion is not only a defiance of God's express commandment ; it is foolish also and worse than futile. The mass of men are and have been Christians in no real sense ; and to rebel or to assert a right to rebel is merely to give increase of opportunity to the wicked. Nothing is so satisfactory to the devil as civil conflict and commotion. No good can come of it ; and in the infernal turmoil it is the innocent, not the guilty, who suffer. The Word of God needs not man's puny weapons ; and God is always on the side of right. If you have faith you will rest content in that knowledge and in quietness and confidence will be your strength. You will, quite simply, obey God's Word, knowing that to use violence is to add evil to evil.

Simple as the view expressed seems to be, it was by no means so simple as it seems. To represent Luther as having taught an unmitigated doctrine of non-resistance, or any doctrine which could logically lead to the establishment of complete absolutism in the State, is to misrepresent him in the grossest manner. It seems strange that anyone who reads his writings without preconceptions should attribute to him any such teaching.

[1] *An den Christlichen Adel.*
[2] *Erwahnung zum Frieden auf die Artikel der Bauerschaft in Schwaben*, 1525.
[3] Letter of March 6, 1530.

Up to 1525, at all events, Luther showed himself as eager to insist on the duty of passive, as on the wickedness and futility of active, resistance. In the treatise *Von Weltlicher Uberkeyt*, published at Wittenberg in 1523, which contains the most complete exposition of his political views that he ever made, he was largely occupied in asserting divinely established limits to all human authority.

With the utmost emphasis he asserted that the civil magistrate as no authority at all in relation to Christian conscience and belief. It is for him to reform the Church ; but it is not for him to say what men shall believe or how they shall worship. That can be settled only by reference to the Scriptures ; and it is assumed, as always, that the Scriptures speak unmistakably. ' The temporal regiment has laws that reach no further than body and goods and what mere things of earth there are besides. For over souls God neither can nor will allow that anyone rule but Himself only.' No one but a fool would, indeed, claim such authority. ' For no man can kill a soul nor give it life nor send it to heaven or to hell.' Princes, he declared, are ' commonly the greatest fools or the worst rogues on earth '. Though evil must not be forcibly resisted, yet ' one must not serve nor follow nor obey it, with one foot or one finger '. If your Prince command you to believe this or that, or to put away your Bibles, ' you shall answer that it becometh not Lucifer to sit next to God. Dear Lord (you shall say), I owe you obedience in body and goods ; command me in the measure of your earthly authority, and I will obey. But if you would take away my belief and my Scriptures, then will I not obey. . . . And if, for that, he take away your goods and punish your disobedience, be happy and thank God that you are worthy to suffer for His Word's sake. Let him rage, the fool ! he will find his judge.' [1]

It might be argued that all that is involved in this fine passage is the assertion of a principle of liberty in religion which, later, Luther himself abandoned. But to say this would be to fall into misunderstanding. Luther was not, here, claiming that anyone has a right to disobey authority in defence of any religious belief he may chance to have. He was declaring only that the truth must, at all costs, be held to and defended. From that assertion he never wavered. The question of how far erroneous beliefs should be tolerated was, to his mind, quite another question. The distinction was not ultimately tenable ; but to his mind it was absolute.

But, in any case, there is far more than this. The principle that we must obey God rather than man covered, for Luther, a formidable array of cases and occasions. The Christian conscience is not concerned only with belief and with forms of worship. It is the ultimate judge of the validity of law, for in it the law of God is apprehended.

[1] *Von Weltlicher Uberkeyt.*

For Luther the limitations of rightful authority arose essentially from the nature of law. We are apt to be misled when we find some-one in the sixteenth century asserting that there is no kind of justifi-cation for any kind of resistance to public authority. We have come to associate the idea of political authority with that of law-making power. That association hardly existed for Luther. If there may be no forcible resistance to a sovereign legislator, that sovereign becomes as ' absolute ' as in the nature of things he can be. But if the sovereign be bound by a law he cannot unmake, the case is very different. Luther knew nothing of sovereign legislators.

In Luther's view human law and government were only needed because men, whatever they called themselves, were not Christians. ' The greater number of men,' he wrote, ' are and always will be unchristian, whether they be baptised or not.' [1] True Christians need no temporal power to rule them ; it is, he says, the temporal power that needs them. The function of the civil magistrate is mainly the administration and enforcement of a law that, for the most part, exists unalterably. Customary or Imperial law, all merely man-made law, is binding only so far as it conforms to two other systems : to that law of God which is expressed in the Scriptures and to that law of God which is written in man's heart and conscience and which Luther calls ' naturlich Recht '. This strictly medieval conception is the groundwork of all Luther's thought on government. Absolute obedience is due to the magistrate in the execution of his proper function and active resistance is forbidden in all cases. But refusal to obey is justified in the case of any order contravening the law of God, which includes the *lex naturalis*. And that law of nature has its voice in the human conscience.

Luther did, indeed, admit that law-making power existed in a secondary sense. Law consists essentially in the Scriptures and in the conscience of man. But the precepts and the principles alike of natural and of scriptural law do require adjustment to a complex of circumstance. Hence arises, for Luther, as for Aquinas, the need of a *lex positiva*. All the same, Luther was impatient and suspicious of all man-made law ; and he disliked the *Corpus Juris Civilis* almost as much as he disliked the Canon Law. Law is, he admitted, neces-sary ; but he was sure there was far too much of it. The mass of man-made law, with its definitions, its subtleties and technicalities, seemed to him useless or worse than useless. Good judges, he declared in 1520, are vastly better than laws, however good. ' Love needs no law.' [2] For the right judging of disputes among men, only a good conscience and love and reason are wanted. In this sense he abounds. If a judge have naught but the letter of the law to aid him, he ' will further nothing but evil '.[3] If a Christian Prince finds himself forced

[1] *Von Weltlicher Uberkeyt.* [2] *Babylonish Captivity.* [3] *Ib.*

to depend upon lawyers and law books, it is like to go ill with his people. He should pray for an understanding heart.

'Without love and natural justice (Naturrecht) you can never be in accord with the will of God, though you have devoured the Jurists and all their works. The more you ponder them, the more will you err. A good judgment must not, and never can come out of books, but can only come from a free mind, as though no books were. Such a free judgment is given by love and natural law, that is full of all reason.'[1]

It is true that Luther does, frequently, in emphatic language, exalt and glorify secular authority, even though at other times and in other places he writes of it with contempt. While in 1520 it was to him too insignificant to be worth resisting, in 1530 he declares that it is a marvel of God's creation.[2] He insisted continually that the Prince, fool or scoundrel as he might generally be, represented God. 'The hand that wields the secular sword,' he wrote in 1526, 'is not a human hand but the hand of God. It is God, not man, who hangs and breaks on the wheel, decapitates and flogs : it is God who wages war.'[3] Luther can hardly have meant that God controls and directs the acts of the magistrate in detail, so that no human responsibility remains. Or was he thinking of the predestination of all things ? But why, then, denounce the Prince who persecutes the faithful as an enemy of God ? When he said that it was God who waged war, did he include war waged unjustly ? Or did he only mean that God has created an authority free to do such things ? Here, as so often, no precise meaning can be given to Luther's whirling words. He was able to use such extravagant phrases and freely to contradict himself, partly because he had no settled or definite conception of the State in mind. He boasted that his teaching had for the first time, given to the magistrate his full right and power.[4] He declared, even, that, since the time of the apostles, there had not been a doctor, a jurist, a writer of any kind, who had succeeded in understanding the nature of secular authority as he himself, at last, by the grace of God, had really succeeded in doing.[5] But it seems remarkably clear that his glorification of the secular magistrate, such as it was, proceeded from his consciousness that only through the support of that magistrate could truly reformed churches be anywhere established ; and that it grew more emphatic with his increasing sense of that necessity, Princes, he says, maintain on earth peace and

[1] *Von Weltlicher Uberkeyt.*
[2] *Predigt dass man Kinder*, 1530.
[3] *Ob Kriegsleute*, 1526, ed. Weimar, XIX, p. 626.
[4] *An einen guten Freund*, 1528, ed. Weimar, XXVI, p. 589.
[5] *Verantwortung*, 1533, ed. Weimar, XXXVIII, p. 102. The passage referred to is quoted in M. de Lagarde's valuable *Recherches sur l'Esprit Politique de La Réforme* (126), p. 209.

order, and it is only in peace and order that the Word of God can be taught and heard. The Prince is the divinely authorized protector of the true Christian life. Where the Word of God is truly preached and safeguarded and heretics and blasphemers prevented from troubling, there, he thought, God dwells as in his own temple. It was only because, and when, he thought thus that he ever glorified the State.

The fact seems to be that only in the most limited sense did Luther recognize the State at all. He had no sort of theory of State-right and no conception of a sovereign law-making power. The State was for him an accidental result of God's command to obey magistrates. By that command, since the jurisdictions of magistrates were territorial, the territorial State was created. It exists, it is true, for the sake of peace and order ; but it was not man's felt need of order that created it. It was constituted simply by God's command and that command was given, it seems, only because men were wicked. Luther seems to have had no conception of the State except as a group or system of governing ' magistrates '. The Prince is usually a fool or a rogue ; but obedience is due to him. His authority is strictly limited by the law of God : by the text of Scripture, that is, and by natural law. Luther's ' theory ' is really simply a theory of the individual in relation to constituted authority. He had no theory of the State at all. The duty of the subject is not really a duty owed to the magistrate : it is a duty to God. But the magistrate must not be forcibly resisted. Rebellion is forbidden by Scripture and violence is never a remedy. On the other hand, of man-made law the less we have the better. We all know what is right and where we cannot see clearly, the Scriptures will guide us. ' Love needs no law,' and, if we were all truly Christians, we should need neither law nor Prince. I think that Luther was about as far from a ' religion of the State ' as it is possible for a man to be. The religion of the State is for those who have no other.

From 1520 onwards, Luther was teaching that it is the duty of secular authorities to undertake the reform of the Church. After 1521 he was asserting that every Prince of the Empire was bound to endeavour to set up a reformed church in his dominions. The question What is the Church ? had then to be faced. Luther's answer to the question was the same, up to a certain point, as that of Calvin. The true Church, to him the Church Universal on earth, consists of those only who know and do the will of the Lord. It has authority in all spiritual matters, but, necessarily, no authority within itself, save that of Christ. In relation to that spiritual world in which it lives, moves and has its being, all its members are priests and kings. But none can know for certain that he himself or anyone else is a member of that Church. It is, doubtless, infallible, but never can it speak a word. All things, the *Defensor Pacis* had laid down, are temporal that have their origin and being in time. Luther seems to have accepted the definition.

So absolutely did he distinguish between the spiritual and the temporal that the realm of the spiritual vanished from sight. Every earthly manifestation of the spiritual life of Christians, words, deeds or institutions, are temporal things and within the jurisdiction of the temporal magistrate. Any visible and organized Church that is soundly based on the Scriptures, in which the pure Word of God is preached and the sacraments duly ministered is, in a secondary sense, a true Church. But so far as it is visible, it is a temporal thing. It is the duty of all secular Princes to establish and maintain such Churches. In doing this righteous work the Prince may organize the Church as he thinks fit in relation to all needs that are earthly and temporal. He may, therefore, dispose of existing Church property as seems best to him, he may appoint to benefice, he may deprive the clergy of all special jurisdiction. All this was taught by Luther with increasingly emphatic decision.

But there was evidently a difficulty. Since no infallible person or body exists, except one that cannot be come at, who is to decide when or where the pure Word of God is taught and the sacraments duly ministered ? Luther answered the question by referring the inquirer to the Scriptures. Unfortunately it was just the meaning or the bearing of the Scriptures that was in question. Implicit in Luther's teaching was the assertion that his own interpretation of God's revealed will, could not reasonably be disputed. But the point especially important to grasp is, that Luther never for a moment admitted that the civil magistrate had any authority whatever in relation to Christian doctrine or the sacraments. He has to maintain true religion and right worship ; but it is not for him to say what is true religion or what right worship.

There remained a pressing question of vast practical importance. Is the Prince bound, in order to maintain true religion, forcibly to suppress false doctrine and false worship within his own dominions ? On this great question of toleration, as we call it, debated throughout the sixteenth century, Luther's utterances, taken as a whole, were not merely incoherent but flatly self-contradictory. Castellion, later, was able to quote him in support of his plea for universal toleration ; while Beza, righteously indignant at such misuse of the great name, was able, as well, to quote him on the other side.

To the question, considered as a practical one, there were three, and only three, possible answers. In the course of the sixteenth century they were all three given. It might be held that the civil sovereign was under a positive obligation to maintain true religion by force and use his sword to exterminate wolves that threatened the fold. This was the view taken by Calvin and his followers and by large sections of the Catholics, usually including the Pope. Or it might be held that, though the secular sovereign had a right to suppress heresy by force, he was under no obligation to do so. It lay with him to ' tolerate ' or not as seem good to him and to ' persecute ' as much or as little as he chose. This, of course, was the view that all governments tended to take. Thirdly it was held, not by isolated thinkers, but by considerable groups of people, that the sovereign was bound to allow his subjects to believe what they could and live and worship accordingly, just as far as was consistent with the maintenance of social order. It must be pointed out that only the second of these positions was consistent with any theory of absolute or unlimited State right. Luther gave the first of these answers to the question and he gave the third. He never gave the second. His inconsistency was due to the fact that on this question, more than on any other, his deepest convictions and feelings were at variance with his sense of what was practically and immediately necessary. His instincts compelled him in one direction ; his increasing sense of danger from the ' Anabaptists ' and of dependence on the Princes, drew him in another.

From 1520 to 1525 Luther spoke for freedom fairly consistently. It may be said that, in those years, he was not merely claiming that which every one must really claim, a right of private judgement for himself, he was claiming the same right for all and sundry. The use of force to propagate the Gospel, he declared in 1522, delights the devil. ' Faith must be voluntary.' [1] In *Von Weltlicher Uberkeyt*, in 1523, he asserted in the strongest language that religious belief is an entirely personal matter and that to make it a subject of legal prohibitions and penalties is unjust and absurd.

' A judge,' he wrote, ' should and must be very certain in giving judgment and have everything before him in clear light. But the thoughts and meanings of the soul can be clear to none but God. Therefore it is futile and impossible to command or to force any man to believe this or that. . . . Thus is it each man's own business what he believes ; and he himself must see to it that he believe aright. As little as another can go to heaven or hell for me, as little as he can shut or open to me heaven or hell, so little can he compel me to believe or disbelieve.'

He went on to point out that the magistrate, by the use of force, can, at most, compel people to say they believe what they do not believe. It is better, he declared, that they should openly err than that they should lie.

' Heresy,' he added, ' can never be contained by force. . . . It is God's Word that must do the fighting ; if that avail not, then will it remain unchecked by temporal powers, though they fill the world with blood. Heresy is a spiritual

---

[1] *Eight Sermons*, 1522. ' I will preach,' he says, ' but I will force no one.'

thing, cut with no iron, burned with no fire, drowned with no water. It is God's Word only that avails. There is nothing that so fortifies faith and heresy as to work against them without the Word of God and by mere violence. . . . For we cannot go about even worldly things with mere force, unless injustice has already been overcome by justice. How much more hopeless the attempt in these high, spiritual matters ! . . . Though we should burn by force every Jew and heretic, yet neither would there, or will there be, one conquered or converted thereby.'

So wrote Luther at his best, and, which is here more important, at the height of his influence. Again, in his circular of 1524, addressed to the Saxon princes, he declared that even Anabaptists should be allowed to preach unmolested. ' All should preach freely and stoutly as they are able and against whom they please. . . . Let the spirits fall upon one another and fight it out.'[1]

And yet, even as early as 1523, Luther declared that the public celebration of Mass is public blasphemy and should be put down by public authority. The gross inconsistency of this declaration, even with his utterances of the same year, was curtly pointed out in a letter written to him by the Elector of Saxony.[2] In 1525 he began to wobble badly under the pressure of circumstances ; and no one who does not know a good deal about the circumstances can realize how severe that pressure was. In that year he declared that the secular ruler must protect his people by force against the dia-bolical activities of the Anabaptists,[3] in flat contradiction of the circular of the previous year. From that time onwards up to 1531 he continued to contradict himself at intervals. In 1527-8 he acquiesced in the taking of severe measures against both Catholics and Anabaptists. Yet as late as 1531, in his Preface to the Shorter Catechism, he says that ' we neither can nor should force anyone into the faith '.

Circumstances were too much for him, and after 1531 he went over almost completely to the side of those who, for one reason or another, believed in the maintenance of pure religion by force. His plea for toleration in religion had never, it seems, been based on any reasoned conviction of principle. His argument was totally unlike that of Castellion or Acontius. It was perhaps because his antipathy to persecution was based on a sense of its futility rather than on a sense of its injustice, that his view on the question was so unstable and altered so quickly under circumstantial pressures. In 1533 he laid down the general principle that it is the duty of the magistrate to use his sword for all it is worth, for the destruction of false doctrine and false worship. To that principle he thereafter fairly consistently

---

[1] Ed. Erlanger, 53, p. 265.
[2] The Elector told him to practise what he preached. Burkhardt, *Brief-wechsel*, p. 76.
[3] *Widder die hymelischen Propheten*, 1525, Erlanger, Vol. XXIX.

adhered. And yet, though he appears to have convinced himself that only by the use of the civil sword against heretics and blasphemers could pure religion actually be maintained, it seems that to the end he must have had misgivings and inward revulsions. In one of his very last sermons, preached in 1546, less than a fortnight before his death, on the parable of the tares, he reverted to his earlier view. It is vain, he then declared, to seek to destroy heretics by force, ' for by human force can we never expel them or make them other than what they are '. The tares only increase for pulling, and Catholics and Anabaptists must be left to grow amongst the wheat until the last harvest.[1]

It mattered, practically, not a jot, except to Luther himself, what view he took on the question. Actually his acquiescence in the measures taken by Princes and cities against Catholics and Anabaptists was, probably, more influential than any of his words. But governments would have found themselves practically forced to ' persecute ' and Protestantism would have developed a coherent theory of their obligation to do so, whatever Luther had said. The fact, in this connection, that needs to be emphasized is the fact that though Luther says so many contradictory things on the subject, there is just one thing that he never says. He says that religious persecution is futile, he even says it is unjust ; he says it is necessary and he says it is a duty. But never for a moment did he admit that it was for the secular sovereign to decide for himself whether to tolerate heresy or not. To him persecution was either altogether a mistake or it was a sheer duty. He never quite knew which it was ; but he knew very well that it was one or the other. To say that the question might practically be decided at the discretion of a political sovereign and for reasons of mere immediate expediency, would have seemed to him something like a blasphemy. This fact, it seems to me, should alone be sufficient to prevent anyone from supposing that Luther believed in the absolutism of the State.

It is not possible by any logical process to derive the idea of absolutism in the State from Luther's writings. The attempt to do so makes pure nonsense of them. It might be argued that to deny a right of forcible resistance in every case, is to make all theoretic limitations to the power of the sovereign practically useless. That is certainly not how the sixteenth century saw it. A student of that century constantly finds people arguing at once that the king's power is strictly limited and yet that his action must not be resisted forcibly. The same view was commonly held by the English Royalists of Charles I's time. Nor is it true that to deny a right of forcible resistance makes all limitations on sovereign authority valueless. Passive resistance, if resorted to by any large proportion of its subjects,

[1] Works, Erlanger, Vol. XVI.

would leave any government powerless.   In 1530 Luther wrote to
the Elector of Saxony that if the Emperor should command the Princes
to persecute their subjects ' because of the Gospel ', the Princes should
leave land and people unprotected and the Emperor unhindered and
should say that if the Emperor would plague their subjects he could
do it himself, but they would have no hand in it.   The Emperor was
to be left to do what, in fact, he would have had no means of doing.
Even though a ruler may break law with impunity so long as he has
the means to do so, it yet remains true, ideally and practically, that
the power of a government is unlimited only so far as it is recognized
as being so.

It seems quite evident that the thought of Luther was essentially
unpolitical.   If he can be said to have had any ideal of the State, it
was a theocratic ideal.   But it would, I think, be truer to say that
he had none at all.   Vaguely there floated before his mind a vision
of a State ruled by the Word of God and by love and reason and
natural law.   Actually he acquiesced in the construction of such
states and churches as the ' Lutheran ' Princes chose to build.   For
his profoundest feeling was that of his early teachers, the mystics,
that in the long run only God's will and God's word counted
or mattered.   Luther represented, incoherently, divergent tendencies
in early Protestant thought, which all found more complete expression
later.   He was in no sense a forerunner of the religion of the State, in
no sense a believer in its absolutism.   Politically he was a forerunner
at once of Calvin and of Knox, of Castellion and the Arminians and
even of the Mennonites.   Calvin's ideal State was a development of
the theocracy vaguely suggested by Luther.   Knox expressed that in
him which had revolted at the godlessness of rulers.   The Anabaptists
voiced his recurrent longings after a perfectly Christian community.
He was never coherent, but he was vastly and variously suggestive.
We may say that Luther sowed the seed of all these different things ;
but we must remember that the things did not actually, or only very
partially, grow from the seed he sowed.   Except accidentally he
has no real connection with any theory of absolute secular sovereignty.
Such a theory, had he ever encountered it, he would have regarded
with abhorrence.   In his teaching of the duty of subject to ruler there
is nothing that is peculiar or distinctive.   There is really nothing
distinctive in his political thought at all, except that part of it which
derived from his mysticism : his profound pacifism, his conviction
that violence was no remedy for anything, his dislike and suspicion
of man-made law, his occasional glimpses of a Christian commonwealth that needed neither law nor magistrate.

The question of a man's influence on thought is always a very
difficult one.   We are apt to forget that one man's influence on
another is a very complex thing.   There are, always, at least two

people concerned. We are apt to forget that the same word or deed may influence two different men in opposite directions. As for the written word, there is a constant tendency to overestimate its power ; a tendency particularly strong in bookish people. There has been a deal of very wild talk about Luther's influence and, at times, really grotesque exaggeration. His influence in Germany and in the lands to the north was great, one way and another ; in the Netherlands it was considerable, in England relatively slight. It was felt in Italy and in Spain, but in France it is, I think, traceable for only a few years. Quite certainly no connection can be traced, as has been suggested, between Luther and Louis XIV.[1] The development that took place in France was completely independent of Luther. In his own lifetime, French lawyers were already expounding a theory of the French State far more absolute and far more coherent than anything ever suggested by Luther. Luther connects no more with Bodin than he does with Machiavelli.

Luther's brave stand against principalities and powers from 1517 to 1521, was potent as an example and as a stimulant all over Western Christendom. It was the interest and the sympathy his conduct aroused and the prestige it brought him, that gave their immense vogue to the treatises of 1520. It was in that year and in the few years immediately following, that his personal influence was greatest. But it is impossible to attribute to his heroic and stimulating example definite results in the world of political thought, or to disentangle his influence from that of other factors and of other men. His influence did not work simply in any one direction nor in any direction was it very definite. It was, certainly, of importance that such a man should have preached, with constant and increasing emphasis, the duty of submission to the civil magistrate and the wrongfulness in all cases of armed resistance and rebellion. Few, indeed, at the time, can have formed any definite notion of Luther's political doctrine as a whole. But what the common man needs and seeks is merely a practical conclusion and rule of life. In Germany, at least, Luther must have done a good deal to strengthen that tendency to regard rebellion against duly constituted civil authority as rebellion against God, which, strong ever since St. Paul's time, was in the sixteenth century becoming stronger than ever it had been. It may be that the strengthening of that tendency was the most important of the directions in which Luther's influence was exerted. But facts do not justify us in saying more than that. Everywhere in the first half of the century the Protestants were preaching the same doctrine. Even the mass of those currently called Anabaptists taught submission

---

[1] 'Had there been no Luther there could never have been a Louis XIV.' The well-known epigram of Dr. Figgis seems to have no relation to fact. See my essay in *Tudor Studies*, p. 102.

to civil authority. Nor was there anything at all distinctively Protestant about that doctrine. The same conclusion was being simultaneously taught, from a very different point of view, in the law
schools of France and Italy. It was asserted by Bishop Gardiner as
well as by Tyndale and as strongly by L'Hôpital as by Calvin.

It is clear, too, that if Luther's influence drew many in the direction of a submissive dependence upon civil authority, he must have
moved many others in a quite contrary direction. His insistence on
the duty of resisting man in obedience to God, his early insistence
on natural priesthood and Christian liberty, above all perhaps his
expressed conviction that a truly Christian community would need
neither law nor magistrate, must have drawn many minds to what
is roughly called Anabaptism. Those who accused him of inciting
to violent revolution were, in spite of his disclaimers, not far wrong.

'I believe,' he wrote in 1520, 'that there is on earth, wide as the world, but
one holy, common Christian Church, which is no other than the community of the
saints. . . . I believe that there is no one blessed who is not in this community.
. . . I believe that in this community or Christendom all things are in common
and each man's goods are the other's and nothing is simply a man's own.' [1]

Luther's thought was nearer that of the Anabaptists than he
himself was aware.

Luther has been far too much identified with the results of the
Reformation in Germany and even in Europe at large. Everywhere
the results of the Reformation were results of an enormous complex
of interacting forces, in which Luther himself could have been, at
most, a not inconsiderable factor. He has been far too much identified
with what is called 'Lutheranism'. Ideally there is little connection
between his teaching and the systems of government that were established in Germany by the Princes he tried to use and who made use
of him. He gave his great name to State-ridden churches along with
but small measure of his great spirit. He ought to have known better
than to have done so; we may, perhaps, say that he did know
better, though he never knew it. His life was a tragedy, that he
never, himself, appreciated.

§ 2. MELANCHTHON

Luther and Calvin set apart, no other man had, in the first half
of the sixteenth century, so great a reputation or so much authority
among Protestants generally, as had Philip Melanchthon. His pronouncements, therefore, on political questions necessarily carried
weight and had influence. But his actual writings can have been known
only to the few. The great mass of them were in Latin and remained
untranslated. This, in the sixteenth century, is always a fact of
some significance. Men who expected or hoped for a large and not

[1] Works, ed. Erlanger, 22, p. 20.

merely for a highly educated audience, either wrote simply in vernacular, as Luther frequently did, or issued their writings in both Latin and vernacular versions as was the regular practice of Calvin. To publish in Latin was perhaps to be read widely but certainly to be read by comparatively few.

Professor in Greek at Wittenberg from 1518, Melanchthon took a weighty and prominent part in the controversies and even in the politics of the Reformation in Germany. His *Loci communes rerum theologicarum* of 1521 was the first systematic exposition of the main points of Lutheran theology. With Luther in 1529, he encountered Zwingli and Œcolampadius at Marburg and he was responsible for the Augsburg Confession of 1530. No one among the German reformers, unless it were Luther himself, was so often consulted or so much deferred to. His fame as an educationalist added much to his fame as a theologian.

But, whatever he was as a theologian, he was vastly more effective as a reformer of education than he was as a politician. He had none of Luther's mysticism, but he had little either of his sense of actuality or of his moral courage. Gentle by nature and retiring, a lover of studious quiet, desirous of dealing charitably with all men, averse to contention and nervous in brawls, he found his world a somewhat melancholy place. His academic habit of thought put him out of court among so many clashing and contradictory passions. His learning and his gravity, his slightly pedantic reasoning, covered often a profound hesitancy and sometimes, it would seem, a profound bewilderment.

For many years Melanchthon followed Luther's strong lead with timidity and hesitation. When Luther turned definitely to the Princes, Melanchthon still followed. For a time the hope of a reform seemed to him to be bound up with the rule of godly Princes. Gradually it was borne in upon him that the Princes were far from godly. He came to think that their falseness and selfish greed were ruining Germany and the Reformation.[1] Thereafter, and definitely after Luther's death, he turned towards the cities, and aristocracy became for him, as for Calvin, the best form of government. But he turned only slightly towards Geneva : it was in such tolerant cities as Strasburg and Basle that he finally saw the best hope of a realization of his dream of reformation. Through all his vacillations he clung obstinately to the ideal of a great German nation united in a German-Reich. It was the strength of the desire in him to see Germany united politically and religiously, that made him so ready, even eager, to effect compromise where there was no ground for compromise, logical or other, and that imposed upon him a policy of

[1] ' Die Sophistik und Schlechtigkeit unserer Fursten,' he wrote, ' richten das Reich zu grunde.'

evasion. To the last possible moment he had hopes of Charles V and when that hope had failed him utterly, he took refuge in the idea of a Germany united under a Collegium of Principalities. His detachment from the cause of the Lutheran Princes was due in great measure to a growing sense that their triumph meant the complete destruction of German unity.[1]

As a political thinker he showed the same tendency to the evasion of difficulties that he showed in politics and, sometimes at least, in theology. In spite of the formal and scholastic method of his exposition, he rarely or never fully faced his question. He constantly takes refuge in vagueness or in statements that no one at the time was likely to deny. There is very little in his arguments or conclusions that can be called original. But his moderation in statement had its value ; and the extent to which he succeeded in formulating or suggesting what became commonplaces of thought in the sixteenth century is even remarkable.

To Melanchthon, as to Luther, the State was formed by, and essentially consisted in, a governing authority. But the State was more to him than it was to Luther, and he gave more thought to it. In his early writings he laid it down that while government is of divine institution (Einsetzung), the magistrate himself is a representative (Vertreter) of the people, created by a delegation of power from the community. He does not explain the ambiguity, stopping, characteristically, half-way to precision. But, later, he arrived at a different conclusion. After 1525, he not only ceased to speak of governmental authority as delegated, but argued positively that it could not be so. The essential feature of political authority, he declared, consists in the right to punish with death. ' Nervus potestatis politicae praecipuus et summus est supplicium capitale.'[2] This power is absolutely necessary to the very existence of government. It cannot be derived from the community itself ; it can only be derived directly from God. Only by special and divine authorization could any man or any number of men have a right to put another to death. It might have been hard, even with the aid of the Scriptures, to show how and when the necessary authorization had been given. But the point hardly, as yet, needed arguing. Melanchthon's position seemed to him to be justified by the assurance that without the right of inflicting capital punishment, no government could exist at all.

His conclusion seems to be that the magistrate represents two things only : the will of God and the need, but not the will, of man. The mere will of man, whatever it be, is irrelevant, since it is incapable of creating authority sufficient. But man needs peace and order for his spiritual life, government answers to that need and God wills

---

[1] For all this see, especially, G. Ellinger : *Philipp Melanchthon*, 1902.
[2] *Philosophiae Moralis Epitomes*, ed. Breitschneider, Vol. XVI.

everything that man needs. Government therefore represents the will of God for man and obedience to the magistrate is a religious duty. It does not matter in this connection what be the form of the government. God approves all forms alike.[1] So far the view expressed was that normally taken and even assumed as a truism, throughout the sixteenth century. Melanchthon went on to conclude further, that rebellion against duly constituted authority is always rebellion against God. Liberty he defined as a state of things in which every man is secured in what is legally his own and the subject is not compelled to anything contrary to law and good morals. Obedience to the magistrate is a necessary condition of liberty. In his refutation of the Twelve Articles of Memmingen, Melanchthon asserted as strongly as did Luther or anyone else, that rebellion is absolutely unjustifiable.

Yet, like Luther, Melanchthon conceived of the rights of rulers as necessarily limited by the natural law and by Scripture. The idea of natural law was as fundamental in his thought as in the characteristic thought of the Middle Ages. If he were less disposed than was Luther to insist on the liberty of obeying God rather than man, yet in some ways he went further than did Luther in limiting the rights of magistracy. Property, he declared, arose, like government itself, under natural law and is protected by natural law. It is a sacred thing and must be respected absolutely. So far from it being true that the property of subjects is at the absolute disposal of the Prince, one of the chief duties of the Prince is the protection of property. As to any power of making law Melanchthon was very vague. But he seems to have thought that customary law was beyond the power of the magistrate to alter. No more than Luther had he any conception of an absolute authority.

There is a difference between Luther and Melanchthon in conceiving of the purposes for which magistracy and the State exist. For Luther magistrates seem to have no other functions than to keep order and establish and maintain a church and a form of worship in accord with the Scriptures. Melanchthon widens the conception. Not liberty nor property nor anything that refers merely to earthly life is, he says, the end of the State. Government exists not so much for ' ventris bona ' as, and far more, for the good that is everlasting.[2] The essential function of government is to maintain, cherish and organize the religious life of the community. His way of putting the matter brings him nearer to Calvin than to Luther. But, like

---

[1] See the *Disputationes de rebus politicis*, ed. Breitschneider, XII, p. 683 et seq.

[2] ' Non tantum ad quarenda et fruenda ventris bona sed multo magis ut Deus in societate innatescat et aeterna bona quaerantur.' So exactly, said Calvin and Beza. *Phil. Moralis Epit.*, Lib. II, ed. Breitschneider, XVI, p. 91.

Luther, he held that it is for the ' Church ', not the magistrate, to declare what is true doctrine and what heresy.

On the question of how heretics should be dealt with he showed hesitancy. In 1530 he was content to lay down that religious professions or preaching that implied or invited sedition could not be tolerated. Later he adopted the view that Luther was at the same time developing. In 1539 he declared that Princes are bound to use force to extirpate heresy. But, shrinking somewhat from the practical results of his conclusion, he endeavoured partially to escape them by means of a distinction. Heresies, which, like Catholicism, erred only by addition, might, he declared, be tolerated in a well-ordered community. But he was quite clear that it was the duty of the magistrate to suppress by force at least all such heresies as blasphemed by denial.[1] His disposition to deal mildly with adversaries seems to have aroused in Calvin and in Beza an irritated impatience.

How far Melanchthon actually influenced the thought of other men it is, of course, impossible to say. He probably did a good deal to make current ideas that are constantly reproduced throughout the century. In any case his significance as a characteristic Protestant thinker of the century is considerable. It may be pointed out that Huguenot thought, so far as there was such a thing, was nearer his than it was to Calvin's. His conception of natural and immovable limits to human authority was reproduced, not only by Huguenot writers, but by very many others and very completely by Bodin. If, as a thinker, he has no great distinction, he was yet very typical. Most striking and curious is the fact that his argument to show that political authority must be derived directly from God and not by any delegation from the community, seems to imply a denial that right or obligation can be created by human will or human need. That assertion, though he did not definitely make it, would link him with the divine right school of French thought, with de Belloy and with Barclay. For the denial that obligation can be created by man lay at the root of the view properly called the theory of the divine right of kings. Yet, of course, that theory as it was developed in France, would have shocked Melanchthon. Like Luther's, his writings were remarkably inconclusive and, like Luther's, they were suggestive. But he was far closer to the norm of sixteenth-century thinking than was the far greater prophet.

[1] *De officio principum*, 1539, ed. Breitschneider, II.

CHAPTER III

THE ANABAPTIST PROTEST

HOW it is best to use the term 'Anabaptism' is not altogether an easy matter to decide. Speaking strictly and with reference to the derivative meaning of the word, it should be used only of those who insisted on an adult baptism as necessary for reception into the Church. But there are serious objections to the use of the term in this narrow sense. Terms are but labels and it would be pedantic so to restrict the use of this one, unless such a use corresponds to a real and sharp division among those who were called Anabaptists. I do not think that this was the case. It is true that no two types of religious men could seem much more unlike than were the philosophic mystic Hans Denck and the lunatic Jan Matthys. The narrow use of the term Anabaptist would exclude both of them. But Denck, it seems, was 'rebaptized', and to say that the fanatics of Münster were not Anabaptists is to ignore altogether the contemporary use of the term. For the sixteenth century it was Matthys and Bockelson and their followers who were the Anabaptists *par excellence*.

'Anno 1524 and 1525 is God's word and the Gospel of Jesus Christ come into all Germany after the Peasants' War.'[1] 'Rebaptism,' in fact, first appears at Zurich in 1525 ; but the little group of enthusiasts who then adopted it and who included Conrad Grebel, Felix Manz and Balthazar Hubmaier, had been gathered at Zurich since 1522. On the other hand, as early as 1521 had appeared the 'prophets of Zwickau', the portentous Nicholas Storch and the yet more portentous Thomas Muntzer. The teachings of these last played a considerable part in the Peasants' Revolt, which was far from being a mere revolt of peasants. It was indeed the part played in that affair by such men as Muntzer and Pfeiffer that turned Luther's semi-sympathetic attitude into one of unmitigated hostility. Quite early, in fact, in the history of the Reformation in Germany, the phenomena roughly classed under the heading Anabaptism begin to appear.

From 1525 onwards there was going on a rapid multiplication of

[1] Beck, *Geschichtsbücher der Wiedertäufer in Osterr.-Ung.*, II, p. 11 (Vienna, 1883). From an Anabaptist writing.

little local religious groups, brotherhoods, congregations or communities, which all alike claimed to possess the true Word of God and all alike denounced Lutherans and Zwinglians no less than Papists. The movement spread through southern Germany and Switzerland and through the Austrian territories to Bohemia and Tyrol and down the Rhine to the Netherlands. The little societies into which these seceders from the main movement were locally divided were often constituted extremely loosely. But they tended from the first to develop a more or less definite constitution, with a ' Teacher ' or ' Shepherd ' or elders, a form of common worship, rules and regulations and a more or less definite creed. There was a great deal of strenuous missionizing. The extent of the journeys of some of the Anabaptist missionaries is astonishing.[1] So strange and formidable seemed the doctrines of these sectaries that persecution of them began very early. Expulsions of the rebaptized took place at Zurich, Basle, Berne and Schaffhausen between 1525 and 1527. In 1527 Ferdinand of Austria issued an edict against Anabaptism and an Imperial mandate of 1528 made rebaptism punishable with death. Protestant sovereigns were not far behindhand and the equivalent decree of the Elector of Saxony was issued the same year. In that year Hubmaier was burned at Vienna and in 1529 Ludwig Hetzer suffered death at Berne. Sebastian Franck reckoned that by 1530 some two thousand ' Anabaptists ' had been put to death. The movement, however, continued to gather strength. It is probable that the chief effect of the persecutions was to strengthen and spread a wild and exasperated hope of a coming reign of the saints and give wide currency to the delusions of Hans Hut and Melchior Hoffmann. From the first there had been a sharp division between those among the Anabaptists who preached a complete pacifism and those who hoped to set up the kingdom of the Spirit by means of the sword of the elect. These latter were always in a minority ; but about 1530 the belief that the day of the Lord was at hand seems to have begun to spread fast along the lower Rhine and in the Netherlands. It culminated in the grand and grotesque attempt to found the New Zion at Münster in 1533. But normal Anabaptism was pacifist ; and this attempt was only an interesting aberration. The capture of Münster by the forces of its outraged Bishop in June, 1535, seems to have smashed the delusion that miraculous assistance was to be looked for and so all but destroyed the physical force party. But it was not in any sense a death-blow to Anabaptism, which continued fruitfully to exist.

However we use the term Anabaptism, it is clear that the Anabaptists of the sixteenth century did not form a sect. ' Sects '

---

[1] Melchior Hoffmann appears at one time or another between 1523 and 1531 to have been at Strasbourg, Amsterdam, Emden, Kiel, Stockholm and in Poland.

formed among them, but even in its narrowest sense the term covers a great variety of opinions. Bullinger enumerates thirteen distinct sects of Anabaptists ;[1] but on his own showing most of them were clearly not what we should call sects. The greatest diversity of views existed among the early Anabaptist congregations. Some denied the divinity and some, apparently, the humanity of Christ. Some believed in the final salvation of all and some in the damnation of all but themselves. Some held that once a man had the gift of the Spirit he could not sin, whatever the form of his act. He was free of all obligations : in particular, perhaps, of the obligation to pay tithe or his debts. But most held merely that such a man would not sin. Many recognized as brethren only such as had been rebaptized ; others were indifferent whether this had happened or not. Some regarded Sunday as an ordinance of Antichrist ; others kept it as a feast day. Some adopted minute regulations concerning dress, food and drink ; others regarded all such things as indifferent. Sebastian Franck declared that there could not be found two Anabaptist congregations which agreed with each other on all points.[2]

All this was in the main a result of the contact of ignorant and totally untrained minds with the Scriptures. Though there were educated and even learned men among the Anabaptists, like Felix Manz and Hetzer, yet the mass of them were certainly grossly ignorant people. Their peculiar opinions, however, were not derived merely from their own reading of the Bible. They were largely derived from, or at all events were at one with, those of various medieval heretical sects. Some of these survived in the early sixteenth century and may have been actually absorbed in Anabaptism. From the fourteenth century onwards small isolated groups or societies had from time to time gathered about some local leader for spiritual edification and as time went on these tended to link up into widespread brotherhoods. Itinerant prophets of a highly unorthodox kind had become numerous long before the time of the Anabaptists. No direct connection has been shown to have existed between such societies and any one Anabaptist group ; but of the connection of ideas there is no doubt. The objection of the Anabaptists to oath taking and office holding and to infant baptism and the notion that Christ did not take flesh from His mother, are all medieval. There is evidence, too, of the influence of Tauler's sermons among them and of the *Theologica Germanica* and the writings of Ruysbroek and the mysterious Merswin. The doctrine of the inner light, which practically allowed free play to every personal idiosyncrasy, would of itself account for much of their diversities and eccentricities. That there was also a large amount of hysteria and even of positive insanity among them is quite certain.

[1] *Der Wiederlaufferen Ursprung*, 1531. [2] *Chronik.*, Bk. III, 1551.

Must we, then, regard the term Anabaptism as merely covering a loose mass of incoherent and unstable opinion or were there any common convictions among the groups called Anabaptist ? The question that, in especial, has here to be asked is whether there existed anything that can be called Anabaptist political theory or an Anabaptist view of the State. In considering this question we must, for the sake of clearness, put aside for the moment the views of that eccentric section of the Anabaptists who hoped to found the New Jerusalem by force. For eccentric that section was. In the main, before and after Münster, Anabaptism was pacifist. It was not, in the main, a positive revolt against the social order, still less against the political order : it was, rather, a way of escape. Each little Anabaptist gathering was a place of refuge from the straitened circumstances and hopeless outlook of the lives of the people who formed it. In it they found a larger life and an outlook on infinity. In it they found a foretaste of the compensation for the wretchedness of earth that they looked for in a hereafter.

The Anabaptists of the straitest sects denied the validity of infant baptism and were ' rebaptized '. They denied, of course, that this second baptism was a rebaptism at all, since the first was null. Their rejection of infant baptism and adoption of adult baptism is the key to their conception of the Church. Infant baptism implied that a child without faith or knowledge or sense of what was happening could be admitted into the Church and become a member of Christ's Body. The Church, therefore, was a formal organization, membership of which did not involve either faith or knowledge. The baptized child remained a member of the Church until, at least, he formally seceded. The Anabaptists will not admit that the Church of God can be any such thing. The Church, to them, consists of those who have faith, those who have been ' reborn ', those, in fact, who have achieved a certain relation to God which can be put in many ways. Such persons, and such persons only, may rightly be admitted into one of the groups of believers of which the Church is composed. Most of the Anabaptists clung more or less closely to the idea of a visible Church. Their visible Church was a group of elect, illuminated persons, a community of saints ; and adult baptism was the sign of admission to it.[1]

It was, practically, just this conception of the Church which separated the Anabaptists most completely from Lutherans, Zwinglians or Calvinists. The ' eglise externe ' of the Anabaptists could not conceivably be a State Church in any sense whatever. No human government could take part in its construction or interfere with it otherwise than harmfully. The civil magistrate, invariably himself

---

[1] The conception closely resembles, but is not quite the same as, that of the English ' Brownists '.

unregenerate, could obviously have no hand in separating sheep from
goats. But perhaps the Anabaptist Church would be best defined
as a congregation of faithful people consciously guided and ruled by
the inner light. Belief in the ' inner light ' [1] seems to have been the
most fundamental of the beliefs that characterized the Anabaptists.
What exactly they believed about it or how much, on the whole, they
believed in it, would be hard indeed to say ; but in one form or another
the belief seems to be common to all of them from Matthys to Denck.
It took, of course, extravagant and grotesque forms. Some of them
received interior illumination by way of ecstasy and vision. Storch
seems to have claimed wholesale inspiration : Muntzer asserted that
he received orders direct from God. With Matthys the belief became
a claim to be a reincarnation of the ' prophet ' Enoch. With Hans
Denck, as with Sebastian Franck, the theory became philosophical
and links them with the medieval mystics and with St. Teresa. Denck
declared that without the ' inner word ' the Scriptures were useless :
and we are told that in some places the Anabaptists burnt their Bibles
on the ground that ' the letter killeth '. ' He who does not know God
from God Himself,' wrote Denck, ' does not ever know Him.' [2] A
man should keep still and listen for that word of God in the soul which
comes to heathen as well as to Christians. For God speaks in the hearts
of all men.

' Oh, my God,' he wrote, ' how does it happen in this poor old world, that
Thou art so great and yet nobody finds Thee, that Thou callest so loudly and
nobody hears Thee, that Thou art so near and nobody feels Thee, that Thou
givest Thyself to everyone and nobody knows Thy name ! Men flee from
Thee and say they cannot find Thee, they turn their backs and say they cannot
see Thee, they stop their ears and say they cannot hear Thee.' [3]

Such a man as Denck can, indeed, hardly be classed with the
Anabaptists, for he can hardly be classed at all.[4] He was, of course,
highly educated. In 1527 he and Ludwig Hetzer published a translation of the prophetical books of the Old Testament, which was the
first German translation made direct from the Hebrew. He was one
of a small group which includes Sebastian Franck, Caspar Schwenckfeld, Christian Entfelden and Johann Bünderlin ; a group which,
it seems to me, links with the Catholic mystics and with the most
profoundly religious people of all times and creeds, rather than with
Anabaptist or any other sects. No one would call Franck an Anabaptist, but his religion cannot be distinguished from that of Hans
Denck. He maintained, like Denck, that unless we listen to the

---

[1] It was called by many names : Das innere Wort (Denck) ; das innere
Licht ; Kraft Gottes ; göttliche Wirkung ; Wort Gottes.
[2] *Vom Gesetz Gottes*, 1526–7.
[3] *Vom Gesetz Gottes*. Quoted by R. M. Jones in *Spiritual Reformers*.
[4] Born about 1495, he died in peace at tolerant Strasburg in 1527.

word of God within ourselves, we can make nothing of Scripture ; 'for everything can be decked and defended with texts '. Plato and Plotinus, he declared, had spoken to him more clearly than ever did Moses. ' I love any man whom I can help,' he wrote, ' and I call him brother whether he be Jew or Samaritan. . . . I cannot belong to any separate sect.' [1]

Caspar Schwenckfeld was a Silesian of noble birth, who passed from Lutheranism into a position quite his own. His conceptions differed in one respect greatly from those of Denck. For him the Word does not come to all alike : it comes only to the elect. But when it does enter a man's soul, the man is transformed and there is a rebirth to righteousness. Such a transformation or ' conversion ' is at once the condition of all understanding of the Scriptures and the condition of salvation. There had once been a visible Church ; but it has altogether disappeared and cannot for the present be built up again. Meanwhile all sacraments are, as it were, suspended : and it does not really matter. God is slowly creating a new humanity ; and when the process has gone far enough there will again be a visible Church on earth. Throughout the ages, as Entfelden finely wrote, the Divine Harvest slowly ripens. ' Time brings roses. He who thinks that he has all the fruit when strawberries are ripe, forgets that grapes are still to come. We should always be looking eagerly for something better.' [2] Schwenckfeld wrote many books and pamphlets and carried on a vast correspondence. His influence spread far and his views seem to be largely reproduced by Coornhert and the Collegiants of Holland.

Denck and Schwenckfeld can hardly be dealt with except in connection with the Anabaptists. It may seem that their religious views are remote from any sort of political theory. But this is hardly the case. The spread of such views tended to undermine belief in the State Churches and Church States of the sixteenth century and everywhere strengthened the tendency towards religious toleration. It is true that for them the State hardly exists at all. They do not seem to condemn it as evil ; they ignore it altogether. This fact does indeed involve a difference between their view and that of the mass of the Anabaptists, who seem to have regarded all coercive government as definitely evil. But in these mystics there was no bitterness, no sense of disinheritance and oppression. Each of them, safe, to use a phrase of St. Teresa's, in his ' interior castle ', could afford merely to wonder at the folly of men. So far as the State exists for them, it is one with the Church, not that is, but that is to be. They look forward to the emergence of a community ruled by the inner light and by that alone. But this is the same with the Anabaptist

---

[1] *The Book of the Seven Seals*, 1539.
[2] Entfelden. Preface to *Von Zerspaltungen*. Quoted by R. M. Jones, op. cit.

masses. It may be said, even, that in this the mystics are at one with the fanatics of Münster, who tried to bring into existence by force that new world of which Schwenckfeld dreamed. From the sublime to the ridiculous is but a step.

For Denck as for Schwenckfeld the Church is, at the moment, an invisible thing. All forms and formulæ were to them things indifferent. Neither baptism nor any other rite or sacrament was necessary to salvation. The Church of the future, says Franck, will dispense with all forms and ceremonies and be governed only by ' the invisible Word of God '. It may be admitted that, practically, there was marked difference between those who believed in a visible Church and those who thought like Denck. But it seems to be illogical as well as inconvenient to separate Denck from the Anabaptists on this ground. The common Anabaptist thought of rebaptism as at once a sign of election or rebirth and as a necessary form of admission to God's visible Church. To Denck and Schwenckfeld the rebirth is all that matters ; and this alone makes a man a member of the Church. The baptism can be no more than a recognition of the fact. Denck and Bünderlin were both ' rebaptized ': Franck and Schwenckfeld were not. If, as a whole, the doctrine of these men resembles St. Teresa's, it resembles still more closely that of the mass of uninstructed Anabaptists. They must, I think, be regarded as philosophic exponents of the ideas underlying the whole Anabaptist movement.

Luther, Zwingli and Calvin alike desired to establish inclusive churches and to support them with civil power, to make admission a matter of form and law and even to enforce membership. Such a Church was to the Anabaptist as bad as the Papal Church and essentially of the same nature. Against any association of the Church with coercive power the Anabaptists protested absolutely. They either ignored the State altogether or conceived it as a hostile or an evil thing. Denck could afford to ignore it : the mass of the Anabaptists could not. They suffered, more or less, under a sense of injustice in the whole social order ; they were exasperated by the treatment accorded to them. Hence they tended to see the State, as they knew it and as we know it, not merely as hostile but as evil. The attitude of the mass of them can hardly be described as merely negative. The belief that all coercive government is evil seems to have been very widespread among them. Both Franck and Bullinger attribute this view to the mass of them. The true Christian, they declared, obeys Christ's command and resists not evil. The use of force is forbidden for any cause and in any direction. This being so, all coercive government and law sanctioned by force is evil. The Magistrate, so far from being a lieutenant of God, is simply the most persistent offender against God's law. They do not merely deny his right to coerce them into religious conformity, they deny his right

to exist at all. They are, by anticipation, Tolstoyan anarchists.[1]
Consistently, therefore, they refuse to maintain by any act the evil
thing, human government. They refuse to accept any civil office;
they refuse to go to law and to war. They refuse even to carry arms :
the sheep, they say, cannot wear the wolves' clothing. Consciously
righteous in a godless world they condemned the whole fabric of
society.

How far this view was consciously taken by the mass of the Anabaptists it is impossible to say; but some such view is attributed
to them by all their hostile contemporary commentators. It was
mainly on the ground of their denial of rightful jurisdiction in the
magistrate that they were everywhere persecuted. It was on this
ground that the mild Melanchthon recommended their suppression by
force. They were persecuted as anarchists rather than as heretics.
But theirs was a religious anarchism : and it was just this fact that
made the problem of dealing with them a difficult one for Protestant
governments inclined to toleration. To say that they were condemned
as anarchists was, really, simply to suppress part of the truth; since
it could be shown that their anarchism was one with their religious
opinions. We prate of religious toleration. as though it rested on
some principle of universal validity. But religious toleration may
be inconsistent with the maintenance of government.

But Melanchthon and others, and in fact all respectable people,
were particularly shocked by another opinion generally attributed
to the Anabaptists : the ' impious dogma ' that Christians should hold
their goods in common. There appears to have been in Moravia
communities of Anabaptists who actually had a common store of
goods from which distribution-was made by an elected official. But
there is little evidence of any organized or systematic communism
among the Anabaptists and none at all that they developed any
conception of a communist State in any sense. I do not see, indeed,
how such an idea could have existed among them. It certainly
could not exist among people who did not believe in coercive government. At most such people could imagine that, in a world ruled
by the Spirit, every one would be ready to share all goods with others.
The ordinary Anabaptist group may have practised such sharing
more or less : there was little enough to share ! In doing so they
were, perhaps, trying to follow the example of the earliest Christians
as recorded in the Acts of the Apostles. But there is no evidence of
any idea of a communism enforced by law. Storch preached that
when the day of the Lord shall have come and the ungodly have disappeared, there will be perfect equality among the surviving elect
and all goods will be in common ; but he preached also that in those
happy days there will be neither law nor authority. He can only

---

[1] Tolstoy's *My Religion* maintains the same thesis.

have meant, if he meant anything, that there would then be universal willingness to share. Muntzer, at Muhlhausen, appears, indeed, to have tried to establish a communistic system by force. But Muntzer was waging war ; he was forming an army. He was under the necessity of feeding his deluded ' troops ' and there is a strong suggestion that his communism was rather a military necessity than expressive of any political or social ideal. Such an ideal does not seem to appear in any of his writings. At Münster communism was little, if anything, more than a system of rationing, forced on the leaders by the stress of blockade : and it appears in fact to have developed along with the increasing stress. No distinct communistic ideal appears in the odd book written at Münster by Bernhardt Rothmann.

The Anabaptists, in fact, do not seem to have developed any distinct conception of a new kind of State, communistic or other. If they recognize any kind of State, it is a kind of ' church ', a Christian brotherhood of the elect and illuminated. When all have been illuminated, or when the ungodly have been otherwise got rid of, there will be, not what we call a State, for there will be no law with sanction, no coercive government, no authority, but a community living peacefully in brotherly love under the universally understood and obeyed law of God. In that perfect theocracy, though there can be no legal communism, yet, in Luther's phrase, every man's goods will be the other's and nothing simply a man's own.

The Anabaptists escaped from a sordid suffering to a suffering for God and for truth. They had been merely oppressed and disinherited : they become outcasts, proscribed, enemies of society ; and are exalted. They are sheep among wolves, conscious of innocence and harmlessness. Government is evil, the whole social order is evil and of the devil. Property, in the sense of a legal right to do with one's own whatever human law does not forbid, is evil. Ranks and distinctions among men are evil : there is no rank before God. Or rather, there is, in reality, one great and sharp distinction among men : the distinction between the ungodly and the called. The Anabaptist escapes from his worldly insignificance into an aristocracy truly divine in origin ; and is content.

Content, as a rule, it seems they were : but it could not be that they should always or all be content. The sense of injustice, economic and social, and the fear, bitterness and horror engendered by persecution, made that impossible. There is no doubt that a sense of injustice, disinheritance and oppression involved in the existing order of society was and had for a long time been widespread over western Europe. It found expression in such writings as the English *Sum of Scripture*, the Scottish *Complaint of Scotland* and the sermons of Guillaume Pepin in France. In Germany and the Netherlands this feeling connected itself more closely than elsewhere with religious conceptions ; and this, perhaps, is the reason why Anabaptism was so distinctively a German phenomenon.[1] To the Anabaptist coercive government might be necessarily wicked ; but actual Princes certainly were. The Anabaptists were willing to share their goods with others ; they could not but be acutely conscious that those who possessed far more, shared with no one. It was declared at Memmingen in 1524 that Heaven was open for peasants but closed to nobles and to clergy. The Anabaptists of St. Gallen were of opinion that the inner light came only to the ignorant and simple. Nicholas Storch included all lords and princes among the ungodly who were, some day, to be destroyed. These lords and magistrates who persecute the saints and oppress the poor, surely the Lord will destroy them ! The transition from pacifism to a belief that the Lord's day was at hand, and from that to the conviction that it had dawned, was not difficult. Yet it is a little strange that while these beliefs spread and became powerful on the northern German Rhine and in the Netherlands, the Anabaptists of southern Germany, after 1525, remained passive. This is perhaps to be explained by the catastrophe of the Peasants' Revolt.

In the first years of the Reform movement in Germany there came to the discontented masses, as indeed to many superior persons, wild hopes of a reform not only of the Church but of the whole social and political structure. These hopes were vividly, if crudely, expressed in the demands made during the Peasants' Revolt : demands for a general redistribution of property and the popular election of all officials and magistrates.[2] They seem to have been for the most part unconnected with anything that can be called Anabaptism or with any kind of religion. The Anabaptists developed hopes of a far more radical and sweeping reformation than was contemplated at Memmingen. Their hopes flared up fantastically at Münster in 1534, and with grotesque and horrible results.

Storch proclaimed, as early as 1521, the approaching reign of Christ and destruction of the ungodly. Both he and Muntzer seem to have come under the influence of Taborite tradition, which was probably still alive in Saxony, as it certainly was in Bohemia. Muntzer, a little later, saw no reason to wait for the new Advent. Apparently the outbreak of the Peasants' Revolt in 1524 was for him a sign that the day of the Lord had come ; and he flung himself fiercely into the rising. But, after Frankenhausen, Melchior Hoffman and Hans Hut proclaimed over wide areas that before long the Lord would give the

---

[1] From the Netherlands Anabaptism spread to England, but most of the Anabaptists of England in the sixteenth century were not English. In France and Italy Anabaptism in the German sense is hardly traceable at all.

[2] See the excellent summary by Prof. Pollard in the *Cambridge Modern History*, II, Chap. 6.

signal for a general rising against the ungodly and miraculous aid to the establishment of the reign of the saints. Then the word comes to Matthys, in Amsterdam, that the time has come : the signal is given through Matthys. From early in 1533 there began a flow of Anabaptists into Münster, proclaimed the New Zion and Temple of Solomon. By February, 1534, Anabaptist government was established in the unlucky city.

But in all that followed, as in what went before, I can find few signs that these aspirants after a better world had developed any clear idea of what they aimed at or any distinct conception of a new order of society. Muntzer's numerous writings are quite singularly barren. His 'communism' at Muhlhausen looks like a mere system of plunder designed to maintain and encourage his supporters : his 'theocracy' was the mere dictatorship of an inspired prophet. He preached the casting down of the mighty from their seat and the exaltation of the humble : he seems to have been animated by a vague vision of a turning of the tables and of the poor and oppressed at last coming into their own. ' The Princes,' he declared, ' are not lords but servants of the sword and may not do as they please but must do right.' Since they will not do right it is for the people to take the sword into their own hands.[1] He is said to have proclaimed, like Hans Hut, that it was God's will that the ungodly should be exterminated by the elect ; but this doctrine does not seem to appear in his writings.

Very little, if anything, can be concluded from the happenings at Münster in 1534–5. Some form of what might be called communism was forced on the leaders by the blockade ; and Anabaptists naturally would give it religious significance. As for their institution of polygamy, it appears to have been a direct result of the fact that after the expulsions of 1534 the number of women in Münster greatly exceeded the number of men and that they were largely unprovided for. It is true that a few people in the sixteenth century argued that polygamy, sanctioned by the Old Testament and not definitely denounced in the New, must be still lawful. It is true, also, that the Anabaptists were exercised about the law of marriage, as they well might be. But it is quite clear that very few of them actually wished to establish polygamy as an institution. The proclamation of Münster as capital of the world, and of Jan Bockelson as King of the World, indicate nothing but an aspiration that remained always vague.

In the book written by Bernhardt Rothmann, entitled *Von tydliker und irdischer Gewalt*,[2] we might expect to find, if anywhere, a distinct

---

[1] *Hoch verursachte Schutzrede und antwort, wider das Gaistlosse sanfftlebende fleysch zu Wittenberg*, 1524.

[2] This book exists, apparently, only in manuscript at Münster. A rather full account of it is given in Jochinus : *Geschichte der Reformation zu Münster*.

vision of the New Jerusalem. Rothmann had been the leader of the Protestant party in Münster in 1531, in alliance with Knipperdolling. Later he adopted the views of the Anabaptist prophets. But his book contains little to any purpose. It was God's will from the beginning, he declares, that men should be subject only to Him. But men were rebellious and set up 'earthly power' and human government; and to save man from utter destruction God acquiesced in their foolish doings. The earthly governments, wicked from the first, grew worse with time. Now the world is suffering under the last and worst of the earthly kingdoms, but 'one may hear the cracking of it'. It is falling and 'with this kingdom shall fall all worldly power; and all its riches, magnificence and show shall be a booty and the true brethren shall divide the booty'. This aspiration is, at least, intelligible.

After the great disillusionment of Münster, Anabaptism seems to have settled into its normal quietism. In the Netherlands it rapidly assumed the form of what came to be known as Mennonism. Menno Simons (1492–1559) had been a priest of the Roman Church. He left the Roman communion in 1536 and in 1537 became minister of a group at Groningen. In the years that followed he did much missionary journeying. The views of the Mennonites concerning government and the State appear to be indistinguishable from those of the mass of the Anabaptists. But Menno taught, quite distinctly, that the commands of the Magistrate must be obeyed if not contrary to the commands of God and that in no case might he be forcibly resisted. The commands of God, however, forbade the taking of oaths or of civil office and forbade the taking of life for any cause whatever. Capital punishment and war, therefore, were alike condemned absolutely. The faithful must refuse any military service. So strong did the Mennonites become that the governments of Holland and of Zeeland exempted them from military service and the taking of oaths before 1580. Elsewhere in the United Netherlands the exemption was only granted on condition of the payment of a special poll-tax. That the Mennonites should have accepted this arrangement makes it doubtful what their theory was. If they really held that the use of force was in all cases unlawful and coercive government, therefore, necessarily evil, they were logically bound not to accept it. They were bound, indeed, to refuse to pay taxes at all to support the evil thing. It looks as though they were only clear that the taking of oaths and of life were forbidden in the Scriptures. It may be that they were too simple to generalize and that they failed altogether to see that to pay the poll-tax was to pay others to kill, and be killed, for them. Had they seen this and acted accordingly they would, indeed, have placed themselves in a hopeless position. It was of very small importance to any government whether they personally served in war or not; but on the question of payment of taxes no government could compromise. Whether they knew it or not, the Mennonites were practically accepting coercive government.

The fact seems to be that the Anabaptists developed, in relation to the State, only a theory of pacifist anarchism. More or less confusedly they taught or implied that all forcible coercive action was evil in its nature. In so doing they disabled government and denied that the State, as ordinarily conceived, has any right to exist. But such a theory becomes altogether unpractical and even wholly absurd unless there goes with it some conception of another kind of order than that involved in the State. This conception, practically at least, the Anabaptists failed to supply. The Anabaptist principle involved toleration, not only of heresy, but equally of theft and murder. To say, like Schwenckfeld, that some day when the work of redemption is complete, a new humanity will include no thieves or murderers, but all will live in brotherly love, offers no remedy for present discontents. Nor does such an assertion seem to give much rational ground for hope. Many have indulged in this dream; but it would be difficult indeed to show that there is or ever has been any appreciable tendency in such a direction. The Münster plan of proceeding, by short cut, to the millennium by way of the extermination of the ungodly, hardly needs comment. If the prophets had not been insane, they would have known that, in such a conflict, it would not be the ungodly who would be exterminated.

I do not think it can be said, even, that the Anabaptists proclaimed any principle of religious toleration, otherwise than indirectly. They denied of course the right of the Magistrate to punish heretics; but they denied his right to punish anyone. Each of the Anabaptist sects tended to regard itself as the true Church and refuse communion with others. They say, says Franck, that God has stopped the ears of all who do not agree with them. They excommunicated, that is expelled, all erring brothers. 'There is a daily purging of members among them,' records Kessler, of those of St. Gall.[1] But in an Anabaptist society what would this expulsion mean for the heretic? It would not mean fire or the gallows: it might mean starvation. I do not think that in a commonwealth of Anabaptists there would have been any real toleration for the heretic.

Yet, however intolerant were actually the mass of Anabaptists, there is no doubt that their ideas made for, and even to a limited extent involved, religious toleration. In the case of those of them who, like Denck, believed only in an invisible Church, this is quite obvious. A government would hardly try to maintain by force an invisible Church: and if it did attempt such a thing it would not be heresy that would be persecuted. But the most important, as the most positive, contribution of the Anabaptists to the thought of the

[1] *Sabbata*, III, p. 232.

sixteenth century, was their conception of the visible Church. This conception outlasted all the earlier forms of Anabaptism and in various modified forms was adopted by many sects of the late sixteenth and of the seventeenth centuries. Whether conceived as composed of persons reborn from above or merely ' covenanted ', the essential fact about this Church was that it was a voluntary association. It has been said that ' Protestantism ' affirmed religion to be wholly a matter between the soul and God. Official Protestantism can hardly be said to have done so ; but Anabaptism did. The fact to notice here is that such a conception of the Church invalidated alike the State Churches and the Church States of the sixteenth century. Though the mass of the Anabaptists saw neither this nor anything else clearly, it involved to some extent religious toleration. If the true Church be a voluntary association, membership of it can neither be enforced nor made to depend on conformity to official regulations. Even Calvinistic discipline might be voluntarily accepted ; but so long as people were coerced into submission to it, the association was not voluntary. But it must be insisted that it is only in a very limited sense that the Anabaptist conception of the Church logically involved toleration. It excluded altogether the enforcement of conformity. But it did not exclude the suppression by force of manifestations of religious opinion judged to be blasphemous, seditious or superstitious. It was as a protest that Anabaptism was above all of value, and in spite of the crudities and absurdities associated with it, its value for sixteenth century thought was, I think, great. It was a protest against all the dominant trends and systems : systems of government and systems of ideas alike. It was indeed a protest against almost everything actual in the sixteenth century. It protested not only against State Churches and Church States but against the current doctrine that the Magistrate could demand obedience as the representative of God. The Anabaptist did not obey the Magistrate as God's lieutenant, but because God had forbidden forcible resistance to evil. But Anabaptism was a protest, too, against the whole actual social order and the doctrine, strong in France and England, that ' divine right ' attached to that also. To the thoroughgoing Anabaptist there was no divine right at all except in the saints, and the actual structure of society was unjust and contrary to the will of God. Anabaptism, in fact, denied the validity of all the dominant conceptions and institutions of the time. In doing so it could not, for all its confusions, but have real value for thought.

CHAPTER IV

CALVIN

§ 1. THE *INSTITUTE*

IN the history of political thought in the sixteenth century, there was no agent of more importance than was Jean Calvin. The Picards, it is said, were a hard-headed, vigorous, argumentative, dogmatic and strong-willed race. Born at Noyon in 1509, Calvin, like Pierre de la Ramée, was a true child of Picardy. In his craving for logical completeness and unity, his love of economy in every direction, including the use of words, his determined lucidity, his purposive concentration and freedom from sentimentality, he was a typical Frenchman. Though the ideal of the State he did so much to propagate was all but dead a hundred years after his death, in 1564, yet at least for the sixteenth century, his teaching was of enormous importance in politics as well as in theology.

He commenced his career as a typical French humanist. The classics and Roman jurisprudence attracted him rather than the Bible. In 1523 he was a student in the College of St. Barbe in Paris. There he had the good fortune of having as tutor Mathurin Cordier, one of the men who did really enlarging and enlightening work in the sixteenth century and who to-day are almost forgotten. There also he gained the friendship of Guillaume Cop, the enlightened physician of Francis I, of Francois Connan, the jurist, and of the great scholar, Guillaume Budé. These men were Catholics or, perhaps, sceptics, but certainly not ' Protestants '. In 1528 Calvin was studying law at Orléans, and next year he continued his legal studies at Bourges, under Alciati. In 1532 he published a commentary on the *De Clementia* of Seneca. The book is merely scholarly and of no marked distinction ; it evinces a scholar's admiration for Erasmus and makes few references to the Bible. So far there is no sign of any special preoccupation with religion.

But it must have been about that time that Calvin began to turn from the classics and the *Corpus Juris* to St. Augustine and the Scriptures. In 1533 he was at Paris again, and there, in the lecture room of Pierre Danès, may have sat on the same benches as Rabelais and Ignatius Loyola. There is evidence that in that year he was thinking seriously about the reformation of the Church. In 1534 he was at Basle, and then and there he may have commenced the writing of the *Institute*.

With the publication of the first edition, or rather of the first version, of the *Institute*, in March, 1536, Calvin began to take rank among the leading exponents of Protestantism. In July of that year he went, for the first time, to Geneva, to work with Guillaume Farel, for the spiritual and political salvation of that city. Under the stress of its struggle with its Bishop and the Duke of Savoy, and of its alliance with Berne, Geneva had developed Protestantism and established itself as an independent Protestant city State after the fashion of Zurich. But the Reformers disapproved of its Zwinglian constitution. Expelled from Geneva in 1538, Calvin, after some wandering, settled for two years at Strasburg. It was during this period that he produced the enlarged edition of the *Institute* in 1539, and the French version of that edition in 1541. Urged in 1541 to return to Geneva, he wrote to his friend Viret that it would be better to die than to be tormented again in that gehenna. But already, in a letter to Cardinal Sadoleto, he had declared himself to be called of God ; and now, without doubt, he believed that God was calling him to Geneva. He went ; and then began that struggle which made of Geneva the pattern State of Calvinistic idealism and which failed only, though completely, to make of it the true centre and capital of an international system of Protestant Churches, united in doctrine and in discipline. The struggle was a long one. It was not till 1555 that Calvin had succeeded in crushing all internal opposition and completely established his system of government. There was nothing so great about the man as that constancy of inflexible and uncompromising will which bore his bodily weakness through all those years of toil and tension.

The literary styles of Luther and Calvin contrast as violently as did the two men. Luther dissipated energy in exaggeration and squandered wealth passionately. As a controversialist he was coarsely and grossly abusive. But Calvin had always the word for what he wished to say. His style was a powerful instrument of his will. Lucid and economical, without superfluous ornament or rhetorical flourishes, logical in arrangement as in argumentation, full of reserve power, at times incisive and familiar, at times gravely eloquent with a restrained passion, Calvin's style, like that of Milton at his worst, was always that of an artist. No one before him had written such French as he wrote. The concentrated energy and lucidity of his style goes far to account for the extent of the influence of his writings.

The *Institution de la Religion Chrétienne* is quite frequently, but very misleadingly, referred to as having been published in 1536. What was published in 1536 was no more than a slight preliminary sketch

of the great work. Calvin was occupied with the *Institute* for more
than twenty years after that. From a little book of six chapters it
grew into a book of eighty chapters ; and the constantly enlarged
versions of it show that Calvin's views developed greatly between
1536 and 1560. Its successive editions contain a history of the growth
of Calvinism. It is necessary to state here the main facts of the
history of a book which, for the sixteenth century, had no equal in
importance.[1]

It seems that it was at first Calvin's intention merely to write a
brief summary of what seemed to him the main points of Protestant
belief. The book was to be a little manual of Protestant theology,
like the *Loci Communes* of Melanchthon, the catechisms of Luther and
the summary of Farel. In October, 1534, came the affair of the Pla-
cards at Paris. Justly incensed, Francis I issued, in January, 1535,
an edict against the Protestants and proceeded to address a letter to
the Imperial Diet charging the French Protestants with seditious
conduct and revolutionary designs. Yet in that very same year the
brilliant and unstable monarch was pressing Melanchthon and Bucer
to come to France and projecting an alliance with the German Lutheran
Princes against the Emperor. It was not even yet certain what
line he would ultimately take. Under these circumstances Calvin
seems to have altered his plan. He resolved to make of his book
at once a defence of the French Protestants and a direct appeal to
Francis. The appeal was made in a dedicatory letter to the King,
austere, dignified, and with a note of menace, which is a landmark
in the history of French prose composition.

The first sketch of the *Institution*, of which the first known issue
appeared in March, 1536,[2] was written in Latin. In October of that
year it seems that Calvin was working at a French version of the book ;[3]
but none ever appeared. But in 1539 he issued, in Latin, a much
enlarged and altered version ; and of this a French version, made by
himself, was printed in 1541. This double edition of 1539–1541,
though far from definitive, is, in more than one way, classical. It
was all but a new book.[4] It formed the basis of all subsequent re-
visions and much of it is verbally reproduced in all the later versions.
Specially important, for France at least, was the French version. It
is worth noting that it was only after the appearance of this, that
Calvin's book was proscribed in France. In 1542 the Parlement of
Paris gave it a magnificent advertisement by ordering its suppression
alike in French and Latin. Copies were publicly burned in Paris.

[1] References to the *Institute*, without reference to any particular version, are
not only unscholarly in form, they are often useless.

[2] It is possible that there had been a slightly earlier impression.

[3] See Hermingard, IV, 86.

[4] If one feels called upon to give a date for the first publication of the
Institute, it would be better to give 1539 than 1536.

Revision after revision followed. Hardly had the 1541 version appeared than Calvin was at work on another. In 1543 was printed a revised and considerably enlarged edition in Latin, and of this a French version appeared in 1545. A new edition was published in Latin in 1550 and in French in 1551 ; but this time the alterations and additions made were inconsiderable. It was not till 1559–1560 that the great work received its definitive and final form, the Latin version appearing in 1559 and the French in 1560. Not only were very large additions now made, but the whole book was re-arranged.[1]

The teaching of Calvin, by word and by deed, involved the construction of a true theory of the State. It was the one theory of the State that was produced in any sense by Protestantism as such. But the Genevan ideal of the State was expressed far more clearly in the constitution that Calvin succeeded finally in getting established in Geneva than it was, at least, in the earlier versions of the *Institute*. In the definitive version of 1559 it is, indeed, expressed clearly enough. It is hardly more than vaguely suggested in that of 1539.

§ 2.   THE DOCTRINE OF NON-RESISTANCE

There were two elements in Calvin's political teaching and, though not logically quite incompatible, they were logically unconnected and practically discordant. He taught that it is the business of government to maintain true doctrine and right worship and to suppress heresy by force ; that the text of the Bible is law for all societies even though the strictly Mosaic law has been abrogated ; that the Church, through its consistories, has power to declare doctrine and authority to bind and to loose ; that it should control and regulate the moral life of the community, feed the sheep and slay the wolves ; and that all mere civil authority should be strictly subordinated to the Word of God as by it interpreted. But he taught also, with the most uncompromising sternness, that forcible resistance to or rebellion against any lawfully constituted civil authority is damnable. And whereas his conception of the ideal Church-State developed only gradually, he taught this latter doctrine explicitly and emphatically from first to last.

It is needful, in the first place, to make it quite clear how explicitly and uncompromisingly, even to the close of his life, Calvin taught this doctrine of non-resistance. The fact that he did so seems to be

---

[1] The French version of 1560 is only partially of Calvin's writing. Much of it is simply reproduced from earlier editions ; but the translation of the additions made in the Latin of 1559 seems to have been done by some careless or incompetent person. M. Lefranc has pointed out that it contains a number of grave errors.

insufficiently realized. Many of the assertions that have been made about Calvin are true enough of that rebellious disciple of his, John Knox, but quite untrue of the master himself. Yet his teaching is as consistent as it is clear. All that was said concerning the duty of subjects in the *Institute* of 1539 is verbally repeated in 1559. The additions then made, except for one ambiguous phrase which appears for the first time and will be referred to later, indicate no change of view. One must keep absolutely separate, as Calvin himself most carefully did, his idea of what the State should be and his idea of what God demanded of all subjects alike. What Calvin, at all events by 1559, was saying, amounts to this. Here, in the *Institute*, we have the true doctrine of the Gospel fully and plainly set forth ; and here, in Geneva, we have such a Church-State as alone is consonant with God's Word. But though these things ought to be universally adopted, inscrutable Divine decree forbids us to use force against any duly constituted political authority, however godless its quality or monstrous its proceedings. To all such authorities we owe complete obedience, as far as the law of God allows. That this was what Calvin consistently taught I do not think that anyone who carefully compares what he wrote on the subject in 1539 with what he wrote in 1559 can have any doubt.

Almost everything that he had to say on the question is contained in the sixteenth chapter of the *Institute* of 1539 and repeated verbally from revision to revision. Calvin conceived of the State as constituted by a grant of authority from God. That grant was made for the sake of man's need. But the State was not a product of man's reason and will. Mere human reason would, it appears, have produced something very different, ' Que scauroit le sens de l'homme produire, si non choses charnelles et folles ? ' [1] He does not say that a right to demand obedience as a duty could nohow else have been derived ; but his language frequently reminds one very strongly of Barclay. Subjects, he says, must obey not out of fear, but as to God, ' d'autant que de luy est la puissance de leur Prince '.[2] No more than Luther did Calvin ask how exactly magistrates came to be where they are. Whatever is established was established by God and that is enough. ' It come not of the perversity of man that kings and other lords have power upon earth : but it comes of the providence and holy ordinance of God whom it has pleased to manage in this fashion the government of men.' [3] Magistrates are the ' vicars ', the ' lieutenants ', the ' ministers ', of God. ' Ils font mesmes et executent

---

[1] *Institute*, 1541, Chap. XV, ed. Lefranc, p. 747. In the Latin of 1559 : ' Quid enim posset parere hominum sensus quam carnalia fatuaque omnia ? ' Ed. 1559, IV, 10, p. 442.

[2] Ib., 1541, XVI, ed. Lefranc, p. 774.

[3] Ib., 1541, ed. Lefranc, p. 756. Ed. 1559, Lib. IV, p. 550.

l'office de Dieu.'[1] Precisely so said the Catholic Royalists of France at the close of the century.

It is always our duty ' nous rendre subjectz et obéissans à quelconques supérieurs qui dominent au lieu où nous vivons '[2] We must show our obedience alike in keeping their laws and in paying the taxes they impose. Mere obedience, indeed, is not enough. There are some who regard magistracy as a necessary evil and obey the magistrate out of mere regard for public welfare. But God demands of us more than this ; we must not only obey, we must hold our superiors in reverence and honour however difficult it may be to do so.[3]

' On ne peut pas résister aux magistratz sans résister à Dieu.'[4] Calvin, anxious as always to avoid ambiguity, stopped one loophole after another. The form of the government, he pointed out, in no way affects the duty of the subject. There is no power but of God. ' Though there be divers forms and kinds of rulers, yet they differ not at all in this, that we must take them all as ministers ordained of God.'[5] And that form, he characteristically adds, ' which is the least pleasing to men is particularly and above all others commended to us, that is the lordship and domination of a single man '.[6] But it is not for man to question providential arrangements. ' Certes, c'est une vaine occupation aux hommes privez, lesquelz n'ont nulle auctorité de ordonner les choses publiques, de disputer quel est le meilleur estat de police.'[7] If there be in the State some fault needing correction, the private person must not agitate about it or take any public action or in any way put his hands to the work ;[8] he should represent the facts to the magistrates who alone have authority to deal with the matter.

' Mais quelqu'un dira, qu'il y a aussi mutuel devoir des superieurs, envers leurs subjectz.' Later we hear a great deal of this from persons called Calvinists, as well as from others, who inferred that failure of the ruler to do his duty released his subjects from theirs. Calvin fully admitted the fact but would have none of the inference. ' Toutesfois si quelqu'un vouloit de ce inferer qu'on ne doibt obeissance sinon à un juste Seigneur, il argueroit perversement.'[9] Men are not to consider how others do their duty, but to look to their own, which is nowise affected by the wickedness of others.

---

[1] *Inst.*, ed. Lefranc, p. 758.   [2] Ib., ed. Lefranc, p. 760.
[3] Ib., ed. Lefranc, pp. 773–774.   [4] Ib., ed. Lefranc, p. 774.
[5] Ib., ed. Lefranc, p. 759. Repeated 1560, Bk. IV, p. 672.
[6] Ib., ed. Lefranc, p. 759.
[7] Ib., ed. Lefranc, p. 759.
[8] ' Lesquelles leurs sont ligées quant à-cela.' Ib., p. 775.
[9] Ib., 1541, ed. Lefranc, p. 786. ' Ab mutuas (inquies) subditis suis vices debent praefecti. Id jam confessus sum. Verum si ex eo statuis, nonnisi justus impervs rependenda obsequia, infulsus es ratiocinator.' Ed. 1559, Lib. IV, 20, p. 560.

The question whether the duty of obedience extended to the case of a tyrannous and unjust ruler and, above all, to the case of magistrates who maintained false religion and persecuted true believers, needed the most explicit answer. No answer could well have been more explicit and emphatic than was Calvin's. He endeavoured to leave no possible doubt about it. Most Princes, he observes, depart from the strait way : indeed that a Prince should do his duty is all but a miracle.[1] Some, without a thought of duty, give themselves wholly to pleasure ; others, greedy of gold, sell right and justice ; others again overburden their subjects with taxes to support their prodigality. Some act like very brigands, wrecking and spoiling, outraging women and brutalizing innocence. 'It is not easy,' he remarks, 'to persuade some people that such are to be recognized as true Princes and obeyed just so far as is possible.' For it must be admitted that in such monsters no one can perceive the image of God or any token of a divine ministry. Men have always hated such tyrants. But one must turn from the contemplation of their iniquities to the Word of God. There we shall find that, though God has empowered magistrates for the benefit of man and has prescribed to them their duties, nevertheless he declares that whatever they are and however they may govern, they hold their authority only from Him. They are responsible to God alone. Such Princes as act justly are very mirrors of the divine goodness ; those who do injustice are raised up for chastisement of the sinfulness of the people. 'But both one and the other alike possess that dignity and majesty which God has given to all lawful superiors.' In the most unworthy magistrate inheres that authority which the Lord gives to the ministers of his justice.[2] If we consider these things there will never enter our minds the foolish and seditious notion that Kings may be treated as they deserve or that because they fail in their duty to us we need no longer be subject to them.[3]

Calvin felt that this assertion needed strong support from the Scriptures. He cited many passages and examples and referred at length to what is told of Samuel, David and Nebuchodonosor. His arguments from the doings or sayings of these persons or from what is said about them, were repeated, wearisomely, to the end of the century.[4]

[1] This remark is an addition to the final version of the *Institute*. It appears on page 672 of the French of 1560.

[2] All this is paraphrased or translated from the *Institute*. See ed. 1541, Lefranc, pp. 775, 776, and ed. 1559, Lib. IV, 20, pp. 558, 559.

[3] 'Nunquam in animum nobis seditiosae illae cogitationes venient, tractandum esse pro meritis Regem : nec aequum esse ut subditos ei praestemus qui vicissim Regem nobis non praestet.' *Inst.*, 1559, Lib. IV, Cap. XX, p. 560. The French has 'folles et seditieuses'.

[4] Very elaborately, of course, by the Catholic Royalist and champion of the divine right of Kings, Alexander Barclay.

We need not discuss the argument, noting only that it was, from his own standpoint, inconclusive. Quite different inferences were later drawn from the same stories. But Calvin left no doubt about his conclusion. It is stated relentlessly.

' Wherefore, if we are cruelly vexed by an inhuman Prince or robbed and plundered by one prodigal or avaricious or despised and left without protection by one negligent : or even if we are afflicted for the Name of God by one sacriligious and unbelieving, let us first of all remember those our own offences against God which doubtless are chastised by these plagues. And secondly let us consider that it is not for us to remedy these evils ; for us it remains only to implore the aid of God, in whose hand are the hearts of Kings and changes of kingdoms.' [1]

Such prayers, he proceeded to show, are not always unavailing. God has, time and again, interposed to free His people from tyranny. Sometimes this has been done by the agency of the wicked : at other times by men specially called and commissioned, like Moses and Othniel. Through such men the King of kings corrected the misdoings of the earthly kings, His unfaithful lieutenants. But he makes it quite clear that it was only a personal calling and exceptional commission that gave Moses and Othniel a right to act.

It is as though Calvin were deliberately barring by anticipation such argumentation as appeared later in the *Du Droit des Magistrats* and the *Vindiciœ*. That, in fact, is exactly what he was doing, whether or no he was distinctly aware of a tendency among his followers to repudiate his doctrine. Not even a persecuting and unbelieving Prince may be forcibly resisted. There is no rightful defence against him but in prayer or flight.

We are all, of course, bound to obey God rather than man. We must be on our guard, says Calvin, lest our obedience to the magistrate lead us into disobedience to God. If the magistrate command us to do what God forbids, his command should count with us for nothing. Whatever the consequences of our disobedience, we are bound in that case to disobey and must be ready to endure all things rather than disobey God.[2] There is, of course, no sort of inconsistency here. Every one who, in the sixteenth century, dealt with this subject, had clearly in mind the obvious distinction between passive resistance or mere refusal to obey, with acceptance of consequences, and active resistance or rebellion. Whether or no active resistance were ever justified, every one agreed that refusal to obey might be obligatory. It is God's command that forbids us forcibly to resist the magistrate and it is God's command that may bind us to disobey

---

[1] *Inst.*, 1541, ed. Lefranc, p. 780. Ed. 1559, Lib. IV, 20, p. 560. The phrase ' si mesmes nous sommes affligez pour le nom de Dieu par un sacrilège et incredule ' is, in the Latin : ' si ab impio denique et sacrilego vexamur ob pietatem '.

[2] Ib., ed. Lefranc, pp. 782, 783.

him. Calvin's view on the question was the same as that of almost all the early reformers.

I can find nothing in Calvin's writings that is inconsistent with this view, unless it be a single phrase that occurs, for the first time, in the final version of the *Institute*. Discussing the conduct of Daniel, he points out that the prophet's refusal to obey a royal edict was justified by its impious character. The King had exalted his horn against God ' et en ce faisant s'estoit demis et degradé de toute authorité '.[1] It might be and it was argued that this phrase would have justified Daniel in doing more than disobey. If the King were, by his impious proceedings, deprived literally of all authority, there would remain no reason why he should not be rebelled against and deposed. God must, if that were so, have withdrawn his mandate. But to suppose that this is what Calvin meant is to suppose that in this passage he flatly contradicted what he had said about persecuting and sacrilegious tyrants only a few pages earlier. To attribute such self-contradiction to Calvin is, I think, absurd. It is simply incredible that by means of this casual phrase he should deliberately have contradicted the tenor of the teaching of his whole life upon the subject. The phrase, it may be admitted, was an unfortunate one : Homer for once was not wide awake. But in this passage Calvin was not dealing with a case of rebellion : Daniel went to the den of lions, but he did not rebel. Authority is a right to demand obedience as a duty : this, at least, is how Calvin and the sixteenth century generally understood it. All Calvin can have meant was that by issuing his impious edict, Darius had deprived himself of all claim to be obeyed as far as the edict went. To suppose that he meant more is to make nonsense of all that he had so clearly and carefully written on the question. Nor can it reasonably be held that Calvin was, for the first time and suddenly, making a distinction between tyrannical acts which merely injure the body and orders which seek to compel a breach of God's law. He cannot have meant that, if a Prince massacre the innocent, though he is certainly breaking God's law, he is not compelling you to break it and you must not rebel ; but that if he orders you to break it, rebel you may. Had he intended to assert so important a proposition, he would assuredly have asserted it in the clearest manner. It may be remarked, also, that an order to massacre innocents would be an order to break God's law ; and

---

[1] ' Cornua tollendo adversus deum, potestatem sibi ipse abrogaverat.' 1559, Lib. IV, 20, p. 561. The Latin, which is Calvin's, is slightly more ambiguous than the French of 1560, which is not his. The passage does not occur in the versions of 1539, 1543 or 1550. But in his *Praelectiones in librum prophetiarum Danielis*, 1561, Calvin repeated the substance of the passage and the crucial phrase appears in a more emphatic form: ' Abdicant enim se potestate terreni Principes dum insurgunt contra Deum.'

Calvin had just been explicitly declaring that against the persecutions of a tyrant the godly have no remedy but prayer. Calvin was incapable of such logical blundering as some of his muddle-headed disciples were fain to credit him with. Yet it must be admitted that there is another interpretation of the phrase in question which is possibly the right one. After Knox's *Appellation* of 1558, with the actual outbreak of rebellion in Scotland and the visible coming of a crisis in France, Calvin may possibly have begun to waver on the question whether resistance by force to an impious and persecuting ruler might not after all be justified. Any the least hesitation, any new-born doubt in his mind on the point, would account for the intrusion into the *Institute* of 1559 of ambiguous and apparently self-contradictory phrases. This, I think, is the utmost concession it is possible to make to those who would represent Calvin as having justified resistance for the cause of religion. Even if that be conceded, it does not in the least alter the main fact. Practically throughout his life Calvin taught a doctrine of absolute non-resistance, qualified only, as it was qualified by every one in the sixteenth century, by an obligation in some cases to a passive disobedience.

That Calvin should consistently have taught such a doctrine may to some seem strange ; but in fact it would have been strange had he not done so. It must be remembered that, after all, insistence on the duty of submission and the wickedness of rebellion was the merest commonplace of the time. Lawyers and divines, Catholic and Protestant, were everywhere, by different roads, reaching the same conclusion. In Calvin's case there were special reasons for that insistence. During the years from 1534 to 1541 he must have been writing under a sense of enormous obstacles. None knew better than he how precarious was the position of Protestantism in France. No one was more aware of the danger of driving constituted authority into hostility. Later his relation to the technically governing body of Geneva was such as would naturally lead him to insist on the wickedness of overt resistance. It is not intended to suggest the least insincerity. I think that Calvin always believed every word he said.

But Calvin did recognize just one possible loophole in the mesh of God's scheme. In some countries or states, he says, there have existed magistrates specially instituted to restrain the doings of the chief magistrate. Such were certain officials of Athens, Sparta and Rome and such, he declares, ' are possibly, nowadays, in each kingdom the three estates assembled '.[1] It would, by hypothesis, be lawful for such magistrates to resist tyrannical action and, therefore, it would be their duty to do so. Failing to do so they would betray the liberty of their people. It must be presumed that, if they do resist, others will be justified, in supporting by force an otherwise

[1] 1541, ed. Lefranc, p. 782. Ed. 1559, Chap. XII, p. 561.

futile resistance, though Calvin refrains from saying so. Two points must be emphasized. Calvin suggests that a real right of resistance may belong in some realms to the estates assembled, but he does not positively say that it is so. And he makes no suggestion that such a right, nowadays, belongs to anyone else.

After the failure of the conspiracy of Amboise, Calvin was charged with having given it his sanction. In April, 1561, he wrote to Coligny on the subject.[1] He had, he said, been asked beforehand whether in view of the oppression of the ' children of God ' in France, active resistance would not be justified. He had answered, he declared, that it were better that all the said children of God should perish rather than that the Gospel should be dishonoured by bloodshed. But he had added that if the Princes of the blood took action to maintain their legal rights and if the Parlements of France joined with them, then indeed all good subjects might lawfully aid them in arms. Asked if action taken by a single Prince of the blood, and he not the first, would suffice to justify such popular support, he had replied that it would not.

There is no reason to suppose, and no likelihood whatever, that in this letter Calvin stated anything but what was true. In his view, apparently, the existence of definite constitutional rights, asserted by all the persons concerned and by the highest judicial authorities, would justify the taking of arms against a sovereign, on behalf of those rights. Nothing less would suffice. Though there is here no reference to Estates, the view is, I think, essentially consistent with what he says in the *Institute*. Whether he would have taken it, however, so far back as 1539 may be doubted. It must be noted that, practically, Calvin's answer amounted to a flat negative. There existed no conceivable chance that all the Princes of the blood and all the Parlements would act together. Calvin's replies were equivalent to telling the Huguenots that nothing that could actually occur would give them a right to take up arms. His opinion, of course, had no appreciable effect on the situation.

That a man of Calvin's legal training and one who most certainly conceived of no earthly sovereignty as unlimited, should hold that the legal constitution of a realm might involve a right under certain circumstances to take arms against the sovereign, is neither surprising nor in any way inconsistent with his general view as to the duty of non-resistance. Luther had finally taken a precisely similar view on the question of the rights of Princes of the Empire. The importance of this letter to Coligny consists in the fact that it furnishes clear evidence that, so late as 1561, Calvin's view on the great question had not changed. The letter amounts to an absolute denial that persecution of true believers gives them any right to rebel. ' Abdicant

[1] Letter in Bonnet, II, p. 382.

se potestate terreni Principes dum insurgunt contra Deum.' But, whatever that means, it is clear that Daniel, had he resisted Darius, would have sinned against God.

§ 3. THE CALVINISTIC CHURCH

A considerable portion of the chapter in the *Institute* upon civil government is taken up with a refutation of Anabaptist views. ' Anabaptists' were asserting that true Christians need no government, that no true Christian can be a magistrate or bear arms or take any share in coercive government, that no Christian may plead in a court of law or prosecute offenders, that, in fact, the command ' Resist not evil' must be literally accepted and obeyed. All these propositions are gravely and carefully refuted by Calvin and shown to be inconsistent both with the Scriptures and with the needs and nature of man. Occasionally, in the course of his argument, he allows himself an expression of contempt. He speaks of people who asserted that all coercive power was evil as ' those who would that men should live pell-mell like rats in straw '.

But he argued the whole matter closely, point by point, and it is significant that he should have thought it worth while to take such views so seriously.

Very vigorously did Calvin assert the need of man for a civil and sword-bearing magistracy. He wrote impatiently of those who said, like Luther, that in a society of true Christians no law would be needed. This is but a foolish dream, he declared, since no such perfection can ever exist among men. To reject government as needless is an inhuman barbarism. Coercive government is no less necessary to man's well-being than food and water, sun and air.[1]

So far Calvin was saying, though with more emphasis and lucidity, little if anything more than was said by Melanchthon. But all this merely led up to an exposition of what the State ought to be. ' Government exists, truly,' he wrote, ' that men may eat and drink.' But it does not exist for mere life only ; it exists for the sake of good life. He did not refer to Aristotle ; and rightly, for his idea of good life was quite unlike Aristotle's. The State exists, he declared,

' that idolatry, blasphemy of the Name of God and against His truth and other scandals to religion, be not publicly set forth and broadcast among the people ; that public peace be not troubled, that each be secured in what is his own, that men's intercourse may be without fraud and violence, in fine that among Christians there may be some public and visible form of religion and that humanity be settled among men.' [2]

Foremost among the ends for which government exists is just the suppression of idolatry and blasphemy. It is the duty of the civil

[1] *Inst.*, 1541, ed. Lefranc, p. 755.
[2] Ib., 1541, ed. Lefranc, p. 755. Repeated in 1560, p. 670.

magistrate to see to it that only the pure Word of God is taught and received : it cannot be for civil authorities to decide what is idolatrous or blasphemous. 'There are,' wrote Calvin, ' as it were two worlds in man' and therefore ' il y a double régime '.[1] God, therefore, for the management of human affairs, has established two authorities, the one spiritual and ecclesiastical, the other ' politic or civil '. Just so it had seemed to Pope Gelasius I, more than a thousand years earlier. Each of these authorities has its own defined and quite separate functions, but for the welfare of humanity they must work in harmony. Neither, of itself, can be held sufficient. There must be an authority with power to say what is truth and what heresy and to declare, in the last resort, what constitutes godly living. That authority can only be the Church.

Ecclesiastical authority may, Calvin declared, be described as ' l'administration de la parolle de Dieu '. The right to administer the Word, and the power to administer it rightly, has been given by God to the pastors of the Church, by whatever name they be called.

' C'est à scavoir que par la parolle de Dieu . . . hardiment ilz osent toutes choses et contraignent toute gloire, hardiesse et vertu de ce monde d'obeyr et succomber à la majesté divine: que par icelle parolle ilz ayent commandement sur tout le monde, qu'ilz edifient la maison du Christ, subvertissent le règne de Satan ; qu'ilz paissent les brebis et tuent les loups : qu'ilz conduisent, par enseignemens et exhortations, ceux qu sont dociles ; qu'ilz contreignent et corrigent les rebelles et obstinez : qu'ilz lient, deslient, tonnent et fouldroyent : mais tout en la parolle de Dieu.' [2]

The whole of this fine passage might have been written by Hildebrand. The ' en la parolle de Dieu ' is, indeed, a saving clause ; but in fact it saved nothing and Hildebrand might equally have so used it. Much ambiguity remained. What, it had to be asked, is this Church that Calvin speaks of ? The answer given by Calvin in 1539 was somewhat vague and inconclusive. But by 1559 his answer had become definite enough for all practical purposes.

He adopted the quite ordinary distinction between the Church invisible and the Church external.[3] The true Church universal and invisible consists only of those who hear the Voice of God and not the voice of strangers, of those only who believe and do the word and the will of the Lord. Every member of that Church has the gift of the Spirit and that Church cannot err. But none can say for certain who belong to it and it can never find collective utterance. That, practically, does not matter.

' Par tout où nous voyons la parolle de Dieu estre purement preschée et escoutée, les Sacremens estre administrez selon l'institution de Christ, là il ne

---

[1] *Inst.*, 1539. End of Cap. XIII, ed. 1559, Lib. IV, 11, p. 447.
[2] Ib., 1541, ed. Lefranc, pp. 725, 726. Ed. 1559, p. 424.
[3] Eglise externe.

faut douter nullement qu'il n'y ait Eglise. . . . L'Eglise universelle est toute
la multitude laquelle accorde à la verité de Dieu et à la doctrine de sa parolle,
quelque diversité de nation qu'il y ait. . . . Que sous cette Eglise universelle,
les Eglises qui sont distribuées par chacune ville et village sont tellement com-
prinses qu'une chascune a le titre et authorité d'Eglise.' [1]

Were it otherwise God's promises to His Church would be of none
effect.

In the sentence last quoted we have the essential declaration that
was not made in 1539. Every local ' Church ', fully and truly based
on the Word of God, has the authority of the Church Universal. No
assertion less audacious would have sufficed for the establishment
of a theocratic government in Geneva. There remained the question
of the right organization of true Churches and the question whether
this could be determined by reference to the Scriptures. Calvin's
answers to these questions in 1539 were rather vague ; by 1559 they
had become fairly precise. It was his contention that the main lines
of the organization of the Church, as God intended it to be, could be
gathered with certainty from the Scriptures. But we are concerned
here with what he had to say of the powers and functions of its
governing bodies.

The Church, he declared, has no power to command ' save in the
name and in the word of God '. No one, however, had ever supposed
otherwise. The Church has no sword and no prisons : but it is part
of its office to establish a moral ' discipline ' for the whole community
and to do this it must needs possess powers of coercion of some sort.
It cannot make law ; but it is the interpreter of the law of God.
Calvin saw the Bible almost as a legal textbook : it replaced, for
him, the *Corpus Juris Civilis*. The text of Scripture is law for all
human societies, though the strictly Mosaic law has been abrogated.
Of all human societies God is the real sovereign. This law of God
it is for the governing body of the Church to interpret. It can declare
what is true and what false, what is right and what wrong. Above
all, practically, it possesses the power of excommunication independently of the civil government ; and in a godly and well-ordered
community, excommunication will involve loss of all civil rights.
The Church claims nothing from the civil magistrate that properly
belongs to him. But the magistrate himself is a member of the
Church and an ordinary though distinguished member. He can
rightly claim no exemption ' from the common subjection of the

---

[1] *Inst.*, 1559, Lib. IV, I, p. 374. Ed. 1560, p. 459. ' Ecclesiam universalem,
esse collectam ex quibuscunque gentium multitudinem, quae intervallis locorum
dissita et dispersa, in unem tamen divinae doctrinae veritate consentit, et ejusdem religionis vinculo colligata est. Sub hoc ita comprehendi singulas Ecclesias,
quae oppidatim et vicatim pro necessitatis humanae rationis dispositae sunt,
et una quaeque nomen et authoritatem Ecclesiae, jure obtineat.' Ed. 1559,
p. 374.

children of God ' and must submit himself to ecclesiastical discipline and censure like every one else.[1] Every member, for instance, of the Supreme Civil Council of Geneva should be liable to excommunication and consequent deprivation of office. By this means the supremacy of the Church would be definitely established. Even so the medieval Popes, in the name of God and the Church, had sought, by the same means, to subject all secular rulers to themselves.

In the final version of the *Institute* Calvin asserted that some kind of aristocracy is the best of all forms of government. Those I deem happy, he declared, who live under such a system ; and went on at once to insist that to attempt to establish an aristocracy by revolt against constituted authorities would be wicked and pernicious.[2] But the word aristocracy had for Calvin no such associations as it commonly had later. His ' aristocratia ' is, in one aspect, a theocracy, in another a government of the godly.

§ 4. THE GENEVAN IDEAL

So said, so done. The transformation of Geneva into Calvin's Civitas Dei was long and hard of accomplishment ; but by 1555 the work was completed so far as it possibly could be. Supreme power in Geneva had by that time been effectively transferred to two bodies, the council of the ministers or pastors of the Church and the Consistory, representing the Church of Geneva as a whole. Neither of these bodies existed till after Calvin's return to the city.

When, in 1536, Calvin first entered Geneva, the city had already succeeded in ousting Bishop and Duke ; and the powers they had held had been taken over by its councils of burgesses. The Protestant Church of Geneva had been organized and was completely controlled by the Supreme Council. Church and State had become one ; and the Council, as representing the whole people of Geneva, spoke and acted in the name of the Church. All this was in accord with the teaching of Zwingli and the actual practice of Zurich and of Berne. ' There exists,' Zwingli had declared, ' no other justice and no other human authority than that of the secular regiment.'[3] Zwingli is no doubt entitled to be styled a religious reformer and, as fully as Calvin, he made the Bible the sole authoritative rule of action and a law book for all societies. But, in effect and in outlook, he was as much a secularist as any religious man can be. He believed in the Church only as existing in and through the State. At Zurich the Council determined forms of worship, appointed ministers and

---

[1] ' Non enim magistratus, si pius est, eximere se volet communi filiorum Dei subjectione, cujus non postrema pars est, Ecclesiae ex verbo Dei judicanti se subjicere : tantum abest et judicium illud tollere debeat.' *Inst.*, 1559, Lib. IV, 11, p. 447.

[2] *Inst.*, 1559, Lib. IV, p. 552.   [3] *Anslegung des 36 Artikels.*

dictated to them, issued excommunications and had established a disciplinary censorship of morals. Geneva was following the example.

In the *Institute* Calvin declared that it is of primary importance that spiritual authority should be completely separated from that of temporal magistrates. 'Ceux qui dépouillent l'Eglise de cette puissance pour exalter le magistrat ou la justice terrienne,' corrupt the sense of the words of Christ.[1] He made it a condition of his return to Geneva in 1540 that there should be created organs for the expression of the judgements of the Church and the exercise of the jurisdiction properly attached to it. Such bodies came into existence in 1541; and from that time forward Calvin persistently endeavoured to make of them the real directive organs of government in Geneva. He encountered considerable opposition, but he was, substantially, successful.

It is, however, of some importance to realize that, to the end, the Supreme Civic Council remained formally supreme. The Church as reorganized by Calvin remained wholly within the framework of the State. Its representatives were public officials. Candidates for the ministry were examined by the body of pastors and, on approval, were recommended by it to the Council for appointment and formal installation in their charges. But it was the Civic Council that, technically, made the appointment, and the minister designate took a formal oath of fidelity to the government of Geneva. The Elders of the Church were, technically, appointed by the Supreme Council from among the members of the various elected councils of burgesses : and they too swore allegiance. It may be said that Calvin confounded Church and State as completely as did Zwingli. But whereas Zwinglian organization left the secular sovereign in real and complete control, Calvin made of the ministers, acting as a body, and the Consistory they dominated, the real masters of Geneva.

God alone is sovereign in Geneva, declares Calvin, and his Word is its law. The interpreters of the Word of God are the pastors and doctors of the Church. All must obey them so long as they speak the Word. If they agree as to what the Word is, who, in Geneva, is going to assert that they do not speak it rightly ? Calvin was insistent that it was the duty of the ministers of the Church to be zealous for the preservation of the authority of the Word. In no case must they suffer the doctrine or the discipline of the Church to be subject to the censure of men. Christ only must be master in his Church.

It is true that the Civic Council has the right to refuse appointment to persons nominated by the pastorate. There is no case of its doing so. Once appointed the pastors are practically irremovable unless their colleagues unite to denounce them. The form of the oath of fidelity they take to the civil authority is itself significant.

---

[1] *Inst.*, ed. 1559, IV, 11, p. 447.

They bind themselves to obey it ' without prejudice to the liberty they should have to teach as God commands them '. They vow so to serve the government and the people of Geneva, that in so doing they shall no way be hindered in their service to God.[1]

Every week the pastors meet in congregation. They do not take confessions, Roman fashion ; they do better. They catechize every one and interfere in every detail of family life. They direct all education. Nor are the elders any check on their activities. The elders, as such, exercise merely judicial and police functions. They have nothing to do with the settlement of doctrinal questions or with questions of principle, though on such questions, if the pastors disagree, they may be consulted. The supreme governing body of the Church is, it is true, the Consistory, in which the lay element of elders outnumber the pastors. But, naturally, since the elders are practically nominees of the pastorate and that their proper functions are strictly subordinate, the pastors dominate the Consistory. This body it is that really governs or at least directs government in Geneva. It has rights of entry into every household and can order arrest. It has definite jurisdiction in a large number of cases. It decides all marriage suits, enforces Church-going, punishes usury and cheating, blasphemy and adultery and any conduct it judges frivolous or profane. It keeps watch for heresy. From 1555 onwards it can excommunicate without seeking approval from any other body. An excommunicated person is deprived of office in the city and banished if he fails to make adequate submission. But the real centre of government is the body of pastors, official interpreters of the law of God. It is for them to decide whether, according to God's Word, this or that should be done. They are able, therefore, to direct public policy and impose on the nominal government submission to the will of God as they understand it.

Calvin conceived that the effective sovereign of the State as it ought to be would be God Himself. The discussion of the nature of law in the chapter of the *Institute* on civil government is by far the weakest portion of that very strong piece of writing. He there laid it down that all human law should be in accord with the law of God as expressed in the Scriptures and with that notion of equity which is the same everywhere among all peoples. But though he speaks frequently of the duty of magistrates to maintain and enforce law, he has practically nothing to say of human law-making. He did not face the question of how far legislative authority exists in the State ; or rather he saw no question to face. He recognized that human law must vary with varying needs, but this seemed to him mere matter of practical detail. All that needed to be done was

[1] *Les Ordonnances Ecclesiastiques de la Ville de Genève*, A. Chauvin, 1561. The text is given almost complete in Cornelius, *Historische Arbeiten*.

to apply the law of God to a tangle of circumstance. The Bible was a digest of divine law and the primary business of government was its explication and enforcement. Law, in all essentials, is made already, once for all. It is for 'the Church' to say what law is needed. The constitution of his ideal State seemed to him to provide for all the law-making that could be required.

Calvin's system has been regarded as democratic, at least in tendency. A system may, of course, tend to produce results radically inconsistent with the ideas and aspirations of its founder and incapable of being logically derived from or reconciled with them. An arbitrary despotism may, in that sense, be democratic in tendency. In no other sense was, I think, Calvin's.

It has been said that he conceived of the Church, democratically, as a voluntary association of individuals. He insisted that all the inhabitants of Geneva should make a confession of faith. Geneva was to be a city of true believers. But what was demanded was subscription to a predetermined doctrine, with the threat of expulsion from the city to back the demand. There need, evidently, be little that is voluntary about an association so formed. Nor can Calvin's organization of government, in the Church or in Geneva, be called democratic in any acceptable sense. So far as there existed a democratic element in his system, it was derived, not from Calvin, but from the old constitution of Geneva which he had, perforce, to accept and to work with. Calvin spoke of his elders as 'representing' the Church. He meant only that they were duly empowered, so far as their authority extended, to speak and to act in its name. He certainly did not mean that they were mandatories of a sovereign people; he did not conceive them as representing a popular will. They were, it was laid down, to be 'gens de bonne et haute vie, sans reproches, hors de tout soupcon, surtout craignants Dieu et ayans bonne prudence spirituelle '.[1] Nor did the elders in any sense govern the Church. As for the all-important ministers, they were formally appointed by an annually elected Council and formally accepted by their congregations. But the appointment by the Council seems to have been almost as completely a fiction as the popular endorsement of it certainly was.

The old law and institutions of Geneva embodied a principle that may be called democratic, and under Calvin's arrangements it became a fiction. He left Geneva far less democratically constituted than he found it.[2]

Calvin's Consistory was, it is true, an elected body and included

---

[1] *Ordonnances Ecclesiastiques.*

[2] ' On croit rêver,' says M. de Lagarde, ' lorsque l'on apprend de M. Doumergue, que " les conceptions calvinistes authentiques " sont, ' à l'origine du système représentatif.' *Recherches*, op. cit., p. 454. I entirely agree.

a majority of lay persons. That it was not elected on a basis that can be called democratic is, it must be admitted, a fact relatively unimportant. But the essential fact is that, under Calvin's system, the machinery of government in Geneva was dominated and directed by a strictly clerical body. It was definitely intended that it should be so. What Calvin provided, or tried to provide, for Geneva was government by an aristocracy of the godly. His system was dominated by a small practically self-electing group of officially ecclesiastical persons. It was their domination alone that gave distinctive quality to the system and it was precisely their domination without which Calvin's ideal could not be realized. Only in a city of the godly could a democratic constitution be compatible with Calvin's aspirations. It might, indeed, be said that Calvin's thought was democratic in that he equalized all men in a common corruption.[1] He did not really do so ; and it was just upon the distinction in his mind between the godly few and the reprobate many, that his system of government was ultimately founded.

In that system the distinction between crime and sin tended to vanish : all crime is primarily sin and all sin offence against the true sovereign. Calvin conceived man as naturally corrupt and evil, a rebel against God. The business of government was to maintain the honour of the Sovereign Deity and enforce His will on recalcitrant man. Obedience to that will must be obtained through force and through fear, if in no other way it could be obtained. Cal·in was strangely preoccupied with the idea of the honour of God. That ' honour ' required that man should be forced to fear, if they could not love. It is saved when men who will not willingly obey are constrained to cower. An important factor in the new constitution and government of Geneva was Calvin's total lack of the saving grace of humour.

§ 5. CALVIN AND MEDIEVAL PAPALIST THEORY

A modern writer, himself a Genevan pastor, has well stated from Calvin's own point of view, the resulting situation. ' L'Etat,' he says, ' est le pouvoir exécutif de la loi divine, l'eglise le pouvoir judiciaire qui determine ce qui est legislation divine et veille à ce que cette legislation soit oberé. L'Eglise interprète et remontre, l'Etat impose l'obéissance par la force ; elle accomplit les fonctions de

---

[1] This, he says, is certain : ' à savoir que l'entendement de l'homme est tellement du tout aliéné de la justice de Dieu, qu'il ne peut rien imaginer, concevoir ne comprendre, sinon toute méchanceté, iniquité et corruption. Semblablement que son coeur est tout envenimé de peché, qu'il ne peut produire que toute perversité. Et s'il advient qu'il en sorte quelque chose qui ait apparence de bien ; néantmoins que l'entendement demeure toujours envelopé en hypocrisie et vanité ; le coeur adonné à toute malice.' *Inst.*, ed. 1541, Chap. II.

l'âme, lui celle du corps.' [1]   It is precisely the conception of Boniface VIII.

Politically Calvin revived for Protestantism the theory of the supremacy of a visible and organized Church. Up to a certain point at least, his conception of the State is that of the Bull *Unam Sanctam.* Medieval theory started like Calvin's, with the posing of two ideally separate and concurrent powers and ended by asserting the supreme sovereignty of one of them. It was not long before this fact was perceived and men began to point out that, from the point of view of secular sovereigns, there was little or nothing to choose between Calvinism and Popery. In fact the Genevan system was necessarily antagonistic to all governments standing on any other basis than its own. By means of his doctrine of the duty of submission to all established governments alike, Calvin temporarily and partially got rid of that dangerous antagonism. But, sooner or later, one way or another, occasion serving, it was inevitable that his followers should repudiate that part of his teaching.

There is, of course, a formal difference between medieval thought and that of Calvin that is not unimportant. The medieval Papalist was thinking of a Church that covered and included many cities and kingdoms and coincided with none of them. It was, therefore, necessarily thought of as existing independently of, and outside of, any one State. From the point of view of any one kingdom or city it was, in spite of its ubiquity, a foreign and external body. The Pope himself was external to all particular states in Christendom. But to Calvin the Church Universal is either a group of localized churches or a thing altogether invisible, apprehended only by faith. His visible Church is bounded by and contained in a single State. The State itself is a church and is under no human external authority. Yet the difference between medieval conceptions and those of Calvin is not really so great as it seems when we put it thus. Medieval thinkers tried, for long, to ignore the actually profound political divisions of Christendom. Persistently they thought of Christendom as an Empire and alongside the Pope set an ideal Emperor. They talked, even in the twelfth century, of a *respublica generis humani* that was also *ecclesia universalis.* They, too, were seeking a reconciling unity, in which Church and State should be one.

Alike Calvin and medieval Papalists asserted that God has endowed His Church with constituted authorities, empowered to speak and to act for it, and that to these belongs the interpretation of His revealed will to men. Whether the Church be conceived of as external to the State or included within it, matters little in this connection. In either case it is for the divinely instituted ecclesiastical authority to decide in the last resort what is right and what wrong in action

[1] E. Choisy : *La Theocratie à Genève.*

and in thought ; and it is, in either case, this same authority which must ultimately control and direct all secular government. It is true that Calvin's pastorate cannot speak with the same authority that belongs to Pope or General Council. They are interpreters of Scripture and not, apparently, inspired interpreters. They are, after all, fallible men. Their authority can only be conceived as absolute on the basis of an assumption that has yet to be considered and that lies at the root of the whole Calvinistic system : the assumption that the meaning of the revelation in the Scriptures is demonstrable and has in fact been demonstrated.

But there are yet more profound differences between the Genevan ideal of the State and any Papalist ideal, than that involved in different modes of conceiving of the Church. Calvin's ideal Church-State rested on a conception of man and of man's needs far narrower than that of Aquinas. Aquinas had conceived the function of secular government to be that of establishing for all such a degree of security and well-being as would liberate men for the pursuit of their true end, under the guidance of the Church. Calvin started with the conception of men as rebels and conceived it to be the business of government to coerce all into at least outward conformity with the divine will. By means of ecclesiastical discipline and control, he attempted to build up the city of God in Geneva, and to realize, as he says, ' in this mortal and transitory life some taste of the immortal and incorruptible beatitude '.[1] The narrow and inflexible character of his idea of righteous living, led him to claim, in practice, for his Church, far more intensive and oppressive rights of interference than were ever, practically, claimed for the Roman clergy. This is not the place for a discussion of Calvin's ethics ; but his ideal of the State cannot be understood without reference to his conception of righteousness in life. It can hardly be denied that he imposed upon Geneva a system of ' discipline ' and a yoke of inhibitions, calculated to thwart individuality, to hamper or frustrate all intellectual effort, to stereotype at once manners and opinions, to make art impossible and to fill life with fear instead of with beauty. The Calvinistic discipline at once hardened and sterilized. It rested on a notion of ' goodness ' having little relation to the real needs and aspirations of humanity.

It is only superficially that Calvin's theory can be identified with Papalist theory of the thirteenth century. Except that both subordinate civil to ecclesiastical power, there is little in common between him and Aquinas. Comparison is not to the advantage of Calvin. The view of the great medieval thinker was far broader, more human and more rational. But it may be noted that a real similarity does exist between the government of Geneva under Calvin and the government of Florence under Savonarola. Savonarola proclaimed Jesus

[1] *Inst.*, 1541, ed. Lefranc, p. 754.

Christ King of Florence and himself governed the city without office, as the inspired interpreter of the Sovereign's will. He endeavoured to effect a compulsory reformation of the morals and manners of the Florentines. He forbade gaming and dancing, closed the drink shops, carried on a crusade against luxury in dress, made bonfires of mirrors and ornaments, musical instruments, books of verses and editions of the pagan classics. Like Luther he denounced Aristotle. He put a stop to classical education and endeavoured to confine the young to a diet of the Scriptures and extracts from the Fathers. He went farther than Calvin.

§ 6. THE BASIC ASSUMPTION

There remains to consider that which, after all, seems to be the central and essential assumption of the whole Calvinistic system. According to Calvin, wherever the Word of God is purely preached and the sacraments duly administered, there is a true Church. The pastors of such a Church have authority to control and discipline, in fact to rule, society ' en la parolle dé Dieu '. There is to be no glossing or addition ; the pastors are simply to expound the Word of God and insist on conformity with it. But who is to say when the Word is purely preached and the sacraments duly ministered ? For it to be possible to say with certainty, either there must exist some- where on earth an infallible authority, or the meaning and implications of the Scriptures must be, if not exactly easy to ascertain, at least strictly demonstrable. But Calvin denied the existence of any infallible authority. There remained only the alternative. It had to be asserted that no sufficiently equipped, rational and earnest inquirer can give to the Scriptures any interpretation differing in any important respect from that given in the *Institute*. Disagreement with, at least, the main conclusions of Calvin, must be held to involve either ignorance or some kind of perversity or dishonesty. Absurd as the assertion might be, it had to be made. For, if the Scriptures be ambiguous, if quite different views may be based on them by honest and competent students, the whole ideal structure of the Calvinist theocracy collapses.

In his preface to the *Institute* of 1539, Calvin remarked that those who are not much exercised in Scripture have need of guidance from those more enlightened. He added that the book he had written was rather God's than his own. ' Dieu m'a fait la grace,' he wrote later, ' de me declarer ce qui est bon ou mauvais.' [1] But, for all his confidence, Calvin never claimed for himself actual inspiration, as did Muntzer and Savonarola. He merely felt certain that he had demonstrated the true import of the Word of God. His view of the matter was expressed in an official declaration of the Council of Geneva

[1] Letter to M. d'Aubeterre, 1553. Bonnet, I, p. 389.

in 1552, to the effect that the doctrine of the *Institute* was the sacred doctrine of God and that no one for the future was to say a word against it. Calvin was apparently incapable of believing that those who disagreed with him could be honest, unless they were simply ignorant. In the *Institute* of 1539 he summarized, rather poorly, the arguments and assertions made by the Romanists in support of their position. But he calmly assumed that their argumentation was insincere. ' Toute leur intention est,' he remarked, ' de ne tenir compte de la verité, pour servir à leur proffit par tout moyen que possible leur est.' That anyone should have written such words in the days of Thomas More and L'Hôpital, Erasmus and Loyola, might be astonishing, were it not that, in religious controversy, as in modern politics, such fatuity is chronic.

To be convinced that you are right is one thing ; to believe that no honest and reasonable person can disagree with you is quite another. It was this second preposterous proposition that was the basis of Calvin's theory as to the duty of the magistrate in relation to heresy.[1] But it was equally needed for his political system as a whole. All the later Calvinists took the same view.[2] The assumption was made by Knox, in his famous interview with Mary Stewart, with the most frank and naïve fatuity.[3] Yet it remains somewhat hard to understand how so severe and logical a thinker as Calvin could come to be possessed by so gross a delusion.

Consideration of Calvin's position in the world of Protestantism throws, however, some light upon this mystery. Calvin was a statesman and a cosmopolitan statesman. During the years from 1538 to 1564 Geneva increasingly became a centre of systematic propaganda. Calvin was increasingly looked to for advice and direction by the Protestants not only of Switzerland and France, but by those of the Netherlands, England and Scotland and considerable part of Germany. His vast correspondence extended to all these lands. It is clear that he was engaged in an effort to get established a great cosmopolitan Protestant Church or system of Churches, united in all essentials, over against that of Rome. It had been possible for Wolsey or Contarini or Luther to dream of a reform of the Church as a whole, without any schism. But, long before 1550, it was manifest that the Papal Church could neither be converted nor destroyed. The attitude of Spain and of the government of France, the Council of

---

[1] See the following chapter.

[2] ' God in these days,' wrote Jewel, ' hath so amazed the adversaries of His gospel and hath caused them so openly and grossly to lay abroad their follies to the sight of all the world, that no man now, be he never so ignorant, can think he may justly be excused ' for not seeing the truth. *Preface of the Defence of the Apology.* Jewel's Works. Parker Soc., III.

[3] See Chap. VI.

Trent and Pope Paul IV, had made that glaringly obvious. On the other hand, Protestantism tended to split up into a multitude of antagonistic sects and of localized churches dominated by secular governments for secular ends. For the arrest of this disintegration two things were needful : firstly a clear and coherent body of doctrine and its acceptance by all Protestant Churches, and secondly an organization of the State such as should everywhere establish the supremacy of the Church. These two things Calvin, in the *Institute* and at Geneva, made a really heroic attempt to provide. One still, occasionally, hears talk of something called ' the Protestant Religion '. Had such a thing ever existed it would have meant the success of Calvin's effort. Writing to Protector Somerset, in 1548, Calvin urged upon him the need of agreement upon ' une somme résolue de la doctrine que tous doivent prescher. Jamais,' he declared, ' l'Eglise de Dieu ne se conservera sans catéchisme.' [1] But it was necessary to be convinced that the interpretation of the Scriptures given in the *Institute* could not reasonably be disputed, before the success of such an effort could even be thought of as possible.

[1] Letter of October 22. In Bonnet.

CHAPTER V

THE TOLERATION CONTROVERSY

§ 1. INTRODUCTORY

THERE seems still to exist an impression, in some quarters, that only a few isolated thinkers in the sixteenth century conceived of legal religious toleration as a thing desirable. That impression is very far from the truth. If, in the sixteenth century, governments and ecclesiastical organizations generally rejected the view that toleration of religious opinion was desirable if not actually obligatory, that was certainly not because such views were not openly maintained. Never has the case for universal religious toleration been more fully presented than it was by Castellion from a religious point of view, and by Acontius from a point of view not specifically religious. Castellion and Acontius were far from being isolated.

It was absolutely impossible in the sixteenth century that the question of how governments should, or had best, deal with religious contumacy, or with ' heresy ', should not be widely debated and from many different points of view. It was a question which, however put, directly and acutely affected the lives of multitudes of men and women all over Western Europe. Every government had to make up its mind at least as to practical action ; and that in face of all manner of difficulties and complications. To the question as a practical one put in general terms, every possible answer, as has already been stated,[1] was given. It was maintained that under some circumstances it was expedient, under others inexpedient, to ' persecute ', and that the ruler had a right to judge and to act at his discretion. It was also maintained that he had no choice about the matter. It was asserted that he was bound to endeavour to stamp out false religion by force, if force were necessary ; it was maintained, on the contrary, that he was bound, morally, to allow people to preach and worship as they pleased, so long as they did not break the peace or incite to breach of it. Often, especially in the second half of the century, the question was put as one of mere expediency, with the assumption that the political sovereign was under no obligation to

[1] See Chap. II, p. 224.

73

do or not do. But there was, also, much controversy on the question as one of duty. ' Toleration ' as a practical solution of intolerable difficulties and ' toleration ' as a general principle of action in relation to religious differences, both appear quite early in the sixteenth century.

If the question be put regardless of circumstance, there can arise no question of expediency. You may ask : ' What grounds are there for treating any religious opinion, or rather the expression of it, as criminal ? ' Or you may ask : ' Is it obligatory on the political sovereign to endeavour to maintain true religion by force, if necessary, against all adversaries ? ' However you put the question, it is not easy to answer, except by means of question-begging assumptions. In any case, no answer that Calvin or Castellion or anyone else could give was of much use to sixteenth-century governments. For what they had to deal with was not religious opinion merely as such. Religious opinion does not exist in a vacuum. It was the practical conclusions that were drawn from, or inseparable from, such opinion that troubled governments. What governments had to deal with were demands that the Mass should be suppressed by force as idolatry, or that monastic or other church property should be confiscated, or episcopacy abolished, or church courts deprived of jurisdiction, or that the canon law should be swept away. There were, of course, other difficulties also. A Catholic government desiring, for any reason, to ' persecute ', might always fall back on the authority of the Pope in self-justification. But there was serious objection to doing so. To persecute on the ground that the Pope orders civil magistrates to destroy heresy raises formidable doubts as to where the Pope's right to give orders ends. Protestant governments could not always ignore the possible effects of their action upon their near neighbours. But, in the main, what sixteenth-century governments had to deal with was a revolutionary effort involving an attack on vested interests in property and jurisdiction. That the attack was made in the name of religion, only made it the more difficult to deal with it effectively. They had not to deal with people humbly asking only to be allowed to worship in their own way undisturbed. Had that been all, we should have heard very little of persecution. But that attitude was not taken by many, nor for long. The Protestants were out to destroy and indeed could hardly build without destroying.

Before ever the storm and stress developed in England, the greatest English thinker of his time summed up the essential features of the position, there as elsewhere.

' In the Land of Nowhere,' says Sir Thomas More, ' it had been established by King Utopus that it should be lawful for every man to favour and follow what religion he would and that he might do the best he could to bring others to his opinion. . . . This surely be thought a very unmeet and foolish thing, and a point of arrogant presumption, to compel all others by violence and threatenings to agree to the same that thou believest to be true.' [1]

The tolerance of the Utopians was not indeed absolutely complete. Belief in man's survival of physical death, and belief in God's government of the world for good, they held to be essential to good citizenship.[2] He who denied these things was, therefore, excluded from all public office, 'howbeit they put him to no punishment, because they be persuaded that it is in no man's power to believe what he list'.[3] Churches in which the services were officially regulated existed in Utopia, but those services were expressive only of what all the sects were agreed upon. Nothing was to be heard in them offensive to any Utopian sect.

Apparently this was the first suggestion of a practically complete legal recognition of diversity in religion, that was made in the sixteenth century. But More knew well that, so far from it being a suggestion of common sense, it was fantastic and impracticable. In his Dialogue concerning Heresies he supplied the corrective. 'Heresies breed disorders and fear of these have been the cause that Princes and peoples have been constrained to punish heresies by terrible death, whereas else more easy ways had been taken with them.' [4] But is such action really necessary ?

'By my soul,' says one of the speakers in the Dialogue, 'I would the world were all agreed to take all violence and confusion away upon all sides, christian and heathen, and that no man were constrained to believe but as he could by grace, wisdom and good works induced and that he that would go to God go on a God's name and he that will go to the devil, the devil go with him.' [5]

This, More answers, is very well, and if heretics would abstain from violence perhaps none would be used against them. But the heretics are not content to argue and to preach ; if they were, the true faith would have nothing to fear.

'But since violence is used on that part and Christ's faith not there suffered to be preached and taken, he that would now suffer that sect to be preached or taught among Christian men and not punish and destroy the doers, were a plain enemy to Christ.' [6]

We are ready, in fact, to abolish the death penalty, but ' que messieurs les assassins commencent '.

'Princes are bound to see that they shall not suffer their people to be reduced and corrupted by heretics, since the peril shall in short while grow to as great,

---

[1] *Utopia*, Clarendon Press, ed. 1895, p. 272.
[2] *Utopia*, p. 274.   [3] Ib., p. 275.
[4] *A Dialogue concerninge hereseyes and matters of religion*, 1528. Works, 1557, p. 274.
[5] *Dialogue*, p. 275.   [6] Ib., p. 275.

both with men's souls withdrawn from God and their goods lost and their bodies destroyed by common sedition, insurrection and open war, within the bowels of their own land.' [1]

The question of how far diversity in religion could legally be tolerated was not, for the sixteenth century, mainly a religious or mainly a moral question. It was a question of public order. The action of sixteenth-century governments, like that of other governments, was determined not by principles, but mainly by the lines of least resistance. Princes and their ministers were, as a rule, little if at all influenced by religious considerations or ideals. They tended, I think, to be as tolerant as they dared be. But how tolerate those who avow their intention of not tolerating us ? How tolerate those who desire not merely to refashion ideas but to demolish established institutions and confiscate property ? The failure of Catherine de Medici to establish two religions peacefully in France illustrates the fact that the intolerance of governments was either a result of the intolerance of sects, or of the fact that the religious reformation desired by one group threatened the material interests of another.

Many people of the present day find it hard to understand how men can ever have thought it right to kill others for their religious opinions. The difficulty seems to be due partly to ignorance of the circumstances under which this was done, and partly to mere emotional revolt. It is, to begin with, not realized that this is not really what was done. I do not mean that such a thing was never done at all, or that there were not, in the sixteenth century, a large number of people willing to do such a thing. But no government ever carried on systematic persecution out of unadulterated zeal for truth or anxiety for the salvation of souls. Men would have to be very much more religious or very much more simple than they ever have been, within historic time, to make religious persecution, in the strict sense, possible. Usually, to say the least, the adulteration was so large in amount that the element of religious motive in so-called religious persecution is barely visible. Not, however, that there was not an excellent case to be made out for religious persecution pure and unadulterated. On the basis of intellectual assumptions current in the sixteenth century, to put heretics to death was a perfectly rational proceeding, and one that needed no special harshness or brutality of disposition. Intellectual assumptions are necessary to any case.

Could a government composed of modern politicians be set to rule under sixteenth-century conditions, I see no reason whatever to suppose that they would act otherwise than did sixteenth-century rulers. I am inclined to think it true that people in the sixteenth century were by temperament and disposition less tolerant than

[1] *Dialogue*, p. 279.

people of to-day. That, I think, is the most that should be said. To imagine that they were very much less tolerant is, I think, a dangerous illusion. We are apt, it seems, to confuse tolerance with mere legal toleration. Tolerance is a mental attitude, while legal toleration may express mere indifference or be a mere counsel of despair.

In the sixteenth century intolerance manifested itself chiefly in connection with religious differences ; and there is, of course, no doubt that we are now far more tolerant of each other's religious, or irreligious, opinions than people were then. There was, then, a widespread belief that there must needs be some sense in which it was possible for governments to maintain true religion and suppress dangerous error ; there was a belief that unity in religion was necessary to national unity and security ; there was a sense that toleration of religious differences might lead to a disintegration of moral standards ; there was also, of course, a tendency to see dissentients as morally perverse. These beliefs and tendencies, except the la st, seem almost to have disappeared. But they have not disappeared because they were unfounded or irrational. Our greater tolerance in respect of religious differences is partly due to their disappearance and partly to many other causes. It is due partly to changes in law, partly to that multiplication of sects which began in the sixteenth century and to which people gradually became so accustomed as to come to think of it as proper and inevitable, partly to simple indifference or scepticism of various kinds and degrees, partly to the fact that religious differences nowadays do not directly threaten anyone's property or personal rights.

But it does not follow, because we are more tolerant of religious difference, that there has been any marked development of a tolerant attitude. Intolerance manifests itself in connection with things in which people, for whatever reason, are passionately interested or with which personal interests are intimately bound up. At the present day, it is manifested most conspicuously in connection not with religion but with politics. The modern politician who asserts or implies that his political opponents are either knaves or fools, might indeed be taken simply as proclaiming himself one or the other. But, unhappily, the case is not so simple. If his utterance be insincere there is, indeed, no doubt about his knavery. But if it be sincere he is not necessarily simply a fool. He is exactly in the position of Calvin. It is unfortunately possible even for a man of great intellectual power to take that absurd view of things. Again, if we look at the action of governments, I understand that neither Italian Fascism nor Russian Bolshevism are distinguished by a tolerant attitude towards political opinion. There is certainly a difference between sixteenth-century intolerance as distinctively religious and twentieth-century intolerance as distinctively political. But the difference is not nearly so great as it might seem. What has to be realized is that, in the sixteenth century, religious opinion was, far more often than not, political opinion also. Had it not been so there would have been little ' religious persecution '.

One hears, sometimes, talk about something called ' the principle of religious toleration '. There seems to be an implication that there is just one ' principle ' on which legal toleration may rationally be based ; but it is not very clear what this is. The phrase appears to be one of those catchwords that are abundant in the structure of what is sometimes strangely referred to as ' modern thought ', and which are useful in saving people the trouble of thinking. We must rid our minds of it if we are to appreciate sixteenth-century thought on the subject. It will be well, also, to refrain, in this connection as in others, from talk about the ' spirit of the age '. I have somewhere read that Beza's *De Haereticis* was an unfortunate aberration on the part of that Protestant champion, due to the spirit of the age. Beza's *De Haereticis* was a controversial work written directly in answer to another, whose author, apparently, had escaped the influence of that spirit. It was also, as it happens, logically derived from Beza's system of ideas. Is there any reason for saying that the spirit of the age expressed itself better in Calvin and Pope Paul IV than in Rabelais or More, Montaigne or Hooker ? All these alike, it should be remembered, were exceptional rather than typical people. But the matter is not worth argument. Such jargon appears to me to be a mere cloak for ignorance or thoughtlessness. There is, really, nothing to argue about.

Certain predispositions existed, in the first half of the sixteenth century, that made, some for, some against, the acceptance of any sort of principle of toleration. There was a certain predisposition to the persecution of religious dissent. This was to some indefinable extent traditional ; not, I think, to any great extent. But people in general were more conscious of, or preoccupied with, religious controversy than earlier ; and that because such controversy was having, or evidently might have, very definite reaction on their own lives and fortunes. Also it was very generally assumed that all the questions raised could be precisely and conclusively answered and that it was highly important that they should be, since one's salvation might depend on believing rightly. There was an intense and quite reasonable reluctance to admit that they were unanswerable. All this naturally gave rise to a disposition to regard it as the business of government to protect people from damning error and its possible earthly consequences, by destroying heresy root and branch.

On the other hand, the tendency of Renaissance culture was towards an acceptance of toleration. What is here meant by the Renaissance is that shift of the point of view which brought earth into the foreground, instead of heaven and hell, and partially, at least, released men from preoccupation with a life hereafter. The period of the Renaissance was one in which men were falling more and more deeply in love with life as they knew it in everyday experience. Human relations became more interesting than man's relatio to God.[1] The Renaissance brought with it increased delight in the things of this world and intense curiosity about it all. This expressed itself in ardent study of classical writings and classical civilization, in scientific exploration and in art which had reference only to earthly values. It expressed itself in varying degrees of scepticism and tolerant morality and, also, in a vision of a reconstructed Christianity which should include the new learning with the old.

Calvin may be said to have effected a clean breach with the Renaissance and with him Protestantism, though not of course all Protestantism, became in a definite sense reactionary. With the Calvinists, preoccupation with man's relation to God was again dominant. It is significant that the classic presentation of the case for the suppression of heresy by force should have come from Calvin himself. That Protestantism as such claimed for the individual a right to form and to express what conclusions he could about religion, is very far from the fact. But such a claim was, at least, implicit in the attitude of the scholars, thinkers and poets who derived from the Renaissance in Italy. It is barefaced in Rabelais and Pomponazzi, and something more than implicit in Erasmus or Etienne Dolet ; it is evident in the Platonizing Christians of the school of Ficino, in Margaret of Navarre and her circle ; it is visible even in the attitude of such cultured princes of the Church as the Cardinals Pole and Sadoleto. All through the century this leaven was working in the lump. It was reinforced by an increasing positive scepticism, which was largely an effect of the impression produced by a multiplicity of sects, all claiming to possess truth more or less exclusively.

It has even been suggested that throughout the first half of the sixteenth century there was a possibility that Pope, governments and reformers alike might agree on some principle of toleration, and that the issue was only really decided by Pope Paul IV and the Council of Trent on one side, and by Calvin on the other. But no pronouncement by the Pope could for long have affected the action of the governments of France and Spain, nor would any action by Calvin have affected that of Lutheran Princes or of England. Nor is it true that Protestantism at large committed itself with Calvin to the doctrine that the civil magistrate was bound to undertake the suppression of false religion. So inconvenient a doctrine was unlikely to appeal to

[1] I am not, of course, expressing any opinion as to whether this was good or bad, gain or loss. My opinion on the point, if I have one, is completely irrelevant to this discussion.

any government unless to one operating on a very small scale. It is true that Protestantism had not before 1553 committed itself to persecution on principle. But neither did it do so later. There were some, though not many, who maintained that Protestantism was bound to assert a principle of toleration or fall into self-contradiction. It may be remarked, too, that by asserting a right of liberty of conscience against the State, the Protestants could have secured a basis for that claim to a right of rebellion which they came to need. It is certainly conceivable that, under altered circumstances, religious Protestantism might have adopted some principle of toleration. But always, in discussing such speculations, one comes finally to the proposition that had things been different, different they would have been. That, obviously, is not worth saying. Yet, certainly, there was for a time, among the early Protestants a rather strong tendency in that direction, as is illustrated by Luther's utterances. It may, indeed, be true that it was chiefly the development of Anabaptism which rendered this tendency abortive. Their doctrine of the inner light, which tended to make even the Scriptures superfluous, their denial of one or other of the doctrines regarded as essential by official Protestantism, their assertion of the freedom of the will, their rejection of civil authority, their supposed advocacy of a community of goods and the extravagances of fanatics like Storch and Muntzer, seemed to threaten to produce social as well as theological anarchy. It was terribly difficult to see how to deal with them. By 1530 it may be said that official Protestantism had committed itself to the suppression by force of Anabaptist congregations. In doing so it had, perhaps, crossed the Rubicon.

Protest was made quite early from the side of official Protestantism against the persecution even of Anabaptists. ' Aequum non est,' Erasmus had written in 1524, 'ut quivis error igni puniatur nisi accedat seditio aut aliud crimen quod leges capite puniunt.' [1] At a critical moment in 1529 Johan Brenz issued a treatise maintaining the same thesis. [2] Brenz distinguished between secular and spiritual sin. The former is that which disturbs the public peace, and it must needs be punished and suppressed by the civil magistrate. But against spiritual sin the sword is worse than useless. Nothing, Brenz declared, following Luther, so much promotes heresy and Anabaptism as the use of the civil sword against them. ' Breviter, incredulitas et haeresis non civilis sed spiritualis gladii poenis subjecta sunt.' He argued that the communism of Anabaptists gave no reasonable ground for taking action against them. It would, he declared, be more reasonable to put monks and nuns to death as communists. If any

---

[1] Letter to George of Saxony.
[2] ' An Magistratus jure possit occidere Anabaptistas.' In *Tractatus Theologici*, 493.

break the civil law or disturb public order, let him be punished, baptized or rebaptized ; otherwise let the sword remain in the scabbard. As chief religious adviser to the tolerant Duke of Würtemberg, Brenz became later so important a personage, that his action at Stuttgart and his declared opinions, gravely embarrassed Calvin and Beza.

It may indeed be said, with at least a good deal of truth, that Anabaptists were persecuted rather as social revolutionaries or anarchists than as heretics. Melanchthon argued that inasmuch as the Anabaptists denied the duty of obedience to magistrates, refused to bear arms and, above all, held the ' impious dogma ' that Christians ought to have their goods in common, their views were essentially seditious. So far as his argument on this subject goes, there is little difference between him and Brenz. Except for the suppression of Catholic practices, regarded as idolatrous, and the persecution of Anabaptists as sedition-mongers, there was, it has been said, very little religious persecution by Protestant authorities before 1553. But how else could it have been ? The confusion of opinion among Protestants made anything else almost impossible until Calvin had formulated a coherent system of Protestant doctrine. It is, I think, true that, down to 1554, the tendency of Protestant authorities was towards toleration of all who were not Catholics or Anabaptists. These, however, are large exceptions ; and it must be remembered that the term Anabaptism covered a multitude of sins. It is manifestly unjust to charge Calvin with having substituted a principle of persecution for one of freedom in religion. None the less is it true that the burning of Servetus at Geneva provoked a crisis, and proved a turning-point in the development of Protestant opinion. Calvin's attitude went far to determine that of large numbers of Protestants.

§ 2. CALVIN AND SERVETUS

In October, 1553, Michael Servetus (Miguel Serveto) was burned at Geneva as a blasphemous heretic. His execution gave him a significance he would never otherwise have acquired. It provoked a controversy which echoed through the remainder of the century and was revived in the most acute form in the Netherlands by Coornhert and the ' Arminians '. It defined an issue never again to be lost sight of. It led to the raising of the question of religious liberty in a form which made escape or evasion impossible, unless by means of a doctrine of unlimited secular sovereignty.

Servetus was a Spaniard and had been born, apparently, in 1509 or 1511. His career had been full of vicissitude and adventure, mental and bodily. In 1531 he had published a book intended to correct what he regarded as erroneous views commonly held concerning the Trinity.[1] In 1542 he had made himself responsible for a book-

[1] *De Trinitatis Erroribus.*

seller's edition of Pagnini's Latin Bible, with rationalizing notes of his own, interpreting prophetic references to Christ as referring primarily to persons and events of the time of the prophecy. His *Christianismi Restitutio* had been printed in 1552. His views seem to have involved an attempt to ' rationalize ' Trinitarian doctrine, and included a denial of Christ as the Eternal Son.[1] He appears to have been a sincere seeker after truth, eager and self-confident and quite extraordinarily imprudent. In the years 1546–1547 he had written to Calvin a series of letters freely criticizing the doctrine of the *Institute*. It has been suggested that, in the trial of Servetus, Calvin was seeking a personal revenge for the lack of deference the unlucky man had shown him. But there is no sufficient reason for imputing such petty feeling to Calvin, and no sort of need to do so. His view of Servetus and of what it was proper to do with him, derived logically and directly from his whole system of ideas.

But it is important to observe that the heresies for which Servetus was condemned, were concerned with questions difficult even to state, remote from the thought of ordinary men, and not necessarily in the least connected with social or political life. It was a case of pure and unadulterated heresy. The views of Servetus on baptism might be, and were, held to associate him with the Anabaptists : but he obviously belonged to a different category. No one could say that Servetus was a danger to the bodies or the goods of men. It could hardly be said that he was a rebel against anything human, but official orthodoxy.

Yet the writings and the conduct of Servetus convinced Calvin that here was the worst kind of heretic. His errors concerning the Trinity were good enough to burn him on : they were far from being all there was against him. He was unsound on baptism, he denied predestination, he was contemptuous of the *Institute*, he had treated the Bible itself as no one could safely be allowed to treat the Bible. His attitude during his trial must have removed any doubts Calvin may have felt ; if he ever felt doubt. His answers to the articles of indictment were contemptuous in form. He told the Genevan prophet that he was talking of what he did not understand, and accused him of deliberate perversion of texts. He alluded to ' savage barking ', and at one moment demanded that Calvin should be made to stand in the dock with him. He was utterly and contemptuously denying Calvin's main pretension : that the full meaning of the Christian revelation had been made clear and undeniable.

That but for Calvin's insistence Servetus would not have been put to death, is clear from the records of the trial. All through, Calvin acted as prosecutor ; and when he knew that an appeal was

---

[1] It may be noted, incidentally, that in the practice of his medical profession he seems to have discovered the pulmonary circulation of the blood.

to be made to the more important of the Swiss churches for their opinion on the case, he wrote beforehand to Sulzer at Basle and to Bullinger at Zurich, to prepare their minds in his sense. The answers officially returned were all ambiguous. Berne expressed a hope that Geneva might be able to fence itself and others against the pestilence of heresy, without doing anything unbecoming a Christian magistracy. Schaffhausen vaguely recommended suppression of Servetus as a blasphemer. Zurich held that the greater severity should be shown because the Swiss churches were reputed to favour heresy. This was a good opportunity to clear themselves; but how it was to be done was not stated. Basle merely recommended that Servetus should be prevented from further troubling the Church. Not one of them definitely declared that the heretic should be put to death. It is clear that misgivings were felt everywhere. Calvin cannot have felt encouraged; but he persisted. It must have seemed to him that it was not merely necessary to make an example, but that the time had come for the assertion of a principle. The timid and the sentimental must be forced to hold to the will of God. Nothing less was at stake than Christianity itself.

Much searching of hearts followed the execution. On all sides there were murmurs, at least, of disapproval. It may have been known at Geneva before the end of 1553 that Castellion was at work, at Basle, on a manifesto for the malcontents. ' For a long time I have known,' wrote Beza to Bullinger soon after the appearance of the *De Haereticis*, ' that abominable things were hatching there.' Calvin's own book suggests similar knowledge. By November, 1553, he had come to the conclusion that he must write in defence of Geneva's action. His book, hastily written, was published at Geneva, in Latin and in French simultaneously, in February, 1554.[1]

In his *Defensio* Calvin confined himself as strictly as possible to defence of the action taken in the particular case. He had to prove that it is part of the duty of Christian magistrates to suppress heresy and punish heretics, and that, at least in extreme cases, the punishment should be death. He had to show that Servetus was one of these extreme cases. Only a short section of the book, ' ubi ostenditur haereticos jure gladii coercendos esse ', deals with the question of

---

[1] The Latin title in full is as follows : *Defensio orthodoxae fidei de Sacra Trinitate contra prodigiosos errores Michaelis Serveti Hispani ; ubi ostenditur haereticos jure gladii coercendos esse et nominatur de homini hoc tam impio juste et merito sumptum Genevae fuisse supplicium.*

The French version bears on its title-page : ' *Declaration, pour maintenir la vraye foy que tiennent tous Chrétiens de la Trinité des personnes en un seul Dieu, par Jean Calvin. Contre les erreurs detestables de Michel Servet, Espagnol. Ou il est aussi montré, qu'il est licite de punir les hérétiques et qu'a bon droit ce meschant a esté exécuté par justice en la ville de Genéve.*'

political principle.[1] By far the larger part is devoted to showing
how monstrous were the heresies of Servetus. The validity of the
principle he was bent on establishing seemed to Calvin so obvious
that it was hardly worth while to argue at length.

He begins by remarking that there are two sorts of people who
deny the justice of punishing heretics by the civil sword. There
are, apparently, no others. Simple and ignorant folk associate such
treatment of heretics with Popery, and do not see the connection
between religion and the sword. Such persons do not understand
the position and may be gently dealt with and instructed. But
there are others whose pretended piety is but a cloak to malice. These
are libertines who would turn all upside down to secure freedom for
their evil wills ; or they are atheists, ' contemners of God ', who hate
the Christian religion and would destroy it.[2] Not for a moment does
he admit that any instructed Christian can sincerely maintain that
people should be allowed to practise and teach what religion they
please.

Brief, magisterial and even contemptuous in tone as is Calvin's
statement of the case, it is lucid and powerful as was everything he
wrote. He had, so far as was possible, to anticipate objections :
and he anticipates the most radical of all. In the preface to his
Latin version of the Bible, addressed in 1551 to Edward VI of England, Castellion had already briefly stated his main contention. All
highly controverted questions of doctrine, he had declared, are difficult
and obscure. For a thousand years and more they have been debated
and no definitive conclusion has been reached. No answer to any
of them is demonstrably true. It is absurd that men should kill each
other for differences of opinion about what cannot be certainly known.

In anticipation, perhaps, of what Castellion might yet have to
say, Calvin went straight to the point.[3] If this be so, he asks, how
is the true Church ever to be discerned, and what religion of any kind
can survive in the world ? What can become of our belief in Christ
or even of our belief in God ? To say that the truth concerning the
nature of Christ and the destiny of man cannot be known, is to say
that God has tried to reveal these things to us and has failed.

' Et quelle opprobre fait on à Dieu en disant qu'il a tellement entortillé son
langage en l'Ecriture sainte, qu'il ne s'est fait que jouer des hommes, leur tenant

---

[1] Ed. of 1554, p. 11 et seq. The reference is always to the original French
edition.

[2] So John Knox, arguing that idolaters should be put to death, refers to
' such objections as men that seek to live as they list do now-a-days invent '.
A Godly Letter to the Faithful in London etc., 1554. Works, ed. Laing, III, p. 197.

[3] He must surely have at least suspected what was coming. He makes a
clear allusion to Castellion, though without naming him. ' Il y a un autre
fantastique qui contrefait le philosophe dans sa tanière,' etc., p. 16.

le bec dans l'eau ! Si nous n'avons religion certaine et resolue en l'Ecriture, il s'ensuivra que Dieu nous a voulu occuper en main par je ne sais quelles fallaces, comme s'il nous parlait des coquecigrues.' [1]

Either there has been no Revelation or the Revelation can be interpreted with certainty, and approximate exactness, on all questions with which it deals or which it directly raises. It was, it seems now, an audacious thing to say. It was almost equivalent to saying that the claim of the Scriptures to inspiration stood or fell with the Calvinistic interpretation. But we may be sure that Calvin was not conscious of taking any risk. Almost brutally, with a contemptuous impatience, he formulated his dilemma.

Calvin anticipated, also, another objection, not radical but of practical importance. It would be said that to assert that it was the duty of the civil magistrate to suppress heresy by force, was to justify Catholic persecution of Protestants. It is somewhat astonishing that a man of Calvin's logical habit should have denied that this was so. But deny it he does and with vehemence ; and all those who followed him, in France, Scotland and elsewhere, continued to deny it. ' God does not command us,' he says, ' to maintain any religion but that only which He has ordained with His own mouth. . . . He condemns the presumption of all those who go about to defend with fire and bloodshed a religion framed to fit the appetites of men.' [2]

If Calvin had said : ' On my own showing the Catholic Prince is justified in persecuting us ; but we, who know we are right, must resist for the sake of truth,' his declaration would have been logically defensible. But he says nothing of the kind. He says in effect : ' The Catholic Prince is not justified because we know we are right ' ; which is sheer nonsense. Later, when the question of the right of a Catholic Prince to persecute came to be discussed among the Huguenots in France, it was invariably answered in the same absurd manner.[3] It might be thought that for Calvin at least such an answer would have been impossible. What made it possible alike for him and for the Huguenots to take such a view, was, I think, their conception of Catholicism. Behind this nonsense is the sense that the Catholic Prince does not really persecute Protestants for the sake of truth or in obedience to God. His pretence of doing so is, in their view, a mere hypocrisy. They see Catholicism as a system expressive on one side of mere superstitious ignorance and on the other of greed and ambition. The Catholicism of the Catholic King was to them the result of an impious bargain between himself and a fraudulent clergy. They will not admit that in the religious sense there exists such a thing as a

[1] Ed. 1554, p. 17.   [2] Ed. 1554, p. 45.
[3] See, for instance, the pamphlet, *Dialogue d'Archon et de Politie* (1576). In *Memoires de l'Estat de France sous Charles IX*, Vol. III.

Catholic government. When Catholic writers express essentially the same view as Calvinists, the Calvinists cannot believe that they are sincere. It might almost be said that when they say : ' You are wrong because we know we are right,' they really mean : ' You are wrong, because you know we are right.'

Thus the way is cleared for the exposition of Calvin's own doctrine. It is true, he says, that the early spread of the Gospel was in no degree due to the use of force. It was decreed that the Gospel should spread by the agency of ignorant and lowly persons, that so the power of God might be made manifest. But the way of life was not barred to kings and princes and magistrates. The turn of these to be called came in due season : and when they entered the Church, they brought with them the powers and the duties of their offices. Then was the power of the sword made a sacred offering to God. ' The advent of Christ changed in no way that which is proper to government nor diminished nor restricted the right function of the Magistrate.' [1]

It is impossible, he argues, to maintain that the Magistrate may punish other malefactors but may not punish heretics. It is true that Christ did not explicitly order the punishment of heretics ; but neither did he give any order for the punishment of murderers. When Christ bade men turn the other cheek to the smiter, it is absurd to suppose that he meant his injunction to apply to the action of public authorities. A private man should forgive wrongs till seventy times seven : but unless all order and government is to cease, the Magistrate cannot do so. The parable of the tares proves too much or nothing to the purpose. Heretics are not the only tares : the tares include all the wicked. ' Ainsi que toutes lois, polices et jugements s'en aillent a val l'eau, s'il faut laisser l'yvraie jusqu'à la moisson.' [2]

What, then, is the duty of the Christian Magistrate ? Though it be true that the Christian religion is maintained by the power of God and triumphs over all enemies, this does not involve that men are not bound to maintain it with what force they have. It must needs be the duty of Magistrates ' de ne permettre que par leur nonchalance les simples et infirmes, desquels il sont ordonnés protecteurs, soyent menés a perdition '.[3] No private man would be excused if he suffered his household to be defiled with blasphemy or allowed any member of it to rebel against God. Yet more wicked would be the conduct of a magistrate who stood aside, useless sword in hand, to see true religion flouted and trampled under foot.

The commands of God, given in the Scriptures, are explicit and decisive. He has made it abundantly clear how those should be dealt with who contemn the word. Calvin refers to various passages of Scripture, and most of his references are very unconvincing. But in the thirteenth chapter of Deuteronomy he found all he wanted.

[1] Ed. 1554, p. 51.   [2] Ed. 1554, p. 36.   [3] Ed. 1554, p. 33.

There it is laid down that if a prophet or a dreamer of dreams entice people to go after strange gods, he shall be put to death ; that if a man's son or brother, wife or daughter, entice him so, he should be ready himself to slay the offender. This might have been enough ; but there is more. If one of your own cities, it is said, abandon the worship of the true God to serve false gods,

'thou shalt surely smite the inhabitants of that city with the edge of the sword, destroying it utterly and all that is therein and the cattle thereof with the edge of the sword. And thou shalt gather all the spoil of it into the midst of the street thereof and shalt burn with fire the city and all the spoil thereof every whit, for the Lord thy God : and it shall be an heap for ever ; it shall not be built again.' [1]

It is clear from this passage, Calvin declares, how little the fancies of our pitiful friends accord with the will of God. Those who say that we, in Geneva, are cruel, must accuse God also of cruelty.

'Whoever shall maintain that wrong is done to heretics and blasphemers in punishing them, makes himself an accomplice in their crime and guilty as they are. There is no question here of man's authority : it is God who speaks and clear is it what law he will have kept in the Church even to the end of the world. Wherefore does he demand of us a so extreme severity; if not to show us that due honour is not paid him, so long as we set not his service above every human consideration, so that we spare not kin nor blood nor life of any and forget all humanity when the matter is to combat for his glory ? ' [2]

It was no sufficient answer to Calvin's argument to say that the Mosaic law had been abrogated. The Mosaic ceremonial law, dealing with mere externals and accessories, could be and, in Calvin's view, had been abrogated. But his point was that the passage he quoted involved the declaration of a principle which, if valid at all, was valid every where and for ever. To say that the massacre of the whole population of an apostate city would be wrong, is either to say that God, on occasion, commands injustice, or to say that God did not write the book of Deuteronomy. Whichever of these things you say, you take your stand openly with the blasphemers.

Calvin, however, guarded against the extreme inferences that might have been drawn from Deuteronomy. Castellion's suggestion that his principles bound him, so soon as he might be able, to organize a campaign of wholesale massacre in France, was not just. He pointed out that God's command does not bind us to slaughter mere infidels like Turks and Jews, or aliens like the people of Catholic countries. It applies only to those who, ' having received the law become apostate'. The magistrate is, apparently, to use his sword only within his proper jurisdiction : he is not bound to go crusading.

[1] Deut. xiii. 15, 16. Authorized Version.
[2] Ed. 1554, pp. 46, 47. Knox made similar use of the same passage in his *Godly Letter to the Faithful*, 1554.

Calvin's general conclusion from all this is, indeed, far more cautious and moderate than might be expected. The magistrate is bound to protect and maintain true religion and to repress and punish heresy. But there are degrees of error : there are heretics and heretics. There are some who need but instruction and warning : there are others who are worthy of punishment but need not be put to death. The magistrate should act with all prudence and moderation and be as merciful as he dare be. He should take action in no doubtful case. One of the marks of the beast on the brows of Catholic sovereigns is their undiscriminating ferocity. But when comes a case of clear apostasy and when the heretic apostate, whose whole attitude is a blasphemy, endeavours to spread in the Church the poison of his damning doctrines, as in the case of Servetus, the magistrate is bound to put the offender to death. Is he to allow the whole body of Christ to be torn asunder rather than cut off a rotten member ? The conclusion, in fact, is not only cautious : it is a little ambiguous. Calvin might be understood as meaning that only in extreme cases should heretics be actually put to death. But he might also be taken to mean that any resolute publisher of heretical views should so be dealt with.

It seemed to Calvin quite clear that to kill people for expression of opinion on questions of religion might be, not merely right, but obligatory. How could he have seen it otherwise ? The system of government and of church discipline which Calvin had built up in Geneva was absolutely incompatible, ideally and practically, with freedom in religion. Calvin thought he knew for certain how men ought to live and what they ought to believe and how they should be governed. A theocratic State such as he was constructing can be based, ideally, only on unity in religion. It involved the submission of all its citizens to ecclesiastical censorship and regulation in every relation of life. But Calvin knew well how difficult it was, even with public authority to back him, with all educational agencies in his hands and with his system of pastoral inspection in working order, to control the workings of the natural man in Geneva. Yet God's law and God's honour demanded that it should be done. Manifestly the government must be armed with power to punish revolt and to punish even with death those who dared to criticize the ideal foundations of his Civitas Dei. The teachings and still more the mental attitude of men like Servetus threatened ruin to the whole fabric. Had it been, indeed, a question of Geneva only, Servetus might have been spared : for, after all, Servetus was, in Geneva, one of those aliens God has not ordered us to slay. But Calvin felt upon him the care of all the Churches. He was working for the establishment of his system in all Protestant countries. It cannot be denied that, from his own point of view, he was right. He would, indeed, have been wrong had he supposed that by burning heretics he could rid the world of heresy. There is nothing to show that he supposed any such thing. But at least he could help to save a remnant : at least he could fence his own city against the pestilence.

Calvin had vigorously presented a strong case and one not easy to meet except by denial of his assumptions. His assumptions were, for the most part, those of common Protestant opinion at the time. But he had presented the case in somewhat summary fashion : it was stronger than he had shown. It was left to Beza to make the statement more complete. Calvin's *Defensio* and the *De Haereticis* of Beza should be considered together : they form a Genevan manifesto. It will be best to defer further comment till we have dealt with what Castellion had to say and with Beza's answer thereto.

§ 3. CASTELLION AND BEZA

At the very time when Calvin was formulating his defence of the burning of Servetus, the *De Haereticis an sint persequendi* must have been in course of preparation. The principal author of this anti-Genevan manifesto, which was partly original composition and partly a compilation, was Sébastien Castellion,[1] assuredly one of the most remarkable minds of the century. He had been born in 1515, of peasant parentage, near Nantua in the French Jura, one of the rudest and most isolated districts of France. At about the age of twenty he had become a student in the municipal Collège de la Trinité at Lyon, then perhaps the most advanced of French schools. As one of a group of enthusiastic young humanists he had doubtless shared their rather vague vision of a reformed and undivided Church, with scholarship and theology, Platonism and Christianity, lying down together in the fold. But the lines of division were being drawn more and more sharply and, like others, Castellion had to make his choice. In 1540 he joined Calvin at Strasbourg and next year went with him to Geneva. As Principal of the College of Geneva he was for a time among the more important of Calvin's fellow-workers. Divergence of opinion between him and the Master made itself felt quickly : Castellion left Geneva and, in 1544, settled at Basle. There followed years of struggle with poverty and of literary and scholarly labour. Castellion's growing reputation secured him, in 1554, the post of reader in Greek at the University of Basle. He was already well known and influential. His Latin Bible, with its remarkable preface, had been published in 1551. But he must have been better known as the author of the *Dialogues Sacrés*,[2] a work which seems

---

[1] For as full information as is possible concerning Castellion's life, see F. Buisson's superb monograph : *S. C. sa vie et son œuvre.*

[2] *Dialogi Sacri, latino-gallici, ad linguas moresque puerorum formandos*, 1542–1545. Castellion's translation of the Bible into French appeared in 1555.

to have been one of the most popular and widely used educational books of the sixteenth century.[1]

The *De Haereticis* of Castellion appeared in March, 1554. The Latin was followed, a few weeks later, by a French version.[2] It was almost entirely Castellion's own work, but he may have had helpers. Lelio Sozini[3] was a suspected accomplice; and so were Martin Borrhée, professor at Basle, and Curione. Yet the book was not unfairly described as a 'farrago'. It began with a preface, addressed to the tolerant Duke of Würtemberg, signed 'Martinus Bellius', but certainly written by Castellion. This preface forms by far the most important section of the book. It is followed by a long series of extracts from the works of other writers, ancient and modern, under the heading 'Sententiae'. The writers quoted in favour of tolerance in religion include some of the early Fathers, but are mostly of the sixteenth century and some of them were still living. Among them are Luther, Erasmus, Brenz, Calvin, Sebastian Franck, Otto Brunsfeld, one of the founders of botanical science,[4] Urbanus Rhegius,[5] Gaspar Hedion,[6] and Conrad Pelican, the great Hebraist, then living, old and honoured, at Zurich. The extracts signed 'Georges Kleinberg', however, appear to be original contributions by a person unknown.[7] The 'Sententiae' are followed by an epilogue, signed 'Basile Montfort', and, like the Preface, certainly written by Castellion.[8]

Castellion's case was not seriously strengthened by the 'Sententiae'. There was nothing to show how far these examples represented the matured opinion of the writers. In one case, at least, it appeared that they did not. It was not even fair to quote from

[1] It went through twenty-eight editions in its author's lifetime and was translated into many languages. (Buisson.)

[2] The Latin version was entitled : *De haereticis, an sint persequendi et omnino quomodo sit cum eis agendum multorum tam veterum tam recentiorum sententiae.* It announced itself as printed at Magdeburg, but was really printed at Basle. 'That Magdeburg, if I am not deceived,' wrote Beza to Bullinger, 'is on the Rhine.' The French version appeared under the title : *Traicte des heretiques, A savoir si on les doit persecuter et comme on se doit conduire avec eux, selon l'avis, opinion et sentence de plusieurs auteurs tant anciens que modernes : grandement necessaire en ce temps plein de troubles et tres utile a tous et principalement aux Princes et Magistrats, pour cognoistre quel est leur office en une chose tant difficile et perilleux.* It was probably published at Lyon : certainly not at Rouen as it pretended.

[3] Uncle of the more famous Fausto.

[4] Died 1534, leaving a great reputation for learning.

[5] Organizer of the Reformation at Luneberg. Died 1541.

[6] Leader of the reformers at Strasbourg. Died 1552.

[7] This unknown may or may not have been David Joris, a notorious Anabaptist, then living under a false name at Basle. His rhetoric and puerile reasoning did nothing to strengthen Castellion's case.

[8] Beza, for a time, believed that 'Basile Montfort' was Curione. (Buisson.)

Luther's *Von Weltlicher Uberkeyt* without reference to the later change in his views.[1] To quote an ambiguous remark of Calvin's was merely absurd. All that was proved was that a number of Protestant divines of weight had at one time or another and in one sense or another declared for toleration. Calvin could not claim to represent the whole body of learned opinion on the subject.

In his preface and in his epilogue to the *De Haereticis*, Castellion stated his views and his argument fully and eloquently. Very soon after its publication he must have got to work on a direct answer to Calvin's *Defensio*. The *Contra libellum Calvini* was written in the course of 1554. But Castellion was unable to secure its publication; and it was not actually published until 1612. The authorities of Basle were not prepared to take any action against him; but neither would they risk an open and absolute breach with Geneva. There is really little in the *Contra libellum* that is not in the *De Haereticis*; but in determining the nature of Castellion's views the two must be considered together.

The preface of the *De Haereticis* addressed to the Duke of Würtemberg opens with an allegory. Suppose, Prince, Castellion asks the Duke, that you had left your people, telling them that some day you would suddenly return and enjoining them to prepare themselves white robes against your coming; what would you do if, on your return, you found that they had paid no heed to your injunction, but had fallen to debating among themselves where you had gone and whether you would return on foot or on horseback, with pomp or without pomp? And suppose you found that they had debated these questions not with words only but with fists and with swords? And what if those few among them who had obeyed your command and got themselves white robes, had been persecuted and put to death by the others? Yet more, what if these wretches pretended that all they had done was done by your commandment? Would you not then judge them worthy of pitiless punishment?

Lengthy and argumentative explanation of the allegory follows. In 1551, in the preface to his Latin Bible, Castellion had already stated his most fundamental contention. The very fact that men have, century after century, disputed and disagreed over free will and predestination, over heaven and hell, over the nature of Christ and of the Trinity and other such obscure matters, and that no agreement has yet been reached, proves that none can be. Nor is any agreement or conclusion upon such questions necessary to man. God is himself veiled in obscurity, but his commandments as to what men should do and should not do are clear. In the Scriptures we

---

[1] About this, Beza is not unjustly indignant. He seems to have regarded the excerpts from Brenz as the most troublesome of the opinions quoted.

find all the certainties we need. It is enough to know that Christ was the Son of God and that His precepts are divine.

' On dispute, non pas de la voie par laquelle on puisse aller à Christ, qui est de corriger notre vie : mais de l'état et office de Christ, a savoir, ou il est maintenant, que c'est qu'il fait, comment il est assis a la dextre du Père, comment il est un avec le Père. Item de la Trinité, de la predestination, du franc arbitre, de Dieu, des Anges, de l'état des âmes après cette vie et autres semblables choses, lesquelles ne sont grandement nécessaires d'être connues pour acquérir salut par foi et ne peuvent aussi être connues si premièrement nous n'avons le coeur pur et net. . . . Lesquelles choses aussi, encore qu'elles fussent entendues, ne rendent point l'homme meilleur.' [1] ' The doctrine of true piety,' he added,[2] ' is that of love for our enemies and of doing good to those who do us wrong, that of hunger and thirst after righteousness. These and such like precepts are clear and certain for us, even though we remain ignorant on all these other obscure points.'

Christ's commandment to men was that they should seek peace and ensue it and live together in love. It is sufficient to know this, if we live accordingly.

What, then, is this ' heresy ' men talk of so glibly and would have suppressed by the sword ? Hardly one of all the numberless sects that now exists but denounces all others as heretical. A man is orthodox in one city and heretic in another : and if you would travel and remain orthodox you must change your religion like your money. Only one conclusion is possible, ' que nous estimons hérétiques tous ceux qui ne s'accordent avec nous en nôtre opinion '.[3] Calvin asserts that the validity of his system is incontrovertible and that all others are in error. But every sect says the same thing. Who made Calvin a judge over us all ? [4] If all be so clear to him, let him at least have patience and allow us time to reach his conclusions. The real heretics, the real rebels against the Church, are the doers of evil, such as are mammon worshippers and persecutors.

From all these considerations, Castellion argues, it is clear that no more can justly be demanded from any man than that he should faithfully endeavour to understand the Word of God and to follow it. It is incredible that the God revealed in the Gospels should demand more. Suppose a man to say : [5] ' I do not believe that men should be baptized till they can give reason for the faith that is in them. I dare not wrong my conscience in this matter lest, by so doing, I offend Christ ; for I must be saved by my own faith and not by the

---

[1] *Traité des Hérétiques*, ed. 1913, Geneva, pp. 12, 13. Beza paraphrases this passage and interjects the exclamation : ' O the gross blasphemy and horrible impiety of Bellius ! ' No one who does not understand his exclamation can understand the Calvinism of Calvin.

[2] *Contra libellum Calvini*, ed. 1612 (29).

[3] *T. des H.*, ed. 1913, pp. 24, 25.

[4] ' Hoc faciunt omnes sectae. Dicit Calvinus omnes errare preter suam. Sed quis nobis eum Judice dedit ? ' *Contra lib.*, ed. 1612 (41).

[5] *T. des H.*, ed. 1913, pp. 16, 17.

faith of another.' If Christ Himself were present and condemned that man to the fire, ' qui est ce qui n'aura Christ pour un Satan ? ' Would not anyone suppose that Christ and Moloch were one ? [1] Does or does not Servetus, Castellion asks, believe what he says ? If you kill him because he says what he truly thinks, you kill him for the truth ; for truth consists in saying what one believes even though one be in error. Or do you kill him because he believes so ? But teach him then to believe otherwise ! Or show us where it is in the Scriptures that we are bidden kill those who think wrongly. Religion does not consist in ceremonies nor in beliefs concerning things beyond human understanding.[2] Righteousness and salvation are independent of all such things. To Calvin's argument from Deuteronomy, Castellion's answer was that by the advent of Christ the whole human outlook has been changed. The Messiah has come and it is He who is our Lawgiver.[3] Are we never to escape from the shades of the Law into the light of the Gospel ?

Castellion argues, also, that persecution is futile ; though he lays little stress on the assertion. Yet it is true, he maintained, that the sword of the magistrate cannot touch men's souls and that religion will be free whether we will or no. Killing a man is not defending a doctrine : it is merely killing a man. One does not maintain one's faith by burning another but rather by being burned for it oneself. He admitted, however, that persons who deny the Resurrection and the immortality of the soul and those also who refuse to recognize any human authority, may justly be forbidden by the magistrate to teach their doctrines and punished, though not with death, if they persist in doing so.

It has, of course, been said that Castellion's thought is astonishingly modern. ' Modern ' it may be called, but there is no cause for astonishment. Castellion was but one of many in the sixteenth century. That his practical conclusion in favour of religious toleration has been accepted by the modern world·is in itself of little or no significance. That conclusion has been reached by many roads. In any case a man's thought is only very partially expressed by his conclusion : it consists essentially in the process by which the conclusion is reached. But it is true that Castellion's argumentation is to a great extent such as might be used nowadays. It might, also, be said that Castellion is ' modern ' in respect of a certain looseness and vagueness in conception and in reasoning and in his evident sentimentalism.

A certain connection plainly exists between Castellion's thought

---

[1] *T. des H.*, ed. 1913, p. 31.

[2] Ib., p. 8.

[3] ' Nobis Messias jam venit Legislator noster, cujus Legi de obedire volumus.' *Contra lib.*, ed. 1612 (125).

and that of the mystics of his own day. He might have said, with
Christian Entfelden, that builders of theological systems are as the
builders of the Tower of Babel. He might almost have said, with
Sebastian Franck : ' Let everyone weigh and test Scripture to see
how it fits his own heart. If it be against his conscience and the
Word within his own soul, then let him be sure he has not found the
right meaning.' [1] He might almost have agreed with Caspar Schwenckfeld that the once visible Church had become invisible. But he was
not a mystic and he made no such drastic assertions. He was an
intellectual sentimentalist.

The weak points in Castellion's presentation of the matter were
fairly obvious and did not escape Beza. The gist of his teaching lay
in two assertions. He asserted, in the first place, that all theological
systems alike were of doubtful validity. Since such systems are
many, all, therefore, are probably erroneous. On this ground alone
religious persecution is absurd. Furthermore, this being so, it cannot
be conceived that God should require more from any man than that
he should do his best to find truth. On this ground, it is declared,
persecution is not only absurd but wicked. Secondly, Castellion declared that Christ, the Son of God, had taught a law of love as the law of
human life : and on this ground also religious persecution is wicked.
But it may be said that the first of these lines of argument proves too
much, while the second proves nothing Castellion, it seems, was
prepared to discard the Old Testament when it did not fit his own
heart. Yet he neither denies its inspiration nor attempts to define in
what sense it is inspired. He declares that men should believe that
Christ was the ' Son of God ' ; and yet, on his own showing, as Beza
pointed out,[2] this phrase has no assignable meaning. The gospel of
love, as he conceives it, seems to him divine in origin : it would have
been hard for him to say why, nor does he attempt to do so. He
comes near to saying : ' The Old Testament is irrelevant and much
of the New Testament is speculative : we have really nothing to go
on but the record of Christ's life and words in the Gospels.' But he
does not say this ; everything is left indistinct. To say that there
was no such thing as heresy came, at least, very near to saying that
man knows nothing for certain and that Christ had merely laid down
a moral law of life, for the validity of which there could be no guarantee
but in experience. Castellion, sincere believer as he undoubtedly
was, does not seem to have seen how fine was the line that divided
him from the pure sceptics.

To Beza, at least, that line was so fine as to be practically non-
existent. His answer to the *De Haereticis* of Castellion was published

---

[1] *Chronica* (1531). Quoted by R. M. Jones in *Spiritual Reformers in the 16th
and 17th Centuries*, p. 50.

[2] Beza: *De Haereticis*, p. 72 of French version.

in September, 1554. It was written in Latin; but a French translation by Nicolas Colladon, one of the Genevan pastors who had subscribed the *Defensio*, appeared in 1560. Theodore de Besze had been born of good family at Vezelai in 1519. He had studied law at Orléans and Bourges and practised it in Paris. In 1548 he had joined Calvin at Geneva and was now teaching Greek in the University of Lausanne. Of all Calvin's personal disciples he was the most able and the most influential, and on his master's death, in 1564, he succeeded to the throne in Geneva, so far as to such a throne there could be any succession. Of all his writings his *De Haereticis* was the most widely known and the most important, excepting, perhaps, his life of Calvin.

The *De Haereticis* of Beza [1] is at once a supplement to Calvin's *Defensio* and a direct answer to Castellion. Just because it answers Castellion point by point and because its statement of Calvin's case is fuller than Calvin's own, it is perhaps the more important of the two. Yet Beza had really little to add to what Calvin had said already. To the main assertions of Castellion, Beza made very definite answers. He saw quite clearly what was the most dangerous of them all. ' If we must put up,' he had written to Bullinger, ' with what this impious man has vomited forth in his preface, what remains to us intact of the Christian religion ? . . . We must wait for another revelation.' [2] He uses almost the same expressions in his book. [3] Castellion's assertions amount, he argues, to a declaration that there has been in effect no revelation at all. It is merely absurd to say that we believe in Christ as the Son of God and yet to say that His relation to God cannot be known. If nothing can be known concerning the Trinity, we cannot know Christ as God. ' Que reste-t-il donc, sinon que tout demeure en suspense ? . . . Il faut certes que la religion Chrestienne s'en aille du tout bas et soit renversée jusqu'au pied des fondements.' [4] If Castellion's view be accepted, no foundation remains on which to rest belief in the validity of Christ's moral teaching. There were few in the sixteenth century who would not have thought that in this Beza was merely stating what was obviously true.

Absurd also is it, Beza declares, to say that the law of love forbids the punishment of heretics, since, if that be so, it forbids equally the punishment of thieves. On this point he has nothing to add to what Calvin had said. But he makes sport with Castellion's ' white robes '.

[1] The full title is as follows : *De haereticis a civile magistratu puniendis libellus, adversus Martini Belli farraginem et novorum Academicorum sectam, Theodora Beza Vezelio auctore.* The French version bears the title : *Traité de l'authorité du magistrat en la punition des hérétiques et du moyen d'y procéder.*
[2] Letter of March 29, 1554. Quoted by Buisson.
[3] *De Haereticis*, p. 63, ed. 1554.
[4] French version, ed. 1560, p. 100. In the Latin ed., 1554, p. 66.

What, then, are they, these white robes and wherein consists their whiteness ? Without faith there is no virtue in man and his every act is sinful. What is the faith of the wearers of the white robes of Bellius ? Mere belief in God is not sufficient : pagans and devils believe in God. The faith that saves involves belief in the whole body of revealed doctrine : and in the view of Bellius there is no such thing. He believes in a whiteness that has no existence.

Beza, like Calvin, proceeds to derive the duty of the magistrate to punish heretics from the nature and end of political society.

'The main end of human society,' he declares, 'is that God be honoured as He should be. Now the Magistrate is set as guard and governor of this society. . . . And though it be his duty, so far as in him lies, to take order that no discord arise among his subjects, yet, since the chief and ultimate end of human society is not that men should live together in peace, but that, living in peace, they should serve God, it is the function of the Magistrate to risk ,even this out- ward peace (if no otherwise may it be done) in order to secure and maintain in his land the true service of God in its purity. . . . And it is impossible that he should so preserve and maintain religion unless he suppress by the power of the sword those who obstinately contemn it and form sects. It remains then to say that those who would that the Magistrate should not concern himself with reli- gion, either do not understand what is the true end of human society or else pretend that they do not.' [1]

His conclusion as to the duty of magistrates is clearly stated.

'Toutesfois et quantes qu'il est besoin pour la tranquillité de l'Eglise, leur devoir est de maintenir par tous moyens a l'encontre de l'audace et malignité des infidèles, des débauchés, des hérétiques, bref de tous ennemies, tant la Parole que les précheurs d'icelle et toute la discipline ecclesiastique.' [2]

To say that it was the duty of the Magistrate to strike with the sword the enemies of ' ecclesiastical discipline ' was to be a little more explicit than Calvin, in the *Defensio*, had been. But from the Calvin- istic point of view this conclusion could not be escaped : rebels against the discipline were in the same category as heretics proper. For the rest Beza's conclusion is the same as Calvin's ; though his statement of it is rather more explicit and uncompromising. Heresy, he declares, if a crime at all, must needs be the greatest of crimes. It is a crime committed directly against God and is more dangerous to society than any other form of lawlessness. It is far worse than parricide.

'Si, avec le blaspheme et l'impieté, il y a aussi l'hérésie, c'est à dire qu'un homme soit possedé d'un mepris obstiné de la parole de Dieu et de la discipline ecclesiastique et se desborde en rage forcené d'infecter mesme les autres, quel crime scauroit on trouver plus grand et plus outrageux ?—tellement certes que si on voulait la ordonner punition selon la grandeur du crime, il ne me semble point qu'on peust trouver torment correspondant à l'enormité d'un tel forfait.' [3]

---

[1] Ed. 1554, p. 186. French ed., 1560, pp. 292, 293.
[2] French version, ed. 1560, p. 42. Latin ed., 1554, p. 29.
[3] Ed. 1560, p. 339.

Those, he declares, who would have it that the magistrate should not punish heretics,

'meprisent la parole de Dieu expresse et machinent une ruine et destruction extrème a l'Eglise.[1] . . . Que s'ils peuvent une fois obtenir une telle licence . . . y aura il meschanceté ou malheurté qu'ils ne viennent à attenter ? ' [2]

That Castellion was substantially in the right, few, nowadays, would deny. Yet, before saying so, it would be well to be clear as to what we mean by being in the right. There is certainly a sense in which Calvin and Beza were not wrong. They saw in the doctrines and arguments of Castellion a solvent of all religious systems of thought. We can see now, that, whether for good or evil, the Reformation as a whole involved rather dissolution than construction. What was happening in the sixteenth century was a disintegration of the Christian system of ideas, which every effort at reconstruction tended to aggravate. Calvin and Beza were conscious, as their language shows, of an abyss opening at their feet. They were not wrong in thinking that if no new authority could be set up to take the place of the old, nothing could arrest that disintegration which, with the multiplication of sects and the open denial of dogma after dogma, was visibly proceeding. Unless Protestantism could pull itself together the battle would be lost ; and lost more completely for Protestantism than for Romanism. The only remedy lay in a universal acceptance of the *Institute* as a sufficient and incontrovertible explanation of the content of Revelation, and a universal submission to the Calvinistic discipline. Freedom of thought and speech had become the enemy as much for Calvin as for the Pope. It was against a rising flood of denial and of scepticism that Calvin and the Pope, alike, stiffened every muscle and hardened their hearts. Neither Calvin nor the Pope was wholly unjustified in thinking that what was at stake was Christianity itself.

§ 4. AFTERMATH

In spite of Calvin's efforts to induce the authorities of Basle to take action against him, Castellion retained till his death, in 1563, his position in the University. Though he had been unable to secure publication for the *Contra libellum Calvini*, he was not even silenced. He continued to expound and propagate his views. In his *De arte dubitandi* [3] he stated his fundamental assertion more clearly than ever before, arguing that all theological systems are evidently open to doubt and that in the free use of reason we have alone the means of arriving at truth. In his *Four Dialogues*, published only in 1578,

---

[1] Ed. 1560, p. 312.   [2] Ib., p. 426.
[3] A small portion only of this work was printed in 1578. As a whole it has never yet been published and exists only in manuscript at Basle.

he attacked the essentials of Calvinistic theology, arguing in support
of free will, the necessary conformity of God's determinations with
human justice and the possibility of salvation for all.   In 1562 was
published his *Conseil à la France desolée*.   It was an appeal to both
sides in a civil war which Castellion seems, naïvely, to have imagined
had originated in mere religious dissension.   The miseries of France,
he declared, are due to the fact that Catholics and Protestants alike
think it their duty to use force to compel others to accept their opinions :
as though, when a sick man refuses food, one should stuff it by force
down his throat.   Both alike are behaving absurdly and trying to do
what is impossible.   The futility of such efforts is manifest :   the
Protestants of France have been persecuted for many years, yet now
they are strong enough to wage war.   Catholics and Protestants
both profess belief in the Scriptures as the Word of God ;   yet they
kill those who only desire to know and obey the Scriptures.   Between
them they will ruin France, but that is all they can do.   There is only
one remedy : to allow every one who believes in Christ ' de servir
Dieu selon la foi non d'autrui mais la leur '.

Nearly all France, thirty years later, was beginning to come to the
same practical conclusion ;   but for the moment, of course, France
paid no heed to Castellion.   Yet he seems to have had adherents at
Lyon and even at Paris, as he had at Berne and at Frankfort.   After
1554 he was in correspondence with many scattered people, not only
in Germany, Switzerland and France, but in the Netherlands and even
in England and Spain.[1]   Two years after Castellion's death there was
published, in 1565, the remarkable book entitled *Strategematum
Satanae*.[2]   Its author signed himself Jacobus Acontius Tridentinus :
his Italian name was Giacomo Contio.   Acontius was in no sense an
ecclesiastic or professed theologian.   He was a military engineer,
who had served under Pescara at Milan and been employed by Elizabeth
in England.   In 1561-2 he was at Basle.   His book is by far the
strongest and most original that was written in support of Castellion's
views during the sixteenth century.

While at Basle Acontius may well have fallen under Castellion's
personal influence : in any case he reproduces much that is in Castellion's writings.   But his point of view is his own and he makes points
that Castellion did not make.   He had had, no doubt, experience of
many sorts of men, which is precisely one of the most disabling lacks
of men who live chiefly in their studies.   His experience had, apparently, convinced him that, whatever man's heart may be, his head is
a poor thing.   Satan, anxious above all to promote discord, hatred
and violence among men, finds in men's religion the eftest way of

---

[1] See Buisson : *Castellion, sa vie et son œuvre*.
[2] An English translation of part of this book (Books I–IV) was published in
1647 or 1648, with a prefatory letter addressed to Fairfax and Cromwell.

doing so. The most effective of his wiles consists in persuading men to persecute and kill each other for differences of religious opinion. And this he finds it easy to do : for the root of the evil is in man himself. To make out what is true, great patience and careful inquiry are necessary : actually, men form opinions hastily and with little or no inquiry at all. Men come to conclusions without knowing how ; and they flatter themselves that their judgements are due to reason or even to divine guidance. 'Most men suppose that they are led by the Word and the Spirit to think as they do in matters of religion,' [1] whereas they are really guided by tradition or by some man's learning or merely by the opinion of the mass of those about them. One doctrine they wave aside, without inquiry, because it is new : for they hate novelties. Another they condemn off-hand as an old error, oft confuted, without pausing to ask whether it be an old truth ill defended. Not only so, but men are angered by contradiction and resent whatever throws doubt on their opinions : they cannot bear to think that their judgements may be wrong.

'When a man is convinced of anything, he cannot but be astonished that there should be anyone who' cannot see what he sees ; and unless, as soon as he has indicated his reasons, his opposite succumb to them, he falls into a passion, as though it were evident that this refusal to be convinced came of mere perverseness and obstinacy ; and so it is odds that he fall to reproach and railing.' [2]

Such, according to Acontius, is the psychological foundation of Satan's strategy.

'If you hear uttered any impious doctrine, what is it that Satan will whisper to you ? He will endeavour first, perhaps, to induce you to approve the heresy. But if he find the doors that way closed : " O abominable wickedness ! " he will cry ; " this wretch deserves that the earth should swallow him up or fire from heaven consume him ! " ' [3] And, since no fire descends from Heaven, he will persuade you, if he can, to set the heretic in earthly fire.'

Now there may be, says Acontius, beliefs that are necessary to salvation, but certainly there are very few. The mass of theological doctrine is mere speculation and that which is merely speculative is vain. If a doctrine has no relation to men's life on earth and means nothing for conduct, it is a thing indifferent and valueless. The less controversy about such matters the better : it is the Devil who stirs up controversy.

Even if a man be convicted of heresy in the highest degree there is no reason for interference by the secular magistrate. Such a man should be excommunicated, that is expelled from the Church, and that ' with signs rather of sorrow than of any anger or hatred '. Interference by the secular magistrate in religious controversies can pro-

[1] *Strategematum Satanae*, Book I.   [2] Ib., ed. 1565, Bk. I.
[3] Ib., Bk. II, pp. 56, 57. The translation is free and omits certain phrases, but is substantially correct.

duce nothing but evil and is radically absurd. It can only mean, practically, two things : that such controversies will be decided by force and, secondly, that they will be decided by the mere mass of opinion. ' Wherever it becomes a custom to decide religious controversies by the sword, there, whoever shall oppose the doctrine, right or wrong, that is generally accepted, will be accounted a heretic and whatever texts or arguments he may bring forward, none but the hangman shall answer him.' [1] The idea that the magistrate should maintain true religion by force is wholly preposterous. It is admitted, Acontius argues, that the Magistrate cannot of his own authority decide what is heresy. It is admitted, also, that he is as a rule quite incompetent to judge in such matters. It is said that he must act on the judgement of the Church. Of what Church ? There are many Churches, all claiming this right of judgement. The magistrate, then, before he can act at all, must decide between the claims of the Churches. But if he be incompetent to judge a charge of heresy, how can he be competent to judge between the Churches ? [2] The very zenith of absurdity is reached when the magistrate interferes, not to punish, but to force men to recant their supposed errors : for then he is merely forcing his subjects to tell lies.

This last apparently conclusive argument could be and was answered in three ways. It could be answered, as it was by the Catholics, by asserting the existence of an inspired authority on earth. It could be answered, as it was by the Calvinists, by asserting that the whole meaning of the Scriptures had been demonstrated and made undeniable. And it could be answered, or rather it could be evaded, as it was by Hobbes, by asserting that heresy meant only what the secular sovereign chose to make it mean.

Acontius goes on to conclude in favour of absolute freedom in religion. The search for truth must needs begin with doubt and the road to truth lies through free discussion and inquiry. If freedom be established truth will be found and will prevail. [3] If the sword of the magistrate be brought into the discussion, it is not true religion that will be maintained but rather the kingdom of Satan.

The book of Acontius was isolated though significant, but from 1554 onwards much trouble was caused to orthodox Calvinists by the spread, locally, of what Beza called ' bellianism '. At Montbéliard, Pierre Toussaint was endeavouring, as Farel put it in 1558, ' castalioniser tout le comté '. For the most part the adherents or disciples

---

[1] Ed. 1565, Bk. III, pp. 143, 144. [2] Ib., p. 161.

[3] ' Qui dubitat, is ad veri inquisitionem exstimulatur. Et, multis inquirentibus, mirum est ni aliquis inveninit. Inventa porto veritate, si disserendi sit libertas, facta sententiarum collatione, illa superior evadat necesse est. Ex quo quidem efficitur cum opinionum de religione libertate consistere Satanae regnum diu non posse.' Bk. VI, p. 268.

of Castellion were more or less completely silenced, though there is some evidence that they wrote when they could not publish. One such writing, printed only in modern times,[1] lays down that Protestantism will fall into self-contradiction if it endeavours to maintain unity in doctrine by force.[2]

But towards 1570, in the Grisons and in the Italian Alps,[3] a strong party openly maintaining Castellion's views was headed by Gantner of Coire and caused much disturbance.[4] Gantner's textbook of arguments was the *De Haereticis* of Castellion: his opponent, Eglinus, relied on that of Beza. In 1573 Pastor Bartolomeo Silvio produced a treatise to show that civil magistrates should not deal with religious error.[5] Far more important was the work of another Italian, Mino Celsi, published at Basle in 1577.[6] Celsi's book was an armoury of arguments for toleration drawn from the writings of Castellion, from the *Strategematum* and from the French *Exhortation aux Princes et Seigneurs du conseil privé du Roi*.[7] It is full of citations and little more than a compilation. But the book showed clearly that Castellion and Acontius had not written in vain.

Castellion was not a prophet in his own country. There is nothing to show that his writings had any influence among the Politiques of France, whose point of view, in fact, was very different from his. But of the importance of his influence in connection with the Arminianism of Holland there is no doubt. From about 1580 there was increasing protest and revolt in the rebel cities of the Netherlands against the efforts of the Calvinist party to establish their discipline and consistory government. A party developed which asserted freedom of the will against Calvin's predestination and adopted Castellion's views as to the wickedness and absurdity of religious persecution. The prophet of this party, from 1580 to his death in 1590, was Dirck Volckentzoon Coornhert. He was a disciple, it seems, of Castellion and of Sebastian Franck, perhaps also of Caspar Schwenckfeld. His religious beliefs resembled those of Franck and Schwenckfeld; but his views on the question of toleration are indis-

[1] The MS. is headed: *Alphonsi Lyncurii Tarraconensis Apologia pro M. Serveto*. It has corrections in the handwriting of Curione. It was printed in the Brunswick edition of the works of Calvin.

[2] This assertion, frequently made in our times, was very rarely made in the sixteenth century.

[3] Trinitarian heresy, Italian in origin, was flourishing aggressively in this region before the death of Servetus.

[4] An account of this interesting affair is given by Buisson.

[5] His treatise was published in 1592, if not earlier.

[6] Under the title: *In Haereticis coercendis quatenus progredi liceat : ubi nominatim eos ultimo supplicio affici non debere, aperte demonstratur.* Another edition appeared in 1584.

[7] 1561. Often attributed, though without sufficient reason, to Etienne Pasquier.

tinguishable from those of Castellion.   Actively, both by speech and writing, he laboured in the cause of religious freedom.   He wrote two treatises on the question, both of which were published only after his death, in 1591 and in 1593.[1]   In 1589 he began, at least, the conversion to his views of the famous Jacobus Arminius.

Arminius (Jacob Hermanns), born in 1560, had become a pastor at Amsterdam in 1588.   Called upon in the following year to refute the heretical Coornhert, he had accepted the task and, as a result, was half converted by the heretic.   In the last ten years of the century Coornhert's views spread steadily.   Later, Arminius, as a professor in the University of Leyden, was, owing to his reputation for learning and the fame of his long controversy with his colleague, Franz Gomar, to give his name to a movement which was strong before he identified himself with it.   How much the influence of Castellion counted for in this movement of opinion is evidenced by the fact that, as it gathered strength, his works were republished in Holland and translated into Dutch.   Complete editions of his writings, including the hitherto unpublished *Contra libellum Calvini*, were printed in Latin and in Dutch in 1611–12.[2]   The *Remonstrance* addressed by the Arminians to the Estates of Holland and Friesland in 1610 is almost pure ' Bellianism '.   A provincial synod held at Delft in 1619 denounced Castellion as the real founder of Arminianism.   To such a title he seems certainly to have a better claim than has Arminius.   It must be noted that, in spite of the Synod of Dort (1618–1619), which witnessed the last real triumph of an expiring Calvinistic theocracy in the Netherlands, the Arminians had, by 1630, secured freedom at least for themselves.   All this belongs to the seventeenth century and cannot be dealt with here.   But it may be pointed out that, in that century, the Arminianism of Holland became an important factor in the mental conflicts of England.   The straight line from Castellion through Acontius to Coornhert, Arminius and Simon Episcopius, may be said to end in England.

---

[1] *Epitome processus de occidendis haereticis*, Gouda, 1591, and *Defensio processus de non occidendis haereticis*, Hanover, 1593.   Coornhert had written a preface for a Dutch version of Castellion's *Four Dialogues*, published in 1580.

[2] On the other hand, the opponents of Arminianism reprinted the *Defensio* of Calvin and the *De Haereticis* of Beza.

CHAPTER VI

THE BREAK FROM CALVIN

§ 1. THE *BEKENNTNIS* OF MAGDEBURG

UP to the year 1550 Lutherans and Calvinists alike preached with rather singular consistency a doctrine of non-resistance to the powers that be. No one ever said that man must be obeyed rather than God; but every one said that, though disobedience might be obligatory, active resistance was always wrong. Revolt against this doctrine began not with Calvinists but with Lutherans.

It is unfortunate that Luther did not live to see the battle of Mühlberg. It would be pleasant and instructive to know what line he would have taken in the circumstances that followed. Up to 1547 Lutherans, at least in northern Germany, had been under no serious pressure. The Lutheran Princes had despoiled the Church with impunity. It seemed, in 1547, that the day of reckoning had come ; and the hearts of the Princes failed them. The position Charles V had established did, indeed, begin to crumble immediately after his victory. His apparent dominance was utterly illusory. But for some three years after the issue of the Interim in May, 1548, it seemed that all Protestant Germany might be compelled definitively to accept the edict. For the Protestantism of southern Germany its effects were, in fact, almost ruinous. Some hundreds of local leaders, ministers and divines, men of merely local importance or men of European fame, like Brenz and Bucer, Osiander of Nürnberg and Blarer of Constance, were driven into exile. It had, so far, been easy and natural for Lutherans to teach and to believe that forcible resistance to impious rulers was never justified. It was far harder to believe that now. Under the new circumstances the Lutherans of Germany began to repudiate the non-resistance doctrine of Luther, just as, a little later, the Knoxian Calvinists repudiated Calvin. Luther himself had indeed asserted a right for the Princes of the Empire to resist the Emperor for the sake of the Gospel. But that right was vested solely in the Princes and derived from their peculiar position in the German Reich. The assertion had become useless ; for the Princes, it seemed, were broken reeds. A new doctrine, a doctrine of a divine right of rebellion, was needed. It was duly produced at Magdeburg.

103

The city of Magdeburg had obstinately refused to accept the Interim. Placed under the ban of the Empire, it was threatened with attack from various quarters. Between May, 1548, and April, 1550, there were published at Magdeburg more than a hundred pamphlets and treatises in defence of the city's attitude. These literary efforts appear to have culminated in the publication on April 13, 1550, of a tract that seems nowadays to be little known,[1] but is of real significance and importance in the evolution of Protestant political thought. It was entitled : *Bekenntnis Unterricht und Vermanung der Pfarrherrn und Prediger der Christlichen Kirchen zu Magdeburg.* The signature of Niclas von Amssdorff, presumably as principal author, was followed by the signatures of eight ministers of Magdeburg. In spite of its clumsiness of phrasing and in spite of much vagueness and confusion, the content of this tract is quite remarkable. To some extent it anticipates both Knox and Goodman and the Huguenot pamphlets of the years after 1572. These anticipations merely illustrate the law that similar circumstances produce similar results. The importance of the Magdeburg treatise consists not so much in them or in its possible positive connection with the French *Du Droit des Magistrats*, as in the fact that it seems to be the first formal enunciation of a theory of rightful forcible resistance by any Protestants who can be called orthodox.[2]

The authors of the *Bekenntnis* began with the usual declaration. Subjects are bound by the command of God to obey their rulers. It is just, they point out, because the subject is bound to obedience only by the command of God, that he is bound to disobey orders that are contrary to God's law.[3] One must not render to Cæsar what is God's. Authority to command is derived only from God. If, therefore, the ruler try to abolish true religion he cannot be held to be acting with any authority at all. So much was being very generally asserted and had been very definitely asserted by Melanchthon.

But the authors of the Magdeburg treatise go much further. They argue that mere passive resistance to a ruler seeking to destroy true religion is not sufficient to satisfy God. In that case the subject is

[1] But see *Die Stadt Magdeburg im Kampfe fur den Protestantismus*, F. Hülsse, 1892. Also the histories of Magdeburg by F. W. Hoffman and Rathmann.

[2] The editor of the *Memoires de l'Estat de France sous Charles IX* referred to the *Du Droit des Magistrats* as a revised and augmented version of a treatise published at Magdeburg in 1550. It seems rather probable that the reference is to this tract of April 13. Both in form and content, however, the Magdeburg treatise differs widely from the *Du Droit*. Sleidan speaks of a treatise published at Magdeburg on March 24, 1550, and gives an abstract of its contents. This treatise of March 24 was entitled *Der von Magdeburg Ausschreiben an alle Christen*, but it contains little to the purpose. Sleidan's abstract refers better to the content of the April tract. See Sleidan, *Commentaries*.

[3] *Bekenntnis*, Part I, Chap. 7.

bound to defend it ' mit Leib und Leben '. For a ruler who attempts
such a thing represents not God, but the devil.

It is impossible, they argued, to believe that God commands non-
resistance in all cases. To believe that, is to believe that in some
cases God wills the maintenance of evil and commands disobedience
to Himself. It can only be the devil who inspires men with such a
belief. God, it is rather confusedly argued, gives authority for the
sake of justice and truth. The very fact that authority is given by
God involves that the authority given is not unlimited. It is incredible
that God has arranged so ill that all good order is left at the mercy
of a ruler's caprice. A ruler who endeavours to destroy true religion
is making war on God, as much as would be the case if he were
attempting to abolish marriage.[1]

The people of Magdeburg were not only concerned to justify their
own resistance : they were anxious also to show that German Princes,
so far from being bound to execute the Imperial ban against them,
were bound to support them against the Emperor. The ' Untere
Obrigkeit ', they declared, holds authority not merely from the
Emperor but directly from God. In proof of this they refer to the
hereditary character of the Princes and to the fact that the death of
the Emperor did not in any way affect the position and authority of a
Prince. Every Prince is bound to protect his own subjects against
attempts to force upon them a false religion. All are bound to resist
such attempts with all the force they have ; but the Prince is bound
above all so to do. For God has given him authority for just this
purpose, that he may defend and maintain right doctrine and worship
and the bodies and lives, the goods and the honour of his subjects.[2]
From this it follows, they declare, that if the Hohe Obrigkeit attempts
by force to destroy true religion anywhere in his dominions, the whole
Untere Obrigkeit is bound, not only to give him no help, but to aid
the faithful against him.

The writers of the *Bekenntnis* were almost wholly concerned with
the justification of forcible resistance to an attempt to abolish ' true
religion '. But they went just a little further, though with caution
and ambiguity. If, they declared, the Hohe Obrigkeit should attempt
by force unjustly to take from his subjects their lives or their liberty
or their property, he oversteps the bounds of his authority and may
rightfully by force be resisted. For since God gives authority for
the sake of justice, there can be no authority to do such things. They
add that, in this case, though resistance by force is justified, there
is no duty to resist. If it be only one's own life or property that is
threatened, it may be more truly Christian simply to suffer. Attacks

---

[1] Part II, 3rd Argument.
[2] He is established for the defence of ' rechte lehr und Gottes dienst, leib und
leben, gut und ehre '. Part II.

on mere life and property are not direct acts of war upon God as is an attack on true religion. In that latter case resistance by force is not merely justified ; it is obligatory.

All the leading ideas expressed in this treatise are reproduced constantly in one form or another in Calvinist writings from 1558 onwards. The notion that just because authority to command is given by God and can only be given by God, it cannot be conceived as unlimited, and the notion that God cannot have commanded non-resistance in all cases because in so doing He would contradict Himself, are the very roots of the 'contracts' of the *Vindiciae*. The assertion of a positive duty of resistance to attacks upon true religion is repeated and expanded by Knox. The assertion that there exists in Germany a magistracy which, though subordinate to the Emperor, yet derives authority direct from God and is therefore bound to maintain justice and true religion even against the Emperor, is made, with the necessary modifications, for Scotland by Knox and for France by Huguenot and by League writers. The Untere Obrigkeit of the Magdeburg tract becomes the 'officiers du royaume' of the *Du Droit*, the 'regni proceres' of the *Vindiciae*, the 'ministri regni' of Boucher. But in saying this much I am not suggesting any causal connection. Even if the author of the *Du Droit* were consciously reproducing some of the contentions of the *Bekenntnis*, he found there only what he was looking for. Knox may well have become acquainted with the Magdeburg tract during his sojourn at Frankfort or Geneva : it may be that this was the very book he gave to Maitland in 1564, with a reference to the list of godly ministers who had subscribed it.[1] It is possible that the reading of it helped him to his own change of view. Even so, to suggest that Knox wrote his *Appellation* as, in any appreciable degree, a result of his acquaintance with this or any other tract, would be entirely absurd.

§ 2. JOHN KNOX

Charles V's attempt to enforce the Interim proved, after all, an utter failure. At least from 1555 onwards Lutheranism was so solidly established in Germany that German Lutherans had no further need to believe in a right of rebellion. The doctrine of Magdeburg was discarded by the Lutheran churches so soon as the storm had blown over. A few years later it was the turn of the Calvinists.

It was not in the regions of Calvinistic domination that any theory of a right of rebellion was wanted ; and it was not there that any was developed. But in Scotland in 1558, and in France later, where the Calvinistic party, with its allies, had become strong enough to take forcible action against a hostile government, there it was needed

---

[1] Knox : *History of the Reformation in Scotland.* He calls it the *Apology of Magdeburg.*

and developed.   In France the repudiation of Calvin's political theory was far more complete than in Scotland, for the French Calvinists, for good reason, never really accepted the political ideal of Geneva. In Scotland, Knox and his followers adhered to the Genevan ideal of State organization and argued from it to a positive obligation to depose idolatrous Princes.

So important was the part played by John Knox in this repudiation by Calvinists of one of the essential points of Calvin's teaching, that he cannot but be regarded as one of the chief personal factors in the history of political thought in the sixteenth century.   For obviously this was a development of extreme importance.   Calvin had formulated a theocratic ideal of the State ; but he had avoided collision with the claims of established secular rulers by a doctrine of submission to whatever powers there be.   Knox taught that it was the duty of the subject to realize the Genevan ideal of the State by force, if force were sufficient.   In doing so he challenged not only or chiefly the claims of Mary of Guise or of Mary Stewart but the claims of all mere secular authority.   From the point of view of governments established on any but a theocratic, one might say an ecclesiastical, basis, Calvinism became the enemy : to Protestant Princes an enemy far more dangerous than ever Romanism was likely to be.   For it was the view of Knox rather than the view of Calvin that tended to prevail among Calvinists after 1560.

We must not, however, overestimate the personal importance of Knox or even of events in Scotland.   It was, actually, in Scotland that the Calvinistic party first found itself in a position to rebel success-fully against constituted authority.   But whenever and wherever that condition had arisen the same thing would have happened. ' Cal-vinism ', in the strictest sense, involved logically no tendency to such rebellion : but, because Calvinists were human, the tendency was inherent in Calvinists.[1]

John Knox had not, and did not need, Calvin's lucidity in thought and in exposition, or Calvin's practical caution and circumspection. Nor had he Calvin's juristic knowledge and training : he never thought in terms of law.   Calvin was coldly intellectual or severely self-restrained :   Knox was hot and violent and impatiently eager. Temperamentally he resembled Latimer or even Luther rather than the great Frenchman.   He was honest and outspoken, even to boorish-ness, and was still more incapable than Calvin of seeing any good in those who did not think with him.   But his violence was more genial than Calvin's coldness and he had, even, a rough sense of humour.

It is a little curious that we do not know when Knox was born.

---

[1] All these terms, Calvinism, Lutheranism, Protestantism, lose their edges when one looks close.   They should be used with the utmost caution : they are pitfalls for the unwary.

It may have been as early as 1505 or as late as 1515. His father
seems to have been some kind of yeoman farmer ; and the son was
able to secure some amount of University education. He had the
advantage of being, like Buchanan, a pupil of John Major.[1] By
1543 he had become a priest, of course of the old dispensation ; but
by 1547 he was a preacher of Protestantism. His dislike of Catholicism
and of Catholics was probably inflamed by his consequent experiences
in the galleys. From 1549 onwards to the end of Edward VI's reign
he was a licensed preacher in England and in 1552 he was offered an
English bishopric, which he wisely declined. Down to the beginning
of 1554, when he went into exile on the Continent, he would seem to
have held quite orthodox views as to the wickedness of rebellion.
The government of Edward VI was not likely to offer a bishopric to a
man unsound on that point. The time was not ripe for rebellion in
Scotland, and in England under Edward VI a doctrine of submission
was greatly needed. But Mary's accession altered the appearance of
things and it seems that Knox at once began to doubt whether it
could be true that one was bound to sit passive under idolatrous
rule. The questions he put to Bullinger in March of that year show
what was in his mind : ' Whether is obedience to be given to a Magistrate who commands idolatry and condemns true religion ? ' and
' To which party should the godly adhere, if a religious nobility resist
by war an idolatrous King ? ' Bullinger's ambiguous and carefully
hedged answers can have given him no comfort.[2] But in the same
year he not only compared Mary Tudor to Jezebel but prayed God to
stir up some Jehu for the general benefit.[3] He was sailing, already,
near the wind.

By 1557 he was becoming more explicit.

' In a few words,' he says, ' to speak my conscience, the regiment of Princes
is this day come to that heap of iniquity, that no godly man can brook office or
authority under them ; but in so doing shall be compelled, not only against
equity and justice to oppress the poor, but also expressly to fight against God
and his ordinance, either in maintenance of idolatry or else in persecuting God's
chosen children. And what must follow hereof, but that either Princes be re-

---

[1] John Major (1470–1550), one of the last of the orthodox schoolmen of the
old style, lectured at Glasgow 1518–1521 and at St. Andrews from 1522 to 1525
and from 1531 to his death. He was the author of numerous works in Latin,
which seem all to have been published in Paris. His best known book is the
Historia Majoris Britanniae tam Angliae quam Scotiae of 1521, of which a translation into English was made for the Scottish History Society in 1892. To
Major all secular authority was derived from the will of the community. But
see Part III, Chap. V, 2.

[2] Questions and answers are given in a letter of Bullinger to Calvin, March
26, 1554.

[3] *A Faithful Admonition to the professors of God's truth in England.* Works,
ed. Laing, III, p. 309.

formed and be compelled also to reform their wicked laws or else that all good men depart from their service and company ? ' [1]

The latter alternative was all that Calvin allowed them : but Knox, clearly, is seriously contemplating the other. But before the end of that year he had gone further. *The First Blast of the Trumpet against the Monstrous Regiment of Women*, published early in 1558, seems to have been written late in 1557.

The main thesis of the *First Blast* is, simply, that whatever law of succession may anywhere exist, no woman can lawfully succeed to a throne. For nothing can make lawful that which God has condemned. The contention is based partly on the Scriptures and partly on the nature of woman, ' weak, frail, impatient, feeble and foolish . . . inconstant, variable, cruel and lacking the spirit of counsel and regiment.' [2] ' Woman in her greatest perfection was made to serve and obey man.' [3] For man to recognize authority in a woman is against nature : for her to assume authority over men is rebellion against God. The consequences of such rebellion against God and nature are, he declares, only too plain in our days : England is handed over to Spain and Scotland to France.

' Doth such translation of realms and nations please the justice of God ? or is the possession, by such means obtained, lawful in his sight ? . . . Will he suffer that the liberties, laws, commodities and fruits of whole realms be given in to the power and distribution of others by the reason of marriage ; and in the power of such as, besides that they be of a strange tongue, of strange manners and laws, they are also ignorant of God, enemies to his truth, deniers of Christ Jesus, persecutors of his true members and haters of all virtue ? . . . For he hath not created the earth to satisfy the ambition of two or three tyrants, but for the universal seed of Adam and hath appointed and defined the bounds of their habitation, to diverse nations assigning diverse countries.' [4]

It is needless to point out the confusions of the argument. But it is noteworthy that this last passage shows that Knox had, at least, a confused notion of ' nations ' as real entities, created by God, constituted by similarity of tongue, manners and laws, each with its own proper boundaries and each with a God-given right to hold its own and not to be ruled by strangers.

No mere legal succession, then, can give anyone a valid title to a throne ; for any law of succession inconsistent with the law of God is invalid. That ' cursed Jezebel ', Mary Tudor, unworthy, even, of the name of woman, [5] is no rightful Sovereign. It is the duty, Knox concludes, ' as well of the Estates as of the People . . . to remove from honour and authority that monster in nature '.[6]

---

[1] This passage occurs in an addition made by Knox in 1557 to a translation of a French *Apology* for French Protestants, for which, also, he wrote a preface. It was, apparently, never published. Ed. Laing, IV, p. 327.

[2] Works, ed. Laing, IV, p. 374.　　　　　[3] Ib., p. 377.

[4] Ib., pp. 411, 412.　　　[5] Ib., p. 411.　　　[6] Ed. Laing, IV, p. 416.

In the *First Blast* Knox had merely asserted a duty of deposing by force any impious ruler who happened to be under ' the malediction and curse pronounced against Woman '.[1] But before the end of the year he went much further. In his *Appellation* of 1558 he broke finally and decisively with Calvin's doctrine of submission. It is possible that, in doing so, he was influenced by the book which Christopher Goodman published that same year. Certain it is that whether Goodman influenced Knox or Knox Goodman, they say exactly the same thing.[2]

' We are persuaded,' Knox had written in 1554, ' that all which our adversaries do is diabolical.' [3] A man who thought like that was hardly likely long to rest content with Calvin's distinctions. Before the end of 1558 Knox felt that the time had come when rebellion against Mary of Guise, Regent in Scotland, might well be successful. Already the covenanted Lords of the Congregation of Jesus Christ were demanding of the Regent freedom of worship for themselves and their adherents. Knox himself had been condemned to death in his absence and burned in effigy. It was against the judgement of the Scottish Bishops that he issued the *Appellation*. Along with the *Appellation* proper, addressed to the nobility and Estates, was printed a letter to the Commonalty of Scotland.[4] It was no appeal to law : it was an appeal for revolt. Knox asserted definitely that rebellion against idolatrous sovereigns was a duty. His later words and writings serve only to amplify his declaration of 1558.

Judged from a legal standpoint the whole argument was absurd. ' Lawful it is,' he declared, ' to God's prophets and to preachers of Christ Jesus, to appeal from the sentence and judgement of the visible Church, to the knowledge of the temporal magistrate, who, by God's law, is bound to hear their causes and to protect them from tyranny.' [5] The prophet Jeremiah was sentenced to death by the priests, the visible Church of his time, and appealed to the Princes. ' This fact and history manifestly proveth . . . that it is lawful for the servants of God to call for the help of the Civil Magistrate against the sentence of death, if it be unjust, by whomsoever it be pronounced.' [6] Manifestly it proved nothing at all. Did Knox mean that God's law makes it obligatory for the civil sovereign to determine appeals against judgements given in ecclesiastical courts ? Did he mean that the civil sovereign had no right to constitute special tribunals to decide

---

[1] Ed. Laing, IV, p. 417.

[2] For Goodman's book see following section.

[3] *A Godly Letter to the Faithful.* Works, ed. Laing, III, p. 198.

[4] *The Appellation of John Knox from the cruel and most unjust sentence pronounced against him by the false bishoppes and clergie of Scotland, with his supplication and exhortation to the nobilitie, estates and communaltie of the same realme.*

[5] *Appellation.* Works, ed. Laing, IV, p. 472.

[6] Ib., IV, p. 473.

finally particular classes of cases ? What is the force of ' servants of God ' and of ' if it be unjust ' ? The confusions are characteristic but not worth dwelling on. ' This is our chief proposition,' he had written a little earlier, ' that in the religion of God, only ought His own word to be considered.' [1] What Knox meant was simply this : that the judgement given against him was clean contrary to the Word of God and that no court could possess a jurisdiction entitling it to give such judgements. In such a case it is for the civil magistrate to protect the condemned and call the judges to account.

But who, in Scotland, was the civil magistrate ? The supreme civil magistrate was the Regent. Knox does not deny this, but he has a confused theory of the Scottish constitution. He might have acquired it from John Major or from David Lyndsay, or from the Magdeburg tract of 1550, or, indeed, from a man in the street. Major had laid down that the King was but a delegate and minister of the community and that power to depose him lay with the Estates. Knox was not so definite. His appeal was to the ' Nobility ', the Untere Obrigkeit, ' ye whom God hath appointed heads in your common-wealth ', [2] rather than to the Estates. He thought, apparently, of civil authority as diffused among a group of nobles, who were God's ' lieutenants '. The Crown had special rights, but the rights of the nobles and Estates derived not from the Crown but from God direct.

As God's lieutenants, Knox argues, certain duties are incumbent on the nobles.

' To wit, first, That in conscience you are bound to punish malefactors and to defend innocents, imploring your help. Secondly, that God requireth of you to provide that your subjects be rightly instructed in his true religion ; and that the same by you be reformed whensoever abuses do creep in. . . . And, last, That ye are bound to remove from honour and to punish with death (if the crime so require) such as deceive the people or defraud them of that food of their souls, I mean God's lively Word.' [3]

From these duties there is no escape possible. ' It will not excuse you . . . to say that ye supposed that the charge of souls had been committed to your Bishops. No, no, my Lords, so ye cannot escape God's judgement,' [4] for ' your Bishops ' can be proved to be but ravening wolves. ' The Reformation of religion in all points, together with the punishment of false teachers, doth appertain to the power of the Civil Magistrate.' [5] But what if the King, or Regent, oppose

[1] Letter to the Regent. Laing, IV, p. 446.
[2] *Appellation.* Laing, IV, p. 480.   [3] Ib., IV, pp. 481, 482.
[4] Ib., IV, p. 484.
[5] Ib., IV, p. 490. So also in the *Confession of Faith* drawn up by Knox and others in 1560. ' Moreover to Kings, Princes, Rulers and Magistrates we affirm that chiefly and most principally the conservation and purgation of the Religion appertaineth, so that not only are they appointed for civil policy, but also for maintenance of the true Religion, and for suppressing of idolatry and super-stition whatsoever.' (Art. XXIV.)

such reformation ? In that case, Knox declares, it being evident that the King is an enemy of true religion, it becomes the duty of God's lieutenants ' to correct and repress whatsoever ye know him to attempt expressedly repugning to God's Word, honour and glory.' [1]

' But this part of their duty,' he goes on, ' I fear, do a small number of the Nobility of this age rightly consider ; neither yet will they understand that for that purpose God hath promoted them. For now the common song of all men is, We must obey our Kings, be they good or be they bad ; for God hath so commanded. But horrible shall the vengeance be, that shall be poured forth upon such blasphemers of God. . . . For it is no less blasphemy to say that God hath commanded Kings to be obeyed when they command iniquity, than to say that God by his precept is author and maintainer of all iniquity.' [2]

Knox was partially anticipating later theory of the Huguenots. But he proceeds to go further than does the *Vindiciae*. This duty of ' repressing ' an impious King is not incumbent on the nobility alone. It is a duty for all. ' The same, I say, is the duty of every man in his vocation.' [3] In his *Letter to the Commonalty* Knox enlarges on this text. ' It doth no less appertain to you, beloved brethren, to be assured that your faith and religion be grounded and established upon the true and undoubted word of God, than to your princes or rulers.' [4] He assures his beloved brethren that if they do not demand for themselves ' true preachers ' and insist on reformation, and if they assist and maintain impious princes, they will perish before God's wrath like the people of Sodom.

It might, perhaps, have been maintained, though unplausibly, that Knox meant that an impious Prince was to be corrected and repressed only by universal passive resistance. But he made it quite clear that he did not mean this. To the *Appellation* and the *Letter*, he appended a statement of the propositions he intended to maintain in the promised but unwritten Second Blast of the Trumpet. There he lays down that no oath can bind any people, that has subjected itself to Christ, to obey and maintain tyrants against God.

' But if rashly they have promoted any manifest wicked person or yet ignorantly have chosen such a one, as after declareth himself unworthy of regiment above the people of God (and such be all idolaters and cruel persecutors), most justly may the same men depose and punish him, that unadvisedly before they did nominate, appoint and elect.' [5]

The words might seem to apply only to elected Princes ; but certainly they were not meant so. Of elected Princes in our sense, Knox knew nothing : he regards recognition as all one with election.

---

[1] *Appellation.* Laing, IV, p. 495.
[2] Ib., IV, pp. 495, 496. One cannot but wonder what Calvin thought of this assertion.
[3] Ib., IV, p. 497.   [4] *Letter.* Laing, IV, p. 527.   [5] Laing, IV, p. 540.

But all this confused argumentation was really needless; for Knox went on to represent the duty of rebellion against idolatrous Princes as involved in, and but a part of, a general duty to kill all idolaters [1] without respect of persons. In this connection he, like Calvin, quotes the thirteenth of Deuteronomy. He was not thinking of Anabaptists or of men like Servetus, but of Catholics. 'No estate, condition nor honour' can exempt the idolater from the punishment commanded by God. Rulers are bound to see to it. But

'the punishment of such crimes as are idolatry, blasphemy and others that touch the Majesty of God, doth not appertain to kings and chief rulers only, but also to the whole body of that people, and to every member of the same, according to the vocation of every man and according to that possibility and occasion which God doth minister to revenge the injury done against his glory, what time that impiety is manifestly known.' [2]

The words might be taken as justifying mere assassination. But Knox, I think, meant only to insist that it was the duty of every member of the community to endeavour to bring about the punishment of idolaters by common action. Arguing with Maitland of Lethington in 1564, Knox explained that by the 'people of God' on whom lay the duty of killing idolaters, he meant 'the people assembled together in one body of one Commonwealth'.[3] But he was quite clear that Kings could claim no exemption. 'I find no more privilege granted unto Kings by God, more than unto the people, to offend God's Majesty.' [4] In the *Appellation* he illustrated his meaning by reference to Mary Tudor. 'I fear not to affirm that it had been the duty of the Nobility, Judges, Rulers and People of England, not only to have resisted and againstanded Marie, that Jezebel, . . . but also to have punished her to the death.' [5]

It follows, of course, that in any commonwealth in which true religion is officially established, idolaters must be punished with death. 'In such places, I say, it is not only lawful to punish to the death such as labour to subvert the true religion, but the Magistrates and people are bound to do so.' [6] In the *First Book of Discipline*, which was mainly the work of Knox, it was laid down that all doctrine repugnant to 'the gospel', that is 'whatsoever men by laws, councils or constitutions, have imposed upon the consciences of men without the expressed commandment of God's word', must be 'utterly abolished from this realm'.[7] As early as 1554 Knox had declared that the

---

[1] 'By Idolatry we understand, the Mass, Invocation of Saints, Adoration of Images and the keeping and retaining of the same: and all honouring of God not contained in his holy Word.' *Book of Discipline*, ed. Laing, II, p. 188.
[2] *Appellation*. Laing, IV, p. 501.
[3] *History of the Reformation in Scotland*. Laing, II, p. 442.
[4] Ib., p. 441.
[5] *Appellation*. Laing, IV, p. 507.   [6] Ib., IV, p. 507.
[7] *Book of Discipline*. Works, ed. Laing, II, pp. 185. 186.

killing of all idolaters was 'the office of every Civil Magistrate within his realm '.[1]

But who was to be the judge of what was true religion and whether Knox himself were a ' true preacher ' or a false ? Always, in sixteenth-century controversies, we came down to this question : and always, from Calvinists, we get the same absurd answer. The whole of Knox's case rested on the assumption that the true religion was ' manifestly known '. If that were not so, if reasonable doubt existed of the validity of his interpretation of the Scriptures, his whole argument became mere nonsense. But Knox had not the least doubt that only ignorance or perversity could disagree with him.

The strength and crudity of this conviction in him may be illustrated by reference to his famous interview with Mary Stewart in 1561, as recorded by himself. He records the ' long reasoning ' he had with the Queen with complete self-satisfaction. Not for a moment did it occur to him that she ended with the best of the argument.

' Ye have taught the people,' the young Queen said to him, ' to receive another religion than their Princes can allow : and how can that doctrine be of God, seeing that God commands subjects to obey their Princes ? ' [2]

Knox answered that ' as right religion took neither original nor authority from worldly princes, but from the eternal God alone, so are not subjects bound to frame their religion according to the appetites of their princes '. From this quite sufficient answer to her question he went on to instance the prophet Daniel and others as justified resisters.

Thereupon the Queen shifted her ground. ' But none of these men,' said she, ' raised the sword against their princes . . . they resisted not by the sword.'

' God, madam,' Knox answered, ' had not given unto them the power and the means.'

' Think ye,' she asked him, ' that subjects having power may resist their princes ? '

He answered fearlessly. ' If their princes exceed their bounds, madam, and do against that wherefore they should be obeyed, it is no doubt but they may be resisted, even by power.'

He went on to explain that if Princes behave like lunatics they should be treated accordingly, bound and cast into prison. ' God craves of Kings that they be as it were foster-fathers to his Church and commands Queens to be nurses unto his people.'

At that the Queen flashed out at him. ' Yea (quoth she), but ye are not the Kirk that I will nourish. I will defend the Kirk of Rome for, I think, it is the true Kirk of God.'

---

[1] *A Godly Letter*, 1554. Laing, III, p. 194.

[2] All the speeches as given are from Knox's *History of the Reformation*. Ed. Laing, Vol. II, p. 281 et seq.

' Your will, madam,' replied Knox, ' is no reason.'

It may be pointed out that she had not given her will as a reason for anything. Knox went on, with what one can only call boorish arrogance, to talk of the ' Roman harlot ' and offered to prove that the Roman Church had ' declined from the purity of that religion which the Apostles taught '.

' My conscience,' the Queen answered simply, ' is not so.'

' Conscience, madam,' said Knox, ' requires knowledge ; and I fear that right knowledge ye have none.'

Her reply to this insolence was quite admirable. ' But,' said she, simply, ' I have both heard and read.' One can imagine the quiet scorn and just lifted eyebrows !

He replied to the effect that she had heard only biased and insincere teachers. And, upon that, she put to him plainly the essential question. ' Ye interpret the Scripture,' said she, ' in one manner and they interpret in another. Whom shall I believe ? And who shall be judge ? '

It seems strange, now, that Knox should have had no sense of the difficulty of the question or of the dangers involved in it from his own point of view. He seems hardly to have understood it. His answer is fatuous in its dogmatic simplicity. ' Ye shall believe God,' said he, ' that plainly speaketh in his word. . . . The word of God is plain in the self ; and if there appear any obscurity in one place, the Holy Ghost, which is never contrarious to himself, explains the same more clearly in other places : so that there can remain no doubt, but unto such as obstinately remain ignorant.' And he went off into an argument about the communion completely irrelevant to the question. But there was, in truth, no more to be said. Mary might well, as on the occasion of another encounter with Knox, have burst into tears. She was up against an impenetrable stupidity.

John Knox was one of those whose minds are powerful without subtlety and who, therefore, are apt to become a prey to illusions which weaker men avoid with a smile. Yet, for all his confusions, he was, perhaps, going deeper than the clever girl who was nominal Queen of Scots. She, a child of the French Renaissance, could no more understand him than he could understand her. He was asserting that there was a written word of God, of which the sense and bearing are plain to those who sincerely seek it. That being so, there can exist no right or jurisdiction in contravention of the Word and the task of Government is to realize the Word in society. Not only must there be a right to rebel against impious government, but rebellion is a duty, and refusal to rebel may entail damnation. This was his way of putting the matter ; and it would merely darken counsel to make him say anything he did not think. But this much at least was implied : that if a people be set upon the realization of righteousness, no law or convention or vested interest can be allowed to stand in the

way and no Prince can claim a right to hinder. It was just this that
the juristic mind of Calvin implicitly but absolutely denied. It was
just this assertion that made of Knox, despite his narrowness and his
harsh and stupid moral code, to some extent at least a liberating force.

It remains only to note that Knox's ideal State was strictly of the
Calvinistic pattern and as much an ecclesiastical State as Calvin's.
In the *Book of Discipline* he laid down that :

> ' Drunkenness, excess (be it in apparel or in eating and drinking), fornica-
> tion, oppressing of the poor by exactions, deceiving of them in buying and
> selling by wrong mete or measure, wanton words and licentious living, tending
> to slander, do properly appertain to the Church of God to punish the same as
> God's word commandeth.' [1]

Courts composed of ministers, elders and deacons, are to have power
to excommunicate, and no one, save his wife and family, is to have
any kind of communication with the excommunicated, ' be it in
eating and drinking, buying, selling, yea in saluting or talking with
him '.[2] The sentence is to be published universally throughout the
realm.[3] Finally, ' to discipline must all estates within this realm be
subject if they offend, as well the rulers as they that are ruled ; yea
and the preachers themselves '.[4] The adjustment in detail of the
Genevan system to the conditions of Scotland was not an easy task
nor could it be done quickly. Knox had stated the principles ; but,
dying in 1572, he had himself little to do with the actual organization
of Presbyterian government in Scotland.

§ 3. GOODMAN

The book written by Christopher Goodman and published at Geneva
in 1558,[5] might almost be regarded as a presentation of the teaching
of the *Appellation* more systematic, if less eloquent, than Knox's
own. Different in form as are the two publications, the similarity of
their content is so great as to suggest intimate connection. Not a
proposition can be found in the *Appellation* which is not in Goodman's
work. Yet Goodman's book was apparently written first.[6] It is

---

[1] *Book of Discipline*, 1560. Works, ed. Laing, II, p. 227.
[2] Ib., p. 230.   [3] Ib., p. 230.   [4] Ib., p. 233.
[5] *How Superior Powers ought to be obeyed of their subjects ; wherein they may
lawfully by God's word be disobeyed and resisted.*
[6] Knox's *Letter to the Commonalty* is dated July, 1558 : the preface to Goodman's book is dated January 1. It is remarkable that both these books as well
as the *First Blast* should have been published at Geneva. In a letter to Sir W.
Cecil (1559. *Zurich Letters*, II, p. 35) Calvin declares that he did not learn of the
publication of the *First Blast* till a year after it had appeared. Beza, writing to
Bullinger in 1566, asserts that both Goodman's book and the *Blast* were published ' without our knowledge ', and that their sale was subsequently forbidden
(*Zurich Letters*, II, p. 34). But Calvin had excused himself to Cecil for not
suppressing the *Blast* when he did hear of it !

possible that Knox was influenced by Goodman; it is possible also that Goodman was little more than a mouthpiece for Knox. For some years they had been closely associated. Goodman was one of that group of English refugees who supported Knox in the ' troubles of Frankfort ' and who adopted a form of worship based on that in use at Geneva, repudiating the official Prayer Book of Edward VI, as containing many things Popish, foolish and unprofitable. Along with Miles Coverdale and Thomas Sampson, he had co-operated with Knox in the production of the ' Geneva Bible '.

It seems probable that Goodman's book had no large circulation.[1] But it is important as showing that the same tendency existed among English as among Scottish Calvinists. Not, of course, that there was, as yet, any chance of successful ' Puritan ' rebellion in England. But, ruined and in exile, bitterly disappointed and exasperated, the refugees from Mary Tudor's England were at least safe at Frankfort or Geneva, Basle, Strasbourg, Zurich or Emden. Exasperation and impunity together might produce the same result as consciousness of power or of opportunity.

Goodman declared, like Knox, that nobles ' were first ordained in realms to stand in defence of true religion, laws and wealth of their nation and to be . . . a bridle at home to their princes in time of peace '.[2] Like Knox, he apparently regards Kings as necessarily elective, in the sense that it is the recognition of their peoples that makes them Kings. Laws of succession must be framed in accord with the laws of God. ' The Word giveth us these notes to know whether he be of God or not whom we would choose for our king.' He must be a man ' that hath the fear of God before his eyes . . . hating unfeignedly all papistry and idolatry '. He must be ' of the brethren ', that is neither a foreigner nor a woman ! And he must not be of such as put their trust in horses.[3]

Kings are God's ' lieutenants ' and ' must be reverenced doing their duty '. But they are also God's subjects and if they abuse their power they must not only be resisted but punished. ' It is not a sufficient discharge for us before God when we deny to accomplish their unlawful demands and threatenings, except we do the contrary, every man in his vocation and office, as occasion is offered and as his power will serve.' [4]

---

[1] Copies have become extremely rare. There is one, perhaps unique, in the British Museum. Yet the book was known to Milton.

[2] *How Superior Powers*, ed. 1558, p. 35. Knox uses the term ' wealth ' in just the same connection. It is equivalent simply to ' weal ' or well-being.

[3] Ib., pp. 50, 51. Robert Parsons, the Jesuit, in his *Conference* of 1594 made, though far less crudely, almost the same assertion from his side. See Pt. II. Chap. X.

[4] Ib., p. 43. Even the phrasing resembles that of Knox.

Mary Tudor, the Jezebel, ought to be not merely deposed but ' punished with death '.[1]

Like Knox, Goodman declares that it is the duty of the common people, no less than of nobles, to resist ungodly Princes. ' They are charged to see the laws of God kept.' [2] Idolatry is to be punished without respect of persons and if the Prince and his magistrates will not put their hands to the plough, the people must do it themselves.

> ' Though it appear at the first sight a great disorder that the people should take unto them the punishment of transgression, yet when the magistrates and other officers cease to do their duty, they are, as it were, without officers, yea worse than if they had none at all, and then God giveth the sword into the people's hand and He himself is become immediately their head.' [3]

This last declaration is more explicit than anything to the same effect in the *Appellation*.

§ 4. PONET

Earlier than either Goodman's book or the *Appellation*, had appeared in 1556, *A Shorte Treatise of Politicke Power*,[4] by John Ponet, another refugee from Marian England. Ponet had been, successively, bishop of Rochester and of Winchester under Edward VI and early in Mary's reign had prudently betaken himself to Strasbourg. Exasperated reflection on the turn things had taken brought him to a practical conclusion which was the same as Goodman's. But he reached it by a different road, and his thought has little resemblance to that of Goodman and Knox. His book links with the *Bekenntnis* of Magdeburg rather than with the *Appellation*. Even more definitely, perhaps, it links with later Huguenot views and with Buchanan. Knox wished to overthrow impious tyrants in order to establish a Calvinistic discipline. In Ponet's book there is nothing distinctively Calvinistic.

The seven chapters of Ponet's treatise are each headed by the statement of a question and some of these questions are fundamental. ' Whereof Politique power groweth, wherefor it was ordained, and the right use and duty of the same.' [5] ' In what things and how far subjects are bound to obey their Princes and Governours ? ' [6] ' Whether it be lawful to depose an evil Governour and kill a Tyrant ? ' [7] His answers are confused but significant.

---

[1] *How Superior Powers*, ed. 1558, Chap. VIII.   [2] Ib., Chap. XIII.

[3] Ib., p. 185. Goodman appeals to ' the people ' rather than to the ' nobles ', and in this he differs from Knox. It is a difference between England and Scotland.

[4] Ponet died that same year. The name is also spelt Poynet. The *Shorte Treatise* was reprinted in 1642 (London).

[5] *Politicke Power*. Heading. Chap. I.

[6] Ib., Chap. IV.   [7] Ib., Chap. VI.

Man, says Ponet, is a being too far gone in corruption to be able to rule himself by his own reason. That he can do so was a vain supposition of the ancient heathen; and their own history shows that they were wrong. Man's action should be directed by the law of God which is the law of nature; but unhappily men will not obey law without coercion. God therefore, for man's benefit, 'instituted politic power' and gave to man authority to make laws for himself and enforce them even by putting offenders to death. Ponet's doctrine seems to be exactly that of Melanchthon. Such authority did not originally exist in man and could not be created by him. It was a special creation; and the announcement of its creation was, apparently, first made to Noah.[1]

But at this point Ponet forsakes Melanchthon. Though all political authority is created by God, God did not settle the form in which it should be exercised. That is left 'to the discretion of the people'.[2] Every one has need of every one else, because 'nature hath made every man apt for all things, but hath made one man more meet for one purpose than another'.[3] The community is a co-operative association for the maintenance of justice and general well-being. It was, therefore, upon the community that God conferred authority; and the community establishes monarchy or democracy or any other form of government as suits it best and alters that form when it thinks fit to do so. Kings are called Gods in Scripture only because the authority they possess comes ultimately from God, not because it was given by God to them. The authority of the Prince is a delegation from the community.

Ponet was strongly of opinion that no wise people would establish monarchy pure and simple. Far preferable is the 'mixed' form of government 'which men by long continuance have judged to be the best sort of all'. By the mixed government he understood some kind of division of sovereignty between a Prince and some sort of Parliamentary body. Such a constitution, he imagined, existed in England, France and Germany. In such States the Prince can never make law of his sole authority. But Ponet is careful to point out that, even in a pure monarchy, the Prince can only make law in respect of 'matters indifferent'; for all Princes are bound for ever by the law of God. In fact, people ought always carefully to consider whether it is right to obey any law that is merely man made. 'It is not the man's warrant that can discharge thee, but it is the thing itself that must justify thee.'[4] Nor is it enough to consider merely whether the man-made law is consistent with the law of God. A man's love and loyalty are due first to God, then to his country, and only last to the King.

[1] *Politicke Power*, Chap. I.   Ponet's reference is to Genesis ix. 5, 6.
[2] Ib., Chap. I.   [3] Ib., Chap. I.
[4] Ib., Chap. IV.

The Prince is only a member of the Commonwealth ; and the Commonwealth can quite well exist without the Prince.[1]

Princes are apt to impose unjust taxes, to tamper with coinage and even to claim that the property of their subjects really belongs to them. All this, Ponet declares, amounts to mere brigandage. When a King speaks of all things within his kingdom as his own, he must be taken as speaking like some great man's steward who says ' my house ' when he means his master's.[2] If he means more than that he is `a robber and a ' tyrant '. The community may always revoke the authority it has given to an unworthy Prince. It is no less, Ponet declares, than a law of nature that evil rulers should be deposed and tyrants punished with death.[3] Even the assassination of a ' tyrant ' by a private individual would, it seemed to him, be justified under some not clearly specified circumstances.[4]

It may be that I have represented Ponet's views as clearer than they were to himself. But he certainly regarded political authority, power that is to create obligation by command and to punish disobedience, as a special creation and gift of God. He implied rather than stated that this authority had been conferred on the community or people and by it delegated in one form or another. He certainly argued that such authority exists only for the sake of justice and general welfare and asserted that the welfare of the community must always primarily be considered. He certainly concluded that rulers who abuse their power may and should not only be disobeyed but forcibly dispossessed of it. All these contentions are essential to a deal of later theorizing and Ponet was, apparently, the first definitely to take this line of argument, unless the authors of the *Bekenntnis* can be said to have done so. On the other hand, all these contentions were ancient and all lay on the surface of things. They were potentially everywhere in the mid-sixteenth century. The significance of Ponet's book consists mainly in its illustration of that fact. For England, however, it had little significance of any sort. So far as Ponet's book was in any sense prophetic, it was prophetic of developments in France. Its denial of the validity of absolute non-resistance doctrine was based on propositions more far-reaching than those of Knox and Goodman.

---

[1] *Politicke Power*, Chap. IV.   [2] Ib., Chap. V.
[3] Ib., Chap. VI.   [4] Ib., Chap. VI.

PART II

ENGLAND

CHAPTER I

PRELIMINARY

THE early Tudor monarchy of England sorely needed a doctrine of a religious duty of obedience to constituted authority. It had, to begin with, to restore order, and to do so it constructed what was practically a new machinery of government out of the wreckage of the fifteenth century. It subjugated or destroyed the old nobility ; it subjugated the Church ; it assisted the spread of national consciousness ; it gave form and meaning to what we know as Parliament. Henry VIII was asserting and realizing a national sovereignty, ' absolute in the sense that it was absolutely independent of anything outside the realm. The need of order and security gave the government immense leverage : but it was difficult to deal with the multitudinous confusion and indiscipline that was the legacy of the fifteenth century. It was yet more difficult to force on a reluctant or indifferent population a change of religious habitudes. But for the dominance of a belief in the wickedness of resistance to constituted authority, the work of the Tudors would have been impossible of accomplishment. It is true that every government in Europe as sorely needed that same belief. England was fortunate. All the factors that gave strength to the new monarchy, the urgent sense of the need of order, the developing and spreading national sense and sentiment, the fear of the foreigner, worked together to ensure belief in the doctrine required.

It will be best at once to insist that the doctrine required was not anything that can accurately be called a theory of the divine right of kings. The doctrine of the religious duty of political obedience as expounded and believed under Henry VIII and Elizabeth, involved no theory of monarchy in especial and no theory of the origin and nature of political authority. It was only out of discussion of the nature of political authority and obligation that any ' theory of the divine right of kings' could possibly arise. But in England, it was only under Elizabeth that such discussion seriously began : under Henry VIII the question was barely touched upon. What was needed under Henry VIII was simply a theory of the duty of the subject as such, towards civil authority, constituted by any means in any form. Even the assertion that monarchy is the best form of government was only occasionally made under Henry VIII or Edward VI. The assertion that monarchy is the only 'natural' form of government was not made till late in Elizabeth's reign. Even that assertion involved no theory of divine right, except in the sense that all that is 'natural' is of God.

To say that God commands obedience to, or forbids rebellion against, any constituted authority, however tyrannical or irreligious, is not to say that authority can only be derived from God. The former of these propositions involves no theory of the derivation of authority. If it were originally derived by delegation from the people or came into existence under a contract, God's command would still hold good. It may be, and it was, conceived that political authority is derived from man's need of it and conferred by man for his own ends ; and that God, thereupon, recognizing man's need, issued his command to obey.

If it were said that a theory of divine right in the king existed in England under Henry VIII, the statement would be undeniably true. But you do not even begin to understand typical sixteenth-century thought till you have grasped the fact that to a vast majority of the thinkers of that period, all right was 'divine'. Right cannot exist on one side without obligation on the other ; and all in the sixteenth century who believed at all in obligation, believed that all obligation was to God. Obligation may be, primarily, to oneself, or to another, or to one's country or to all mankind ; but it must ultimately be to God. It was inconceivable that there could be any obligation merely to man. For this reason, and for no other, it may be said that all right is divine.

The King's right is, of course, divine; so are the rights of his subjects, if they have any. All magistrates have divine right ; if they had not they would have none at all, for there would be no obligation to obey them. You may obey the magistrate from fear or from hope, or in your own interest ; if you disobey you perhaps act foolishly and certainly you take a risk. But, if the magistrate have no divine right, if God be indifferent whether you disobey or not, then it is your own affair simply. You are the judge, in that case, and your conscience need not be troubled, whatever you do. And divine right does not attach only to magistrates. Rank shares divinity with the prince and rights of property, too, are sacred or 'divine'. Even the right of rebellion is conceived as a divine right, arising from a breach of obligation : unless, indeed, rebellion be conceived as a positive duty, in some cases, as it was by Knox. Theories of divine right exist everywhere in the structure of sixteenth-century thought. But to speak of this way of thinking as a ' theory of the divine right of kings ' is evidently absurd. It must be remembered, too, that the king's right is not necessarily unlimited because it is divine. Such phrases as ' vicar ' or ' lieutenant ' of God imply no theory as to the extent of the prince's rights. It is quite possible to argue, as was done in France, that just because the prince is a lieutenant of God he may be forcibly deposed if he act in a manner unbecoming God's representative. Only if an unqualified right to demand obedience as a duty has been specially created by God in the prince, need his authority be regarded as unlimited and indefeasible.

It may be said that the difference between the assertion that God has forbidden rebellion against the Prince in any case and the assertion that the Prince holds of God an unlimited authority, is practically unimportant, since, in practice, the two doctrines will come to the same thing. But this is not true : actually in the sixteenth century, it did not come to the same thing. The practical importance of the distinction lies in the fact that the one assertion leaves open a door to questions, while the other shuts it. If you say simply ' God has forbidden rebellion against constituted authority ', there is nothing to prevent your asking whether the command was really intended to apply to all cases and to admit of no exceptions. In order to answer that question, you will have to consider how the authority you are to obey came into existence and why. And you may inquire whether God's command does not of necessity imply conditions. If you conceive that authority is derived from need and established by consent or delegation, you will easily find reason to believe that the duty of obedience has limits. This is exactly the course that thought often followed in the sixteenth century. Almost every one agreed that obedience to constituted authority was normally a religious duty. The question was whether forcible resistance is not in some cases justified. But if the authority you have to obey was in no sense created by you and if its right to command be altogether independent of your will and your desires, then no need or desire of yours can diminish that right or give you a right to rebel. The door is slammed in the face of question. This did not happen in England.[1] In England at the end of the century the door is still open and the questioning had begun.

Under Henry VIII and indeed to the end of the century it was, from the point of view of the government and its active supporters, needful to lay all possible stress on the religious character of the duty

---

[1] It did not actually happen in France either. Doors of this sort can never be really closed.

of obedience and the essential wickedness of rebellion. But there was no need for the elaboration of any new theory, even in relation to the Church. The requisite material was all there to hand, a legacy of the Middle Ages which the Tudors had only to adopt and adapt. William of Occam had asserted the need in every community of a single sovereign and laid down that society which civilly has one head and ecclesiastically has another is in a dangerous condition. ' Illi qui non habent unam regem,' he had written, ' non sunt unum regnum.' [1] Wyclif had defended a doctrine of secular sovereignty unlimited save by something called natural law ; and to him, as to the early Fathers of the Church, a king is a vicar of God. The *Defensor Pacis* had declared that no coercive power belongs rightly to the clergy and that neither Pope nor clergy can rightfully speak or act for the Church. It is true that the theories of the *Defensor* or of Occam were not exactly what was needed. They went much too deep and too far ; nor were they easily comprehensible. The *Defensor* was the work of men who had no belief in Christianity ; and what Occam and Wyclif believed is highly problematical. There is no divine right of any sort in the *Defensor* and the King is, whatever else he may be, a mere instrument of earthly needs. The theory the Tudor government required had to be easily intelligible and had to be religious, for it had to be popular. What was wanted was an exclusive stress on certain features of medieval theorizing.

The doctrine that it is a duty to God to be submissive to constituted human authority must not be confounded with the theory of the relation of Prince to Church developed under the Tudors. A theory of royal supremacy in ecclesiastical causes may be said to imply a theory of the duty of obedience ; but the former is not implied in the latter. Belief that the civil magistrate must be obeyed in all things consistent with the law of God, obviously does not involve that the law of God allows of his supremacy in the Church. The former belief was held as strongly by Catholics in France as by Protestants in England. It was, no doubt, above all in relation to Henry VIII's Reformation of the Church, that the religious duty of submission needed emphasizing. This is why that duty was preached and insisted upon in England chiefly by the government itself and by the active supporters of or sympathizers with its religious policy, by lawyers and officials and more or less Protestant divines. The association in England of such teaching with Protestantism was accidentally inevitable. In France, for similarly circumstantial reasons, it was associated, for long, with Catholicism. These terms, Protestantism and Catholicism, are, in this connection, irrelevant.

[1] *Dialogue.* Pars III, Tr. II, Lib. III, c. 19. And see the whole section.

CHAPTER II

THE DOCTRINE OF NON-RESISTANCE

IT was a very simple doctrine concerning the duty of subjects that was being taught in England under the Tudors. It was, under Henry VIII and Edward VI, almost but not quite Lutheran. Luther had taught simply that God forbids forcible resistance to the magistrate in all cases, and commands positive obedience to him except where He forbids it. In England the doctrine was not quite so simple as that. Luther, in Germany, could see nothing but a confused complex of magistracies in indeterminate relation to each other. The Emperor could not be for him what the King was to Tyndale or Cranmer. A German nationalism, had it really existed, must have supported Charles V : it would have been Catholic like the nationalism of France. But in England in 1529 there already actually existed clear outlines of a national State, and along with this a national sentiment and desire for complete independence. Tyndale's patriotic sentiment found an English commonwealth ready-made. It needed only the repudiation of Papal claims and a full assertion of the principle that the clergy are subjects in the same sense as other men, to make England stand forth as a fully-developed secular State, ' absolute ' in the sense that it was ideally self-sufficient and independent of all external jurisdiction, as unhampered by ecclesiastical pretensions as by the *Corpus Juris Civilis*. The English reformers had before them a national and political ideal as well as one that was religious. It is a special peculiarity of English Protestantism that from the first it was allied and associated with national sentiment. It was the realization of the national State in fact and in law that was the work of the government of Henry VIII. But even before its full realization, Englishmen were able to see the state as much more than a mere system of magistracy. ' This realm of England is an Empire ' expressed what was implicit in the minds of Englishmen long before the formula was officially adopted. The realm of England was to Englishmen of Henry VIII's reign a true commonwealth, united under a law that was wholly its own and under a crown which had no superior. There was an element in English feeling and belief on the question of political obligation which was not present in the teaching of Luther.

'The office of a magistrate,' wrote Hooper, 'is the ordinance of God.'[1] I quote these words, written under Edward VI, because they put briefly what was constantly being said, before and after. As a rule there is no attempt to explain what such phrases mean ; and when the attempt is made, nothing is explained. Whatever exactly is meant, since the office of a magistrate is an ordinance of God, you may say that the King, as chief magistrate, is God's vicar or God's lieutenant. These phrases, too, are constantly used, and with variations. 'The King,' says Gardiner, 'yea, though he be an infidel, representeth the image of God upon earth.'[2]

Such phraseology was as loose and ambiguous as it was ancient. The language used would sometimes seem to point to the existence of some theory of the origin of political authority. By some writers stress was laid on the establishment of a King by God's direct action among the Jews.[3] But no inference from the fact was drawn by these writers as to the origin or the form of civil government. They were concerned only with the power over the priesthood that was given by God to the Jewish King. The fact is that in England, till late in the century, no one was much interested in the question of the origin of political authority. Political authority is felt to be necessary ; it is sanctioned in the Old Testament and in the New ; it represses the evil-doer and secures peace and order and so subserves the purpose of God for man ; it is, therefore, however it came to be there, an ordinance of God. I do not think that anything more than this was meant. It is true that the Elizabethan Homily *Against Disobedience and Wilful Rebellion* asserted that ' when mankind increased and spread itself more largely over the world, He by his holy word did constitute and ordain in cities and countries several and special governors and rulers '.[4] Here the declaration that the office of a magistrate is the ordinance of God takes the form of a statement of presumed historical fact. It may be that the drafters of a Homily published only in 1571 had a suspicion that some such assertion was needed, logically or practically. The assertion is made ; but nothing is made of it. The writers merely point out that this means that political authority ' cometh not ' by chance nor of mere self-assertive ambition.

It must be observed that while German and French writers, at

[1] *Annotations in the thirteenth chapter to the Romans.* Later writings of Hooper : Parker Society ed., p. 103.

[2] *De vera obedienta, oratio.* Printed, first, in 1535. An English version appeared in 1553.

[3] Especially in the *De vera differentia.* See p. 160.

[4] *Against Disobedience and Wilful Rebellion.* Homilies. Ed. by J. Griffiths for Oxford University Press, 1859. Sermon I, p. 547. This particular Homily appeared for the first time in 1571 and was considered important enough to be first issued separately.

least of the mid-sixteenth century, in discussing the duty of the subject, very generally speak of ' the magistrate ', English writers usually speak of the Prince or simply of the King. They were thinking of England, and about other countries they knew little. But they did not mean to convey the idea that monarchy is the only form of regiment ordained by God, or even that God especially favours it. Hooper carefully explains that the powers St. Paul referred to in the thirteenth of Romans ' be not only kings and emperors, but all such as be appointed to any public office and common regiment, either for a king, where as is a kingdom, or in the place of a king, where as the state of the commonwealth is no monarchy '.[1] ' All kings, queens and other governors,' declares the Homily of 1571, ' are specially appointed by the ordinance of God.'[2]

It was really almost unnecessary to say that magistracy was an ordinance of God, or that, by the mouth of St. Paul, God commanded obedience to the powers that be. If every one did not really believe these things, at least no one denied them. What was necessary was to insist that God forbids active resistance or rebellion in all cases whatsoever. ' Though the magistrates be evil and very tyrants against the commonwealth,' wrote Cranmer in 1549, ' yet the subjects must obey in all worldly things.'[3] ' Such subjects,' declares the Homily of 1571, ' as are disobedient or rebellious against their princes, disobey God and procure their own damnation.'[4] Even Robert Barnes, a too faithful disciple of Luther, who was hanged for sedition in 1532, admitted that ' the Scripture commandeth us to obey to wicked Princes '.[5] ' What true English heart,' he added, ' would think but that the King's request was both godly and lawful ? ' The words are far more significant than were the assertions for which he was hanged.

It was not of course said by anyone that you must or may obey the King rather than God. All agree that commands contrary to God's law must be disobeyed. In the book of Homilies issued under Edward VI this principle is asserted emphatically :

' It is intolerable ignorance, madness and wickedness for subjects to make any murmuring, rebellion or insurrection against their most dear and most dread sovereign Lord and King, ordained and appointed by God's goodness for their commodity, peace and quietness. . . . Yet let us believe undoubtedly that we

---

[1] *Annotations in the thirteenth chapter to the Romans*, ed. Parker Soc., p. 101.

[2] *Against Disobedience.* Sermon I, p. 549, ed. 1859. All my references are to this edition.

[3] *Notes for a sermon on the rebellion of* 1549. Printed in Parker Soc. ed. of Cranmer's Works, II, p. 188.

[4] *Against Disobedience.* Sermon I, p. 549.

[5] *Supplication unto the most gracious Prince, King Henry VIII.*

may not obey kings, magistrates or any other . . . if they would command us to do anything contrary to God's commandments.' [1]

But however unpleasant the consequences of such disobedience may be, they must be borne with. There must be no active resistance. Latimer, preaching in 1552, stated the matter forcibly and simply :

' Be ye subject to all the common laws made by men of authority ; by the king's majesty and by his most honourable council or by a common parliament : be subject unto them, obey them, saith God. And here is but one exception, that is, against God. When laws are made against God and his word, then I ought more to obey God than man. Then I may refuse to obey with a good conscience ; yet for all that I may not rise up against the magistrates nor make any uproar ; for if I do so, I sin damnably. I must be content to suffer whatsoever God shall lay upon me.' [2]

The practical conclusion is stated clearly and semi-officially in the publication often referred to as *King Henry's Book*.[3] There the command : ' Honour thy father and thy mother ' becomes an order to obey magistrates. ' No subjects,' it is declared, ' may draw their sword against their prince for any cause whatsoever.'

' Obedience is due,' wrote Gardiner, ' but how far the limits of requiring obedience extend, that is the whole question that can be demanded.' [4] It was, in fact, the question that was being demanded everywhere throughout the century. But in England there seems to have been little question that obedience was always due, except when it conflicted with positive commands of God. ' What manner of limits are these that you tell me of,' asks Gardiner, ' seeing that the Scripture hath none such ? ' Extraordinarily emphatic was the language of William Tyndale, the man whose translation of the New Testament became the basis of our Authorized Version. ' He that judgeth the king,' wrote Tyndale in 1528, ' judgeth God ; and he that resisteth the king resisteth God and damneth God's law and ordinance. . . . The king is, in this world, without law, and may at his lust do right or wrong and shall give accounts but to God only.' [5] The words seem to repre-

---

[1] *An Exhortation concerning Good Order and Obedience to Rulers and Magistrates*, ed. 1859, p. 112. This Homily was printed as early as 1547 and appears in all later editions of the *First Book*. It reads rather like a rough draft of the Homily of 1571 against disobedience.

[2] *Sermons on the Lord's Prayer*, IV, p. 371. Ed. Parker Soc.

[3] *A Necessary Doctrine and Erudition for any Christian Man*, 1543. It was a revision and enlargement of an earlier work, *The Institution of a Christian Man*, published in 1537 ; the result of a commission issued to Cranmer and others in 1540.

[4] *Concerning True Obedience*, 1553, p. 22.

[5] *The Obedience of a Christian Man*, ed. 1582, p. 32. Ed. R. Lovett (1888), pp. 90–92. Published at Marburg, where Tyndale was living under the protection of Philip of Hesse. All Tyndale's writings were printed in exile. The full title of the book is : *The Obedience of a Christian Man, and how Christen rulers ought to govern, wherein also (if thou mark diligently) thou shalt fynde eyes to perceave crafty conveyance of all jugglers.*

sent an extreme view and can hardly be paralleled from any other English writings before the reign of James I. Tyndale was probably saying more than he really meant.[1] Latimer refers to Parliament ; Hooper explains that the king is bound by the law of the land.[2] When, in Tudor England, a writer insists that God forbids any sort of rebellion against constituted authority, we must not suppose that he thinks of the English King as what we call an ' absolute ' monarch. Whether he uses the term ' magistrate ' or whether he speaks of ' Prince ' or ' King ', the meaning is generally, if not always, the same. Probably the writer would have agreed with Fortescue or with Sir Thomas Smith that the power of the King in England is ' dominium politicum et regale '. Far more probably he was not thinking in terms of law at all. He was simply anxious to emphasize the wickedness of rebellion against lawful authority. The term, ' the Prince,' does not necessarily refer exclusively to the monarch. It seems to be used to mean the highest civil authority, however constituted. ' When I speak of a Prince,' says the Scottish lawyer, Sir Thomas Craig, at the very end of Elizabeth's reign, ' I mean a Prince in the Parliament or Great Court of the kingdom.' [3]

Like Luther, the English writers see very good reasons for God's command to obey ; and they see more reasons for it than were seen by Luther. In the first place they insist that disobedience to the lawful magistrate or rebellion against the Prince is unlikely to produce anything but disorder and misery. ' Naturally there is in every man,' says Hooper, ' a certain desire of liberty and to live without subjection and all manner of laws except such as please himself.' [4] There exists, therefore, a constant tendency towards anarchy. The King, says Tyndale, ' though he be the greatest tyrant in the world, yet is he unto thee a great benefit of God '. For one tyrant is far more bearable than many tyrants and even the worst keeps order, ' neither suffereth any man to poll but himself only '.[5] All through the century one finds people expatiating on the horrors that follow rebellion ; especially in connection with the disturbances of 1549 and 1569. In 1549 Sir John Cheke, tutor to Edward VI, enlarged at length upon the subject.[6] ' A rebel is worse than the worst prince,'

---

[1] He violently attacked Henry VIII's proceedings in the matter of the divorce in his *Practyse of Prelates* (1530).

[2] *Annotations in the thirteenth chapter to the Romans.* Parker Soc. ed., p. 101.

[3] *Concerning the Right of Succession to the Kingdom of England,* ed. 1703, p. 123. The book was originally written in Latin but seems to have been published, for the first time, only in 1703, in an English version. See Chap. X.

[4] *Annotations.* Parker Soc. ed., p. 103.

[5] *Obedience of a Christian Man,* ed. 1528, p. 33. Ed. R. Lovett, p. 93.

[6] In a treatise entitled *The Hurt of Sedition : how grievous it is to a Commonwealth* or *The True Subject to the Rebel.* Holinshed inserted it in his Chronicles and it was reprinted in 1641.

declared the Homily of 1571, 'and rebellion worse than the worst
government of the worst prince.'[1] How monstrous is the wickedness
of those who 'rob, spoil, destroy and burn in England Englishmen!'[2]
At the very end of the century Sir John Hayward was writing more
coolly and with less sense of danger, but saying the same thing.

'The vices of any prince,' he wrote, 'are not sufficient of themselves to overthrow a state, except thereupon rebellion be raised which will draw all things
into confusion. . . . By obedience a few particulars remain in danger; by
rebellion, all. . . . It is a rule in reason, a trial in experience, an authority
confirmed by the best, that rebellion produceth more horrible effects than either
the tyranny or insufficiency of any prince.'[3]

Along with this sense of a constant danger of disorder and its
ruinous consequences, went a perception that, if once any sort of
right to rebel were recognized, the danger would be greatly increased.
How can such a right conceivably exist or in what form can it possibly
be recognized ? The answer to these questions seemed to thinking
Englishmen of the sixteenth century so axiomatic that the questions
are hardly asked save by implication. 'Is it the office of subjects,'
asked Cranmer, 'to take upon them the reformation of the commonwealth, without the commandment of common authority ? '[4] If the
realm be in any sense a 'commonwealth', how can it be so ? If
rebellion be rightful for any cause, who is to judge when the moment
has come ? No one in England would have asserted for the
'nobility' or for any class of officials, for any 'proceres' or 'officiarii
regni', a right to judge and to give the signal. Under Henry VIII
it is constantly and emphatically declared that such rights of rule
and jurisdiction as are possessed by subordinate magistrates or by
landlords, are rights created by the King or by the law. 'They rule
but by law,' wrote Cheke; 'if otherwise, the Law, the Council, the
King taketh away their rule. . . . There can be no just execution
of laws, reformation of faults, giving out of commandments, but from
the King. For in the King only is the right hereof, and the authority
of him derived by his appointment to his ministers.'[5] It seemed no
less clear that no right of judging whether or when rebellion were
justified could be recognized in subjects in general. 'What a perilous
thing were it to commit unto the subjects the judgement which prince
is wise and godly and his government good and which is otherwise.'[6]
Ever it is the worst men who are most inclined to rebellion. 'Whatsoever the prince be or his government, it is evident that for the most

---

[1] Sermon I, p. 553.   [2] Ib., p. 558.
[3] In Hayward's *Answer to the First Part of a certain Conference*, 1603, ed.
1603, Chap. IV, L. 3. For Hayward, see Chap. X.
[4] *Sermon on Rebellion*. Works, Parker Soc., p. 193.
[5] *The True Subject to the Rebel*.
[6] *Against Disobedience*, 1571, I, p. 547.

part, those princes whom some subjects do think to be very godly . . .
some other subjects do take the same to be evil and ungodly. . . .
If, therefore, all subjects that mislike of their prince should rebel, no
realm should ever be without rebellion.'[1] The ' common-sense ' view
thus presented in the Homily of 1571 was the view generally taken.
The question whether anything ever justifies rebellion and if not,
why not, is not being really faced. In England, all through the
Tudor period, thinking people are unwilling to admit that there is
any real question about it. In this respect England differed strikingly
from France, and even from the German countries. Perhaps the
most striking peculiarity of England in the sixteenth century was the
general refusal to admit that any case can be made for a right of
rebellion. Only very late in Elizabeth's reign is the question seriously
taken.

It is highly significant that from the time of Henry VIII onwards
great stress is laid on the notion that England is environed about
with enemies : French or Scots or Spaniards. It is believed, too,
that the foreign enemy has papist friends within the gates. Under
these circumstances rebellion, it is declared, is not only wicked but
foolish and suicidal. ' It is an easy thing to break a whole fagot
when every stick is loosed from another.'[2] ' God,' wrote John Fox
in 1576, ' hath so placed us Englishmen here in one commonwealth,
also in one Church, as in one ship together : let us not mangle or
divide the ship, which being divided perisheth. . . . No storm so
dangerous to a ship on the sea, as is discord and disorder in a weal
public.'[3] This sort of feeling remained strong throughout the
century.

The Homily of 1571, *Against Disobedience and Wilful Rebellion*,
is the completest expression of what might be called the Tudor theory
of the duty of subjects in a commonwealth. It summed up what
had been said during the previous reigns, and enlarged upon it, if it
added little. Cranmer had declared that you could see in history,
sacred and profane, what God thinks of rebellion, by noting the
calamities that constantly fall on rebels. Edward VI's *Exhortation
concerning good order*[4] repeated this ; the Elizabethan Homily enlarged
on the text. We can all see how grievous is the sin of rebellion, if we
do but consider ' the heavy wrath and dreadful indignation of Almighty
God against such subjects as do only but inwardly grudge and
murmur against their governors '.[5] References follow to incidents
recorded in Exodus and Numbers. ' Turn over and read the histories
of all nations, look over the chronicles of our own country, call to

---

[1] Ib., I, p. 549.   [2] Cranmer, *Sermon on Rebellion*.
[3] Preface to the 1576 edition of the *Acts and Monuments*. (*A Protestation
to the whole Church of England*.)
[4] *First Book of Homilies*, 1547.   [5] Sermon IV, p. 583.

mind so many rebellions of old time and some yet fresh in memory, ye shall not find that God ever prospered any rebellion against their natural and lawful prince.' [1]

If all do not agree in this historical generalization, all agree in the sentiment and the perception. Even the Elizabethan Puritans, rebels as they were logically and potentially, never claimed a right of rebellion. ' If the Prince commands anything contrary to the word of God,' wrote John Udall in 1590, while actually under sentence of death for sedition, ' it is not lawful for subjects to rebel or resist, but with patience and humility to bear the punishment laid upon them.' [2] Had the Puritans been in a position to rebel with any chance of success their views would have been different ; but it was as it was. To the end of the century the chorus sang the same tune. It is true that the loudest voices in that chorus were those of officials and clergy ; but I think it is also true that they voiced a national sentiment. When the finest of all the passages in the Homily of 1571 was read in church, I think that nearly all the listeners felt solemnly and sympathetically thrilled :

' He that nameth rebellion, nameth not a singular and one only sin, as is theft, robbery, murder and such like ; but he nameth the whole puddle and sink of all sins against God and man, against his prince, his country, his countrymen, his parents, his children, his kinsfolks, his friends and against all men universally ; all sins, I say, against God and all men heaped together, nameth he that nameth rebellion.' [3]

Real conviction is needed for the writing of a passage like that. But the strength of the English conviction of the wickedness of rebellion was not in the main derived from religion or from any theory of divine right. It was derived from the sense of the need of order, from the sense that the welfare and very existence of the commonwealth was bound up with obedience to authority, from the sense of danger from foreign enemies ; from, one might say, the common sense of the English people, or at least of its upper classes. Obedience to the Prince was, it is true, conceived as a duty to God : a divine right to command is vested in the ' common authority '. This was believed ; but it was believed because men felt that magistracy was so urgently needed that this must be true. It was not believed because of anything St. Paul said. The thirteenth chapter of the Epistle to the Romans contains what are perhaps the most important words ever written for the history of political thought. Yet it would be a gross mistake to suppose that men, at any time, took their political opinions from St. Paul. The Tudor theory of subjection was fundamentally utilitarian : it has strict reference to immediate expediency

---

[1] Sermon IV, p. 583.
[2] Udall's *Confession.* See Neal, I, p. 452.
[3] Sermon III, pp. 573, 574.

and to time and place. At the end of Elizabeth's reign it was, on the whole, just the most thoroughly religious people, Catholic or Puritan, who were nearest to revolt. Even their resentment was aroused, not by the conception of the magistrate as a divine ordinance, but by the assertion of his supremacy in the Church.

CHAPTER III

THE VERY AND TRUE COMMONWEAL

§ 1. INTRODUCTORY

THE expression of political thought in England, at least down to Elizabeth's reign and even to the end of the century, was, for the most part, inextricably entangled with religious controversy. Thinkers were concerned chiefly with the question of the nature of the Church and its relation to civil authority, as they had been in the Middle Ages. Even the question of the nature of political obligation was discussed chiefly in this connection. But under Henry VIII and Edward VI political thought was also taking another and quite different direction. The conception of an ' absolute ' national sovereignty was developed mainly in connection with the Reformation : the conception of the Church of England as an aspect of the commonwealth presupposed a conception of the commonwealth. This idea of a Christian commonwealth, inherited from the Middle Ages, was being explored without specific reference to the Church. Men were considering the actual structure of society and asking how its parts are related and what binds it together and what should be its animating purpose. In this there was nothing whatever that was new. It is true to say that, under Henry VIII and Edward VI, there was formed a conception of what the commonwealth should be, or, if you like to put it so, of what it really is. It would be more fully true to say that medieval conceptions received at that time a fresh expression. The writers who furnished that expression were, in the main, reproducing medieval conceptions of the meaning and purpose of the social and political order and of the duty of every man in his station to see to it that his activities were strictly related to that end. So only could he be justified and so only serve the purpose of God. England in the sixteenth century was passing through an economic as well as a religious revolution. The idealists of the mid-century, therefore, tended to see in co-operation for economic purposes the immediate object of the social and political structure. But that tendency, too, is visible earlier ; and as fully as Aquinas or St. Antonino of Florence, they found in religion the unifying and defining and animating purpose of society.

The writings of these idealists were, it is true, to a great extent, merely a protest against what was happening ; against the greed of landlords and commercial persons, against ' usury ' and enclosure and rack renting and the attack on copyhold tenure. That protest was, to a considerable extent, ill-informed and its economic theories were crude and more or less fallacious. For all that, its dream of a perfectly co-operating commonwealth, which was a part of the rich medieval legacy, was fairly coherent and substantial. It is perhaps due to the fact that it was developed in protest, that we do not find definite expression of it before the latter part of Henry VIII's reign. There is, of course, one partial and magnificent exception : the *Utopia* of Sir Thomas More, published as early as 1516. But More was isolated not only, or chiefly, by time. The nature of that isolation of his and the relation of his thought to that which appears after 1530, must be discussed later. For the moment we must pass him by.

In order to exhibit clearly the nature of the ideal that was constructed, one must first consider certain notions concerning society, that were very widespread in the sixteenth century and not only in England. The religious duty of obedience to the Prince was constantly associated with the conception of a similar duty in relation to every recognized form of authority in human society. A divine right was attached, not only to the Prince, but to the father in the family, the landlord on his estate, even to the common employer of labour. The idea seems to have been generally, though not necessarily, connected with a conception of the actual social order as having been arranged or ' ordained ' by God. God has not merely ordained princes and other governors to rule and give law to their people ; He has so constructed society, at least in England and presumably, with differences, elsewhere, that whatsoever section or aspect of it be regarded, we shall find ordained superiors and ordained subjects, the one bound to rule for the welfare of the other, the other loyally to obey. Just as the Prince should be obeyed in all things lawful by God's law, so the inferior should obey his immediate superior in all things lawful by the law of the Prince. Increased emphasis on the Prince alone separates all this from medieval conceptions.

' Standeth it with any reason,' wrote Cranmer, ' to turn upside down the good order of the whole world, that is everywhere and has ever been, that is to say the commoners to be governed by the nobles and the servants by their masters ? ' [1] Sir John Cheke, in the same connection, argued in the same way. Because men are not equal, says Sir Thomas Elyot, ' therefore God hath ordained a diversity or pre-eminence in degrees to be among men for the necessary direction

[1] Answer to the articles of the rebels, 1549. Works, Parker Soc., ed. Cox, II, p. 185.

and preservation of them in conformity of living '.[1] High degree, involving superior wealth, involves also fitness to rule ; and this is the reason why high degree exists. ' It is only a public weal, where, as God hath disposed . . . understanding, is also appointed degrees and places according to the excellency thereof ; and thereto also would be substance convenient and necessary for the ornament of the same, which also compasseth a reverence and due obedience to the vulgar people or commonalty.' [2] Elyot is sadly confused, but he meant what Cranmer said when he declared that ' gentlemen ' were fitter for authority than ' villains '. ' Take away gentlemen and rulers and straightway all other falleth clearly away and followeth barbarical confusion.' [3] In a commonwealth, says Cheke, addressing the rebels of 1549, ' one kind hath need of another and yet a great sort of you more need of one gentleman than one gentleman of a great sort of you.' [4] In Starkey's *Dialogue* one of the speakers defends the law of primogeniture on the ground that if estates in land were divided, the people would be deprived of their natural heads. ' The maintenance of these heads is the maintenance of all civil order and politic rule here in our nation.' [5]

The whole social order is regarded as representing arrangements made or brought about by God for the peace and well-being of men. The idea is frequently expressed by the use of the word ' vocation '. A man's social position or occupation is represented as his ' calling ' : we still use the word without any clear sense that it originally meant a calling by God. It is every man's duty to labour in his vocation and be obedient to his superiors. So he does his duty in that state of life to which it has pleased God to call him. It almost seems sometimes that the duty of obedience extends even to submission to illegal exactions and proceedings. This view would of course be irreconcilable with any conception of law as representing the authority of the Prince. But I do not think that any English writer of this period intended to forbid the inferior to appeal to law against his superior. It is merely insisted that he must not defend his rights by the use of force. The right to use force belongs to the Prince only. ' To revenge wrongs is, in a subject, to take and usurp the office of a King and consequently the office of God.' [6]

' When I consider and weigh in my mind all these commonwealths, which nowadays everywhere do flourish,' declared the greatest English

---

[1] *The Governour*, 1531, ed. H. H. Croft, 1883, I, p. 209.

[2] Ib., p. 8.

[3] Cranmer's *Sermon on Rebellion*. Works, Parker Soc., II, p. 196.

[4] *The True Subject to the Rebel*.

[5] *Dialogue between Cardinal Pole and Thomas Lapset*, 1536. E.E.T.S., ed. S. J. Herrtage, pp. 110, 111.

[6] Robert Crowley : *The Way to Wealth*. Select Works, ed. J. M. Cowper or the E.E.T.S., p. 134.

thinker of the age, ' so God help me, I can perceive nothing but a certain conspiracy of rich men, procuring their own commodities under the name and title of the commonwealth.'[1] The conception of the social order, with its gross inequalities of possession and of opportunity, as having been divinely ordained and established, so that those who have little or nothing are called by God not only to accept their inferior position and straitened means, but to reverence and obey those who have much, might, if it stood alone, be taken as justifying More's famous and terrible judgement. Very often, no doubt, it did stand alone, without other implication than that of a right to possession absolute on one side and a duty of submission absolute on the other. But, logically, standing thus alone it became mere nonsense ; and this was as obvious then as now. The very fact, it was perceived, that God had ordained the main features of the social structure, implied that the welfare of all alike is the purpose of these arrangements. God could not have ordained such a conspiracy as More spoke of ; he had ordained rather a ' conspiring together in all virtue and honesty '.[2] ' Hath God put immortal souls in none other but such as be possessioners in this world ? ' asked a pamphleteer.[3] Evidently it could not be so. Society must be thought of as a co-operative association in which the duty of every member to the whole is primary. This is, above all, what the political idealism of the time insisted upon.

It was, in fact, usually in connection with the idea of society as divinely ordered, that the conception of a ' very and true commonweal ' was developed. In that perfect commonwealth, waste and dishonesty and mere self-seeking disappear and every member of the community works single-mindedly for the common good. How far the conception may have been derived from Plato or how far the later writers were influenced by More, it is not possible to say. But I doubt, at least, whether Plato had any part in it. Such a conception might simply and easily have developed on the basis of medieval thought, joined to a heightened and diffused sense of the nation as a community and to an acute sense of the economic stresses of the time. Putting More aside, the two writers who expressed most fully the idea of a ' true commonweal ' are Thomas Starkey and Robert Crowley. But Starkey, like More, is in some respects isolated. Neither of them believed that man was bound by God's ordinance to any particular form of social or political organization. Crowley, on the other hand, like Cranmer and Cheke and Elyot and Forrest, believed in a divine right to rule vested in noblemen and gentlemen, as well as in the Prince. In this respect Crowley is more typical than

---

[1] *Utopia*, II, 9. Clarendon Press ed., p. 303.
[2] Starkey's *Dialogue*, E.E.T.S., p. 10.
[3] *Supplication of the poore commons*, 1546.

are the more deliberate and analytical thinkers. Because his view is more closely connected with the current thought of the time than was that of the earlier writer, Starkey, I shall deal first with the true commonweal as visible in his writings. But it is by no means only in his writings that it is visible. It is indicated or implied in many others.

§ 2. THE IDEALISM OF ROBERT CROWLEY [1]

Alike in his conception of what a Christian commonwealth should be and in his attitude towards the commercialism that seeks in all transactions the greatest possible profit, Crowley was at one with medieval schoolmen and with such medieval economists as St. Antonino of Florence. His earnestness gave vividness and freshness to his expression of old ideas, but the very last thing that can be claimed for him is originality. It seems, indeed, that in the first half of the sixteenth century, almost every one who thought about landownership and trade and money-making from a religious standpoint, was saying much the same thing. Luther had denounced idlers and money-makers as pests of society, had referred to the taking of interest on loans as an invention of the devil, and had denounced trade in luxuries and combinations for profit-making.[2] ' Love thy neighbour as thyself ' and ' What ye would that men should do unto you, do ye also unto them,' were to him the rules that should govern all traffic. The observance of them, he thought, would get rid of all difficulties. ' Then no law books nor courts nor judicial actions would be required ; all things would quietly and simply be set to rights, for every one's heart and conscience would guide him.'[3] Luther was but reproducing, crudely and emotionally, the thought of medieval schoolmen. ' He who has enough to satisfy his wants,' had written Henry of Langenstein in the fourteenth century, ' and nevertheless ceaselessly labours to acquire riches, either in order to obtain a higher social position, or that subsequently he may have enough to live without labour, or that his sons may become men of wealth and importance, all such are incited by a damnable avarice, sensuality or pride.'[4]

[1] Robert Crowley, or Crole, born about the year 1518, set up as a printer in London in 1549. He printed his own writings and the latest production of his press is dated 1551. In that year he took orders and abandoned printing for preaching. During Mary's reign he was in exile at Frankfort ; under Elizabeth he became Vicar of St. Giles, Cripplegate. He was deprived as a result of his objection to the surplice. He published numerous tracts in prose and verse and died in 1588.

[2] *Von Kaufshandlung und Wucher*, 1524. Works (Weimar ed.), Vol. XV. In his *De Regno Christi*, Bucer urged that persistent idlers should be dealt with penally, that just prices should be fixed by law, and that schools should be established for every town and village. He also pathetically suggested that only pious persons should be allowed to engage in trade.

[3] *Grosser Sermon von Wucher*, 1520. Works (Weimar ed.), Vol. VI.

[4] Quoted by R. H. Tawney in *Religion and the Rise of Capitalism*, p. 35.

Crowley's view was the same. He expressed it variously and vigorously and it stands to the credit of his intelligence that he emphasized what was, practically, the main point of contention. Aquinas had laid down two principles : that a contract or bargain is only just when both parties gain equally and that property must be regarded as a stewardship or trust. To Crowley the very roots of the evils he denounced, the most anti-social and damnable of errors, was the belief that a man has a real right to do as he wills with his own. ' If the possessioners,' he'declared, ' would consider themselves to be but stewards and not lords over their possessions, this oppression would soon be redressed. But so long as this persuasion sti.keth in their minds : It is mine own, who should warn me to do with mine own as myself listeth ? it shall not be possible to have any redress at all.' [1] All through his writings he was asserting and applying this principle. ' If there were no God,' he says, getting near the heart of the matter, ' then would I think it lawful for men to use their possessions as they list.' For Christians such a view is not possible. God has not given their property to possessioners in the sense in which the law gives it. Ownership as conceived in law must be taken only as a convenient fiction.

It follows that a man should not aim at ' rising ' in the world nor should he aspire to grow indefinitely richer. Indeed any increase in his wealth that comes naturally from his labour in his vocation ought to be used for the benefit of his poorer neighbour. The business of the merchant is, not to make all the profit he can for himself, but simply to provide needful things for others as cheaply as he can do it.[2] The business of the landlord is to rule justly and to assist his neighbour. If he seek to enrich himself by enclosing or by raising rents, he will surely be damned. Greedy landlords and commercial profiteers or ' usurers ', were at this time being denounced with the utmost freedom and violence of language. ' The rich man,' says Hooper,[3] ' so encroacheth, gathereth together and obtaineth so much into his own hands, that he alone possesseth the earth, liveth thereby and his poor neighbour ready to die for lack. . . . These men, except they repent, cannot be saved.' Here Cranmer and Tyndale, Hooper and Latimer, Becon and Lever are at one with Crowley, Starkey and More. They all express a sense that in a Christian commonwealth lust of wealth and riotous living are alike damnable. Appeal was made to Henry VIII to put a stop to such wickedness. ' Employ your study to leave him (Prince Edward) a commonweal to govern and not an

---

[1] *The Way to Wealth*, 1550, ed. E.E.T.S., p. 157. So in the *Sum of Scriptures* : ' He that is rich and liveth of his rents, may not use or spend his goods as he will, but thy goods belong as well unto the poor as to thee.'

[2] *Voyce of the Laste Trumpet. The Merchant's Lesson*, ed. E.E.T.S.

[3] *Later Writings*. Parker Soc. ed., p. 97.

island of brute beasts, among whom the strongest devour the weaker.'[1]
' Neither the Church of England nor a Christian Commonwealth,'
declared Martin Bucer, ' ought to tolerate such as prefer private gain
to the public weal, or seek it to the hurt of their neighbours.'[2]

Crowley conceived of the structure of society as ordained by God
and therefore not to be altered without impiety. Wealth, and especially land as the source of wealth, has been portioned out by God among
a relatively small number of ' possessioners ' and these persons thereby
become fit and able to govern under the Prince and it is intended by
God that they shall do so. But it is clear that the system must be
worked as God intends it shall be. ' The end why all men be create,'
wrote Crowley, in the doggerel verse he apparently considered suitable
for popular consumption, ' as men of wisdom do agree, is to maintain
the public state in the country where they shall be.'[3] Gentlemen
and possessioners generally, must, like common folk, regard their
stations as callings from God and labour in their vocation for the
common good, on pain of damnation. All men alike, Crowley continually insisted, must think first of the commonweal and every man
should regard his business or his property as a public trust, almost as
public office. In other places than Utopia, More had declared, ' men
speak still of the commonwealth but every man procureth his own
private wealth '.[4] Starkey had said the same, but had added that
' every man knoweth, as I think, they should above all regard the
commonwealth '. Crowley insisted that possessioners should regard
themselves as stewards of public property. ' Thou art a man,' he
wrote, addressing ' gentlemen ' or landlords, ' that God hath set to
rule the rout in thy country, wherefore thou hast need for to get good
knowledge, rather than money.' Having acquired good knowledge,

' thou shalt perceive thou hast no time to spare and spend in banqueting, for
though thou watch till it be prime, thou shalt have enough to doing. Thou shalt
not find any leisure to dice, to card or to revel, if thou once do take a pleasure
in using thine own calling well. . . . Thou shalt have delight in nothing, saving
in doing thy duty ; which is, under God and thy King, to rule them that thou
dost dwell by.'[5]

' Consider,' says Crowley, addressing landlords, ' that you are but ministers
and servants under the Lord our God and that you shall render a strait account
of your administration. . . . We are all one man's children and have by nature
like right to the riches and treasure of this world. . . . By nature you can
claim nothing but that which you shall get with the sweat of your faces. That

---

[1] *Supplication of the poore commons*, 1546.
[2] *De Regno Christi*, 1557. Quoted by Mr. Tawney in *Religion and the Rise of
Capitalism* (1926), p. 63. Bucer's book was written during his residence in
England from 1549 to his death in 1551. A French translation of it appeared
in 1558 and a German in 1563.
[3] *The Voyce of the Laste Trumpet*, 1550.
[4] *Utopia*, Clarendon Press ed., p. 299.
[5] *The Laste Trumpet. The Gentleman's Lesson*, ed. E.E.T.S., pp. 91, 92.

you are lords and governors therefore, cometh not by nature but by the ordinance and appointment of God.'[1]

He meant that the position of landlords was not one that had arisen inevitably from a natural superiority in them ; but that God had specially entrusted land to them as stewards and trustees for the rest of the community. ' You have their inheritance and do minister unto them. The whole earth by birthright belongeth to the children of men. They are all inheritors thereof indifferently by nature.'[2] These arrangements, he says, very inadequately, have been made by God ' because the sturdy should not oppress the weak and impotent '. This it seems is, nevertheless, just what is happening. But Crowley is well aware of that ; and he becomes prophetic. ' The mystical body of this most noble realm '[3] will go to wrack if any of its members be unjustly ruined. He makes a violent attack on extortionate clergy and on the legalizing of ' usury ' by the Act of 1545. ' If you let these things pass and regard them not, be ye sure the Lord will confound your wisdom. Invent, decree, establish and authorize what you can : all shall come to naught.'[4]

The fundamental fact is, it was declared, that the Christian commonwealth must be knit together by love among its members. Nothing less will suffice to bring about real co-operation and general well-being.

' Love,' wrote Sir John Cheke, ' is not the knot only of the Commonwealth, whereby divers parts be perfectly joined together in one politique body, but also the strength and might of the same, gathering together into a small room with order, which, scattered, would else breed confusion and debate.'[5] ' There is perfect civility,' wrote Starkey,[6] ' there is the true commonweal, where as all the parts, as members of one body, be knit together in perfect love and unity, every one doing his office and duty, after such manner that, whatsoever state, office or degree any man be of, the duty thereto pertaining with all diligence he busily fulfill and without envy or malice to other accomplish the same. . . . And so thus,' he concludes, ' when every part, after this manner doeth his office and duty . . . with perfect love and amity one to another, one glad to succour and aid another as members and parts of one body ; to the intent that after this worldly and civil life here peaceably passed and virtuously spent, they may, at the last, all together attain such end and felicity as, by the goodness of God and ordinance of nature, is determined to the excellent dignity and nature of man. Then shall there be established and set in such a multitude of people so governed, so ruled, with such policy, that thing which we have so long sought, that is to say a very and true commonweal.'[7]

---

[1] *The Way to Wealth*, ed. E.E.T.S., p. 163. The distinction between that which arises inevitably and so is ' natural ' and that which is specially ordained by God, is constantly made.

[2] Ib., ed. E.E.T.S., pp. 163, 164.   [3] Ib., ed. E.E.T.S., p. 175.
[4] Ib., ed. E.E.T.S., p. 175.   [5] *The True Subject to the Rebel.*
[6] *Dialogue*, ed. E.E.T.S., pp. 54, 55.
[7] Ib., ed. E.E.T.S., pp. 54–56. In Utopia ' the whole island is as it were one family or household '.

It was a dream, this vision of a happy commonwealth knit together by the amity among its members, kindled to a perfect co-operation by love of the weal public and one's neighbour. It was a dream of what might be under existing conditions, if all men did their ' duty '. Crowley was afflicted with no doubts about that duty, and he hoped, at least, that if only the matter were put clearly before them, men would see it and do it. He failed, and all those who at the time thought like him failed, to see that principles once fairly easy of application had in process of time become increasingly difficult practically to apply. He made no attempt to show how his principles were to be applied to the new conditions that were being established by capitalistic enterprise, large scale trading and international finance. Of what was behind the developments he bewailed he shows no understanding. But he was sure that all the devices of the wicked for mere personal gain would ' come to naught '. Here lurked another fallacy. One may grant that in a sense he was right ; but the prospect of failure in that sense would not seriously have alarmed those he denounced, even had they understood it. Crowley had few positive suggestions to make for remedy. What was wanted, it seemed to him, was a change of heart or a realization of God's purposes. ' Seek ye first,' he might have quoted, ' the kingdom of God and his righteousness and all good things shall be added unto you.' But were those good things in truth the good after which his greedy bankers and traders, landlords and speculators, were grasping ? Crowley was asking men to be other than they are. His ideal was conservative in that it involved a stereotyping of the social structure. It was, even, reactionary in the sense that it aimed at restoring a state of things vaguely supposed to have existed in a happy past. And like much that is called reactionary, it was revolutionary. At this distance it may be felt as pathetic. Commercialism was spreading, the old religion 'of Christendom was disintegrating, the dominant trends were in directions wholly different. Yet it is curious to note how many of the sentiments, complaints and suggestions of these social idealists of the mid-sixteenth century have been repeated from that day to this. In that modern world that was coming the dream was to revive and to persist. It takes many forms but is, itself, perennial.

§ 3. STARKEY'S *DIALOGUE*

Crowley's appeal was not to government. It would seem to be implied in his writings that no redress of the evils from which society suffered was possible without a change of heart. His appeal was to the moral and religious consciousness. Starkey's *Dialogue* presents the view that redress is largely a question of organization and that governmental action can do much to create the very and true commonweal. The treatise includes a series of sweeping and far-reaching practical proposals for reform.

Little is known of Thomas Starkey beyond the superficial facts of his career. He was born some time between 1490 and 1500. He graduated at Oxford and became a Fellow of Magdalen, where he lectured on natural philosophy. His connection with the Poles began in 1531 and for some two years, perhaps, he was in the service of Reginald Pole in Italy, probably as chaplain or secretary. By 1534 he was back in England and acting as chaplain to Pole's mother, the Countess of Salisbury. He became a royal chaplain, and in 1535 was commissioned to write to Pole with the object of ascertaining his views about the divorce and persuading him to return to England. The result of these overtures was untoward both from Starkey's point of view and that of Henry VIII. Pole's reply took the form of his treatise, *Pro Ecclesiasticae Unitatis Defensione*, published in 1536. Yet Starkey did not lose his royal chaplaincy, and later the King rewarded his efforts by making him Master of Corpus Christi. He preached before the King only a few months before his death in 1538.

The *Dialogue between Cardinal Pole and Thomas Lupset* must have been written between 1536 and 1538 inclusive. Its form is accurately indicated by this title. Lupset, Lecturer in Rhetoric at Oxford, had been a friend both of Starkey and of Pole and was dead. His part in the dialogue consists mainly in making objections which, subsequently, he drops or withdraws.[1] The main contentions of the Dialogue are represented as being Pole's. It is impossible to say, even with any certain degree of probability, how far this is really the case. There is little in the Dialogue which might not have come from Pole, and there are opinions expressed in it which strike one as more likely to have been Pole's than Starkey's. But there is nothing in it which might not have come from Starkey's own mind simply. In any case he must surely have sympathized with the views expressed, and he certainly well understood them. One would like to know whether and how far the Dialogue expresses the views of Reginald Pole, but, however interesting, the question is not of importance. Pole himself, of course, had no chance of disclaiming : he can never have heard of Starkey's audacity. Neither Starkey nor anyone else published the Dialogue till 1871. Yet it is by far the most remarkable piece of writing concerned with politics that was produced in England under Henry VIII, with the exception of More's *Utopia*.

The Dialogue begins with an attempt by Lupset to persuade Pole that it is his duty to give his life to politics and the service of his country. For a man in Pole's position there can be no higher duty and no life so useful. This was a view very generally held at the time

---

[1] It is hard to imagine why he was introduced, unless it were that Starkey did not wish to represent himself as accepting Pole's conclusions.

and it is constantly implied in other writings. Pole, however, objects and his objections are noteworthy though they are not pressed. He feels by no means sure that the life of study and contemplation is not in any case higher than the active political life. He expresses, even, a doubt of the value of the life of ' civility '. It seems to him, sometimes, that man was not born for civilization, ' but rather to live in the wild forest, there more following the study of virtue, as it is said men did in the golden age '.[1] It may well be that Reginald Pole, aristocratic scholar of the Renaissance, already disillusioned, had actually expressed such thoughts in Starkey's hearing.

But these sceptical suggestions are quickly discarded and serious discussion begins on the main question of the Dialogue : ' what is the very and true commonweal, wherein it standeth and where it most flourisheth '.[2] At once it is laid down, doubtless with reference to Plato and More, that what is wanted is not a picture of an impossibly beautiful commonwealth inhabited by impossibly wise and virtuous persons. What we have to consider is ' the nature of our country, the manner of our people ', remembering that this is the material we have to work with. In the Dialogue as a whole two questions are dealt with : firstly, what is the nature of the true commonweal ? and secondly, how can such a commonweal be established in our own country of England ?

For complete well-being, it is declared, man as an individual needs bodily health, ' convenient abundance of all worldly things ', children and friends who are, very properly, included under the heading ' riches ', and finally and above all honesty and virtue.[3] Over-great wealth is always dangerous, and wealth and authority combined without virtue are ' plain destruction ' to a man. Neither health nor wealth are of any value without virtue, which is that which directs to the right use of them. On the other hand, real poverty, or the lack of what all men need, cramps the mind and is a great evil. It is not, Pole is made to insist, a question of happiness, still less of pleasure. Wealth is not desirable because it can procure ' pleasure ', but because it gives freedom and power to help others. In More's *Utopia*, the chief gain resulting from the organization that produces abundance for all with short hours of labour, was represented as being ' the free liberty of the mind and garnishing of the same '[4]

Now the commonwealth is composed of individuals and therefore resembles an individual. Fanciful comparisons follow and it is concluded that the needs of the individual must be the need of the commonwealth. Upon which Lupset remarks that, if this be so, the commonwealth will be best served by every man doing the best he

---

[1] *Dialogue*, ed. E.E.T.S., p. 9.   [2] Ib., p. 131.
[3] Ib., pp. 35–37.
[4] *Utopia*, p. 152. All the references are to the Clarendon Press edition.

can for himself without any regard to others. It is merely, and inadequately, answered that while ' overmuch ' regard for self is destructive to the commonwealth, ' mean and convenient regard thereof maintaineth the same '.[1] Lupset, apparently, was content with this admission.

The commonwealth, then, must first of all be healthy. This involves a high average of individual healthiness and a right ratio of population to means of subsistence. This right ratio can only be. maintained by effective co-operation and the action of government. But health also involves beauty or harmony : that is a due proportion between parts. There will not be in a healthy society numerically more craftsmen or more husbandmen than are required. Further, the true commonweal must be ' rich ' . it must possess ' friends, riches and abundance of necessaries '. Cramping and demoralizing poverty, ' the mother of envy and malice, dissension and debate', must not exist within it. It needs friends also, like the individual. If a country be surrounded by foes, ' I cannot see how that country can long flourish in prosperity '.

Finally, what corresponds to ' virtue ' in the individual is, firstly, ' good order and policy, by good laws established and by heads and rulers put in effect', and, secondly, religion. What is, above all, required is that ' this multitude of people and whole commonalty, so healthy and so wealthy . . . may with due honour, reverence and love religiously worship God . . . every one also doing his duty to other with brotherly love, one loving another as members and parts of one body '.[2] Such a society, it is implied, could not lack good laws and good policy.

' A time there was, Master Lupset,' says Pole, ' when man, without city or town, law or religion, wandered abroad in the wild fields and woods, not otherwise than you see now brute beasts to do.' [3] In this condition he ' long continued and many years ', till he came at length to some order and civility and so gradually, ' in long time by little and little ' to the civilization that now is.[4] Many types and modes of government arose among men during this long process and no one type, it is suggested, can be regarded as primitive. Monarchical, aristocratic and democratic forms of society were developed ' according to the nature of the people '.[5] Like Bodin, later, Pole thinks that some peoples are best suited by monarchy, while others ' can in no case suffer the rule of one '. But, unlike Bodin, he does not think that rejection of monarchy implies an inferiority in the people. All forms of government are alike good, he declares,

---

[1] *Dialogue*, p. 33. [2] *Ib.*, p. 51. [3] *Ib.*, p. 52.
[4] No clearer statement of a belief in progress could well be made. Starkey put the idea of a presocial condition more significantly than did Buchanan.
[5] *Dialogue*, p. 53.

' so long as they which have authority look not to their own singular profit nor
to the private weal of any one part more than to the other, but refer all their
counsel, acts and deeds to the common weal of the whole. . . . As to dispute,'
he adds, ' which of these rules is best . . . me seemeth superfluous, seeing that
certain it is that all be good and to nature agreeable ; though the one be more
convenient to the nature of some people than the other.' [1]

For forms of government, in fact, let fools contest. ' The end of
all politic rule is to induce the multitude to virtuous living ' ; [2] to such
religious and brotherly co-operation, that is, as has been shown to be
necessary in the true commonwealth. ' To the aid and setting forward '
of such a true commonweal ' every man for his part, by the law and
order of nature, is bounden ; which hath brought forth man for this
purpose and this end : that after such manner he might live a civil
life, ever having before his eyes the common weal, without regard of
his own vain pleasures, frail fantasies and singular profit '.[3]

Lupset's comment is, that if such be the true commonweal, all
actual commonwealths are sadly deficient. He is told that this is
true but that, nevertheless, things are better now than they ever yet
have been. Man had to learn contempt for mere earthly prosperity
before the true commonweal became possible. He has not yet fully
learned his lesson. Men do not yet see clearly that by their stupid
selfishness they injure or endanger themselves.

Now comes the question : how is England to be brought to true
well-being ? There has been, latterly, it is agreed,[4] actual loss of
population ; and yet there are still among us hordes of idle people
and of people ill occupied. There are troops of idle servants and of
priests, monks and friars, ' nothing but burdens to the earth '. In
every order and degree there are such people, ' to the commonweal
utterly unprofitable '.[5] More, bolder than Starkey, or more radical
than Pole, had spoken explicitly of noblemen and gentlemen, living
' in rest and pleasure, nothing profiting, yea much annoying the weal
public '.[6] Ill occupied, and as burdensome to the commonwealth as
the mere idlers, says the Pole of the *Dialogue*, are ' those which busy
themselves in making and procuring things for the vain pastime and
pleasure of other ',[7] who contribute to pleasure of the body and do
nothing for the dignity of man's nature. ' Consider with yourself,'
More had said, ' of those few that do work, how few to be occupied
in necessary works. For where money beareth all the swing, there
many vain and superfluous occupations must needs be used.' [8]

Lupset objects to the implication that all men ought to work

---

[1] *Dialogue*, pp. 53, 54.   [2] Ib., p. 54.   [3] Ib., p. 57.
[4] This illusion seems to have been very general.   [5] *Dialogue*, p. 77.
[6] *Utopia*, p. 52. Becon classed the landed gentry as the worst of idlers ;
more greedy and useless even than monks. *Jewel of Joy*, 1553.
[7] *Dialogue*, p. 80.   [8] *Utopia*, p. 146.

productively, remarking that the labour of some only will suffice to keep many at liberty and ease. ' This is spoken, Master Lupset,' Pole answers, ' even as though you judged men to be born for to live in idleness and pleasure. . . . But, Sir, it is nothing so ; but, contrary, he is born to labour and travail . . . and not to live as an unprofitable weight and burden of the earth.' [1]

But there is, in England, far more than this that needs remedy. Our public policy is in some respects absurd and in others wicked. We export cattle and corn and wool and get in return only such rubbish as wine and silk.[2] Clerical immunities are preposterous : crime in clergy should, if anything, be punished more severely than in others.[3] But our criminal law is stupidly and wickedly severe, especially to theft, as More had declared yet more emphatically.[4] Pole suggests that it would be better in the case of a first offence ' to find some way how the man might be brought to better order and frame ',[5] than to hang him out of hand. ' Most part of the world,' More had said, ' are like bad schoolmasters, readier to beat than to teach.' [6] ' What other thing do you than make thieves and then punish them ? '

All classes of English people, it is declared, are in all manner of ways, in building and clothes and food, extravagant and wasteful. Workmen are lazy and negligent and as extravagant as their betters. ' The people of England is more given to idle gluttony than any people of the world.' [7] Then, too, our nobility and clergy, and of course our people in general, are badly educated. Our schools are insufficient, our Universities need reform ; there is general ignorance, even of the Bible. Yet more serious are the antagonisms of class that exist among us. Laity grudge against clergy and commons against gentry : it is a disease that threatens destruction to all good civility. But the very root of all evils is the fact that all men seek their own profit without regard to their neighbours. Landlords care only for rent and prelates for the wool of the flock.

All these things, and others, have to be altered before England can become a very and true commonweal. ' Much easier it is to spy a hundred faults in a commonweal than to amend one ' ;[8] yet the remedy is to a great extent within the power of government. Our country and people are, after all, such ' that they may be brought well to all good civility '.[9] A large number of positive proposals are made. Marriage should be encouraged, bonuses given to large families and bachelors should be taxed. Rents should be regulated by law,

---

[1] *Dialogue*, p. 78.
[2] Ib., p. 97. Lever denounced merchants who served 'foolish men's fancies'. *Sermons*, ed. Arber, p. 131.
[3] Ib., p. 139.   [4] *Utopia*, pp. 58–61.
[5] *Dialogue*, p. 120.   [6] *Utopia*, p. 45.
[7] *Dialogue*, p. 87.   [8] Ib., p. 143.   [9] Ib., p. 68.

and government should limit the amount of cattle rearing and organize all crafts by means of official agents. Towns should be cleansed and ' gentlemen ' compelled to build houses in them. Schools should be multiplied and the most promising young scholars should be sent up to reformed universities. Special schools should be established for the ' nobility ' and for the training of clergy. Law should be codified and simplified.

But to this programme Lupset makes the objection that you cannot make men virtuous by regulations ; for virtue essentially consists in knowing and pursuing the good without fear as a motive. ' Except we find some other mean whereby man may come to this his perfection, all our communication, we think, is void and all law without effect.' [1]

' Master Lupset,' Pole justly answers, ' you enter now into a great matter.' He proceeds to admit that man cannot be coerced into virtue, but argues that law and its enforcement can assist in creating a habit and a bent.[2] He confesses, however, that law alone will be insufficient. The defect of law must, and can only, be supplied by religion. But here also something can be achieved by governmental action. Government should take measures to secure for us a more learned and religious clergy, should establish public religious services in English and should allow the Bible to be translated. More had suggested ' that the scriptures might without great peril and not without great profit, be brought into our tongue and taken to lay men and women both '.[3] ' I never read in no stories,' Pole is made to say, ' of greater blindness ' than the opinion that this would destroy religion.[4]

It was an enormous undertaking that Starkey makes Pole demand of the English government. But it must be noted that all the evils he mentions are denounced by other writers of the time and that all or nearly all the proposals he makes for reform are suggested in other writings of somewhat earlier or later date.[5] What is peculiar to Starkey's *Dialogue* is the suggestion that, before it can reasonably be hoped that what is needful will be done, the constitution of the English monarchy itself needs reconstruction. In the actual English system

---

[1] *Dialogue*, p. 206. [2] Ib., p. 206.
[3] *A Dialogue concerning heresyes and matters of religion*, 1528. Works of More, ed. 1557, p. 186.
[4] *Dialogue*, p. 212. Whatever the attitude of the Pope, the desire to have the Scriptures in vernacular seems to have been widespread among educated Catholics. ' Vehementur ab istis dissentio,' Erasmus had written, ' qui nolint ab idiotis legi divinas literas in vulgi linguam transfusas.' (In prefix to his Greek text of the New Testament, 1516.)
[5] Many of them are to be found in William Forrest's *Pleasaunt Poesye of Princelie Practise*, written under Edward VI and edited for the E.E.T.S. by S. J. Herrtage. But Forrest's verse is anything but pleasant : it is worse than Crowley's.

of government there is no guarantee for and little likelihood of ' good policy '. The constitution itself must be reformed.

' It is not unknown to you, Master Lupset,' says Pole, ' that our country hath been governed and ruled these many years under the state of princes, which, by their regal power and princely authority, have judged all things pertaining to the state of our realm to hang only upon their will and fantasy.'

But the idea that the Prince may

' rule all things according to his will and pleasure, is without doubt and hath ever been the greatest destruction to this realm, yea and to all other. . . . For, Master Lupset, this is sure and a gospel word, that country can not be long well governed nor maintained with good policy where all is ruled by the will of one, not chosen by election but cometh to it by natural succession ; for seldom seen it is that they which by succession come to kingdoms and realms are worthy of such high authority.' [1]

The declaration thus emphatically, if rather confusedly, made, is insisted upon at considerable length. ' What is more repugnant to nature than a whole nation to be governed by the will of a Prince ? . . . What is more contrary to reason than all the whole people to be ruled by him which commonly lacketh all reason ? ' [2] If the ruler be of exceptional wisdom and virtue, the absolute rule of one becomes, indeed, a ' most perfect and excellent state of policy ' ; but if he be not so, it is of all ' the most pestilent and pernicious state '.[3] Unlimited power is ' the open gate to all tyranny '.[4] To believe that God ordains tyranny as a punishment for men's sins is mere superstition : ' this agreeth nothing with philosophy nor reason, no nor yet to the doctrine of Christ and good religion '.[5] Tyranny is the greatest of social evils and cannot come from God. ' Better is it to the state of the commonweal to restrain from the prince such high authority, committing that only to the common counseyl of the realm and parliament, assembled here in our country.' [6]

' It is not man that can make a wise prince of him that lacketh wit by nature. . . . But this is in man's power, to elect and choose him that is both wise and just and make him a prince and him that is a tyrant so to depose.' [7] It may, sometimes, be reasonable to delegate an unlimited authority to an elected Prince. But, Pole concludes, if monarchy is to be hereditary, the power of the monarch should always be strictly limited. Here in England, it is said, no change is needed for the present, since we happen to have just now a noble and wise Prince.[8] But Pole suggests that, when Henry VIII dies, Parliament should either elect a King ' which should not rule and

---

[1] *Dialogue*, pp. 100, 101.　　[2] Ib., p. 107.　　[3] Ib., p. 102.
[4] Ib., p. 103.　　[5] Ib., p. 167.　　[6] Ib., p. 102.
[7] Ib., p. 167. In Utopia the Prince is elected for life ' unless he be deposed or put down for suspicion of tyranny ' (*Utopia*, p. 136).
[8] Ib., p. 105. Pole, surely, would not have said this.

govern at his own pleasure and liberty, but ever be subject to the order of his laws ', or, if hereditary succession be maintained, as may practically be best, then to the new King should be joined a permanent council, 'not such as he will', but approved by Parliament, without consent of which nothing can be done.[1]

Lupset is represented as being astonished at these views, but as having few objections to make, beyond the obvious objections to elective monarchy. He remarks, indeed, that Pole's scheme would involve frequent meetings of Parliament, ' which were no small trouble to the commons of this realm '.[2] But he is finally reduced to an amazed silence ; and his silence is significant. He has nothing to say about scriptural commands to obey the powers that be [3] and makes no objection to the assertion that a tyrant may rightly be deposed, or to Pole's clear implication that a people may, through the action of a representative body, at any time change an hereditary into an elective monarchy or presumably into any other form of government.

It is clear that, to Starkey-Pole, kings and other governors are in no sense ' specially appointed by the ordinance of God '. The position of the Prince is of mere human ordinance and the form of governmental institutions should be simply determined by the end in view. It is clearly implied that the people of any commonwealth may freely choose and change the form of its government. England has fallen into the mistake of allowing too much power to the Prince and this mistake should now be corrected. The Prince has no absolute right to his position. The author of the *Dialogue* has a conception of what constitutes a true commonwealth and considers that to the attainment of that ideal all men's efforts should combine and all other things be subordinated. Just because the end of the commonwealth is perfect welfare in virtuous communion and harmonious co-operation, the determination of all arrangements for achieving the end is assumed to lie with the community as a whole. It is implied that there can be no such thing as an absolute right to rule and that all actual authority is delegated.

These views are surprising if they be regarded as those of Thomas Starkey, chaplain to Henry VIII and Master of Corpus Christi College, Oxford. But regarded as the views of Reginald Pole, the friend of Contarini and Sadoleto, Vittoria Colonna and Morone, they are not surprising. Not only was the idea of the Prince as delegate a common-place of Roman law, but the view expressed in the *Dialogue* could be

---

[1] *Dialogue*, pp. 168, 169. With the details of Pole's projected constitution we are not concerned.

[2] Ib., p. 105.

[3] The absence from the *Dialogue* of reference to the Scriptures is one of its striking features.

derived from late medieval thought and in fact is medieval thought. Sir John Fortescue had taught that the King is a delegate : [1] in Starkey's *Dialogue* the delegation becomes one which may at any time be resumed. The contrast indeed, between the view Starkey expressed and that of the writers who preached politics from the thirteenth chaptér of Romans, is not so great as may appear. Either Starkey or Pole would no doubt have accepted the dictum that the office of the magistrate is the ordinance of God and probably both would have said that God forbids rebellion. But to them, apparently, the highest authority is that of the commonwealth itself, expressed, for England, in ' the common counseyl and parliament '. Or rather, perhaps, the highest authority is the divine law which is the law of man's nature and bids him strive after the perfect commonwealth.

It was not on the basis of the assumptions of Starkey's *Dialogue* that opposition to Tudor orthodoxy in politics developed in sixteenth-century England. It is true that the *Dialogue* does anticipate to some extent what was freely asserted in France after 1570. But the French thought is more logically formal and complete. In the *Dialogue* little is argued and much assumed ; and the author is more concerned with practical remedies for admitted evils than with any fundamental question. In this respect it may, perhaps, be regarded as characteristically English. But the positive feature of the *Dialogue* that is peculiarly English is that conception of the very and true commonweal which it shares with Crowley, and we may say with More. Nothing at all closely resembling it was developed in France.[2] Bodin's conception of the ' république bien ordonnée ' perhaps comes nearest to it. Yet Bodin had no vision of a people united in love and amity as members of one body, ever having the commonweal before their eyes, without regard of their own vain pleasures. To Bodin the problem was, first of all, one of the recognition of political authority. In the *Dialogue* the problem is how to secure the co-operation of all classes for general welfare : and love and religion are the factors depended upon, as much as, or more than, regulation or political reform.

What, perhaps, strikes one most in reading the *Dialogue*, as in reading Crowley and More, is that society is regarded mainly as an association for economic purposes. All the stress is laid upon the question of how to get rid of waste and idleness and selfish greed and competition, how to abolish poverty and secure for all a competence

---

[1] ' Ad tutelam namque legis subditorum ac eorum corporum et honorum rex hujusmodi erectus est et hanc potestatem a populo effluxam ipse habet, quo ei non licet potestate alia suo populo dominari.' *De laudibus legum Angliae*, XIII, ed. Amos, p. 221.

[2] Unless it be the strange vision of a reformed France described by Rauol Spifame in the *Dicaearchia* of 1556.

suitable to the dignity of human nature. Nothing is more distinctive of English thought in the sixteenth century than the tendency to think in terms of economics. This is evidenced by a large number of writers who express little or nothing that can be called political thought. In reading Starkey's *Dialogue* or even the *Utopia*, one gets an impression that even love, even religion, are thought of as serving, mainly, an economic purpose.

In literature, at least, the ideal of the very and true commonweal flourished only for a few years. It was partly due to the fact that it was born of economic crisis, that the vision faded so quickly. Under Elizabeth political thought, so far as it was not concerned with the question of royal supremacy in the Church, took directions barely indicated in earlier Tudor writings. Yet, to the end of the century, we find as it were echoes of the thought of the idealists of the early days of the Reformation, when men were still under the illusion that the restoration of true religion was going to produce a world in all respects better than the old. In the writings of Thomas Wilson, Nicholas Heming, Miles Mosse and Henry Arth [1] every form of what they call ' usury ' [2] is denounced, in gross and in detail, with much argumentative appeal to authorities and to canon law. Desperately these writers went on repeating old formulæ about just prices and just bargains and the responsibilities of property. They can have had little hope. Faint and far off to them was the very and true commonweal. They were doing little more than protest against the commercialism of a world that regarded them not. To that new world of commerce and finance the old formulæ seemed inapplicable or had no meaning at all. Wilson, in 1572, spoke of the sin of usury as ' rank throughout all England ' ; [3] he did not know of any part of Christendom ' so much subject to this foul sin. It will,' he declared, ' be in the end the undoing of all, if it be not looked to in time.' ' Men of wealth are now wholly given everywhere altogether to idleness, to get their gain with ease and to live by lending upon the only sweat and labour of others.' The modern merchant, in his dialogue, has the assurance to ask the frank question : ' What man is so mad to deliver his money out of his own possession for nought ? ' ' I do verily believe,' cried the worthy Doctor, ' the end of this world at hand.' On the false supposition that there ever had been such a world as the one he looked back to, its end had certainly come. The

---

[1] Wilson : *A discourse upon Usurye*, 1572. Heming : *The Lawfull use of Riches*, 1598. Mosse : *The Arraignment and Conviction of Usurie*, 1595. Arth : *Provision for the Poore, now in penurie*, 1597.

[2] This vague term is used much as we use, with even greater vagueness, the word ' profiteering '.

[3] Wilson : *Discourse upon Usurye*, 1572. The quotations are all, except for the Merchant's question, from the dedicatory epistle to Leicester. Wilson was a Doctor of Civil Law and a Master of the Court of Requests.

tendency to think economically persisted in England ; but that earlier vision of a harmonized economic and religious co-operation from which waste and mere profit-mongering should have been eliminated, seems to have faded quickly and for a time to have disappeared. It passed away with the passing of conditions it had assumed as static. Rather perhaps it had been essentially but a protest ; and it perished in the triumph of that against which it had protested in vain.

§ 4. UTOPIA: THE ISLE OF NOWHERE

The ' fruitful, pleasant and witty work, of the best state of a public weal, and of the new isle, called Utopia ',[1] written in Latin and published at Louvain in the year 1516,[2] was, for sixteenth-century England, the earliest expression of that same dream. I deal with it last because, logically considered, it lies beyond the point that was reached later. Crowley felt bound to accept the form of society as it stood, for it was to him of divine ordinance. Starkey was at least convinced that the existing form of society must, substantially, be accepted, if one wished to get anything done. But for the very practical character of his thought, he too might have sought his remedy in some kind of communism. As it was, he proposed that government should determine rents and organize industry through officials. But More had felt no need of accepting anything as it stood, because in truth he had no hope of getting anything done. It is essentially this lack of faith in the possibility of actually constructing a very and a true commonwealth, that isolates More and separates him from Crowley and Starkey. Crowley declared that the very root of all evil is the notion that a man may do as he wills with his own. Starkey hoped to find remedy and establish the true commonwealth by means of religion and reasonable and thorough regulation. Twenty years before Starkey and Pole, More had come to the conclusion that the mass of men will never become religious, that law can be but a palliative, and that, while private property exists, it is vain to hope that men will think they have no right to do as they will with their own. The inference was obvious : only in a land such as never was and such as is nowhere nor will be, can the perfect commonweal exist. With an irony and in a fantastic form that betray his scepticism, More set forth his dream of that Utopia.

It is a mistake to regard More's *Utopia* as an isolated work of

[1] Title-page of the second edition (1556) of Ralph Robinson's translation, first published in 1553.

[2] More's European reputation secured for his book a vogue on the continent it seems to have lacked in England. By 1520 editions had been published at Paris, Basle and Vienna. A German version appeared in 1524, an Italian in 1548, a French version in 1550. No English translation appeared till 1553. In the same year was printed a Dutch version.

imagination. The thought of its first ' book ' is in close accord, up
to a certain point, with that of Crowley and of Starkey's *Dialogue*.
More is preoccupied with the same evils that are denounced by the
later writers : the stupid brutality of criminal law, the excesses of
sheep-farming,[1] idleness and frivolity, extravagance and waste, unjust
and unnecessary poverty, prevalent selfishness and greed. But so
little hope had More that any change for the better could be effected,
that he had really no remedial measures to propose. His book became
a simple indictment of society. Where Crowley saw religion as a
lever, More saw a vast and stupid, conservative inertia. Every
proposal for change is always opposed, simply as suggesting something
new.

' These things, say they, pleased our forefathers and ancestors ; would God
we could be so wise as they were : and as though they had wittily concluded the
matter and with this answer stopped every man's mouth, they sit down again.
As who should say it were a very dangerous matter, if a man in any point should
be found wiser than his forefathers were.' [1]

While the *Dialogue* saw possibilities of large reconstruction by
governmental action, More saw Princes ' employ much more study
how by right or by wrong to enlarge their dominions, than how well
and peaceably to rule and govern that they have already ' : [3] Princes
who suppose that the property of their subjects is to their own
advantage.[4] If the *Utopia* be a fairy tale, it is the saddest of fairy
tales. More himself says that he had ' taken great pains and labour
in writing the matter '.[5] It was, obviously, so. The book amounts
to an indictment of humanity almost as terrible as *Gulliver's Travels*,
though wholly without Swift's savagery of resentment.

It is excessively difficult to get any change made, and yet every-
thing needs to be changed. Among the nations of Christendom
More's traveller cannot find ' any sign or token of equity and justice '.[6]
The rich men who control things

' invent and devise all means and crafts, first how to keep safely, without fear of
losing, that they have unjustly gathered together, and next how to hire and abuse
the work and labour of the poor for as little money as may be. These devices,
when the rich men have decreed to be kept and observed under colour of the
commonalty, that is to say also of the poor people, then they be made laws.' [7]

In Starkey's *Dialogue* it was implied that More had disregarded
the actual. But it was the Pole of the *Dialogue* who idealized Parliament, satisfied with the fiction of the common law as to its representa-

[1] On this particular point there is a difference of opinion. The passage in the
Utopia in which More speaks of sheep devouring men and houses and cities is
very well known. In the *Dialogue*, when Lupset attacks enclosure, Pole expresses the view that more sheep are wanted.
[2] *Utopia*, p. 40.   [3] Ib., p. 38.   [4] Ib., pp. 91, 92.
[5] Ib., Preface, p. 12.   [6] Ib., p. 300.   [7] Ib., p. 304.

tive character. He had founded on it a great hope of reconstruction. More was possessed by no such illusion and had no such hope.

' The whole wealth of the body of the realm,' declared an anonymous writer, ' cometh out of the labours and works of the common people.' [1] More's thought was the same. Usurers become rich ; but ' labourers, carters, ironsmiths, carpenters and ploughmen ', all those who do the necessary work ' that without it no commonwealth were able to continue and endure one year ', all these labour all their lives for a pittance, with nothing before them but an ' indigent and beggarly old age '.[2]

For this injustice and absurdity there is, it is asserted, but one conceivable remedy. ' Where possessions be private, where money beareth all the stroke, it is hard and almost impossible that there the weal public may justly be governed and prosperously flourish.' [3] For ' where every man's goods be proper and peculiar to himself ' and where every man ' draweth and plucketh to himself as much as he can ', there will a few ' divide among themselves all the whole riches ' and ' to the residue is left lack and poverty '.[4] So we reach the conclusion : ' I do fully persuade myself, that no equal and just distribution of things can be made nor that perfect wealth shall ever be among men unless this propriety be exiled and banished.[5] . . . Christ instituted among his all things common ; and the same community doth yet remain amongst the rightest Christian companies.' [6] The evils resulting from private ownership may, indeed, be ' somewhat eased ' by law and regulation, but ' that they may be perfectly cured . . . it is not to be hoped for, whiles every man is master of his own to himself '. [7]

All this is asserted by the mouth of More's imaginary traveller, not in immediate connection with the account of the isle which is Nowhere, but in the far more significant discussion that precedes that account. In his own person More makes the usual objections. ' Men shall never there live wealthily where all things be common.' [8] Men are driven to work by hope of gain for themselves : under communistic conditions every one will idle. The dilemma is stated, but it is not resolved. It was hardly worth while attempting to resolve it ; so obvious was it that the remedy proposed by the traveller, Hythloday, was impossible of application. To the doubts expressed by More, Hythloday can only answer that, if he knew the island of Nowhere,

[1] *How to Reform the Realm in setting them to work to restore Tillage, c.* 1535. Attributed uncertainly to Clement Armstrong. Reprinted in *Tudor Economic Documents* (Tawney and Power), Vol. III. See p. 115.

[2] *Utopia*, p. 301.   [3] Ib., pp. 104, 105.   [4] Ib., p. 106.

[5] Ib., p. 107. In the Latin: ' Adeo mihi certe persuadeo, res aequabili ac justa aliqua ratione distribui, aut feliciter agi cum rebus mortalium nisi sublata prorsus proprietate, non posse.' Ed. 1516.

[6] Ib., p. 269.   [7] Ib., p. 109.   [8] Ib., p. 109.

he would know better. Coming after all that has gone before, the answer is as sad as it is witty. It was no answer at all; and it reveals at once the fallacy of what follows. Proof of the assertions made in the first book of the *Utopia* is supplied in the second by means of a picture of an imaginary commonwealth, in which communism has actually resulted in all but complete contentment, prosperity and stability. The picture, obviously, is a mere assumption of what has to be proved. So conscious was More of the fallacy that, when he came to describe his island of the blessed, he let fancy loose and became little more than ingenious. He makes, it is true, in the course of this account certain far-reaching suggestions ; [1] but for the most part it seems to be calculated rather to amuse than to suggest. It appears, too, after all, that this particular land of heart's desire is not, on close acquaintance, so very attractive. ' So must I needs confess and grant,' More concludes, ' that many things be in the Utopian weal public, which in our cities I may rather wish for than hope after.' [2] Many things, perhaps ; but surely not those houses all alike, those people so much alike that they are content hardly to differ in dress, that monotony of grave entertainment and garnishing of the mind. But it did not matter. More knew that his Utopia was nowhere and proved nothing. He had declared in effect that, men being what they are, there is no conceivable remedy for social evils except, at all events, one that cannot be adopted ; and as to that one, that it is doubtful what, in any case, the result of its adoption would be. His book is the work of a sceptic in politics, though of a sceptic whose mind rests in religious faith. The real land of More's heart's desire was not of this world. It was Crowley and Starkey who were the idealists in politics : it was More who had kept to the actual. His Utopia is a *reductio ad absurdum* of their very and true commonweal. He had written the last word first.

---

[1] Some of these must be referred to later.   [2] *Utopia*, p. 309.

CHAPTER IV

THE THEORY OF ROYAL SUPREMACY UNDER HENRY VIII

THE Tudor government undertook the task of forcing upon a necessarily more or less reluctant population a change of religious habits. It was an operation that was gradually and most skilfully performed. But it was an operation of great difficulty. Henry VIII had with him the great prestige already attaching to the successful new monarchy and the generally hearty support of the landed and moneyed classes except in the far north. He had behind him the old eagerness to appropriate Church property which, according to Bodin, was the main factor in the Reformation everywhere. He had with him the new national consciousness and the old and widespread dislike of Papal interference and jurisdiction. He found leverage in the grievances of the clergy against the Pope, of seculars against regulars and of laity against clergy. He had with him the sense, widespread among the more educated of the laity, that clerical ascendancy in school and college was obstructive and obscurantist, and that an ignorant clergy, for grossly material and selfish purposes, was pandering to and making use of a mass of popular superstition. For all that, the difficulty of effecting the great change was enormous.

In that difficulty the Pope counted for little. The claims of the unreformed Papacy were, as things stood, the weakest point in the Catholic position. The fact that those claims conflicted with the nationalist sentiment and dislike of foreign interference strengthened the hands of the government. Henry VIII had not to meet or to fear any serious opposition based on the conception of a great Christian commonwealth centralized at Rome. That particular ideal, which had for a very long time been in a very low condition, was practically dead when the Reform Parliament met in 1529. To educated Catholics the recognition of Papal supremacy in the Church might seem for many reasons absolutely essential : its necessity was certainly not appreciated by the mass of everyday Catholicism in England. Even among educated Catholics there seem to have been few in England or in France who were prepared to admit that Papal headship of the

Church meant much politically. The difficulty did not lie here : it arose from the fact that the mass of the population was still ' Catholic ' by habit and tradition and vaguely Catholic in sentiment. It cannot be doubted that the religion of the masses in 1529 must be labelled Catholic if it is to be labelled at all. Catholics by understanding conviction seem to have been relatively so few that there was no danger from them : their conversion was most improbable but they were helpless.[1] What was, first of all, needed was some kind of theory which would enable the mass of semi-Catholics to discard their semi-belief in Papal claims, which they had always disliked and never really understood. The dead weight of Catholic habit and tradition fixed a limit to the extent of the government's action under Henry VIII.

Henry VIII, therefore, with that just sense of actuality which distinguished him and his great daughter, broke with Catholic tradition little more than was necessary for the assertion of the supremacy of the Crown in all causes and over all persons ecclesiastical. Far more was involved in this than an assertion that Papal claims were completely invalid. Equally had it to be maintained that the clergy possess no rightful jurisdiction or coercive authority except such as may be derived from the Crown, and that the clergy, as such, have no right to speak for or to govern the Church. In these assertions there was nothing whatever that was strictly new. They had all been made, quite explicitly, two hundred years earlier. They were part of the great and varied legacy of the Middle Ages.

So far the assertions made were simply negative. Taken by themselves they afforded no ground for any theory of royal supremacy. They could be made from a point of view that denied the need of any legal recognition of any ' church ', or which denied that ' the church ' really existed at all. The expression of such opinions could hardly even be tolerated. It had to be officially admitted that the Church is needed and must be recognized as really existing in some sense. The question is : how should it be governed ? It was argued that God never intended to establish any centralized government of the Church Universal, or that the Church should be governed by the clergy. But it had also to be shown that what God did intend was that the government of the Church should be in the hands of the final civil authority. It had to be maintained that the general duty of obedience and non-resistance to the secular magistrate extended even to questions of religion. It had to be shown that God intended that a national king should rule a national church.

Effective proof of these propositions would certainly have been difficult had there not existed a strong predisposition to believe them. The arguments of the supporters of Henry VIII's Reformation were

---

[1] The nature of the Catholic protest, so far as it concerned politics, will be considered later. See Chap. VI.

undeniably strong up to the point at which mere negatives became worse than useless. When positive conclusions had to be established there appears a tendency to adopt the method of proof by bald assertion.

This statement is formally true ; and nevertheless it grossly misrepresents the fact by ignoring that which was the essential contention of the English supporters of royal supremacy. It is important to realize what that contention was, even though to do so we have to read their works. Badly as they state the case, it comes out clearly enough. We have to remember that Protestantism in the sixteenth century was generally actually Christian. The controversialists, for the purposes of controversy, had a right to assume as true what nobody openly denied. They assumed the truth of the revelation in the Scriptures ; they assumed also that right faith and the due ministration of sacraments have, to say the least, a value for salvation ; they assumed that Christ had founded a visible Church. They proved to their own satisfaction that neither Pope nor clergy have any claim to govern the Church or to speak in its name. They proved that God never intended that the Church should have a single head or a centralized government. If, then, the civil magistrate has no right to order the Church, what remains but a descent to chaos ? But religion is not of value only to the individual ; it is essential to the existence of ordered society. It seemed totally incredible that God had provided no means whatever of ordering His Church. He must therefore have intended from the first that the government of the Church should be in the hands of the civil magistrate. Just because God did not give power to the clergy to rule the Church he must have intended this. Therefore it is that, from Sampson and the *De Vera Differentia* onwards to Jewel, Horne, Bilson and Bridges, the ecclesiastical champions of the royal supremacy were so anxious to prove that the Pope and clergy had usurped powers which were originally in the hands of secular princes and magistrates. The whole point of the tedious historical argumentation is lost, if we do not see what was, all the time, at the back of the writers' minds. For, obviously, the alleged facts proved nothing of themselves to the purpose. But since it was incredible that God had not, from the first, provided means for the government and ordering of the Church, the question of how the Church had in the earliest times been governed, logically became important.

The Pope and the bishops, says Tyndale, have taken the sword out of the hands of temporal rulers and reduced them to something like impotence. ' Kings they are, but shadows ; vain names and things idle, having nothing to do in the world but when our holy father needeth their help.' [1] They have come to be little more than

---

[1] *Obedience of a Christian Man*, ed. R. Lovett, p. 102.

'hangmen unto the pope and bishops'. But it is clear from the Scriptures that God intended all ecclesiastics to be as fully subject to the civil magistrate as are other folk. There should be 'one King, one law'. The function of the clergy is merely to preach the word and minister the sacraments. Similarly, Simon Fish, in the *Supplication for Beggars*,[1] declared that the clergy 'exempt themselves from the obedience of your grace' and 'translate all rule, power, lordship, authority, obedience and dignity from your grace unto them'. This sort of grossly exaggerated language was common. The conclusion was clear enough. It was the duty of secular Princes to resume the power God originally gave them, and to rescue their people from the tyranny of pope and clergy.

It is worth while to look a little closely at the argument of an anonymous work that may, for shortness' sake, be referred to as *De Vera Differentia*.[2] This book sums up and includes most of what was said, on its author's side, under Henry VIII. The claims of the Pope having been rather quickly disposed of, the writer goes on to assert that the Church, as such, has no power to make law and no coercive authority, 'no power to constrain or to punish'. It is clear that, here, when he says the 'Church' he means the clergy. The argument is, of course, scriptural; but little ground is stated for this last assertion, except that Christ's kingdom is not of this world; an inconclusive phrase that was continually quoted.[3] There follows an argument from the Old Testament which we meet with very frequently, in France as in England. God, it is asserted, gave power to Jewish kings to see that divine law was kept; He authorized them to appoint and to punish and depose priests. It is clear that, in God's own kingdom of the Jews, the clergy were subject to the King; and no ground exists for saying that under the new dispensation the Church is any more independent of secular authority than it was then. We need not be troubled about what Canon Law may say, since the Church

---

[1] *A Supplicacyon for the Beggars*: addressed to Henry VIII in 1529 by Simon Fish, 'gentleman, of Gray's Inn'. It is a grossly and unscrupulously libellous attack on the clergy, which justified the indignation expressed by Sir Thomas More in an answer called *The Supplication of Soules*. Fish declares that the clergy are ready to do with Henry VIII as they did 'unto your noble predecessor King John . . . such a righteous king'. He exhorts the King to despoil the monasteries and 'set these sturdy lobies abroad in the world'. The work has been edited for the Early English Text Society by F. J. Furnivall.

[2] *De Vera Differentia Regiae Potestatis et Ecclesiasticae, et quae sit ipsa Veritas ac Virtus utriusque*, 1534. Attributed, without certainty, to Edward Fox, who became Bishop of Hereford in 1535. An English translation by Henry, Lord Stafford, appeared in 1548 and was dedicated to Somerset.

[3] The Jesuit, Santarelli, explained this phrase as meaning that the Pope derived authority directly and solely from God and not from anything in this world. *Tractatus de Haeresi*, I, 32 (1625).

never had any rightful power to make law.[1]   St. Paul's text in Romans
can only refer to the civil ruler ; and he excepts no one from the
obedience he demands, ' neither Peter nor Paul, nor priest nor bishop,
nor cardinal nor patriarch nor Pope '.[2]   The author agrees with
Gardiner that, searching the Scriptures for proof of the validity of
Papal claims, one finds nothing but testimony to the authority of
Princes over priests.[3]   It is, even, absurd to maintain that the secular
magistrate has no authority in relation to things spiritual.   For it is
the function of civil authority to punish evildoers ; and what does
this involve if not spiritual jurisdiction ?   It is clear, he concludes,
that the care of the Church of God must from the beginning have been
committed to the civil magistrate, and that he will have to make
account for it to God.   This indeed, in the words of the translation,
is ' the proper and chief use of Princes '.

The gist of the argument is clear enough and is very simple.   It
can be shown from Scripture that the Pope's claims are wholly unfounded and that the clergy have no claim to any coercive authority.
There remains only the ' Prince '.   God must have intended to commit
the ordering of the Church to Princes, and we find in the Old-Testament
that in fact he did so ; and we know what St. Paul said.   We may
say, therefore, with Cranmer, that ' all Christian Princes have committed unto them immediately of God the whole cure of all their
subjects, as well concerning the administration of God's Word for the
cure of souls, as concerning the ministration of things political and
civil governance '.[4]   Latimer, characteristically, warned Henry VIII
that his position as Head of the Church was likely to be ' a chargeable
dignity when account shall be asked of it '.[5]   By most of the writers,
in this sense, in Henry VIII's time, little or nothing is added to the
argument of the *De Vera Differentia*.   Sampson's *Oratio* adds nothing
but a rather neat expression of the conclusion.[6]   If you would obey
the Word of God, it is the King you must obey, not the Pope, who is
not even mentioned in the Scriptures.

From the views thus expressed it followed that right to control
the Church had always lain with the King and that the actual power
the Pope possesses, or had possessed, in England may be described

---

[1] ' Constat Canones necessitate neminem obligare.'

[2] *De Vera Differentia.*

[3] *On True Obedience.*

[4] Answers to questions put to the bishops in 1540.   See A. J. Mason's *Thomas
Cranmer*, pp. 102–3 (1898).

[5] *Sermons*, Parker Soc. ed., p. 152.

[6] *Oratio quae docet, hortatur, admovet omnes potissimum Anglos regiae dignitati
cum primus ut obediant*, 1533.   Richard Sampson, an old agent of Wolsey's, held
successively many high ecclesiastical preferments, presented the opinions of the
Universities on the divorce question in 1530 and became Bishop of Chichester
in 1536.

either as a usurpation or as having been derived from grant or acqui-escence of the Crown. Henry VIII is merely resuming the ancient powers of the Crown in England. The writer of a treatise of 1538 undertook to prove that the supremacy assumed by the King ' had always been in his most noble progenitors '.[1] This assertion was constantly made and was officially adopted. The Acts of Supremacy were professedly Resumption Acts. Gardiner says that the Acts of the Reform Parliament only established for the King power that was his already. In the *Reformatio Legum Ecclesiasticarum*, drawn up by Cranmer late in the reign of Edward VI,[2] it is definitely declared that all ecclesiastical jurisdiction is derived from the Crown and that it is for the Sovereign to decide, in the last resort, what is heresy. In the discussion in Parliament on the Act of Supremacy in 1559, it was maintained that English common law had always held that ecclesiastical courts, and even the Pope himself, derived their jurisdic-tion from the Crown.

Historically, then, and legally and by God's ordinance and even by the very nature of a commonwealth, the King in England must rightfully be Supreme Head, or, if that title be reserved for Christ, at least Supreme Governor of the Church. But, this being so, what is the Church and what becomes of the Church Universal ? It was an awkward question, but it had to be answered. What is the Church ?

' Is it not,' wrote Sir Thomas More, ' this company and congregation of all those nations that . . . profess the name and faith of Christ ? By this Church we know the Scripture and this is the very Church ; and this hath begun at Christ and hath had him for their head and St. Peter, his vicar, after him and head under him and alway since, and successors of his continually ; and have had his holy faith and his blessed sacraments and his holy scriptures delivered, kept and conserved therein by God and his Holy Spirit. And albeit some nations fall away, yet likewise as how many boughs soever fall from the tree, though there fall more than be left thereon, yet they make no doubt which is the very tree, although each of them were planted again in another place and grew to a greater than the stock he came first of ; right so, while we see and well know that all the companies and sects of heretics and schismatics, how great soever they grow, came out of this church that I spake of, we know evermore that the here-tics be they that be severed and the Church the stock that they all came out of.' [3]

If More were right, obviously no King of England could be Head of the Church, and though the Church is in England, there is no

---

[1] *A Treatise proving by the King's Laws.*

[2] Edited by Cardwell. Oxford, 1850.

[3] *A Dialogue concerning heresyes and matters of religion*, 1528. Works of Sir T. More, ed. 1557, pp. 185, 186. I have turned a few commas into semicolons. It is a reproach alike to our historical sense and to our literary sense that no complete edition of the works of More has been published since 1557. There is a good edition of this *Dialogue* recently published by W. G. Campbell (Eyre & Spottiswoode, 1927).

Church of England. A new, or another, conception of the Church was evidently required. In the *De Vera Differentia* no attempt was made to supply one. There, as often, the question is shirked through an identification of ' the church ' with the clergy. It had to be maintained that the Church Universal is a system of separated, national or State churches.

The Church of England, says Gardiner, is ' nothing else but the congregation of men and women of the clergy and of the laity, united in Christ's profession '.[1] The Church of England, in fact, is one aspect of the realm, and to say that the King is head of the realm but not head of the Church, either means something evidently absurd or means nothing at all. But Gardiner's assertion did not go far enough. It assumed that ' Church of England ' meant something more than Church in England ; which, after all, was the question.

But Gardiner's inadequate assertion officially received its logically necessary expansion in the *Necessary Doctrine and Erudition for any Christen Man*, issued in 1543. It was there explained that the Church Catholic is a group of localized Churches, each with its own proper head, more or less different in form, but united by true Christian profession and the fact that all their members are alike called of God. ' As they be distinct in places, so they have distinct ministers and divers heads in earth . . . yet be all these holy churches but one holy church catholic.' [2] The unity of the Church Catholic involves no common organization or common sovereign ; it consists simply in a common profession of essential doctrine, ' the one doctrine of the Scriptures '. The ' churches ' of Italy and Spain are specifically mentioned as united with that of England in this common profession. Slight diversities count for nothing. But it is the duty of every Christian to adhere to the Church of his own land and live in obedience to his Prince, the head of his branch of the Church Catholic. The Church Catholic has no need whatever of any common Head. To acknowledge a single ruler for the whole Church Catholic, declared Thomas Starkey, would be as inconvenient as to recognize the Emperor as supreme secular ruler in Christendom.[3]

It must be noted that the view thus officially expressed differs from that of Luther and of Calvin, both of whom conceived the Church Universal as an invisible thing. In the *Erudition* it appears as a group of quite visible Churches, each governed by its own natural and secular head and united by a common profession of the essentials of the Christian religion. The later development of the English

---

[1] *Concerning True Obedience*, 1553, p. 20.

[2] *A Necessary Doctrine and Erudition*, 1543, p. 15 B. The same view is expressed in John Bekinsau's work : *De Supremo et Absoluto Regis Imperio*, 1546.

[3] *Exhortation to Christian Unity*, 1534.

Reformation made this view hard to hold. Under Henry VIII it was not yet difficult to maintain that the churches of England and Spain were united in a common profession.

But to what extent and with what, if any, limitations, is the King to be conceived as having right to govern and order the Church ? How much is involved in royal supremacy ? This is the main question that was raised for England by the action of Henry VIII's government. It was on this point that all the controversy under Elizabeth really turned. As time went on the Pope and his claims became, for England, more and more a kind of Aunt Sally at which every one contemptuously threw any kind of rubbish. But the controversy concerning the nature of royal supremacy in the Church became ever more serious. Lawyers might be, and were, inclined to put the whole question as one simply of jurisdiction ; but behind the question of jurisdiction there was, evidently, the question of the Sovereign's authority in relation to strictly religious belief. It could not be escaped or for long evaded. The repudiation of Papal did not logically involve the recognition of Royal Supremacy. It seemed at first, no doubt, that the one did necessitate the other. Practically that was so ; but only on the assumption that the Church was to remain one body inclusive of the nation. But no sooner has the recognition of royal supremacy been made, than doubts and difficulties appear. It was indeed a long journey from the Catholic conception of the Church to the conception of a national church ruled by a civil sovereign. To religious minds it might seem, as more and more it came to seem, a passage from Scylla to Charybdis.

Under Henry VIII the question was generally either shirked or was not clearly seen. If any answer is given, it is usually prudently vague. Much is implied and no one quite knows what. Henry accepted and attempted to safeguard with penalties the doctrinal system of Rome and the traditional organization of the Church, as far as that could be done with the Pope left out. He retained transubstantiation and the confessional system and *jure divino* episcopacy. The retention of all this suggested that the tradition of the Church was still to be taken as authoritative in all that did not concern the claims of the Papacy. There were, of course, also the Scriptures, by which every one professed to hold himself bound. Yet it seemed to lawyers that the power Henry was claiming in ecclesiastical causes was strictly unlimited. In the fine and characteristic speech the King made in Parliament in 1545,[1] he rebuked the laity in general for jeering at preachers and speaking slanderously of bishops.

' If you know surely,' he continued, ' that a bishop or a preacher erreth or teacheth perverse doctrine, come and declare it to some of our council or to us,

---

[1] In Hall: *Chronicles*, 1548, pp. 261, 262.

to whom is committed by God the high authority to reform and order such causes and behaviour : be not judges yourselves. . . . Although you be permitted to read Holy Scripture . . . in your mother tongue, you must understand that it is licensed you so to do only to inform your own conscience and to instruct your children and family, and not to dispute and make scripture a railing and a taunting stock against priests and preachers.'

The King, it is implied, may forbid the reading of the Scriptures and, where the meaning of the Scriptures is doubtful, it is for the King alone to decide what the meaning is. The secular ruler, it appears, is to decide all controverted questions of doctrine, to determine what of tradition is sacred and what worthless, to decide, in fact, what are the essentials of the Christian religion.

Of all the writers of Henry VIII's time the lawyer, Christopher St. Germain,[1] expressed most clearly the nature and implications of the change that the Tudor government was bringing about. In his writings the right, not of the King simply, but of the supreme civil authority, to decide for every one all controverted questions of religious belief, is much more than implied. It is natural that the assertion should have been made by a lawyer and not by a theologian. Cranmer and Fox and Hooper and Gardiner and Sampson and Bekinsau were theologians or, at least, ecclesiastics. They saw, or tried to see, in Henry VIII's Reformation a reformation of religion, and to them the royal supremacy was an instrument for religious reform. They concerned themselves with the invalidity of Papal claims rather than with the question of what was implied in the royal supremacy they needed. None of them really faced the issue.

St. Germain of course took the view that all punitive and coercive power, all property and office and all rights and claims connected with them are 'temporal' things. All temporal authority belongs to the Crown and, if it has been granted away, may be resumed. By the Act of Supremacy the King 'hath, as I take it, no new power given him in anything'.[2] Any privileges or exemptions that the clergy legally enjoy by virtue of custom or acquiescence, must be conceived as derived from the Crown and if they prove detrimental to the commonwealth, may and should be abolished.[3] Like all other English

---

[1] St. Germain was a lawyer of considerable repute. He was born c. 1460 and died in 1540. For the most part he kept clear of politics and he collected a large legal library. By 1536 he was sufficiently prominent to be denounced by the northern rebels. He is now chiefly known through his controversy with Sir Thomas More.

[2] *An Answere to a Letter.*

[3] *Treatise concerning the division between the spiritualtie and the temporaltie,* c. 1532; p. 34. The book is an attack on the clergy, rather than what it pretends to be. In the admirably acute and effective *Apology* which he wrote in answer to it, More justly pointed out that St. Germain had made a long series of charges against the clergy, not in his own name, but in that of a public most of whom had never heard of them.

' Protestant' writers of the time he does not admit that any sort of case can be made out for the Pope.

All this, coming from a ' Protestant' lawyer, is matter of course at the time. The only distinction St. Germain can claim is that of having faced the fundamental question as to how much was involved in royal supremacy. How much is included in that ' administration of God's¹ Word' which is a function of the Crown ? It was comparatively easy at the moment, and it was highly convenient, to assume that no reasonable doubt existed as to what God had said. The assumption could not be maintained in the face of increasing controversy over every article of the faith. St. Germain frankly put the essential question : ' Who hath power to declare and expound Scriptures ? ' ¹

St. Germain may claim merit for having seen that here was the crucial point. He saw, too, that an answer was not easy ; but he made a serious attempt at an answer. Lawyer-like, he inclines to put the question as a question of where the right lies to determine what is heresy. But the question is not altered by this way of putting it ; since power to determine what may not be believed is power to determine what must be.

It is admitted, he argued, that it is for the Church Catholic to declare the truth concerning the faith. If the clergy of themselves formed the Church, there would then be no doubt that the decision of all controverted questions concerning the faith lay with the clergy. But, actually, the Church consists of the whole body of professing Christians. The Church Catholic has, itself, no common organization and no common head : for all practical purposes every localized or national Church is a Church Catholic. The Church Catholic of England consists of all professing Christians within the realm and the natural and only possible head and representative of this body is the King. Just because the people of a realm constitute a Church, it follows that the King or other legal representative of that people can speak and act in the name of the Church and expound Scripture. ' If the emperor, kings and princes, with their people, as well of the clergy as of the lay fee, make the church . . . then may the emperor, kings and princes with their people expound it.' ² The conclusion is obvious and inevitable. In all cases of theological ' variance ' or dispute as to the meaning of the Word of God, it is for the civil sovereign to decide the question authoritatively. All that is wanted to decide religious controversies is a legal decision.

St. Germain admitted that it might be held expedient to make over the right to determine doctrinal questions to the clergy, as a body of experts. But he argued that to do so would be highly imprudent.

¹ *Answere to a Letter.* Heading of Chap. VII.
² *An Answere to a Letter.*

The clergy may be comparatively learned, but quite certainly they are biased. They are likely to maintain their own honour 'under a pretence to maintain the honour of God'.[1] The ill results of leaving it to the clergy to decide what is and is not heresy have been shown by experience.

In the realm of England, according to St. Germain, the representative of the Church is not the King merely and alone. It is the King 'with his people' who have the authority of the Church; and this, for England, means the King in Parliament. The right of the King in England, he explains, is *jus regale politicum*, and this signifies that he 'may make no law to bind his subjects without their assent'.[2] Convocation 'representeth only the state of the clergy'. The King in Parliament, on the other hand, represents the 'whole Catholic Church of England'. St. Germain appears to attribute to the King in Parliament a quite unlimited authority. 'It is holden,' he says, 'by them that are learned in the law of this realm that the parliament hath an absolute power as to the possession of all temporal things within this realm . . . to take them from one man and give them to another, without any cause or consideration, for if they do it, it bindeth in the law.'[3] Because Parliament represents the whole Church, which is the whole realm, its authority is that of the Church and extends to spiritual things. In one place, indeed, St. Germain says that no law made by man is binding unless 'consonant to the law of God'.[4] But since Parliament can decide authoritatively what the law of God is, the restriction becomes unreal. It is for 'the King's Grace and his Parliament'[5] to expound the Scripture and decide all religious controversies in the last resort.

What will become, under these circumstances, of that unity of the Church Universal which consists in agreement on the essentials of the faith St. Germain did not pause to inquire. The English Church is Catholic because it holds these essentials. But what is or is not essential is to be determined by the King in Parliament. It may be that, in time, the English Church may become the only true Church Catholic. That eventuality would, I think, have been contemplated by St. Germain without the least tremor.

Evidently it was not easy for theologians to come to such a view as this. They could not be expected to do so quickly, if at all. Under Henry VIII and Edward VI they may perhaps be said to have been feeling their way towards it; but they certainly do not state it. There was doubt in their minds on this point, as on many others. Whether

---

[1] *An Answere to a Letter.*   [2] Ib.

[3] *Treatise concerning the division*, p. 24.

[4] *Dialogus de fundamentis Legum Angliae et de conscientia*, 1523 (?). This subsequently appeared in an English translation, with additions.

[5] *Treatise concerning the division*, p. 21.

Henry VIII himself believed in transubstantiation and *jure divino* episcopacy may be doubtful; but certainly his reforming clergy can only have half believed in these things. Like Luther, the early reformers of England knew better what they did not believe than what they believed.[1]

Yet the implications of the assertion of royal supremacy could not logically be escaped. St. Germain has the merit of having perceived that you could not have the thing both ways. Royal Supremacy need not mean the supremacy of the King simply; but it must mean a right to decide all doctrinal questions or it meant nothing at all. It may be said that St. Germain anticipated the view officially adopted under Elizabeth. In her reign the clergy may be said to have been uneasily reconciling themselves to the new theory. That reconciliation was never anything like complete.

[1] Cranmer's perplexities are obvious. Latimer apparently believed in transubstantiation down at least to the death of Henry VIII. But he must have felt doubt before that event.

CHAPTER V

THE SUPREMACY OF ELIZABETH

THE early Tudors were engaged in releasing England from its ' liberties ', and the greatest of these were those attached to the Church. ' They did it by means of Parliament and could not have done it without.'[1] Along with the development of the theory of royal supremacy in the Church there went necessarily what Professor Pollard has called ' a novel theory of an omnicompetent crown in Parliament '.[2] It was not the need of an anti-Papal theory that was the driving force in that development. Nothing was easier than the formulation of anti-papal theory ; and no mere anti-papal theory involved any sort of royal supremacy in the Church. The great Tudor sovereigns were creating a national State and a national government. To that creation the repudiation of papal authority was incidental, and the establishment of national control of the Church a necessity of the moment So the Tudor Reformation involved the evolution and the partial acceptance of a theory that made of Church and State two aspects of one thing, the Commonwealth. Under Henry VIII that identification was already being made by lawyers, if not by theologians. Unfortunately the theory of royal supremacy involved that for all practical purposes the decisions of Parliament on religious questions had to be taken as though they were infallible. Whatever was the case with the theologians, the Tudor lawyers seem to have found no difficulty here. They revered the common law ;[3] they did not revere the Church and they cared little, or nothing, for theology. They accepted, without misgiving, the idea of a High Court of Parliament delivering final judgements on questions of religious belief. ' The Parliament,' remarks Sir Thomas Smith, ' legitimateth bastards, establisheth forms of religion, altereth weights and measures.'[4] To him, apparently, it did not

---

[1] Pollard : *Evolution of Parliament*, p. 175. [2] Ib., p. 215.

[3] In his *Dialogues*, St. Germain, very confusedly but almost completely, identifies the English common law with what he calls the law of reason ; another name, he explains, for the law of nature. See McIlwain's summary of his incoherencies in *The High Court of Parliament and its Supremacy*, 1910.

[4] *De Republica Anglorum*, 1583, ed. L. Alston, p. 49.

seem at all strange that weights and measures and forms of religion should be prescribed and defined by the same body for the use of all.

The lawyers, indeed, had their own difficulties with the theory of royal supremacy. How far did the spiritual supremacy vested in the Crown extend ? Lawyers held that the power of the King in civil affairs was limited by the common law ; but in spiritual causes it seemed that there was nothing to bind him. It was not easy or comfortable to recognize the existence of an unlimited jurisdiction in spiritual causes, while denying it in civil causes. Already under Henry VIII, Lord Chancellor Audley indicated the difficulty and the danger. He insisted that the King's doings as Supreme Head of the Church ' be restrained to spiritual jurisdiction ', and that it had been provided that no spiritual law should be valid if contrary to common law or act of Parliament. ' And if this were not,' quoth he, ' you bishops would enter in with the King and by means of his supremacy, order the laity as ye listed. But we will provide (quoth he) that the præmunire shall ever hang over your heads ; and so we laymen shall be sure to enjoy our inheritance by the common law and acts of Parliament.' [1] On behalf of a monarch vested with the full spiritual supremacy, as on behalf of a Pope, it might well have been argued that all mere civil law was absolutely subject to his determinations. Elizabeth, of course, was too wise and prudent to make such a claim. Yet the danger was visible. It was, perhaps, chiefly on that account that lawyers were inclined, like St. Germain, to hold that supremacy in the Church lay, not with the monarch alone, but only with the Crown in Parliament.

Even so they were in a difficulty. If the common lawyers did not doubt the omnicompetence of Parliament as a High Court, they certainly doubted its omnipotence as a legislative body. They were, at least, reluctant to admit that there existed any power radically to alter the sacred rules of the common law. They were inclined to assert the existence of law that was ' fundamental ' [2] and unalterable. So it was that they tended to become jealous and suspicious of the practical exercise of the Crown's ecclesiastical supremacy. After 1585, when the commission for causes ecclesiastical was passing more and more under episcopal control and developing into a regular court of ecclesiastical law, the common law judges began frequently to interfere with its action by writs of prohibition. So commenced that process which was to bring about that strangest of alliances, the

---

[1] Recorded in a letter of Stephen Gardiner to Protector Somerset, 1547. This was printed in the first edition of Foxe's *Acts and Monuments*, 1563 ; and reprinted in Cattley's edition of that work, 1837, 1839. See Vol. VI, p. 43.

[2] This term of French law seems not to have been used in England before James I. In 1604 the Speaker of the House of Commons referred to the common law as ' not mutable '. In 1607 King James spoke of the term as used of common law.

alliance between the Puritan parties and the common lawyers. The firs literary sign of the coming alliance seems to have been an anonymou treatise published in 1589 or 1590.[1] When, in 1604, William Stoughton dedicated his *Assertion for true and Christian Church policie* to the common lawyers of the realm, that alliance was maturing. All through the later years of Elizabeth's reign, the common lawyers were claiming that it is for civil courts to define the limits of ecclesiastical jurisdiction and, therefore, the practical limits of the royal supremacy as established under Parliament.

Just as it seemed to the lawyers that royal supremacy in spiritual causes might wreck the common law, so, to others, it seemed to threaten the destruction of religion. It was possible under Henry VIII to see in the Royal Supremacy an instrument for the salvation of souls and the construction of a truly Christian commonwealth. It was possible to believe that popular Bible reading would produce general agreement about true religion. It became, under Elizabeth, more and more difficult to hold such views. Increasingly apparent was it that, while royal supremacy involved a power to determine the form of religion for every one and in every sense, that power was being used for quite earthly ends. Visibly the government was seeking lines of least resistance and not, unless with extreme indirection, the salvation of souls.

For many reasons Elizabeth's settlement of the Church had to be far more distinctively ' Protestant ' than Henry VIII's had been. The Mass became officially, at least by 1571, a ' blasphemous fable and dangerous deceit '.[2] Transubstantiation, denial of which had, by act of the infallible Parliament of 1539, been punishable by death, now became ' repugnant to the plain words of Scripture ' : [3] purgatory and invocation of saints were now ' fond things, vainly invented '.[4] The Pope became more, and worse, than a mere usurper of royal jurisdiction. But, no more than Henry VIII, did Elizabeth see reason for structural alterations in strictly ecclesiastical organization. It has been pointed out that the retention of old forms of Church government to some extent disguised the character of the Elizabethan settlement. Much, too, of the language officially or semi-officially used to explain or justify the arrangements, was mere repetition of that used under Henry VIII. Elizabeth's Act of Supremacy was an act restoring to the Crown ancient jurisdiction. Christ, it was declared, had expressly forbidden the clergy to assume any kind of worldly dominion and, in particular, ' did forbid unto all eccle-

---

[1] *A petition presented to her Most Excellent Majesty.* Matthew Sutcliffe's *Answer to a Certaine Libel supplicatorie or rather Diffamatorie*, was an answer to it from the point of view of Whitgift (1592).

[2] *Articles of Religion*, XXXI.

[3] Ib., XXVIII.   [4] Ib., XXII.

siastical ministers dominion over the Church of Christ '.[1] Clergy
ought, ' specially and before others ', to be obedient to their princes.
As for the Bishop of Rome, he is ' none other than the bishop of that
one see and diocese and never yet well able to govern the same '.[2]
In 1585, Bilson carefully repeated all the old assertions.[3] It is for
the secular sovereign to establish and maintain right forms of
worship and true religion. All the old arguments, assumptions and
ambiguities were reproduced. They became part of an established
convention.

But a great change had come about and, disguised as it might be,
the main facts stood out ever more clearly. Henceforward the form
of ecclesiastical organization and government, the forms of ritual and
common prayer, the existence of episcopacy, were to be wholly dependent upon the determinations of the civil sovereign. Bishops hold
such authority as they possess by virtue of a royal commission and
for no other reason, exactly as do justices of the peace. Recognition
of the royal supremacy and attendance at the authorized and official
church services becomes a test of loyalty. The government makes
use of bishops and ecclesiastical commissioners to enforce those tests.
The High Commission is an instrument of the Council. And more
and more apparent was it that he who determines the form, determines the substance.

Power to ordain sacraments and power arbitrarily to dictate
doctrine were indeed officially disclaimed. It was fully admitted
that the Supreme Government of the Church was bound by the text
of Scripture. Yet, if you accepted the Elizabethan system, you
could not deny that it was for the Queen, or for the Queen in Parliament, to declare authoritatively what doctrines and what sacraments
are indeed in Scripture. ' The Word of God cannot speak,' said
Bishop Andrewes to Henry Barrow : ' which way should it decide
our controversies ? ' Law recognized that the determinations of
civil authority concerning religious belief and observance, must be
consistent with the Word of God ; and law proceeded to assume that
they always were so. The authority of the Scriptures became a kind
of legal fiction. But the lawyers went even further ; as indeed they
could not help doing. They maintained that appeal to the text of
Scripture was, if not quite irrelevant, at least not admissible. John
Penry complained [4] that if one were summoned before judges or royal
commissioners for the cause of religion, these authorities declared
that the question whether this or that were supported by the Word of
God was not before the court. All they had to do was to see to it that

---

[1] *Homilies. Against Disobedience*, V, p. 589.   [2] Ib., p. 599.
[3] *The True Difference between Christian subjection and unchristian rebellion*,
1585.
[4] In his petition to the Queen, written in 1592.

the Queen's law was not broken and that her supremacy was recognized in word and in deed.

However reluctantly and with whatever misgivings, the official theologians and ecclesiastical apologists for the royal supremacy were bound to come into line. There were, under Elizabeth, many such defenders of the position.[1] The earlier were concerned with defence against Romanist criticism ; the later writers had to deal mainly with Puritanism. Long before the end of Elizabeth's reign it should have been clear that the ' Puritans ' were far more formidable foes than ever the Catholics were likely to be. Putting Hooker aside, as quite peerless, the ablest of all these controversial writers was, I think, Whitgift. He had not Hooker's philosophic breadth nor his calmness nor his patience nor his subtlety, nor did he attempt to consider things so deeply. He was, therefore, all the more typical of Elizabethan orthodoxy. But it is remarkable how much of his argumentation, especially that of his very able *Defence of the Answer*, was incorporated into Hooker's great book. Particular importance attaches to his views because of his highly representative character as an Elizabethan churchman. His chief controversial treatises were, however, published before orthodox Elizabethanism, in his person, ascended the throne at Canterbury.[2]

Whitgift's point of view, even in 1572, was that of a statesman and not that of a philosopher. Though he was, I believe, an honest and a religious man, he was less concerned about religious questions than about the maintenance of social order. In this he was typical not only of orthodox Elizabethanism but, it may be said, of Elizabethan England. His object in writing was to meet specific objections made by the ' Puritans ' to the organization and character of the Church of England and to point out the dangerous implications of their argument. He was one of the first in England to point out that Puritans were like Catholics in denying to civil magistrates authority in relation to the Church. We cannot find in his writings any philosophic exposition of the theory of the royal supremacy. But he expressed vigorously the ordinary views of the orthodox and the

[1] Jewel, Horne, Whitgift, Bilson, Bridges, Cosin and Bancroft may be mentioned. Jewel's *Apology for the Church of England* was first published in 1562 ; his *Defence of the Apology* appeared in 1567. John Bridges, Dean of Salisbury, published, in 1587, a bulky *Defence of the Government established in the Church of England*. ' Oh ! read over Dr. John Bridges, for it is a worthy work.' Anyone who attempts this feat will feel the point of Martin Marprelate's jeer.

[2] The *First* and *Second Admonitions to Parliament* appeared in 1572 and Whitgift's *Answer* came out the same year. Then followed Cartwright's reply ; and Whitgift's *Defence of the Answer* was published in 1574. He became Archbishop in 1583. His predecessor, Edward Grindal, belonged to the group of Marian exiles who became bishops after Elizabeth's succession and whose sympathies were with Geneva and ' Puritanism '.

arguments of his *Defence of the Answer* were constantly repeated in other writings for the next twenty years.

Here, in the Church of England, Whitgift argued, we have ' all points of religion necessary to salvation . . . as purely and perfectly taught as ever they were in any Church sithence the Apostles' time '. That being so, it is merely mischievous to raise all manner of unnecessary questions and attack the Church as by law established, because on points of detail you mislike its arrangements. Question and difficulty may arise concerning essential articles of faith; but where ' things indifferent ' are concerned there should be no question at all. In every Christian Church, the Word must ' be truly taught, the sacraments rightly administered, virtue furthered, vice repressed and the Church kept in quietness and order ' : [1] to all this the Scriptures bind us. But where the Scriptures are silent or where legitimate doubt exists, there the Church is free. Every particular Church [2] has a right to order as it will its own form and ceremonies, its own method and system of government, except so far as these things are definitely determined for it by the text of Scripture. There is ' no one certain and perfect kind of government prescribed or commanded in the Scriptures to the Church of Christ '.[3] It is therefore for the supreme ecclesiastical authorities to arrange the government of the Church ' according to the state of times, places and persons '.[4] But Church and State cannot be separated. Whitgift makes the essential assertion boldly. ' I perceive no such distinction of the commonwealth and the Church that they should be counted as it were two several bodies governed with divers laws and divers magistrates.'[5] It follows that it is for the civil sovereign to order the form of the Church and its ceremonial and services. But Whitgift went further. ' The continual practice of Christian Churches, in the time of Christian magistrates, before the usurpation of the Bishop of Rome, hath been to give to Christian princes supreme authority in making ecclesiastical orders and laws, yea and that which is more, in deciding of matters of religion, even in the chief and principal points.'[6] What can be ' the chief and principal points ' if not the articles of faith ? So, then, the difficulty about these disappears also : for England any such difficulty will be solved by the Queen in Parliament. So too, there-

---

[1] *Defence of the Answer*. Preface. Parker Soc., I, 6.

[2] By a ' particular Church, we understand every particular kingdom, province or region which by order maketh one Christian society or body '. This is from the Discourse prepared by Jewel, Grindal and others for use in the abortive discussion arranged for at Westminster in 1559.

[3] *Defence of the Answer*. Works, Parker Soc., I, p. 182.

[4] Ib., Preface, I, 6.

[5] Ib., I, p. 21. The passage occurs in the introductory ' Answer to the Epistle '.

[6] Ib., III, p. 306.

fore, the criticisms and questionings of the Puritans are not only mischievous but seditious, and involve an attack on the Crown itself and on the principle of order. The tendency of such seditious cavilling is towards sheer anarchy. On this Whitgift enlarges, comparing the Puritans with the Anabaptists of Germany. Bancroft, later, put the same point with epigrammatic vigour. No petty Pope, says Martin Marprelate, speaking of bishops, is to be tolerated in a Christian commonwealth : and he explains that a petty Pope is one who assumes the same authority in ecclesiastical matters as the Pope of Rome had had. But this, says Bancroft, is just what Her Majesty has done. The Puritans are bound to complete the syllogism. ' Her Majesty is a petty Pope. Therefore Her Majesty is not to be tolerated in a Christian Commonwealth.' [1] ' This judgement doth but begin at the house of God and it will proceed further to the overthrow of all government.' [2] Bancroft's *Dangerous Positions and Proceedings,* published in 1593,[3] was designed to convict the Puritans out of their own mouths of subversive and treasonable intentions.

In assuming the essential identity of Church and Commonwealth, Whitgift and Bancroft were assuming all that they had to prove. The proof of the proposition was left to writers like Bridges and Bilson, who could convince no one. The assumption made, it was easy to show that to declare that the ' tyrannous lordship ' of bishops ' cannot stand with Christ's kingdom ',[4] to describe the authorized Prayer Book as ' culled out of the vile Popish Service Book ',[5] to speak of ' our English Church unreformed ',[6] was seditious language, calculated to bring Queen and Parliament and so all law into contempt. But the assumption made involved much more. It involved either the belief that Queen or Parliament could pronounce infallibly on the articles of the Christian faith or the belief that one was in duty bound to accept their pronouncements and act on them, right or wrong.

[1] *A Sermon preached at Paules Crosse,* 1588, p. 68. Martin's actual words are : ' Those that are petty popes and petty Antichrists ought not to be maintained in any Christian Commonwealth. . . . Therefore no Lord Bishop . . . is to be tolerated in any Christian Commonwealth.' ' The Epistle ': first of the Marprelate tracts, 1588.

[2] Ib., ed. 1588, p. 89.

[3] Two editions were printed within a year and the book was widely read. It gives a history of the Presbyterian movement in England and is full of quotations from Puritan tracts and letters.

[4] *An Admonition* to the Parliament, 1571. Attributed to John Field and Thomas Wilcox : but others probably had a hand in it.

[5] *The Second Admonition.* 1572. Often attributed to Cartwright. But the style is not his and is hardly distinguishable from that of the first Admonition. He may have revised it. See R. Bayne's edition of Book V of the *Ecclesiastical Polity.* Introduction.

[6] Anthony Gilby : *A View of Antichrist, his Lawes and Ceremonies, in our English Church unreformed.* 1571. Gilby was probably one of the authors of the Admonitions.

' These things are commanded by act of Parliament and in disobeying the laws of your country, you disobey God,' says a Master of Requests to a recalcitrant of 1573.[1] It would appear, therefore, that God may command you to say you believe what you are sure is not true and may command you to obey the Queen's orders even though they be contrary to His own. But neither Whitgift nor Bancroft nor indeed any Elizabethan Churchman went so far as to say these things. They did not, I think, dare to see all that was involved in their own argument. In the argument of Whitgift and of Bancroft, all the stress is laid on the seditious and dangerous nature of opposition to the determinations of civil authority as to ' things indifferent '. The Puritans, of course, did not admit that either surplices or bishops were things indifferent : nor did they admit that even an act of parliament could make of a thing indifferent for the religious conscience, anything but an indifferent thing. In controversy over the question of what things were indifferent, Whitgift was at least equal to his adversaries. But he was not really facing the main question which, after all, referred to things which no one would have called indifferent.

The difficulty in which religious and conforming persons were placed by the doctrine of royal supremacy is well illustrated in Thomas Bilson's *True Difference between Christian Subjection and Unchristian Rebellion.*[2] The unfortunate author could do little more than state a paradox. In every Christian commonwealth, he says, Princes ' command for truth '. It is their right and their duty to legislate ' for the true service and worship of God ' and ' to plant and establish the Christian faith in their realms by their princely power '.[3] God has charged all Princes with the maintenance of true religion and they have full authority ' to forbid, prevent and punish in all their subjects . . . schisms, heresies, idolatries '.[4] But he admits that the prince has no other means of discovering true religion than all men have ; and he admits, therefore, that the prince's decisions cannot be regarded as a rule of faith. ' Never man of our side affirmeth any such thing.' Princes, evidently, may err and ' that Princes may prescribe what faith they list, what service of God they please . . . is no part of our thought, no point of our doctrine '. This is explicit ; but what ' our doctrine ' is remains obscure. ' And yet,' he goes on, ' that Princes may by their laws prescribe the Christian faith to be preached, the right service of God to be used . . . this is no absurdity in us to defend.'[5] Does, then, the royal supremacy

---

[1] See the examination of a certain Mr. White, given in Neal, ed. Toulmin, I, p. 280 n.

[2] Published 1585. It was written in answer to William Allen's *Defence of English Catholics* (1584). Bilson became Bishop of Worcester in 1596 and of Winchester in 1597.

[3] *True Difference*, 1585, p. 123.

[4] Ib., p. 129.   [5] Ib., p. 217.

mean no more than that the Prince is bound to establish a certain known and undeniably right faith and service ? That is just what the Puritans were saying. Princes, Bilson admits, may make laws ' against God and His truth '. All that he is sure of is that, in this case, there is no rightful remedy. ' All their subjects . . . must obey them commanding that which is good in matters of religion and endure them with patience when they take part with error.' [1] Even while defending the actual ecclesiastical system by law established, Bilson was breaking away from the doctrine of royal supremacy as based on a strict identification of Church and Commonwealth.

The question of the nature and rightfulness of episcopacy bulked very large in the controversies of Elizabeth's reign and with good reason. The continuance of the institution under the royal supremacy suggested, as Professor Pollard has remarked, that the bishops still held authority ' by virtue of the ancient derivation '. It was just this suggestion that roused suspicion, resentment and hostility among the Calvinistic. Had Elizabeth called her bishops superintendents or simply royal commissioners, their hostility to the institution would have been mitigated, at least for a time. On the other hand so startling a change of names would have antagonized a much larger number of people. But from the point of view of Elizabeth and her ministers and her first bishops, the abolition of episcopacy would not, ideally, in any way have altered the character of the Elizabethan Church. To Cranmer and to Latimer and their colleagues under Edward VI, episcopacy had been an allowable institution and no more. ' I refer the standing or falling altogether to your own considerations, whether Her Majesty and you will have any archbishops or bishops or how you will have them ordered,' wrote Matthew Parker to Burghley.[2] Parker was a moderate man ; but some of Elizabeth's first bishops would have liked to see the name abolished, if not, quite, the thing. Episcopacy, later, is merely an arrangement the Queen has chosen to make. ' The Bishops of this realm,' wrote Whitgift, ' do not . . . nor must not claim to themselves any greater authority than is given them ' by statute. ' For if it had pleased Her Majesty, with the wisdom of the realm, to have used no bishops at all, we could not have complained justly of any defect in our church.' [3] John Hammond, Chancellor of the diocese of London, writing to Burghley in 1588, puts the points clearly.[4] ' The supreme civil magistrate,' he remarked, ' in every country, may appoint under officers in the execution of that government which he hath in ecclesiastical causes, as well as he may do in civil matters.' The only doubt is as to whether such office may be conferred on ' ministers of the Word and Sacraments '.

[1] *True Difference*, 1585, p. 213.   [2] *Parker Correspondence.* Parker Soc., 1853, p. 454.   [3] See Strype's *Life of Whitgift*, III, 222.
[4] *Hatfield Callendar*, III, No. 754, pp. 369, 370.

' But as I think this charge may be in some manner committed to ministers of the Word, so am I out of doubt the same so done is but an human ordinance and may not be entitled to any greater authority, nor otherwise said to be of God's ordinance, than the office of civil magistrates be.'[1] It was, in fact, the official view that episcopacy was a ' thing indifferent '.

Down to 1570 this was hardly questioned in Protestant England. Episcopacy was objectionable, perhaps, because of its associations and suggestions ; it was not asserted that it was an absolutely unrighteous arrangement. But in 1570 began, at Cambridge, an attack on the institution as disallowed by the law of God, and therefore beyond the power of any ruler rightfully to establish. From that time onwards, with increasing assurance and vigour, the ' Puritans ' denounced episcopacy as positively antichristian. They asserted that a form of government for the Church was definitely prescribed in the Scriptures and that this form was not, in any sense, episcopal. They were told that they were factiously objecting to a mere name. The Bishop was but a minister of the Word acting under a civil commission from the Queen for her ecclesiastical business.[2] In denouncing episcopacy as established in England they were denouncing not the Papistical institution going under that name but, simply, the royal supremacy. It was, of course, also asserted that, while the Scriptures do not bind us to adopt any particular form of Church government, what they suggest is not Presbyterianism but episcopacy. ' A very strange matter if it were true,' said Bancroft, ' that Christ should erect a form of government for the ruling of his church to continue from his departure out of this world until his coming again : and that the same should never be once thought of or put in practice for the space of fifteen hundred years.'[3] For the Puritan platform, wrote Hooker, ' no age ever had knowledge of it but only ours . . . neither Christ nor his Apostles at any time taught it but the contrary '.[4] From about 1585 the apostolic origin of episcopacy is being more and more insisted upon ; and this was the prelude to an important development of opinion.[5]

' The fundamental contention underlying the Elizabethan settlement,' says Professor Pollard, ' was that a national church had the right to determine its own faith, ritual and organization.'[6] The

---

[1] Hammond goes on to repeat, almost verbatim, the words of Whitgift quoted above.

[2] See the curious argument between Barrow, Greenwood and Sperm in *A Collection of Certain Letters and Conferences lately passed betwixt certain preachers and two prisoners in the Fleet*, 1590.

[3] *Sermon preached at Paules Crosse*, 1588, pp. 10, 11.

[4] *Ecclesiastical Polity*, Book III, 10.

[5] The significance of this is dealt with later.

[6] *Political History of England*, Longman, 1910, Vol. VI, p. 210.

words need and merit close attention. This national church was conceived as but an aspect of the commonwealth and it could only determine these things through the civil sovereign and by law. This meant that one must adhere to the faith and conform to the ritual and accept the ecclesiastical organization prescribed by the Queen or Parliament, or be disloyal and be treated as disloyal. Parliament became, necessarily, a High Court for the definition of Christian faith. Constant repetition of the assertion that the sovereign is bound by Scripture served but as an anodyne for the conscience. It should have served for nothing, since, in the last resort, it was for Parliament to interpret Scripture. Evidently the conception is political and evidently it is not religious. Put in its extreme logical form, as it was put by Hobbes, it is a negation of religion. It refers to the need of order in society, to the sense that rebellion is the greatest of crimes against one's neighbours, it refers, if you will, to the need of union in religion. What it does not refer to is the need for religious truth. Religion is conceived as a function of social order ; and such a conception could satisfy no religious man. The principle involved that the determination of public authority, that is of the commonwealth itself, is binding on all subjects, even in matters of religious faith, and irrespective of the truth of the doctrine officially proclaimed. It may be possible for a man ' religious ' in some sense to say that ; but certainly no man could say it who believed that salvation depended in any degree on believing rightly. And in fact no one did quite say it. ' No man of our side affirmeth any such thing.' But when Whitgift says he can see no real difference between Church and Commonwealth, when Hooker says that the law as determined by public authority is the act and deed of every member of the Commonwealth, they have come very near to committing themselves to the Hobbesian doctrine.

At the beginning of the reign of Elizabeth there existed absolutely valid practical objections to any attempt at a logical reconstruction of the English Church or definition of its distinctive character. Except among a few convinced Calvinists there seems, indeed, to have been little sense of any sort of need of any such thing. The official religious reformers, from Cranmer to Parker, seem naïvely to have supposed that an open Bible and free discussion would rapidly bring all men to the same conclusions. The one thing immediately necessary was to abolish the Roman system : the new system could be left in vagueness till a general conviction of true religion had come about. Parker and Elizabeth, therefore, agreed very well in practice : he with her, because he believed that Bible reading would produce something like unanimity ; she with him, because she was aware of vast differences of opinion to be conciliated.

But the result of Elizabeth's wisdom and Parker's simple faith, was a construction vague and incoherent, ideally and in law, and disorderly in practice. From a religious point of view the Elizabethan settlement settled nothing. The right of the national church to determine its own faith and form was asserted; and its actual determinations were merely negative. The one positive doctrine essential to and distinctive of the Elizabethan church system was the doctrine of royal supremacy. The Elizabethan church had no defined constitution, form or character. It was designed to include as many irreconcilable views as could possibly be included. It may fairly be said that the Elizabethan Church had no definite doctrinal position, no distinctive theology, no law that anyone could ascertain for certain and very little either of discipline or of order. The theology of Whitgift, as of most of Elizabeth's earlier bishops, seems to have been substantially Calvinistic. But it would be hard logically to extract any definite doctrinal system from the Elizabethan Book of Common Prayer and Articles of Religion. The law of the Church of England when Elizabeth died was contained in certain Acts of Parliament, Articles, Advertisements, Injunctions and Canons. It was, as has been said, a thing of 'scattered fragments, more or less contradictory and of questionable legality'.[1] Were the Queen's Injunctions of 1559 superior in force to the Canons of 1571, which had behind them only the authority of convocation? What force was added to the Canons of 1597 by the Queen's approbation and confirmation? The Advertisements of 1564 were issued on the sole authority of the Commissioners for Causes Ecclesiastical and remained without royal confirmation. Whitgift's regulations for ecclesiastical courts were issued in 1587 of his sole authority as Archbishop: so also were the Articles of 1593. It is strictly true to say that, on very many points of practical importance, no one knew or could know what the law of the Church was. Nor would the government, while insisting on the recognition of royal supremacy, practically insist on conformity to such law as there was. Elizabeth, in her wisdom, would neither govern the Church herself nor allow her Bishops to do so. ' To sign the required papers under compulsion when confronted by the Bishop . . . to read the greater part of the Prayer Book, to wear the surplice occasionally, to say nothing in open derogation of the Church or of the royal authority . . . this was Elizabethan conformity.'[2] Even this amount of conformity was far from being always forthcoming from Elizabeth's ministers of the Word. It might be said that the English people was asking its government to give it the bread of life from the Scriptures and that it was given something about as nutritive as a stone. No one could say precisely what it was that the Church was supposed to teach, unless it were the doctrine of royal supremacy.

[1] R. G. Usher: *The Reconstruction of the English Church*, 1910, I, p. 196.
[2] Ib., I, p. 207.

And no one quite knew what that was. So thought the Puritans and so, also, it seems, thought Bancroft. But if they, in a sense, were right, Elizabeth, in another, was right also. For it was not that spiritual bread for which the mass of English people were asking.

The constant resolution of the great Queen neither to allow of definition, nor strictly to enforce conformity, delayed the development of the disastrous struggle that came later. Even so, before the end of her reign, most of the more profoundly and intelligently religious people of the time were revolting or protesting, it might be only half-consciously, against her system. On the one hand the Puritans were attacking not only its details but its ' fundamental contention '. On the other, among the supporters of the system, there was developing a revival of the claim to *jure divino* authority in the episcopate, which, as was pointed out at the time, was radically incompatible with the theory of royal supremacy.

The Puritan assertion that episcopacy was absolutely disallowed by the Word of God was met, first, by an assertion that, so far as any particular form of church government was suggested in Scripture, it was episcopacy that was indicated.

In his famous sermon of 1588 Bancroft went a step further. He definitely claimed that episcopacy had been established in the Church ' even since the Apostles' time '.[1] In 1590 appeared a book by Adrian Saravia, attempting to prove that episcopacy was of apostolic if not actually of divine institution.[2] In 1593 Bilson boldly asserted the derivation of episcopacy not merely from apostolic times but from Christ Himself. He spoke of the vocation of bishops ' immediate from Christ, not from men or by men '.[3]

A superficial view of the facts might suggest that this development was due mainly to mere exigencies of controversy. But there was no logical necessity for such a development. It had to be shown that no definite form of Church government was prescribed in Scripture : that done the authority of bishops could be derived quite simply from the royal supremacy. The significant fact is that such a derivation came to be felt as unsatisfactory or as dangerous. More or less clearly it was seen that such a defence of the institution as it stood, involved recognition of a royal supremacy unqualified and unlimited.

---

[1] *A Sermon preached at Paules Crosse*, 1588, p. 99.

[2] *De Diversis Gradibus Ministrorum Evangelii.* Saravia was a Spanish Fleming, a refugee in England and a friend of Hooker. He spoke of the Roman Church as ' mater nostra '. An English translation of his book appeared in 1592.

[3] *The Perpetual Government of Christ his Church.* Prefatory epistle. In the fifth book of the *Ecclesiastical Polity*, Hooker speaks of the degrees of ' bishops, presbyters and deacons, which had their beginning from Christ and his blessed Apostles '. Chap. 78. Works, Clarendon Press, II, p. 482.

The development was no doubt partly due to the desire of the Bishops to strengthen morally a position that was weak in law. There can have been few positions less enviable than that of an Elizabethan bishop, placed between the devil of Puritanism and the deep sea of secularism, called upon to deal with an ignorant and refractory clergy and armed with totally insufficient powers, harassed by the Council and by the lawyers, savagely abused and maligned and hampered at every turn by his own poverty and that of the despoiled church. But it would be ridiculous to attribute the revival of the claim to *jure divino* authority simply to the bishops themselves. It arose, immediately, from moral revolt against the disorder and incoherence of the Elizabethan Church, from a sense that royal supremacy had failed to produce any real settlement and a sense that a great wrong was being done to religious life in England. But its root, I think, lay far deeper. From the beginning of the reign the Elizabethan Church had included two very different forms of religious consciousness. The one was the Protestantism of Calvin and of Knox, of Geneva or of Scotland, the other was derived from that Catholic tradition which Elizabeth's arrangements modified but did not kill. The one developed into a ' Puritanism ' that became more and more definite in aim and more and more antagonistic to the Church established. The other developed, far more slowly, into an Anglican Catholicism. This latter development, in many ways retarded, can hardly be said to find quite definite expression before the reign of James I ; but its beginnings, at least, are visible under Elizabeth.

No sooner had Bancroft suggested that bishops might be held to possess authority not altogether derived from the Queen, than it was pointed out by Sir Francis Knollys that to say ' that the superiority of Bishops is God's own institution . . . doth impugn Her Majesty's supreme government directly '. Sir Francis, then Lord Treasurer of the Household, was one of those of Elizabeth's ministers who contrived to combine a thoroughgoing belief in the royal supremacy with Puritanic sympathies. It would be well, he wrote to Burghley in 1589, that the bishops should be made to acknowledge in some further manner, that they possessed no authority ' but such as is to be derived unto them directly from Her Majesty's supreme authority and government '. He pointed out that if the authority of the bishops were held *jure divino*, it was meaningless to say that they held it from the Queen, since in that case the Queen would only have conferred what she could not have withheld. If, in fact, bishops derive authority direct from Christ and the Apostles, then the Queen is not ' the only supreme governor of this realm . . . in all spiritual or ecclesiastical things or causes '.[1]

[1] Letters of Knollys to Burghley, 1589–1590, printed in *Strype Annals,* I and IV.

Knollys was right.   A new line of attack on the royal supremacy was developing.   A new crack had opened in the crazy structure of the Elizabethan Church.   It was left to the Stuart Kings to widen that crack, to accept the divine right of bishops and ally themselves with the new High Church party ;   and so to bring about the alliance of Puritans and common lawyers against the claims of the Crown.

CHAPTER VI

THE LAWS OF ECCLESIASTICAL POLITY

IT was, presumably, the calm sanity of his outlook that earned for Richard Hooker the almost ludicrously inadequate epithet ' judicious '. The epithet suggests that his contemporaries were far from appreciating his immense superiorities. Not merely as a controversialist but as a political thinker, he was incomparably the greatest Englishman of the sixteenth century and on the Continent had few compeers. For breadth of view, combined with intellectual honesty and detachment, he had no serious rival save Bodin. For fairness and courtesy in controversy only Cardinal Bellarmine was his equal. Among learned or controversial or philosophical books, no literary style is comparable in excellence to his, save the totally dissimilar style of Calvin.

Hooker's great work, *The Laws of Ecclesiastical Polity*, was designed to show that Puritan criticism of the Elizabethan Church was unsound in substance and in detail and that Puritan refusal to conform to the ecclesiastical law of the land could not rationally be justified. It was addressed specifically to the Puritans from the first word to the last. The first four ' books ' were published in 1594, the fifth in 1597. The sixth, seventh and eighth books appear to have been completed before Hooker's death in 1599. But they are wholly or partially lost to us. What purported to be the sixth and eighth books appeared in print for the first time in 1648, the seventh only in 1662. The so-called sixth book may be of Hooker's writing, but, except for the first two chapters, it is certainly not the sixth book of the *Ecclesiastical Polity*. The seventh and eighth books, as we have them, represent only a first rough draft ; and how far that has been faithfully reproduced, how far re-written or added to, none can tell with certainty. The eighth book, with which we are here particularly concerned, may at least be taken as substantially representing Hooker's thought and contains much that one feels almost sure was written by him as it stands. But if Walton's story of how the completed manuscript of these last books was deliberately destroyed, by a Puritan named Charke, be true, then even Puritanism never destroyed anything more worth keeping. The loss or partial loss of these books in their finished form is one of the greatest that English scholars and lovers of literature have suffered.[1]

Much of Hooker's great work is occupied with the details of Puritan criticism. But his main purpose was to show that the claim of the Puritans to disobey the law of the Church was inconsistent with the nature of politic society and involved a denial of political obligation. He was therefore forced to begin with an exposition of the nature of law. In his preface he describes his first ' book ' as an introduction ' declaring what Law is, how different kinds of Law there are, and what force they are of '.[2] But, since he was concerned above all with the nature of positive or man-made law, it was not enough to define the senses in which the term Law was used. He had in that same ' introduction ' to consider the origin of politic society and government and the ground of political obligation. The essentials of Hooker's political philosophy found expression therefore in his first book and in his preface. In most of the remaining books he was occupied chiefly in dealing, point by point, with specific Puritan contentions. But since he had to justify his conception that ecclesiastical law, except so far as it was directly determined by Scripture, was ultimately of the same nature as civil law, he was compelled to discuss the question of the nature of the ' Church '. His views on this subject were expressed chiefly in the third and in the eighth books. In that unlucky eighth book he dealt directly with the nature of the Church of England and with civil supremacy.[3]

Hooker, it must be remembered, wrote after the publication of Bodin's *Republic*, after that of the *Vindiciae*, after Buchanan. His was the latest or almost the latest of the more important expressions of political thought in the sixteenth century. Yet to none of the earlier writers does he seem to owe anything directly. It is even, perhaps, a little singular that the influence of Bodin, so apparent in other English writers of the last years of the century, should be untraceable in Hooker. He owed far more to Whitgift than to any writer of the Continent. Hooker, in fact, was intensely and typically English. Not only did he deliberately set himself to deal minutely with circumstantial aspects of the position in England, but in doing so he displays a very English caution. He had none of Bodin's love of generalization and none of Calvin's audacity of logic. He was shy

[1] For the evidence as to the fate of Hooker's manuscripts and the facts concerning the publication of the last three books of the *Ecclesiastical Polity*, see Preface to Keble's edition of the works of Hooker and the Appendix to Walton's *Life* (1665), printed in that edition. See, also, Hooker in *Dict. of Nat. Biog.* All my references are to the Clarendon Press edition, 1888.

[2] *Eccles. Pol.*, Preface. Clarendon Press ed., 1888, p. 172.

[3] In reading this eighth book one seems constantly to hear the voice of Hooker with a distinctness that is exasperating, since one can never be sure of the words.

of logical abstractions. He saw the search for the ideally best as a likely road to ruin. What we have to do, he says, is to see to it ' that when the best things are not possible, the best may be made of those that are '.[1] To say that things should be thus and thus and that therefore we must have them so, is absurd.

' In polity, as well ecclesiastical as civil, there are and will be always evils which no art of man can cure, breaches and leaks more than man's wit hath hands to stop.' [2]

There are few principles that are absolutely valid in relation to actuality.

' They that walk in darkness know not whither they go. And even as little is their certainty, whose opinions generalities only do guide. With gross and popular capacities nothing doth more prevail than unlimited generalities, because of their plainness at the first sight : nothing less with men of exact judgment, because such rules are not safe to be trusted over far.' [3]

What Hooker sought was conclusions of practical value which should commend themselves irresistibly to the reason or the common sense of men of his own time and place. For all his breadth of view, his sweet reasonableness and admirable dialectic, and in spite of his realization that no conclusions whatever could be established until certain fundamental questions had, in some fashion, been answered, he was never quite the complete philosopher. He glossed over or passed over in silence difficulties for which he had no solution ; he refused to ask questions he was wise enough to know he could not answer. For all that he was one of the very few political thinkers of the century who tried definitely to connect his political philosophy with a view of the universal order.

All through his exposition of the nature and connection of the different kinds of Law, Hooker follows Aquinas very closely. His categories are almost exactly those of the great medieval thinker, though his terminology is somewhat different. We are not concerned here with his explanatory discussion of what he terms the Eternal Law, from which all things derive, or of what he calls the Law of Nature. But we are concerned with his explanation of what he terms the Law of Reason,[4] both because this conception is common to most writers of the sixteenth century and because Hooker, like others, found in it a constant limit to all rightful human authority.

The Law of Reason, says Hooker, ' is the law whereby man in all his actions is directed to the imitation of God'. Argumentative explanation of this utterance follows. All action whatever must

[1] *Eccles. Pol.*, V, 9, p. 36.
[2] Ib., p. 38.   [3] Ib., p. 39.
[4] The Law Naturalis of Aquinas. Hooker sometimes uses for it the term 'Law of Human Nature '.

necessarily refer to an end ; [1] and that end is necessarily conceived as a ' good ' to be obtained or to be preserved. ' God alone excepted, who actually and everlastingly is whatsoever he may be and cannot hereafter be that which now he is not, all other things besides are somewhat in possibility which as yet they are not in act.' [2] All other beings have a sense of their own imperfection and ' covet more or less the participation of God himself '.[3] Every man desires to perfect himself in some sense or relation : man, we may say, desires perfection in every sense and without limit.   ' To will is to bend our souls to the having or doing of that which they see to be good.' [4] The world is governed by a will to goodness or a will to more perfect life. It is always some good that the will seeks ; ' for evil as evil cannot be desired : if that be desired which is evil the cause is the goodness which is or seemeth to be joined with it '.[5] Sin consists essentially in the wilful preference of a lesser to a greater good.   ' The object of Will is that good which Reason doth lead us to seek.' Reason is the director of man's will, by discerning that which is good.   ' For the laws of right doing are the dictates of right reason.' [6]

How are these laws to be known ?   An object is not good because it is desired, though it is desired because it seems good.   Goodness to Hooker was of course an absolute reality.   In the complex of the actual it is bound up with its contrary, so that that which is evil rather than good may be seen as good.   Nothing, in Hooker's view, is wholly evil.   ' Because there is not in the world anything whereby another may not some way be made the perfecter, therefore all things that are, are good.' [7]   ' There is a soul of goodness in things evil.' But how is reason to discern ?   Action which is in harmony with the Eternal Law, that is with the will of God for his creation, is good action.   But of the Eternal Law man can know little and that little but partially.   How is man to find out what is goodness in action, what things are to be done ?

It is possible, Hooker held, to arrive at valid conclusions concerning what is good, by examination of the ' causes whereby it is made such '. But he does not give us the demonstration, remarking that it would be long and difficult and unsuited to the capacity of ' this present age, full of tongue and weak of brain '.[8] But what is goodness in action may be known, not exactly indeed, but sufficiently for practical purposes, without any such painful inquiry.   ' The most certain token of evident goodness is, if the general persuasion of all men do so account of it.' [9]   In this matter *vox populi* is veritably *vox Dei.*   ' The general

---

[1] ' Omne agens agit propter finem,' says Aquinas.
[2] *Eccles. Pol.*, I, 5, p. 215.   [3] Ib., I, 4, p. 215.
[4] Ib., I, 7, p. 220.   [5] Ib., I, 7, p. 223.
[6] Ib., I, 7, p. 221.   [7] Ib., I, 4, p. 215.
[8] Ib., I, 8, p. 226.   [9] Ib., I, 8, p. 226.

and perpetual voice of men is as the sentence of God himself. For that which all men have at all times learned, nature herself must needs have taught.' [1]

But we must at least see grounds for believing in this general voice of 'nature'. 'The Law of Reason or Human Nature is that which men by discourse of natural reason have rightly found out themselves to be all for ever bound unto in all their actions.' [2] Upon what data are men supposed to have reasoned ? The Christian world has of course the Scriptures as an infallible guide. But Hooker believed that man may know what is good even without the Scriptures. 'Those men which have no written law of God to show what is good or evil, carry written in their hearts the universal law of mankind, the law of reason, whereby they judge as by a rule which God hath given unto all men for that purpose.' [3] What man has reasoned on are those intuitions of the Eternal Law which his conscience gives him. The basis of the law rational is 'an infallible knowledge imprinted in the minds of all the children of men, whereby both general principles for directing of human actions are comprehended, and conclusions derived from them'. [4] Implanted in every man are intuitions as to what is in harmony with the purpose of God in creation. It is because this is so that the 'general and perpetual voice of men' may be taken as a practical and infallible guide. By reasoning upon his intuitions as to right and wrong, man can deduce general principles or rules of action which constitute the law of reason. All that is necessary for that demonstration which Hooker did not think it necessary to give, is the assumption that the voice of conscience is the voice of God.

The whole theory is of course medieval : it is substantially the theory of Aquinas. But, with certain qualifications, it may be said that this theory of a law of nature or reason, based on intuitions assumed to be at once valid and universal, was generally held throughout the sixteenth century. Hooker's statement of it is much fuller than is to be found elsewhere in writings of the period ; [5] but the theory is expressed, more or less crudely, or referred to as undeniable, by writers of almost every kind of opinion. It was the absence of any such conception in Machiavelli that made him unintelligible to most people. The theory was held by Catholics more clearly and consistently than by Protestants, but it is in no way distinctive of the Catholic point of view. Hooker's law of reason is Luther's *natur recht* and Bodin's *loi naturelle*. Few English Protestants of the period would have denied its validity. Sceptics apart, if anyone in Elizabethan England denied it, it was the Puritans.

---

[1] *Eccles. Pol.*, I, 8, p. 227.   [2] Ib., I, 8, p. 233.
[3] Ib., I, 16, p. 281.   [4] Ib., II, 8, p. 334.
[5] It is interesting to compare Hooker's exposition with that of Suarez in his *Tractatus de Legibus ac Deo Legislatore*, 1613.

Calvinism did, indeed, tend to deny the validity of any law of mere reason. The Calvinistic insistence on the Scriptures and nothing but the Scriptures and the Calvinistic conception of man as powerless of himself for any good, led Calvinists to regard with distrust all reasoning save reasoning on the text of the Scriptures. Some of them, in spite of Calvin's example, even deprecated thaf. In England the Puritans talked as though human reason, divorced from Scripture, could find no assurance of anything whatever. They quoted St. Paul's warning against philosophy [1] and pointed out that heretics had always been given to much reasoning. Unfortunately, as Hooker remarked, ' there is as yet no way known how to dispute or to determine of things disputed, without the use of natural reason '.[2] It was just because his Puritan opponents seemed to be maintaining that man could know nothing of goodness or of God but by the text of Scripture, that Hooker judged it necessary to confront them with a reasonable exposition of a theory generally accepted.

Under the heading of positive or man-made law, the *lex humana* of Aquinas, Hooker goes on to consider the origin and nature of ' politic society '. Understanding of this, he observes, is necessary to an understanding of the nature of human law and authority. The laws of reason ' do bind men absolutely, even as they are men, although they have never any settled fellowship, ne'er any solemn agreement amongst themselves what to do or not to do '. [3] Hooker was not much concerned about the exact process by which politic society came into being ; but he expresses himself clearly enough as to the causes in general which brought it into existence. There are two general and immediate causes of man's settled fellowship : his natural sociability and his insufficiency in isolation to provide himself with things needful ' for a life fit for the dignity of man '.[4] All men desire happiness and complete happiness is not possible until men can live according to the dictates of right reason without impediment. Happiness is not, of course, for Hooker, measured by material prosperity. ' Of earthly blessings,' he says, ' the meanest is wealth.' [5] ' The gross and bestial conceit of them which want understanding is only that the fullest bellies are happiest.' [6] It does not, however, matter to his argument that a considerable part in the construction of politic society must have been played by them which want understanding. In any case property to some amount and as much security as possible [7] are needed for that life which befits the dignity of man. In those times ' wherein there was as yet no manner of public regiment established ', impediments to virtue must have been numerous and insecurity extreme. Hooker had no illusions about the natural goodness of man.

[1] Col. ii. 8.   [2] *Eccles. Pol.*, III, 8, p. 379.
[3] Ib., I, 10, p. 239.   [4] Ib., I, 10, p. 239.
[5] Ib., V, 76, p. 445.   [6] Ib., V, 76, p. 447.   [7] Ib., I, 10.

' We all make complaint about the iniquity of our times : not unjustly ; for the days are evil. But compare them with those times, wherein there were no civil societies . . . and we have surely good cause to think that God has blessed us exceedingly and made us behold most happy days.' [1]

' This was the cause of men's uniting themselves at the first in politic societies, which societies could not be without government, nor government without a distinct kind of law from that which hath been already declared.' [2] Security and property involve such law and co-operation must needs be organized. Authority, that is a right to command, which is a right to make law, had to be recognized, if only for limited ends. As soon as it is recognized, the body politic is in being. Men always knew that they had a right to defend themselves against injurious violence, that no man had a right to pursue his own ends to another's injury, that it was right and rational to combine against such offenders and also that no man could rightly be judge in his own cause. [3] ' To take away all such material grievances, injuries and wrongs, there was no way but only by growing upon composition and agreement amongst themselves, by ordaining some kind of government politic and by yielding themselves subject thereunto.' [4] For it was apparent ' that strifes and troubles would be endless, except they gave their common consent all to be ordered by some whom they should agree upon : without which consent there were no reason that one man should take upon him to be Lord or Judge over another '.[5]

As to the form or manner in which this common consent was given Hooker's language was ambiguous. ' All public regiment of what kind soever,' he says in one place, ' seemeth evidently to have risen from deliberate advice, consultation and composition between men.' [6] But in another place he speaks of politic society as founded upon ' an order expressly or secretly agreed upon, touching the manner of their union in living together '.[7] Hooker was not attempting to give definition to what evidently could not be defined. He avoids the mistake of supposing a formal contract. What he insists on is, simply, that political authority can only be rationally conceived as derived from what he calls consent. To a modern reader his meaning might perhaps have been clearer had he used the word recognition. It is clear that his ' consent ', though it may be given deliberately, need not be formally given ; it may be given ' secretly '. But if it were not given at all there could be neither government nor body politic. It is implied all through that the two things are inseparable.

Since all governing authority rests upon, and is in fact created by, recognition or consent, the constitution of the body politic may take

<hr>

[1] *Eccles. Pol.*, I, 10, p. 241.   [2] Ib., I, 10, p. 239.   [3] Ib., I, 10, p. 242.
[4] Ib., I, 10, p. 241.   [5] Ib., I, 10, p. 242.
[6] Ib., I, 10, p. 243.   [7] Ib., I, 10, p. 239

on any form. It is not improbable, Hooker suggests, that Fatherhood, which involved a natural authority within the family, may have suggested monarchy and that the earliest forms of government were monarchical. ' Howbeit over a whole grand multitude . . . and consisting of so many families . . . impossible it is that any should have complete lawful power, but by consent of men or immediate appointment of God.' [1] Nor is monarchy ' the only kind of regiment that hath been received ', for ' the inconveniences of one kind have caused sundry others to be devised '.[2] He recognizes, too, that forms of government may change and have changed.

' At the first, when some certain kind of regiment was once approved, it may be that nothing was then further thought upon for the manner of governing, but all permitted unto their wisdom and discretion which were to rule ; till by experience they found this for all parts very inconvenient. . . . They saw that to live by one man's will became the cause of all men's misery. This constrained them to come unto laws, wherein all men might see their duties beforehand and know the penalties of transgressing them.' [3]

Hooker did not, I think, intend.this passage to be anything but vague.[4] At first there was no law but the ruler's will : anything might be treated as an offence and punishment was arbitrary. Then the body politic ' comes ' unto laws ; and evidently these laws bind the ruler. It is not clear how they are made, but there is certainly a change in the manner of governing. Since the form of government is created by recognition, it must change as the form of recognition changes. There is no question of ' contracts ' or of breach of contract.

To Hooker, as to Bodin, the essential feature of the body politic was its right to make law. There can be no sort of body politic or government without it. Whence is that right derived ? ' Out of the precepts of the law of nature,' says Hooker, translating Aquinas, ' as out of certain common and undemonstrable principles, man's reason must necessarily proceed unto certain more particular determinations : which particular determinations being found out according unto the reason of man, they have the name of human laws, so that such other conditions be therein kept as the making of laws doth require.' [5] But society needs much law that cannot be arrived at by deduction from the law of nature. ' All laws human,' says Hooker, ' be either such as establish some duty whereunto all men by the law of reason did before stand bound, or else such that make that a duty now that before was none.' [6] Whence does the

---

[1] *Eccles. Pol.*, I, 10, p. 242.
[2] Ib., I, 10, p. 243.　　　　　　　　　[3] Ib., I, 10, p. 243.
[4] He was repeating, perhaps unconsciously, what Buchanan had said in his *De jure regni apud Scotos* ; and, equally, what Cicero had said in *De Officiis*, Lib. II.
[5] *Eccles. Pol.*, III, 9, p. 381.　　　　　　[6] Ib., I, 10, p. 248.

body politic derive this power to create obligation ? Hooker's answer to the question was implied rather than stated. The right is derived from the need of it.

' Unto me it seemeth almost out of doubt and controversy, that every independent multitude, before any certain form of regiment established, hath, under God's supreme authority, full dominion over itself. . . . God, creating mankind, did endue it naturally with full power to guide itself in what kind of societies soever it should choose to live.' [1]

So far, be it observed, from the right being created by any kind of contract, it exists in every independent multitude before ever the body politic comes into being. This conception is essential in Hooker's political philosophy and it separates him definitely from the later contractualists. It provides also an answer to the divine right theorists, who contended that no amount of human agreement could create obligation or give a right to create it. The establishment of the body politic is necessary to man's well-being. But a right to make law is implied not only in the existence but in the construction of the body politic. God, therefore, who wills the well-being of man, must be supposed to have endowed with the necessary right every potential body politic. ' Those things without which the world cannot well continue, have necessary being in the world.' [2]

' By the natural law . . . the lawful power of making laws to command whole politic societies of men, belongeth so properly to the same entire societies, that for any prince or potentate, of what kind soever upon earth, to exercise the same of himself and not either by express commission immediately and personally received from God or else from authority derived at the first from their consent upon whose persons they impose laws, it is no better than mere tyrany.' [3]

Legislative power rightly belongs to the whole community and must be conceived as conferred by the whole community upon some person or body. Laws made by such a properly constituted authority are laws made by the whole community by which it is empowered to act. ' Laws they are not therefore which public approbation hath not made so.' [4] But it matters not a whit whether you, Dick or Harry, personally approve of any enactment.

' Approbation not only they give who personally declare their assent by voice, sign or act, but also when others do it in their names, by right at the least originally derived from them. . . . In many things assent is given, they that give it not imagining that they do so, because the manner of their assenting is not apparent.' [5]

Your consent has created the authority which commands your obedience.

[1] *Eccles. Pol.*, VIII, 2, p. 343. [2] Ib., VIII, 4, p. 380.
[3] Ib., I, 10, p. 245. [4] Ib., I, 10, p. 246.
[5] Ib., I, 10, p. 246.

'To be commanded we do consent, when that society whereof we are part, hath at any time before consented, without revoking the same after by the like universal agreement. Wherefore as any man's deed past is good as long as himself continueth : so the act of a public society of men done five hundred years sithence, standeth as theirs who presently are of the same societies, because corporations are immortal.' [1]

In the phrasing of this last sentence Hooker lapses a little towards that quasi-legal formalism that was to become common later. But what else could he consistently have said ? It seemed to him that the conception of organized society involved that of an obligation to obey its dictates. Social life and every form of co-operation are bound up with the obligation to obey law. Positive law must be conceived as the command of a general will with reference to good. 'A Law is the deed of the whole Body Politic, whereof if ye judge yourselves to be any part, then is the Law your deed also.' [2] By acceptance of membership of society your assent to its actual constitution is given. The murderer hangs by his own will. 'Laws that have been approved may be again repealed and to that end also disputed against. . . . But this is when the whole doth deliberate what Laws each part shall observe and not when a° part refuseth the Laws which the whole hath orderly agreed upon.' [3] Once authority has been established by consent the right to command must be held to be vested permanently in the ruler so created. If any man may refuse obedience simply because he disapproves of the command, no right to command can be said to exist at all. Unless it were strictly demonstrable that 'the Law of Reason or of God doth enjoin the contrary', it was impossible, Hooker thought, to recognize a right to disobey law. 'Because, except our own private and particular resolutions be by the law of public determinations overruled, we take away all possibility of sociable life in the world.' [4] The forms of government established are revocable by general agreement, but until that agreement be reached, the right to command must remain.

To Hooker a right to make law for its own good is inherent in every potential community. This right is limited absolutely by the revealed law of God and by the law of reason : the making of law inconsistent with these could be to no man's good. Thus limited the right may be and for practical purposes must be conferred upon some sort of legal sovereign. There is no reason why this sovereign should be a monarch. 'That the Christian world should be ordered by kingly regiment, the law of God doth not anywhere command.' [5] But whether sovereignty can be conferred upon limiting conditions or whether a right to make law can be conceived as being limited by agreement, Hooker can hardly be said to have inquired. In some

---

[1] *Eccles. Pol.*, I, 10, p. 246.   [2] Ib., Preface, V, 2, p. 164.
[3] Ib., V, 2.   [4] Ib., I, 16, p. 282.   [5] Ib., VIII, 2, p. 346.

places he does indeed use language that seems clearly to imply that he thought it might be so. ' Touching kings which were first instituted by agreement and composition made with them over whom they reign, how far their power may lawfully extend, the articles of compact between them must show.' [1] He speaks too of ' power . . . limited before it be granted '. Is this power the power to make law ? The question is not faced and the phrases used are ambiguous. [2] Hooker was really concerned only to show that refusal to obey duly constituted authority is justified only when the command given is demonstrably contrary to the law of God or the law of reason. If an ' absolute monarchy ' be duly constituted, the edicts of the monarch are, he says, true laws. Edicts manifestly injurious or unjust may rightly be disobeyed on the ground that they are inconsistent with the law of reason. But in Hooker's system there is no ground for a claim to a right of forcible rebellion in any case. He did, indeed, just touch on the question. After remarking that ' dominion ' resides fundamentally in the body politic itself and derivatively in its legal representative, he asks the question : ' May then a body politic at all times withdraw in whole or in part that influence of dominion which passeth from it, if inconvenience doth grow thereby ? ' But his answer was : ' I do not see how the body should be able by any just means to help itself.' [3] He could not, consistently, have given any other. Tyrannous government might indeed produce a general agreement that the form of the government needed to be changed. That, he thought, had happened in the past when ' to live by one man's will became the cause of all men's misery '. In that case, the form of the general recognition or consent which created the authority that has become oppressive, having changed, the manner of governing will inevitably undergo a corresponding change, with little or no friction. But there seems to be no question here of what is called rebellion, though there is, certainly, some ambiguity. Authority seems to be conceived as simply ceasing to exist when society as a whole refuses to recognize it. Certainly there is no question of breach of a ' contract '. To read contracts into Hooker is, I think, at once to misapprehend and to belittle him. Hooker saw the establishment of government under a contract as a possible thing but no more. His view may be said to resemble that of Locke only if you strip Locke's Essay of its verbiage about contracts.

All this, for Hooker, merely led up to his demonstration that the Puritans had no justification for claiming a right to disobey the law of the Church as established in England. The validity of the argument of his first book being assumed, he had, in order to prove this, to show

---

[1] *Eccles. Pol.*, VIII, 2, p. 350.

[2] The phrases, too, occur in the eighth book and are only doubtfully Hooker's.

[3] *Eccles. Pol.*, VIII, 2, p. 350.

two things. He had to prove that the ecclesiastical law of England as it actually stood, was in no way inconsistent with the law of God revealed or with the law of reason. He had also to show that for England, Church and Commonwealth were essentially identical; and that therefore ecclesiastical law, established under the royal supremacy, was as binding as other law and for the same reasons. The greater part of the *Ecclesiastical Polity*, after the first book, is taken up with the proof of the first of these two propositions : but it is with the proof of the second that we are concerned here. It is unfortunate that it was only in his eighth ' book ' that Hooker dealt directly with this. But the argument of that eighth book, as we have it, is so completely consistent with the view he takes throughout, that I refer to it without hesitation.

Hooker went at once to the essential point by remarking that his Puritan opponents ' make a necessary separation perpetual and personal between the Church and the commonwealth '.[1] He grants at once that a church as such and a commonwealth as such, are distinguishable things. But ' we say that the care of religion being common unto all societies, politic, such societies as do embrace the true religion have the name of the Church '.[2] ' If the commonwealth be Christian, if the people which are of it do publicly embrace the true religion, this very thing doth make it the Church.'[3]

' As a politic society it doth maintain religion ; as a church that religion which God hath revealed by Jesus Christ.'[4] ' We hold, that seeing there is not any man of the Church of England, but the same man is also a member of the commonwealth ; nor any man a member of the commonwealth which is not also of the Church of England . . . so, albeit properties and actions of one kind do cause the name of a commonwealth, qualities and functions of another sort the name of a Church to be given unto a multitude, yet one and the selfsame multitude may in such sort be both, and is so with us, that no person appertaining to the one can be denied to be also of the other.'[5]

So, he sums it up fearlessly, ' with us one society is both Church and commonwealth '.[6]

Hooker proceeds to argue that the view thus clearly stated is the only view it is rationally possible to hold of such a society as that of England. Another view might be possible if Church and Commonwealth were absolutely distinguishable by reference to their ends. But they cannot be so distinguished. It would be monstrous to say that a commonwealth exists only for temporal or material ends.

' As by all men the kingdom of God is first to be sought for, so in all commonwealths things spiritual ought above temporal to be provided for.[7] . . . A

---

[1] *Eccles. Pol.*, VIII, 1, p. 328.
[2] Ib., VIII, 1, p. 329.   [3] Ib., VIII, 6, p. 402.
[4] Ib., VIII, 1, p. 329.   [5] Ib., VIII, 1, p. 330.
[6] Ib., VIII, 1, p. 340.   [7] Ib., VIII, 1, p. 332.

gross error it is to think that regal power ought to serve for the good of the body and not of the soul; for men's temporal peace and not for their eternal safety.' [1]

A commonwealth, in fact, is, or should be, always a kind of Church : if it be Christian it is a true Church. In such a commonwealth as that of England, it is impossible, Hooker argued, even to conceive of the Church as a distinct body. ' If all that believe be contained in the name of the Church, how should the Church remain by personal subsistence divided from the commonwealth, when the whole commonwealth doth believe ? ' [2] Conceivably it could only be so if the Church consisted of the clergy alone.

It might be said that the validity of the whole argument rests on a legal fiction or that Hooker was arguing in a circle. According to the law made by the commonwealth every member of it is also a member of the Church and ' the whole commonwealth doth believe ' : therefore we cannot separate Church and Commonwealth and the law made by the commonwealth is law for the members of the Church ! But to put it thus would be to misapprehend Hooker's meaning. When he said that ' the whole commonwealth doth believe ' he was thinking not of any legal fiction but of what seemed to him an actual fact. Certainly it was not true that the whole commonwealth believed what Hooker believed. He did not say it was. He meant only that the whole commonwealth believed in what he called ' the very essence of Christianity ',[3] those essential doctrines common to the Church of England and the Church of Rome. This was substantially true : it was hardly unreasonable to ignore a silent scepticism.

To Hooker most religious controversy turned either on things indifferent or on questions that could not be demonstratively answered. The Puritans, of course, denied both these assertions. They denied that such things as the use of the surplice were things indifferent and they seemed to have believed that saving faith involved the acceptance of Calvinistic theology. To them, therefore, it was grossly untrue to say that ' the whole commonwealth doth believe '.

But if the validity of the view stated by Hooker be admitted, then, on the premises established in the first book of the *Ecclesiastical Polity*, his conclusion follows unescapably.

' The parliament of England together with the convocation annexed thereunto, is that whereupon the very essence of all government within this kingdom doth depend ; it is even the body of the whole realm ; it consisteth of the king and of all that within the land are subject unto him, for they all are there present. . . .[4] Touching the supremacy of power which our kings have in this case of making laws, it resteth principally in the strength of a negative voice,' but,

---

[1] *Eccles. Pol.*, VIII, 3, p. 363.   [2] Ib., VIII, 1, p. 334.
[3] Ib., III, 1, p. 339.   [4] Ib., VIII, 6, p. 408.

'to define of our church's regiment, the parliament of England hath competent authority.' [1]

This must be so : for if Church and Commonwealth be one, the Parliament of England, 'the body of the whole realm', must also represent the Church. Our ecclesiastical law, therefore, not being inconsistent with the law of God or of reason, is derived

'from power which the whole body of this realm being naturally possessed with, hath by free and deliberate assent, derived unto him that ruleth over them. . . . . So that our laws made concerning religion, do take originally their essence from the power of the whole realm and church of England.' [2]

Which was to be shown ! Hooker, at long last, had come to St. Germain's conclusion ; and he had given it as broad a base as possible. He had not set out to defend the actual arrangements of the Elizabethan Church as the best conceivable. He had not asserted that the judgements of public authority need be right judgements or even that they actually were right. It was better, he thought, that erroneous judgements should be accepted than that vain contention should arise about things indifferent or things indeterminable.[3] He had set out to prove, only, that the Puritans had no rational justification for refusal to conform to law. Yet, for all that he had so strictly limited his theorem, he had evidently, after all, failed in his attempted demonstration.

It is a little strange that a man so genuinely religious should not have seen that he had proved either too much or nothing at all. He had distinguished between what he called the ' essentials of the Christian religion ', on the one side, and things indifferent or indemonstrable on the other. Upon the validity of these distinctions rested all his assertions as to how far refusal to conform was or might be justified. Yet he could not have drawn the lines he assumed to be there ; and he should have known that neither he nor anyone else could do so. What were the essentials of the Christian religion ? There was hardly a single doctrine associated with Christianity that was not, at the time he wrote, being denied by one sect or another. Then, as now, it would have been impossible to arrive at any definition of ' essentials ' which would have been accepted by all who professed themselves Christians. Would Hooker have denied that Socinians were Christians ?

Again, his argument for the impossibility of separating Church from State in England, rested upon the assertion that ' the whole commonwealth doth believe '. Presumably it was in the essentials of the Christian faith that the whole commonwealth was supposed to

[1] *Eccles. Pol.*, VIII, 6, p. 411. The words may not be Hooker's ; but the thought must be his.
[2] Ib., VIII, 6, p. 412.   [3] Ib., Preface, 6.

believe. Even in Hooker's own sense, whatever exactly that was, the proposition was not strictly true. There was, evidently, too, the possibility that a time might come when it would be very far from the truth. In any case, Hooker should have known that to his Puritan opponents the assertion was not true at all. Much that they regarded as essential, Hooker regarded as indifferent : much that they were sure was proved, he was sure could not be. He had laid it down that, in questions of religion, no man can be justified in defying the determinations of public authority, unless he can prove to demonstration that he is right. But that was precisely what the Puritans alleged that they could do. Hooker had admitted that men should not be required to ' yield unto any thing other assent than such as doth answer the evidence '.[1] The Puritans maintained that they were required to yield assent to propositions which could be proved to be false. It is difficult to see how Hooker could have hoped to convince them. His demonstration broke down at the last moment. For if the whole commonwealth doth not believe, how can it, as a Church, have authority to bind the consciences of its believing members ? How can it, even, be regarded as a Church ?

[1] *Eccles. Pol.*, II, 7, p. 323.

CHAPTER VII

THE CATHOLIC PROTEST

RATHER singularly small was the amount of literary protest from the Catholic side against the action of Henry VIII's government. This was so not merely because protest was dangerous and because, for one reason or another, the upper class was supporting the government. Though the England of 1529 was vaguely and confusedly Catholic, its Catholicism was not intelligent enough to be very greatly disturbed by the repudiation of Papal claims and the assertion of a royal supremacy in the Church. So long as the old services and the bulk of the old formulæ were retained, people in general were not acutely conscious of the nature of the change that was being effected. The dissolution of the monasteries stirred popular feeling far more than did the Act of Supremacy. The government of Edward VI did indeed create a somewhat dangerous position and provoke reaction. But Mary Tudor lost her chance.

In 1559 the position was not radically different from what it had been in 1529. ' Protestantism ' in some sense may have been more prevalent ; anti-Papal sentiment was certainly stronger than it had been. But the thoroughgoing Protestants were still a small minority. The mass of the clergy were certainly Catholic. In January, 1559, the Lower House of Convocation almost unanimously declared for the Roman doctrine and for transubstantiation. The mass of the laity were Catholic rather than Protestant ; but their religion was largely a matter of forms and habits and associations. As under the steady pressure of government and establishment new habits and associations were formed and as the older generation died out, the mass of the English people conformed to the new arrangements. The transition was made easy by the strength of nationalist and anti-foreign sentiment.

But though the mass of the people gradually ceased to be in any sense ' Catholic ', Catholicism, far from dying out, was revivified under Elizabeth. In England, as elsewhere, Catholicism was forced by opposition to clarify itself and look to the grounds of its faith. The fact, too, that the English Catholics drifted gradually into the position of a persecuted sect, could not but intensify English Catholicism since it did not destroy it. At the end of Elizabeth's reign a Catholic must not attend mass, becomes a felon if he harbours or assists a Catholic priest, incurs a præmunire if he contributes money for any Catholic purpose, is forbidden to go more than five miles from his home if he will not go to church. If he be a priest he commits treason by mere presence in the realm. Yet, for all that, not only was the number of Catholics in England still large in 1603,[1] but there were priests, more or less hidden, in almost all districts. In Northumberland and North Yorkshire, Cumberland and Lancashire, Catholics preponderated : they were strong in North Lincolnshire, Derby and Cheshire and Cornwall. In many districts it was hard or impossible to get law enforced against them at all. The Jesuits had divided England into ecclesiastical districts, had established priests in permanent cures and had organized hiding-places and secret chapels.

Naturally the amount of literary expression of the views of English Catholics increased under Elizabeth. But, after the first year or so of the reign, it became practically impossible for Catholics resident in England to express their views in print, except by printing abroad. Consequently the English Catholic protest against the Elizabethan system was expressed mainly in the writings of Catholics in exile. This is an unfortunate fact, since men, suffering from the bitterness of exile and subject directly to Roman and Jesuitical influence, naturally developed a point of view that was cosmopolitan rather than English. As time passed there was increasing divergence between the views of English Catholics in England and the views expressed on their behalf by their spokesmen on the Continent. The degree of this divergence is hard to determine.

It is hard, if not impossible, to disentangle the Catholic protest against the political theory of royal supremacy from the case presented for the claims of the Roman Church generally. But even under Henry VIII we find that the main points insisted upon by the later English Catholics were made or suggested.

' Admit there were, sir,' said Sir Richard Rich, the King's Solicitor, to Sir Thomas More, ' an Act of Parliament that all the realm should take me for the King, would not you, Master More, take me for the King ? ' ' Yes, sir,' quoth Sir Thomas More, ' that would I.' ' I put the case further,' quoth Master Rich, ' that there were an Act of Parliament that all the Realm should take me for the Pope ; would then not you, Master More, take me for the Pope ? ' ' For answer,' quoth Sir Thomas More, ' to your first case, the Parliament may well meddle with the state of temporal princes : but to make answer to

[1] Prof. Usher estimates the number of professed or secret catholics in England in 1600 as not fewer than 750,000.

your second case, I will put you this case. Suppose the Parliament would make a law that God should not be God, would then you, Master Rich, say God were not God ? '

This little passage of arms, recorded by Roper,[1] very neatly illustrates at once the point of view of the Tudor lawyer and that of the convinced Catholic. More died not in defence of extreme Papal pretensions, but because he could no more admit that an act of parliament could make Henry VIII Pope, than that an act of parliamant could make him God. Pole, in his *Pro Ecclesiasticae Unitatis Defensione*,[2] tried to show that the assertion of royal supremacy meant denial of the unity of the Church and was equivalent, even, to a declaration that the Church Universal had no substantial existence. So it seemed to More also ; [3] but to him it seemed to go further yet, even to a negation of religion. Between them More and Pole furnished the texts on which later Catholic writers enlarged.

Of all men living at the time, Thomas More was best fitted to present the Catholic case against royal supremacy in the Church. It is unfortunate that he made no full statement of his position. But it must be noticed that in one of his writings he struck at the root of the assumptions on which the religious political theories of the Protestants professed to be based. Tyndale and Cranmer, like Luther, were appealing to the Scriptures against the claims of Pope and clergy. Their assertion that Papal claims were wholly invalid and that no coercive power belongs rightly to the clergy was professedly based on what they found in the Bible. The inspiration of the Scriptures was assumed. In his *Apology* of 1533 More made a point which seems never to have been adequately answered.

' The Church was gathered and the faith believed,' he wrote, ' before ever any part of the new testament was put in writing. And which writing was or is the true scripture, neither Luther nor Tyndale knoweth but by the credence that they give to the church. . . . Which is this word written Tyndale cannot tell but by the church. . . . Why should not Luther and Tyndale as well believe the Church, in that it telleth them this thing did Christ and his Apostles say, as they must believe the Church (or else believe nothing) in that it telleth them this thing did Christ's evangelists and apostles write.' [4]

Deny the authority of the Church and there remains no reason for believing the canonical Scriptures to be inspired. ' There is like surety and like certain knowledge of the word of God unwritten as there is of the word of God written, sith ye know neither the tone or the tother to be the word of God but by the tradition of the Church.' [5] Protestants, he added, have nothing to say to this. What, in fact, they often

---

[1] In his *Life* of More, written under Mary, but printed only in 1626.
[2] Published in 1536.
[3] See the passage on the Church already quoted.
[4] *Apology*, Works, 1557, p. 852.   [5] Ib., p. 853.

did say was that it was evident to all who read them that the Scriptures came direct from God.[1]

It may be noted, in passing, that, in the same treatise, More raised the question whether it were reasonable or safe to recognize, in the Crown or in Parliament, a right to confiscate ecclesiastical property.

'If any man would give him the counsel to take away man's land or good from him, pretending that he had too much or that he useth it not well or that it might be better used if some other had it: he giveth such a counsel as he may, when he list, and will peradventure after, stretch a good deal further than the goods or possessions of spiritual men.'[2]

Such a principle involves that the sovereign is not bound to respect the property of any man, clerical or lay. On the fundamental question suggested, no controversy ensued in England. But, later, Hooker and Bancroft agreed with Puritan writers as to the iniquity of the spoliation of the Church under Henry VIII.

From the time of More and Pole onwards, what English Catholic people, under Henry VIII and Elizabeth, felt or saw, was, that if the Church Universal has no Head but one in heaven, there is, on earth, no Church Universal. It is this point, first of all, that the later writers insisted upon. If every secular sovereign be rightfully supreme head or governor of the Church in his dominions, there is no Catholic Church: nothing is left, as Cuthbert Scot said in 1559, but a number of quite separate and independent churches.[3] In the absence of any common authority, there is nothing to prevent these separate churches from drifting further and further apart, till the imaginary bond of common Christian belief shall have practically disappeared. How can a Church Catholic, that can do nothing to prevent this happening, be said to exist at all? The door is open wide to every kind of heresy and irremediable division.[4] The whole system of Christian belief will be shattered into fragments. Royal supremacy, wrote William Allen, 'is a thing most monstrous and unnatural, the very gap to bring any realm to the thraldom of all sects'.[5] The Church Universal, Scot argued, must needs be strictly international, must have its own centre and its own government, altogether separate from any secular State.

[1] So Calvin, in a characteristic passage: 'Quant à ces canailles demandent dont et comment nous serons persuadés que l'Ecriture est procédée de Dieu si nous n'avons recours au degré de l'Eglise: c'est autant comme si aucun s'enquerait dont nous apprendrons à discerner la clarté des ténèbres, le blanc du noir, le doux de l'amer.' *Inst.*, 1559-60, Chap. VII. More takes his place among ces canailles.
[2] *Apology*, pp. 881, 882.
[3] Marian Bishop of Chester. See his speech of March 18, 1559, in Strype: *Annals*, I, Pt. 2, App.
[4] See speech of Nicholas Heath, Marian Archbishop of York, in Strype: *Annals*, I, Pt. 2.
[5] *A True, sincere and modest defence of English Catholiques*, 1584, p. 7.

This was the main contention, in relation to politics, of almost all the English Catholic writers of the century : of Pole and Sanders,[1] Feckenham [2] and Stapleton, Harding [3] and Cardinal Allen. The essential positive assertion is that the Church, so far from being in any sense, anywhere, identical with the commonwealth, is an altogether separate body with its own special form, organization and government and its own special rights and powers. It is a flat denial of the fundamental contention of Tudor nationalism.

Incidentally it was, of course, argued that, since the Church has real existence as an organized body distinct from any one commonwealth, the Parliament of England has no conceivable claim to confer supremacy over any part of the Church on anyone. ' No earthly commonwealth,' wrote Allen, ' can give or confer it to their prince, because they cannot give that which they have not by any natural faculty.' [4] He argued that, all the ecclesiastical legislation of England since 1558 being invalid, it was absurd to say that Catholics were disloyal for denying its validity.

The main fact is that all these English Catholic writers, from More and Pole, to Sanders and Allen, were making of the question at issue a question of the preservation of the Christian religion. It was not, to them, in the main, a question of Papal claims or a question of how far the Church should direct or control secular policy. ' Now and ever,' wrote Allen, ' when the superiority temporal hath the pre-eminence and the spiritual is but accessory,

[1] Nicholas Sanders left England in 1559 and became professor in theology at Louvain, the chief centre of English Catholics in exile. His *De Visibili Monarchia Ecclesiae* was published in 1571: his *De Origine ac Progress schismatis Anglicani* in 1585. This later work, very widely read and very fiercely attacked, goes, so far as Sanders was concerned, only to 1558 : it was continued by Edward Rishton. Sanders, in England, was renamed Slanders ; but his work is no more slanderous or inaccurate than that of other fervid partisans. He accompanied Spanish troops to Ireland in 1579 and died there in 1581.

[2] John Feckenham, last Abbot of Westminster, produced in 1559 a *Declaration of scruples and staies of conscience touching the Oathe of Supremacy*. To this an elaborate Answer was written by Robert Horne, Elizabethan Bishop of Winchester. Feckenham and Thomas Stapleton, who had joined Allen at Douai, published a *Counterblast* in 1567.

[3] Thomas Harding, exile at Louvain from 1559 to his death in 1572. He carried on controversy with Jewel from 1564 to 1567.

[4] *An Apology and true Declaration of the institution and endeavours of the two English colleges, the one at Rome, the other now resident in Rheims*, 1581, p. 41 B. William Allen (1532–1594), Principal of St. Mary Hall in 1558, went into exile at Louvain in 1561. In 1568 he succeeded in getting established a seminary or college at Douai for the purpose of maintaining a supply of instructed priests for England. The College, transferred to Rheims 1578, is said to have sent a hundred priests to England before 1580. The aims of this institution were in no direct way political or even missionary. After 1579, however, under the influence of Robert Parsons, Allen's activities became more and more political. He became a Cardinal in 1587.

dependent and wholly upholden of the other, error in faith is little accounted of.' [1]

Under such conditions there will always be ' more ado about Cæsar's tribute than about God's due '.[2] Elizabeth's government maintained that it took no action against Catholics simply on the grounds of their erroneous beliefs. Either, Allen argued, they know ' our religion is true ' or else, ' that they care not for it nor what we believe, no further than toucheth their prince and temporal weal '.

None of these Catholic writers put his case as strongly or as lucidly as it might have been put. They suggest far more than was clear to themselves. But they did see clearly enough, that no secular government was likely to concern itself very seriously with questions of religious belief. They laid, too, great stress on the obvious fact that no commonwealth or Prince can be regarded as infallible. That being so, they argued, it is impossible to maintain that any political sovereign has any real authority in matters of faith. To hang on the will of a Prince for our religious belief, says Allen, were ' the pitifullest hazard ' and no greater absurdity can be imagined than ' to believe what our temporal lord and master list '.[3] They felt that to believe that the civil sovereign may determine for its subjects all questions of religious belief must be, in the long run, to have no religious belief at all.

The Church is ' a spiritual and mystical commonwealth ',[4] wholly distinct from the secular State and of different nature. It is bound to keep the form Christ gave it, which was in no sense chosen by or derived from popular consent or ordinance. So far from supremacy in causes ecclesiastical being involved in the position of a temporal Prince, such supremacy is utterly incompatible not only with the existence of a Church Universal, but with any religion whatever. If the religion of a community were to be dictated by political authority, what would happen ? Just so far as that authority succeeded in enforcing uniformity it would, in the long run, destroy religion. If none of the Catholic apologists actually say this they yet all seem to imply it.

The position and powers of the Pope were conceived as giving practical and effective unity to the Church. But as to the extent of Papal power in relation to secular government or secular rulers, there was, in the sixteenth century, no one theory that ought to be called ' Catholic ' ; there was, that is, no theory on which Catholics were agreed. Bellarmine's Disputationes were disapproved of by Pope Sixtus V ; but the claims made by Bellarmine on behalf of the

---

[1] *A True, Sincere and Modest Defence of English Catholics*, 1584, p. 60. This was written in answer to the tract entitled *The Execution of Justice in England*, attributed to Burghley.

[2] *Defence*, p. 77.   [3] *Apology*, p. 34.   [4] Ib., p. 40 B.

Papacy were repudiated by the French Gallican Catholics as strongly as by Protestants. The notion that a Catholic always in his heart believed that the Pope had power to depose a King, was a delusion deliberately, even though not dishonestly, fostered by Protestant controversialists, who should have known better. It seems impossible to arrive at any definite conclusion as to what the mass of English Catholics thought about the Pope. But quite certainly, I think, their views did not coincide with those expressed by English Catholic refugees. Sanders argued zealously for the validity of the bull of Pius V excommunicating and deposing Elizabeth [1] and did his utmost from that time onwards to bring about a crusade against his heretic fellow-countrymen. Allen, under the influence of Robert Parsons, adopted the same attitude at least after 1585 ; and in 1587 wrote to Philip II exhorting him to undertake the invasion of England.

The writings of Cardinal Allen exhibit the view that was afterwards more clearly and fully expressed by Bellarmine. The temporal kingdom is a thing wholly different and separate from the Church. It stands on its own base and has no necessary dependence on ecclesiastical authority. But it must needs be subject to the Church in things spiritual. The authority of the secular ruler of a Christian community is conditional on his maintaining true religion or at the very least on his refraining from persecuting those who adhere to it. The highest interest of man is salvation and the Church and the Pope exist for the salvation of men. The Pope, therefore, is divinely commissioned to take any action that is necessary to maintain the true faith and secure the salvation of peoples. ' Where the temporal power resisteth God or hindereth the proceedings of the people to salvation, there the spiritual hath right to correct the temporal and to procure by all means possible that the terrene kingdom give no annoyance to the state of the Church.' [2] Unless such power be recognized there can be no guarantee either for the faith itself or for the freedom of true believers. ' God had not sufficiently provided for our salvation and the preservation of his Church and holy laws, if there were no way to restrain apostate Princes.' [3]

' If these high tragical powers should be permitted to him to exercise,' the author of *The Execution of Justice in England* had written, ' there should be no empire, no kingdom, no country, no city or town, be possessed by any lawful title longer than one such, only an earthly man, sitting, as he saith, in St. Peter's chair at Rome, should, for his will and appetite . . . think meet and determine.' [4]

---

[1] The bull of February 25, 1570. *De Visibili Monarchia Ecclesiae*, 1571.
[2] *True, Sincere and Modest Defence*, 1584, p. 99.
[3] Ib., p. 114.
[4] *The Execution of Justice in England*, 1584 (?). Printed in the 1587 edition of Holinshed, Vol. III, p. 1363.

Allen answers that this notion is a mere bogy ' fit only to fear babes '. The Pope ' may only intermeddle indirectly with temporal princes, as he is the chief officer under Christ and hath charge of their souls '.[1]

But he adds that, as chief under Christ, it is the Pope's duty to see to it that all Princes rule for the good of the Church and the salvation of their subjects. ' The Protestants,' he preposterously declared, ' plainly hold in all their writings and schools . . . that Princes may for tyranny or religion be resisted and deprived. We and all Catholics likewise affirm ' the same.[2] But he argued that it is very much safer to leave judgement as to when a Prince should be deposed to the Pope, than to leave it to the aggrieved people themselves.

Considering the content of the Bull of 1570 the inference from these views seemed to be formidable both for Elizabeth and for the English Catholics. But the mass of the Catholics resident in England do not seem to have accepted the doctrine of Allen and Bellarmine concerning Papal authority. They remained for the most part, throughout the reign of Elizabeth, English in sentiment rather than Catholic. The mass of them seem to have been as resolved as were their Protestant fellow-countrymen to submit to no kind of foreign dictation or interference and never to accept in place of Elizabeth, or after her death, a Catholic sovereign representing France or Spain. The efforts of the Jesuit missionaries in England after 1580 seem to have been, in some considerable degree, successful in revivifying Catholic faith and even in giving a certain amount of organization to the Roman Church in England. But in so far as these efforts were directed to stirring up rebellion against Elizabeth or on behalf of a Catholic claimant after her death, they were completely unsuccessful. Politically the chief results of these efforts were to increase the sense of danger from Catholicism alike in the government and among the people at large ; and to make the lot of the English Catholics far harder in the later years of Elizabeth's reign than it had been earlier. It became, indeed, very hard ; but the persecution of Catholics as potentially if not actually seditious, had the effect not of bringing about a desperate Catholic rebellion, but of arousing hatred of the Jesuits among the English Catholics. Towards the end of the reign certain English Catholics resident in England were loudly asserting their loyalty and their disbelief in any Papal power to release them from allegiance to Elizabeth and expressing in violent language their detestation of the Jesuits.

' However we dissent from the State in the profession of our religion,' wrote Christopher Bagshaw, ' yet we are Her Majesty's born subjects and vassals and ought not, for any cause, to withdraw in that respect our duties, love and allegiance from Her Highness or our native country : much less to slander or seek

---

[1] *Defence of English Catholics*, p. 118.   [2] Ib., p. 121.

the cruel overthrow of both, as our traitorous adversaries of the society, not a deed of Jesus but of the Devil, and their adherents have done.' [1]

'We all of the secular clergy,' wrote a Catholic priest, '*una voce* do utterly disclaim and renounce from our hearts both archpriest [2] and Jesuits as arrant traitors unto their Prince and country: whom to death we will never obey: no, if the Pope's Holiness should charge us to obey in this sense, to advance an enemy to the English Crown, we should never yield to it: as by no law of nature or nations or of man to be compelled thereunto: no more than to commit adultery. incest or to murder ourselves, our children, our parents.' [3]

The author or authors go on to say that were the Pope himself to send an army to establish Catholicism in England by force, they would be ready to risk their lives in defence of Queen and country. 'For we are throughly persuaded that Priests of what order soever, ought not by force of arms to plant or water the Catholic faith.' [4] Jesuit activities in England were such as would in any case have aroused bitter opposition among the seculars; and to some extent account for the violence of the language used. But it is clear that, in 1601, a considerable section, at least, of the English Catholics, would gladly have repudiated the Papal claim to be able to release them from allegiance, if by so doing they could have obtained toleration for Catholic worship.[5] Bancroft was probably right in thinking that it needed only concessions and conciliatory action to make the mass of English Catholics soundly loyal. As early as 1584 William Allen had argued that Elizabeth's government, from its own point of view, was making a great mistake in not granting toleration to Catholic worship.

The views of Sanders or of Parsons or Allen and of Bellarmine on the Papal claim to the right to depose Princes and release subjects from their allegiance, were not, it seems, those of the mass of English Catholics. The conception of Christendom as a great commonwealth of peoples or of states, held together and ultimately directed to a common end by a Church, which is in them all but of none of them, made even less appeal, it would seem, to English than it did to French Catholics. That conception, medieval in origin and fully expounded by Bellarmine was, in the sixteenth century, Jesuit rather than

---

[1] *A True Relation of the faction begun at Wisbech*, 1601. Quoted by T. G. Law in *A Historical Sketch of the conflicts between Jesuits and Seculars in the reign of Queen Elizabeth* (1889), p. 96.

[2] This, of course, is not the Pope!

[3] The title of the tract, from the prefatory epistle to which these words are taken, is itself significant: '*Important Considerations, which ought to move all true and sound Catholics, who are not wholly Jesuitical, to acknowledge without all equivocations, ambiguities or shiftings, that the proceedings of Her Majesty and of the State with them, sinse the beginning of Her Highnesse reigne, have been both mild and mercifull*,' 1601. By William Watson and, apparently, other priests.

[4] *Important Considerations*, 1601, p. 37.

[5] The hope that, through Bancroft's good offices, they would be able to arrive at such an accommodation, no doubt added emphasis to their utterances.

Catholic. What English Catholicism was asserting was that there is no valid basis for Christian belief or security for its continuance, apart from the authority of the Church Catholic. ' The highest and deepest end of any Commonwealth is Cultus Dei.' But to say that a national government, representing a national Church, may define its own faith and enforce conformity to the views it chooses to adopt, is destructive of and implies, even, a negation of, religion. For, obviously, the civil sovereign is not infallible, and equally obvious is it that he will, in general, seek not truth but lines of least resistance. The claim of a national government to represent a ' church ' is absurd.

The book in which occur the words last quoted was written by Robert Parsons, the Jesuit, under the name of Doleman.[1] Of some importance at the time of its publication, and provocative of elaborate refutations, it was not for the most part, in the least representative of the views of English Catholics. Nor was it directly concerned with the Tudor doctrine of royal supremacy. All the same, the most striking and the only at all original feature of this work, is its insistence on the doctrine that every man is in duty bound to put his personal religion before everything else.[2] The appetite of man's soul can only be satisfied by the attainment of ' some infinite, endless and immortal object '.[3] In that connection what sovereigns or law may say, is obviously and completely irrelevant to the issue.

' Supposing there is,' wrote Parsons, ' but one only religion that can be true . . . and, moreover, seeing that to me there can be no other faith or religion available for my salvation than only that which I myself do believe, for that my own conscience must testify for me or against me : certain it is that, unto me and my conscience, he which in any point believeth otherwise than I do and standeth wilfully in the same, is an infidel. . . . I affirm and hold that for any man to give his help, consent or assistance towards the making of a king, whom he judgeth or believeth to be faulty in religion . . . is a most grievous and damnable sin to him that doth it, of what side soever the truth may be.' [4]

Parsons had definite and immediate practical purposes in writing thus : but whether he believed what he said or not does not in the least matter. He was asserting that it was a man's duty, under all circumstances, to act consistently with the faith that is in him, whatever it may be, right or wrong. Catholic or Protestant, a man has no right to give his conscience into the keeping of the State. His phrases give a significance that would, at the time, have been new to many, to the old saying that one must obey God rather than man. But if this were generally recognized as true, what would become of the claims of national sovereigns to establish forms of religion ? ' Were this rule of Doleman strictly observed,' says Craig, ' there

---

[1] *A Conference about the next Succession to the Crown of England*, 1594. Its main contentions are dealt with in another connection.

[2] It was the doctrine of the Catholic League of France.

[3] *Conference*, 1594, p. 204.   [4] *Ib.*, p. 216.

should not be one born for some ages that could be made King by the whole commonwealth.'[1] Indeed what way could there be out of the impasse so created except the toleration of all forms of religion ? And if it were the duty of every man to stand by his faith and refuse dictation, it would seem that it must be the duty of the ruler to tolerate. This was not the conclusion Parsons was hoping for ; but he might have found it difficult to escape the implications of his own words.

It has been said that Puritans and Catholics alike were contending for liberty of conscience. To put it so seems misleading if not altogether untrue. They were contending for the liberty of their own consciences, not for those of other people. Both were, most of them, ready and eager to see the civil sword used for the establishment of the ' true religion ', which was simply their own, and the destruction of all other. What they both claimed was freedom to dominate. So far as they were concerned it was merely an accident in the vast process of things, that their efforts to free themselves helped to enlarge human freedom. Had Parsons had his way and England become subject to a Spanish Catholic, had Travers succeeded in getting his ' discipline ' established, there would have been far less freedom in England than there was under Elizabeth. The establishment in law of intellectual freedom and of freedom for the religious consciousness, was the triumph not of Peter or of Paul, but of Gallio. For the purchase of freedom perhaps no price is too heavy ; but a price had to be paid.

[1] *Concerning the Right of Succession.* See Chap. X.

CHAPTER VIII

THE PURITAN PROTEST

§ 1. THE CALVINISTS

IT was, for obvious reasons, unlikely that opposition from the Protestant side to the action of the government would become serious during the early stages of the Reformation in England. But it is significant that quite early in the process we find Robert Barnes making some of the assertions that were constantly insisted upon by the Elizabethan Puritans. He declared that no ecclesiastic ought to be allowed in any case to exercise any civil jurisdiction and he declared that ecclesiastical law made concerning things indifferent in religion need not or should not be obeyed.[1] But his confused protest was quickly stifled. Tyndale, from his exile, might view the proceedings of the government with very mixed feelings ; but for the most part religious Protestants were supporting the government and trying to push it forward on the way it should go.

Yet in spite of all reasons for silence there developed among enthusiastic Protestants a strong sense that the action of Henry VIII's government was not inspired by the Scriptures, that motives were at work which could not justify themselves to any religious consciousness, that little good was likely to ensue to the cause of true religion from the measures taken, that the setting up of secular rulers as final authorities on religious questions involved something like denial of revelation, that the last state of things might be worse than the first. The Act of Six Articles was, of course, a terrible blow to their hopes. Bitter, too, was the resentment and disappointment at the way in which monastic property was disposed of. In 1542 Henry Brincklow complained that the Church was then worse served and the poor more neglected, than in the days of the Papal Antichrist.[2]

---

[1] *Men's Constitutions Bind not the Conscience*, 1532. Printed in the *Whole Workes of Tyndale, Frith and Barnes*, 1573. Barnes declared that if the King forbade reading of the Bible he must be disobeyed. He reflects Luther's aversion to law and lawyers.

[2] *Complaynt of Roderyck Mors*. Geneva, 1542, ed. J. M. Cooper (1884), for E.E.T.S., Chap. 14.

'This is the thirteenth article of our creed added of late,' he wrote, 'that whatsoever the Parliament doth, must needs be well done and the parliament, or any proclamation out of the parliament time, cannot err. . . . If you have given the same authority unto the parliament that the papists gave to their general councils, that is that they cannot err . . . if this be so, it is all in vain to look for an amendment of anything, and we be in as evil a case as when we were under the Bishop of Rome.' [1]

Far more violent was the language of Anthony Gilby, writing in exile in 1558, in denouncing the doings, not of Mary, but of Henry VIII.

'There was no reformation but a deformation,' he wrote, 'in the time of that tyrant and lecherous monster. The boar, I grant, was busy rooting and digging in the earth and all his pigs that followed him. But they sought only for the pleasant fruits that they winded with their long snouts : and for their own bellies' sake they rooted up many weeds ; but they turned the ground so, mingling good and bad together, sweet and sour, medicine and poison, they made, I say, such confusion of religion and laws, that no good thing could grow, but by great miracle, under such gardeners. . . . This monstrous boar must needs be called the Head of the Church, displacing Christ our only Head. . . . Wherefore in this point, O England, ye were no better than the Romish Antichrist.' [2]

But before Gilby wrote his *Admonition,* he had become, in connection with the 'troubles of Frankfort ',[3] a prominent member of a definite group which might be called the embryo of the Puritan party under Elizabeth. Among the hundreds of English refugees at Frankfort there arose angry contention on the question whether they were bound, in their exile, to adhere to the Prayer Book set forth by the government of Edward VI. Their fellow-refugees at Strasburg and at Zurich thought they were. But some of those at Frankfort, headed by Knox, maintained that the authorized services were in many respects unprofitable, marred by human inventions and, in fact, distinctly Popish. They appealed to Calvin and he supported them. The result was a schism in the English congregation. Outnumbered at Frankfort, the Nonconformists, Gilby and Goodman [4] among them, went to Geneva. There, in 1556, they published *The Form of Prayers and Ministrations of the Sacraments* they had adopted, *as approved*

---

[1] *Complaynt of Roderyck Mors,* ed. 1884, p. 35.

[2] *An Admonition to England and Scotland to call them to repentance.* First published along with Knox's *Appellation.* Printed in Laing's edition of the works of Knox, IV, App., pp. 563, 564. After Elizabeth's accession Gilby returned to England and obtained the living of Ashby-de-la-Zouch. Thereafter he violently attacked the ordinances of the Church he no doubt supposed himself to be serving. He died, undeprived, probably in 1585.

[3] A *History of the Troubles of Frankfort* was published in 1575.

[4] Goodman's *How Superior Powers ought to be obeyed* and Ponet's *Treatise of Politique Power* were also products of this moment. These have already been dealt with. Goodman's views were repudiated by the Elizabethan Puritans and Ponet's have little or no connection with theirs.

by the famous and godly learned man, John Calvin.   It was just such
a book as the Elizabethan Puritans craved for.

The significance of these apparently trivial events is clear enough
on consideration.   These English Protestant refugees were certainly
in revolt against the doctrine that in matters of religion Parliament
‘ cannot err ’.   Their objections to the Prayer Book of Edward VI
were, in detail, almost exactly the same as those the Elizabethan
Puritans made to her modified version of it.   Finally, some of the
members of this Geneva group, like Gilby, Sampson and Goodman,
returned to England on Elizabeth’s accession, accepted office or
benefice under her and helped to form a nucleus of Nonconforming
clergy.   The views of the Disciplinarians under Elizabeth coincided
closely with those of Knox’s followers at Frankfort and Geneva.

It was only under Elizabeth that Protestant opposition to the
action of the Crown in relation to religion and Protestant protest
against the doctrine of royal supremacy was very seriously developed.
It may here be noted that, though Luther had been a power in England
under Henry VIII and Edward VI, he had little or no influence on the
later Puritan thought.   The influences under which it shaped itself
came from Geneva and from Zurich and from the Scotland of Knox
and Andrew Melville.

The ambiguities associated with the word ‘ Protestant ’ are endless.   But whatever the Elizabethan Church was, it was certainly
not Catholic, officially or in structure.   It is equally certain that it
was not a fully ‘ reformed ’ Church in the sense of Calvin or of Knox.
Elizabeth’s government undertook the task of constructing a national
Church that should include in its membership Calvinist and conforming
Catholic, Parker and Gilby, the sceptic and the indifferent, the just
and the unjust.   Therefore there must be no definition or if, for seemli-
ness, some were wanted, at least none that defined ; there must be
as little break with tradition as possible ; there must be no rigid
enforcement of conformity.   Under these circumstances a Protestant
revolt of some sort was inevitable.

The Elizabethan government, at starting, found itself confronted
with the awkward fact that, with a single dishonourable exception,
every Bishop in England refused to accept the revived royal supremacy.
It had no choice but to fill their places with men who had proved their
probable loyalty by service under Edward VI or by exile under Mary.
A considerable proportion of the new bishops were returned refugees.[1]
These men regarded the system now established with hardly less dislike than did the mass of semi-Catholics.   But they accepted the royal
supremacy in accepting their positions.   They became royal officials
for the government of the Church.   They had to reconcile their

[1] Grindal of London, Pilkington of Durham, Sandys of Worcester, Park-
hurst of Norwich, Cox of Ely, Horne of Winchester, Jewel of Salisbury.

Calvinism with the doctrine of royal supremacy; and there is no reason to doubt their success. But it was impossible that the generality of those who thought like them and who accepted inferior posts or none at all, should be equally successful. Probably they all hoped at first, and even for long, that the original settlement would be developed into something definitely and coherently Calvinistic. Some of them seem to have imagined that the transition would be easy, so sure were they that only ignorance stood in the way of a general adoption of their opinions. ' God in these days hath so amazed the adversaries of his gospel,' wrote Jewel in 1567, ' and hath caused them so openly and grossly to lay abroad their follies to the sight and face of all the world, that no man now, be he never so ignorant, can think he may justly be excused ' for not seeing the obvious.[1] Exasperating disillusionment was bound to follow.

In 1561 Thomas Sampson and Lawrence Humphreys,[2] at Oxford, took the lead in starting what is called the Vestiarian controversy, which continued to rage almost to 1570, if it can ever be said to have ceased. It began with a revolt against the use of the surplice. It was argued that, if the surplice were a thing indifferent, then its use ought not to be enforced to the restriction of Christian liberty. It was, also, asserted that the surplice was not a thing indifferent, because it had been ' consecrated to idolatry '. In either case, it was implied, it is beyond human right to make its use compulsory and, law or no law, the bishops have no right to enforce it. This was but a beginning. Rapidly there developed, on similar grounds and with similar arguments, an attack on very many particulars of the official Prayer Book, on the use of the ring in marriage and of the cross in baptism, on the observance of fasts and saints' days, on choral services and the use of organs, on compulsory kneeling at communion as suggesting divine presence in the elements. All these things were denounced, with increasing violence as marks of the beast and remnants of idolatry.

' It is judged,' Hooker could say truly in 1597,[3] ' our prayers, our sacraments, our times and places of public meeting together for the worship and service of God, our marriages, our burials, our functions, elections and ordinations ecclesiastical, almost whatever we do in the exercise of our religion according to laws for that purpose established, all things are some way or other thought faulty, all things stained with superstition.'

Most of those who, in the early days of the Vestiarian controversy, denounced this or that particular disposition of authority as idolatrous, did not admit, or see, that they were attacking the royal supremacy. They were capable of saying in the same breath that the Queen is not

---

[1] Preface to the *Defence of the Apology*. Works, Parker Soc. ed., III.
[2] Sampson was Dean of Christchurch and Humphreys President of Magdalen.
[3] *Eccles. Pol.*, Book V. Clarendon Press ed. (1888), II, p. 26.

a governor of the Church and that they are loyal subjects.[1] When they are told that in refusing to wear the surplice they are denying the royal supremacy, they bewilderedly protest. To them royal supremacy meant simply a right to enforce the determinations of Scripture which, to them, were beyond all doubt. What they understood as the law of God was to them necessarily the law of the land. Law made by Parliament in contravention of God's law, they refuse to admit can be law at all. They simply do not understand how it can be said to be so without blasphemy. They were in revolt, not only against the royal supremacy, but against the conception of an absolute law-making power. It would be more accurate to say that no such conception existed in their minds.

So long as attack was concentrated on points of detail and grievances were not generalized, it was not, indeed, very clear what was happening. All those who came to be called ' Puritans '[2] objected to a number of rites, ceremonies, observances and arrangements established by law ; but many of them, apparently, went no further. When they were given the choice between deprivation and wearing the surplice, most of them chose to wear the surplice, at least now and then ; and, perhaps, conscientiously explained to their congregations that they wore the abominable rag only because they would otherwise not be allowed to preach the Word. Hooker's saying that ' obedience with professed unwillingness to obey is no better than manifold disobedience ',[3] left their withers unwrung, for the law he referred to did not bind their consciences. Professor Usher has pointed out that they seem to have held the view, common in the later Middle Ages, that, so long as a man conforms outwardly, he may think what he pleases. They seem to have believed that it was their duty formally to adhere to the Church of England they denounced and they felt horror at the idea of separating from it. Obviously it was their interest to feel like that. But they felt also that they were called upon to leaven the lump.

But on this road there was no stopping-place. By 1570 the disillusionment must have been fairly complete : it was evident that the Queen had no intention of allowing a handful of Puritans to dictate its religion to the nation. Accordingly in 1570 began a further development of the position. What distinguishes the Puritans who merely objected to this, that and the other, from the later Disciplinarians, is that the former had not grasped or accepted in its completeness, the Calvinistic ideal of the commonwealth. No one in England maintained that ideal, even indefinitely, before 1570. But the group that appeared in Cambridge that year, whose prophets were Cart-

---

[1] See the examination of a certain Axton in Neal, I, 211.
[2] The term seems to have been first applied to them in 1566.
[3] *Eccles. Pol.*, V, Clarendon Press ed., Chap. XXIX, II, p. 138.

wright and Travers, had in view the transformation of the Church of England into something essentially like that of Scotland. With them the denial of royal supremacy in the Church, implicit in the Puritan attitude from the first, became explicit, however they might try to disguise the fact from themselves or from others. The failure to convince the nation that the English Church was still ' unreformed ' and the exasperated disappointment that failure aroused, drove the Puritans into an attack on the royal supremacy as direct as they dared make it.

The passing in 1571 of an Act for the reformation of ' certain disorders touching ministers of the Church ', appears to have produced the first *Admonition to the Parliament,* printed at the end of that year or early in the next. It is commonly attributed to Field and Wilcox ; but Bancroft [1] seems to have thought that Sampson and Gilby and others had a hand in it and was probably right. It went rapidly through four editions. It is not surprising that it should have created a stir : it marks definite revolt against the Elizabethan Church system as a whole and resembles a declaration of war. A Second Admonition followed hard on its heels.[2] The controversy that arose directly out of these manifestoes continued, with increasing bitterness, for nearly ten years.[3] In 1573 appeared the *Ecclesiasticae Disciplinae et Anglicanœ Ecclesiae . . . explicatio* of Walter Travers ; [4] and an English version of this, probably by Cartwright, was issued in 1574.[5] Travers and Cartwright had supplemented the onslaught made in the Admonitions by a full statement of what the Church ought to be. Henceforward, the Puritans, or a section of them, have a definite programme to work for.

Under Grindal as Archbishop, from 1575 to 1583, there seems to have occurred a marked increase in the number of Puritan and more or less nonconforming ministers of the Church of England. Puritan activity began now to express itself in Parliament : an attack on the

[1] See his *Survey of the pretended Holy Discipline,* 1593.

[2] The Second Admonition is often attributed to Cartwright. Mr. Bayne in his edition of Hooker's Fifth Book, expresses the view that it is not Cartwright's, though he may have revised it. It was probably written by the authors of the first, of which it is a mere amplification. Whitgift remarked truly that an answer to one was an answer to the other.

[3] Whitgift's *Answer to a certain Libel* appeared before the end of 1572. In 1573 was published Cartwright's *Replye to an Answere* and Whitgift's *Defence of the Answere* came out in 1574. Cartwright issued a Second Reply in 1575 and, in addition, *The Rest of the Second Reply* in 1577. To these last Whitgift made no answer ; but later Hooker considered them both.

[4] This is the work most properly referred to as *The Book of Discipline.* There has been considerable confusion in the use of this term, which appears on no title-page.

[5] *A full and plaine declaration of Ecclesiastical Discipline out of the word of God and of the declining of the Church of England from the same,* 1574.

bishops and their administration was made in Parliament in 1580. After that year began what has been called the ' Presbyterian movement '. Even if by ' party ' is only meant an unorganized group of people of substantially identical views, the people called Puritans under Elizabeth can hardly be regarded as ever having formed a party. But those of them whose views were represented by Cartwright and Travers, the Disciplinarians or Presbyterians, seem to have obtained some degree of organization as a party before 1585. Out of a more or less organized effort to introduce, locally, a Presbyterian system under the existing law,[1] sprang the petitions to Parliament of the years 1584 and 1586.

It should, indeed, have been obvious that such an effort must fail. A tendency to split up had appeared in the party already. Robert Browne had broken away from the main movement at least by 1582 and was preaching congregationalism and denouncing the orthodox disciplinarians. The petitions failed to produce the least concession and the result was increased exasperation. In 1588 appeared the first of the series of Marprelate tracts. Effective suppression by the government of the classis system followed. By 1592 such organization as the disciplinarian party had obtained was completely broken up. The execution of Barrow and of Penry in 1593 marks the close of very serious Puritan agitation under Elizabeth. The government had, at last, put its foot down heavily.

Puritan argumentation would seem to start with the assertion that the form of Church government is prescribed in Scripture. ' The discipline of Christ's Church that is necessary for all times,' wrote Cartwright, ' is delivered by Christ and set down in the Holy Scriptures.'[2] It was declared to be demonstrable that some such form of ecclesiastical organization as that set forth in the *Explicatio* of Travers, was alone in accord with the word of God. Christ had arranged that all ecclesiastical power should lie with assemblies of elected ministers and elected elders, parochial, provincial or national. To constitute a Church without elders is, according to Cartwright, to rebel against God.[3] These consistories are to deal with ' the order of divine service, sermon, prayers, sacraments, marriages and burials ', and also with such things ' as pertain to the oversight of every one and their particular deeds '.[4] The elders are to know ' every particular home and person ' and the consistories must have disciplinary powers

---

[1] The *classis* appears about 1581. Its appearance was followed by an attempt to arrange for ' provincial ' synods. See Usher, *Presbyterian Movement*. By far the greater part of England must have been quite unaffected by and even unaware of the ' movement '.

[2] *A Directory of Church Government*. Written by Cartwright but apparently not published till 1644.

[3] Cartwright's First Reply to Whitgift.

[4] *A Directory of Church Government*.

to enforce at least outward conformity to the laws of godly living. Power to excommunicate must belong to them and excommunication must involve serious civil consequences. Persons who contemn such censures, say the authors of the Second Admonition, are guilty of a kind of blasphemy and for them the civil magistrate shall provide some sharp punishment. God, Cartwright points out, no longer punishes rebels against ecclesiastical authority as he punished Korah : therefore the magistrate should be the more severe and exacting on behalf of the Church and hold a ' harder hand ' than ever.[1] The existence of such disciplinary power in its consistories is essential to the structure of a true Church.

All this the Puritans declared, with perfect assurance, is derived from the Scriptures. How did they come to believe this ? Evidently the argument from Scripture as to the form and the powers of the ecclesiastical government cannot have been the real starting-point of their thought. They found in the Scriptures what they looked for.

Different minds may, of course, have travelled different roads to the same conclusions. But it seems that Puritan thought may be said to have started with a conception of the function of the Church. They conceived the Church as God's instrument for the sanctification of human life. Ecclesiastical organization exists to secure right preaching of the Word and right administration of the Sacraments and for the establishment of a moral discipline for all. Every earthly kingdom should be a *regnum Christi* and it is the business of the Church to see that it is. To think thus was to come easily to the conviction that the form of Church government will be found to be defined in Scripture. ' Either hath God left a prescript form of government for the Church under the New Testament,' wrote Udall : ' or he is less careful for it now than he was under the law . . . but he is as careful now for his Church as he was then : therefore hath he left a prescript form to govern it.' [2] This syllogism seemed sufficient. Sure, already, of finding a ' prescript form ' of Church government. in the Scriptures, they turned to the Scriptures and found it. God, intending to work for the sanctification of society through the Church, could not have left the form of it at the mercy of civil rulers who, obviously, might be ungodly persons.

What they found was determined for them partly by their own experiences in England and partly by the teaching and example of reformed churches in other lands, as in Geneva or in Scotland. These other churches were at least trying to perform the functions proper

---

[1] *The Second Replie*, 1575.
[2] *A Demonstration of the Truth of that Discipline which Christ hath prescribed in his Word, for the government of his Church, in all times and places until the world's end*, 1590.

to a Church. On the other hand, it was evident that the Elizabethan Church was not doing so and, as things stood, could not do so. Under the royal supremacy no real effort was being made to establish a kingdom of Christ. Royal supremacy tolerated the appointment of parochial ministers by the evidently ungodly; it had left its clergy practically without disciplinary powers; it worked through bishops who represented either mere civil authority or idolatrous associations, and through a clergy for the most part too ignorant to be allowed to preach; it admitted to its communion the just and the unjust; it had established forms of public prayer full of vestiges of the old superstition. The ideal of a sanctified society rightly ruled for the glory of God could never by such methods be realized. It seemed evident that if the Church were to perform its proper function, it must be released from mere civil control, from the control of those who did not think first and last of the glory of God. It must be so organized that its government shall be in the hands of the godly.

The account of Puritan thought so far given is evidently incomplete. In what consists sanctification and who are the godly? It is not enough to say that the godly are those who believe substantially the doctrine of the *Institute* and see in the glorification of a jealous God the purpose of society. The Puritan's conception of the Church was absolutely bound up with a system of moral values which answered these questions for him. It was just his own inadequate ideas of value that he conceived it was the main function of the Church to represent and to impose. But his valuations could be accepted only by persons of similarly narrow sympathies and defective perception and afflicted with a similar incapacity for enjoyment.

But what then, after all, in Puritan conception, was the Church? The marks of a true Church are the possession of sound doctrine and right form of government and disciplinary powers. But what constitutes membership of the Church? It is significant that Puritan writers constantly use the term Church to signify simply an ecclesiastical organization for government, as though the Church consisted of its consistories; exactly as Romanists often used the term as though the Church consisted of its clergy. Cartwright speaks sometimes as though every parish were a 'particular church'. On the other hand, the mass of the Puritans, as distinct from the Congregationalists, cling to the idea of a church of the nation. It is the function of the civil magistrates, says Cartwright, translating Travers, ' to set in order and establish the state of the church by their authority and to preserve and maintain it '.[1] It is their business to see to it ' that the service of God be established as he hath appointed and administered by such as ought to administer the same '. It is th.

---

[1] *Full and plaine Declaration.*

duty of Parliament, declared the Second Admonition, ' to have all reformed according to the word of God '.

Just because it is the duty of every government to establish a true Church in its dominions, the Church of England must be in some sense national. There was, for the Disciplinarians, no question of tolerating heretical or idolatrous sects. They assume that for England there can only be one Church. It follows that every member of the commonwealth will be a member of the Church even though, rather probably, an excommunicate member. Yet they endeavour to establish a distinction between Church and Commonwealth. Cartwright, in his First Reply, makes it a subject of accusation against Whitgift that he can see no real difference between the two. The Church, he explains, exists for the sake of the inward, civil government for the sake of the outward man. The Church, says Travers, is concerned only with spiritual ends and needs and the care of souls ; while the civil magistrates care for the body. But they admit that the distinction is not absolute. It may fairly be said that Puritan writers tried to effect an ideal separation of Church and Commonwealth and did not succeed in doing it.

' If all that believe,' says Hooker, ' be contained in the name of the Church, how should the Church remain by personal subsistence divided from the commonwealth, when the whole commonwealth doth believe ? ' [1] The obvious retort was that the whole commonwealth doth not believe and that no legal fiction as to common belief can constitute a true Church. The Puritans felt this strongly and said it. But they were evidently in a difficulty. It was useless to say that the Church itself can settle all questions as to its membership, unless you were prepared to say that the Church consists of its governing bodies. But even by saying that, you merely slipped from one difficulty to another. Ministers and elders are alike to be elected and the Church is national : its final authority is a national synod. The language sounds democratically : yet it is certain that nothing can have been further from the desires of the Disciplinarians than to see democratic election of ministers and elders established in a national Church. They must have been aware that such elections would, in some parts of England, be more likely to result in a revival of the Mass than in the establishment of a godly discipline. To suppose that the Puritans conceived of a democratic government of the Church is to misunderstand their thought completely. What they aspired to was the establishment of government by the godly of the ungodly multitude they habitually denounced. Evidently, in their system, votes must be confined to the godly, to those who in the full spiritual sense were members of the Church. From their point of view the

---

[1] *Eccles. Pol.*, Book VIII, 1. Works, Clarendon Press, 1888, Vol. III, p. 332. These may not be Hooker's own words, but the thought seems to be his.

supremacy of the multitude would have been likely to produce results even more disastrous than did the royal supremacy. The language of Puritan writers on this question of an ecclesiastical electorate is habitually, perhaps carefully, vague. But it is clear that, had the Church of their dream been actually established, some method of granting certificates of godliness would have had to be contrived.

The fact is that the Puritans were not really concerned to effect an ideal and absolute separation of Church and Commonwealth. They separated absolutely the ecclesiastical from the civil organization of the commonwealth and they proceeded to subordinate the latter to the former. In their ideal commonwealth the action of civil government is controlled and directed by an ecclesiastical organization. They begin, like Calvin, by distinguishing between Church and State and, like him, they end by creating a State ecclesiastical.

It is the duty of civil magistracy to establish the Scriptural Church and maintain with the sword the power of its consistories. In this sense, and in this sense only, the Puritans acknowledge a royal supremacy. No strictly ecclesiastical jurisdiction rightly belongs to civil magistrates. Not only must they not rule the Church, they must obey it. ' Neither let the magistrates think,' writes Cartwright, translating Travers, ' that . . . they are to be exempted from this precept and commandment of the apostle, who chargeth every one to be subject to those who in the Lord are set over them ' : the ministers, that is, and elders, who represent the Church. ' They must also as well as the rest submit themselves to be obedient to the just and lawful authority of the Church. For seeing they rule not as they themselves list . . . but only according to this word and commandment, is it not meet that even kings and the highest magistrates should be obedient unto them ? ' [1] Magistrates, wrote Robert Browne,

' have no ecclesiastical authority, but only as any other Christians; if so be they be Christians. . . . For who knoweth not, that though Magistrates are to keep their civil power above all persons, yet they come under the censures of the Church if they be Christians. . . . For all powers shall serve and obey Christ, saith the Prophet.' [2]

All the Puritan writers agree that magistrates, and even the Prince himself, must be subject to excommunication. On this point Cartwright was explicit.[3] The Church, said Barrow, in answer to this very question as to the Prince, ' ought to have judgment ready against every transgression, without respect of persons '.[4]

[1] A full and plaine Declaration, 1574, p. 185.
[2] A Treatise of Reformation without Tarrying for anie, 1582.
[3] See his First and Second Replies to Whitgift.
[4] The Examinations of Barrow, Greenwood and Penry, 1593. Harleian Misc., II.

'It is true,' wrote Cartwright, 'that we ought to be obedient unto the civil magistrate, which governeth the church of God in that office which is committed unto him and according to that calling. But it must be remembered that civil magistrates must govern it according to the rules of God prescribed in his word, and that as they are nurses, so they be servants unto the Church, to submit their sceptres, to throw down their crowns, before the Church, yea, as the Prophet speaketh, to lick the dust off the feet of the Church.' [1]

He proceeded to explain that he did not mean much by this Hildebrandine rhetoric ; and one is left a little doubtful what he did mean. But he explained, also, that it is a gross error to suppose, like Dr. Whitgift,

'that the church must be framed according to the commonwealth and the church government according to the civil government ; which is as much as to say, as if a man should fashion his house according to his hangings, when as indeed it is clear contrary, that as the hangings are made to fit the house, so the commonwealth must be made to agree with the church and the government thereof with her government. For as the house is before the hangings, and therefore the hangings . . . must be framed to the house . . . so the church being before there was any commonwealth and the commonwealth coming after, must be fashioned and made suitable unto the church. Otherwise God is made to give place to men.' [2]

The Church is 'the foundation of the world' and the commonwealth is built upon it.[3] All states, as Udall wrote, must be ruled by the Word 'and not the word by them and their policies'.[4]

The Disciplinarian Puritans were convinced that the realization of their ideal commonwealth, disciplined and directed by councils of the godly, was a plain command of God. Elizabeth's government was obviously setting at naught God's commands. Those among the Puritans who abandoned, at least for the time, the hope of seeing England become such a commonwealth and who adopted the Congregationalist conception of the Church, agreed with the rest that the Elizabethan Church was unscriptural, to say the least, if not positively antichristian. 'You pretend a reformation,' wrote the authors of the Second Admonition to Parliament, 'and follow not the word of God.' It was dangerous to say such things and most of the Puritan writers show caution. But the finer and more fearless spirits drew the necessary conclusions and stated them uncompromisingly, even though the doing so might lead them to the gallows.

'England,' wrote the fervid Welshman, John Penry in 1599, 'has refused the Gospel, saying : I will not come near the Holy One and as for the building of his house, I will not so much as lift up a finger for that work. Nay, I will continue the desolations thereof. And if any man speaketh a word in behalf of this house or bewaileth the misery of it, I will account him an enemy to my state. As for

[1] *Replye to an answere*, 1573, p. 180.   [2] *Ib.*, p. 181
[3] *The Second Replye*, 1575.
[4] *The Demonstration of Discipline*, 1590. Preface.

the gospel, I have already received all the gospels and all the ministries that I mean to receive . . . a gospel and a ministry that will stoop unto me and be at 'my beck, either to speak or to be mute, when I shall think good.' [1]

From the point of view of any Puritan this language, though rhetorical, was an accurate statement of the case. A Catholic might have said the same thing.

'They confess,' wrote Browne, with the same thought in his mind, 'that Christ ought to reign over them, yet they reign without Christ and have sent an embassage after·him, saying, We will not have this man to reign over us, except our magistrates will suffer him or make him to reign. Yea, we will have none of his Discipline, except our Parliaments decree that we shall have it.' [2]

Henry Barrow declared that the Elizabethan Church was subject unto an antichristian and ungodly government ; [3] and he agreed with Penry that conformity to such a church is utterly unlawful. [4]

'The last days of your reign,' wrote Penry, addressing Elizabeth directly, 'are turned rather against Jesus Christ and his Gospel than to the maintenance of the same. . . . The practice of your government sheweth, that if you could have ruled without the gospel, it would have been to be feared whether the gospel should be established or not. For now that you are established in your throne, and that by the gospel, ye have suffered the gospel to reach no further than the end of your sceptre.' [5]

Penry was in agreement with Cardinal Allen. Royal Supremacy tends to the destruction of religion, for civil government cares not what we believe ' no further than toucheth their prince and temporal weal '. [6]

'The Magistrate's commandment,' wrote Browne, ' must not be a rule unto me of this and that duty, but as I see it agree with the Word of God.' [7] ' If we cannot have your favour,' wrote Penry, ' but we must omit our duty towards God, we are unworthy of it ; and by God's grace we mean not to purchase it so dear.' ' But, Madam,' he continued, ' we must needs say that if the days of your sister Queen Mary and her persecution had continued unto this day, that the church of God in England had been far more flourishing than at this day it is.

---

[1] *Reformation no Enemy. A Treatise wherein is manifestlie proved*, etc., 1590. Preface. It was natural enough to interpret this passage as referring personally to Elizabeth. But Penry said and probably meant ' England '.

[2] *A Treatise upon the 23 of Matthew.* 1582.

[3] *A Briefe Summe of the causes of our separation*, 1591 (?).

[4] See *Penry's Historie of Corah, Dathan and Abiram*: printed 1609. The opinion that it is unlawful ' to communicate in any action of religion ' in the public services as established by law, is, he says, regarded as seditious. What, he asks, if it be true ? He did not see that its truth or falsehood was irrelevant to the question.

[5] From a ' petition ' to the Queen written in Scotland in 1592 and neither completed nor published. The words above given were quoted as part of Penry's indictment.

[6] See *supra*, p. 204.

[7] *A Treatise of Reformation.* 1582.

. . . The whole truth we must not speak ; the whole truth we must not profess. Your state must have a stroke above the truth of God.' [1]

Penry and Browne saw very clearly what they saw at all. It was perfectly true that, in their sense, England had refused the gospel and declared it would not have that man to reign over it. It was true that Elizabeth was reigning and that she suffered the gospel, as they understood it, to reach no further than her sceptre. But neither Penry nor Browne had any understanding of how this came to be so. They were sure that they knew ' the truth of God '. Quite sincerely they ascribed opposition to mere ignorance or sheer wickedness. They really could not understand how anyone could disagree with them.

Men who thought like this would probably, had circumstances favoured such courses, have come, like Knox, to the conclusion that armed rebellion against antichristian government is not only right but a duty. But the Elizabethan Puritans consistently repudiated any such view. They did, at times, use language that seemed menacing. The more ardent of them could hardly but believe that God would somehow intervene and deliver his people from oppression. ' Look to yourselves,' cried Martin Marprelate to the bishops. ' I think you have not long to reign.' [2] They prophesy plagues for the nation's unfaithfulness.[3] If England continues to refuse the gospel, says Penry, God will ' enter into judgment with the whole land ' and ' make his sword drunk with the blood of our slain men '.[4] But how this is to be brought to pass they do not know : it will not be by them. They all seem sure that actual rebellion against the constituted authority of the magistrate is absolutely forbidden by God in all cases. To the end they remain good Calvinists. Cartwright and Travers refrain from the slightest suggestion that there can, under any circumstances, be a right to rebel. All seem to agree that ' for procuring reformation of anything that we desire to be redressed in the state of our church, we judge it most unlawful and damnable by the word of God to rebel, and by force of arms to seek redress thereof '.[5] Extremists like Udall, Penry and Barrow explicitly disavow any claim to make use of force. Private persons, wrote Barrow, ' however they

[1] Petition to the Queen : quoted on his indictment. John Penry, born in 1559, was hanged in 1593. For a full account of his career and writings see the very interesting biography by W. Pierce : *John Penry* (1923). Mr. Pierce thinks that Penry's trial was conducted in a grossly unfair manner. This seems to be the case ; but that his whole attitude was technically seditious there can, I think, be no doubt. He was suspected of being the author of the Marprelate tracts and certainly had a hand in the printing of them.

[2] *The Epistle*, 1588.

[3] In the *First Admonition* and other places.

[4] *Reformation no Enemy to the State*, 1590. Preface.

[5] *Letter of the Puritan Ministers, imprisoned, to Her Majesty*. 1592. Neal's *Puritans*, Toulmin ed., App.

ought to refrain and to keep their souls and bodies undefiled from all false worship which is imposed . . . yet ought they not to stretch forth their hand by force to the reformation of any public enormities, which are by the magistrate's authority set up '.[1]

The Disciplinarian Puritans recognized in a sense, which was not that of the law, a royal supremacy. They regarded it as a duty incumbent on the civil magistrate to plant a true Church and maintain with the sword the plain determinations of Scripture. They demanded, as of right, that the civil sword should be used to enforce their ecclesiastical discipline, and give effect to their excommunications. They held that it was the duty of the civil magistrate to suppress false religion and false worship. They did not, therefore, completely separate Church from State : they desired to make of civil power a sword in the Church's hand. This, perhaps, was the real reason why they conceived the Church as national.

On the other hand, their religious consciousness was intense ; and this made it impossible for them to admit that the magistrate had any right to dictate to themselves in matters of faith and worship.

' It is allowed and commanded to Christian men,' wrote the authors of the Second Admonition, ' to try all things and to hold that which is good, whosoever forbid without exception, Prince or other : so that if we examine everything done in this Church of God in England . . . and hold that which is good, though the law be offended, that Law is to be reformed and not we to be punished.'

It may seem strange that they did not see clearly that in making this claim for themselves, they were bound to make it also for those who disagreed with them ; or else to claim infallibility for their own personal judgements. But they did not see it. What they thought they saw, was that the determinations of Scripture were perfectly clear to all reasonable and instructed persons. They were able, therefore, to claim that, while the law must not punish them, it should punish others who also, but falsely, imagined that they held that which is good. Men had a right to search the Scriptures, but no right to come to conclusions different from theirs. The mass of the Puritans reconciled their claim to freedom in religion with their conception of the functions of civil government, by subordinating civil government to the Church of their own construction.

The fallacy should have been obvious : and, to some of the Puritans themselves, it came to seem obvious. As ' Doleman ' said, ' to me there can be no other faith or religion available for my salvation than only that which I myself do believe '.[2] Implicit in the attitude of the Disciplinarians was the assertion that it is the bounden duty of every man to hold by his personal religion and act in accordance with it, whatever happens and whether he, actually, be right or wrong. It was just this sense that religion is personal and compelling or nothing

[1] *The Platform*, 1590.　　　　[2] See *supra*, p. 208.

at all, that was developed into a theory of the Church by the separatists who were called ' Brownists ' and for whom ' Congregationalists ' is the more accurate and comprehensive name.

§ 2. THE CONGREGATIONALISTS

The ideas of these separatist Puritans, who broke with the orthodox Disciplinarians, had no direct bearing on political theory. But they expressed in a simplified form, the radical objection of Puritans and Catholics alike to the doctrine of royal supremacy and their conception of a ' church ' at least suggested a principle of tolera-tion. Without the co-operation of the civil magistrate the Disciplin-arians could not conceivably realize their ideal of a Church-State. The Brownists would not tarry for the magistrate. Browne agreed with Doleman. He and those who thought, or who felt, like him, formulated a conception of the Church which differed from that of the Disciplinarians, in that it absolutely disassociated the idea of the Church and the idea of the State.

Since religion consists essentially, asserted the Congregationalists, in the establishment of a relation between the individual soul and God, it is fallacious to suppose that civil power can ever create a real church. To say that it is the duty of the civil magistrate to establish the true Church by law and by force, is mere nonsense ; for the thing simply cannot be done. ' No Prince can make any a member of the Church,' says Barrow. It is a most false and pernicious doctrine ' that a Christian prince which publisheth and maintaineth the gospel, doth forthwith make all that realm, which with open force resisteth not his proceedings, to be held a Church '.[1] ' To compel religion, to plant churches by power and to force a submission to ecclesiastical govern-ment by laws and penalties,' says Browne writing of civil magistrates, ' belongeth not to them . . . and neither to the Church.' No disci-pline worth having can be maintained by such means.

' Concerning ecclesiastical discipline,' wrote Browne, ' some are deceived and do mistake it, for it is not that civil discipline nor bodily punishing, nor outward forcing of good and bad. . . . I say and have always said that, whoso hath the word of God and doth live according to it, he hath the discipline, government or kingdom of Christ.' [2]

Robert Browne, the remarkable man who gave his name to a number of separatist congregations who repudiated it, was born at

---

[1] *A Briefe Discoverie of the False Church*, 1590. Henry Barrow was hanged in 1593 after long imprisonment : a martyr to his convictions, like Campion. His conception of the Church seems to be substantially the same as Browne's ; but there is no evidence that he had read Browne's writings and he always dis-claimed the connection. For a good account of him see F. J. Powicke : *Henry Barrow, Separatist.*

[2] Letter to Mr. Flower, 1589. Published in 1904, under the title *A New Year's Gift.*

Tolethorpe, in Rutland, about the year 1550. He was not the earliest in time of Elizabethan separatists. Quite early in the reign a Nonconformist church, apparently ' Brownist ' in type, had been formed in London, with one Richard Fitz as its minister. In 1567 some of the members of this congregation were arrested. It was probably others of them who, in 1571, in a petition to the Queen, spoke of themselves as ' a poor congregation whom God hath separated from the churches of England '.[1] But Browne was the first to give full expression to the Congregationalist ideas. He took a degree at Cambridge in 1572 and seems to have developed his characteristic views after 1578. The classis at Bury, in which he was the leading spirit, seems to have developed into a Brownist ' church ' : and in 1581 he and his adherents emigrated to Middleburgh. There, in 1582, his three most important treatises were published.[2] Subsequently, after the break-up of his congregation, he had unpleasant experiences in Scotland ; and what he saw there of Presbyterian discipline must have confirmed his already expressed opinions. After his return to England, his activities brought an excommunication upon him. In 1591, he, very surprisingly, became rector of Achurch, a little village in Northants, not far from Oundle. He remained there, as rector, uncharged and unmolested till his death in 1633 ; and during all that time he published nothing. There is reason to believe that he had not changed his opinions. But that long silence is intriguing.[3] Whatever be the fact, Browne was certainly the most vigorous and expressive of the early Congregationalist writers.

To wait the magistrate's good pleasure is mere unfaithfulness. The magistrate can do nothing worth doing ; but any group of true believers can form a true Church here and now. ' Where find they,' wrote the author of a tract that may or may not be Barrow's, ' that either our Saviour Christ or his Apostles sued to parliaments or princes for the planting or practising of the gospel ? '[4] It is absurd to suppose that the kingdom of God needs to be so established that men may say, ' Lo the parliament or Lo the bishops decrees ! ' ' The kingdom of God shall be within you.'[5] ' The Lord's people is of the willing sort. They shall come unto Zion and enquire the way to Jerusalem, not by force or compulsion, but with their faces turned thitherward,'[6] wrote

[1] For these early separatists see W. Pierce : *Historical Introduction to the Marprelate Tracts* and *John Penry.*

[2] *A Treatise of Reformation without tarrying for anie, A Treatise upon the 23 of Matthew,* and *A Booke which showeth the life and manners of all true Christians.*

[3] Browne was, by marriage, a distant relative of Burleigh, who probably secured for, or presented him with, his rectory. It is possible that he developed some kind of mystic quietism.

[4] *Four principal and weighty Causes of Separation.* Published for the Congregational Historical Society, 1906.

[5] *Treatise of Reformation.*   [6] Ib.

Browne. ' Faith is a conscience of our redemption and happiness in Christ, whereby we wholly yield up ourselves unto him in all newness of life.' [1] It is just such a yielding up by a group of faithful people that constitutes a ' church '. ' The church,' wrote Browne, ' planted or gathered, is a company or number of Christians or believers which, by a willing covenant made with their God are under the government of God and Christ, and keep his laws in one holy communion.' [2]

These early Congregationalists did not agree with the continental Anabaptists in insisting on adult baptism ; nor did they agree with them in condemning all coercive government as evil. Browne and the rest specifically recognize in the civil magistrate a right to punish, even to death, for civil offences. But they agree with the Anabaptists, or with many of them, in conceiving the Church as essentially a voluntary association, or congregation of persons united in faith, who have no Lord of their spiritual life save Christ. The Church is to govern itself on the basis of a common faith and understanding of the will of God. It must needs have power to excommunicate, that is to expel, its own members : and it needs no more. It is necessarily self-governing, independent of all civil power and needing no help from it. There can be, in relation to it, no such thing as royal supremacy. The Church is completely disassociated from any commonwealth and, so far as it can be said to be localized at all, it is localized only accidentally. At Bury or at Middleburgh, in London or Amsterdam or Leyden, it is the same Church. That being so, the Church makes and can make no claim to control the lives or the religious observances of those who are outside its covenanted unity. ' We leave it free to them,' says Browne, ' to follow or not to follow our ways and doctrine, except they see it good and meet for them.' [3] Obviously a church so constituted could do nothing else, since it had completely disassociated itself from the source of coercive power.

In connection with Anabaptist ideas, something has already been said on the question of how far such a conception of the Church logically involved a principle of toleration. It did certainly involve that civil power should not be used to compel anyone to become a member of, or conform to the practices of, any particular church. But it did not necessarily involve that it is not the duty of the civil magistrate to suppress by force idolatrous or blasphemous or even simply erroneous forms of doctrine and worship. It is obvious that before the civil

---

[1] Browne : *True and Short Declaration*. Reprint of 1882, p. 10.

[2] *Booke which Showeth*. Definition 25. John Robinson, head of a congregation at Leyden, wrote in 1610 as follows : ' A company consisting though but of two or three separated from the world, whether unchristian or antichristian, and gathered into the name of Christ by a covenant made to walk in all the ways of God known unto them, is a Church and so hath the whole power of Christ.' *Justification of Separation from the Church of England*, 1610.

[3] *True and Short Declaration*. Reprint, 1882, p. 9.

magistrate can do so, he must determine what doctrines are idolatrous or blasphemous. If we assume that he cannot do that, nothing remains but that he shall tolerate all religious associations that do not conflict with merely civil law. If, on the other hand, we assume that what is idolatrous and blasphemous is demonstrable by the Word of God, there remains no ground for saying that the civil magistrate should not suppress by force such forbidden opinions and practices. This latter assumption it is that seems to have been made by Disciplinarians and Congregationalists alike. The early Congregationalists could therefore maintain, at once that the civil magistrate should not plant churches by power or compel submission to ecclesiastical discipline, and yet that it was his duty to suppress false religion.

This, precisely, is what they habitually did assert. It has been held that they were, incidentally, announcing a principle of religious toleration. But they did so only in the sense that it was possible, starting with their conception of the Church, to conclude in favour of a general toleration. That was not their own conclusion. ' It is the office and duty of Princes,' wrote Henry Barrow, ' most carefully to advance and to establish in their dominions the true worship and ministry of God and to suppress and root out all contrary.' [1] He was of opinion that ' blasphemy and open idolatry ' should be punished with death.[2] Whether Browne would have gone as far as this seems uncertain. He never specifically claimed that the civil magistrate should undertake the suppression of false worship, though his attitude seems to imply that he thought such suppression would be a righteous work. In any case no principle of toleration can be found in his writings. He would, I think, have disapproved of Castellion's views almost as strongly as did Calvin. When he said that the Lord's people are of the willing sort and that it is not the business of the magistrate to compel religion, he meant what he said and no more. He asserted that religion is and must be independent of State law. Faith cannot be commanded and law and force can establish only a fictitious church. The ' Brownists ' were sure that they had the truth and therefore they demanded toleration for themselves. Browne demanded no more ; and that he demanded no more separates him absolutely from the Disciplinarian Puritans and orthodox Calvinists generally. But when he said ' we leave them free ', he was speaking simply of his ' church '. He was not saying that the magistrate should leave all men free to form whatever sort of religious associations they might please. It is unlikely that any such notion ever entered his mind. What Browne taught was, that it is worse than useless for the magistrate to set about planting churches by law, because

---

[1] *The Platform*, 1590.
[2] *Discoverie of the False Church*, 1590, p. 220.

the result of so doing is that all sorts of people who are not real believers become members of a ' Church ' that is thereby rendered fictitious. A true Church is composed of the faithful and believing. We, say the Brownists, have the truth ; and if the magistrate were, like us, faithful and believing, though he would compel no one to join our communion, yet he would most certainly use his sword to suppress manifest idolatry and false worship that dishonours God. In 1596 a congregation of exiles at Amsterdam, describing themselves as ' falsely called Brownists ', published a *True Confession* of their faith.[1] In this they declared that ' it is the office and duty of Princes and Magistrates, to suppress and root out by their authority all false ministries, voluntary religions and counterfeit worship of God '.[2] There is nothing in the writings of Browne himself that is inconsistent with this assertion. Rather we may say that the declaration made by Ainsworth's congregation exhibits the natural tendency of Browne's teaching.

The ' church ' of the Brownists was essentially a self-governing congregation. Yet Browne's programme provided for ' synods or meetings of sundry churches ' ; and he apparently regarded the findings of such synods as superior in force to those of any particular church.[3] It seems that in the perfected commonwealth of the early Congregationalists, there would be a number of independent though connected ' churches ', unconnected with the civil government and asking nothing from it except the suppression of forms of religion unlike their own.

Recognition that it is not the duty of the civil magistrate to establish and maintain true religion by force, was, practically, a step in the direction of religious toleration. But it was a step that went half-way only, if that ; and the ' Brownist ' congregations had no intention of going further. There remained the duty of the civil government to suppress forms of religion demonstrably idolatrous or false. This involved the assumption that the false and the true could be infallibly discriminated ; and it is true that this assumption could not in the long run be maintained in the minds of most people. It is also true that, once the mass of people gave up the belief that government could maintain true religion by law, no government was likely to refuse to tolerate religious bodies on the ground that their religion was false. The influence of the early Congregationalists was one of the factors working to bring about legal religious toleration. But this fact is really irrelevant to a comprehension of their ideas. To say

---

[1] This was many times reprinted before 1614, both in English, Latin and Dutch. The head of this congregation was Henry Ainsworth. The whole text is given in Williston Walker's *Creeds and Platforms of Congregationalism.* 1893.

[2] *A True Confession*, etc., 1596. Art. 39.

[3] *True and Short Declaration.* But Browne's language on the subject is excessively vague.

that they held or expressed a principle or a theory of religious toleration, appears, on reference to their writings, to be simply untrue.

§ 3. PURITANS AND CATHOLICS

' Suppose the Parliament would make a law that God should not be God,' said Sir Thomas More, ' would then you say God were not God ? ' ' The magistrate's commandment,' wrote Robert Browne, ' must not be a rule unto me of this and that duty, but as I see it agree with the Word of God.' [1] English Catholics and English ' Puritans ' disagreed about many or perhaps most things, but in one thing they agreed ; and the agreement was fundamental. They agreed that to identify Church and State is to identify religion with law and make the command of a sovereign a rule of faith. They agreed that religiousness is a relation of the soul to God and is not a relation of the soul to the State. Both would have agreed that, in the words of Professor Pollard : ' It is the essence of all religion that man's relation to God and conscience makes his relation to the state conditional and not absolute ; and the absolutism of the state is a form of pagan idolatry. Man is a great deal more than a political animal.' [2] To both of them, though they had different conceptions of the ' church ', the preservation of true religion was dependent on the church's independence. Catholics and Disciplinarian Puritans, holding alike that it was the duty of the civil magistrate to maintain true religion and that the critical determination of what constitutes true religion lay with an independent church, both claimed for the Church the final word in the direction of secular government. The Congregationalists, insisting that to constitute a true church by legal arrangements is impossible, limited the action of the magistrate to the suppression of manifestly false religion. All of them, though they neither knew it nor intended it, were helping to create an impossible position, from which legal religious toleration was the only way of escape.

[1] *Treatise of Reformation.*   [2] *Evolution of Parliament*, 1920, p. 345.

CHAPTER IX

THE QUESTION OF TOLERATION

§ 1. THE STATE OF THE CASE

NO controversy developed in England during the sixteenth century as to the rightfulness or expediency of general religious toleration. From time to time suggestions were made that it was unreasonable or unjust to punish people for their religious opinions, that nothing is gained by doing so and that trouble would be saved by not doing so. Such suggestions passed almost unnoticed. It is only towards the end of the century that we can see that the question is beginning to be regarded as a practical one and discern signs of the coming controversy.

This fact is at first sight a little surprising in view of the acuteness of controversy on the subject on the Continent and in view of the development of Nonconformity and the difficulty, under Elizabeth, of establishing any sort of order in the religious life of the community. But Continental controversy had little or no effect in England. Anthony Brown, Lord Montague, speaking in Parliament in 1563, declared that

' naturally no man can or ought to be constrained to take for certain that that he holdeth to be uncertain: for this repugneth to the natural liberty of man's understanding: for understanding may be persuaded but . not forced. . . . When there be many opinions of the one side and of the other,' he added, ' it is reason that the thing be doubtful, till all opinions come to one.' [1]

This sounds like an echo of Castellion ; but Castellion's writings seem to have been hardly known in England until published in Holland early in the next century. The influence of Bodin is traceable after 1580 ; but conditions in France differed so greatly from those of England that the argument from expediency that there seemed overwhelmingly strong, had little weight here.

If the Arminian controversy, in its early stages, aroused little interest in England, that was partly because England had developed already its own kind of Arminianism.   Under Henry VIII the doctrine of. the royal supremacy had been an instrument of nationalization,

---

[1] Speech in Strype : *Annals*, App., p. 443.

an instrument for the demolition of Papal jurisdiction and the liberties
of the clergy. Under Elizabeth it enabled the government to make
a settlement, so indefinite doctrinally and so traditional in form, that
conformity became possible for the great mass of the nation. It was
used to minimize friction and the danger of conflict between religious
parties. The Elizabethan settlement, and perhaps the administration
of the law still more than the law itself, was practically a great step
in the direction of religious toleration, whatever a handful of harassed
Puritans or a minority of Catholics might feel about it. Mere opinion,
it may fairly be said, was no longer punished by death. So little
was defined that only the most clear-cut dogmatism could find much
to quarrel with ; so much was traditional that it was possible to feel
that things were improved but not radically changed ; so lax was
administration that it was possible for men like Anthony Gilby and
Robert Browne to hold benefice in a church they denounced as idolatrous. The Supreme Governor, whose function it was to define and
maintain true religion, maintained without defining. The one thing
that could not be tolerated was denial of the royal supremacy. The
good sense of the government went far to prevent the question of
toleration from becoming practically acute.

Such a settlement was possible partly because there was little
disposition in England to take ' heresy ' very seriously. The tradition
of the common lawyers was against doing so and their jealousy of
ecclesiastical jurisdiction was a practical hindrance. Very few would
have denied that the public profession or exercise of false religion
ought to be suppressed by public authority ; but the view ordinarily
taken on the subject was not that of Calvin and Beza.

' To Princes,' wrote Bilson, ' who bear the sword and are God's Lieutenants
not only to procure peace between men but also by laws to maintain religion . . .
we neither bid nor dispraise moderate correction when need so requireth ; only
we would have such as stray from truth corrected, not murdered. For it never
pleased any good men in the Catholic Church that heretics should be put to
death.' [1]

There was little or no disposition to put into practice the precepts
of the book of Deuteronomy. It was felt, indeed, that to allow officially
of two or more religions would be a dangerous impiety. ' I reckon,'
wrote Bilson, ' it cannot stand with a Prince's duty to reverse this
heavenly decree, " Thou shalt worship the Lord thy God and Him
only shalt thou serve," with establishing two religions in one realm.' [2]
But there was a very general willingness to treat most of the subjects
of religious controversy as things indifferent. English people : in
general seem to have been of the opinion of Acontius that, while
there may be beliefs necessary to salvation, there must be very few.
Fundamentally important in the situation were certain implications

---

[1] *True Difference*, 1585, p. 19.   [2] Ib., p. 21.

of the theory of royal supremacy. It logically involved a claim that the Crown was free to tolerate as much, or as little, as it pleased. That, in itself, was a denial of the assertion that it was the absolute duty of the civil ruler to suppress false religion and worship. It is true that professed believers in the royal supremacy often made this assertion. But the two notions were inconsistent. To say that the determination of all ecclesiastical or religious questions lay with the civil sovereign and yet that the sovereign could not determine what was tolerable and what intolerable, would have been absurd. A national ' church ' that could determine its own faith and ritual and interpret Scripture could certainly also determine how the law of God bade it deal with heresy. The conclusion could not be escaped ; and it was certainly the view taken by the government itself. The author of the essay called *The Execution of Justice in England*, Burleigh himself or another, defended the government against the charge of persecuting for the cause of religion.

' Though there are many subjects known in the realm,' he wrote, ' that differ in some opinions of religion from the church of England and that do also not forbear to profess the same, yet in that they do also profess loyalty and obedience to Her Majesty and offer readily to Her Majesty's defence, to impugn and resist any foreign force, though it should come or be procured from the Pope himself : none of this sort are for their contrary opinions in religion persecuted or charged with any crimes or pains of treason, nor yet willingly searched in their consciences for their contrary opinions, that savour not of treason.' [1]

Whatever be the value of his argument concerning the actual dealings of the government with the Catholics, the importance of the principle he announced by implication was great. ' It is not nor hath been for contrarious opinions in religion or for the pope's authority alone . . . that any persons have suffered death since Her Majesty's reign.' Positively he plumes himself on the alleged fact. Not only was there a clear implication that the civil sovereign was free to tolerate dissent in religion, but it was even implied that it was only reasonable and just to do so when it could be done with safety.[2]

The theory of royal supremacy did indeed itself involve an implication that the power of determining religious controversies should be used only for secular and political ends, and with reference merely to the temporal needs of the commonwealth. It could rightly be used to prevent the development of factions tending to disorder, and to reconcile as far as possible conflicting beliefs. It might, perhaps, reasonably be used to suppress manifestations of opinion offensive

---

[1] *The Execution of Justice in England for maintenance of publike and Christian peace, against certeine stirrers of sedition, and adherents to the traitors and enemies of the realm, without anie persecution of them for questions of religion*, 1584. In Holinshed, III, p. 1360, 1587.

[2] Exactly similar is the view expressed in a letter of Walsingham which seems to have been actually drafted by Francis Bacon in 1589. See Spedding : *Life and Times of Francis Bacon*, I, p. 42.

to the great majority of people. It could not rationally be used for definition of true belief or the suppression of mere error unless Parliament were indeed infallible. This conclusion could be escaped only by those who really believed that all relevant questions could be answered for certain by reference to Scripture. Reluctant as men might be to accept it, they seem to have been half-conscious of what was really undeniable. This, perhaps, is why people were so ready to accept ambiguity and incoherence and why it was sought to show that royal supremacy did not really involve a power to define the faith. And once the illusion vanished that all difficulties could be solved by reference to Scripture and once it was admitted that the royal supremacy existed only for temporal needs, the straight road to toleration lay wide and open. The mere difficulty of refusing to tolerate would alone, in the long run, be sufficient to drive the government to take that road. Tentatively, under pressure of circumstances, the Elizabethan government had already started on it.

How far it would be able to continue along that road was doubtful. The Puritan conception of a Church-State, ruled for the glory of God by an ecclesiastical organization, was a barrier in the way. So, in less degree, was the conviction of the Brownist Independents, that at least blasphemy and idolatry should be suppressed by force. Even the Anglican supporters of royal supremacy were beginning to develop a conception of a national church under an episcopacy of divine right. So long as Elizabeth lived, the road that led to toleration was kept open. She struck at those who attacked and denied the royal supremacy ; but it was just those who denied it who were trying to close the road. But, when the great Queen died, another way was taken. ' I will have one doctrine and one discipline, one religion in substance and in ceremony,' announced James I at Hampton Court in 1604. ' That it is one of the principal parts of that duty which appertains to a Christian King,' he wrote, ' to protect the true Church within his own dominions and extirpate heresies, is a maxim without all controversy.' [1] The phrase ' without all controversy ' was singularly inept ; but the King's acceptance of this principle of Calvinism again closed the road, for a time.

It may be said that, under Elizabeth, the people who stood most in need of toleration, the Puritans and the Romanists, were absolutely debarred by their own distinctive ideas from adopting any principle of toleration. Cardinal Allen pleaded for toleration for the Catholics on the ground that it was impolitic to persecute them : [2] and that

---

[1] *A Declaration against Vorstius.* Works, p. 349.

[2] This is true ; but is put in a manner unfair to Allen. He went further, declaring that it is simply wrong to force men into unconvinced conformity. ' No Jew, no Turk, no Pagan, can by the law of God, nature or nations be forced from the name and possession of his own sect and service.' *True, sincere and modest defence,* 1584, pp. 7 B, 8.

was little to the purpose. The Puritans pleaded for toleration only
for themselves and simply on the ground that they were right. That
was not to the purpose at all. But, for the mass of the people, who
were neither Romanist nor Puritan, there existed, in England as
elsewhere, good reasons against the acceptance of any principle of
toleration and a grave difficulty even in conceiving such a principle.

It was one thing to compromise or to take refuge in ambiguity ;
it was quite another to say that it is not the duty of the magistrate
in any sense to maintain true religion. Yet this, it seemed, had to
be said before any principle of toleration could be held valid. But if
religious truth were in any degree ascertainable, how could this be
said ? ' We agree,' wrote Hooker, ' that pure and unstained religion
ought to be the highest of all cares appertaining to public regiment.' [1]
Must not the magistrate, even for the sake of mere peace on earth,
maintain it against all assault ? ' The very worldly peace and prosperity, the secular happiness, the temporal and natural good estate
both of all men and of all dominions, hangeth chiefly upon religion.' [2]
In the sixteenth century men were convinced, even men little preoccupied with religion believed, that, again in Hooker's words, ' the
safety of all estates dependeth upon religion '.[3] This ' safety ' to Hooker
indeed meant far more than it did to most men.

' This singular grace and pre-eminence,' he wrote, ' religion hath, that either
it guardeth us as a heavenly shield from all calamities, or else conducteth us
safe through them and permitteth them not to be miseries ; it either giveth honours, promotions, and wealth, or else more benefit by wanting them than if one
had them at will ; it either filleth our houses with plenty of good things, or
maketh a sallet of green herbs more sweet than all the sacrifices of the ungodly.' [4]

Few, doubtless, understood it in this sense ; but if in any sense
safety depended upon religion, the magistrate must maintain it.

' No religion,' wrote Hooker, ' can wholly and only consist of
untruths ; '[5] and therefore every religion is of value. But men
instinctively feel, he declared, the immense importance of possessing
true religion.[6] There existed, indeed, a very general suspicion, if
not conviction, that the possession of untrue religion made a man, in
the long run, anything but safe. If, therefore, true religion could
at all be found, government must maintain it. And how in any sense
maintain it, if not by the use of force ? To deny that the magistrate
ought to suppress any religious profession as erroneous, seemed to
imply that he could never reasonably hope to distinguish truth from
error. But this was to admit that the truth of no doctrine, the validity
of no sacrament, could be demonstrated. Few religious men of the

---

[1] *Eccles. Pol.*, Bk. V, 1. Clarendon Press, ed. II, p. 13.
[2] Ib., Bk. V, 76, pp. 444, 445.
[3] Ib., VI, p. 18.   [4] Ib., V, 76, p. 454.
[5] Ib., V, 1, p. 19.   [6] Ib., V, 1, p. 16.

sixteenth century could find it in their hearts to make that terrifying admission.

Here was the main intellectual difficulty. Few people, perhaps, saw it distinctly ; but they saw other things. If this admission were made what results would follow ? ' Is it meet,' asked Whitgift, ' that every man should have his own fancy and live as him list ? ' It was the prospect of men living as they listed that frightened him. How would it be possible to maintain order in society, if men of the strangest religious opinions are allowed to live in accordance with them ? If the expression of opinion and the formation of organized sects be in no way limited, will not the result be the disappearance of any common standard of conduct and an anarchy in action as in ideas ?

There was the sense, too, that religious unity was needed to assure national safety and that rebels against the royal supremacy and its determinations were aiding and abetting enemies abroad. How was it possible for any nation to maintain itself in a hostile world if it were divided within into factions upon the most important of all issues ? The constant seeming menace from abroad associated national sentiment in the closest manner with the notion that it was the government's business to maintain, not so much truth, as unity in religion. Men conformed out of mere loyalty, because to them, though they might not know it, the highest duty was to the nation. The religious dissentient, however much he might protest his loyalty, was always necessarily, it was felt, disloyal. Apart, even, from any danger from the foreigner, what horrors might not ensue from the unfettered development of religious differences ? Englishmen had before their eyes the awful example of France. If absolute unity were unattainable, at least no one must be allowed openly to oppose the determinations of national authority. As Bilson said : ' Princes must either not meddle with matters of religion at all or else of necessity they must command and afterwards punish if their commandment be despised.' [1]

It has to be remembered, also, that there of course existed, on all sides, the constant tendency of the human mind to resent disagreement and to regard those who differ from ourselves as foolish or perverse or wicked. ' There is no prince or private man so foolish,' wrote William Thomas under Edward VI, ' as if it lay in his power, would not compel the whole world to believe as he doth.' Why should he wish to do anything of the kind ? Is it because, as Thomas suggested, he fears the enmity of those who will regard him as outside the pale and as one with whom no faith need be kept nor code observed ? Is it because, as Acontius suggested, he feels his confidence in his own judgements to be shaken by another's denial ? Or is it, ever, because he would fain save the world by force from damning error ?

[1] *True Difference*, 1585, p. 205.

In any case, though Thomas exaggerated even grossly, he was pointing to what is probably as much a fact in the twentieth as it was in the sixteenth century. Men have to learn not to resent contradiction ; and when the proposition in question is one that seems of the utmost import, the lesson is hard to learn. That which has convinced me, ought, it seems, to convince all others or, alternatively, it ought not to have convinced me. The alternative may seem intolerable.

The belief that it must, surely, be possible for government to maintain true religion ; the fear lest religious dissension should endanger the national independence ; the sense that toleration might result in a moral disintegration ; the tendency to see rebels against the mass of opinion as perverse ; all these, added to the fact that a system had been established allowing a wide freedom and to the fact that those who most loudly demanded toleration for themselves were just those who most strictly denied it to others, seem to explain why it was that no principle of toleration was ever fully formulated in Elizabeth's England. Yet circumstances were tending to produce a practical conclusion in favour of toleration at least on grounds of expediency. As early as 1562, in a remarkable speech made in Parliament, a certain Mr. Atkinson argued for toleration and prophesied its coming. Speaking against the imposition of the oath of supremacy under penalties, he said that he did not profess to know much about the Scriptures but that what would happen was evident. Men would simply perjure themselves and, ' if any were rebellious before, now will his heart become more rebellious for that he is forced to perjury '. It was unjust, he implied, to treat men whose attitude was determined by religion, as mere criminals. ' Remember that men that offend in this way, offend not as murderers and thieves do . . . but through conscience and zeal, at least through opinion of religion.' Toleration, he declared, must come. ' And when we have all done, to this we must come at last. We see in Germany, where, after so long contention, so great destruction and waste . . . at last they are come to this point, that the papist and protestant can now quietly talk together and never fall out about the matter.' He added that, ' though you may like these doings, yet it may be that your heirs after you shall mislike them '.[1]

If very few were prepared to go as far as this, yet some such views must have tended to become increasingly common. In 1571 a Mr. Aglionby of Warwick argued in Parliament [2] that though it might be reasonable to compel people to go to Church, it was unjust to force them to receive the communion. ' There should be,' he declared, ' no human positive law to inforce conscience ; and he quoted Cicero :

[1] See the whole speech in Strype : *Annals*, I, App. The passages quoted are on pp. 454, 455.
[2] D'Ewes, I, p. 177.

' Qui Deum non curat hunc Deus ipse judicabit.' In the same debate one finds a Mr. Norton saying that ' where many men be, there must be many minds, and in consultations convenient it is to have contrary opinions . . . thereby the rather to wrest out the best ' •

At the end of Elizabeth's reign a deadlock was visibly threatened. Deep divisions of Protestant religious opinion of the most serious kind had already developed. It had become quite manifest that Bible reading and controversy were not going to produce unanimity. The maintenance of true religion was likely to prove in the future a more and more troublesome and dangerous business. From the beginning of the reign the government had really been trying to evade it ; but mere evasion was becoming more difficult. It was beginning, also, to be seen that certain of the arguments against toleration might cut both ways. France was an awful example of the results of religious division : it might also be regarded as an example of the result of trying to maintain true religion by force. The effort had all but ruined it ; and now, in the last years of Elizabeth's reign, a toleration settlement had commenced to bring peace and recovery. National unity in religion might strengthen the national front against foreign enemies. But it had begun to be doubtful whether the effort to maintain it might not prove to be more weakening than mere disagreements about religion themselves could be.

It is, accordingly, towards the end of Elizabeth's reign that we find the most striking manifestations of a tendency in the direction of a general religious toleration. It is a somewhat striking fact that, in 1601, a partial and conditional toleration of Catholic worship was being projected. ' I muse they are so senseless,' Father John Mush had written in 1599, ' as not to think upon some toleration with conditions.' [1] Bancroft, Bishop of London since 1597, was actually thinking upon that very thing. He had come to the conclusion that the mass of the Catholic laity and secular priests in England would be willing to forswear belief in the Papal claim to depose Princes or interfere with a succession to a crown, in return for a measure of toleration. With a view to bringing about such a compromise he was negotiating in 1601 with the heads of the anti-Jesuit party. This would, in his opinion, have secured the loyalty of the mass of English Catholics and rid the country of a real danger. We are not concerned here in any way with the question of policy : what has to be noticed is that a mere question of policy it was. Bancroft saw no theoretical objection to such an expedient arrangement. But this was to say that the Crown was free to tolerate two religions in the realm ; and if two, then more than two. Whatever motive induced Elizabeth finally to refuse to accept Bancroft's suggestion, it

---

[1] Quoted in Law's *Jesuits and Seculars*, 1889. Mush was a missioner from the English college at Rome.

certainly was not the sense of an obligation to make no terms with idolaters.

But the most important illustrations of a tendency as yet still feeble, are to be found, towards the end of Elizabeth's reign, in the writings of Hooker and in a remarkable pamphlet by Edwin Sandys.

§ 2. HOOKER

Hooker made no direct pronouncement as to how such as stray from truth should be dealt with. One feels, in reading him, that had the correction of them been left to him, it would have been of the mildest character. But the manner in which he identifies Church and Commonwealth and his conception of positive law, made it impossible for him to say that rebels against the system of the national Church should not be punished. To say that Parliament hath competent authority ' to define of our churches regiment ',[1] is not, indeed, the same as saying that Parliament is competent to decide questions of faith. But though Hooker denied that power to ' decide the questions which rise about matters of faith ' belonged to the sovereign in his own proper person,[2] he did not deny that it belonged to the Crown in Parliament.

No man, he declared, can have a right to defy the determinations of national authority on the strength of alleged special enlightenment in himself or in another.[3] ' Neither wish we,' he wrote, ' that men should do anything which in their hearts they are persuaded they ought not to do.' [4] It is never allowable to obey a command clearly contrary to the law of God. But unless a man can prove to demonstration that he is right, he has no right to disobey on that ground.

' An argument necessary and demonstrative is such, as being proposed unto any man and understood, the mind cannot choose but inwardly assent. Any one such reason dischargeth, I grant, the conscience and setteth it at full liberty.' But ' is it meet that when publicly things are received and have taken place, general obedience thereunto should cease to be exacted, in case this or that private person, led with some probable conceit, should make open protestation, Peter or John disallow them and pronounce them naught ? ' [5]

It is sometimes better, he added, that an erroneous judgement should be accepted than that contention should arise. Only the loyal acceptance of the final judgement of national authority can lead to peace.

Peter and John, therefore, according to Hooker, had clearly no positive right to air their religious views on all occasions. And yet, if we do not wish that they should do anything that they are persuaded in their hearts they should not do, how are we to correct their vagaries ? They may be persuaded in their hearts that they ought not to keep

[1] *Eccles. Pol.*, Bk. VIII, 6, p. 411.   [2] Ib., Bk. VIII, 1.
[3] Ib., Bk. V, 10.   [4] Ib., Preface, 6.   [5] Ib., Preface, 6.

silence.[1] Hooker was clear that to reason must be the final appeal. ' It is not required,' he wrote, ' nor can be exacted at our hands that we should yield unto anything other assent than such as doth answer the evidence which is to be had of that we assent unto.' [2] Peter and John then, it appears, must be reasoned with. If they continue to refuse assent, how can we exact obedience from them or for what can we punish them, unless for their stupidity ?

Hooker could, partially at least, have escaped from his logical difficulties, by saying that though law made should be obeyed, law limiting the liberty of man's religious consciousness should not be made. He never did say this ; but it seems that any man seriously influenced by his writings would be likely to come to some such conclusion. Heretics, he says, embrace ' the very principles ' of Christianity and ' err only by misconstruction '. No one except such as are not Christians, is altogether outside the Church.[3] The Church of Rome is not antichristian ; it is a true Church. He argued elaborately, in a famous sermon, that Roman Catholics and even an honest Pope, might be saved.[4] The conclusion of that sermon is finely characteristic.

' Ye are not now to learn that as of itself it is not hurtful, so neither should it be to any scandalous or offensive in doubtful cases, to hear the different judgments of men. Be it that Cephas hath one interpretation and Apollos hath another ; that Paul is of this mind, that Barnabas of that ; if this offend you, the fault is yours. Carry peaceable minds and you may have comfort by this variety. Now the God of peace give you peaceable minds and turn it to your everlasting comfort.'

Hooker might, consistently, have said that men should be left free to come honestly to such conclusions as they could : he did, in fact, almost say so. But he did not think that men should be allowed to adopt any conclusions they pleased. He makes a distinction ideally valid but practically impossible to work with. It seemed clear to him that, through ignorance and vanity, through prejudice derived illogically from association, through partisan passion, and desire for domination and from yet meaner motives, men were asserting against the determinations of public authority, opinions either demonstrably false or at best only probably true. He could not admit their right to do so.

' The public power of all societies,' he wrote, ' is above every soul contained in the same societies. And the principal use of that power is to give laws unto

---

[1] Cartwright had headed his Second Reply to Whitgift with the words : ' Ye that are the Lord's remembrancers keep not silence.'

[2] *Eccles. Pol.*, II, 7, p. 323.   [3] Ib., III, 1.

[4] *A Learned Discourse of Justification.* The proposition aroused the astonished indignation of Walter Travers, the Puritan, who in his *Supplication made to the Councell* in 1586, described it as ' absurd '.

all that are under it ; which laws in such case we must obey, unless there be reason showed which may necessarily inforce that the Law of Reason or of God doth enjoin the contrary. Because except our own private and but probable resolutions be by the law of public determinations overruled, we take away all possibility of sociable life in the world.' [1]

Loyalty to the society in which and by which we live, demands that in things indifferent, or uncertain, we shall accept its decrees. A man who without demonstrative reason, refuses to do so, is punishable justly ; and this cannot be denied, without also denying that there is any human power to make law.

This great thinker knew that the final appeal must be to human reason and not to law. He believed that human reason could establish certainties on the basis of a belief in the Christian revelation. Those certainties might be few : he was aware that on most contraverted questions no demonstration was possible. He was ready, therefore, to allow and even to approve of large differences of opinion. He had freed himself from any inclination to ascribe wickedness to those who disagreed with him. What he was not ready to allow of, was rebellion against the determinations of public authority on questions concerning which no demonstration was possible. Controversy over such questions seemed to him worse than useless : its effect was merely to increase unbelief. ' There can come nothing of contention,' he said, ' but the mutual waste of the parties contending, till a common enemy dance in the ashes of both.' [2] Yet he declared that it should not be exacted of any man that he should give his assent to propositions not justified to his reason by the evidence. To say that was, in effect, to say that the body politic had no right to impose opinions concerning religion upon anyone. But Hooker's distinction between reasonable and unreasonable opinion and his failure to see that practically there was no way of drawing a line between them, prevented him from drawing that conclusion. That failure was characteristic : he believed too much in human reason. He did not, therefore, see his way to advocating complete legal toleration in religion. But his whole attitude suggested it. He saw truth in all religions and good in all seeking after truth. He knew that men should not do things which they were convinced they ought not to do and that they should not perjure themselves by saying they believed what they did not believe. Any man deeply influenced by his teaching was likely to come to the conclusion he had just failed to reach.

§ 3. EDWIN SANDYS

Edwin Sandys, a son of the Archbishop of York, had been a pupil of Hooker's at Corpus Christi, Oxford, and later maintained close relations with his old tutor. In 1593 he and George Cranmer, another

---

[1] *Eccles. Pol.*, Bk. I, 16, pp. 281, 282.   [2] *Discourse of Justification.*

favourite pupil of Hooker, started on a grand tour on the Continent. Sandys travelled in France, Italy and Germany and did not return to England till 1599. Apparently he brought home with him the manuscript of his *Relation of the State of Religion*.[1]

In this remarkable essay Sandys does not appear as an advocate of the legal toleration of different religions. He did not see any clear need of such a recognition of hopeless division. What he hoped to forward was the coming of rational agreement about religion and the acceptance of differences of opinion in a rational charity. His hope of so happy a consummation was but very faint; but at least he hoped to show that the mutual hatred of rival churches was founded on ignorance, prejudice and passion. He was convinced that the desire of the sects to destroy or disable each other was unchristian and irrational. His travels on the Continent had, no doubt, taught him much; his intercourse with Hooker had taught him more.

Sandys saw Europe and the countries of Europe divided by religious feuds, so fierce that everywhere public order was, at least, menaced. Everywhere Catholics anathematized Protestants and Protestants reviled Catholics and each other. Such feuds had already broken up Germany and almost ruined France. It seemed to Sandys that there was little rational basis for these devastating divisions and none for the passions generated in connection with them. Roman Catholicism, he pointed out, so far from being antichristian, is a religion with excellent points and essentially Christian. He had been struck by what he saw of Catholic devoutness in Italy and by its effects on character and conduct, in spite of what he regarded as the idolatry involved. He expressed a sense of the practical value of the Catholic system of confession and penance and could almost wish to see it adopted in 'reformed' churches.[2] 'Conscience,' he remarked, 'in what religion soever, doth ever in the mists of error breed an honestness of mind and integrity of life in whom it settleth, of so divine and pure virtue is the love of the Creator, which is the ground of all that merit the name of religion.'[3]

But Roman Catholicism is arrogantly dogmatic and intolerant. The Roman Church claims infallibility and regards all outside its own communion as lost souls. Catholics are forbidden to pray with

---

[1] *A Relation of the State of Religion and with what Hopes and Fears it hath been framed and is maintained in the severall States of these Western parts of the World.* Written in 1599 and dedicated to Whitgift: published 1605 without the sanction of the author, who obtained its suppression. A copy in the British Museum has corrections in his handwriting. A new edition was published in 1629 under the title *Europae Speculum* and was three times reprinted before 1640. In 1625 had appeared an Italian translation, with some additions, by Paolo Sarpi: a French translation was made from this in 1626. A Dutch translation, suggested by Grotius, was published in 1675.

[2] *Relation of the State of Religion*, 1638, p. 30.　　　　[3] Ib., p. 254.

Protestants, though both pray to the same God. They may not even say the Lord's Prayer together or so much as a grace before meat.[1] Catholics are forbidden to read Protestant writings, and the result is that never a Catholic ' conceiveth rightly of any almost of the Protestant positions '.[2] And the Protestant attitude is almost, if not quite, as absurd. Each side habitually and grossly exaggerates the misdeeds of the other and the importance of its errors. Both sides completely ignore what they have in common. They read each other's writings, if at all, not to find points of agreement but to pick holes and to detect falsehoods. Both sides write in hatred and passion and freely and absurdly attribute to each other sheer malice and wickedness. ' How can these courses stand with the principles and rules of that religion, whose root is Truth, whose branches are Charity, whose fruits are good deeds ? ' [3] Than such passions there is ' no such enemy to the finding out of truth '.[4] On both sides we find the controversialists ' preferring their third rate syllogisms to the peace of the Church and the happiness of the world '.[5] The Protestants are as dogmatic as the Catholics.

' Let them look with the eye of charity upon them as well as of severity, and they shall find in them some excellent orders for government, some singular helps for an increase of godliness and devotion . . . and contrariwise in themselves, looking with a more single and less indulgent eye than they do, they shall find that there is no such absolute and unreprovable perfection in their doctrine and reformation as some dreamers . . . do fancy. Neither ought they to think it strange they should be amiss in anything, but rather a very miracle if they were not so in many.' [6]

Reason suggests that on many points of religious controversy no certainty is attainable. Wise and ' moral ' men ' think not these diversities of opinion of any such moment, as that they ought to disjoin those who, in the love of God, in the belief of the fundamental articles of the Christian faith, in integrity of life and honesty of conversation . . . remain united '.[7]

All through the essay the question is put as one for all Western Christendom. Nowhere does Sandys refer to the particular circumstances existing in his own country. ' The greatest desire I have in the world,' he wrote, ' is to see Christendom reunited in the badge of their profession . . . and that without the ruin and subversion of either part.' [8] Unity in essentials, it is implied, substantially exists already : it needs only to be recognized. The problem is how to

[1] Ib., p. 149.   [2] Ib., p. 151.   [3] Ib., 1638 ed., p. 156.
[4] Ib., 1638 ed., p. 116.   [5] Ib., 1638 ed., p. 248.
[6] Ib., 1638 ed., p. 282.
[7] Ib., 1638 ed., p. 262. Precisely the same practical conclusion was reached in the *Heptaplomeres* : except that Bodin went further and left out, as needless, any belief in the Christian faith.
[8] Ib., 1638 ed., p. 288.

induce the churches to recognize their essential unity and crediting
each other at least with honest intent, to agree to differ on what is
not fundamental. From the European point of view the greatest
obstacle in the way consists in the uncompromising attitude of the
Roman Church and its arrogant claims. He proceeds to make a
suggestion that he might have found in More's *Utopia*. If the Catholics

'should but join with the Protestants in such service of God as are allowed by
both, this concurring with them in some actions might abate the utter dislike
which they have now of their whole way. . . . For factions, as by disparity
they are raised, so by strangeness they are continued and grow immortal, whereas,
contrariwise, they are slaked and made calmer by intercourse, by parley they are
reconciled, by familiarity they are extinguished.' [1]

But that any kind of unity or agreement could actually be brought
about Sandys had no real hope. Argument, he points out, is altogether
unavailing. Neither side will argue except in the hope of completely
converting the other.[2] A union in charity is conceivable ; but charity
is just what is lacking. Compromise is impossible, for the Roman
Church will certainly not compromise, even if other churches would
consent to do so. Compromise is impossible unless, indeed, it were
forced on all churches alike by the concerted action of the governments
of Christendom. There exists in Christendom a common basis of
belief and upon this Sandys suggests a church might be constructed
' to be established so universally in all Christian dominions, that this
all Christians should necessarily hold '.[3] The construction of such
a truly Catholic Church might conceivably be the work of a General
Council. But, this being impracticable, ' it remains that Princes take
the matter in hand and constrain the Pope and others to yield to
some accord '.[4] Such action would be supported everywhere by all
moderate persons ' who affect a quiet world and peace above glorious
troubles ',[5] and would relieve governments themselves of great part
of their difficulties. But this, he confesses, is a mere ' cabinet discourse of speculative consideration ' : it is useless to put your trust
in Princes.

' Take them as they are and as they are like to be, being brought up in the
midst of their factions and their flatteries where they seldom hear truth . . . the
world may hold itself reasonably happy and content if the civil state be upheld
in any tolerable terms and not think that they should care greatly for reforming
the church and much less for the uniting of the State Ecclesiastical, the dissen-
tions whereof daily serve so many men's turn.' [6]

Thus the conclusion is reached : our hope must be that God will
effect what to man's wit seems impossible and ' extend his compas-

---

[1] *A Relation*, 1638 ed., p. 152.　　　　[2] Ib., 1638 ed.
[3] Ib., 1638 ed., p. 285.　　　　　　　　 [4] Ib., 1638 ed., p. 293.
[5] Ib., 1638 ed., p. 263.　　　　　　　　 [6] Ib., 1638 ed., p. 294.

sionable and helping hand over his miserable, defiled, disgraced Church, persecuted abroad and persecuting herself at home '.[1]

It was, presumably, a result of his continental experience, that Sandys wrote as though the question were essentially one of the reunion of Christendom. It was hardly worth while to point out that that was impossible. But for all his talk about reunion, his essay was in the main simply a plea for the making on all sides of reasonable admissions. He asked that it should be recognized that true Christians might honestly and rationally differ on every controverted question of the moment and that, so much being undemonstrable, to claim sole possession of saving truth was radically absurd. He asked that the churches should give each other credit for a sincere endeavour to compass truth. The tolerance for which he pleaded was an attitude of mind ; and its general adoption would have made legal toleration a matter of course. Though Sandys did not advocate mere legal toleration, he had gone to the root of the matter. It was just the refusal to make reasonable admissions that constituted the difficulty.

There were two things that Sandys was not prepared to tolerate. One was, apparently, the expression of views positively anti-Christian ; the other was the arrogant claims that made toleration impossible. But all through the treatise it is clearly implied that it is not the business of governments to maintain by force any one form of Christianity. It is, rather, the business of governments to compel the sects to respect each other. Sandys seems to have perceived, what was certainly the fact, that it was not governments that insisted on persecuting. What made it difficult or impossible for governments to be tolerant was the refusal of the sects either to tolerate or merely to be tolerated. He rightly put the problem as one, not of how to induce governments to tolerate sects, but of how to induce sects to tolerate each other.

Mere legal ' toleration ' may express mere indifference to religion or it may be a counsel of despair. It does not necessarily imply the existence of such toleration as that of Sandys. It does not involve the general acceptance of anything that can be called a principle. Sandys was no prophet : the tolerance he pleaded for remained and remains uncommon. His treatise, nevertheless, foreshadowed, for England, the controversy of the seventeenth century. But its bearing on the actual situation in England was only indirect. Later, during his honourable career as a Parliament man under James I, Sandys exhibited a pronounced hostility to Catholicism. It is possible that the life of practical politics blunted the fine edge of his perceptions and weakened his grasp of principle. But even in 1599 he had seen Catholicism as the chief obstacle to that union in reasonable charity that he desired. What he hated in Romanism was its intolerance. He was right in thinking that it was not the attitude of governments

[1] Ib., 1638 ed., p. 309.

so much as the attitude of religious bodies that needed changing ; but he was wrong if he supposed that, in England, Catholicism was the main obstacle. Perhaps it was so on the Continent : it was not so in England. Nor was it the doctrine of royal supremacy that barred the way. Whatever James I might think or intend, the Crown in England was in no sense logically bound to the maintenance by force of any form of religion. For England, apart from a general reluctance to make necessary admissions, it was Puritan idealism and the idealism later represented by Laud, that blocked the road to legal toleration.

CHAPTER X

THEORIES OF THE CONSTITUTION AND OF SOVEREIGNTY

§ 1. BEGINNINGS

BEFORE the reign of Elizabeth English thought seems to have concerned itself very little with questions as to the nature of political authority or with questions as to what sovereignty is or where it should, or does, reside. The earlier writers, almost all of them, were content to say vaguely that constituted authority was ordained of God. They insisted on the duty of obedience to it and they discussed the relation of the Prince to the Pope or to the Church. Some concerned themselves with the conception of society as a co-operative association for common welfare in a form ordained by God. They denounced social abuses and suggested remedies, but usually took the government for granted. Even under Elizabeth, controversy turned mainly on the meaning and implications of Royal Supremacy in ecclesiastical causes. Indeed, for the first twenty years of her reign, writers on politics were concerned with little else. A change begins to be discernible about 1580.

Argument in favour of monarchy as the best and most natural form of government is to be found, however, under the earlier Tudors. But there was then neither much of it nor much in it. It is to be found in the strangely popular work of Sir Thomas Elyot, entitled *The Governour*.[1] Elyot regarded aristocracy and democracy as alike tending naturally to disorder. 'The best and most sure governance is by one king or prince, which ruleth only for the weal of his people.' This was not saying much : Elyot was aware that his good Prince might not be easy to find. Indeed, his book, like many others in the sixteenth century, was chiefly concerned with the formidable list of admirable qualities required to make a good Prince. The demand

---

[1] Elyot (1490 c.–1546) held various more or less important official posts at one time or another and twice served as ambassador to Charles V. He produced a number of moralizing works and a Latin-English Dictionary. *The Boke named the Governour* was published in 1531 and was frequently reprinted up to 1580. It was dedicated to Henry VIII. Elyot borrowed freely from Patrizi's *De Regno et Regis Institutione* and from the *Institutio* of Erasmus.

for so many virtues might well have induced scepticism of the value
of princely government actually and in general. But Sir Thomas
seems to have felt no doubt. Nor is his argument, if it can be called
one, merely utilitarian. He suggests that the constitution of the
heavenly hierarchy and that of the beehive, afford ground for thinking
that monarchy is the best form of government. But, like Starkey
and most of the other writers of his time, he was more preoccupied
with the constitution of society than with the constitution of government. 'The public weal,' he wrote, 'is a body living, compact or
made up of sundry estates and degrees of men, which is disposed by
the order of equity and governed by the rule and moderation of
reason.'[1] Public order, he insisted, is founded on 'faith', not, that
is, religious faith, but fidelity to contract and to law. 'Without
faith a public weal may not continue. . . . Since faith is the
foundation of justice, which is the chief constitution and maker of a
public weal, faith is the conservator of the same.'[2] The most
important thing, in fact, about a public weal is not the form of its
government.

Less typical than Elyot's was the attitude of William Thomas,
another official personage, who served as Clerk of the Council under
Edward VI.[3] Discussing the question 'whether it be better for a
commonwealth that the power be in the nobility or in the commonalty',
he concluded that, of the two, it had better be in the nobility,
but that it were still better vested in a Prince. 'He that hath,
thinketh he cannot safely enjoy his own if he get no more; and he
that hath not must of necessity seek to have.'[4] The antagonism
between these desires he saw as a difficulty only to be overcome by
the supremacy of a Prince. Still more sure was he that the rule of
the commonalty is the worst possible. 'The multitude utterly knoweth
nothing.' It is fickle and passionate; 'if they once attain the power,
they destroy both the nobility and themselves'; wherefore 'it is
impossible any estate should long prosper where the power is in the
commonalty'.[5] The tyranny of a Prince is more tolerable than any
other; and a good Prince will protect his commons against the tyranny
of nobles, even while not allowing them so much 'as to talk of the
Prince's causes and of the reason of laws'.[6] All this is commonplace.
What really distinguishes Thomas is that his writings contain no
reference to the law of nature or to the Scriptures and the fact that

[1] *The Governour*, ed. 1880, I, p. 1.   [2] Ib., II, p. 258.
[3] Thomas lived for some time in Italy, made translations from Italian and
himself published in Italian a book in defence of Henry VIII. His essays,
written for the edification of Edward VI, remained unpublished till 1774. He
was hanged for connection with Wyatt's rebellion in 1554.
[4] *A discourse made for the King's use whether it be better, etc.* In Strype,
Memorials, II, 2, App. Works, 1774.
[5] Ib., Works, 1774, p. 165.   [6] Ib., p. 169.

he was not thinking merely of England. He treats the question of the best form of government as one of practical expediency only. This much he may have learned from Machiavelli, to whom he frequently refers. He had certainly studied both the *Discorsi* and the Prince. He drew up a list of eighty-five questions which he offered to elucidate for the benefit of Edward VI ; and the bulk of these are simply formed from the chapter headings of the Prince and the *Discorsi*.[1] It is, however, quite inaccurate to say that he represents the views of Machiavelli. His practical conclusion was the reverse of that reached by Machiavelli in the *Discorsi* and his attitude generally is Italianate rather than Machiavellian. He insisted on the need, on occasion, of craft in practical politics ; but he disclaimed any wish to defend the doing of what is really wrong. ' He is to be esteemed,' he remarks, ' the wisest and happiest man that, in proceeding, maketh least discords with time.' The Prince must trim his sails to the wind, altering as the occasion requireth ; but, ' I mean not that any man should vary in amity, turn from virtue to vice or alter in any such thing as requireth constancy '.[2] Like others, he saw in Machiavelli only what he wanted.[3] The views of Thomas were probably shared by many ; those of Elyot are more representative, as the popularity of his book seems to testify. But the writings of neither have any great significance. English thought was hardly as yet concerning itself with the questions they suggested.

From the time of Edward VI to the year 1581 almost all writers who dealt in any sense with political problems were either preoccupied with the Church or with the evils of ' usury ' or were merely repeating the old formulæ about the wickedness of rebellion. The *De Republica Anglorum* of Sir Thomas Smith is an exception and is by far the weightiest pronouncement of those years that is unconcerned with the Church. Next to it in weight and significance is the Homily of 1571.

It is a little difficult to characterize the change of direction that occurred in English thought in the later years of Elizabeth's reign without exaggeration of its extent and import. People, we may say, began to speculate about the origin of political authority and the nature of political obligation, about the question as to the ideally best form of government and the question as to where sovereignty lay in England and how much was involved in it. It does not seem, however, that there was much such speculation till the last years of

---

[1] They may be read in Strype, *Memorials*, II, Pt. I. In his *History of Italy* Thomas relied entirely on Machiavelli for the story of Florence.

[2] Whether it be expedient to vary with time. Works, p. 134.

[3] The earliest reference to Machiavelli in English writing appears to occur in a letter written from Padua in 1525 to Cromwell. See J. W. Horrocks : *Machiavelli in Tudor Opinion and Discussion*, 1908.

the reign. What there was of it, also, if we put aside Hooker, was timid and inconclusive and more or less incoherent. But before the end of the reign attempts were made to prove that monarchy is the best form of government and peculiarly in harmony with nature. It was even suggested that monarchy is the only form of government that can be regarded as definitely ordained of God. Along with this went an apparently increasing disposition to say that the Prince is accountable to God only for his actions. That, of course, had been said earlier ; it was said now with a more definite suggestion that whatever limits to the Prince's right may ·be imposed by laws of God or of nature, it is not limited by human law or by any institution. We may, perhaps, say that out of the earlier Tudor doctrine of the duty of obedience and the conception of royal supremacy in the Church, there was being evolved a theory of absolute monarchy. After 1580 the influence of Bodin becomes marked and may have been partly responsible for a tendency to attribute unlimited powers to the sovereign monarch. But, on the other hand, not a single English writer of the reign of Elizabeth does actually claim unlimited powers for the monarch. The only writer of English who does so is King James VI of Scotland. English thought was not really moving in the direction of a belief in absolute monarchy. There was a certain tendency in that direction ; but counter tendencies also were gathering strength.

It was in 1581 that appeared a book by a certain Charles Merbury which, though trivial and confused, was the first English writing to show the influence of Bodin and marks a new departure.[1] It would seem, indeed, that the publication of Bodin's *Republic* in 1576 must be seriously regarded as one cause of the new directions taken by thought in England towards the end of Elizabeth's reign.

Merbury discussed the question as to the best form of government and dealt, incidentally and confusedly, with the question of what is implied in sovereignty. He admitted that there existed three types of well-ordered commonwealths. An oligarchic kind of democracy, in which ' a number of good men and men of reasonable wealth do jointly bear rule together ', or an aristocracy of ' a few of the best and choicest persons ', may both be decently successful. His reasons for concluding that monarchy is better than either, appear to be reasons of expediency only, though it can hardly be said that he gives any. But he insists, using Bodin's terms, that, in a monarchy, the Prince must possess what is called in Latin *majestas* and in French *souveraineté*, that is, ' power full and perpetual over all his subjects in general

---

[1] *A Briefe Discourse of Royall Monarchie as of the best Common Weale.* ' Monarchie royale ' is a term used by Bodin of a certain type of monarchy. Merbury states that at the time his little book was published, he had recently returned from France.

and over every one in particular'.[1] ' Neither is he countable of such his government saving to God and his conscience.' Nobles and ' estates ' in a monarchy can only have a ' voice deliberative '. All this looks as though it were taken straight from Bodin, but if Merbury had really read the *Republic* he had not, it would seem, understood it. At most he took from Bodin only what he could fit in with English custom. Bodin had seen the power of making law as the essence of sovereignty : Merbury's ' full and perpetual power ' did not, apparently, include any power to make law. He evidently regarded England as a monarchy : yet ' our Prince,' he says, ' is subject unto laws both civil and common, to customs, privileges, covenants and all kinds of promises, so far forth as they are agreeable unto the law of God '.[2] He speaks of ' his power and authority in allowing and disallowing of matters propounded to be laws ',[3] with the clearest implication that the Prince cannot make law himself of his sole authority. Merbury copied from Bodin and left out the main point. His feeble book is but slightly indicative even of a tendency.

The tendency to see in monarchy the one form of government that is ' natural ' and approved by God, and the tendency to suggest or even positively to assert that the rights of the sovereign monarch are unlimited by human law or institution, found definite literary expression only late in Elizabeth's reign. The publication of Doleman's *Conference* in 1594 provoked replies of great significance. That of Peter Wentworth, published in 1598, is comparatively very unimportant. But in 1603 Sir John Hayward published an *Answer* which, I think, expressed the views of a large number of people at the time and certainly a view very widespread later. About the same time the Scottish lawyer Sir Thomas Craig produced a somewhat remarkable book in the same general sense, which seems never to have been published as written. And in 1598 appeared King James's *Trew Law of Free Monarchies*, which, written in Scotland, expressed a certain tendency of English thought in an extreme form. None of these writings has any value as philosophy ; none of them presents a distinct and coherent theory. It is hard to know in what order it is best to deal with them. Hayward is especially interesting because he expresses to a very large extent the views of Royalists pamphleteers of the period of the coming Civil War. The book of King James is interesting, I think, chiefly, because of the contrast it offers to the views of Hayward and Craig. It is only by comparison that the significance of these writers in English thought can really be extracted. Hayward and Craig must be compared with Doleman on one side and with King James on the other. On the whole I think it will be most convenient for purposes of comparison to deal first with the views of King James.

---

[1] *Briefe Discourse*, 1581, pp. 40, 41.   [2] Ib., 1581, p. 44.   [3] Ib., p. 51.

§ 2. KING JAMES OF SCOTLAND

The *Trew Law of Free Monarchies* was published in 1598.[1] It is significant that the only writings in English of the period of the reign of Elizabeth that definitely formulate a doctrine of absolute monarchy, were written by a Scot in Scotland and by a man who suffered from the drawback of being himself a King. They cannot be taken as representing the views of any considerable number of people either in England or Scotland. They represent rather the sort of view that was beginning to be dominant in France. But it may be remarked that King James gave to Elizabethan official phraseology a meaning that for the mass of English people it had never had. In a royal declaration, issued in 1585, Elizabeth had spoken of Princes as ' not bound to yield account or render the reasons of their actions to any others but to God '; and of herself as holding dominion ' immediately of the same almighty Lord and so therefore accountable only to his Divine Majesty '.[2] That the monarch in England was not personally accountable for his actions to anyone was matter of English law, and no one denied it. To say that he held his throne immediately of God was a comforting assurance of the absolute independence of the nation. The phrase expressed for the mass of Englishmen not the absolutism of the monarch, but the ' absolutism ' of the nation. When King James founded on the familiar phrases conclusions they would logically bear, he was listened to with astonished resentment. That, nevertheless, the *Trew Law* expressed a real tendency of thought in England is shown by the readiness with which its doctrine was taken up and further expounded immediately after 1603. The view expressed by James affords, too, a significant contrast with the far more typically English view that was expressed by Hayward.

The views of King James perhaps underwent some alteration after his coming to England; and certainly the *Trew Law* should be read in connection with his published speeches. But it is impossible by any process to extract from his writings and speeches any distinct theory either of Kingship or of the State. Indefinitely he may have been influenced by what he knew of the writers of France of the later sixteenth century. He seems to have got something from Blackwood and something from Barclay. He may have derived suggestions from Bodin. If so, he only half understood them: his view is quite

---

[1] It was of course included in the complete edition of the works of King James in 1616. An earlier written work of James, the *Basilicon Doron*, had expressed the same sense of divinity in Kings that we find in the *Trew Law*; but need not be particularly considered, since it expresses nothing else and that only fragmentarily.

[2] *A declaration of the causes moving the Queene of England to give aid to the defence of the people afflicted and oppressed in the Low Countries.* October, 1585. Printed in Holinshed, III, 1587.

unlike that of Bodin.   Much of what he had to say is merely rhetorical and conveys little but his sense of his own importance.   He was fond of argumentation and prided himself on his cleverness in dialectic ; a sure sign, this, of the second rate.   But there is little argument in the *Trew Law*, and what there is, is singularly futile.   That the book expresses a tendency rather than a theory should be evident to anyone who reads it carefully.

In early ages, James admits, men sometimes chose kings for themselves.   ' Yet these examples,' he declares, ' are nothing pertinent to us,' because our kingdom of Scotland ' began in a far contrary fashion '.[1]   The kingdom of Scots was, it appears, founded by a certain Fergus, who came out of Ireland with a great number with him and made himself master of the country,. till then inhabited only by a few barbarians.   From this fact James draws the astonishing conclusion that

' the kings therefore in Scotland were before any estates or ranks of men within the same, before any Parliaments were holden or laws made ;   and by them was the land distributed, which at the first was whole theirs, states erected and discerned and forms of government devised and established.   And so it follows, of necessity. that the kings were the authors and makers of the laws and not the laws of the kings.' [2]

The argument is historical if anything ; but it is hard to see what meaning James can have given his words.   Was Fergus a King before he came to Scotland ?   How came it that his followers recognized the conquered land as belonging ' whole ' to Fergus ?   Did the invaders bring with them no sort of law ?   If Fergus were an absolute monarch before he left Ireland, then the origin of his monarchy was wholly independent of his conquest of Scotland.   These questions are, of course, only worth asking because James should have asked them himself.   That he did not do so leaves his assertions meaningless.

James seems to conceive the King of Scotland as primarily an owner by conquest.   But apparently he owns not only the land but the people who live on it.   ' As ye see it manifest that the King is over-lord of the whole land ; so is he Master over every person that inhabiteth the same, having power over the life and death of every one of them.' [3]   Can this power be derived from his ownership of the land ?   Or was it recognized from the first in Fergus : and if so, why ?   A just King, says James, will not take the lives of his subjects without a clear law ; ' yet the same laws whereby he taketh them were made by himself or by his predecessors '.[4]   He is not bound by the law ' but of his good will '.[5]   We begin to see that Fergus has

---

[1] *Trew Law.   Political Works of James I.*   Harvard Press, 1918, p. 61.   My references are all to this edition.

[2] Ib., Works, p. 62.   [3] Ib., Works, p. 63.

[4] Ib., p. 63.   [5] Ib., p. 63.

really nothing to do with the matter and that the argument is not historical. Vaguely James conceived that an unlimited authority over persons and property might be and had been established in Kings by conquest : that successful wars of conquest had led somehow to the recognition of unbounded authority in a monarch. Still more vaguely he conceived that there must be, somewhere, in all societies, a law-making power without assignable limit, an unrestricted right to command involving obligation to obey. But he states no such proposition. That England and Scotland are ' free monarchies ' and that in them such power lies with the King, he asserts quite clearly. But his attempted explanation of the assumed fact is feeble and incoherent. He really does nothing but emphasize in every way that occurs to him the idea of an unlimited royal authority.

'Kings are justly called Gods,' he said in a speech in Parliament in 1609, 'for that they exercise a manner or resemblance of Divine power upon earth. For if you will consider the attributes to God, you shall see how they agree in the person of a King. God hath power to create or destroy, make or unmake at his pleasure, to give life or send death, to judge all and to be judged or accountable to none : to raise low things and to make high things low at his pleasure, and to God are both soul and body due. And the like power have Kings : they make and unmake their subjects : they have power of raising and casting down : of life and of death : judges over all their subjects and in all causes and yet accountable to none but God only. They have power to exalt low things and abase high things and make of their subjects like men at the chess.' [1]

It would seem to be implied that wherever monarchy exists, this is the King's position. But actually James never committed himself to that assertion. He is doing little more than claim an unlimited authority for himself, first as King in Scotland, then as King in England.

A King's power resembles that of God : but, so far, no connection has been shown, or even asserted, to exist between the King's power and Divine will. But an attempt to connect them is made. God instituted monarchy among the Jews and gave Saul power to act tyrannically and to his people no right to depose or resist him. That ancient Jewish monarchy ' ought to be a pattern to all Christian and well-founded monarchies '.[2] No Christian people nowadays ought to ' claim to that unlawful liberty which God refused to his own peculiar and chosen people '. So it appears, after all, in spite of the earlier assertion that absolute monarchy in Scotland originated in conquest, that the King is to be obeyed, not as the successor of Fergus or of William the Conqueror, but because his commands are ' the commands of God's minister ' and because he is a Judge ' set by God over them having power to judge them, but to be judged only of God '.[3] It is a matter of course, then, that active resistance to the

---

[1] Speech of 21st March, 1609. Works, pp. 307, 308.
[2] *Trew Law.* Works, p. 59.   [3] Ib., p. 61.

King is always wicked. James felt himself logically entitled to go further.

‘ It is atheism and blasphemy to dispute what God can do : good Christians content themselves with his will revealed in his word. So it is presumption and high contempt in a subject, to dispute what a king can do or say that a king cannot do this or that ; but rest in that which is the king’s revealed will in his law.’ [1]

Yet, except that God established an unlimited monarchical authority among the Jews and that the Scriptures consistently forbid rebellion, absolutely no reason is given for these assertions. James is credited, sometimes, with having expounded a theory of the divine right of Kings ; but I do not see in what sense he can be said to have expounded any theory whatever, unless it were a theory of the English, or of the Scottish, constitution. He had really no explanation to offer of what he asserted as a fact. He was, indeed, conscious of the danger of attempts to explain. ‘ That which concerns the mystery of the King’s power,’ he wrote, ‘ is not lawful to be disputed ; for that is to wade into the weakness of Princes and to take away the mystical reverence that belongs unto them that sit in the Throne of God.’ [2]

The words last quoted give the key to his idea and to his attitude. They express his sense that the existence of unlimited monarchical power could not really be explained : it could only be referred to the mysterious will of God. God had willed that it should exist ; he had created it among the Jews and the language of the Scriptures implied always that rebellion against a king is rebellion against God. James did not say or imply that politic society rests on an obligation to obedience that was specially created by God and could nohow otherwise have been created. He did not say that right to command involving obligation to obey had been conferred by God only on patriarchs and Kings. These assertions were suggested in France earlier and in England, in Overrall’s *Convocation Book*, a little later : they were not made in England during the sixteenth century. James had no positive theory : he did not approve of Overrall’s statement of the case and told him that he had ‘ dipped too deep into what all Kings reserve among the arcana imperii ’.[3] He believed that it was a Christian’s duty to accept the fact that God commands unlimited obedience to Kings. But he felt that it was dangerous to pry into the matter and dangerous to attempt definition. That way lay all the heresies. His writings express an unexplained sense of divinity in Kings, but they express no theory of divine right. He was not only a king himself, but he was well aware of the ugly possibilities of argumentation.

---

[1] Speech in Star Chamber, 1616. Works, p. 333.   [2] Ib.
[3] Letter to Abbot, 1606. In Wilkins’ *Concilia*, IV, 405.

§ 3. HAYWARD AND CRAIG

Far more in accord with ordinary English opinion were the views
expressed in Sir John Hayward's *Answer* of 1603.[1] Towards the end
of Elizabeth's life, the question of succession seemed to have become
exceedingly serious. Hayward's main purpose in writing was to show
that James of Scotland had an absolute right to succeed. The same
thesis was elaborately maintained by Sir Thomas Craig in a book
written about the same time, that remained unpublished.[2] Both
deemed it necessary to expound the nature of monarchy in general
and of English monarchy in particular ; and they expressed substantially the same view and used much the same arguments. Both
show clearly the influence of Bodin. The two books together give
very full expression to a view typically English, utilitarian and illogical,
and very widely held in the seventeenth century.

Both Hayward and Craig endeavoured to show that of all possible
forms of sovereignty, that of a single person can alone be called
'natural'. The reasons Hayward gives for thinking so might have
been derived from Bodin. Sovereignty consists in a right to command.
'But obedience cannot be performed where the commandments are
either repugnant or uncertain : neither can these inconveniences be
any ways avoided but by union of the authority which doth command.'[3] If sovereignty belongs to many and the many are knit in
one will, then, indeed, the commands of the sovereign will be neither
inconsistent nor vague. But this is unlikely ; ' and the more they
are who join in government the less natural is their union and the
more subject to dissipation '.[4] A union of many wills, so far from
arising inevitably, that is ' naturally ', is unlikely to occur at all ;
while if very many are concerned, such a union becomes practically
impossible, unnatural, that is, in the highest degree.

Craig argued differently to the same conclusion. He maintained
that, starting with the family, monarchy arose inevitably from the
nature of man, his needs and his associations. ' By the only instinct
of nature, by mere inclination and choice of the mind, men embraced
monarchy for their own safety. . . . Reason which governs in men
aims always at monarchy, as the most certain form of government.'[5]
Aristocracies and democracies are merely accidental results of tyranny

---

[1] *An Answer to the First Part of a certaine Conference concerning Succession.*
[2] This book, originally in Latin, exists only in an English translation published in 1703. *Concerning the Right of Succession to the Kingdom of England* is
the translator's title. The dedication to King James is dated January 1, 1603.
Craig was an eminent lawyer, author of a standard work on Scottish land law,
entitled *Jus Feudale*. Like Hayward's, his book was designed as an answer to
Doleman.
[3] *An Answer*, 1603. I.B.   [4] Ib.
[5] *Concerning the Right of Succession*, 1703, p. 16.

by monarchs and reaction against it. ' Natural ' is that which is absolutely involved in the nature of man and his permanent environment, as monarchy, by Craig, is conceived of as being. But the degeneration of a monarch's rule into tyranny is not ' natural ' but accidental, ' so that these aristocracies and democracies were not instituted from any natural cause '.[1] Hayward pointed out that monarchy is the form of government that has prevailed always almost everywhere in the world. Only in Europe, he says, have other forms been tried in some places, and of these, ' some are already returned to a monarchy and the residue in their time will do the like, even as all others have done which have been before them '.[2] The fact of itself suggests not only that monarchy is ' natural ', but that it is the most practically efficient form of government. The argument was, already, an old one in France.

Hayward argued, not merely that hereditary monarchy is practically by far the best of all forms of monarchy, but that when once it has been established, the right of the heir under the law of succession becomes quite absolute. So sacred is the right of the heir, he declared, and so important is it to all mankind that it should be kept inviolate, that any people that disregards it commits an offence against all other states which affords just ground for war. ' For as in the state any man may accuse upon a public crime, so in the state of the world any people may prosecute a common offence.' [3] The same assertion had been made by John Leslie, Bishop of Ross, writing in 1580 on behalf of the claims of Mary Stewart and her son. Hayward saw, however, a certain difficulty. Rebellion or conquest may result in the displacement of a dynasty : is it to be said that no later king of the new dynasty has any right to command ? His answer was that ' the successors of a usurper by course and compass of time may prescribe a right, if they who have received wrong discontinue both pursuit and claim '.[4] He did not stop to examine the implications of that assertion. Craig argued the question more elaborately but very confusedly. As a lawyer he saw that the main question may be put thus : in an hereditary monarchy can the established law of succession be altered by any enactment ? His answer was that it could not. He seems to have thought that the right of the nearest in blood to inheritance, whether to property or a crown, is quite absolute under ' natural ' law and argues that a statute debarring the rightful heir from succession to a crown would be of the same nature as a statute arbitrarily depriving a man of his inheritance in property. It would be a mere act of robbery and a breach of natural law. Peter Wentworth, in 1598, had argued the matter differently. Parliament, he admitted, may deprive private persons of their property. But, he wrote, ' if

[1] Ib., p. 15.   [2] *An Answer.* I.C.
[3] Ib., I.E.   [4] Ib., 3.

all the people of the whole realm by common and voluntary consent, for themselves and their posterity, do transfer and surrender the government of themselves and their state into the hands of some chosen man, to be governed by him and his heirs for ever, according to such and such laws,'[1] it cannot reasonably be maintained that there remains in anyone a right to alter the arrangement. He concluded definitely that the right of succession is ' a thing impregnable by any Parliament '.[2]

The whole argument, alike of Hayward and of Craig, involves that monarchy is a human institution and ' ordained of God ' only as is everything else. It develops ' naturally ' from human need and its usefulness is its justification. Rebellion against a tyrannical prince, Hayward argued, is never worth while. It is always a crime against society. ' By obedience a few particulars remain in danger; by rebellion, all.'[3] Yet, after all this, he suddenly informs us that ' it is God only who seateth kings in their state ; it is he only who may remove them '.[4] The assertion is not in any way linked with his argument. Confusion is confounded by the remark that any liberty or authority which originally belonged to ' the people ' may be annihilated by common consent or by prescription or by conquest.[5]

With precisely similar inconsistency, after asserting that monarchy is rooted in man's instinct and reason, does Craig declare that ' monarchy was from the beginning of God's appointment and brought in by him as the true expedient for obliging his people to live orderly '.[6] The two assertions might of course be reconciled ; but apparently they were not. In one place Craig tells us that the first Kings ' were chosen' by the consent of the people ' : in another he declares that ' Kings owe it not to the people that they are kings but to God '. He was aware of at least a seeming inconsistency. God, he says, confirmed the arrangements that the people had already made. He does not explain why an institution that arose under God's own law of nature needed any special confirmation or what could be added to it thereby.

Appointed or confirmed by God as he may be, natural and necessary sovereign as he is, the monarch of Hayward and of Craig is far from being an ' absolute ' monarch. Both these writers seem vaguely to conceive that an absolute right to command is needed and that this right cannot be subject to definite limitation ; but they will not accept the consequences. Hayward's language on the subject of the sovereign's powers is indeed less explicit than that of the Scottish lawyer and he uses phrases which might seem to imply the attribution to his Prince of an unlimited authority.

---

[1] *A Discourse containing the Author's opinion of the true and lawful successor to Her Majesty*, 1598, p. 50. It was written as an answer to Doleman in 1594.
[2] Ib., p. 56.   [3] *An Answer.* 4.L.   [4] Ib., 2.
[5] Ib., 1.D.   [6] *Right of Succession*, 1703, p. 10.

'No prince is sovereign who acknowledgeth himself either subject or account-able to any but to God. . . . If a prince doth profess that he will bear him-self regardful of the accomplishment of the laws, he doth not condition or restrain himself . . . being tied thereby to no scanter scope than before . . . the authority ceaseth not if performances do fail.'[1]

For all that, it appears that the sovereignty of a Prince does not, or need not, include any power to make law of his own sole authority. 'Parliaments in all places,' he says, 'have been erected by kings.' But he says also that the manner of law-making is determined 'by the particular laws and customs of every nation, in which the consent of the prince, either secret or express, sometimes only is sufficient, always principally doth concur'.[2]

Hayward may possibly have felt a doubt as to whether his Prince might not be entitled to abolish altogether the Parliament his pre-decessors had erected. Craig, certainly, felt no such doubt. He inclined to the view that, if there be any unlimited sovereignty, it lies only with the Prince 'in the Parliament or Great Court of the Kingdom'. Certainly it is only in Parliament that the Prince is a legislator; 'because otherwise he cannot make a law that obliges the subjects nor impose taxes upon them'.[3] In Britain, he says, 'the Monarchy is tempered with something of Aristocracy and Democ-racy' and no taxes can be imposed 'without public consent'.[4] But, in fact, Craig was very far from asserting the absolutism of the Prince even in Parliament. He raises the question whether the Prince in Parliament can 'by any new statute take away or destroy the common and municipal law of a kingdom'.[5] Not only did he deny flatly that Parliament was competent to empower Henry VIII to settle the succession by will; but he seems to have felt serious doubt how far any law-making power existed at all.[6] Yet Craig was even more emphatic than Hayward in denying to the subject any right of forcible resistance to the King's acts. Kings are accountable to God only and subjects 'may complain to God against the iniquity of their king, but not to any other'.[7] In the passage that immediately follows this remark it seems to be implied that even though the King should slaughter the innocent and spoil his subjects of their goods, there must be no rebellion. The King has no right to tax his subjects 'without public consent', yet, if he 'spoil' them, there is, apparently, no remedy.

It is impossible, Craig argued, rationally to hold that a King is

---

[1] *An Answer*, 5.   [2] Ib., 2.F, p. 39.   [3] *Right of Succession*, p. 123.
[4] Ib., p. 162.   [5] 1 Ib., p. 123.
[6] Craig, in the manner of Bodin, to whom he frequently refers, speaks of 'fundamental laws . . . of the same date and establishment with the king-dom', which can certainly in no case be altered (Chap. 15). But, of course, the phrase is not Craig's, but that of his translator.
[7] *Right of Succession*, p. 189.

subject to deposition on the ground of tyranny. The question who is to try him on such a charge is unanswerable. Nor can the charge even be properly made. To say that the commonwealth itself may accuse and judge its sovereign is absurd ; ' for the commonwealth is only a mute body which can do nothing of itself. If nothing be done until the Commonwealth accuses, all kings may rest securely and without fear on their thrones.' [1] If, for any reason, a King become unpopular, the ' mob ' would always be quick to declare him a tyrant ; and if such a judgemènt should be held to justify rebellion, government would become ineffective and even impossible. No State can be stable or quiet if it be admitted that forcible resistance to the sovereign is ever justified.

If what King James suggested rather than expounded is to be called a theory of the divine right of Kings, then Hayward and Craig were certainly not exponents of that theory. James may be said to have claimed for the King, simply as God's representative, all powers whatever : he can make law of his sole authority, the lives and property of all his subjects lie at his mercy and to question his authority or seek to limit it, is a kind of blasphemy. Yet even James did not really quite say as much as this ; and no one in England, before Elizabeth's death, said anything like it. Hayward and Craig agree that the King is sovereign and that he is God's minister and delegate, accountable to God only, that he may not be resisted or, in any case, deposed. But to them there is nothing really mysterious about kingship. They were at great pains to explain that it arose naturally everywhere in the world, from the needs and the experience of man. They believed that something called sovereignty, concerning which their thought was vague, must be recognized somewhere and is best recognized in a single person. They believed that the English King possessed this sovereignty. But when they sought an explanation they turned to Bodin and not to Barclay. Nor did they accept the doctrine of Bodin. Their sovereignty did not include the power to make law. Their King is not a sovereign in the sense of Bodin.

§ 4. DOLEMAN : AND HAYWARD AND CRAIG

It is a fact that Hayward and Craig agreed far more with their adversary, Doleman, than they did with King James. ' Doleman ', or Robert Parsons, like Hooker, laid down [2] that it was man's natural sociability, added to his feebleness in isolation, that had driven him to create and to accept authority. The institution of government arose inevitably and being from nature is from God. So far he was in fairly exact agreement with Craig and Hayward. But he asserted that no particular form of government was specially of divine insti-

---

[1] *Right of Succession*, p. 16.

[2] *A Conference about the next Succession to the Crowne of England*, 1594.

tution. ' These particular forms are left unto every nation and country to choose that form of government which they shall like best and think most meet for the natures and conditions of their people.' [1] Here, verbally at least, he parts company with them : for they wished to have it both ways. Monarchy, Doleman declared, has been proved by experience to be the best form of government ; but the powers of the monarch should always be limited by law, as in fact they are in England. England is a ' mixed ' monarchy. In this, in spite of his talk about the institution of monarchy by God, Craig agreed with Doleman.

What has to be kept in mind, Doleman argued, is that Kings exist at all, solely for the welfare of their subjects. That being so, if a King do not respect the laws of his monarchy or observe the implied conditions on which his authority is held, he may lawfully be deprived of his crown, ' upon just and urgent causes and by public authority of the whole body '.[2] It is merely absurd to say that authority having been delegated to a King, the people can have no right to take it from him. A commonwealth exists ' for justice and order ' : and no delegation of authority can rationally be conceived except as having strict reference to those ends. The assertion that a King may always do as he wills and that the very property of his subjects really belongs to him, ' overthroweth the whole nature of a commonwealth itself '.[3] If a Prince, he concluded, do not govern religiously, equitably and lawfully, not only may he be deposed but evidently for the salvation of the commonwealth, he ought to be.[4] The same principles apply to the heir to a crown. Laws of succession vary from country to country ; and that fact alone proves that all laws of succession are of merely human origin. No mere law of succession, therefore, can give to anyone an absolute right to succeed. Religion being the most important of all considerations, the lack of religion in an heir at law is the best possible ground for excluding him from succession. For ' no reason or law, religion or wisdom in the world can admit such persons to the government of a commonwealth by whom no good but destruction may be expected to the same '.[5]

There is far less difference between the views of Doleman and those of Craig or of Hayward than either of the latter were willing to admit. To all three monarchy was derived from human need of it. Doleman declares that all forms of government alike develop thus naturally and ' being from nature are from God '. Craig asserts that only monarchy develops ' naturally ' : it alone therefore is from God. But the difference between them here does not amount to much, since Craig's monarchy does not or need not, and even should not, involve complete sovereignty in the monarch. Doleman draws the conclusion that a

[1] Ib., p. 73.
[2] Ib., p. 68.
[3] Ib., pp. 32, 33.
[4] Ib., p. 73.
[5] Ib., p. 1.

King who turns tyrant may be forcibly deposed. Craig refuses to admit this, but he argues the case as a lawyer or on mere grounds of expediency. His language about the King as God's lieutenant has no real connection with his main assertions. Like much of such language in the sixteenth century it exhibits little but a conventional piety.

Doleman concludes, further, that the heir to a throne may always be set aside if public welfare imperatively demands that course. Craig argues that to deprive any heir of his inheritance is contrary to natural law. But he does not dream of asserting that laws of succession were established by God. There is, in fact, no absolute antagonism between the views of these writers. But Doleman wished to secure a Catholic successor to Elizabeth ; while Craig and Hayward alike simply could not believe that any Catholic or Spaniard had any right to become King of England. That inability seems to have been general among Englishmen, then and later.

§ 5. *DE REPUBLICA ANGLORUM*

Hayward and Craig had apparently accepted the notion that full sovereignty must exist somewhere. But they had not really accepted or even understood it : when they came to the point, they higgled and hedged. In spite of Bodin they saw the English Constitution as what was called a ' mixed ' monarchy. It was the ordinary view at the time. Sovereignty was conceived in England as shared or as divided. It was not really, in Bodin's sense, conceived as existing at all. There was no distinct recognition of an absolute law-making power. To the question : Where does full sovereignty lie ? the answer could only be : Nowhere. Merbury and Craig both made that answer by implication. Where resides power to make law ? The answer is : In many places, according to the purpose and nature of the law to be made. Where is absolute power to make law ? No one was willing to admit that such power existed. Parliament is a High Court : not the only High Court, yet the highest. It can decide what law is ; but how far it can make law is a question. Law is conceived, especially by lawyers, as ruling all : King and Parliament interpret and apply.

Yet it had become or was becoming possible, before the end of the reign of Elizabeth, to see supreme power as residing in the Crown in Parliament and there only. Such a view, though something, at least, very like it, had been taken long before by the idealist lawyer Fortescue, it had been barely possible to hold under Henry VIII. But the Tudor government had made of Parliament something very different from what it had been at the commencement of Henry VIII's reign. It had begun to feel itself representative of a nation : it had begun to claim as of right what the Crown had given to it. The legend that

England had always been a Parliamentary monarchy was growing up. The common lawyers were becoming increasingly hostile to the exercise of royal power in Star Chamber or Council of the North or courts spiritual. The conception of the King in Parliament as the only proper law-making body was striking root. At the end of Elizabeth's reign it was on the point of being said that there are no limits to royal authority, that England, in Fortescue's phrase, is a *dominium regale* pure and simple and that all law proceeds from the King. But no one says so under Elizabeth. On the other hand, it was actually being said, or at least very strongly suggested, that England is a *dominium politicium et regale* and that supreme power resides only in the Crown in Parliament.

By far the most important exponent, during the reign of Elizabeth, of the view of England as a mixed monarchy, was Sir Thomas Smith. He was a man of the most varied learning, accomplishments and experience. At the time he commenced his famous book he was Elizabeth's ambassador to France : before that he had been in turn a University professor, a Dean, Provost of Eton and Secretary of State under Protector Somerset. He had lectured at Cambridge on natural philosophy, on Greek and on civil law, having taken a degree in law at Padua. He took priest's orders in 1546, but, after 1559, seems to have forgotten the fact altogether. The loss of his various posts under Mary was but a temporary eclipse. He served as ambassador in Paris from 1562 to 1566, and it was during those years that at least the first draft of the *De Republica Anglorum* was written,[1] though it was not published till 1583. Many editions rapidly followed. Sir Thomas was sworn of the Privy Council in 1571 and made Secretary of State in 1572. He died in 1577.

Sir Thomas was not a philosopher. He was a man of affairs, a jurist, a scholar, a man of the world of practical politics. He was struck by what seemed to him the dissimilarity between the law and constitution of England and that of continental countries and in particular of France. He tells us that the chief purpose of his book is ' to see who hath taken the righter, truer and more commodious way to govern the people '.[2] Actually there is very little comparison in the book and nothing to show that he knew much of the constitution or law even of France.

After remarking that commonwealths are conventionally divided into three types, according to whether ' one, few or the multitude rule ', Sir Thomas proceeds at once to assert that actually it is very

---

[1] It would seem, though it is not certain, that towards the end of his days, he added to his book a good deal from William Harrison's *Description of England*.

[2] *De Republica Anglorum*, III, 9, ed. L. Alston, p. 142. All my references are to this valuable edition.

rarely that any of them do so simply. ' You must not take that you shall find any commonwealth or government simple, pure and absolute in his sort and kind.' [1] All or nearly all actual constitutions are of the mixed type. England is an excellent example.

' The most high and absolute power of the realm of England consisteth,' says Sir Thomas, " in the Parliament.' An Act of Parliament, he goes on to explain, ' is the Prince's and the whole realm's deed : whereupon justly no man can complain, but must accommodate himself to find it good and obey it '. Parliament

' abrogateth old laws, maketh new, giveth orders for things past and for things hereafter to be followed. . . . All that ever the people of Rome might do . . . the same may be done by the parliament of England, which representeth and hath the power of the whole realm both the head and the body. For every Englishmen is entended to be there present . . . from the Prince to the lowest person. And the consent of the Parliament is taken to be every man's consent.' [2]

For England it is Parliament, with or including the Prince, that makes law and imposes taxation. To do these things, it would seem, requires the whole power of the realm and that whole power is not in the Prince alone. We must connect all this with Smith's definition of a commonwealth as ' a society or common doing of a multitude of free men collected together and united by common accord and covenants among themselves, for the conservation of themselves as well in peace as in war '.[3] It might seem to follow that every man's consent is needful for the making of law within a commonwealth.

Was Sir Thomas asserting full sovereignty, or sovereignty as full as that of Bodin, for the Parliament of England ? To say so would misrepresent his thought.[4] It must be remembered that he was not concerned with what may be and little with what should be.[5] He was asking simply how England was actually governed. He found that it was governed by the Prince but that, normally at least, the Prince made law and imposed taxes only in Parliament. He explains that while the making of laws and the providing of money is done by the Prince in Parliament, the management of foreign relations and of official appointments is by the Prince alone.[6] He never explicitly says that the Prince can neither make law nor impose taxes of his own will simply. He was not, I think, prepared to say what the Prince could not do. He might have said that what really rules is custom ; but he did not say so. Nor does he seem to have been clear

[1] *De Rep.*, I, 6, p. 14.
[2] Ib., III, 1, pp. 48, 49.   [3] Ib., I, 10, p. 20.
[4] Maitland, however, thought that he was. See *Const. Hist.*, ed. 1920, p. 254 and p. 298. One must hesitate to disagree.
[5] He speaks slightingly of Plato's and More's Utopias : ' feigned commonwealths, such as never was nor never shall be '. III, 9, p. 142.
[6] *De Rep.*, II, 4, p. 63.

as to the nature of the law-making power of Parliament. He appears to confuse the making of law with a final judgement as to what is law. Parliament was to him ' the highest and most authentical court of England ',[1] and from Parliament's decision as to what is the law there is no appeal. He did not clearly distinguish between legislative and judicial power : he did not distinctly see law as simple command. It might be gathered from the *De Republica* that England was governed not so much by the Prince or by Parliament as by courts of law. Yet even though it be true that ' for him Parliament was still primarily a court ',[2] it must be added that it was certainly an omnicompetent if not an omnipotent court.

Sir Thomas never uses the word ' sovereignty ' and, had he been asked where sovereignty lay in England, he would have said it was in the Prince. To him ' the highest and supreme authority ' is that ' which doth control, correct and direct all other members of the commonwealth '.[3] This, it may be said, is just what Elizabeth was doing. But the Sovereign to Sir Thomas is not the law-maker and in his view ought not to be. He associates ' absolute ' monarchy definitely with tyranny, saying that ' uncontrolled authority ', necessary in war, is in peace very dangerous both to monarch and people and asserting that ' for the most part they who have had that absolute power ' have become very tyrants.[4] Sir Thomas seems to have seen no reason why law-making should not be the function of a specially constituted body completely impotent in many relations.

Sovereignty, in fact, ought to be divided and commonly is. To say that such a division of power cannot exist is mere nonsense, for it evidently does exist, talk about sovereignty as you will. Sir Thomas was looking at a very complex thing, compounded of law and custom, tradition, habit, institutions and detailed arrangements and he tried to describe it as it was. He did so with a sense that it was quite admirably adapted to its purpose. To say that in a well-ordered State there must be a sovereign power, *legibus solutus*, definitely vested somewhere, struck him, if he ever thought of it at all, as simply untrue. His well-loved England was proof to the contrary. He seems to have

---

[1] *De Rep.*, II, 2.   [2] MacIlwain: *The High Court of Parliament*, p. 127.
[3] *De Rep.*, I, 1, p. 9.
[4] Ib., I, 8. The Chapter is headed: ' Of the absolute King.' Sir Thomas uses the word absolute in three different senses. Speaking of a Court, and especially of the High Court of Parliament, he uses it, as does Lambard, to signify that its decisions are not subject to appeal. A Court may be absolute even though its jurisdiction be very limited. A King or a kingdom is absolute if completely independent of all foreign powers. This is the ordinary sixteenth-century use of the term—and carries no reference to the position of the King in his own country. Thus Smith speaks of early Kings in England as ' each absolutely reigning in his country '. But in this particular chapter the ' absolute king ' is clearly one who possesses all powers.

been profoundly aware that human institutions will not actually fit into logical categories. The constitution of any State was, he insisted, a natural product. ' The mutations and changes of fashion of governments in commonwealths be natural. . . . According to the nature of the people, so the commonwealth is to it fit and proper.' [1]

The negative aspect of Sir Thomas's views is possibly even more significant than their positive aspect. Sir Thomas never refers to God as the author or giver of authority ; nor does he ever refer to the Scriptures or even to natural law in any sense. He has, apparently, no conception of divine right in the Prince or in anything else. Governments and constitutions develop naturally out of need and are good or bad as they serve their purpose and suit the character of the people. They exist for commonly understood ends and their authority, it is implied, is derived from the need of society to take thought for its own welfare. Authority, in fact, is derived quite simply from the need of it. There was no question or difficulty about it in the very British mind of Sir Thomas.

But there was a doubt in his mind which one hardly expects to find in a high officer under the Tudors. The views of Sir Thomas in general led him to be slightly unsound, from the Tudor point of view, on the question of the rightfulness of rebellion.

' When the commonwealth,' he observes, ' is evil governed by an evil ruler and unjust . . . if the laws be made, as most like they be, always to maintain that estate : the question remaineth whether the obedience of them be just and the disobedience wrong : the profit and conservation of that estate right and justice or the dissolution : and whether a good and upright man and lover of his country ought to maintain and obey them or to seek by all means to abolish them.' [2]

It is not a question, apparently, of whether mere disobedience is allowable but of whether the just man should seek ' by all means ' to abolish the laws that maintain such an estate and endeavour its dissolution. Can Sir Thomas have meant all lawful means ? But how, in such an estate, could there be any ? The question appears to be frankly, if long-windedly, put : but it is not frankly answered. ' The learned,' says Sir Thomas, ' will judge in each case according to the purpose of the doers and the estate of time then present.' It would seem to be implied that rebellion may be justified by circumstance. The implication is rather confirmed than weakened by the remark that ' certain it is that it is always a doubtful and hazardous matter to meddle with the changing of the laws and government or to disobey the orders of the rule or government which a man doth find already established '.[3] It is clear that Sir Thomas, good Elizabethan Churchman as he was, had not been notably impressed by the official argument of the Homilies.

[1] *De Rep.*, I, 15, p. 28. [2] Ib., I, 5, p. 10. [3] Ib., I, 5.

It is apparent how closely the view of Sir Thomas Smith agrees with the view of the constitution of the English monarchy that was, later, suggested, rather than expounded, by Hooker. Hooker placed legislative power in full Parliament and regarded the monarch as bound by law in his executive capacity.

'Though no manner of person or cause,' he wrote, 'be unsubject to the king's power, yet so is the power of the king over all and in all limited, that unto all his proceedings the law itself is a rule. The axioms of our regal government are these: lex facit regem; the king's grant of any favour made contrary to the law is void; rex nihil potest nisi quod jure potest.'[1]

Smith would surely have agreed.

In the writings and the Parliamentary activities of Peter Wentworth, we find a view perhaps still closer than Hooker's to that of the unphilosophic Sir Thomas. But in Wentworth the tendency towards a conception of Parliamentary sovereignty is yet more pronounced. 'The power of Parliament,' Wentworth declared in his *Discourse*,[2] 'is appointed by God, as the power next to himself to reform and redress wrongs and outrages which cannot be holpen by other means and by good and wholesome laws to procure the peace and wealth of the Republic.' The Prince, on the other hand, he also 'the ordinance not of any man but of God', is God's deputy 'for the maintenance of his truth and to minister justice according to the good and wholesome laws of that land over which he doth place him'.[3]

Here the Prince seems to appear definitely in a merely executive capacity, though there might be some difficulty about the maintenance of God's truth. But law-making, it seems, belongs only to Parliament as a whole. Such a conception, or any near approach to it, involved as corollary the assertion of a right to free speech in Parliament. Wentworth's Parliamentary career was largely devoted to that assertion. If law were to be made for redress of grievances and wrongs only in Parliament, it followed that in Parliament there should be complete freedom to discuss, to propose and to offer advice to the Prince, upon any and every subject. Not only would its work otherwise be hindered, but a right in the Prince to forbid or set limits to discussion is inconsistent with the conception that legislative power resides only in Parliament. All this, of course, is theory of the English constitution rather than of anything else. But behind it all is a notion, perhaps rather vague, though it is not vague in Hooker, that power to make law belongs rightly and essentially to the community

---

[1] *Eccles. Pol.*, VIII, 2, p. 353.
[2] *A Discourse containing the Author's opinion of the true and lawful successor to Her Majestie.* Written in 1594 as an answer to Doleman and published in 1598 after Wentworth's death. For Wentworth's views see the article by J. E. Neale in *English Hist. Rev.*, April, 1924.
[3] *Ib.*, pp. 45, 46.

itself. That power is claimed for Parliament on the ground, as Smith put it, that ' every Englishmen is entended to be there present '. The conflict of the next century was clearly coming, even though no one under Elizabeth seems to have foreseen it.

§ 6. CONCLUSION

At the end of Elizabeth's reign there existed a tendency to assert that the recognition of an absolute legal sovereignty, definitely seated, was necessary to the well-being of society. It was no more than a tendency and it was not very strong. Full sovereignty might be thought of as vested in the monarch alone or in the Crown in Parliament. Visibly there was a movement in both these directions. But far stronger was the tendency to illogical compromise. Full sovereignty might, of course, be attributed to the monarch without any sort of theory about divine right. The phrase ' the theory of the divine right of Kings ' has been used far too loosely and with curiously little consideration. It has been used, sometimes, as though it had no assignable meaning or as though it referred to a mere unexplained sentiment. If either were the case, it would be difficult to find a reason for using it at all. But it is hardly the case. At the close of the sixteenth century a theory was being developed which may, with sufficient accuracy, be termed ' the theory of the divine right of Kings '. But it was not formulated in England in the sixteenth century and it was hardly more than strongly suggested even in France.

Any theory which can accurately be dignified by this hackneyed phrase must, it appears to me, satisfy two conditions. It must, in the first place, have specific and exclusive reference to monarchies. Throughout the sixteenth century it was being taught that God has forbidden resistance to all properly constituted authorities, so that the duty of obedience to them is a duty to God and the right to demand it may be called a divine right. To call this doctrine a theory of the divine right of Kings, as though it referred to Kings only, would be inaccurate and misleading : to call it ' the ' theory would be simply absurd. The theory of the divine right of Kings must assert that God intended mankind to be governed by monarchs and himself established monarchies and monarchies only. In the second place, while admitting, as it could not avoid doing, that a people can and does confer actual coercive power or force, the theory must assert that moral obligation to obey the monarch is the result of a divine grant of real authority. It must deny that such obligation could possibly be created by any human arrangements. A King, of course, needs absolutely that popular recognition which confers force ; but the real authority of the monarch, that is his right to demand obedience as a duty, is created and conferred by God and could not otherwise exist at all. The theory is that which asserts that no right or duty can be created out of a supposition or a sense of need; that no majority can impose on a man an obligation that did not exist before; that unless God has granted authority to demand obedience, no such authority exists; and that actually the divine grant of it has been made to Kings only. This is the theory suggested, at least, in France by Barclay and De Belloy. I do not see in what sense anyone not prepared to make these assertions can be called a believer in ' the theory of the divine right of Kings '.

To say that the King is God's vicar or lieutenant or, like Peter Wentworth, that the Prince is an ordinance ' not of any man but of God ', certainly does not imply belief in any such theory. The phrase is piously utilitarian. Obedience is due because the Prince, presumably, acts in the sense of God's will. It is, perhaps, due only so far as he so acts. As for the constantly repeated declaration that rebellion against constituted authority was always wicked, not only had it no necessary reference to Kings but it could be and was made on the purest grounds of expediency. It does not necessarily imply any theory at all of the nature or the origin, or even the extent, of the authority against which rebellion is forbidden. All these formulæ imply no more than that all obligation is ultimately to God.

None of the English Elizabethan writers are willing to admit, or do actually conceive, that any absolute and unlimited authority exists. Some of them seem half to believe that it ought to exist; they do not see how it can. It may, perhaps, be said that they feel, obscurely, that though monarchy arose out of need and circumstance, yet obligation to obey can only be to God. But they do not see the point clearly. The Scottish lawyer, Craig, says that monarchies alone arose directly from the will of God : but this only because they alone arose ' naturally '. I cannot find anything that ought to be called a theory of the divine right of Kings in Elizabethan writings. I do not find it even in the writings of King James, which seem to me to express no theory at all.

Under Elizabeth the sense of the wickedness of rebellion was kept vivid by the sense of danger from France or from Spain, by the rebellion of 1569 and the plots that centred round Mary Stewart, by the fear of Catholic rising stirred up by the Jesuits and by the awful example of France. Towards the end of her reign men were beginning to ask what was the nature and source of that authority which must not be resisted. They were also beginning to ask where it really lay. The relation of the Crown to Parliament and to law was becoming a question. Theories were in course of formation ; but not one received clear expression. Such as they were they pointed forward in various directions, to Eliot and Prynne, Ferne and Filmer. Soon after the accession of James we begin to find more definition. It might be argued that the first expression in England of the theory of the divine right of Kings appears in 1606 in Bishop Overrall's *Convocation Book*. But even there it is indefinite. Overrall does indeed assert quite definitely that God originally gave authority always and only to single individuals, patriarchs or Kings, and that all non-monarchical forms of government are perverted or degenerate, mere results of the unruliness of man. What is vastly more important is that he does appear to imply that while ordered society rests upon an obligation to obedience, that obligation could never have existed had it not been specially created by God. But it is only by implication that he can be said to make that essential assertion ; and one is doubtful whether he really meant to make it. The theory of the divine right of Kings, in the only sense I can give to the phrase, belongs to the seventeenth century and not, even in France, to the sixteenth. In England I know, at present, of no full expression of it earlier than the writings of Sir Robert Filmer. Even Filmer was not too clear about it. Nor was Filmer at all representative of typical royalist thought in his time. His view was certainly not that of the mass of the royalist writers of the period of the Civil War.

PART III

FRANCE

CHAPTER I

PRELIMINARY

IN Germany, owing largely to the chaotic nature of its political constitution, the controversy of the sixteenth century was, from the first, and remained, far more religious and juristic than political. The issues were, it is true, largely political and the results more political than religious. But the political issues of the conflict were difficult to disentangle at a time when nobody knew whether Germany were a monarchy, an aristocracy or a federation. Controversy turned mainly on questions of theology and questions as to the nature of the Church or on the question of the legal relation of Princes of the Empire to the Emperor. The main political question that was raised was as to the rights and duties of secular rulers in relation to religion and the Church. In England the main question in debate was of the import and implications of the conception of a national Church under royal supremacy. It was a conflict between modes of thought all but frankly and simply political and utilitarian and modes of thought essentially religious. There, too, the controversy turned largely on religious beliefs. But in France, from beginning to end, the controversy was far more political than religious.

At the commencement of the sixteenth century, France, though far more settled than Germany, was yet, in many respects, chaotic. In every part of its territory, the action of the central government was limited or obstructed by clerical, noble, provincial and communal privilege or custom. All powers were already claimed for the King; but his recognized positive rights varied from province to province. The centralized machinery of administration, so far as it existed, was at once extremely insufficient and very imperfectly controlled. Law varied from province to province and even from town to town. Though France was very conscious of its Frenchness, yet popular sentiment was very largely local rather than national. All through the century men talk of going out of Guienne into France.

The connection of many of the frontier provinces with the monarchy, though in nearly all cases old in one sense, was really comparatively very new. It was only in the mid-fifteenth century that the English had been driven from Normandy and Bordeaux ; it was only after war (1574-6) with the Count of Armagnac that Louis XI had been able to take effective possession of Guienne. In Languedoc the royal authority, nullified by the English war, had been re-established only under Charles VII. Old French Burgundy had been recovered for France after the battle of Nancy and Brittany had become part of the kingdom in any real sense only in 1493. Provence had come to the Crown only in 1486. The reconquest of France under Charles VII and Louis XI was not only recent, it was incomplete. In almost all these newly acquired territories the King had been forced to admit that he could not tax save under a grant from the Estates of the province. So far was this from being a fiction that it was hard to induce them to pay anything. Each of them, too, was left with its own Parlement, a supreme court with far more than judicial powers, completely independent of that of Paris. The French monarchy of 1500 was an invasive and aspiring rather than a governing power.

Under such circumstances the centralizing policy of Francis I and the increasing taxation of his reign was bound to provoke resistance and to afford fine opportunities for ambitious great nobles. There followed, also, the spread of Calvinistic Protestantism over wide areas, especially in the south and west. French Protestantism allied itself with provincial and municipal resistance to the action of the government, with growing exasperation at the increase of taxation and with a faction of great nobles, to form the Huguenot party. The Huguenot was very far from forming a merely religious party.

Rebellion followed. In 1562 began a series of desolating civil wars. Centralized government practically disappeared and France all but broke up. Castellion's prophecy that the contending parties would ruin France was very nearly fulfilled. It is probable that only the deaths of the last Valois Kings without children and the fact that Henry of Navarre was at once the military chief of the Huguenots and a man of something like genius, prevented a disruption of the kingdom. Even so, the civil wars resulted in terrible devastation, impoverishment, misery and demoralization.

Alongside the fighting developed a great controversy with pen and ink. Just as in the English civil war of the next century, the political pamphlet literature of the period after 1562 is very great in amount. Men of all sorts, clerics, nobles, scholars, bourgeois, even poets, plunged into the controversy on one side or another. For every one was vitally interested. In times of security political thought tends to be superficial and to express mere acquiescence in existing facts. Fundamental questions as to the nature of governmental authority are either not raised at all or are shelved with unexamined catchwords. It is even comfortably assumed that they have been satisfactorily answered. The amount and the seriousness of the thought devoted to the nature of the State seems to tend to vary inversely with the sense of security. When government breaks down and the country is infested with marauding bands of ruffians and no one's life, property or honour is safe, it is perceived that these questions need an answer. So it was in sixteenth-century France, when it became a question of reconstructing government. So it was in England in the seventeenth century ; and so it may be again. In the latter half of the sixteenth century France became a great factory of political ideas.

What was formally in question for France was the nature of the French monarchy. There was little question made of where legal sovereignty lay. It lay with the King or, as some said, with the King and the Estates of the realm. But the question was of the nature of this sovereignty. It was a question that referred to the foundations of the monarchy historical and ideal, to its ' fundamental laws '. It was a question of the ideal relation between the King of France and his subjects and so necessarily of the relation between government and subject. It involved the determination of the relation of the King to tradition and custom, to law, to the Church and to religion. The question whether the sovereign has a right, or is bound, to put down heresy by force or whether men ' for the cause of religion ', have a right to rebel, are here subsidiary. The controversy in France turns on the larger question whether the subject may rightfully, for any reason or cause, forcibly resist the King. Though at the end of the century the ' constitutional ' or rather the customary theory of the monarchy was by no means dead, though Parlements and municipalities and provincial estates continued an obstructive resistance in the name of customary rights, till late in the seventeenth century, we may say that the answer was in the negative. The Catholic League represented a last desperate attempt to establish a divine right of resistance.

Throughout the sixteenth century, in spite of all checks and set-backs, in spite, or rather because, of the Huguenots and the League, two things were growing in the mind of France. In the first place was growing a sense of the need for recognition of a single will as supreme and endowed with power to make law absolutely : in the second the conception of this needed sovereign power as ordained and directly created by God as His agent for the welfare of society. The *princeps* in whom France is coming to believe, whom Huguenots as well as Politiques see in Henry IV, is not the *princeps* of Roman law, a delegate with all the powers of a sovereign people, but a King who owes his throne to God's arrangements and his powers to God's gift. It is, strictly, a religious conception, though its effective basis was utilitarian. In spite of all opposition France was making for itself a national government. More and more clearly it appeared that only the recognition of a single will as supreme could give France unity or peace or order. It seemed so to many early in the century and to the mass at the end. This was only to be expected, for, in fact, it was so.

CHAPTER II

LE GRANT MONARCHIE DE FRANCE

ONE who wishes to understand the development of political thought in France in the sixteenth century can do no better than begin by studying *Le Grant Monarchie de France* of Claude de Seyssel. De Seyssel's view was that of an ex-minister of Louis XII, at one time Chancellor of France, at another ambassador to England, a bishop and a scholar, a man of long and varied experience in the affairs of Church and State. It was the view, too, of a man of acute intelligence and observation and of much common sense. *Le Grant Monarchie* was written during his retirement after the death of Louis XII, apparently in response to a request for counsel from the new King. It was published in 1518. It has been said that we can gather from this book how France thought of herself and her political constitution at the commencement of the sixteenth century.[1] This observation is so far true that much of the controversy that followed can be read as a commentary on or an expansion, on one side or another, of the views of Seyssel.

Yet the contrast between Seyssel and Barclay is very pronounced. In view of what followed, the most striking thing about Seyssel's book is the absence from it of any reference to divine right. His grant monarchie rests not on divine right in any sense or degree, but on custom and expediency. He is one of the few writers of the sixteenth century, outside Italy, who show clear signs of having been influenced by Machiavelli.[2] From the Florentine writer he had learned something, from his own experience, much more. To Seyssel government was simply a practical problem of how to maintain peace and order and justice. He recognized customary rights without inquiring into their nature: with other kinds of 'right' he did not concern himself. A great deal, he remarked, in his preface, has been written to little purpose about the best form of government. Men arrange things in their own minds as they wish them to be and picture a society of sensible and virtuous beings, ruled as such beings might

[1] A. Jacquet in *Revue des Questions Historiques*.
[2] Many of the sixteenth-century writers who refer to or attack Machiavelli do not even show any real acquaintance with his works.

be. But this is not helpful. Actually no one is so sensible or so virtuous as these writers seem to think men are ; nor is any State, big or little, regulated and managed solely by reason. Seyssel was determined to consider only the actual. Like the practical man he was, he probably thought that once you get among abstractions you never quite know what you are talking about. What is wanted above all is a government that can govern.

Yet the question as to the best form of government did trouble him a little. He felt by no means sure that it was monarchy. To monarchy, he pointed out, there are grave objections. So much depends on the King ; and the King may be and probably is, more or less incompetent.[1] Good Princes are rarities. It would seem that the best form of government should be an aristocracy. By ' aristocracy ', he explained, he meant, not the government of an hereditary group, but a government of notable and eminent persons based on some system of election. But, owing to the perversity of man, such a government is practically liable to corruption ; it tends to become a close and selfish oligarchy.[2] He concluded in favour of hereditary monarchy as the form of government least liable to degeneration and most practically effective. For, he pointed out, men find it more easy and natural to obey a single chief than to submit to control by a group of any sort.[3]

But monarchy to Seyssel was only out of doubt the best form of government when it was such a monarchy as that of France. France, he felt sure, was the best governed country in the world. What made the government of France so admirable and satisfactory was just the fact that the King of France was checked and restrained on all sides by customary law and customary rights. Seyssel saw the French constitution as a system of checks and balances producing a real equilibrium. He saw France as a system of customary rights, of liberties and franchises belonging to classes and groups, cities and provinces, under an hereditary monarch who was bound to respect all such customary rights as part of the constitution of the monarchy. The function of the King was to exercise a general controlling and directive power and to reform abuses. In one passage Seyssel speaks of the King as making law.[4] But it is clear that he thought of law as made only to supplement defects or correct manifest abuses. Existing law he conceived as something that should not be, or even as something that could not be, altered. He certainly had no notion of an absolute law-making power residing in the King or anywhere else. He would probably have regarded the question of how far the

---

[1] *Le Grant Monarchie*, II, Chap. 2. [2] Ib., I, Chap. 1.

[3] This observation is repeated by later pamphleteers after 1560 and, in particular, by Louis le Roy.

[4] *Le Grant Monarchie*, II, Chap. 4.

King could make law as one of those questions that should never be asked.

Seyssel's 'great monarchy' was not 'constitutional' in the ordinary sense in which that term is used. He did not regard States-General as even a part of the constitution of France. If, he says, it be a question of general legislation, it is sometimes expedient to summon to council, along with the notables and high officials, ' a few people from the cities and chief towns of the kingdom '.[1] This is his only reference to States-General. He insists that it is wholly desirable that the King should hold councils for the discussion of all important questions and should never act hurriedly or on impulse ; but he never suggests that the King is positively bound to listen to anyone. There seem, indeed, in his system, to be no strictly legal limits to the King's powers.

Yet, if there be no legal limits, there are real limits. The beauty of the French monarchy consists in the fact that it is ' refrenée par bonnes lois, ord nnances et coustumes, lesquelles sont établis de telle sorte qu'à peine se peuvent rompre '.[2] The King is under three kinds of restraint. In the first place France is a Christian and, what is more, a religious country. The consequence of this is that an openly irreligious King would be generally hated ; and accordingly the King is under a practical obligation to live outwardly like a Christian and refrain from tyrannous and unjust behaviour. If he does not do so any ordinary priest may rebuke him ' to his beard '.

In the second place the King is restrained by his own judicial machinery. The Parlements, Seyssel says, ' ont esté instituez principalement pour cette cause et cette fin, de refrener la puissance absolue dont vouldroient user les rois '.[3] To these High Courts the King himself is subject ' quant à la justice distributive '. But he is careful not to say exactly in what the restraining power of the Parlements consists and does not even mention their claim to veto royal edicts by refusing registration. Always, when it is a question of defining limits to the royal authority, Seyssel becomes studiously vague. It is possible that he said less than he meant : it is more likely that he did not wish to admit that there existed quite definite and strictly legal restraints on the action of the Crown.

But the third kind of restraint is the most important of the three and appears, indeed, really to include the second. The King of France is restrained by all that complex of ancient law and custom which is of the essence of the monarchy. Even though there be no legal reason why he should respect it, yet, in fact, he must. These ancient ordinances ' ont esté gardés pour tel et un si long temps que les princes n'entreprennent point d'y déroger, et quand le vouldroient

---

[1] *Le Grant Monarchie*, II, Chap. 4.
[2] Ib., I, Chap. 8.   [3] Ib., I, Chap. 10.

faire l'on n'obeist point à leurs commandement '.[1] Under such restraints and ' subject to his own law ', the King is far better honoured and obeyed than would be the case were he simply absolute.[2]

The ambiguities are deliberate. The strength of the French monarchy as Seyssel saw it, lay in the inconsistencies of its constitution. On the one hand we have a King able to cope with all emergencies because his powers have no legal limit. On the other hand we have a people so happily wedded to its ancient customs that it is impossible for the King to disregard or to destroy them. All that is needed to make the system work is justice and reason and goodwill, such as France found in Louis XII.[3] It might be said that his idea of the sacredness of custom, his idea of group rights as absolute, lasted on in France into the seventeenth century, and was, in fact, the most obstinate enemy the monarchy had to deal with, retaining its vitality long after constitutionalist and contract theories had gone into limbo. But to put the matter so would be inaccurate. Seyssel had no idea of group-rights as absolute : he seems to have had no conception of ' absolute ' rights at all. To him the problem was simply one of how to secure and maintain order and justice : and he saw safety only in adherence to custom and tradition.

Seyssel's theory of the constitution of France seems to express a momentary equilibrium of forces under Louis XII. Local and class privileges, the right of nobles and of clerical property to exemption from tailles, the rights of local Parlements and provincial estates, had been more or less definitely recognized. For the moment it did actually seem that the constitution of France was such as Seyssel described it as being. It seemed to be so to so acute an observer as Machiavelli. In his *Discorsi* he speaks admiringly of the French monarchy, ' which enjoys complete security for this only reason, that its kings are bound to compliance with an infinite number of laws upon which the well-being of the people depends '.[4] Yet Louis XI had already represented the idea of a *Princeps* whose will is law throughout his dominions. Fifty years later men saw in that monarch an innovator who began the destruction of that ancient constitution which Seyssel had described.

The optimism of Seyssel is, in fact, rather astonishing. For all his positivism his picture is as sanguine and idealistic as Fortescue's account of the constitution of England. His implication that custom and tradition ruled France, allowed nothing for changing circumstances. He was aware of a tendency to change, but he saw in it only a tendency to degeneration. Yet he ought to have seen that so delicately balanced a structure as his could not in any case last. Introduce into this system

---

[1] *Le Grant Monarchie*, I, Chap. 11.   [2] Ib., I, Chap. 12.
[3] Seyssel's admiration for his old master was unbounded.
[4] *Discorsi*, I, Chap. 16.

the idea of positive right or the idea of unfettered law-making power and the whole structure goes to pieces. Once the question of legislative power is definitely raised, the main question comes to be as to where such power resides. There is in *Le Grant Monarchie* no suggestion that it can reside anywhere but in the King. On the other hand, insist that customary rights are absolute and you will have a legally limited monarchy which will be nearer Seyssel's than the other, but will not be his. Both these things were to happen or had happened already in 1518. Under Francis I the Crown developed afresh an aggressive and centralizing policy, which threatened alike seigneurial, ecclesiastical, municipal and provincial ' liberties ' ; and along with this there developed a theory of royal absolutism.

CHAPTER III

CONSTITUTIONAL THEORIES

§ 1. ABSOLUTIST THEORY

IT was chiefly in the law schools of France that the absolutist theory of the monarchy was formulated under Francis I and Henry II. In the first half of the century the most important of these schools was that of the University of Toulouse, even though Alciati and Duaren and, later, Doneau and Cujas, all taught at Bourges.[1] The study of the *Corpus Juris* was beginning to proceed upon new lines. The new school of jurists, of whom Jacques Cujas was the greatest representative, sought to connect Roman law with the actual life and institutions of the time in which it developed, and thought of it, not as a system of law for all times, but as one which could only be understood in relation to the state of society which had produced it. The public lecturing of Cujas only began in 1554, but ever since the publication in 1514 of Guillaume Budé's great treatise, *De Asse et Partibus*, French scholarship had been taking an antiquarian and historical direction. The work of Cujas was only part of the effort of French scholars to reconstruct Roman society and its history. It must be noted that the growing ascendancy of this new school of jurists tended to diminish the influence of the *Corpus Juris* on the political thought of the period by exhibiting it as belonging essentially to the past. In 1567 Bodin complained that too exclusive an attention was given to Roman law : what was wanted, he declared, was rather a comparative study of all legal systems. The point is neatly illustrated by Cujas' own refusal to apply the results of his historical studies to the politics of his own day. ' Nihil hoc,' he would say, ' ad edictum praetoris.'

It would be easy to exaggerate the influence of the writing and lecturing of the French ' civilians '. They can have directly influenced few beyond professed law students. This, however, certainly does not mean that their influence was unimportant. Lawyers played a great part in shaping the policy and the theory of the monarchy in the sixteenth century, as they had done all through the later Middle

---

[1] Both Doneau and Cujas were pupils of Toulouse.

Ages. It is significant that the Parlement of Toulouse, fed by the law school of its University, early became a champion of the King's claim to almost unlimited rights, while the Parlement of Paris, in which city the law school was unimportant, tended to take a very different view. Without doubt the work of the French civilian jurists did much to establish the idea of a law-making *princeps*, a supreme and sovereign will.

That this idea was to some extent derived from, that is, to some extent a direct result of, the study of Roman law, is no doubt true. But the influence of such study on its votaries was not a simple thing. Two conceptions were found in the *Corpus Juris* : the conception of a sovereign law-making *princeps* and the conception of the *princeps* as delegate of a sovereign people. The stress might be laid on one or the other, or even alternately on both. The study of the *Corpus Juris* did not necessarily turn men into royalist absolutists. ' In the beginning of things,' says Alciati,[1] ' Kings were not established by divine decree but by popular consent.' His pupil, François Connan, laid down that if a king by hereditary right should defy human and divine law, 'tyrannus expellendus est'.[2] Doneau[3] seems to have seen in the institution of royal absolutism a mere matter of expediency. The opponents of absolutism could have found texts on their side in the writings of these jurists had they looked for them : as in fact some did.[4]

But to explain the fact that an absolutist theory of monarchy developed in the France of Francis I, it is in no way necessary to refer to the *Corpus Juris*. If literary ' sources ' of the conception of a law-making sovereign are required they can be found elsewhere. All through the later Middle Ages such a conception had been in process of formation. It had, even, been fully formed. The bull of Pope Boniface VIII, called Sacrosanctae Ecclesiae, issued in 1298, had spoken of the Pope as one ' qui jura omnia in scrinio pectoris sui censetur habere '. The same Bull had laid down, with regard to local customary law, that whatsoever the Papal Sovereign permits he must be taken as commanding ; which is precisely what the absolutist lawyers of the sixteenth century say of the King in France. All that the jurists, or anyone else, needed to do was to take over the Papalist conception and apply it to their national King. But they need not even have gone to Papal Bulls. They had little need to add to, or to alter, what they could have found in the writings of Wyclif or Occam, Dubois or Marsilio. Italy, too, in the fifteenth century, it may be noted, had developed a conception of a Prince ruling absolutely as the representative of God. A book written in

---

[1] Andrea Alciati, 1492-1550. *De verborum significationibus*, 1529.
[2] *Commentaria Juris Civilis* (1558), I, 8.
[3] Hugues Doneau (Donellus), 1507-1591.   [4] Especially Salamonius.

this sense by an Italian Bishop, describing the King as an image of God, had become well known in France before the year 1500.[1]

The fact is that the French lawyers of the sixteenth century were only continuing the work done by their predecessors from Beaumanoir to Jean de Doyat. From the time of Louis IX onwards the lawyers of France had been constantly engaged in an effort to extend the power of the Crown in every possible direction. They had gone to Roman law chiefly to look for weapons against the antagonists they recognized as most formidable: feudalism and the Church. They were concerned, at first, not with theories of sovereignty but with questions of jurisdiction and procedure and the legal principles governing these. Under Louis IX they had laid down two great principles, without as yet explaining their implications. 'Toute justice émane du roi,' declared Beaumanoir; and. 'Fief et justice n'ont rien de commun.' In relation to the Pope they were maintaining already a kind of 'Gallicanism'. Under Philip IV the doctrine that the King possesses all powers was all but proclaimed. It would probably have been formally asserted much earlier than it was but for the interference of the Hundred Years War. During the revival of the almost wrecked monarchy, in the fifteenth century, the influence of the lawyers steadily revived. Louis XI adopted their point of view and governed through them. They proclaimed, then, that the King is direct lord of all land and of all persons. The conception of an absolute power inherent in the Crown and limited only by law which forbade the King to destroy his own position, had been implied from Philip IV's time onward. As the actual power of the King increased in the latter half of the fifteenth century, the hopes of the lawyers grow bolder and their claims took a wider sweep. When, in connection with the edicts of Francis I, they used, for the first time, the formula: 'Car tel est nôtre bon plaisir,' they were but going a step further than their predecessors had dared to go. They saw, then, the promised land close in front of them. It was not nearly so close as they imagined.

Students and bookish people generally are far too ready to trace ideas and ideals to literary sources. Ideas are begotten of circumstance on the human mind, and rarely, if ever, is their source to be found in books. What books supply is chiefly forms and conventions of expression. They furnish categories and classifications and, perhaps, 'arguments'; they supply needed contrasts and parallels; they suggest ways of putting things. But the continuity of political thought arises from the continuity of circumstance. It would be meaningless to say that had there been no such thing as the *Corpus Juris*, the ideal of a royal absolutism would have developed in six-

---

[1] *Speculum Humanae Vitae*, by Rodericus Sancius, Bishop of Calahorra. It was printed at Paris in 1472 and at Lyons in 1477.

teenth-century France precisely as it did ; because, had there been
no such thing, France and all Europe must have been quite other
than it was.   But we may say that the immense and increasing confusion and the felt need of order are alone enough to account for the
genesis of the ideal and for its ultimate triumph.   If the theory of
absolutism came first from the lawyers, that is not because the lawyers
were students of Roman law, but because, as lawyers, they were
above all preoccupied with the idea of law and of law-making power
and because they were seeking legal remedy for devastating disorder
and confusion.

The conception of the King as an absolute monarch was, with
the lawyers of the first half of the sixteenth century, rather an ideal
than a principle.   It did not bind them to assert that the political
sovereign must everywhere possess unlimited powers or even to assert
that monarchy is generally the best form of government.   In fact
they did not go out of their way to make any such rash assertions.
They were thinking of France and of France only, or they were commenting on the Digest and only on that.   But concerning what was
right and best for France they had little doubt.

In any case it was not the Roman conception of sovereignty that
was being elaborated, but the conception of a monarch ruling as a
vicegerent of God, independently of any popular will or consent.
For, in the sixteenth century, once expression was given to the idea
of a *princeps* to whom unlimited obedience was due and who had
power to make law for all, this conception had to be shown to be in
accord with the will of God.   Inevitably the Prince delegate was
transformed into the Prince of divine appointment.   The tendency
to this transformation is apparent from the first, even among the
lawyers.   When a jurist is not merely commenting on the Digest
but writing specifically of the kingdom of France, he tends to represent
the King's absolute authority as derived from God simply.   The
study of Roman law helped the lawyers to see law-making power as
the very essence of sovereignty and suggested to them the embodi-
ment of such sovereignty in the King of France ; but they tended
from the first to substitute the idea of Divine sanction for the idea of
delegation.

The *Jura regni Franciae* of the lawyer, Jean Ferrault, published
under Louis XII, was probably the first book published in sixteenth-
century France to claim for the King rights almost unlimited.   Almost
but not quite unlimited : for all the writers of this school of the first
half of the century insist that there exist in France ' fundamental '
laws which the King is bound to respect.   In the view of the royalist
lawyers there are just two things the King cannot do.   He cannot
alter the ' Salic ' law of succession and he cannot ' alienate domain '.
As to the Salic Law it may have seemed only logical to say that a

Prince who succeeds to the throne only by virtue of a specific law of succession cannot himself alter that law. This was at least clear : but in what exactly alienation of domain consisted was a question on which different views were taken. The principle was an old one : it had been broadly asserted by the States-General of 1439. It was generally understood to mean that the King could not alienate revenue-bearing property attached to the Crown : and in this specific sense it was maintained by Bodin at the Estates of Blois in 1576. It was sometimes interpreted as meaning that the King could not cede any territory within his jurisdiction. But the royalist lawyers tended to give the rule as restricted a meaning as possible. By the end of the century they were interpreting ' domain ' as referring neither to property nor to territory but only to the sovereign power itself. Never at any time do they see ' fundamental law ' in the claims made by Parlements or Estates ; and they tend to see it only as rules which prevent the King from destroying his own sovereignty.

More significant than the work of Jean Ferrault is the *Regalium Franciae* of Charles de Grassaille,[1] published in 1538. In this book we see the Roman *princeps* in process of being metamorphosed into the vicegerent of God. The King of France is described as ' imperator in suo regno ' ; he is also described as ' quidem corporalis Deus '. He cannot alter the law of succession or alienate domain ; but all other powers are definitely attributed to him, including unlimited rights of legislation and taxation. All jurisdiction belongs to him and he can suppress all inferior jurisdictions. De Grassaille was an extremist and Bodin's theory of the French monarchy, compared with his, might be described as constitutionalist. But his view was typical of that taken by lawyers before 1562, and not by lawyers only. In 1555 the lawyer-poet, La Perrière, attacked Seyssel for saying that an element of aristocracy existed in the French constitution. ' Les parlements ne brident point nos rois, ains nos rois les brident.'[2] In the *Livre des dignités* of the lawyer Vincent de la Loupe we read that the King can make war or peace, impose taxes and make law as seems good to him, ' et tout ce qu'il dit est estimé comme une loi et venant de l'oracle d'un autre Apollo '.[3]

For these royalist lawyers the claims of the Church and of the Pope of course involved a difficulty. They were almost all of them professed Catholics. But they seem to have been prepared to claim

[1] Born 1495 ; died 1582. He studied law at Toulouse and became a royal magistrate at Carcassonne. His *Regalium Franciae libri duo, jura omnia et dignitates Galliae regis continentes*, originally published at Lyon, was republished at Paris in 1545 along with Ferrault's *Jura regni Franciae*.

[2] *Le Miroir Politique*, 1555. An odd and very silly book. La Perrière acquired an ill-founded reputation as a poet and man of learning.

[3] *First and second book of dignities*. Published in Latin in 1551 and in French in 1560.

that the King was for all practical purposes head of the Church in France. The clergy are his subjects, says De Grassaille : he can tax them and he can confer ecclesiastical office : the Pope may excommunicate him but can neither depose him or place an interdict on his kingdom. Du Moulin goes further. He argues elaborately that the King has authority and jurisdiction over all the clergy of his dominions ' de droit divin ' and can regulate by ordinance the discipline and government of the Church. ' It is certain that the King of France, sovereign lord in his kingdom, has no less power than had Justinian the Great or other Emperors in their Empire.' [1] Still further went Claude Gousté in a remarkable though confused book published in 1561.[2] According to this writer, ' Dieu élit le roi et le peuple établit et crée,' [3] and as a result the King is ' premier après Dieu ' and the Pope, it seems, counts for practically nothing. The ordinances of the King are to be accepted by every one, including the clergy, ' as though they had been sent from heaven '. There no longer exist any such priests as appear in the Old Testament. ' Levi est passé et la famille de Levi, ensemblement toutes choses vieilles.' Christian Kings have, therefore, Gousté asserts, full power and authority ' in the ecclesiastical state ' ; and if any dispute arises concerning religion, it is for the King to decide the matter. In ecclesiastical councils it is the King who should preside. Throughout the book the claims of the Papacy are almost entirely ignored. The later Gallicans went no further.[4]

§ 2. OPPOSITION THEORIES

If a King, declared Guillaume Budé, disregards his own ordinances and acts contrary to equity and reason, he is guilty of a kind of *lèse majesté* ; nevertheless Kings ' ne sont sujets ne aux lois ne aux ordonnances si bon ne leur semble '.[5] It is for the King alone to judge what is equitable. This kind of language is so common under Francis I that one might suppose that the theory of a divinely bestowed and all but unlimited authority in the King was already dominant in France. It was not so. Behind all such talk and in spite of the lawyers, there existed a widespread and growing resentment of the aggressive and centralizing action of the government. The concordat of 1515, the restriction of seigneurial and ecclesiastical juris-

[1] Charles Du Moulin : *Traité de l'origine, progres et excellence du Royaume et Monarchie des François*, 1561, p. 68.
[2] *Traité de la puissance et authorité des Rois*, 1561.
[3] Almost the phrases of the *Vindiciae*, etc. ! ' Ostendimus Deum reges elegere . . . populum reges constituere.'
[4] This book was no doubt written in defence of the toleration policy the government was developing in 1561.
[5] *Enseignement et Exhortement pour l'Institution d'un Prince*, ed. Lyon, 1547, cap. 30.

diction by the ordinance of Villers-Coterêts, the attack on municipal liberties in the ordinance of Crémieux, above all, perhaps, the great increase of taxation and the persistent effort to compel grants from provincial Estates, resulted in the development of an opposition that nearly wrecked the monarchy. From about 1535 Protestantism of Calvinistic type was spreading steadily.[1] It was one form that was taken by the growing discontent and irritation, especially in *pays d'état*; and if Genevan influence counted for much in it, the increase of taxation and the attack on municipal freedom probably counted for more. In any case, French Protestantism, as it developed and spread in spite of spasmodic persecution, allied itself inevitably with groups and classes concerned mainly or merely with the defence of local or class privilege.

De Seyssel had implied, though he had not exactly stated, that the complex of restraints on the royal will which actually existed, were to be taken as essential parts of the constitution of the French monarchy. He had seemed to imply that the King was bound by custom to govern with the advice of councils of magnates or notables. He had declared that the Parlements existed to act as a check on the action of the King. The aggressive policy of the Crown after 1515 produced a hardening of all these implications. It began to be asserted definitely that the monarchy is limited absolutely by law at once customary and fundamental. Under Francis I began a new systematic study of that mass of customary law which was in the main the real law of actual France. The *Premier Commentaire sur la Coutume de Paris* of Charles Du Moulin, greatest pioneer of this kind of legal research, was published in 1539.[2] Such studies tended to emphasize the sacredness, the ' divine right ' of custom, and represent it as having originated independently of the Crown. They produced a school of lawyers who defended the claims of provinces and of cities against the monarch.

If the action of the Crown were to be conceived as limited by customary rights, the limitations were not the same for every part of France. Customarily the King had more power at Amiens or Bourges than he had at Nismes or Rouen. This fact, coupled with the strength of merely provincial patriotisms, tended to make opposition to the Crown local rather than national, and so in the long run ineffective. It was difficult to frame, even ideally, any sort of ' constitutional ' theory of the French monarchy that would not conflict with the claims of Languedoc or Provence. A sovereign States-General

---

[1] Protestantism, of course, appears in France earlier. But it was only after 1535 that it began to establish itself solidly in towns. The Ordinance of Crémieux was issued in 1536.

[2] Du Moulin inquires into the origin of customary law and suggests its codification and unification.

would have been almost as objectionable as the .sovereign monarch of Grassaille from the point of view of Grenoble or Montauban. Yet constitutionalist theory developed in France before 1560, based either on the assertion of the existence of an ancient constitution which the King has no right to alter, or simply on belief in customary rights, as ancient and as sacred as the monarchy itself. But while the theory of royal absolutism was taking clear and definite shape in the hands of the jurists, the rival theories remained almost formless and quite incoherent. France in the mid-sixteenth century did not lack a theory of its constitution to oppose to that of royal absolutism : the mischief was that it had too many such theories. The claims made for the Parlements and for particular provinces were in conflict with those .made for States-General. Yet it is true that, in 1560, France was on the eve of a constitutional conflict similar to that which tore England in the following century : and a conflict which did not end for France with Henry IV or even with Richelieu. But in England the issues were relatively very simple. There opposition to the claims of the King focussed naturally in Parliament. There was no such single focus in France. In France the struggle is so complicated and confused, and the theories of the constitution so diverse and incoherent, that it is hard to disentangle any distinct constitutional issue at all.

A conception of the power of the Crown, or of any possible sovereign, as necessarily limited by something described as natural law was, it must be noted, very general, even among lawyers. No one attempted to formulate this law of nature or to say definitely in what ways it restricted governmental action. It is almost always referred to in discussions of the question, but often, it seems, little or no meaning is attached to it. Often, however, the assertion of limitation on this ground is quite emphatic. ' En choses qui sont de droit divin ou naturel,' says Du Moulin, ' le prince même souverain ne peut proceder sinon comme la verité lui commande : autrement ce qu'il fait est du tout nul.' [1] Commands contrary to the 'law of nature', it is declared, must be disobeyed as much as commands 'contrary to the direct word of God. Connected with this general notion was the old idea that law, to be valid and binding, must be directed to the general welfare.[2] ' La fin de la loi,' wrote François Grimaudet, ' est le bien public . . . et si les édits sont faits en la faveur et utilité de ceux qui commandent ou d'aucuns particuliers, ne sont Lois.' [3] Such language is common. This way of seeing things was, at least, a bar to the acceptance of any theory of absolute sovereignty in the King or anyone else. The idea of natural law connected itself, also, confusedly,

---

[1] *Traicté de l'origine . . . du Royaume des Francais*, ed. 1561, p. 70.
[2] The connection appears in Aquinas and in the *Defensor Pacis*.
[3] *Opuscules Politiques* : published 1580.

with the idea of the sacredness of customary right, and added extra weight thereto.

But apart from particularist claims and the general notion of customary rights as absolute, what may be called constitutionalist theory tended to focus on two points : the idea of the Parlements as instituted to restrain the action of the Crown, and the idea of the States-General as representing all France. The Parlements of France were bodies possessed of great authority, traditionally and morally as well as legally. A hundred years after the time of Francis I, Richelieu wrote of them as those great companies on whose attitude the contentment or discontent of the masses chiefly depends. In addition to their strictly judicial functions they exercised very large powers in connection with police and censorship of morals and the Press. They were totally unrepresentative bodies, not merely because they were not elective and tended in fact to become close hereditary corporations, but because they were composed of lawyers. They were strongly royalist in sentiment and inclined to be hostile to all claims made against the Crown other than their own. But their own claims to strictly political power were formidable. It was claimed for the Parlement of Paris that it and not the Estates represented the ancient assemblies of the Champs de Mai.[1] It was in connection with the all-important matter of law-making that the claims of the Parlements were specific. It was admitted even by the King that mere publication of a royal edict did not make law. Before an edict became law it had first to be formally accepted and registered in the Parlement possessing jurisdiction in the district to which it applied. Before it became law for all France it must have been registered by all the Parlements. The famous Edict of Nantes was registered at Paris in 1598 : but it was not law for all France till ten years later.[2] Whether registration could be absolutely refused was the essential question. There was a theory that the Court had an absolute right to refuse : there was also a theory that if the King directly commanded registration the Court must obey. The language used by writers of the sixteenth century concerning this question is usually vague and suggests a shrinking from any positive assertion. ' Les édits ordinaires,' wrote Michel de Castelnau, ' n'ont point de force s'ils n'ont été reçus et vérifiés ès Parlements, qui est une regle d'Etat par le moyen de laquelle le roi ne pourrait, quand il voudrait, faire des lois injustes.' [3] But few venture to be so explicit : neither the King nor the Parlement of Paris itself, spoke or acted consistently. Refusal to register royal edicts was actually frequent ; sometimes the

---

[1] See Etienne Pasquier : *Recherches de la France*, I, ed. 1560.

[2] The Parlement of Rouen registered the edict for Normandy only in 1608.

[3] Memoirs. See Fustel de Coulanges in *Revue des Deux Mondes*, October, 1871.

King gave way and sometimes he treated the refusal as an offence against his sovereignty. In 1527 President Guillard, acting as spokesman for the Parlement of Paris, told Francis I that to dispute or raise a doubt concerning royal authority would be a sacrilege ; ' et savons bien que vous êtes par sus les lois et que les lois et ordonnances ne vous peuvent contraindre '.[1] But in 1561 it told the King that he had no right to grant liberty of public worship to heretics, since his coronation oath bound him to destroy heresy in his kingdom. It is doubtful, on the whole, whether, at least before 1562, the Parlement of Paris ever meant to claim a right to veto royal edicts simply because it disagreed with the policy involved. But it appears to have regarded itself as the guardian and interpreter of a traditional constitution and to have claimed at least a right to refuse registration to edicts it judged inconsistent with this. Quite certainly it held that if the King, by threats or violences, compelled a reluctant registration, he was acting ' unconstitutionally '. After 1562 it becomes bolder and the theory that a right to veto royal edicts was vested in the Parlements hardens. The Estates of 1576 gave a general support to the claim ; while those of 1588 explicitly demanded that the Court should never be compelled to register. The long conflict over the registration of the Edict of Nantes shows that the claim was still very much alive at the end of the century. It was, in fact, alive very much later. A declaration that if the King directly commanded registration the Court was bound to obey was the substance of Richelieu's edict of 1641 That edict was declared null and torn out of the registers during the Fronde, on the ground that its registration had been forced. It was necessary to re-enact it so late as 1670.

The claim of the Parlements to veto royal edicts tended, it must be observed, not only to place sovereignty actually in their hands,[2] but to divide France permanently. It tended to make the Parlement of Rouen sovereign in Normandy, that of Rennes in Britanny, that of Bordeaux in Guienne, that of Toulouse in Languedoc, that of Aix in Provence, that of Grenoble in Dauphiné and that of Dijon in Burgundy! It was partly, at least, for this reason that the claim never received any great amount of support. But there were other reasons. The noblesse were at once jealous and contemptuous of the claims of gens de robe ; while the Huguenots were hostile to bodies that were one and all Catholic. Not only so, but the Parlements themselves were all more or less dominated by the ideal of a national government. Their claims were in conflict with their ideal. They were in conflict also with the claims made on behalf of States-General.

The claim that the sovereignty of the King was shared in by the

---

[1] Isambert: *Recueil general des anciennes lois françaises*, Vol. XII, p. 277.
[2] This tendency was clearly pointed out in the preamble of the Code Michaud in 1629.

assembled Estates of the realm was, of course, a very old one. So far back as 1356 it had been formally declared that the King, even in the most pressing circumstances, could impose no tax without consent of the Estates. Actually it had only been at the feeblest moments of the monarchy, during the Hundred Years War, that States-General had ever looked like acquiring a definite place in the constitution. So irregular and occasional had been its meetings in the last two hundred years that neither its forms of procedure nor the relation to each other of its three orders had become really fixed. No one in the sixteenth century seems to have known for certain what consent of the Estates meant.[1] In spite of all this there was, for some time after 1550, an increasingly strong tendency to regard States-General as an essential part of the ancient constitution of the monarchy. Commines, in his memoirs, had asserted that the King could tax only with consent of the Estates. It was declared that in the good old times it had always been so. The States-General of 1560–61 showed itself definitely hostile to the theory of royal absolutism. The Third Estate declared that one of the chief causes of the troubles of the time was the abandonment of the ancient practice of assembling the Estates regularly. At Pontoise in 1561 the Noblesse and the Third Estate joined in demanding that all taxes should be voted by the Estates and no war undertaken without their consent. At Blois in 1576 these demands were repeated and fourteenth-century practice was appealed to. The Estates of 1483 had demanded that meetings should be held every few years : this demand was repeated at Blois. It was declared, too, at Blois, that the King should be held bound to act in accordance with any demand made by the three Estates together, and that an edict issued with the sanction of States-General could not, without its sanction, be revoked. After 1560 the theory that sovereignty lay with the King and the Estates jointly was, for a time, more and more frequently maintained. There arose, even, a tendency to claim that ultimate sovereignty lay with the Estates and that the King was subordinate to them. Such views were held by Catholics as well as by Protestants. Hotman in 1573 was only trying to prove a theory as to the ancient constitution of France that existed long before he wrote and was in no way specifically associated with the Huguenot party. The strongholds of the view that the Estates shared sovereignty with the King were the municipalities, Catholic or Protestant. The association of the theory with the Huguenots and the League only served to discredit it.

It is true, however, that the view that national sovereignty lay essentially with the Estates was held only by a few of any party at any time. Even the view that the Estates shared sovereignty with

[1] At the Estates of Blois in 1576 the Clergy declared that two of the orders could not bind the third.

the King never received any great amount of support. This was so because no powerful party or faction had anything to gain by the establishment of such theories. The nobles on both sides were always more or less hostile to any such view, and so also were the higher clergy. The Huguenot party, even apart from its nobles, had nothing to gain by the establishment of a claim to sovereignty for States-General, in which a Catholic majority was assured. Had there been any party in France which saw in the sovereignty of the Estates a means of establishing its own domination, a theory of the sovereignty of ' the people ' expressed through representatives would have been developed and adopted by that party. Such a theory was in fact developed both in the *Franco-Gallia* and by the prophets of the League.[1] But Hotman's doctrine never for a moment became the doctrine of the Huguenot party, and within a few years was utterly repudiated by it.

France in 1560 was even further from accepting the doctrine of an unlimited sovereignty in the King than it had been in 1540. Before that idea, even in a form not quite absolute, could be accepted, many obstacles had to be removed. The idea of a law of nature limiting all governmental action, the idea of the sacredness of customary rights, the claim of the Parlements to veto royal edicts, the conception of States-General as sharing in sovereignty, all stood in the way. There was a widespread feeling that the Crown had broken with tradition and was endeavouring to destroy the ancient constitution of the monarchy. None the less strong was this feeling because no one could give any clear account of that imagined ancient constitution. It was conceived after the fashion of Seyssel or, though somewhat vaguely, after the fashion of Bodin or of Hotman. But the disposition to assert some theory of limitations against the absolutist lawyers seems to have been very general. No one before 1562, or even for some years after, spoke definitely of any right of active and armed resistance to the Crown.[2] But that was already bound to come : and when it came it was on behalf of a traditional constitution of the realm that a right of rebellion was claimed.

It may seem that these last few sections have been concerned not with political thought proper but with mere aspects of French constitutional theory. But it is impossible, or rather it would be absurd, to separate these things. It was on the basis of the ideas current before 1560 concerning the nature of the French monarchy that the theories of the following period were developed ; nor can they really be understood without reference to this complex. It was only with the outbreak of civil war in 1562 that the controversy

---

[1] See Chap. IV, 4, and Chap. VI.

[2] This is not quite true. It seems that in 1560 certain priests were already preaching that a King who favours heresy may be forcibly deposed.

became acute and searching. From that time forward men were forced, more and more, into consideration of the foundations and meaning of politic society. Doctrines based on mere tradition, precedent and custom became evidently insufficient. Principles of universal application had, if possible, to be found and asserted. But before proceeding to these developments it will be well to give particular attention to the views expressed by Chancellor L'Hôpital, the most outstanding figure in French politics in 1561, on the eve of the great controversy.

§ 3. MICHEL DE L'HÔPITAL

In the years 1560–61 the government of France, directed by Catherine de Medici, was endeavouring to avert civil war by the establishment of a partial and localized toleration of heretical or ' reformed ' worship. L'Hôpital, as Chancellor, expounded and defended the new policy in a series of remarkable public speeches.[1] Incidentally he set forth his views of the nature of the French monarchy and laid down certain general principles. A lawyer and a humanist, who regaled himself in leisure moments with the composition of Latin verses in the fashionable manner, a friend of scholars and of poets, he was a statesman rather than a politician and a seer rather than a man of affairs. But he saw much further than the practical men of the moment. It was said of him later that he was the real founder of the party of the Politiques ; and it has been said, recently, that the Politiques were the founders of the ' modern state '. Whatever exactly this may mean, it is certainly true that L'Hôpital's utterances in 1561 were prophetic. Thirty years later France was becoming convinced that he had been right.

L'Hôpital's conception of the nature of the French monarchy resembled that of Grassaille rather than that of Seyssel. The King, he declared, holds his crown ' not of us but of God and the ancient law of the realm '.[2] He is sole lawgiver and himself ' legibus solutus '. It is the duty of his subjects to obey all his commands, ' c'est à dire ses lois, édits et ordonnances, auxquels tous doivent obéir et y sont sujets, excepté le roi seul '.[3] He can make or abrogate every sort of law so long as he does not contravene positive commands of God.[4] Parlements may give advice or delay his legislation ; they have no right of veto. States-General have no power but to present petitions. The subject is never justified in rebellion, whatever the King may do.

---

[1] L'Hôpital's views are expressed not only in his speeches but in various scattered writings, collected in Dufey's complete edition of his works (1824). The most important of these are the unfinished *Traicté de la reformation de la Justice* and the *Mémoire sur la necessité de mettre un terme à la guerre civile*, 1570.
[2] Speech of December 13, 1560, at Orléans.   [3] Ib.
[4] Speech at St. Germain-en-Laye, August 26, 1561.

' Il n'est loisible au sujet de se defendre contre le prince, non plus qu'au fils contre son pere . . . soit que le prince et magistrat soit mauvais . . . ou soit qu'il soit bon.'[1] Tyrannicide is abominable and honoured only by heathens.

L'Hôpital's view of the King's constitutional position is not, in fact, distinguishable from that of the civilian lawyers of Toulouse or Bourges. He has introduced into the system of Seyssel the conception of a sovereign law-making power. But he was not content, as they were, with the mere assertion of an unlimited right to command. Like Seyssel, he regarded custom and tradition with the greatest respect and held that innovation was dangerous. On the ground that it is of the highest importance that the King should be in close touch with his people, he argued that States-General should be summoned frequently.[2] Law varies with the particular circumstances of different times and places, but ' reason ' must always be the soul of it, else it will perish. For it must needs rest on ' la justice divine ' and on ' le droit naturel ', which is the same for the savages of America as for the Christians of Europe.[3] It is for the King to make such alterations in law as are from time to time required, even as a seaman trims his sails to the wind.[4] Evidently he was a little afraid of this law-making power that he recognized.

But of the practical necessity of such a recognition he was convinced. He asserted that the King held his authority from God : but it was not upon this that he laid stress. He saw in the recognition of the King as a real sovereign, with power to make law and to determine all questions without appeal, the only hope of peace and order in France. In this he anticipates Bodin. Of all evils, he declared, civil war is the worst. Better that a man should suffer every kind of injury than be a cause of civil war.[5] It is for our own sakes, he insisted, that we ought to obey the Prince and hold in horror all faction and sedition, remembering that the Prince exists for the sake of his people as a shepherd for the sake of his sheep. Internal peace, order and unity is the grand object to be achieved, and recognition of full sovereignty in the King the only means of its achievement.

It is on his defence of the policy of toleration which the government had at the moment adopted, that the later fame of L'Hôpital has chiefly rested. But that he should have seen in a measure of legal toleration the only way of escape from prolonged anarchical confusion and war, is not in the least surprising. Many others who saw the same thing preferred the grim alternative : but many also drew the same conclusions as did the Chancellor from the rather obvious fact. There was already in 1560 a quite considerable body

---

[1] Speech of December 13, 1560.   [2] Ib.
[3] *Traicté de la reformation de la Justice.*
[4] Speech of June 18, 1561.   [5] Speech of December 13, 1560.

of opinion in favour of the policy of the government and views in effect similar to those of L'Hôpital were vigorously expressed in the assemblies of Estates and Notables held in 1560–61. Jean de Montluc, Bishop of Valence, pointed out that the ' malady ' of heresy had become universal in Christendom and that so far persecution had but aggravated the situation.[1] Charles de Marillac, Archbishop of Vienne and a friend of the Chancellor, spoke in the same sense and added that reform of the Church itself could alone bring back the heretics into the true faith.[2]

In 1561 was published the *Exhortation aux Princes et Seigneurs du Conseil privé du Roi* which was referred to by Castellion and has been attributed to Etienne Pasquier.[3] The author argued that the state of the country required the establishment of two Churches in France and that there was no reason why such an arrangement should not be made. The Huguenot party, he declared, was as powerful as its enemies and its ruin could be compassed only by the ruin of France. It is well to amputate a diseased member, but it must be done in time ; when the disease has spread far, amputation means death. Religion may be a necessity of social order ; but all that is necessary is ' une générale et conforme apprehension de la crainte Divine et terreur du Jugement de la vie seconde en tête '. The author denounces the Pope as mainly responsible for heresies, and the preachers on both sides as the chief authors of tumult and sedition.

L'Hôpital was one warning voice among many ; but his voice was far-reaching and he presented the case for toleration far more completely than did anyone else in France at the time. Logically, as well as by his official position, he was bound first of all to deal with the assertion, made by a section of the Catholic clergy and by the Parlement of Paris, that the King had no right in any sense to legalize heresy. It is his manner of dealing with this assertion that is above all important : for here was indeed the key of the whole position. To declare baldly that the King's rights being unlimited, he had a right to tolerate or to persecute as he pleased, could have satisfied no one. L'Hôpital was confronted with two propositions : that justice required the punishment of heretics and that the maintenance of

---

[1] *Apologie contre certaines Calomnies* (1562), an anonymous tract attributed to Montluc. See also his speech of August 21, 1560, given by De Thou.

[2] Speech at Fontainebleau, August 23, 1560, given in full by Regnier de la Planche : ed. Pantheon Litt., p. 352, etc. Marillac argued in favour of frequent assemblies of Estates. See P. de Vaissière : *Charles de Marillac* (1896).

[3] *Exhortation aux Princes et Seigneurs du Conseil privé du Roi, pour obvier aux seditions qui semblent nous menacer pour le faict de la Religion*, 1561. It is included in the *Mémoires de Condé*, Vol. II, p. 613. Attributed to Pasquier chiefly on the authority of Pierre Pithou. But see article by A. Chamberland in Vol. I of *Revue d'Histoire Moderne et Contemporaine.* I entirely agree with the author that the pamphlet cannot be Pasquier's.

true religion is a primary function of government. Boldly he denied them both. Justice, he declared, does not demand the punishment of those who act according to their consciences, without injury to others. He did not say, or imply, that under all circumstances the treatment of religious opinion as criminal would be unjust; he only said that the King's duty to do and maintain justice does not of itself involve any such action. The maintenance of peace, order and justice, this is the essential function of government and the King is and can be bound to nothing else. He stands above and outside all groups and parties and sects, a supreme and final arbiter of all disputes. It is not for him to take sides with one party or another, religious or otherwise. It is his business to care impartially for the interests of all his subjects alike, irrespective of their religious opinions. Who, after all, knows what is heresy ? ' You say your religion is the better and I say mine is. Is it any more reasonable that I should adopt your opinion than that you should adopt mine ? ' [1] It is not the King's duty to compel either to give way : his duty is to see to it that the safety and welfare of the whole people is not destroyed by factions.

It would be quite wrong to represent L'Hôpital as saying that to the State, as such, religious opinion is a thing indifferent. He made no such absurd assertion. He felt profoundly that it was an evil and a dangerous thing that there should be two religions in the realm. Nothing divides men, he declared, as does religion. A Frenchman and an Englishman of the same religion are nearer together than two men of the same city whose religions differ.[2] Infinitely better would it be were there in France ' une foi, une loi, un roi '. It seemed to him almost impossible that men of different religions should live together in peace.

But he argued that, as things stood, toleration had become a mere necessity, if peace and order were to be maintained. The question for us now, he declared, is not of what is the true religion but of how men are ever to live together in peace. If the country is to be saved from anarchy we must all try to be patient and forget our differences and remember only that we are all Christians. ' Otons ces mots diaboliques, noms de partis, factions et seditions : luthèriens, huguenots, papistes : rechangeons le nom de chrètiens ! ' [3] Persecution has been tried and has failed utterly. ' Le couteau vaut peu contre l'esprit.' [4] A great rebellion can hardly be put down by force and, could it be done, the doing were worse than useless. The results of war would be mere devastation and a growing contempt for the royal authority, upon obedience to which the whole social order depends. If, by the use of overwhelming force, heresy could be

[1] Speech of December 13, 1560. [2] Ib. [3] Ib.
[4] Ib. ' Il ne faut point faire état de la force, sinon de celle qui est la servante de la raison.' *Traicté de la reformation de la Justice.*

utterly destroyed in France, liberty would perish with the heretics.
' Si on veut venir à borner la liberté de si etroites barres que la religion
et l'âme n'y soient point comprises, c'est pervertir malignement et
le mot et la chose même.' [1] Liberty has perished if men are not free
to seek God in their own way. ' Que reste-t-il à perdre apres cela ?
. . . La liberté et la vie vont d'un meme pas ; la liberté est l'élément
hors lequel nous ne vivons plus qu'en langueur.' [2] There was for
L'Hôpital no sort of inconsistency between the idea of liberty and the
idea of royal absolutism. The one indeed, for him, depended on the
other. He would have agreed heartily with what was written by
a French royalist forty years later : ' Tel crie Liberté, Liberté ! qui
ne sait que c'est. . . . La liberté n'est autre chose qu'une légitime
puissance que chacun a de disposer du sien à son plaisir . . . ce qui
ne peut être sans sureté, ni la sureté sans l'authorité publique, ni
l'authorité sans puissance, ni la puissance sans obéissance et commandement.' [3]

The ideal which L'Hôpital was setting before France was that of
a national government without legal limitation to its powers : a government not independent of religion, for the King holds authority from
God, still less indifferent to religious opinion, but seeing in the maintenance of peace, order and justice its essential function and owning
a duty to secure as far as possible the welfare of all its subjects, irrespective of creed. Unity in religion is, according to him, in the highest
degree desirable ; but where it does not exist a government which
attempts to establish it by force is failing in its duty and promoting
the disorder it exists to prevent. No Calvinistic Huguenot could
have accepted such a declaration ; and few convinced Catholics
could easily have persuaded themselves that this could be true. But
after long experience of those evils of which L'Hôpital forewarned
his countrymen, France as a whole was to come round substantially
to his opinion.

§ 4. RAOUL SPIFAME

There is just one French writer of the period before 1560 who
can hardly be placed in connection with any development, or with
any school, of political thought in France. If he is to be classed
at all it must be with writers of Utopias. Yet his was not a Utopia
and, though his thought was not wholly unlike Starkey's, it was very

---

[1] *Discours sur la pacification des troubles*, 1568. Also published as *Mémoire
addressée à Charles IX et à Catherine de Medicis sur la necessité de mettre un
terme a la guerre civile*, 1570.

[2] *Traicté de la reformation de la Justice.*

[3] *Parenetic ou Discours de remonstrance au peuple francais sur le suject de la
Conspiration contre l'Estat*, by P. Chevalier, 1602. The ' conspiracy ' was, of
course, that of Biron.

unlike that of More. He was, in his way, an economist before Bodin and an extreme ' Gallican ' who outdid in advance Servin and Pierre Pithou. He was a dreamer and something of a prophet and apparently a little crazy. But the world might perhaps do better with more of his kind of craziness.

Raoul Spifame was born about the year 1500 and came of a family which had for long belonged to that highly important section of the middle classes which managed the King's finance and filled the legal profession.[1] He himself studied law in Paris and was called to the Bar of the Parlement in 1524. It is unfortunate that about the career of this remarkable personage very little has been made out. A strange and pleasing tale is told of the odd results of what is alleged to have been his astonishing personal resemblance to King Henry II, who was his junior by nearly twenty years. Accustomed to be addressed by sportive companions as Sire and Your Majesty, Raoul, it is said, developed the delusion that he was actually the King. As a consequence he was shut up in Bicêtre as a madman in 1554. But later, we are told, the real King Henry transferred him to a royal château de plaisance where, by royal order, he was treated as the King he believed himself to be. Unfortunately I can find no reason whatever for believing this improbable story,[2] though the form of Raoul's book bears it out. But it seems that Raoul was on the list of avocats practising before the Parlement of Paris in 1562 and that, in his later years, he made himself conspicuous by insisting on wearing the scarlet robe that had gone out of fashion. Even the date of his death appears to be uncertain.[3]

However little can be discovered about the career of Raoul Spifame, we have his solitary book, which is all we really want. The book appeared anonymously and without date. It must have been published between 1554 and 1560 and is stated to have come forth in 1556. It is entitled *Dicaearchiae Henrici regis*,[4] but is written in French. It consists of a series of what are nominally royal edicts, supposed

---

[1] His father, Jean Spifame, seigneur de Passy, near Varennes, held the rather important office of ' trésorier de l'extraordinaire des guerres ' and was, no doubt, well to do. M. Nys states that Raoul was born at the château de Passy.

[2] Why this tale was admitted into the *Nouvelle Biographie Générale* is a mystery. The only reference given is to Gerard de Nerval: *Les Illuminés*. Some information about Raoul is given in Loisel's *Dialogue des Avocats du Parlement de Paris*. An account of him appears in the *Memoirs of the Académie des Inscriptions et des Belles Lettres*, Vol. XXIII, p. 271 (1756). There is another in Moreri's *Grand Dictionnaire Historique* (1759). There is also a modern life of him by E. Nys (1890).

M. Nys did not believe the tale of Raoul and King Henry but has not succeeded in discovering much.

[3] It is given as 1563 and as 1565.

[4] The full title is: *Dicaearchiae Henrici regis Christianissimi Progymnasmata*.

to be issued in due form by King Henry.[1] There are 309 of them. Raoul seems to have planned to issue five hundred ; but the remainder, unhappily, never came to light. They may have been written in the madhouse : several of them order the immediate release from confinement of Raoul Spifame.

Madhouse or not they form a really remarkable collection. In one respect, at least, Raoul was a Frenchman of his time ; but even in that respect he was a fanatical extremist. He was a single-minded and zealous believer in monarchic absolutism in general and the absolutism of the King of France in particular. He speaks of the ' Imperial and Pontifical Majesty ' of the King of France and compares his ' temporal and spiritual sovereignty ' with that of ancient kings of Egypt and of Rome, ' qui simul erant Reges et Pontifices '.[2] He gives some reasons for the faith that was in him, which Bodin and Le Roy would have approved. He remarks that, originally, France was governed in a democratic fashion, but experience having shown that this did not work well, sovereignty was transferred to a Prince. But his chief reason for believing in monarchy pure and simple was that a monarch ought to be able to decide quickly and quickly get things done. In large assemblies, he says, and even in oligarchies, decision is slow and difficult. In France the interference of the Parlement of Paris has been a constant hindrance to getting things done. The Estates have been a still greater nuisance. Some, he remarks, would make States-General the sovereign, but such an arrangement would amount to mere ' dissipation et confusion ' of the sovereignty and lead to a struggle for mastery among the Estates. All this appears in the preamble of one of his ' arrests ',[3] which goes on to anticipate Richelieu by enacting that henceforth royal edicts shall be registered and published as law as soon as signed, without remonstrance or any sort of interference from Parlements. All the same, at the very end of his book, he added a word of warning. ' Il n'est Prince qui ne se pense tel et en tient la parole et fait les oeuvres.'

There was so much, in Raoul's opinion, that wanted doing at once ; and only a King possessed of all powers could be conceived as at all likely to undertake the task. What he wanted the King to do is set forth in his edicts. They are arranged in no order, or rather they are not arranged at all. Had Raoul grouped his edicts under appropriate headings, such as The Church, Education, Public Health, Justice, Paris and so on, this would at least have made easier the task of a reader. He deals with all these matters and many more, issuing his edicts, evidently, as ideas occur to him, now on one subject,

---

[1] More than one antiquarian or ' historian ' of the eighteenth century took them to be actual royal edicts.
[2] *Dicaearchiae.* Preface.   [3] Arrest 19.

now another. All of them are drastic, some are prophetic and some are a little crazy.

We need not stay over the craziness, but even in that there is method. It was crazy to enact that all men over twenty-five and all girls over fourteen were to be married within three years.[1] It was a little crazy, though it would have pleased Bodin, to ordain that all children, every evening before going to bed, should ask parental blessing on their knees.[2] It was a little crazy to issue an edict ordering, on the ground that death is advantageous to man and to Christians desirable, that for the future there should appear no sign of mourning at funerals, but, on the contrary, signs of joy and thankfulness to God.[3] It was, perhaps, a little crazy to provide that what he calls a martyrology of all soldiers who died in their countries' wars should be officially made and preserved.[4] It may have been crazy to ordain that a company of musicians should play for the public enjoyment twice every day, in the court of the king's palace, and to enact detailed arrangements for the ordering of music in churches, ' to serve as well for a school of music as for devotion '.

Whatever one may think of these enactments, the edicts issued by Raoul about the Church are certainly remarkable. Under them all fees for the administration of sacraments are abolished,[5] no person is to hold two benefices,[6] bishops are to reside in their dioceses [7] and inspect all monasteries and, what is more, are to preach regularly on pain of being deposed.[8] In these enactments Raoul was only complying with a widespread and insistent demand ; but he went very much further. By one of his edicts all ecclesiastical jurisdiction is confiscated and taken over by the Crown, the clergy being reminded that it is held only by grant from the King and at his pleasure.[9] By another it is decreed that no benefice is to bring to its possessor more than twelve thousand livres tournois a year. All surplusage is to be confiscated to the Crown and used to form a pension fund.[10] Raoul announces his intention to establish, by his pontifical power, a single form of church service for the whole kingdom.[11] But a great evil remained ; and was drastically dealt with. The King has been informed that there exists in France an extravagant number of idle and unattached clergy. It is enacted, therefore, that all clerks unbeneficed, unemployed and without property, shall be deprived of orders and made over to the municipal authorities to be set to work ' comme serfs publics ', though their work is to be paid for.[12] If they will not work they are to be banished France. No special animus against the clergy is shown, for all persistently unemployed

---

[1] *Dicaearchiae*, Arrest 53.   [2] Ib., Arrest 90.   [3] Ib., Arrest 14.
[4] Ib., Arrest 14.   [5] Ib., Arrest 81.   [6] Ib., Arrest 46.
[7] Ib., Arrest 31.   [8] Ib., Arrest 245.   [9] Ib., Arrest 70.
[10] Ib., Arrest 70.   [11] Ib., Arrest 121.   [12] Ib., Arrest 70.

idlers are to be similarly dealt with.[1] Mendicant friars are to be set to harvesting.[2] There is to be no interference by the Pope with these measures or with anything else. Special edicts provide that henceforth a member of the royal family shall act as Vicar-General at Avignon and that the powers and rights of the Pope, so far as France is concerned, shall be transferred to the Archbishop of Lyon to be exercised by him in perpetuity.[3] Some similar arrangement might conceivably have satisfied Henry VIII of England.

Yet more revolutionary were Raoul's edicts concerning agriculture and property in land. It grieved him to think of scarcity while land went uncultivated or badly cultivated. All that was to be remedied, and without the least respect for the sacred rights of proprietors. Raoul shows a consciousness that his remedial measures might arouse opposition and asks people to remember that the power of the King is an infinity.[4] All land uncultivated, he decreed, may be squatted on and worked by the first comer. When this happens the owner has a right to buy out the squatter; but if he does not do so within three years, the squatter becomes the owner.[5] This was Raoul's first idea on the subject: later he had another. By edict he establishes Chambers of Agriculture for every part of France, with power to take over for nothing not only all uncultivated but all badly handled land. These chambers were to oversee all agricultural operations and see to it that all land was used to the best advantage, ' and not at the ignorant will and personal appetite of the owner '. If their directions were not followed they were to confiscate. They were to have special powers for the making of roads and pathways and for the punishing of cattle stealers and of those who cast spells on cattle.[6]

There was not very much, apparently, that Raoul would have left as it was. He established a new police for Paris with a commissioner for each quarter; he ordered the laying out of public gardens and the construction of new bridges and quays; blind alleys were to be abolished and slaughter-houses to be moved outside the city; stray dogs were to be destroyed.[7] He undertook elaborate reform of hospitals,[8] insisting on the isolation of infectious cases and compelling all monasteries to assist. Justice is to be administered gratuitously to all; the épices are abolished and an effort is made to cut down the exorbitant charges made by lawyers and doctors.[9] It is a matter of course that law was to be unified for all France and also weights and measures.[10] No one was to hold more than one office

---

[1] *Dicaearchiae*, Arrest 50,
[3] Ib., Arrests 153, 177, 180.
[5] Ib., Arrest 113.
[7] Ib., Arrests 291, 292.
[9] Ib., Arrest 21.

[2] Ib., Arrest 256.
[4] Ib., Arrest 185.
[6] Ib., Arrest 185.
[8] Ib., Arrests 1, 44.
[10] Ib., Arrests 196, 198.

under the Crown.[1] Raoul established a school in every parish to which all children were to go at the age of six and, to the poor at least, this education was to be given without payment. He even made arrangements for the free lodging of poor children in the school buildings. This is to be done, he says, ' because the said teaching is due to them ' and to make them pay for it would be simony and might altogether exclude the poor,' ' lesquels ordinairement profitent plus en lettres et vertus que ne font les enfans des riches maisons '.[2] Further, the municipalities are bound to find work for all who apply for it, but such applicants are, prudently, only to be paid at three quarters the usual rate.[3] Retreats are to be provided for all disabled soldiers.[4] A copy of every book published is to be placed in the royal library. The year is to begin on January 1st.

It is no matter for wonder if this man were really confined in a madhouse. He was considering things with a freedom from the usual assumptions and associations that must have stamped him crazy. Yet it is assuredly not the things he desired to get done that afford ground for calling him insane. What perhaps may here justify the use of that ambiguous epithet is not what he saw but what he did not see. One of the most striking features of his book is the fact that he does not even refer to the Huguenots. The questions that were to disturb men's minds and disorganize society for the next half-century hardly, it seems, existed for him, On the one side he saw an all-powerful King, on the other things that needed to be done. But while he wrote, France was drifting steadily towards civil war. He shows no consciousness whatever of the danger or the causes of it. He wanted the King to do what it might well have cost him his throne to attempt. Actually the monarchy, in 1560, was on the verge of a collapse. One would like to know whether his vision of possibilities was in any way modified by the events of 1562. That he should have imagined that any King could at such a time undertake the reforms he desired is the only real reason we have for regarding him as insane. Manifestly he was a man obsessed ; yet one may pardonably prefer his obsessions to Calvin's. It is, in any case, worth remembering that in the France of 1560 there was such a man. The fact cannot be without significance. Eccentric as Raoul was, or crazy if you will, it is incredible that there were not many who would at least have gone a long way with him.

[1] *Dicaearchiae*, Arrest 46. [2] Ib., Arrest 143.
[3] Ib., Arrest 50. [4] Ib., Arrest 294.

CHAPTER IV

THE HUGUENOTS AND THEIR ALLIES

§ 1. PRELIMINARY

W E have now to deal with that great controversy that animated France from about 1560 till the triumphant entry of Henry IV into a converted Paris. Many issues were involved in it and many were the points of view that found expression. Some of those view-points were not distinctively religious in any sense at all. Yet, to a great extent, both sides grounded their argumentation on a religious or theocratic conception of the State. Because that was so, both sides appealed, habitually, to the Scriptures. It could hardly have been otherwise, seeing that Catholic and Protestant alike, for the most part, held that all real authority is derived from God and that all real obligation is to Him. It would, indeed, have been possible to argue for the divine right of this or that without reference to the Scriptures. But it would have been harder to do and far less effective when done. Both sides consciously appealed to a mass of ignorant and not very intelligent people. Since the Protestants appealed to the Bible, needs must the Catholics have done so ; since the royalists appealed to them, rebels had to do the same. So both sides made all the use they could of Samuel and Saul and David and Daniel. One wonders a little, finding in pamphlet after pamphlet the same manifestly inconclusive arguments, why it was that neither saw the futility of it all. For, evidently, Saul and David were as much use to one side as to the other. It seems, indeed, to be the case that, as time went on, there was relatively less of argumentation from the text of Scripture. Yet, at the very end of the century, Alexander Barclay was going, wearisomely and exhaustively, over the trodden ground.

It is the views and theories set forth on the Huguenot side of the controversy that are first to be considered. It may be said at once that nothing that should be called ' the political theory of the Huguenots ' ever, in fact, existed. The attitude of the Huguenots as a party is one thing in 1562, another in 1567. In the period of desperation and experiment after 1572, what may, rather roughly, be called two distinct theories were set forth by Huguenot writers. Neither of them can be said ever to have been accepted by the party as a whole and after 1588 both were altogether repudiated. Nor were these theories, in the main, either new or distinctively Protestant. There was nothing either new or definitely Protestant in Hotman's *Franco-Gallia* or in the *Réveille Matin* : and little that was either in the theory summed up in the *Vindiciae*. The theory of the *Vindiciae* is medieval rather than Protestant. The Huguenots were not the first to develop a theory of a right of rebellion for the cause of religion. Knox, at least, had done that earlier. Nor was such a view distinctively Protestant in the sixteenth century. The Catholics of the League did the same thing, with quite equal sincerity.

If there be any theory which was characteristic of the Huguenots as a religious party, that is of French Calvinism, it was simply the theory that it is the duty of the Prince to establish Calvinistic doctrine and discipline or, at the very least, to tolerate their existence. But it is a fact of the greatest importance that the French Calvinists, and *a fortiori* the Huguenot party, never really adopted the Genevan ideal of the State. Knox in 1558 was enunciating, in defiance of Calvin, a theory which, if accepted by them, would have completely justified in their own eyes the rebellion of 1562. But the Huguenot party was only very partially a religious party. Lambert Daneau, one of the most learned and able of Huguenot pastors, a man, according to Beza, ' incredibilis laboris et diligentiae', upheld, during his absence from France, the strict theory of political Calvinism. The magistrate, he declared, should maintain if it exists, establish if it does not exist, re-establish if fallen, the true Calvinistic faith and discipline and suppress by force all heresy and idolatry.[1] But it was at Leyden, in opposition to Coornhert and the city magistrates, that he maintained this doctrine. I know of no similar writings published in France. Even the most convinced French Calvinist could not imagine France organized like Scotland. To have set up such an ideal would have hopelessly split the Huguenot party and deprived the Calvinists of most of their allies. Could anyone in his senses suppose that the Prince of Condé would endeavour to set up the government of consistories ? It might have been possible, perhaps, after 1572, to establish a strictly Calvinistic system of government in Languedoc. But the Genevan ideal could be realized in France locally only, if at all : and to realize it even so, the French Calvinists must have become separatists in the completest sense. But though they allied themselves with, and shared in, separatist provincial feeling, they never completely committed themselves to definite separation. They were too French. At heart, as they showed finally, they believed in France and in its monarchy. They ended by accepting mere toleration from

[1] See his *Politices Christianae*. He was absent from France 1572–1583. In 1582 he published, in Dutch, a violent attack on the heresies of Coornhert.

a Catholic monarchy claiming absolutism by divine right. From a point of view strictly Calvinistic, that was nothing less than defeat. The development of the whole controversy is one of the most striking examples of the way in which men adjust their theories at once to their desires and to circumstance. As circumstances changed so did Huguenot, and so did Catholic, opinion. One of the most acute and unbiased of contemporary observers noted and commented on the fact.

'Voyez,' wrote Montaigne, 'l'horrible impudence de quoy nous pelotons les raisons divines et combien irréligieusement nous les avons rejetées et reprises selon que la fortune nous à changés de place en ces orages publics. Ceste proposition si solennelle : s'il est permis au sujet de se rebeller et armer contre son prince pour defense de la religion, souvienne vous en quelles bouches cette année passée, l'affirmative d'icelle estoit l'arc-boutant d'un party, le negative de quel autre party c'estoit l'arc-boutant : et oyez à present de quel quartier vient la voix et instruction de l'une et de l'autre et si les armes bruyent moins pour ceste cause que pour celle-la.'

Accurately as these words apply to France in the sixteenth century, they have a far wider application. But Montaigne hardly seems to see that the process by which men persuade themselves of the truth of some principle that justifies them in doing what they wish to do, involves no conscious insincerity.

§ 2. BEFORE 1572

The ' confession ' issued by the Huguenot synod held in Paris in May, 1559, endorsed the political faith of orthodox Calvinism. ' We hold,' it declared, referring to the civil magistrate, ' that his laws and statutes must be obeyed, that we must pay tribute and tax and all other duty and bear the yoke of subjection with frank willingness, even though the ruler be unfaithful.' This declaration seems to have expressed the general attitude of French Protestants up to that moment. It was on the point of changing ; yet some years were to pass before any right of rebellion was claimed. Before the end of that same year began an outpouring of Huguenot pamphlets, appeals, denunciations and apologies, that continued till the end of 1560 and the accession of Charles IX. These writings express, mainly, simply an acute exasperation that becomes almost hysterical after the failure of the conspiracy of Amboise. Most famous of them is Hotman's *Epître au Tigre de la France*. Violent and rhetorical, abusive and vague, it is highly typical, and from our point of view quite worthless. But from other pamphlets certain positive contentions may be gathered, in spite of confusion and ambiguities. It was the Guises and not the King, who were denounced. The Guises, it was asserted, had usurped power and were ruling unlawfully. It seems to be implied or assumed that they had constituted a Regency. No Regency, it was declared, can lawfully be established save by the act of States-

General nor can Regency be held by foreigners. The Guises are mere foreign usurpers, tyrants 'ab titulo'. It is lawful to overthrow them by arms if any Prince of the Blood sanction the enterprise.

It does not seem worth while to discuss these contentions which appear to have little or no basis either in law or fact. Actual Huguenot rebellion may fairly be said to have begun with the seizure of churches and church property and the expulsion of Catholic clergy and monks in Languedoc and Guienne, after the failure of the conference at Poissy in 1561. But, after Vassy, the appearances of things were changed. With the entry of the Duke of Guise into Paris, it became possible to maintain that Charles IX and his mother were prisoners. The Huguenot pamphleteers of 1562 declared that their party was fighting for the King against the Guises. Condé proclaimed that his object was to set the King at liberty and assist him to enforce his edicts. It was their very loyalty that had led them to take up arms. Coligny presented an address repudiating any claim to rebel for any cause whatever. One and all utterly disclaim any right to rebel for the cause of religion. . Some of the writers did, indeed, suggest that the party was fighting in defence of the fundamental laws of the monarchy and on behalf of the constitutional rights of Princes of the Blood. But this contention, with its implication of right, remained vague. All that the writers seem quite sure about is that they are not rebels. The emphasis with which they repeated and amplified this assertion and protested their entire loyalty, seems to indicate that they were conscious of a certain lack of plausibility.

In 1567 Huguenot writers could no longer even pretend to believe that the King was a prisoner or in danger. Forced to find some kind of justification for rebellion against a government which had been doing its best to secure toleration for them in face of enormous difficulties, they still continued to disclaim religious motive or sanction. They fell back on the claim, already suggested in 1562, that they were fighting in defence of the ancient laws and liberties of their oppressed country. Condé's proclamations declared that he had taken arms on behalf of the whole French people, irrespective of religion. The pamphleteers of the party, from 1567 to 1570, maintain that they are fighting against despotism. France, it is declared, was constituted as a 'mixed' monarchy.

'L'intention du peuple français et gallique n' pas été par la loi royale du pays de souffrir un roi tyran ni qui usât d'absolue puissance contres toutes lois, et fit toutes choses à son plaisir. . . . Les rois n'ont pas levé tailles et autres tributs et impôts en la France sans le consentement du peuple, qui est argument que la monarchie française est composée d'aristocratie et du populaire état.' [1]

---

[1] Discours par Dialogue, sur l'Edit de la révocation de la paix, 1568. The passage is quoted by P. F. Méaly in Les Publicistes de la Reforme, p. 116.

The King is charged with endeavouring to subvert the ancient constitution and with disregard of rights as divine as his own. Such conduct, it is implied, gives the subject a right to defend his rights by force.

But some of the pamphleteers of those years go a little step further. It must have been felt, one would suppose, by many, that in appealing to the tradition of an ancient constitution, they were not on firm ground, historically or legally. Some principle was needed to supplement the constitutional argument. A good deal of stress, therefore, was laid upon the general notion of a reciprocity of obligation between King and people. To break faith with his subjects, to whom he is bound ' par obligation naturelle et réciproque ', turns a King into a mere ' tyrant '.[1] It is implied, though not yet clearly stated, that the duty of obedience is conditional always on the proper use of authority. Already, before 1570, the Huguenot apologists are seeking a new formula. They have not yet found the blessed word ' contract '.

Charles IX may be a tyrant ; all the same, the Huguenot writers of these years were continually protesting their loyalty and their respect for the King, while denouncing his advisers. ' Nous n'avons changé,' impudently wrote a pamphleteer of 1568, ' ni de volonté, ni de nos premières propos, contenant que nous voulons rendre obéissance à nos supérieurs.'[2] As Pierre de l'Estoile remarked later of the people of La Rochelle : ' Ils se déclarent très humbles serviteurs du roi, pourvu qu'on fasse ce qu'ils veulent.' It was equally true of both sides.

So far as the attitude of the Huguenots in 1568 was sincere, it was the attitude of nobles and aggrieved municipal magistrates, rather than of convinced Calvinists. There were very many among them who thought much of threatened customary rights and privileges and very little of religion. In 1568 the magistrates of La Rochelle issued a declaration to the effect that Kings who behave as enemies of God are not true Kings but merely private persons. The views of the strict Calvinists can never have coincided with those of the mass of the nobles, who, for one reason or another, supported the party. There was, no doubt, a tendency among the thoroughgoing Calvinists to take up a Knoxian position. It is even a little surprising that so few signs of that tendency appear before, or even after, 1572. By the party officially and as a whole, the Knoxian position was completely repudiated, at least up to that year.

§ 3. THE EFFECTS OF THE MASSACRES OF 1572

The massacres of 1572 produced a change in the situation that was greater morally even than materially. The Crown had, appar-

---

[1] *Discours par Dialogue.* Quoted by Méaly, op. cit., p. 112.
[2] *Contrepoison à l'avertissement sur le pourparler,* 1568.

ently, decided on a policy of extermination. Protestants therefore, it seemed, must now either submit or leave France or be killed ; or they must resist as Protestants and for the cause of religion. One result of the massacres was an immense exasperation ; another was that the direction of the party fell for the time into the hands of the Huguenot towns, in which the strictly religious element, if not dominant, was at least far stronger than among the nobles. For a time there was a strong feeling that, for Protestants, the struggle had become one for existence. It is a striking fact that a good many of the pamphlets published in the year that followed August, 1572, alleged ' necessity ' as a sufficient justification under the circumstances for armed resistance. Self-preservation, it was argued, is a natural right. Taken too literally the argument was logically unsound ; since self-preservation of a sort could be secured by submission and conformity. But we may fairly assume that behind the assertion was the sense that a man who allows threats to silence his conscience has in no real sense preserved himself. There was a sense, too, that only continued war could force upon the Crown a peace that would be kept. That feeling was expressed in a curious ' sonnet en parodoxes ' that seems to have been widely circulated :

' La paix est un grand mal, la guerre est un grand bien.
La paix est nôtre mort, la guerre est nôtre vie.

. . . .
Paix est propre au méchant, la guerre au vrai chrétien.' [1]

It must have been difficult to see what attitude it was practically best to adopt and opinion among the Huguenots was clearly divided. To have set up the standard of the Genevan ideal would have been practically to declare for separation and would have alienated the nobles and the Bourbons. A tendency in that direction was indeed manifested in certain writings as well as in the new organization that took shape in Languedoc. But the party could not have been held together on such a programme and the league of Huguenot towns stopped just short of a declaration of independence. There was, in truth, no need of any radical change of front. All that was needed was definition, expansion and systematic presentation of the ideas suggested by the writers of the late civil war. All that happened was that certain tendencies, apparent before 1572, became strongly emphasized, certain ideas, held in solution earlier, now crystallized into definite shape. Hotman in 1573 was but trying to prove historically assertions made in 1568. The authors of the *Du Droit* and the *Vindiciae* were doing little more than elaborate the assertion freely made by the pamphleteers from 1567 to 1570, that the duties and obligations of Prince and People are reciprocal.

The terrible events of August, 1572, led at once to a violent out-

[1] Printed in *Mémoires de l'Estat de France sous Charles IX.*

break of pamphlets. On the Huguenot side many of them, as in 1560, express little more than an exasperation that tends to become hysterical.[1] Now, for the first time, attacks of extreme violence were made in print on the King personally. It was declared that his assassination would be just and laudable. Wild projects circulated on paper. Nicolas Barnaud produced a scheme for a federal organization of Huguenot towns after the Swiss pattern.[2] The author of the *Réveille Matin* [3] advocated the complete dethronement of the Valois and was apparently ready to recognize even the Duke of Guise as King if he would guarantee toleration. He called for a league of all Protestant princes, princesses and potentates to assist the Huguenots and save Protestantism in France, and declared that, if the tyrant could not actually be deposed, at least total repudiation of his authority would be justified. *La France Turquie* [4] suggested the formation of an association for the refusal of all taxes ; a suggestion made long before in La Boëtie's *De la Servitude Volontaire*.[5] In *Le Tocsin* of 1577 [6] the Swiss and the English were appealed to and Paris was described as the great Babylon. It was remarked by the author that, if the early Christians had not rebelled against Cæsar, that was only because they were not strong enough to do so. Much more significantly, he declared that the constitution of a model State is to be found in the Old Testament : that of the monarchy of the Jews in which the King was restrained by prophets acting under the inspiration of God. But suggestions of this sort were few. The mass of Huguenot opinion was adverse to government by any kind of prophets. With one exception the writings so far mentioned only vaguely suggest any kind of theory, constitutional or other. But out of a tumult of ambiguous voices certain ideas were emerging into at least partial definition. It remains to deal with the more important writings of this period : and first with the *Franco-Gallia* and the *Réveille Matin*.

§ 4. HOTMAN AND THE *RÉVEILLE MATIN*

Both Hotman's *Franco-Gallia* and the anonymous *Réveille Matin* differ essentially from the tracts of the *Mémoires de l'Estat* and from the *Vindiciae*, in that the views expressed or implied in them are

---

[1] Far the finest expression of this exasperation is *Les Tragiques* of Agrippa d'Aubigné, originally written, apparently, in 1577, though revised and enlarged later and not published till 1616.

[2] *Dialogue auquel sont traitées plusieurs choses advenues aux Luthériens et Huguenots de la France*, etc., 1573.

[3] See *infra*, p. 311. The author may have been Barnaud.

[4] *La France Turquie, c'est à dire Conseils et Moyens tenus par les ennemis de la couronne de France, pour réduire le royaulme en tel estat que la tyrannie turquesque*, 1575.

[5] For La Boëtie, see p. 313. His essay was not published till 1576 but appears to have circulated in manuscript.

[6] *Le Tocsin contre les massacreurs et auteurs des confusions de la France*, 1577.

strictly political or juristic and are not radically concerned with any religious conceptions.[1] They are distinguished further by the fact that they express rather a theory of constitutional rights than a theory of the State in general.

The *Franco-Gallia* of François Hotman was published at Geneva in 1573.[2] Born at Paris in 1524, Hotman was already eminent as a jurist and in 1567 had succeeded to the chair of Cujas at Bourges. He had been in the employment of the Bourbons since 1560 and had been one of Condé's advisers in 1567. In 1572 he had narrowly escaped death and by the end of that year he was at Geneva. It is possible that it was in some degree due to his counsels that his chiefs, in 1567, had adopted the attitude of defenders of constitutional rights. In any case, in his exile at Geneva, he set himself to prove that they had been justified in doing so. His book has been described as a manifesto of the Huguenot party. But, regarded as a manifesto of the party, it was belated : it should have been published in 1568. The time was already in the past when any such theory as his could be of much use to the Huguenots.

The *Franco-Gallia* is in form a treatise on French history and constitutional law ; but it is written with passionate and elaborated rhetoric. It is a very angry essay on the constitutional history of France. It has been lauded on the ground that Hotman here made use of the historical method of approach to politics. But it is just the use made of history that condemns the book. If Hotman were trying to prove from historical records that, legally or not, the King was rightfully subordinate to the Estates, as representing the sovereign people of France, he was doing a merely absurd thing. For, in the nature of things, no such proposition can be proved from history. If he were trying to prove that the history of France showed that sovereignty had always legally belonged and still did belong to States-General, then, obviously, he could not escape the historical method, any more than any other lawyer arguing from precedent. Unfortunately his documents proved nothing of the sort. Hotman's history is a mass of inaccuracies, confusions and misunderstandings. Nor can it be said that no more truthful presentation of the history of France was possible at the time. Belleforest's *Grandes Annales*,[3] written partly to refute Hotman, was not, perhaps, much better as

---

[1] This fact is pointed out and laid stress upon by G. de Lagarde in a recent and valuable work : *Recherches sur l'Esprit Politique de la Reforme* (1926, Paris). The author even suggests that the *Du Droit des Magistrats* may have been written partly in order to counteract the influence of a work so secular and uncalvinistic as the *Réveille Matin*.

[2] *Franco-Gallia seu Tractus isagogicus de regimine regum Galliae et de jure successionis.* A second edition, with a translation by Simon Goulart, appeared in 1574 ; and an enlarged edition, in Latin, in 1576.

[3] *Grandes Annales de la France.* 1579.

history than the *Franco-Gallia*. But Du Haillan's *Histoire Générale* [1] was in every way far superior. It can hardly be said that Hotman used the historical method in a manner worthy of a disciple of Cujas. He sketched the constitutional history of France with the object of showing that, from the time of pre-Roman Gaul, the sovereignty of the people, expressed through a national representative body, had always been recognized, except during an insignificant period of Roman rule. Pre-Roman Gaul he identifies with the kingdom of France and he represents the Franks as deliverers from Roman tyranny. He maintains that the right of the representative body, under whatever name, to make law, to appoint magistrates, to create a regency, to elect and depose the King and to confer the crown, was continuously recognized till towards the end of the fifteenth century. He denounces the claim of the Parlements to any share in political sovereignty as baseless and wrongful.

Hotman did not tell his readers what inferences they were expected to draw from all this nor how exactly the facts as stated bore on actual conditions at the moment. In his preface he declared that Frenchmen could find remedy for present ills only in reform along the lines laid down by the wisdom of their ancestors : so only could they recover ' ce bel ancien accord qui fut du temps de nos pères '.[2] This does not take us very far. But the main assertion and the main implication of his book were clear enough. Hotman implied that sovereignty naturally resides in the people and is naturally expressed through some sort of representative assembly ; and he asserted that this fact had been practically recognized in law throughout the history of France, until these last times. For the implied proposition no grounds were given : it was not, in fact, even stated. For the second the argument was worthless, as was seen even at the time.

The *Franco-Gallia* has, I think, been greatly overrated. It may be said that Hotman was attempting to justify, by reference to history, the attitude taken up by the Huguenot leaders in 1567. It might equally be said that he was trying to justify the attitude of the Estates at Pontoise in 1561. He was trying to prove historically the validity of a theory or tradition that had existed for long inside and outside the Huguenot party. In doing so he had given it a precision that perhaps it had not possessed earlier. That his book created a considerable flutter is true ; and this was due perhaps as much to his reputation as a jurist as to its content. That it exercised any profound influence on Huguenot or on French thought in general, it is impossible to believe. French thought after 1573 was certainly not moving in the direction

[1] Bernard Girard, du Haillan : *Histoire générale des rois de France*, 1576. His view of the constitution of the monarchy closely resembles that of Seyssel.
[2] French version, 1574. In *Mémoires de l'Estat*, 1578.

of a recognition of the sovereignty of States-General.   It is true that for a few years after that date a tendency to claim something like supreme authority for States-General was more manifest than it had been earlier.   But that tendency was more manifest on the Catholic than on the Huguenot side.   It might even be suggested, though with little plausibility, that the attitude of the Estates of Blois in 1576 was influenced by the *Franco-Gallia*.   But, only a few years later, the trend of both Huguenot and Politique opinion was in quite another direction.   In truth Hotman's constitutional theory was of little use to the Huguenot party at any time.   When, in the next few years, Huguenot writers repeat the historical fictions of the *Franco-Gallia*, they do so, as a rule, in a perfunctory manner, making no attempt to connect them with their main argument.   After 1573 the pretence that the Huguenots were fighting to maintain or restore an ancient constitution had worn so thin that it did not even deceive themselves.

In recent times Hotman's book has been commended largely on the score of its implication of an ultimate sovereignty in the community as a whole.   Whatever merit may attach to the making of this assertion, it was certainly no new one.   It is, indeed, somewhat remarkable that Hotman did not state distinctly this ancient proposition.   But he must have been aware that to a considerable section of his party, language about the sovereignty of the people had to be carefully guarded, if it were not to give offence.   He did, in fact, go out of his way to suggest that he meant nothing objectionable.   A King, he says, ought always to be restrained by the authority ' des gens des bien et d'honneur comme representant la personne du peuple, lequel les commet à cela et leur donne cette puissance '.[1]   Evidently this can hardly refer to States-General.   These ' gens de bien et d'honneur ', who permanently represent the people, are surely the same as the officiarii regni and proceres of the *Du Droit* and the *Vindiciae*.   The suggestion conveyed in Hotman's vague phrases was perhaps of more practical value for the Huguenot party than anything else in his book.

That suggestion became more definite in the *Réveille Matin des Français*, which appeared in two parts, the first in 1573, the second in 1574.[2]   It has been conjectured that it was the work of several authors ; and this might at least explain its confusion of topic and arrangement.   It is the community, the writer or the writers declare, that confers power, and power is conferred on a King conditionally.

---

[1] *Franco-Gallia.*   French of 1574.   Chap. I, p. 12.   In the Latin : ' quo de causa optimatum et delectuum auctoritate, quibus eam potestatem populus permittit, tanquam fraena coercendus est '.
[2] *Le Réveille Matin des Français et de leurs voisins composé par Eusebe Phila-delphe Cosmopolite en forme de Dialogues.*

No people has ever been or will ever be so foolish, as to set up a supreme magistrate with absolute authority to do whatever he pleases. Sovereignty was not conferred upon the King alone : a portion of it, or a share in it, was given to a number of magistrates whose ordinary functions are subordinate. It is the right and the duty of such magistrates to resist tyrannous action on the part of the monarch. Who exactly, in France, are such magistrates and whether they possess this right of resisting tyranny collectively or individually and how the duty of ordinary folk is affected by their action, these points are not elucidated. What the writer is quite clear about is, that the obligations of ruler and subject are what he calls reciprocal : in other words, that the subject's duty of obedience is conditional on the ruler's at least attempting to do his duty. Like Hotman, the author believed in an ancient constitution in which this principle was practically embodied. That constitution has recently been subverted ; but it may and should be revived. It is futile to argue that even though the absolute authority now claimed for the King were originally a usurpation, it has become by continuance established in law. For there can exist no prescription against the rights of the people.[1] When a King becomes a tyrant and treacherously massacres his subjects, like Charles IX, he may rightly be deposed and even justly assassinated.

Except for the still vague assertion that there exists a class of officials who represent the community and share in sovereignty and are entitled, somehow or other, to keep the King within due limits, there is nothing in all this but an expansion of the suggestions in earlier Huguenot writings. The *Réveille Matin* is a hotch-potch of ideas current among the Huguenots at the moment, unsystematically presented and all rather vague. It is, perhaps, especially remarkable in that the view presented was almost unconnected with any form of religion. But its practical conclusion was more drastic and uncompromising than any reached before 1573.

§ 5.· THE *MÉMOIRES DE L'ESTAT*

The views expressed in the *Franco-Gallia* and the *Réveille Matin* link up, to a certain extent, with a fairly coherent theory of the origin and nature of political authority and of the relation between Prince and People, developed in a series of pamphlets, before the publication of the *Vindiciae contra Tyrannos* in 1579. The political theory expounded in the *Vindiciae* was, in fact, in all essentials, fully developed before the publication of that work, in which it was, as it were, summed up and fully and systematically presented. To that theory Hotman

---

[1] 'La prescription contre les droits du peuple est invalide.' The phrase is repeated in the *Vindiciae*. 'Adversus populum non praescriptio.' The writers could have found it in William of Occam.

really contributed nothing ; while the *Réveille Matin* made towards it only rather crude suggestions. Hotman's view of the constitution of France and its history was, indeed, more or less definitely adopted by the group of writers concerned ; but it was in no way essential to their view and was unconnected with their argument.

These writers were concerned, not with any questions of legal right, history or precedent, but with the fundamental question of the nature of political authority and the extent of the obedience due to it. All of them approached the problem from a point of view definitely religious. The religion of all of them was, presumably, Calvinistic ; but their political theory derived not from Calvin but from the thought of the later Middle Ages.[1] As political thinkers they were far nearer to William of Occam than they were to Calvin. Their reasoning is of a kind which Calvin had condemned and their conclusions involve flat contradiction of Calvin's positive teaching. Calvin had thrown over all the traditional medieval teaching which limited the duty of obedience by reference to a law natural or to the nature of man-made law. The Huguenots, after 1572, were reviving the older mode of thought, they were turning back to Nicholas of Cusa, to William of Occam, even to Aquinas. But the effort to reconcile a mode of thought, and premises, derived from these sources, with Calvinistic faith and the needs of the Huguenot party, necessarily produced a certain incoherence.

Mémoires de l'Estat de France sous Charles IX is the somewhat misleading title of a collection of writings published by Simon Goulart in 1576.[2] Its publication is a far more significant fact in the history of Huguenot political thought than is that of the *Vindiciae*. There in, in fact, hardly a contention, hardly even an argument, in that pretentious book which is not to be found in the earlier pamphlets. The Memoirs included all the most important Huguenot writings dating after 1572 with the exception of the *Réveille Matin*. It included, also, the *Discours de la Servitude Volontaire* of La Boëtie, which now appeared for the first time in print though probably written before 1550.[3]

It seems necessary to add a few words concerning this exercise in rhetoric by a gifted young student who knew his Seneca. Not only was La Boëtie not a Huguenot, but his essay contains no direct reference to the state of France under Charles IX and no kind of theory

[1] On this point see G. de Lagarde's *Recherches sur l'Esprit Politique de la Reforme*, pp. 265–268.

[2] A second edition, ' revue, corrigée et augmentée,' appeared in 1578 and is the one usually referred to. That of 1576 seems to have become a very rare book. Feugère, in his edition of the works of La Boëtie, says that he could not find a copy. There is no copy of it in the British Museum ; but there is one in the London Library. The additions made in 1578 were of small importance.

[3] La Boëtie died in 1563. *See* Feugère.

of government. It is an essay on 'tyranny' in general, why it is endured and how maintained and how easily it might be overthrown. 'Tyranny' here means, apparently, a government directed entirely for the gratification and entertainment of a governing person or group. La Boëtie wrote as though he imagined that such governments were quite ordinary and prevalent phenomena. There is a constant implication that Europe is now governed by tyrants, but no positive statement to that effect. The instances given are all from ancient history. He makes no definite application of his views to the France of his own day and never even refers to religious persecution. But the essay gave a general support to the Huguenot pamphleteers by its insistence that natural law and natural rights justified forcible resistance to tyrannous government. Incidentally the *Contr' Un* [1] was an essay on the natural liberty, equality and fraternity of man. Nature,

'le ministre de Dieu et la gouvernante des hommes,' says the author, 'nous a tous faits de même forme et, comme il semble, à même moule, à fin de nous entre conoistre tous pour compagnons ou plutôt frères . . . elle a montré en toutes choses qu'elle ne voulait tant nous faire tous unis que tous uns : il ne faut pas faire doute que nous ne soyons tous naturellement libres, puisque nous sommes tous compagnons ; et ne peut tomber en l'entendement de personne que Nature ait mis aucun en servitude, nous ayant tous mis en compagnie.'

But this sort of language served no Huguenot purpose. It served, in truth, no purpose at all at the time, though, one day, it might come to do so.

The writings included in the *Mémoires* of 1576 almost completely anticipate the *Vindiciae* of 1579. To isolate the latter is a mistake and gives a wrong impression. It should be considered along with the writings which it at once expanded and reduced to order. Its superior importance is hardly at all due to any originality, but primarily to the fact that it states the case of the earlier writers more completely and systematically than was done by any one of them. There is another reason also for considering all these writings together, so far as that is possible. The points on which they differ among themselves are of some significance.

§ 6. THE *MÉMOIRES* AND THE *VINDICIAE* [2]

The most striking and significant of the writings that appeared in the *Mémoires* of 1576 are the *Du Droit des Magistrats sur les sujets* and the *Dialogue d'Archon et de Politie*. Available evidence points

---

[1] This sub-title of the essay did not appear in 1576.

[2] *Vindiciae contra tyrannos, sive de principis in populum populique in principem legitima potestate, Stephano Junio Bruto Cella auctore.* Basle, 1579. A French translation appeared in 1581.

to an almost unavoidable conclusion that the *Du Droit*,[1] published anonymously, was actually written by that veteran champion of Calvinism, Theodore de Beza. That Beza should, at this crisis, have produced an essay in flat contradiction of his master's teaching and in equally flat contradiction of earlier utterances of his own, is not really surprising. But it is certainly an extreme case of the way in which the political views even of the most faithful followers of Calvin adjusted themselves to circumstances. Beza was a Frenchman ; and the emotional stresses aroused in him by the massacres of 1572 and by the critical position of Calvinism in France in the years that followed, sufficiently explain a quite honest change of view. The *Dialogue* between Archon and Politie,[2] inferior to the *Du Droit* in completeness and coherence of statement, is perhaps in some ways more typical and the author saw points that were missed by his fellow-writers.

All these writers, from the author of the *Du Droit* to the author of the *Vindiciae*, agree with one another and, indeed, with almost every one else in the sixteenth century, that the obligation to obey constituted political authority is an obligation to God and that rebellion is, normally, rebellion against God. The author of the *Archon et Politie* was at great pains to explain away the Biblical texts that were used to prove that rebellion is wicked in every conceivable case : but that God normally requires obedience to Princes it would never have occurred to him to deny. It may be noted also that all of them were inclined to allow that monarchy is at once practically the best form of government and the form most clearly approved of in Heaven. The *Du Droit*, indeed, suggests a doubt. ' Since the world was,' says Beza, almost in the words of Calvin, ' if we consider even the best of Kings, we shall not find one who did not abuse his position.' Monarchical government tends rather to the ruin than to the conservation of peoples ' unless it be bridled in such sort that the great benefits that may come of it be gathered in and the wondrous harm prevented '.[3]

However that may be, they all assert vigorously that there exists no absolute sovereignty save that of God. From this they draw directly the conclusion that the rightful power of all magistrates must,

[1] It seems to have been first written in Latin, but to have been first printed in French in 1574. De Thou's statement on this point is probably correct. The editor of the *Mémoires* makes the strange assertion that, in its original form, it was published at Magdeburg in 1550. To what confusion this assertion is due is not clear. The essay has no vital connection with the Magdeburg tract of April 13, 1550, already dealt with, and certainly with no other that is known. But there is sufficient resemblance to allow one to suppose that Beza had the Magdeburg tract before him while writing.
[2] This has an alternative title : *Dialogue de l'autorité des Princes et de la liberté des peuples*. In *Mémoires*, Vol. III, 1576.
[3] *Du Droit*, Mem. II, p. 757, ed. 1576.

in the nature of things, be limited. ' It is God alone whom we are bound to obey in all cases without exception.' [1] Kings are bound not only by the commands verbally given in the Scriptures, but also by that natural law which is, equally, the law of God. ' The Prince is subject to the law divine written and to that natural law of equity imprinted in the hearts of all men.' [2] Here, as almost everywhere, the *Vindiciae* follows suit. God reigns *per se*, *Kings per Deum* ; their jurisdiction belongs to God and they are his delegates. There can be no such thing as unlimited human authority. God recognizes Kings as his agents and has, indeed, created them ; but ' magistrates were created for the people and not the people for magistrates '.[3] This last medieval commonplace is repeated again and again by the various writers and in almost the same words.

From these propositions, which no one was likely flatly to deny, we pass to the essential contentions. It is not quite easy to see what these were. The writers were not very sure about it themselves.

God, they agree, makes of Kings his agents and ministers for general welfare : they are ' given by God for our good '.[4] None the less do these writers agree with the author of the *Réveille Matin*, that all princes and magistrates were established by a common consent of the people. Some peoples have established monarchic, some aristocratic, some democratic forms of government ; but every particular constitution owes its being at every moment to the will of the people. So had declared the writer of the *Réveille Matin* ; and Beza and the rest agree. So absolutely is this the fact, says Politie, that even in a monarchy hereditary by custom, a King should be regarded as elected.[5] Though nominated by God as the heir of Saul, David only became King by the free choice and consent of the people.

They agree, too, with the *Réveille Matin*, in thinking that no people would be so foolish as to vest unlimited authority in anyone.[6] There was never a monarchy, rashly declares the writer of one pamphlet, without some kind of representative body to act as a check on the King. The institutions of France, he argued, of themselves imply a right of rebellion under certain circumstances.[7] The authority of all magistrates being derived from the people and held conditionally,

---

[1] Opening of the *Du Droit*.　　　[2] *Dialogue*, Mem. III, p. 113.

[3] The phrase is at least as old as Aquinas. It occurs in Pasquier's *Pourparler du Prince*, 1560. It was, in fact, the merest commonplace at the time.

[4] *Dialogue*, Mem. III, p. 96.

[5] Ib., Mem. III, p. 97. The *Vindiciae* repeats this.

[6] There is confusion here : since, on their own showing, the thing could not be done.

[7] *Réponse sur la question à savoir s'il est loisible au peuple et à la noblesse de resister par armes à la felonie et cruauté d'un seigneur souverain.* Mem. III, p. 229.

' il s'ensuit que ceux qui ont eu puissance de leur bailler telle autorité, n'ont eu moins de puissance de les en priver '.[1] Among the Jews ' Dieu temoignait par la bouche du sacrificateur qu'il les reconnaissait pour son peuple ; le roi promettait de regner selon Dieu, et le peuple, suivant cela, de lui obeir '.[2] Everywhere magistrates were originally established ' avec pactes et obligations reciproques '.[3]

None of these writers, with the partial or possible exception of him of the *Vindiciae*, conceived of any definite ' contract '. What they were asserting is simply that political authority was established in answer to recognized needs and that the ends for which government was established involved absolutely a limitation of the rights of any possible sovereign. The limits of the subject's duty of obedience are and must be determined by the ends for which political sovereignty was instituted. The duty of obedience is, in other words, conditional on the sovereign's acting in the sense of the need that created him. From the mere fact, which no one denies, that the Prince exists for the sake of his people, it is inferred that the people may depose a Prince whose action is inconsistent with the purposes for which alone he exists. Just so had Gerson and Pierre d'Ailly argued that the Pope's power must needs be limited by the ends for which the Church exists.

So far the view presented is intelligible enough ; but now arises a difficulty. All these writers insist that though the Prince is an agent and delegate of a sovereign people, he is also an agent and a delegate of God. In the *Vindiciae* the notion is formally emphasized to the point of paradox. ' Deus reges instituit, regna regibus dat, reges eligit ; populus reges constituit, regna tradit, electionem suo suffragio comprobat ! ' The phrases were apparently intended to throw light on the matter : it can hardly be said that they do so. It would appear, if the words mean anything, that the populus may reject the King appointed by God. It is not easy to see why God is brought into the business at all. God, it might be said, created the need to which government corresponds and created man with power to deal with his need. But to say this would be merely to say that God created whatever is. God wills peace and order among men and therefore the government set up by the people represents God's will. Certainly the writers all had this in mind ; but they must have meant more than this. For this alone affords no ground for saying that God institutes and appoints Kings.

In what sense then, for these thinkers, did God create the King ? Why did they feel bound to make this assertion ? None of them seem clearly to have known : certainly none of them clearly state the

---

[1] *Du Droit.*

[2] *Dialogue.* This is pompously expanded in the *Vindiciae*, in which the alleged fact becomes a ' foedus ' or a ' pactum '.   [3] Ib., Mem. III, p. 98.

reason. It was, I think, because all of them, rightly or wrongly, conceived of obligation as arising only in reference to some final end and purpose in life. There can be, they felt, no obligation that is merely to man. My need, of itself, cannot create for another an obligation to God. Hence, though the people could set up a government and endow it with force, they could not give it real authority. They could not create an obligation to obey it, for all obligation is to God.

Their theory, then, may be stated as follows : Any actual Prince receives his office and his actual power from the people. But the real authority attached to that office, the obligation to obey the commands of the Prince, is derived not from the people but from God.

In the view, or the sense, that the authority of the Prince is created by God, the Huguenot thinkers were at one with the believers in absolutism by divine right. It is just at this point that the two diverged. The authority attached to kingship is conferred by God, but, say the Huguenots, it is conferred only for the benefit of the people and therefore conditionally. If any King act in a manner destructive of the people's welfare, he has, in the language of the *Vindiciae,* broken his covenant with God. In such a case the people may and should deprive him of the office which the people conferred.[1]

The so-called ' contracts ' of the *Vindiciae* signify this and little, if anything, more. It is doubtful, at least, whether the word ' contract ' should be used in translating the phrases of that book. The author uses, indiscriminately, the word pactum and the word foedus, as though both meant the same thing. But while pactum was a term of law and properly signified contract, the word foedus signifies alliance or treaty. Of both terms alike, as used in the *Vindiciae,* the vaguer word covenant would seem to be the better translation. The author of the *Vindiciae* did not himself attach any very definite meaning to his terms and certainly did not intend to suggest that his pactum was something quite definite, rigid and enforceable. His own account of its terms makes that clear.

He does not seem quite to know whether there are two contracts, or covenants, or three. Obviously it did not matter. There is the ' duplex foedus ' between God, Princeps and Populus and there is another pactum between Prince and People only. The first of these, whatever it is, is clearly not a contract in the strict sense. Under it the Prince binds himself to serve and obey God purely, according to his Word and to see to it that the People does the same. The People binds itself to the right and proper worship of God before all

---

[1] So Nicholas of Cusa, in his *De Concordantia Catholica,* had declared that all authority is held ultimately from God but immediately from man ; that the Pope's authority rests on the consent of the Christian community and that the Pope is Vicar of the Church rather than of Christ.

things else. The Prince is to answer to God for the People and the People for the Prince. If the People desert God the Prince will be held responsible : if the Prince turn traitor the People is responsible for suffering it. Under the second ' contract ' the Prince binds himself to rule ' justly ' and to respect and maintain the rights of every one ; the People binds itself to obedience so long as he does so and no longer. This ' contract ', it is important to observe, is not conceived as necessarily historical or formal or as necessarily expressed at all in words. It may be tacit ; [1] but whether express or tacit, it cannot by any process be cancelled. Why not ? Because, in the first place, it is not a contract at all. It is a mutual obligation arising from the nature of things and from the will of God. The words pactum and foedus would seem to imply a conscious and deliberate act of will. But what is a tacit ' contract ' ? It is surely evident that the writer was thinking simply of a moral obligation. His pactum does not, like a contract, depend on man's volition. It is something that exists necessarily and universally.

The pamphlets of 1576 had asserted that the Prince is bound to rule justly and to serve God and that he ought to be resisted and even deposed if he definitely and consistently refuses to do so. The author of the *Vindiciae* was not content to declare that the Prince was bound ; he declared that the Prince had bound himself by a pactum. The difference is merely verbal : both meant the same thing. The pactum of the *Vindiciae* is one that cannot be cancelled even by the agreement of both parties ; and it is one that, whether expressed or not, exists always. There is, really, nothing voluntary about it. On the author's own showing the pact was not made either by Prince or People. It expresses nothing but the immutable will of God. It is not very clear what the author thought was gained by putting it as he did. Whoever he was,[2] he was gathering up the content of the earlier pamphlets and presenting it in a logical order and with a great parade of precision. He had really little to add to what had been said already ; but he was bent on giving to the theory increased definition and an exactitude that could not be given. By his talk about contracts he succeeded in emphasizing the idea of reciprocal obligation and especially the obligations of the Prince. Perhaps

---

[1] ' Inter reges et populum mutua obligatio est, quae sive Civilis, sive Naturalis tantum sit, sive tacita, sive verbis concepta, nullo pacto tolli, nullo jure violari nulla vi rescindi potest.' *Vindiciae*, ed. 1660, Amsterdam, p. 232. ' In constituendo principi intervenit foedus inter ipsum et populum, tacitum, expressum, naturale vel etiam civile.' (Summary of the conclusions under *Tertia Quaestio*.)

[2] Who was ' Junius Brutus ' is a vexed question on which there is no need to enter here. Judging from what I know of his writings I do not believe that the *Vindiciae* was the work of Duplessis Mornay, in spite of his wife's statement. Nor am I in the least convinced that Hubert Languet was the author.

this was all that he aimed at doing. His ' duplex foedus ' emphasized
the notion that a Catholic Prince who persecutes true religion, has
forfeited authority and may justly be resisted and deposed. His
language is in keeping with the pretentious character of the whole
book, which professes to be demonstrative ' geometrarum more '. In
posing the second of his questions, as to whether it be lawful to resist
a Prince who is violating God's law and wrecking the Church, the
author had the audacity to declare that, owing to its delicacy, no one
had yet made more than a passing reference to the problem. Did
he wish it to be supposed that he had never even read the pamphlets
of 1576 ? [1]

§ 7. THE DIVINE RIGHT OF REBELLION

In every kingdom, says the *Vindiciae*, drawing an inevitable
conclusion, the true lord and sovereign is the People.[2] If the King
becomes a tyrant he commits treason against his lord and is a rebel
against his sovereign. But under what circumstances exactly does
a Prince become a tyrant ? When is a King not a King ? It is well
to say that the Prince is bound by natural law and justice, is bound
to work for the welfare of his subjects and to serve God. It is well
to say that his authority is limited by the ends for which it exists.
It is well to say that where private are put before public ends, there
is tyranny.[3] But who is to judge, in any one case, whether the conduct of the Prince amounts to a breach of the conditions on which
he holds authority ? Or who is to say whether a ' contract ', avowedly
unwritten and indefinite, has been broken or not ? Does the right
of judging and of revolt belong to all and sundry and, if not, to whom
does it belong ? To these momentous questions similar answers
were returned by the *Vindiciae* and by the earlier pamphlets.

It is carefully explained that there are two quite different kinds
of tyrant.[4] But about one of these, about the tyrant who has no
just title to his throne, there is little to be said and no real question.
It is every one's duty to resist usurpation. Rebellion against a
tyrant of this species is always justified : he may even rightly be assassinated. The fact that among the Jews killers of tyrants of this
class were specially commissioned by God only proves, says the
author of the *Du Droit*, the faint-heartedness and stupidity of the
Jews.[5] The serious question is concerned with legitimate princes.

[1] Just possibly he had not. The preface to the *Vindiciae* is dated 1577.

[2] ' Deinde probavimus, reges omnes regiam dignitatem a populo accipere ;
populum universum rege potiorem et superiorem esse ; regem regni, imperatorem
imperii supremum tantum ministrum et actorem esse ; populum vero vere
dominum existere.' *Vindiciae*, ed. 1660, p. 264.

[3] ' Ubi utilitas publica praevalit, rex et regnum : ubi propria, tyrannus et
tyrannis.'

[4] The distinction is at least as old as Bartolus.   [5] *Du Droit*, Mem. II, p. 741.

Who is to judge whether a legitimate prince has become what the *Vindiciae* calls ' tyrannus exercitio ' and to whom belongs the right to take action against him ?
More or less elaborately the writers contrast the true King with the Tyrant. They are careful to point out that one swallow does not make a spring.[1] David was guilty of abominable outrages, but David was not a tyrant.[2] An occasional murder or so may be passed over. Princes are but men ; and if a Prince behave tolerably we may think ourselves lucky, says the *Vindiciae*. The Tyrant is one who rules habitually without regard to law, justice or piety. He is at enmity with God and man.[3] The true King diligently studies the Word of God : the Tyrant speaks of God only to blaspheme. The true King loves to hear the truth : you tell the truth to a Tyrant at your peril.[4] In the characterization of the good King the author of the *Vindiciae* exhibits some slight orginality, due to his personal aristocratic bias. The Tyrant, he says, prefers persons of low or unknown birth to his nobles : the good King cherishes his grands seigneurs as himself and sees in them the friends of his kingdom.[5] But all this does not help much towards an answer to the questions that must be answered.

It might be supposed that the answer would have been that it is for the People both to judge and to act. In a sense this was the answer that was given : but our authors distinguish. They distinguish absolutely the right to judge from the right to act on the judgement. They contemplate the possibility of a position in which no action is justified against one who is, nevertheless, a ' manifest ' tyrant. The right merely to judge could, in fact, hardly be denied to anyone. Every one may judge : and the writers show little or no sign of any sense that the question might be difficult. Any may judge and can ; but it is not for every one to act on the judgement. All agree that the private man, the individual subject as such, has no right to take action on his own judgement. The right of active resistance is conceived as belonging not to individuals but to communities. The simple subject is bound to submission by the law of God and by his own consent. He must not obey commands contrary to God's law nor must he participate in tyrannical action, but, says the *Du Droit,* ' Il n'est licité à aucun particulier d'opposer force à la force du Tyran de son autorité privée.' ' Celui qui a été avoué de son peuple, nonobstant qu'il abuse de son droit, retient toute fois ce fondement d'autorité qu'il a sur ses sujets particuliers.' Were it otherwise, he adds, the remedy would prove worse than the disease, ' et surviendraient

[1] ' Una hirundo non facit ver.' The very phrase is used in this same connection by the author of the *De Justa Reipublica* of 1590.
[2] *Du Droit*, Mem. II, p. 775.   [3] *Vindiciae*.
[4] *Dialogue*, Mem. III, p. 144.   [5] *Vindiciae*, ed. 1660, p. 239.

mille Tyrans sous ombre d'en vouloir empêcher un '.[1] All agree that
the right to take action against the Tyrant belongs to communities
as such. It does not belong to any mere multitude of individuals.
Considered as a mass of individuals the People is but a monster,
with a million heads and no sense. The community can only act
through representatives. Who or what is it that possesses the right
to speak and act for the community ?

The answers given to this question vary slightly in form but
in substance are similar. To have declared that the right belonged
solely to the Estates of the realm assembled, might have been a logical
but would have been a sadly unpractical answer. The Estates had
the fatal defect of meeting only when summoned by the presumed
Tyrant. Permanent representatives of the community, able to act
for it at any moment, had to be found. They were found in magistrates, in nobles, in regni proceres.

All holders of public office, declared the *Du Droit*, must be regarded
as officers of the kingdom rather than of the King. They ' ne dépendent proprement du soverain mais de la soveraineté '. Each of them
shares in sovereignty and each of them is sworn and bound to maintain
law and justice. Their duty so to do includes a duty to resist by
force, if necessary, the ' sovereign magistrate ' who acts as a tyrant.
All ' Dukes, Counts, Viscounts, Barons and Chastelains ' belong to
this class of officers of the kingdom : they were, originally, ' magistrates ' pure and simple, and still retain their old rights. There are
yet other magistrates ' ordonnés pour servir comme de bride et de
frein au souveraine Magistrat '. He was thinking, probably, of the
Parlements of France, but he does not specify. Over and above all
this the Estates assembled possess an indefeasible right to depose
a tyrant. The sovereignty of the people is conceived as delegated
to and divided among a group of magistrates and nobles.

' Il y a un mutuelle obligation entre un Roi et les officiers d'un Royaume :
duquel Royaume tout le gouvernement n'est pas mis entre les mains du Roi,
ains seulement le souverain degré de ce gouvernement, comme aussi les officiers
inferieurs y ont chacun leur part selon leur degré et le tout à certaines conditions
d'une part et d'autre.' [2]

If the sovereign magistrate disregard these conditions, it is for the
inferior magistrates to protect the people against his tyranny and
raise the standard of revolt.

The language of the *Vindiciae* is similar. The author says plainly
that when he speaks of the ' populus ' he really means those ' qui
universum populi coetum representant '. These are the magistrates
and ' proceres ', delegated and established by the people with a share
in sovereignty. They include all officers of the crown, all city magistrates, grands seigneurs, Parlements and deputies of town or province.

[1] *Du Droit.* Mem. II, p. 492.   [2] Ib., Mem. II, p. 749.

They are the guardians and guarantors of the compacts on which political society is based.[1] The confused nature of the answer is already obvious. It would have been difficult for the writers to say what they meant by the word ' represent '. In what sense did nobles and Parlements, city magistrates and Estates all alike represent the community ? What ground was there for regarding the nobles or the Parlements of France as ' representing ' anything ? But, even taking the answer as it stands, a difficult question at once arises. Did this strangely miscellaneous crowd collectively ' represent ' the people or did each member of it sufficiently represent the whole community ? Did the right of rebellion lie with every ' chastelain ' and with every Parlement ? An attempt was made in the Vindiciae to answer this question. But the answer it gives is hopelessly ambiguous. Only on one point was the author quite clear. Any magistrate or group of magistrates, he lays down, standing at the head of and therefore ' representing ' a distinct community within the kingdom, such as is a province or a town, may resist tyranny on behalf of the community for which he is locally responsible : and that even though all the rest of the kingdom side with the tyrant. In particular the magistrates of any town may establish true religion within their walls and resist by force all attempts to introduce idolatry. Such action being taken it will become the right and even the duty of the inhabitants of that town or province to draw the sword in support of the conscientiously rebellious magistrate. Whether persons not of that town or province may, in such a case, do the same is not, however, made clear. But we are told elsewhere that if any one of the ' principal officers ' of the kingdom raise the standard of revolt, then all may join him and feel that they fight for God.

The author of the Vindiciae apparently, at times, saw France as a sort of federation of communities each with its own law and magistrates and each with its own independent right to defend itself against tyranny. It would appear that there was not, after all, a single pactum between the King and people, but a pactum between the King and every such community. Every community that can be seen as distinct, is conceived as having rights against the common sovereign. It is this conception that gives to the Vindiciae one of its chief claims to originality. But it would be easy to claim too much on this account. The conception was really, as things stood, almost inseparable from the widespread conception of ancient custom as sacred and immutable. It corresponded to a considerable extent to the actual condition of France. The author of the Vindiciae was conscious of a difficulty. He did not see how it could be said that a small group of nobles or a city magistracy represented the people of France. But it was easy

---

[1] ' Hujus vero foederis seu pacti, regni officiarii vindices et custodes sunt.' Vindiciae, p. 294.

and natural to see La Rochelle or Montauban as distinct communities, with their own laws and their elected magistrates; for such in fact they were. If magistrates derived their right of revolt against tyranny from their representative character, it was reasonable, he felt, to claim for the magistrates of Nismes or for the Estates of Languedoc the full rights of representatives of a ' populus '. The conception had the additional advantage of fitting exactly the needs of the Huguenot party. But no stress is laid qn it. No attempt is made to work out a conception of a Federal State consisting of communities each with its own rights. Most of the language of the *Vindiciae* is inconsistent with any such conception of the State.

There is no question in any case of a counting of heads or votes. The Huguenot pamphleteers are quite free from any superstition about numerical majority. No one even suggests that it is only for a majority of the regni officiarii to give the signal for revolt. The author of the *Archon et Politie* dialogue does indeed suggest that there is a question. Archon asks whether, supposing that a majority of his people support the tyrant, the minority can have a right to rebel. Politie answers stoutly that right is right and injustice, injustice. The opinion or the action of a majority as such can make no difference. The majority may go to perdition as it pleases. Life and honour and salvation must not be surrendered to a majority.[1] But this is, practically, only negative. To the question who it is has the right to give the signal for general rebellion, we are left without any definite answer.

Suppose a ' manifest tyrant ' whose iniquities are supported or connived at by all the officiarii regni without exception : what is to happen ? The case is not, indeed, likely to occur, if any one of these officers may initiate rebellion. Perhaps this fact helps to account for the answer given to the question. The people, says the *Du Droit*, have, in that case, no remedy but in repentance, patience and prayer. The *Vindiciae* abounds in the same sense. If private persons drew the sword without due authorization, they are guilty though their cause be just. They are bound to wait for the command of all, that is of those who represent the whole body of the people in kingdom, province or town, or at the least of one of these, before taking any action against the Prince.[2]

King and officers of the kingdom alike were established by the community for its own benefit. The King is bound absolutely by the purposes for which he was set up. No less absolutely are the

[1] *Dialogue*, Mem. III, p. 136.
[2] ' Singuli denique principem non constituunt, sed universi. Itaque universorum, eorum, inquam, qui universos in regno, regione, urbere quae regni partem faciat, representant, jussum expectent oportɜt, aut unius saltem ex illis, antequam adversus principem quidquam moliantur.' *Vindiciae*, p. 287.

magistrates bound to resist tyranny. On this point all the writers are emphatic. So expressly is it the duty of the magistrates to resist a tyrant, says the *Vindiciae*, that they have no possible excuse for not doing so. But if the magistrates, nevertheless, fail in their duty, the community has no remedy against them. It may not rise and depose its magistrates. It can speak and act only through them. That pactum between Prince and people, it appears, was badly drawn. It has made the magistracy the judge of the King's action without appeal and has disabled the people from taking any action against an unfaithful magistracy. Evidently it was drawn by the governing class itself.

There is no frivolity in putting the matter in this way : it expresses, crudely, the real fact. The *Vindiciae* proclaimed the sovereignty of the people. We must guard against the absurd notion that this phrase has always the same meaning or even necessarily any meaning. What does it signify in the *Vindiciae* ? The people is sovereign in the sense that all governmental action must be referred to the general welfare. Again, it is sovereign because political authority can only be conceived as originating in its needs and as resting on its recognition. This is meant and no more than this. The populus is not conceived as in any sense a sovereign agent. It can act only under orders and direction. It has no will of its own ; it does not even recognize its own needs ; it does not know its friends from its enemies ; it does not know itself ; it knows nothing. But in every populus there exists an upper stratum which is self-conscious and intelligent. Just as, in medieval conception, the ecclesia was the whole body of the faithful, but the sacerdotium alone its thinking and active agent, so now the State is conceived as a community which can think and act only through its upper classes. Every populus, then, has its natural representatives, and the sovereignty of the people, conceived as acting, lies wholly with these. This, it is true, is not how the Huguenot writers put the matter. They speak always of official persons and of nobles : of persons, that is, either holding some kind of jurisdiction or some kind of recognized superiority. But definition had to be arrived at : and it would have been no more possible then than now to define ' upper classes '. In France, indeed, the class of nobles was inclined to claim that it alone ' represented ' the people. The Huguenot writers claim a share in active sovereignty for the aristocracy of the towns also.

But before the theory could be said to be intelligible, yet another difficulty had to be met. All these writers, from the *Réveille Matin* to the *Vindiciae*, habitually speak of the King as bound to respect positive law. He is bound to think of law as ' lady and mistress ', and if he breaks law habitually he becomes a ' tyrant '. But what, then, is the source of law and what gives it validity ? If the rights of the King include the right to make what law he pleases, even the most wrong-headed of tyrants might well dispense with breaking law. He has only to alter or repeal it when it stands in his way. The question as to law-making power was, of course, fundamental: but only the authors of the *Archon et Politie* and the *Vindiciae* seem to have seen this at all clearly.

The view of ' Politie ' was that law-making power can exist at all only within narrow limits. There are, he says, three kinds of law. There is natural law ; there is a law of nations which binds all peoples alike and determines the relations of individuals of different nations ; and there is the law which is peculiar to particular States. Natural law is divine ; its content is everywhere apparent to human reason and on it ' dépendent le droit des gens et le droit civil '. This natural or divine law determines in all cases what is just or unjust. There is no difficulty, to his mind, in determining the limits of human legislative power. ' On aura pour régle certaine les lois divines et l'equité naturelle.' Every human ordinance inconsistent with natural law is null. It is not a question of what the Prince thinks good or of what the mass of people desire. ' La force d'un vrai loi le doit emporter sur la volonté du peuple.' In the main, in fact, law has been made by God and there is little left for the human legislator to do. The Prince may and should bring the law of his particular community into harmony with natural law and he may make such legislative adjustments and alterations as occasion requires. Having conceded this much the author felt that it was too much. He adds that the Prince has no right to make violent or drastic changes in law ' without the common consent of those most interested in the matter '.[1]

It is important to realize that this way of thinking of law and of legislative power was, in the sixteenth century, not only common but perhaps more common than any other. The author's phrases had for long been commonplaces. But this medieval view of the matter, whatever might be said about it theoretically, was from the point of view of a practical lawyer, all but meaningless. The author of the *Vindiciae* shows an awareness of this fact. He refused to concede to the King, as such, any law-making power at all. His language indeed is, here as elsewhere, confused. He speaks of law as ' an instrument given by God for good government '. But he says, also, that Kings receive law from the people. ' Law,' he says, ' is an apprehension of intelligence or rather a body of such apprehensions.' [2] It is ' the reason and wisdom of thinking men gathered into unity '.[3]

---

[1] *Dialogue*, Mem. III, pp. 116, 117.

[2] ' Lex est mens vel potius mentium congregata multitudo.' Ed. 1660, p. 158. Translation is not easy. The French version of 1581 gives : ' La Loi est une intelligence ou plutôt un amas de plusieurs entendements ' (p. 138).

[3] ' Lex est multorum prudentum in unum collecta ratio ot sapientia.' Ed. 1560, p. 157.

It is, in fact, as the *Defensor Pacis* had averred, a judgement of the community as to what is required for general welfare. As such it cannot be changed by a mere royal edict. It can be changed only by a common consent. That common consent can be given by the community through its representatives. He arrives, thus, at the conclusion that law can only be made by the King with the assent of the Estates of the realm. So, it seems, he comes back to the conclusion of the *Franco-Gallia*. Legal sovereignty lies with the King and the Estates jointly. But he was not claiming for the King ' in Parliament ' an unlimited power of law-making. His belief in natura¹ and divine law forbade that absolutely. His assertion, in fact, was mainly negative. He was merely saying that law could not be changed at all without a general consent.

There remained the question whether rebellion is justified for the cause of religion. There could, surely, be no doubt that a Prince who persecutes true believers and endeavours to destroy the true Church, is the very worst sort of tyrant. It is inconceivable that authority to do so could be derived from God or man. Yet there was, here, a certain difficulty ; and all the writers showed that they felt it, even though none but the author of the *Archon et Politie* definitely expressed a doubt. None of them could say that a King who ' persecutes ' for the cause of religion is necessarily a tyrant. On the contrary, they all agree that it is the duty of the Prince to maintain true religion and to use force if necessary to root out false doctrine and idolatry. The true end of government, says the *Du Droit*, is not the peace and quiet of this life but the glory of God.[1] It follows that it is the duty of all those in authority to maintain the right service of God by all means in their power. In the *Vindiciae* the Prince ' contracts ' with God to do this very thing : it might be held that, under the ' contract ' he might justly be deposed if he does not persecute ' idolaters '. But, if this be so, how can the persecution of any particular religious group give it a right to rebel ? Archon, in the Dialogue, asks the question. Catholic Princes, he points out, hold that their religion is the true one and claim that in persecuting Protestants they are doing their duty. When Politie replies that it is for the Church to determine from the Scriptures what is heresy and for the King to act on that judgement, Archon ventures to remark that that, precisely, is what Catholic Princes are doing. The question is fairly stated ; but it is not answered. Politie answers the question only by begging it, exactly as Calvin and Beza had done long since. The author of the *Vindiciae* begs the question without even asking it. He seems not to have seen the difficulty. But it is a little curious that Beza, in the *Du Droit*, denies that mere ' persecution ' could give the faithful a right to rebel. On this point, at least, he remained a strict Calvinist.

---

[1] Beza was repeating both himself and Calvin.

He asserts, merely, that rebellion is justified on behalf of forms of worship authorized by law ; and that this was the case with the ' reformed religion ' in France. He was a better Calvinist than lawyer. It was not quite enough to argue that the Huguenots were justified in rebelling; it was desirable also to show that they were justified in seeking aid from foreigners. Ever since the Huguenot chiefs had, in 1562, agreed to hand over Havre to Elizabeth of England in return for armed assistance, the party had constantly endeavoured to obtain foreign aid. Bands of German ruffians, politely presumed to be of the true religion, had assisted vigorously in the devastation of France. It was, indeed, hardly worth while to try to persuade Protestant princes in general that it was their duty to assist the Huguenot party. Such an enterprise had not the smallest chance of success. The *Réveille Matin* sorrowfully admitted as much. But it was worth while to try to persuade the French people, who had suffered from such pious invasions, that the party was justified in bringing them about. The demonstration was undertaken in the *Vindiciae*. It put the question : ' Whether neighbour Princes are bound to give aid to other's subjects, persecuted for the cause of true religion or oppressed by manifest tyranny ? ' [1] On general grounds of duty to God and one's neighbour, he asserted, the answer in both cases must be affirmative. There is but one true Church and injury done to the least of its members is injury to the whole body. All Christian Princes are bound to safeguard, not only the Church in their own dominions, but the Church Universal. To abandon one part of it to the enemy is to betray the cause. As to the case of mere manifest tyranny, what has to be considered is that all men are of like nature, that justice is the same for all and that a tyrant is a common enemy of mankind.

' Piety bids us maintain the Law and the Church of God : justice demands that we bind the hands of the tyrant who would destroy all right and all good government : charity requires that we lend a hand to lift up the fallen. Those who make no account of these things would drive piety, justice and charity from the world, that they be no more heard of.' [2]

The writer seems to have been unaware how far-reaching was the principle he had laid down.

§ 8. THE THEORY OF THE *VINDICIAE*

The theory of the *Vindiciae*, which is also, in all essentials, the theory of the *Du Droit* and of the *Archon et Politie* dialogue, is a theory of the nature of political sovereignty. Any possible political sove-reignty, it is declared, is bound by the law of its own nature and its nature is and must be determined by the ends for which it was created. It was established by the community to meet certain needs and to

[1] *Vindiciae. Quarta Quaestio.*   [2] Ib. Last words of the book.

realize certain objects of desire. What these needs were is not made very clear : it is clear only that they were universally felt and recognized. According to the *Vindiciae* the chief of them were the protection of property and defence against external enemies. It is important to observe that the community is conceived as existing before the establishment of the sovereign. Nothing is said as to the form in which it existed ; but since property existed in it there must also have existed some kind of law, though this, perhaps, was only the law natural. In what sense or manner the community was capable of action is not made clear : it is clear only that it was capable of action. It is not even clear that the establishment of a ' sovereign magistrate ' was to the writers the same thing as the first establishment of co-operative coercive government. Some of the language used almost suggests that they conceived of a community, in which law and ' magistrates ' already existed, setting up a ' sovereign magistrate ' as an additional institution. But on all possible questions concerning the origin and nature of the community which sets up political sovereignty, these writers have practically nothing to say. There is, if you will, in the *Vindiciae*, a ' contract ' between people and ruler : there is no suggestion of a social contract. Something is assumed and one does not quite know what. It might be said that the whole theory is baseless.

It would be wrong to say so. When it was said that the sovereign was constituted by the people, all that was meant was that imperative need necessarily brought about his establishment. When it was said that the people is ' par dessus le roi ' [1] or that the people is the sovereign, all that was meant was that government exists for the general welfare and that all power depends on the recognition of authority. May we say that when a contract between King and people was spoken of, this meant only that such recognition carries with it, always, implied conditions ? We cannot say quite that. The use of such terms as pactum and foedus seemed to imply that political sovereignty was established by a deliberate act of will and with a consciousness of the ends to be realized through it. This, whether he exactly meant it or not, is, practically, what the author of the *Vindiciae* contributed to the theory by his use of the word pactum. And this, it would seem, is the essence of what is loosely called the ' contract theory '. The contribution made by the *Vindiciae* was in one sense important. In the seventeenth century it became fashionable, among certain groups, to refer all questions concerning the rights and obligations of sovereigns and peoples to a fictitious contract. But how far the *Vindiciae* can be held responsible for that fashion is a question which belongs to the history of thought in the seventeenth century.

---

[1] *Vindiciae*, ed. 1581, p. 105. ' Cum reges a populo constituantur, omnino regni videtur, populum universum rege potiorem esse.' Ed. 1660, p. 116.

Had this been all, we might have said that the theory of the *Vindiciae* eliminates divine right. It did, of course, nothing of the kind. On the contrary, the whole theory depends on its conception of God's will and of God's law. Rebellion against a sovereign who is doing, or even trying to do, his duty is declared to be rebellion against God. For it is God alone who gives the sovereign a real right to demand obedience, even though his power to enforce it is derived directly from the people. In setting up a sovereign the people has, logically, bound itself to obedience though only conditionally. But the people could not create an obligation. All obligation is to God. Even the right of resistance is a 'divine right'. It arises because God, like the people, granted authority only on conditions; for, again like the people, God wills the general welfare.

Sovereignty is bound and limited by three things. It is limited by the law of nature, which is nothing else than the sense, assumed to be the same in every man, of what is right and what is wrong. Sovereignty, we may put it, is limited by the moral consciousness of the community. The sovereign is bound also by positive law which is not of his creation. Law, so far as it is not simply divine in origin, is a judgement of the community as to justice and welfare. It cannot, by its nature, be altered at the will of any one man. The making or the alteration of law requires a general consent. Finally, the sovereign is bound by the law directly given in the Scriptures: and this, to the Huguenot writers, means that he is bound to maintain what they call the true religion, assumed to be a fixed and known quantity. If a King persistently disregard any of these obligations he becomes a 'tyrant': that is, he loses his God-given authority, the obligation to obey him ceases and he may rightfully be rebelled against and deposed.

The right of resistance to tyranny belongs to the community as a whole. How is it to be exercised? When they come to answer this question the Huguenot theorists are at a loss to know what to say. The exigencies of their party were altogether too much for their reasoning powers. Their answer is absurd. It means, if it means anything, that any one of the *regni proceres* or *officiarii* may pronounce the King a Tyrant and initiate rebellion. They shrink from saying this outright: but what else were they saying? They might have said, with some show of reason, that only some kind of representative body could declare a King a tyrant and levy war against him. But they knew that States-General was of no use to them. Their theory on this matter was adjusted to and determined by the needs of the Huguenot party. The preface to the French version of the *Vindiciae* claimed that its author had had no desire to favour any party. It is difficult to suppose that he could have even hoped to be believed. But there is, of course, no reason to suspect either the author or his translator of dishonesty.

It must be understood, however, that the author of the *Vindiciae* was in no way logically bound to say that the community could express itself only through the majority of some kind of representative body. There was nothing in his theory from which such a conclusion could be drawn. Whether the laws of God or of nature or positive law is being habitually broken or not, was to his mind a question of fact simply. The opinion of a mere majority, as such, on the subject, is completely irrelevant. The truth is that his theory did not furnish any basis for an answer to the question : how is the will and judgement of the community to be expressed ?

Whatever importance ultimately attaches to the theory of the *Vindiciae*, its importance for the sixteenth century and for France in particular was small. The book had far more influence in the seventeenth than in the sixteenth century and far more in England than in France. Its vogue in France lasted only a few years. Barclay, at the end of the century, classes Junius Brutus with Buchanan and Boucher as the chiefs of the ' monarchomachi '. In England the book had become fairly well known before 1600 and Whitgift refers to it as dangerous. But its doctrine was completely abandoned by the Huguenots within a few years of its first publication ; and the general trend of thought in France was in a wholly different direction. If the book was influential anywhere in the sixteenth century, it was in the Netherlands. On the other hand, in England, in the seventeenth century, the *Vindiciae* had considerable influence. References to it are very frequent and its statements and arguments are constantly repeated. So late as 1683 it suffered the honour of being publicly burned by the University of Oxford.[1]

The most original contributions made by the *Vindiciae* to the theory of sovereignty developed by Huguenot writers after 1572, were, not its suggestion of formal ' contracts ', but its suggestion of a federal system based on recognition of the rights of natural communities and its theory as to the nature of law. The first of these, later developed by Althusius, was not followed up by the author : it appears almost accidentally. The second was medieval and, in the sixteenth century, had been more than anticipated by the writer who called himself Marius Salamonius. In fact, substantially, the whole theory of the Huguenot writers may be said, with certain qualifications, to have been developed and supplemented, partly by Salamonius and partly by Buchanan, before the appearance of the *Vindiciae*. The views of these rather isolated thinkers are so intimately connected, ideally, with those of the Huguenot writers, that it seems practically desirable to deal with them at once.

[1] Along with the *De Jure Regni* of Buchanan and the political works of Milton.

CHAPTER V

SALAMONIUS AND BUCHANAN

§ 1. SALAMONIUS

THE *De Principatu* [1] of Marius Salamonius was published at Rome, 'cum privilegio summi pontifici,' as early as 1544. The author appears to have been a Spaniard and no more than that is certainly known about him apart from his writings.[2] The book is in the form of a discussion between a Lawyer, a Philosopher, an Historian and a Theologian. In the main it consists in an argument between Lawyer and Philosopher as to the meaning of the Lex Regia and whether and in what sense the Prince is *legibus solutus*. The Historian contributes to the discussion some indifferent and irrelevant 'history'. The Theologian contributes nothing. He makes long speeches which are listened to, in presumably respectful silence, by the Lawyer and Philosopher, who then continue with their argument as though nothing had happened. It might almost seem that the Theologian is introduced to show that theology has nothing to say in the matter. The Scriptures contribute nothing to the argument. The only 'authority' in any sense recognized is that of the *Corpus Juris*.

The whole discussion is abstract in form and ancient or mythical history alone is used in illustration. No reference is made to the conditions of any particular country of the sixteenth century nor is there any sign that the author was preoccupied with the practical politics of any country. He exhibits a strong personal dislike of cruel punishments and public executions, and he shares the feelings and the views of Machiavelli about mercenary and national armies. He betrays, otherwise, no particular concern with any immediate and practical questions.

The argument is concerned with the right interpretation of the Lex Regia, that is with the nature of the delegation of sovereignty made by the people to the Prince. But it is not particularly concerned

---

[1] *Marii Salamonii Patritii Romani de Principatu. Libri Septem.*
[2] He was of course a Catholic and may have been a Jesuit. The book begins with a letter addressed to the Pope. There seems no reason to suppose that Marius Salamonius represents the author's real name.

with the power and position of the titular Emperor. When particular reference is made to the Holy Roman Emperor or to the Empire, the terms Princeps Romanus or Populus Romanus are always used. The argument refers to an unqualified Princeps and an unqualified Populus. Yet it would seem to be assumed that the nature of sovereignty in general can be arrived at through an interpretation of the Lex Regia. To put it thus, however, is not fair to the author. The assumption made is, that every one agrees that the Prince is a delegate of a sovereign people. The question at issue is, how much is involved in the delegation.

The Philosopher maintains that a Prince who does not hold himself to be bound by positive law, as well as by natural and divine law, is nothing else than a tyrant. Lawyer and Philosopher agree without difficulty that every Prince is bound by natural and by divine law. There is no question about this ; and neither of them seem to regard the matter as practically important. What they differ about is the nature of positive law. The Lawyer contends that there must always in every State exist some law-making authority and that law-making power cannot be limited. This power has been conferred by the People on the Prince and the Prince has therefore become *legibus solutus*, so far as positive law is concerned. He admits that sovereign authority originated ' hominum conventionibus ' [1] and that the Prince is an agent and delegate of the people ; but he insists that the delegation of authority was complete. He quotes Ulpian to show that the essence of the Lex Regia was a delegation to the Prince of power to make or unmake law at will. But he makes the dangerous admission that there might exist agreements come to by the community as a whole which, in spite of the subsequent delegation, could not be abrogated save by common consent. But no particular interest attaches to the views of the Lawyer. They were only such as were being taught in the law schools of Italy and of France under Francis I. The importance of the De Principatu consists in the views propounded by the Philosopher.

The Prince is a delegate and an agent of the People. This fact of itself implies, argues the Philosopher, that the right, authority and power of the People is greater than that of the Prince, the creator being always and necessarily greater than the creature. All magistrates are servants of the People and the Prince is but a perpetual magistrate. Even though, technically, law-making power belongs to the Prince, yet the People is always the real legislator. For government, to be just, must always be ' omnium consensu et ad populi utilitatem '. A Prince who makes or unmakes law against the will of the people must needs, therefore, be a tyrant. He can have no right to do such things. It is incredible that any people should have

---

[1] *De Principatu*, ed. 1544, p. 11.

authorized a Prince to rule it in a manner contrary to its will and interests.[1]

The view taken of law appears to be precisely the same as that of the *Defensor Pacis* of 1324 and as that taken in the *Vindiciae*. It is, essentially, a judgement of the community as to justice and commodity, that cannot conceivably be changed at the will of one man. But Salamonius goes further. He supplies, what is lacking in the *Vindiciae*, a conception of what constitutes a populus. A populus is constituted by a common agreement or understanding which expresses itself in law. Law is the bond of society. The laws of a community, he declares, must be regarded as ' pactiones ' between its members. They form the terms of association into what is called a State. ' Lex inter ipsos cives pactio quaedam est.'[2] There can be no kind of society or association among men except upon understood terms and conditions : in civil society these are properly called laws.[3] Any association involves the recognition of mutual obligations : and this recognition issues in law. All citizens are bound by the law because all citizens, as such, have assented to the terms of association.[4] In vain does the Lawyer object that a man cannot bind himself. Every man, it is answered, remains bound so long as he voluntarily remains a citizen. It is, also, rather obscurely, suggested that he is bound to obey the law by his own desire for liberty. For law is the condition of liberty.

The Philosopher then proceeds to argue that the People cannot be conceived as having delegated to anyone a right to destroy the bonds and the conditions of its own existence. Furthermore, as the Father of a family is a member of the family and as the captain of a ship is a member of the crew,[5] so the Prince himself is a citizen (*socius*) and bound by the terms of association as are all other citizens. Those terms, summed up, amount, it is declared, to this : that no citizen shall be neglectful of what concerns the common welfare. The Prince, therefore, to whom, above all, is committed the charge of the common welfare and whose position requires that he, above all, should set a good example, is even more straitly bound than anyone else.[6]

Salamonius has something to say also concerning the ends of political association. It exists not merely to secure means of life but for the achievement of good life. Government, therefore, should

---

[1] Exactly as in the *Réveille Matin*.   [2] Ed. 1544, p. 19.

[3] ' Pactiones hujusmodi nonne recte societatis leges dicuntur ? '

[4] But there is nothing whatever in all this that is new. Salamonius might have taken it direct from Chap. XIII of Sir John Fortescue's *De laudibus legum Angliae*, published in 1537, though written before 1471. Salamonius is only stating more distinctly the idea there rather obscurely expressed. Fortescue uses the phrase : ' Lex vero, sub qua coetus hominum Populus efficitur.'

[5] These analogies are favourites with French writers of the second half of the century. They appear in the *Vindiciae*.

[6] Ed. 1544, p. 22 B.

seek to promote virtue by rewards and punishments. The latter method of promoting virtue is, the author thinks, much overdone. No other conclusion is drawn from the Aristotelian commonplace except that it is highly important that the Prince himself should be virtuous.

Two kinds of 'tyrants' are distinguished, as in the *Vindiciae*. There is the tyrant who 'non legitime principatum ineat', who, in fact, has received no delegation at all. And there is the tyrant who 'in administranda justicia deficiat'.[1] To govern justly is to govern according to the will and in the interests of the people. Law is an expression of that will : and so we return to our original declaration that a Prince who holds that he is not bound by law is a tyrant.

The practical conclusions drawn from all this are lame and impotent in the extreme. One might have expected the author to conclude, as does the *Vindiciae*, that law can only be changed by a common assent. But Salamonius was, it seems, conscious that all the laws of a State could hardly be regarded as involved in the original pactio. After all, he admits, the Prince can make law. He is bound ' by all those laws by which the general welfare is secured . . . nor does it lie in his power to abrogate arbitrarily laws rightly established, unless with just cause '.[2] But who is to say which are the laws on which the general welfare depends ? The Prince, it is said, may and should make new law when it is expedient to do so in the common interest ; remembering always that no law can be valid that is contrary to nature or to the custom of the country or directed to any private or personal end. But who is to judge whether a new law will work for the general good ? If the Prince himself be the only judge the theoretical limitation of his power practically disappears.

Nor does Salamonius give any explicit answer to the question : What is to happen when the Prince becomes a tyrant ? There seems to be an implication that, in that case, the People may resume its sovereignty and depose its unfaithful delegate. But no explicit statement is made to that effect. Actual rebellion is never mentioned. The fate of the tyrannical Prince is discreetly veiled.

Like the author of the *Vindiciae*, Salamonius·may be said to have formulated a contract theory. But between the two there are two important and radical differences. On the author's own showing the so-called contracts of the *Vindiciae* are not voluntary agreements. They derive not from the will of the parties but from the will of God and are not therefore, in any accurate sense, contracts at all. In the *De Principatu* God is not a party to the contract and this, perhaps, is the most remarkable thing about it. In the second place, the contract of Salamonius is not between Prince and People : the Prince is a mere delegate. He is bound by the contract only as a citizen and as

---

[1] Ed. 1544, p. 24 B.   [2] Ib., p. 27 B.

all citizens are bound. The contract is a social contract, not a contract for government. It consists in an understanding among the individual members of any political entity as to the terms of their association. This understanding, according to Salamonius, is expressed in the law of the State. The society that establishes legal sovereignty is conceived as formed by an agreement among individuals which may be termed a *pactio*. It seems probable that the author of the *Vindiciae* did not know the *De Principatu*, which was published in France only in 1578. Had he known it, he might have tried to fortify his position with yet another ' contract '.

The theories of Salamonius and of the Huguenot thinkers were alike based on a groundwork of medieval thought and it was owing to this that they had much in common. But they were thinking of different things and in different ways. Salamonius was concerned with the problem of the nature of law and of law-making. The Huguenots were concerned, primarily, with justification of their own attitude towards constituted authority. It might be said that, by adding the suggestions of the *Vindiciae* to those of the *Principatu*, it would be possible to arrive at the two contracts of Locke. It would be not only possible but very easy, on condition that one ignored the essentially religious character of the conceptions of the *Vindiciae*. It might, also, be said that this was what was actually done in the seventeenth century. It was not done earlier : and the fact that it was, in a sense, done in the seventeenth century, has little to do with Salamonius or the *Vindiciae*.

§ 2. BUCHANAN

The connection between the Huguenot thinkers and Salamonius is somewhat remote : their connection with Buchanan is far closer. George Buchanan was born in Scotland in 1506 and died, in Scotland, in 1562 ; but he was vitally connected with France. He was never concerned with French politics nor had he ever any connection with the Huguenot party. Nevertheless, his thought is French rather than Scottish ; and if he were a Calvinist in any sense he was certainly not, politically, a Knoxian. Almost all the most formative years of his intellectual life, from the age of nineteen onwards, were passed in France. He was in France from 1525 to 1535 and again from 1547 to 1552 and thereafter in France again till 1561.

His teacher at St. Andrews in his early student days was John Major : and it has been pointed out that he might have derived his political theory substantially from that remarkable man. It is curious that no one seems to have reckoned Major among the leading political thinkers of the early sixteenth century. He was that ; but he was also a medieval schoolman of fifteenth-century type. Little originality can be claimed for him ; yet he was teaching, before 1525, all the political doctrine that is really essential in the later Huguenot thought. Between the later Middle Ages and the *Vindiciae*, Major's writings are a very definite link. He taught in Paris as well as in Scotland ; and it might be conjectured that his influence counted for something in the evolution of political thought in France and not only among the Huguenots.[1]

Major taught that all civil authority is derived from the will of the community as a whole. The essential sovereignty of the people is, he declared, ' inabrogabilis '. A King is merely a delegate and an agent. Arbitrary power to levy taxation should, he remarks, never be allowed to a King unless in case of special emergency. If a King go out of bounds or misuse his power and prove incorrigible, he may rightfully be deposed and even put to death. The deposition of a King should, indeed, be brought about only by lawful authority and not by mere violence. But it may always be rightfully effected by the Estates of the realm. In his History of Great Britain,[2] Major had maintained that these principles had always been recognized in the constitution of the Scottish monarchy.

It has been said that both Knox and Buchanan held the views of their tutor, John Major. But I can detect no real resemblance between the views of Knox and Buchanan. Both justified rebellion against the Queen of Scots ; but that fact is a mere accident of circumstance. They did so on grounds entirely different. The same practical conclusion may easily be reached by men whose thought has as little as possible in common.

How far Buchanan's bias was shaped as a boy under John Major, it is impossible to say. He seems to have broken with his old tutor soon after 1525. There was probably little sympathy between the two at any time. In any case Buchanan developed not on the lines of the schoolmen but as a humanist. As a teacher in the colleges of Ste Barbe and Le Moine in Paris, as professor of Latin at Bordeaux and Coimbra, he passed his life on the Continent in the society of scholars, teachers and literary men of the French Renaissance. Adrien Turnèbe and Muret were his colleagues at Le Moine ; he was intimate with Andrea de Gouvea, with Elie Vinet, the mathematician, with the elder Scaliger and the poet Saint Gelais and with Charles du Cossé, Comte de Brissac, to whose son he became tutor. Almost all his close friends in France were, or called themselves, Catholics ; but he was on friendly terms with Hubert Languet and with Beza. During a sojourn in Scotland from 1537 to 1539 he made violent literary attacks on monks in general and Franciscans in particular. He was arrested as a ' Lutheran ' in Scotland in 1539 and imprisoned as a suspected heretic

---

[1] Major was teaching in Paris from 1493 to 1518 and again from 1525 to 1531. He died in 1550. All his writings seem to have been published in France.

[2] *Historia Majoris Britanniae et Scotiae*, 1521.

at Lisbon in 1551. But he does not seem definitely to have attached himself to any Protestant church until in 1562, in Scotland, it had become merely prudent to do so. It was among the humanists of France that the mode of thought which led to the production of the *De Jure Regni* must have been fully formed. As De Thou wrote of him, Buchanan, Scottish by birth, was French by adoption.

Buchanan acquired a great and a European reputation both as a scholar and a poet ; above all, perhaps, as a practical master of the Latin language.[1] So much a master of Latin was he, that he was able to develop in it a style distinctively his own and much admired by contemporaries. The vogue of the *De Jure* in the sixteenth century seems to have been largely due tó its Latinity and the reputation of the author.

When we, nowadays, turn to the book, we are likely to be a little disappointed. There is not much to be found in it except some ancient wisdom and a confused and partial anticipation of the theory adopted or developed by the Huguenots after 1572. An anticipation, so far as it goes, it seems to have been, though the fact is of no real importance. The *De Jure Regni apud Scotos* was published only in 1578 ; but it seems to have been written a good deal earlier, and perhaps before 1570,[2] in order to justify to Europe the dethronement of Mary Stewart. That the book could not have been published in Scotland so early, it is easy to believe. Buchanan absolutely ignores the grounds on which Knox justified rebellion ; while of the Genevan ideal of what the State should be, there is no trace in his book. Even the success of the actual publication [3] and the reputation of the author could not long conceal the fact that Buchanan's point of view could hardly be reconciled with Presbyterianism. In 1584 the *De Jure* was condemned by the Scottish Parliament to be purged of the ' offensive and extraordinary matters ' therein contained.

The *De Jure Regni* is cast in the form of a dialogue between Buchanan himself and a very feeble personage called Thomas Maitland. This method of discussing social or political problems was very commonly made use of in the sixteenth century, especially in France. It has been used frequently, then and since, agreeably to cover a multitude of defects. It enables a writer neatly to evade difficulties and to conceal weak points in his case behind the obliging obtuseness of the other party to the discussion. A treatise in this form may be easily readable, may be amusing, may even, perhaps, be dramatic ; but it

---

[1] Henri Etienne spoke of him as ' easily the foremost poet of his age '. There seems to have been confusion in his scholarly mind between scholarship and poetry.

[2] See lives of Buchanan by D. Macmillan and P. Hume Brown, and Epist. XXIV in Ruddiman's edition of Buchanan's works.

[3] There were three successive editions in three years.

will rarely present anything but a statement so one-sided as to be philosophically worthless. The use of it invites suspicion. It is clear, Buchanan declares, that Kings exist only for public purposes. They must, originally, have been established by an act of the people. Under the law of nature, no man may rightfully assume any authority over his fellows; but the people by giving authority to one of its own members could create a King. It would have been wholly irrational to give to this King an unlimited authority, seeing that a King must needs be a man. Still, in the beginning, this unreasonable thing may have been done. If so, the mistake would quickly have been discovered. The remedy was to bind the King by law.

How exactly this was or could be done is not made clear. Buchanan seems to have thought of law as necessarily made by enactment of some representative body or by the 'people' itself. 'A law is a decree made by the people at the instance of the proper authority.'[1] He seems even to have regarded some sort of plébiscite as required. The act of a representative body should, he says, be referred to the people for their sanction.[2] But all through the most critical portion of his argument it is impossible to be sure what exactly he is talking about. What has been and what should be and what necessarily is, are hopelessly confused. The King, it is clear, can have no powers except such as have been conferred upon him. Either the power to make law was never given to him or, if it were ever given, it was withdrawn. The 'people' at all events can always make law; and the laws it makes bind the King.

The King is a delegate and an agent and is responsible to the community that created him. The rightful power of the people is superior to that of the King. The same rights and jurisdiction which the King has over any individual of the community, are possessed by the mass in relation to the King. Whatever powers have been given to the King, may rightfully, for good cause, be taken from him and resumed by the people. In all States alike, it is declared, this principle holds good. The rights of the people are inalienable.[3] It does not matter that power may have been granted hereditarily. In Scotland, at

[1] 'Probes definitionem legis a jure consultis positam ? Qui legem esse aiunt quod populus scivit, ab eo rogatus cui rogandi jus est.' De Jure, ed. 1579, p. 67.

[2] 'Ego nunquam existimavi universi populi indicio eam rem permitti deberi. Sed ut prope ad consuetudinem nostram ex omnibus ordinibus selecti ad regem in consilium coirent. Deinde ubi apud eos factum esset, id ad populi indicium deferretur.' Ed. 1579, p. 32.

[3] 'Nos autem id contendimus, populum, a quo Reges nostri habent quicquid juris sibi vindicant. Regibus esse potentiorem; jusque idem in eos habere multitudinem, quod illium singulos e multitudine habent. Omnes nationes sentiun⁺ quicquid juris alicui populus dederit, idem eum justis de causis posse reposcere. Hoc civitates omnes semper jus retinuerent.' Ed. 1579, p. 80.

least, it is doubtful how this was. But even if it were so given it may still be taken away. Kings are hereditary only under law made by the people and the people can repeal law. It would appear from this that the King has no part at all in legislation.

'Mutua igitur Regi cum civibus est pactio.' It may be remarked that a ' contract ' must needs be mutual and there is no point in saying that it is. I do not think that Buchanan meant anything more by this phrase than was asserted in the *Du Droit* and in the *Archon et Politie*. The conclusion is stated clearly and forcibly. A King who disregards the understanding on which he was created, may be said to break an implied contract, becomes a tyrant and forfeits all his rights. A King who rules without regard to public interests or who assumes powers not given to him and disregards law, should be regarded and treated as an open enemy of God and man. War against a tyrant is the justest of all wars and not only his outraged subjects but every human being has a right to slay the tyrant.

No argument from the Scriptures is used in support of these contentions. It is only the compliant Thomas Maitland who appeals to the Scriptures. Buchanan merely occupies himself in pointing out their irrelevance. If St. Paul tells us to pray for tyrants, that does not mean that we may not depose and punish them. If there be no instance in Scripture of a King deposed by his own subjects, that does not prove that no King should be deposed. Criminal Kings ought to be punished like other criminals. 'There is nowhere any particular privilege granted in that respect to tyrants.' In this passage alone can Buchanan be said to show any trace of Knoxian thought.

Political authority can be rationally conceived only as derived from the people and held conditionally. The people is the lawgiver and the King must rule in its interests and be bound by its law or be justly deposed. Beyond these assertions there is little, so far, that is clear and explicit. But there remain two propositions which are distinctive of the *De Jure Regni* as compared with the *De Principatu* or the *Vindiciae*. If Salamonius may, rather absurdly, be said to have contributed a ' social contract ' to the theory of the *Vindiciae*, Buchanan may be said to have contributed two things : a theory as to the origin of the social contract and an assertion that the will of the people is naturally expressed in the act of a numerical majority.

There is no social contract in Buchanan, but there is a theory as to the origin of politic society. Men, it is declared, originally lived solitary or in herds, in huts or in caves of the earth, vagrant and lawless.[1] It was not merely for the sake of material advantage that

---

[1] ' Putasne, tempus quoddam fuisse cum homines in tuguriis atque etiam antiis habitarent; ac, sine legibus, sine certes sedibus, palantes vagarentur ? ' Ed. 1579, p. 8.

they formed themselves into co-operative societies. The cause of their association in communities is far more ancient than any perception of utility, the bond between them far more venerable.[1] Mere self-interest would never, indeed, have brought them to co-operate. If each man cared for himself only, this would dissolve rather than found society.[2]

Men were brought into co-operative association partly by an innate propensity to associate with beings of their own kind and partly by natural law.[3] The law of nature is that illumination of our minds by God, by which we distinguish right from wrong.[4] Men are united by a natural love for each other's society and by a natural sense of mutual obligation. Both are implanted by God in all men : and, therefore, we may say that politic society is founded by God. Nothing is more acceptable to Deity than those associations of human beings that are called States (civitates).[5] It is rather as though he were saying : In this sense, and in this sense only, is God the source of political authority. All the rest is the work of the people. And this, by implication, is just what he was saying. He was not, indeed, saying much more. What we have here is a suggestion as to why the herd takes action. But, as in the *Vindiciae*, there is no suggestion as to how it acts or how exactly the lawless herd is formed into an association for co-operation.

The assertion that the act of a majority may and indeed must be taken as the act of the people, is made quite explicitly.[6] The people, it is pointed out, is never unanimous ; and this fact is apparently regarded as sufficient ground for declaring that the majority can speak for the whole. But no connection is established between the fact alleged and the conclusion, which, actually, remains quite groundless. It is even meaningless ; unless it means, simply, that a majority can always impose its will on a minority : and that is both irrelevant and untrue. The principle that the act of a numerical majority may be taken as the act of a community naturally commends itself to practical politicians and was one of the great practical discoveries of medieval lawyers and governments. But the practical possibilities of this legal fiction are here irrelevant. Why the act of a majority should be ideally conceived as the act of the whole, when, on the face of it, it is not so, is not made clear. There is a passage in the *De Jure* in which Buchanan avers that a number of men see more and see better than any one man. Individuals, he says, possess each a degree of

---

[1] ' Sed est congregagandorum hominum causa longe antiquor et communitatis eorum inter ipsos multo prius et sanctius vinculum.' Ed. 1579, p. 9.
[2] Ed. 1579, p. 9.   [3] Ib., p. 10.
[4] Ib., p. 11. ' Nihil aliud intellegi volo, quam lucem animis nostris divinitus infusam.'
[5] Ib., p. 11.   [6] Ib., pp. 87, 88.

virtue which, being accumulated, constitute a virtue transcendent.[1] These are given as reasons for legislation by an assembly rather than by a single person. They do not help much here. If two heads be, quite necessarily, better than one, it must be admitted that one hundred and one heads will be better than one hundred. But the argument sounds suspiciously like a *reductio ad absurdum*.

It would be possible, out of all these writings, to construct a theory of society and of government more complete than appears in any one of them. It is possible to take Buchanan's conception of the state of nature, to add to it the ' social contract ' of Salamonius and to establish the theory of the *Vindiciae* on both. It is true, roughly speaking, that these different conceptions were finally, in one form and sense or another, brought together. But it is only superficially true ; and the fact has no great historical significance. No one did it in the sixteenth century and in the seventeenth no one did it, or tried to do it, accurately. To add the theory of the *Vindiciae* to the rest, the whole theory must be made strictly ' religious '. The social contract of Salamonius would have to cease to be a voluntary contract and be made to arise inevitably from natural law and the will and act of God : otherwise there would be incoherence. It must be pointed out, also, that Buchanan's identification of the will of the majority with the will of the people cannot be reconciled with the theory of the *Vindiciae*. It is, in fact, flatly contradictory of the views of the Huguenot writers. To ' add ' it to the *Vindiciae* would disintegrate the whole structure. The views of these ' monarcho-machi ' [2] are strictly irreconcilable.

Buchanan's reputation remained great throughout the seventeenth century and his writings, or some of them, were still well known in the eighteenth.[3] Any influence he had upon political thought belongs rather to the seventeenth than to the sixteenth century and, as in the case of the *Vindiciae*, is far more apparent in England than elsewhere.[4]

---

[1] Ed. 1579, p. 33.

[2] The use of this monstrous term is sometimes convenient : but it must not be taken as indicating any profound resemblance between the views of the writers referred to.

[3] Dr. Johnson declared that he was the only man of genius Scotland had ever produced.

[4] An English translation of the *De Jure Regni* appeared in 1680, and a second edition of this in 1689.

CHAPTER VI

THE CATHOLIC LEAGUE AND ITS ALLIES

§ 1. THE LEAGUE

FROM 1562 to 1572, Catholic absolutists and Catholic believers in limited or constitutional monarchy, alike saw the Huguenots as rebels and separatists, in spite of their vehement denial of these charges. The division of parties in France appeared, superficially, to be simple. On one side were the Catholics, on the other the adherents of the 'reformed religion'. For the most part the Catholic pamphleteers of this first period of civil war maintained a divine right and non-resistance doctrine which falls to be explained later. But after 1572 and still more completely after the death of Charles IX in 1574, the Catholic party split up. A large section of the Catholic royalist party had always been far more Catholic than royalist. Every royal edict under which a partial and localized toleration of Protestantism had been formally established, had been denounced from Catholic pulpits from 1560 onwards. Under Henry III those of the Catholics who had all along seen in the 'wars of religion' religious wars, developed theories of popular or of democratic sovereignty and maintained a right of rebellion against impious and 'tyrannical' princes.

The definitive starting-point of this development was the formation of the united League of 1576. It was a matter of course that it was joined by very many to whom religious feeling was a counter in a game and by many whose objects were in no sense religious. It is true that its formation was the work of men who were certainly not religious enthusiasts. But it would be a mistake to regard the Catholic League as in the main, or even to any very large extent, a mere result of the ambition and influence of the Duke of Guise. The Duke was a man of great capacity and strength of character, bold and wary, astute and unflinching. 'Lui seul est toute la Ligue' wrote of him, in 1588, the most clear-sighted and fair-minded of all the writers of that troubled time.[1] But the Duke could not make bricks without

---

[1] *Excellent et libre Discours sur l'état présent de la France*, 1588. By Michel Hurault, a grandson of Chancellor L'Hôpital. It contains far the best contemporary appreciation of the situation that I have come across.

straw. The tendency towards the formation of leagues for the defence of ' true religion ' against the organized assaults of ' heresy ' or ' idolatry ' was inherent in the position of Catholics and Protestants alike. Local Catholic leagues had come into existence as early as 1567. But, even apart from the merely personal motives that played so large a part in it and did so much to wreck it, the League was not merely religious. Two things constituted its strength : the belief that true religion was in danger and the belief that the national unity had already been gravely compromised by the grant of privilege to the Huguenots. The two beliefs generally coexisted ; but they were separable. It may be that the League represented as much nationalist as religious feeling ; and that it is just this fact that made it possible for Henry IV to bring about its rapid disintegration. Soon after the battle of Ivry a position was reached in which it was increasingly obvious that the unity of the kingdom could only be re-established by the acceptance of the Huguenot leader as King. When that moment arrived the nationalist element in the League went over to the Bourbon, as town after town was doing before 1593. For the simply religious opposition Henry provided a bridge of escape from the wreck by a nominal ' conversion ', that saved many faces while it deceived only the most ignorant. ' Over that bridge only the most honest and fearlessly logical could, in the end, refuse to go. Yet Henry's carefully prepared and beautifully timed ' conversion ' was far more than a fire escape. It was a public recognition that the League had been right, at least to some extent. It was true, after all, that the King of France must be a Catholic.

Between 1576 and 1585 the principles of the League were not fully or clearly stated, nor was any theory developed that can be identified with it. But from the first it was, by its very nature, hostile to any theory which placed supreme direction absolutely in the hands of the King. A Leaguer might see the constitution of France as Seyssel had seen it or he might conceive, like Bodin, of a monarchy at once absolute and yet limited by fundamental laws, or he might hold a constitutional theory and claim a share in sovereignty for the Estates. All these views were, in fact, represented in the League, as among the Politiques. But the principles of the League forbade acceptance of any theory of unlimited powers in the King or of non-resistance in all cases. The assertion of a right, if not a duty, of rebellion against a King who compromised with heresy was implied in its whole attitude.

From the first it aimed at forcing the King's hand. Henry III had good reason for hostility to the League apart from his jealousy and fear of the Duke of Guise.

In its earlier years the League tended to adopt a constitutional theory and to claim sovereignty, or at least a share in sovereignty, for the Estates of the realm. That view of the position was indicated in the first League declaration in 1576. It was expressed at the assembly of Estates held that year at Blois and still more emphatically at the assembly of 1588. In 1588 the demand was made that the King should recognize a right of armed resistance to the levy of any tax not authorized by the Estates. An odd and elaborate book, the *Miroir des Français*, published in 1581 [1] and impertinently dedicated to Catherine de Medicis, asserted roundly that the Estates could lawfully depose the King for violation of the law of the land. For all that, it can hardly be said that the League developed any sort of definite theory before 1585. As a body it was merely asserting that it was the bounden duty of the King to root out heresy and denying, by implication at least, his claim to absolutism.

It must, however, be noticed that the view that sovereignty resided essentially in the Estates of the realm continued to be held by many Leaguers after 1585, was frequently expressed in League writings and was maintained by one of the League's chief literary champions, the redoubtable Jean Boucher. The King, declared a League pamphlet of 1589, must obey the Estates just as a Pope must obey a General Council. [2] If the remonstrances of the Estates prove altogether unavailing, rebellion is justified. The King, says another pamphleteer, must do nothing contrary to the will of the Estates. [3]

It has frequently been said that the League took over from the Huguenots the theories of Hotman and of the *Vindiciae*. Such a way of putting the matter, though it expresses some of the truth, appears very crude when the facts are looked at carefully. That when, after the declaration of Péronne in 1585 and again after the murder of Guise, the League stood committed to rebellion, there were put forward on its behalf theories resembling those of the Huguenot writers is, of course, true and is not at all surprising. The position of the League in 1589 was sufficiently like the position of the Huguenot party in 1573 to produce like effects. To some extent there was, on the part of League journalists like Louis Dorléans, a conscious adoption of theories from the enemy without any real conviction, merely to hoist the heretics with their own petard. But only a mind with a strong Protestant bias could suppose that the League writers were, on the whole, less sincere than those on the Huguenot side. The adoption by the Leaguers of theories justifying rebellion was certainly not so quick or so complete a change as was the abandonment of such theories by the Huguenots at this very time. Nor is it accurate to say that the League advocates simply restate in their own terms the

---

[1] Under the name Nicholas de Montand.

[2] *Causes qui o t contraint les Catholiques à prendre les armes.* Republished in *Mémoires de la Ligue*, Vol. III.

[3] *De la puissance des rois, contre l'usurpation du titre et qualité de roi de France par le roi de Navarre.* 1589.

theories of Huguenot writers. There were different opinions among the Leaguers as there were among the Huguenots. It might be said that the only thing they really agreed upon was that unity in religion must be maintained at all costs. Actually they did not even agree on that. Even when the League writers come nearest to the theory of the *Vindiciae*, the resemblance is somewhat superficial. League theory tended to be more democratic than Huguenot theory and also to be more theocratic.

A significant parallelism exists, in certain respects, between the history of the League and that of the Huguenot party. From 1562 to 1572 the Huguenot party was led and dominated by nobles and during those years its political theory was constitutional and not radical. As a result of the massacres of 1572, its direction fell, at least for some years, into the hands of the governing bodies of towns and there followed a development of far-reaching theories of sovereignty. The history of the League exhibits similar phenomena. From 1576 to 1585 the League was dominated by nobles and during that period its political thought tended to take the form of a theory of the constitution. After 1585 and still more completely after the death of the Duke of Guise in December, 1588, the mass of the lesser nobles, alarmed and disgusted, withdrew their support. The League became essentially a league of towns, centred in Paris. Mayenne's failure or refusal frankly to recognize the fact was one cause of its break-up. The development of radical League theories of sovereignty followed on the change.

§ 2. THE PAMPHLETEERS OF THE LEAGUE

From 1585 onwards the war of pamphlets raged more and more hotly for some years. From the numerous writings on behalf of the League one gathers that many and wide differences of opinion existed among Leaguers. It is not very easy to detach what is significant. In the League pamphlets there are reflections of the *Vindiciae* and repetitions of the *Servitude Volontaire*. Louis Dorléans, one of the most effective of the League pamphleteers, a smart journalist, to whom any stick was good enough for beating a heretic dog, made jeering allusions to Huguenot theory.

'They cannot complain,' he wrote, 'if we mete to them the measure they mete to others. . . . In their *Franco-Gallia*, one of the most detestable books that ever saw the light . . . they pretend that it is lawful to choose a King to one's own taste. Let the heretics know, then, that the King of Navarre is not to our taste; and so let him stay in his Béarn.' [1]

Great efforts were made to persuade the nobles that their position was in no way threatened by the League. The other side was trying hard to persuade them of the contrary. The Huguenots were declared

---

[1] *Avertissement des catholiques anglais aux catholiques français*, 1586.

to be plotting the establishment of a republic and to be as much enemies of the nobles as of the King. ' Jamais ferme hérétique n'aima les princes,' wrote Dorléans. It is not the League, it was asserted, that is the cause of our troubles. Heresy is the root of the evils from which France has suffered so long. With the spread of heresy things have gone from bad to worse. Heresy and rebellion go always together, for rebellion against the Church leads to rebellion against the Prince.[1] ' Cette maxime,' declared Pierre d'Espinac, Archbishop of Lyon, ' est toujours vraie, que, où le crime de lèse-majesté divine ne sera puni, là le crime de lèse-majesté humaine viendra à n'être plus crime.'

Whatever *ad hoc* arguments the League pamphleteers may use, they all come back to religion. Agreement in religion is the only solid basis of any State : there can be no real unity without it. This and not any theory of sovereignty in the Estates or in the ' people ', is the essential declaration of the League. The assertion was not borrowed or in any sense derived from Huguenot theory. It might have been derived from Geneva ; it could hardly be derived from the *Vindiciae*. Actually it was developed, just as was the Genevan ideal, from the religious consciousness of a party. Just because ' true religion ' is the real bond of society, the King of France must be a Catholic and it must, also, be his duty to extirpate heresy. It was a *non sequitur* ; but the Leaguers argued, just as the Calvinists argued, on the assumption that theirs was the one true religion. The recognition of a heretic prince is forbidden absolutely by divine law, Dorléans declared ; [2] while the Salic Law is not even Christian in origin. That the King must be a Catholic, it was declared, is a ' fundamental law ' of the French monarchy, and the most fundamental. The Salic Law must be set aside if need be. No Catholic could accept a heretic King without thereby becoming a traitor to France as well as to the Church. So, in 1590, the Sorbonne solemnly declared that to assist Henry of Navarre was mortal sin. The Crown is not, and cannot be, simply and strictly hereditary. What makes a King is the consecration bestowed by the true Church : so declared Mayenne himself in December, 1592. ' Jésus Christ vaincra,' cried one of the pamphleteers, ' Jésus Christ régnera, Jésus Christ sera roi de France et y aura son lieutenant, rendant sa justice, toujours très chrétien.' [3]

Many of the League pamphleteers spoke of a ' contract ' between King and people. Some give the right of declaring the King a tyrant to the Parlements ; others, after the fashion of the *Vindiciae*, place it with a noble and official class. Most of them assert that the people

[1] *Remontrance du clergé de France*, 1585. In *Mémoires de la Ligue*, I, p. 247.
[2] *Apologie ou défense des catholiques unis les uns avec les autres contre les impostures des catholiques associés à ceux de la prétendue religion*, 1586.
[3] *Avertissement des avertissements au peuple très chrétien* : signed Jean de Caumont Champenois. 1587.

are, in some sense, sovereign. There was a fairly general agreement among them that a King, being established by the people for the common benefit, may always be rightfully deposed for doing injury to the kingdom. What they had chiefly in mind was what they regarded as the greatest injury that could be done to a kingdom : the establishment within it of two religions. Their talk about sovereignty of the people seems to have meant very little : even less perhaps than it did for the Huguenots. Many of them, to say the least, would have repudiated any claim to a right of rebellion against an orthodox King. But because religion seemed to them to be the only sure basis of peace and order and the only bond of real union, it followed for the Leaguers, quite simply, that a King who is a heretic or who allies himself with heretics, may and should be deposed. Some of their writers concluded further that it is always the Church that must say the decisive word.

A vivid picture of the views and emotional attitude of a religious Leaguer is presented in the remarkable pamphlet entitled *Dialogue entre le Maheustre et le Manant*, which was written certainly between Henry IV's conversion and his entry into Paris.[1] The ' Maheustre ' stands for a Politique, or Catholic supporter of Henry ; the Manant [2] represents the religious element in the League. Though writing from the point of view of a Politique, the author does justice to his opponent and actually appreciates his point of view. In a sense the Manant is allowed, even, to have the best of the argument ; though he is forced to admit that nothing short of miraculous intervention can save his party from destruction. The writer shows a sense of the paradox and the tragedy of the situation.

It is impossible, declares the Manant, that a heretic should be a legitimate King. As well or better make a King of a brigand ; a thief at least knows he does wrong, a heretic does not ! Henry of Navarre is of a religion different from that of the mass of his subjects : that fact alone is sufficient. The first of the fundamental laws of the French monarchy is that no heretic can be King. Two religions cannot coexist peacefully. A heretic King is bound to persecute Catholics : if he did not do so he would prove himself worse than a heretic ; he would be an atheist. As to Henry's conversion he will have none of it. ' Les parois ne font les Catholiques.' It is incredible that there has been any real conversion and a man does not become

---

[1] Acc. Weill it was published 1593. It is attributed, without certainty, to Pierre Pithou, one of the principal authors of the *Satyre Menippée* and author of the famous and important tract *Les Libertés de l'Eglise gallicanes* (1594). It was printed in late editions of the *Satyre Menippée*, but is not included in the original publication.

[2] The origin of the word is uncertain. ' Manant ' was a contemptuous term applied to Leaguers.

a Catholic by saying he is one. It cannot be the will of God that Catholics should submit to have a heretic King : that would imply that God willed the damnation of men. God condemns heretics : there can, therefore, be no obligation to obey a heretic. It is useless to say that only recognition of Henry can give peace and order to France. It may be true ; the unhappy Manant admits that it seems to be true. But it is mere blasphemy to prefer worldly goods to the plain will of God. No good, he implies, can really come of doing so. These stalwarts of the League seem to have felt that the real unity of France was being sacrificed for a unity merely mechanical and a peace merely external. In vain is the Manant forced to admit that his party is hopelessly divided, betrayed by its leaders, rapidly disintegrating. Challenged to say on what, under these circumstances, he can found any hope, he repeats simply : ' God ! God ! God ! '

§ 3. JEAN BOUCHER AND THE *DE JUSTA REIPUBLICAE*

The pamphlets written between 1585 and 1594 give a far more accurate and complete idea of the views and attitude of Leaguers in general than do the more elaborate expositions of political doctrine that were published in defence of the League. The most elaborate and famous of these apologia were the *De Justa Reipublicae christianae* of unknown authorship and the writings of Jean Boucher. Of the preachers of the League at Paris Boucher seems to have been by far the strongest. Born at Paris in 1551, he died only in 1646 ; and the length of his life is matched by the verve and vigour of his writing. He was a man of considerable learning, Doctor in Theology of Paris and Prior of the Sorbonne. He could express himself freely and vigorously in Latin and still more vigorously in French. It was the energy of his style as preacher and writer that gave him influence. His style has an uncommon directness, a wealth of illustration, an oddly Rabelaisian quality, enormous verve. He was coarsely ironical and brutally calumnious. Very few political partisans can ever have lied with such verve and such audacity. Yet, for all his mendacity, he seems to have been an honest fanatic. At least he refused, finally, to make his peace by eating his words and from his exile in the Netherlands continued to denounce the impostor on the throne of France.

Whatever may be thought of Boucher's power of expression, he was certainly not a serious thinker. It is impossible to derive from his writings any coherent theory whatever. He seems to have thought that it did not matter what he said, so long as he gave the adversary something to answer and supporters something to hold by. He defended the position of the League on every ground at once without regard for consistency. What he represents is, in fact, the confusion of opinion among the Leaguers.

In 1589 he published the *De justa abdicatione Henrici tertii*.[1] The form of the book was scholastic and logical, but its content is quite incoherent. He asked four questions and answered them all affirmatively. Can either the Church or the People rightfully depose a King ? Ought Henry III to be deposed by the Church ? Should he be deposed by the People ? Is it lawful to take arms against him without waiting for an act of formal deposition ?
The important question was, of course, that which was put first. It is characteristic of Boucher that he put two distinct questions as though they were one. He answers them, however, separately. He declares Kings ' a populo constitutos esse ' ; and because the People ' constitutes ' it can depose. There can be no such thing as absolute hereditary right to a Crown. All the regular commonplaces are solemnly restated. There is nothing that might not have been written, say by John Major.
On the other hand, the power of the Pope is represented in this book as limitless. He has power ' regni jura immutare, leges abrogare '. He can release a people from its allegiance, he can order it to depose its King, he can even, apparently, dispose of the crown as he pleases. What becomes of the sovereignty of the people under these circumstances is not explained. But Boucher has the adversary both ways and is content.
In 1594 he published, at Paris, a volume of sermons.[2] The view set forth in this book is less incoherent than that of his first production, but entirely inconsistent with it. The Pope, now, almost completely disappeared. The nature of his authority is described in language so ambiguous and deliberately involved that it is not possible to extract from it anything definite. The meaning of this change is only too clear. Henry of Navarre's conversion dated from July, 1593 ; and the Pope was not now likely to be of any further use to the League. On the other hand, the sovereignty of the people, vaguely asserted in the earlier treatise, was now definitely declared to reside, for France, in States-General. The people of France has chosen to establish a monarchical form of government. Monarchy is, in fact, Boucher declared, ordinarily the most useful kind of arrangement that can be made. That does not affect the principle that the people can always depose its King and even, it is implied, abolish its monarchy, ' étant en tout veritable que c'est des peuples que sont les rois et non des rois les peuples. Veu que le peuple est la base sur laquelle le roi pose.' [3] There is nothing especially sacred about a royal family. ' Il n'y a rien de moins en l'âme du moindre de tout

[1] A second and large edition was printed at Lyon in 1591.
[2] *Sermons de la simulée conversion et nullité de l'absolution de Henri de Bourbon.*
[3] Ib., ed. 1594, p. 250.

ce peuple qu'en celle du plus grand monarque.' But it is the Estates of the realm that represent the people and speak for it. ' Ce sont eux en qui, naturellement et originairement, reside la puissance et majesté publique.' [1] Originally they elected the King ; they can always depose him or change the order of succession. Their power is declared to be inalienable.

Boucher's fame or notoriety was sufficient, later, to secure for him the honour of Barclay's special attention ; but the case for the League was put far better by the author of the *De Justa Reipublicae*.[2] It was not put as well as it might have been by anyone.

There is something of the same incoherence in this book as in Boucher's *De justa abdicatione*. But it is less complete and better concealed.

Civil society and civil authority alike, the author asserted, originated in the needs of man. The State is a natural development. It is necessarily for the community itself to determine the form of its own government. The right to do so, and equally the right to elect its king and to depose him, is derived from the nature of things as established by God and from the fact that man is rational.[3] Man necessarily wills government and the form of government is determined by man's reason. Kings and all other magistrates exist for common and recognized purposes, which may be summarized as the freedom and security of their subjects. The rights of Kings must needs be limited by the ends for which they exist. No King can rationally be conceived as possessing a right to defeat the purpose he represents. Nor can any King claim that he cannot be deposed because he succeeded to the throne by absolute hereditary right : for no King can rationally be regarded as succeeding by an absolute right. No man is King unless and until the people approves his succession. Apparently this approval is conceived as being given at the coronation : it is declared that anyone who asserts that he is King before coronation becomes, by that alone, a ' tyrant '. It is further declared that the people's approval need not be given unconditionally. The sovereign people may impose on its King any condition it pleases in return for recognition. Just as it is and must be for the people to determine its form of government, so it is for the people to determine the nature

---

[1] *Sermons*, ed. 1594, p. 249.

[2] *De justa reipublicae in reges impios authoritate, justissimaque catholicorum ad Henricum Navarreum et quemcunque haereticum a regno Galliae repellendum confederatione.* Paris, 1590. Published under the name Rossaeus. It has been attributed to Guillaume Rose and to William Reynolds, and even to Boucher. The authentic utterances of Rose do not suggest that he was capable of it ; and there are grave objections to the authorship of Reynolds. Labitte did not think it was by either. A second edition appeared in 1592.

[3] ' Principum electio fluit a natura quam Deus condidit et a ratione quam Deus homini infudit.'

and limits of the King's authority and to alter it or suppress it as it pleases.[1]

But government came into existence not merely for the needs of bare life but also for the sake of good life. Hence it is part of the function of government to maintain true religion and to suppress heresy. A King who refuses to do so is defeating one of the main purposes he was established to serve. It is clear that to the mind of the writer, toleration of heresy is destructive of unity in the State. The Huguenots, he declares, are no more truly French than are the Turks : a Calvinist is French but as a dog may be.[2] He will not even admit that a Calvinist is a Christian. ' Paganismus multo magis cum religione christiana convenit, quam calvanismus ! ' [3] He pointed out too, as Andrew Blackwood had done earlier,[4] that Calvinism is as radically hostile to any mere secular authority as ever was the Pope.

So far we have a theory which resembles that of the *Vindiciae*, relieved of its suggestion of formal ' contracts ' and relieved also of its ambiguous and aristocratic conception of the People as agent. But, so far, there is no positive suggestion as to how a tyrannical King is to be dealt with. As soon as this question arises the author becomes confused. He does not, like Boucher, in his sermons, place sovereignty with the Estates, nor does he suggest that power to act for the people belongs to any class. The question is not directly stated or answered ; but it would appear that it is the Church and, presumably, finally the Pope, that represents the ' people '. Excommunication, it is declared, carries deposition with it and it is a duty to take arms against a heretic King. The connection between these two propositions is not stated. A King, it is clear, may be deposed for other crimes than heresy. One ought not to act hastily ; but when it is certain that the community (respublica) is resolved to treat the King as a tyrant, then anyone may kill him. Yet it is said also that no one ought to do so until the Church has given the signal which makes the act rightful. The Church is to judge whether any given King deserves to be deposed either as a heretic or, apparently, on any other ground.[5] There is to be no rebellion unsanctioned by the Church. And yet the author declares, like Knox, that a heretic King, like any other heretic, may be killed by any one.[6]

Boucher had finished off his treatise on the deposition of Henry III with a panegyric of his murderer, Jacques Clément. The author of the *De Justa Reipublicae* was of the same spirit. To him the assassin

---

[1] *De Justa*, ed. 1592, p. 104.   [2] *De Justa*, Chap. VI.
[3] Ib., Chap. V.   [4] In *De Vinculo Religionis*, 1575.
[5] ' Ecclesiae sententia in rege tyrannica deponendo maxime attendenda.' What is the force of ' Maxime ' ?
[6] ' Rex haereticus ut alius haereticus cuivis occidendus.'

was 'innocentissimus et praeclarissimus juvenis . . . Spiritu Deo impulsus et armatus'. Just so, earlier, Huguenot writers had justified and acclaimed Poltrot, the murderer of the first great Duke of Guise, and had congratulated Henry III on his assassination of the second. Royalist opinion in the sixteenth century seems to have been more shocked by the justification of such murders than by the justification of rebellion. But, in all cases, the same doctrine that was held to justify the one, justified the other. In the writings of the ' monarcho-machi ' the justification of the assassination of a ' tyrant ' is only a minor and contingent incident of their theories of a right of rebellion.

Constitutional theories of the monarchy of France, the theory which placed sovereignty in the Estates or in the King and Estates jointly, the theory that the Parlements of France, instituted to prevent tyranny, could give a final judgement whether or no the King had become a ' tyrant ' ; the conception of the King as delegate of a sovereign people and responsible to it, or as bound by a ' contract ' ; the idea that rebellion may be not merely a right but a duty ; all these find expression in League writings. None of them were, in any sense, new : all of them in substance if not quite in form, were medieval. But from the babel of utterances, one conception emerges which was certainly characteristic of the League : the conception of national unity as necessarily based upon, and indeed essentially consisting in, unity in religion. The inference drawn from it, that the political sovereign is bound to suppress heresy by force, did not strictly follow. It seems to have involved the unjustified assumption that there is always a remedy for a disease. But, however practically important and however false that inference, it could not affect the question of the validity of the conception. It is unfortunate that the partisan writers of the League, confused by passion or suffering from the incompetence of insincerity, were none of them equal to the task of presenting the conception adequately.

§ 4. THE LEAGUE AND THE JESUITS

That religion is the only sure basis of order and the only bond of real union in society and that it is therefore the duty of the sovereign to extirpate heresy, these were the main assertions of the League. Most Leaguers went no further. But, seeing that by religion, the League understood only that of the Catholic Church, these conten-tions inevitably raised the question of the relation between the Papacy and the sovereignty of France. How far is the Crown of France necessarily subordinate to the Church and the Pope ? What are the limits of Papal power ? Has the Pope rightful authority to depose the King of France and if so under what circumstances ? For the Huguenots these questions did not arise ; but no clear-headed and honest Leaguer could escape them. It could not be simply argued that, because the Pope can decide in the last resort what is heresy, therefore it was for the Pope alone to authorize rebellion against a heretic King. Once heresy is defined, the question whether a particular person is a heretic may be easy for anyone to answer. In the case of one notoriously, and even avowedly, a heretic, no Papal pronounce-ment could be needed or could in any way alter the position. It could not be held that it was the Pope's declaration that made a heretic into a heretic. In 1593 the Sorbonne declared that Henry's conversion was a mere imposture and that even were the Pope to recognize him, Catholics must still reject his claims. On the other hand, it could be and was argued by Leaguers that the Pope had a right to depose for heresy and that, if he did so, good Catholics must accept his decision.

The excommunication of Henry of Navarre by Pope Sixtus V in 1585, led at once to controversy. The *Brutum Fulmen* of Hotman and the *Apologie Catholique* of Pierre de Belloy, in 1585, were followed, in 1586, by the *De Summo Pontifice* of Bellarmine.[1]

This was but the beginning of a long controversy, that continued for many years after the entry of the triumphant excommunicate into Paris and belongs, indeed, even more to the seventeenth than to the sixteenth century. That controversy was concerned, not in any way directly with the position of the League, but with the general question of the relation of the Catholic Church to the Catholic State and particularly with the claims of the Papacy. The Papalist writers, even in the first stage of the controversy were not, of course, necessarily Frenchmen or specially interested in France. They were, nevertheless, allies of the League, if somewhat dangerous and suspect allies.

This controversy led to elaborate restatements of the Pope's position and claims, chiefly by Jesuit writers and to a restatement of the medieval conception of a great Christian commonwealth. The idea of a commonwealth of Christendom which, essentially, is the Church, of which the head is the Pope and in which every King is a subordinate member, found expression in writings on behalf of th League. It is confusedly implied in the *De Justa Reipublicae*. ' Ce que la Ligue pense, dit, fait et respire,' wrote Boucher, ' n'est autre chose que l'Eglise.'

But by the defenders of the League in France, Papalist views

---

[1] *De Summo Pontifice* is the general title of the *Tertiae Controversiae Generalis* of Vol. I of Bellarmine's *Disputationes de controversiis christianae fidei*, published in 1586. This title appears in the original edition and in the *Opera Omnia* of 1620. Maffei in his edition of the Disputationes adopted the title *De Romano Pontifice*. Bellarmine's *Tractatus de Potestate summi pontifici in rebus tem-poralibus* is a separate work, published in 1610, and is a later development of the same controversy.

were only partially accepted, if at all. The strong nationalist element in the League was adverse to any general acceptance of them. The Manant of Pithou's Dialogue speaks of the fact of Henry's excommunication as a technical bar to his succession, but makes little of it and never suggests that it forms the groundwork of his own attitude. Nor do the ordinary League pamphlets suggest any such view. Most of the Leaguers would have maintained that their opposition to Henry was justified quite independently of any action taken by the Pope. Most of them, probably, would have denied that it was for the Pope to settle, in any sense, a question of succession to the throne of France. The Jesuits in France were active in support of the League, but they did not control it. There was no reason why a Leaguer should not be a ' Gallican '. Strong Papalist views were, of course, held by some Leaguers. The author of the *De Justa Reipublicae* seems to have been Papalist after the fashion of Bellarmine ; and in Jean Porthaise, Bishop of Poitiers, the League possessed a sorry champion of the most extreme Papalist views. A volume of sermons published by this equivocal personage in 1594,[1] claims for the Pope an absolute and unqualified dominion in temporal things. Both swords, it proclaimed, belong to the Church. The Pope can depose a King not only for heresy but for tyranny and even for ' fainéantise '. All secular authority is held from the Church and derives its validity from Papal sanction. The sovereignty of the people is no more real than that of the King. But very few among the Leaguers held any such view.

Jesuit thinkers, writing while the League yet flourished or after it had collapsed in ruin, may be said to have made out a better case for the League than was made by the Leaguers themselves.

There may be said to exist ideally, a close connection between the attitude of the League and Jesuit Papalist theory ; though its connection with the actual views of Leaguers is relatively very slight. The theory of Bellarmine provided sufficient justification for the action of the League and to some extent helps towards an understanding of it. But fundamentally the League was nationalist and not Papalist. Its essential contention referred not to a commonwealth of Christendom but to a national State. The Jesuit theorists did not represent it. Yet certainly they must be regarded as having given it support ; nor is it wholly accidental that Papalist theory was being developed afresh alongside the activities of the League. The theory of Christendom as set forth by Bellarmine may naturally be considered in connection with it.

---

[1] *Cinq sermons . . . esquels est traité de la simulée conversion du roy de Navarre.* After Henry's entry into Paris the author changed his opinions. He is said to have had, even, the stupid impudence to assert that by ' King of Navarre ' he had meant Philip II. See Ch. Labitte : *De la democratie chez les prédicateurs de La Ligue.*

§ 5. THE CHRISTIAN COMMONWEALTH

The most remarkable attempts at an ideal reconstruction of a Christian commonwealth, within the limits of the sixteenth century, were the work of Bellarmine and Luis Molina. The work of Mariana was perhaps rather new construction than reconstruction ; and he demands to be separately considered. The translation of the thought of Aquinas into terms of the new political conditions by Francesco Suarez, falls outside my arbitrary limits.[1] His great *Tractatus de Legibus ac Deo Legislatore* was published only in 1612. It is a somewhat significant fact, and greatly to the credit of the Order, that all the really considerable writers engaged in such restatement of medieval conceptions, both in the late sixteenth and earlier seventeenth centuries, should have been Jesuits.

The Jesuit thinkers of the sixteenth century have, with the partial exception of Mariana very little claim to originality. But they were highly intelligent and lucid and logical in exposition. They took broad views and were, on the whole, far more detached and coolly reasonable than the mass of the writers on political topics at the time. Their writings, at their best, are even quite remarkably impersonal. They were apparently aware that reasoning can but be disordered by the intrusion of ephemeral interests and passions.[2]

It must be remembered that, in the late sixteenth century, claims were being made for the Pope, by Jesuit as well as other writers, more extravagant than had ever, perhaps, been made in the Middle Ages. In a book published at Padua, in 1599, it was asserted that the whole world belonged to the Pope, that, for us on earth, the Pope is equivalent to God and that Kings are his valets.[3] The writer of a thesis presented to the Sorbonne, in 1594, declared like Jean Porthaise, and in flat contradiction of Bellarmine, that all civil authority is held of the Pope ; that the Church has two swords and allows the use of one of them to secular magistrates.[4] A pamphlet published by French Jesuits in 1595, claimed for the Pope an absolute and unqualified sovereignty everywhere and in all relations.[5] Pope Sixtus himself would seem to

---

[1] This may be unfortunate, But if one does not draw one's necessarily arbitrary lines ruthlessly, one could never stop at all.

[2] In a well-known essay on political theories of the early Jesuits, published in the *Transactions of the Royal Historical Society* (New Series, XI), Dr. Figgis ironically remarked : ' Fools they were not. Were they all knaves ? It seems doubtful.' Evidently only ignorance allied with prejudice could suppose that Bellarmine and Molina and Suarez were ' knaves ' !

[3] *De Potestate romani Pontificis adversus impious politicos*, signed Alexandre Carrerius.

[4] These propositions were promptly condemned by the Parlement of Paris and the author made an apology. See F. T. Perrens : *L'Eglise et L'Etat en France sous le règne de Henri IV et la Régence de Marie de Medicis.*

[5] *Avertissement aux Catholiques.* Printed in *Mémoires de Condé,* Vol. VI.

have disapproved of Bellarmine's moderation and placed, or intended to place, the first volume of his Disputationes on the Index. It must not be supposed that all Jesuit writers of the sixteenth century presented the same view. Yet, in spite of the disapproval of Pope Sixtus, Bellarmine's doctrine tended to become generally accepted by the Jesuits and, in the seventeenth century, substantial agreement among them seems to have been reached.[1]

The endeavour of the Jesuit writers was, it must be admitted, to a considerable extent futile. No restatement of the Pope's relation to Christendom conceived as a political entity, could affect the fact that Christendom was no such thing. It never, in fact, had been. The medieval ' Empire ' had never, at least since the ninth century, been anything but a fiction. It was a fiction, however, that appealed to the imagination and to the aspirations of many. But so long ago as the very beginning of the fourteenth century, John of Paris and Pierre Dubois had seen and had said that the Empire was unreal and could hardly be. otherwise. In the sixteenth century it appealed to no one. It had shrunk into a germanic confederation, which itself, by the end of the century, was largely fictitious. Whatever reality the Christian commonwealth had ever had, was given to it by the Church. But the Church had gone to pieces. The Pope could no longer even be supposed to be the actual head of Christendom. But he might still, conceivably, be the head of a group of Christian states. It was not so much the fact that many Christian states had broken altogether with the Papacy, as the attitude and policy of Catholic governments and Catholic nationalists that made a revival of any kind of real Papal supremacy impossible *in rebus temporalibus*.

To the Jesuit thinkers the Empire is dead and the Papacy remains alone. Western Christendom has become a group of secular states independently ' absolute ' in all temporal concerns. There is no longer, even fictitiously, a temporal head of the Christian commonwealth. Yet the Christian commonwealth still exists and must always exist, ideally if not actually. There are, it is true, Protestant states which have broken away from that Christian commonwealth which is constituted by the Catholic Church. But the Catholic Church remains, nevertheless, and therefore the Christian commonwealth.

The theory that has now briefly to be set forth is that which appears in the writings of Robert Bellarmine.[2] Molina, at the end of the century, was substantially, though not quite completely, in agreement with him and added but little. In 1586 Bellarmine, not yet a

---

[1] A large majority of the writings quoted or referred to in Dr. Figgis's essay belong to the seventeenth century.

[2] His actual name was, of course, Bellarmino. Born in 1542 he attached himself to the Jesuit Order in 1560. He became a Cardinal in 1599 and died in 1621.

Cardinal, was already recognized by Protestants as the most formidable of Catholic controversialists. He embarrassed opponents by a care and moderation in statement and by a fairness and evenness of temper, which made it difficult to be rude to him. By far the greater part of his life was spent in his native Italy and he had no personal connection with France till sent there by Pope Sixtus in 1590 and attached to the Papal embassy. From 1576 he had held the Chair of controversial theology at Rome; and his lectures there grew into the *Disputationes*. With the subject of the position of the Pope in the Christian commonwealth he dealt in the first volume of that work in 1586. In 1587 he published, under the name Franciscus Romulus, an answer to Belloy's *Apologie*.[1] The statement of his theory was completed by the publication of the *Tractatus de potestate summi pontificis in rebus temporalibus, adversus Gulielmum Barclay*, in 1610.

What gives, or should give, effective unity to the Christian commonwealth, is the God-given authority of the Pope, ' pastor gregis totius et Praepositus toti familiae et caput vice Christi totius corporis Ecclesiae'. The Pope derives his authority not from man, not even from the Church,[2] but from Christ directly. He has the cure of all souls and is the infallible judge of all that is done on earth. It is his business to act as overseer of the whole Christian commonwealth and it is his right and his duty to correct and direct the action of all secular magistrates.[3] For it is his function to see to it that men are not governed in such manner that their final salvation is imperilled. This does not mean, it is carefully explained, that God has given to the Pope any authority in concerns merely temporal. The Pope has no power to make law or to abrogate law concerned merely with earthly and bodily welfare. But he has and, by reason of his position, must have, authority to set aside, or altogether abrogate, any law by which men's spiritual welfare is endangered. So, also, the Pope has no authority arbitrarily to depose Princes at his discretion. He can act only ' ad finem spiritualem '. Yet, if the spiritual welfare of subjects require the deposition of their Prince, the Pope has a right to depose him. Were it otherwise there would be no sort of guarantee that men should be ruled and guided in a manner consistent with the meaning and purpose of life. Here, as to the medieval thinkers, is the root of the matter. The end and purpose of man's life, realizable only in another world, is the same for all men. Government must needs refer to that end or be altogether senseless and destructive. It is for the spiritual power to direct the temporal ' ad finem spiritualem aeternae vitae '.

---

[1] *Responsio ad praecipua capita apologia, quae falsa catholica inscribitur, pro successione Henrici Navarreri in Francorum regnum.*

[2] See Molina: *De Jure et Justitia*, 1599. Tract' II, Disp. 26.

[3] ' Dirigere et corrigere potestatem politicam.'

There is no ground, Bellarmine declares, on which this can reasonably be disputed. Secular authority is, it is true, independent of the Church in origin. But it cannot be independent of the end and purpose of life, nor can that purpose be rationally conceived as referring to mere circumstantial needs or to anything merely temporal. Temporal authority is not held from the Pope, but neither is it held directly from God.[1] ' Non enim potestas nisi a Deo,' says Molina ; but the authority of a temporal ruler is held from God, only in the sense that every man holds from God his life and all that he has. Civil authority was created by the community itself for the sake of its own temporal welfare. The secular State is founded only on man's needs in this world. It develops from the nature of man and his circumstances and refers only to earthly good. The Prince, therefore, is a delegate and a minister of the community. To him has been delegated by the body of his subjects ' dominium jurisdictionis ad jus illis dicendum, eosque defendendum et gubernandum in commune bonum '.[2]

But his authority must needs be held conditionally and can never be unlimited.[3] As well say, declared Bellarmine in the *Responsio*, that no man may for any cause be deprived of life or goods, as that no King may for any cause be deposed. The mere fact that a Prince is Christian binds him to serve and defend the faith ' sub poena regna perdendi '. There is, normally, for all of us, an obligation to God to obey the Prince ; but in the case of a heretic Prince no absolute obligation can exist.[4] All men are equal before the Pope and in divine law there is no respect of persons. ' Si id exigat finis supernaturalis potest summus Pontifex deponere reges.'[5]

Molina asserted quite distinctly that a people has a right, under appropriate circumstances, to depose its delegates. He seems even to have thought that it is not strictly accurate to say that the Pope can depose. It is the Respublica itself that deposes a Prince, though it may be bound to do so by the Pope's decision. But neither he nor Bellarmine were concerned to show what, in general, would justify the deposition of a Prince by his subjects. What they wished to show was that the constitution of the Church and its necessary relation to the Christian State and to the Christian commonwealth of states, involved a right in the Pope to depose heretical princes or bar the

---

[1] This had been asserted by Diego Lainez, second General of the Jesuits, in his *Disputationes Tridentinae*.

[2] Molina : *De Jure*, Tract II, Disp. 23, p. 116.

[3] Ib., Tract II, Disp. 33.

[4] ' Non licet Christianis tolerare Regem infidelem aut haereticum, si ille conetur pertrahere subditos ad suam heresim, vel infidelitatem, at judicare an Rex pertrahat ad haeresim, necne, pertinet ad Pontificem . . . ergo Pontificis est judicare, Regem esse deponendum vel non deponendum.' *De Summo Pontifice*, Bk. V, cap. 7. *Opera Omnia*, ed. 1620, I, p. 903.

[5] Molina : *De Jure*, Tract II, Disp. 29.

succession of a heretic to a throne. No more moderate statement of the case could well have been made by ultramontane Catholics.

The Jesuit writers taught, with more or less distinctness, that the Prince is a delegate of a sovereign people, holding his authority conditionally and liable to deposition. They taught that secular authority is created by the act or by the recognition of the community itself. The Huguenots, or some of them, after 1572, made the same assertions. The doctrine that a heretic or idolatrous or infidel Prince, who endeavours to force on his subjects his own religion or irreligion, may rightfully be deposed by force was the doctrine alike of Knox and of Bellarmine and of the *Vindiciae*. Similar assertions made by Leaguers in France might as well have been derived from one as from another. But in truth all these propositions could all be derived either from the *Corpus Juris* or from medieval writings. In the sixteenth century the validity of these assertions was altogether denied by very many. But the conception was always to hand, here, there and everywhere. There was not the least reason for anyone to go for it to any particular book. Jesuit writers, concerned to maintain the right of the Pope to depose heretic Princes and seeing in the extension or revival of Papal authority the best hope of salvation for Christendom, naturally tended to adopt it. They were certainly not less sincere than other controversialists.

They had to meet the assertion that Princes derived authority straight from God. They met it either with the old commonplace that civil authority is derived from the populus or, in some cases, by boldly declaring that all earthly authority is derived from the Pope. To credit them with any originality in the matter is absurd, except so far as all sincere, personal beliefs are original. The value of their work consisted partly in its lucidity and coherence and partly in their insistence on the conception of a Christian Commonwealth. But to speak thus of the Jesuit writers of the sixteenth century is to ignore the most original thinker among them, Juan de Mariana.

§ 6. MARIANA

Juan de Mariana, born in 1536, studied at the most splendid educational foundation of the Renaissance, the University of Alcala, taught at Rome and had Bellarmine as a pupil, taught at Paris from 1569 to 1574 and passed the rest of his life in study and in writing at Toledo, till his death in 1624. The first part of his elaborate *Historiae de rebus Hispaniae* was published in 1592 and his view of the constitution of Spain was derived from, or reinforced by, his studies in Spanish history. His *De Rege et regis institutione* was published in 1598 and rather strangely dedicated to King Philip III.

Mariana's *De Rege* is a philosophical treatise on the origin and nature of the State : it is also an essay on the constitution of Spain.

He cannot be regarded as a typical Jesuit thinker. His originality, indeed, consists largely in his departure from ordinary Jesuit modes of thought. It may fairly be said that the Jesuit writers of the sixteenth century agreed generally on two points. They agreed in conceiving Christendom, or at least Catholic Christendom, as a commonwealth united by recognition of a common purpose in life of which the Pope was the real head and in which all kingdoms and kings were subordinate to the spiritual authority, *ad finem spiritualem*. This conception was consistent alike with the most extreme Papalist views and with such a view as that of Bellarmine. They agreed, further, that secular Princes do not hold their authority directly from God. But Mariana was a patriotic Spaniard and a nationalist. While holding, like Bellarmine, that the authority of the Prince is not derived immediately from God, he denied, at least by implication, that Christendom is any sort of commonwealth. His book contains few references to the Pope ; and he may, not improbably, have shared in some degree the anti-Papal sentiment that had long characterized the Spanish Church. Before the end of his life, his orthodoxy was seriously questioned and he left behind him, in manuscript, a treatise in which he criticized the government of his Order. He thought in terms of National States and not in terms of Christendom. He may, I think, have been influenced by Italian thought and rather, perhaps, by Botero than by Machiavelli.

Mariana attempted to establish his theory of political authority on a conception of the State of Nature, that is on a conception of the manner of the State's origin. The State of Nature might be conceived as having actually existed in an unhistorical past ; and in that case we should be dealing with actual origins. But it might, also, be conceived as a mere pictorial representation of the nature of man, as seen apart from all such accidents as social organization and law. Man in the State of Nature would then be man stripped of all the clothing time has put upon him, divested of all the specific habits and notions that belong to particular times, thrust outside all circumstance that is not permanent, at once an absolute and a mere potentiality. Nothing of man would then remain but that which is at all times. The question, of course, arises whether anything would remain. However this may be, it did actually become a fashion, in later times, to construct ideal states with these attenuated beings of the state of nature. But this was not the thought of Mariana. He seems to have imagined that he was dealing with actual origins. If you deal with actual origins it is, to say the least, difficult to show that they prove anything.

Mariana's idea of the State of Nature was similar to that suggested by Buchanan ; but he was far more explicit than Buchanan had been. There was a time, he says, and he meant there actually was a time, when men lived without law or government and therefore without rights of property. They lived then as the animals live : in fact, they were animals ; he implies, quite distinctly, that they were not fully human. This condition, he thought, had certain, not small, advantages. Cheating and lying were then unknown among men. Why this should have been so is not very clear. It could hardly have been so merely because no property ' rights ' existed ; for, law or no law, two men could not eat the same apple, nor could opportunities for trickery well have been absent. Perhaps it was that, at this stage, man's intellect was too feeble for deliberate trickery. But man, says Mariana, is at once a poor weak creature and yet one afflicted with far more wants than other animals. Fear and desire and need drove men to group themselves in societies and to co-operate for self-protection.[1] Such grouping, he imagined, involved the recognition of private rights of property ; and once such rights were recognized the selfish cupidity of man grew apace, till lying and cheating became as common as they now are. The consequence of this was an increasing elaboration of law and stringency of repression, until at last man was as much vexed by his laws as by his vices.[2]

Mariana, like Bodin, regarded the family, substantially as we know it, as simply ' natural ' and existing, without law, in the State of Nature. The further grouping that took place was conceived, therefore, as a grouping of families. Perhaps it was for this reason that he imagined that the first form of government established was a vaguely unlimited monarchy. But Mariana conceived, like Buchanan, that it was quickly found that this did not work ; and as restraining law developed, the restraint of law was imposed on the ruler as on the ruled.

The point is that any and every form of governmental authority originated as a response to need and was derived from the will of a self-protective society. Mariana considered that his account of the origin of society proved this to be universally true. Men have forgotten, perhaps, or been imposed upon ; but no change in the character of human association has taken place since those earliest days of humanity. This, be it observed, is implied absolutely in the argument. He put it, therefore, that the authority of any Prince must be held to originate in a grant made by the community and that this grant cannot rationally be conceived as having been unconditional. Whether

---

[1] ' Sic ex multarum rerum indigentia, ex metu et conscientia fragilitatis, jura humanitatis (per quam homines sumus) et civilis societas, qua bene beateque vivitur, nata sunt. . . . Omnis que hominis ratio ex eo maxime pendet, quod nudus fragilisque nascitur, quod alieno praesidio indiget atque alienis opibus adjuvari opus habet.' *De Rege*, ed. 1599, pp. 21, 22.

[2] ' Legum multitudinem tempus et malicia invexit tantam, ut jam non minus legibus quam vitiis laboremus.' *De Rege*, ed. 1599, p. 23.

or no in a particular case any kind of formal grant was ever in fact
made, does not affect the contention. The grant is made perpetually
from day to day. It cannot be unconditional, because the will that
makes it is directed to limited ends.

Salamonius and others had declared that no people would be
insane enough to create a right to defeat its own will. Mariana was
more explicit. He declared, boldly and indeed rashly, that the
community must be held always to reserve to itself the right to legislate
and the right to tax, and further that both the form of religion and,
in a monarchy, the law of succession, must be held to be fundamental
and unalterable arrangements. Those powers which the community
reserves to itself can only, according to Mariana, be exercised by a
representative assembly. The existence of such a body he seems to
have regarded as involved necessarily in every political association ;
presumably because, without it, the community would have no means
of expressing its will.[1] It is implied that if, actually, it has disappeared,
there has been usurpation. The ' Estates ' of the realm share sovereignty with the monarch ; but with them lies the last word and
it is their will that must prevail, because they represent the will that
created the monarch. Evidently Mariana, like Buchanan and like
Molina,[2] accepted the view that the will of the people is sufficiently
expressed by a majority.

He proceeded to draw the conclusion, that if the Prince overstep
the limits of his authority, he may rightfully be restrained by force,
warred upon and deposed and killed. But individuals as such must
not take action on their own initiative. Initiative lies with the
Estates. It is for the representative body to say whether the Prince
has become a tyrant and a public enemy. Mariana laid down definitely
that if the Prince defied the Estates or if he refused to allow them to
meet, there could then be no doubt that he was a tyrant. When,
either by his own action or that of the Estates, the Prince has become
a manifest tyrant, not only may he be deposed by force but he may
be killed by any private citizen. With much elaboration Mariana
argued that tyrannicide is justified in anyone and by any means,
except by poison : and even poison may be used so long as the tyrant
is not made to kill himself with it.[3]

There was, of course, in this assertion of a general right of tyrannicide, nothing whatever that was new. The strange thing is that
Mariana seems to have been more concerned to prove a common
right to kill tyrants than to prove a right to depose by force, though,

---

[1] He might have derived this from Huguenot writings ; but of course he
did not.

[2] See Tract II, Disp. 23, of the *De Jure.*

[3] It is odd to find this muddle-headed quibble in the work of a man capable
of such fearless reasoning.

of course, he asserts both. It may be that he felt strongly that, under some circumstances, the most effective and least risky method of dealing with a tyrant would be murder. But it looks as though the moral question involved interested him extraordinarily. Mariana seems to have seen what Buchanan did not see, that to say that a King may be rightfully deposed does not involve that any private person may rightfully kill him. Buchanan seems to have imagined that the mere fact of tyranny made killing no murder. Mariana, it appears, had doubts ; and it was these doubts that he set himself to resolve in his famous sixth chapter. His reputation suffered by reason of his moral scruples. The importance he apparently attached to what was really a detail, gave a weapon to the enemies of his Order and helped to discredit his work.

It was a fashion with sixteenth-century writers who wished to prove a right to rebel against and depose tyrannical Princes, to give examples of actual Princes who had been deposed by force. What these instances were supposed to prove, or why they were supposed to prove anything, was not made clear. In pamphlet after pamphlet they appear as mere irrelevancies. Mariana ingeniously argued that the numerous recorded depositions of tyrannical rulers pointed to a sense everywhere prevailing that authority is held on conditions and that tyranny justifies rebellion. The origin of society may be forgotten and its nature, therefore, not understood, but the ' voice of nature ' in our minds is never stifled. It speaks in our obscure souls of the originally conditional grant of authority and tells us that tyranny need not be endured. Nature does not allow us to be deceived. We discern tyranny and our right to depose the tyrant, just as we distinguish right from wrong.[1]

It should go without saying that, to Mariana, an attempt by the Prince to alter the form of religion established, would be tyranny. But what if there develops among his people a new form of religion ? Mariana did not suggest that the mere toleration of such heresy would be tyranny ; and in this he differs from the League. But he argued that it would be highly impolitic and dangerous ever to tolerate two religions in one ' province '. The inevitable hostility of the two religions to one another must needs create enormous friction and difficulty. If, when he used the word provincia, he was thinking of the bundle of unlike provinces that constituted the kingdom of Spain, and when he wrote, included Portugal, he must, it would seem, have been ready to accept the establishment of two religions even within Spain. In any case he did not assert that there is only one religion which should anywhere be established. He contemplated with

---

[1] ' Et est communis sensus quasi quaedam naturae vox mentibus nostris indita, auribus insonans lex, qua a turpi honestum secernimus.' *De Rege*, ed. 1599, p. 74.

equanimity, the establishment of different religions under different jurisdictions. All that he insisted on was, that unity in religion is all but necessary, if peace and order are to be maintained. Here, at least, his thought is one with that of the League. Heretics, he says, cannot be trusted to keep faith. The remark looks like a slip : for on his own showing, ' heresy ' may mean different things in different countries. But perhaps his real thought was that the partisans of different religions would never keep faith with each other. He had ample reason for thinking so. It that were so, every compromise would be unstable and the fact would constitute a serious obstacle to the attainment of peace.

Mariana had the, perhaps somewhat doubtful, advantage of writing after the League and after Buchanan and the *Vindiciae*. It might be said of him that he presented all that was essential in the thought of Huguenots and Leaguers more completely and coherently than ever they did themselves. Like the Huguenots, he asserted the necessarily conditional character of all human authority : like the Leaguers, he asserted, though less emphatically, that national unity is dependent on unity in religion. His thought was nearer to Buchanan's than to that of the *Vindiciae* ; but Buchanan's thought, compared to his, was thin and conventional. The *Vindiciae* is confused by partisanship and by the idea of the sovereignty of a Calvinistic God. Mariana escaped both the partisanship of the *Vindiciae* and the passionate confusions of the Leaguers. It might be said that he made a better case both for Huguenots and Leaguers than they made for themselves. But it needs to be noted that Mariana's theory would not have justified Huguenot rebellion. He claimed a natural sovereignty for Estates and placed the right to initiate rebellion absolutely with them. In this he is completely at variance with the *Vindiciae*.

If not a great thinker, Mariana was, at least, comparatively detached. His thought was not seriously confused or distorted by passion or by party. He was more dispassionate than the author of the *Vindiciae*, more subtle than Buchanan and had more imagination than either. His sensible views on economics, his acute sense of the ill results of a depreciation of coinage, his advocacy of a poor law system for Spain, do not fall to be considered here but illustrate at once his patriotism and his perspicacity. But the structure of his thought is medieval. Perhaps the most original thing in his book is the dim vision of man emerging from the semi-brute of the State of Nature into a consciousness of himself and of right and so into full humanity.

For all the likenesses that exist between the thought of the *De Rege* and of the *Vindiciae* or of the *De Justa Reipublicae*, it would seem that Mariana's thought is really profoundly different from both. The difference may roughly be expressed by saying that Mariana conceived the State in no sense as theocratic. It is perhaps significant that for him the inner light by which we know right from wrong was *vox naturae* rather than *vox Dei.*[1] He agreed with the League writers that national unity depends on unity in religion ; but his argument went no further. It was not unity in ' true ' religion that was needed : Mariana, apparently, perceived that any religion might serve the purpose. The State might flourish in unity on a false religion. But there is an implication more fundamental. To say that the Prince does not hold his authority directly from God was, in 1598, a mere commonplace. What Mariana implies distinctly is, that political authority needs no further justification when it corresponds to general needs and is directed by the will of the community. In thinking thus he resembled Buchanan, but was far from the thought of the *Vindiciae* and yet further from that of the League. Mariana was a Jesuit and, orthodox or not, no doubt a sincere believer. He recognized in the Church a rightful, if shadowy, power of direction. Yet he conceived the State as something that had grown out of the nature of men and things and that justified itself by the felt need of it. With whatever inward qualifications, he was accepting the national and secular State, resting on mere earthly needs and on the will to peace and security, as something complete in itself, potentially and logically independent of any Church. Mere reaction from and weariness of strife, a growing scepticism and the obvious failure of the theocrats to realize any-thing but dissonance, tended, in the sixteenth century, to produce this mode of thought. Mariana, it seems to me, links with Bodin and the Politiques as well as with the League. His thought was prophetic, or ominous, of what was coming.

[1] He may have learned to think thus from Vasquez.

CHAPTER VII

THE DIVINE RIGHT OF KINGS

§ 1. INTRODUCTORY

THE theory of royal absolution expounded in the law schools of France under Francis I tended from the first to dissociate itself from the *Corpus Juris* and to substitute for a theory of delegation a conception of the King as holding his authority directly from God. This conception is the very essence of what is called the theory of the divine right of Kings. Whether it would have become predominant in France, but for the disturbance caused by the Huguenots and the disorganization, misery and ruin produced by the civil wars, is one of those questions on which speculation is vain. All we can say is that, but for the Huguenots, opposition to the Crown would have taken a ' constitutional ' form simply and the King's claims would have been resisted only in the name of established custom or local privilege or on behalf of a claim to a share to sovereignty for the Estates or for the Parlements of the realm. In that case the struggle would more nearly have resembled that which was fought out in England in the next century. What would have been the issue in France it is not possible to say certainly. But it would probably have been impossible for the opposition to combine on any single point and against a divided opposition the Crown should have been assured of triumph in the long run. The fact really seems to be that only recognition of practically unlimited powers in the King could have given peace and order to France. If that were so, the recognition would have come. The permanent will to security would have won its usual victory and would have developed a theory to fit its exigences. It is possible even that, under such circumstances, the triumph of the monarchy would have been more rapid than actually it was, though this, certainly, is dubious. Certain it is, in any case, that Huguenots and factious and self-seeking grands seigneurs on both sides, between them drove France to find a refuge from chronic disorder in the recognition of the absolute authority of a sovereign will. It was the civil wars and the prospect of civil war interminable that made France royalist.

A ' Royalist ', in the sense of a supporter of the Crown against the Huguenot party, might, in 1562 or in 1567 or even in 1588, desire to establish the Estates in a share in sovereignty ; or he might be a believer in a monarchy limited by custom and unable, at least, to raise taxes at pleasure. The Politiques of Henry III's time were, in fact, inclined to adopt some theory of limited monarchy. But in the stress of the struggle after the death of Henry III, when it was visibly a question of how government was ever to be re-established at all and of whether the unity of France could ever be restored, all theories of limitation tended to sink into the background or even to disappear altogether. Already in 1589 the Huguenot writers themselves were declaring that there can never be any justification for rebellion. More and more dominant became the sense that only in recognition of the King's power as unlimited was there any guarantee for security. That recognition took the form of a theory of divine right in the King and it could have taken no other.

There is danger, however, of overstating the case. By the end of the century, indeed, very few would have maintained that the Estates of France possessed any rights not derived from the King or shared his sovereignty in any sense. Yet, on the other hand, the claim of the Parlements to put a veto on proposed royal edicts was by no means dead ; while the claims of provinces and of classes to customary rights independent of the will of the Sovereign, remained almost as strong as ever. It must even be said that the Edict of Nantes created a new privileged class, new privileged localities and a new 'fundamental' law. There was a great deal of very hard work yet to be done before all opposition was overcome. Yet the decisive battle had been fought and complete victory was only a question of time and persistence. Barclay's *De Regno* of 1599 was at once a summary of earlier writings and a summary of the conclusions to which France was coming. Richelieu, Bossuet and Louis XIV were in sight already.

§ 2. ROYALIST OPINION TO 1572

The royalist or anti-Huguenot publications of the years from 1562 to 1570 were, in themselves, journalistic and trivial scribblings. Yet they have considerable significance. The main issue raised by the opposition was constitutional. The Huguenots claimed that they were defending a traditional constitution : but they carefully refrained from attempting definition. No one quite knew what they supposed themselves to be defending. For the most part their adversaries countered by simply declaring that the King is the direct representative of God in his kingdom and that, consequently, tradition or no tradition, armed rebellion against him amounts to sacrilege. In a pamphlet that seems, in spite of its stupidity, to have attracted a significant amount of attention, it was proved from Scripture that even a heretic

King must not be forcibly resisted.[1] Yet it must not be supposed that these writers regarded the King's powers as unlimited. All of them would probably have denied that the King could abolish the Salic Law or alienate domain : some of them, probably, would have gone much further. It may be hard to reconcile the opinion that the King has no absolute sovereignty, that he cannot do this and that and is bound by custom, with the opinion that armed resistance to what he does is always unjustifiable. But it is quite certain that both views at once were held by many Frenchmen in the sixteenth century, as they were by many Englishmen in the century following.

The royalist pamphleteers were expressing a sense that the disorder and ruin caused by rebellion can never be justified. As early as 1562 it was argued that the only alternative to permanent anarchy and general brigandage was the recognition of an unlimited duty of submission.[2] Who is to give final decisions if not the King ? asked a pamphleteer of 1569. How is it possible to have a government of as many people as there are opinions, when there are about as many opinions as heads ?

Other perceptions, other fears, were also expressed in the Royalist writings of these years. In 1567 the Huguenots were charged with the design of breaking up France and establishing some sort of Genevan or Swiss republic. The accusation that they were engaged in this ' dammee entreprise ' was made by the King himself in a declaration of September, 1568. More telling, perhaps, was the argument of a pamphlet published in 1568 at Lyon.[3] The writer argued that if the King cannot secure obedience, assuredly nobles can expect none from their ' subjects '. The Huguenot ministers, he declared, hate all nobles and teach that their privileges are naught but human inventions without warrant in the Scriptures, which make all men free. There is no mention of gentilshommes in Scripture, they say, and they say also that nothing is to be allowed of that is not expressly approved in Scripture. It is quite likely that a few Huguenot ministers were saying these things ; but the Huguenot party most certainly stood for no such principle nor was ever likely to. Yet the writer expressed a feeling and a perception that was probably widespread among the class concerned. Monluc in Guienne regarded the Huguenots as a town party aiming at the domination of the countryside and the destruction of the noblesse. There was just enough truth

[1] *Remonstrance salutaire aux dévoyéz.* By Canon Thomas Beaux-Amis, 1567.

[2] Du Préau : *Harangue sur les causes de la guerre,* 1562.

[3] *Avertissement à la noblesse tant du parti du roi que des rebelles et conjurés,* 1568. Referred to by G. Weill : *Les Théories sur le pouvoir royal en France pendant les guerres de religion* (1891), p. 75.

in the charge to make it bite. Later the same charge was brought, both by Politiques and Huguenots, against the League.

Already, therefore, before 1572, the Royalists were saying that there was no alternative to anarchy but unlimited submission, that rebellion bringing ruin on all alike, cannot possibly be justified, whatever the legal and constitutional limits of rightful royal action may be; that noblesse and monarchy stand or fall together. Insignificant as are in many ways the Royalist writings of these years, one can gather from them what were the main factors in the conversion of France to a theory of divine right absolutism. But no such theory was as yet fully formulated or defined. Few denied a divine right in the King; but this did not involve absolutism.

§ 3. THE POLITIQUES

After 1572, however, there came a change in Royalist as in Huguenot opinion. Many, indeed, of the Royalist pamphlets of the following years were of the same character as those published earlier. There was a great deal of argumentation from Scripture to show that Kings must never be forcibly resisted. Much was made of Nebuchadnezzar and, on both sides of the controversy, Samuel's remarks as to what might be expected from a King, were regularly quoted.[1]

But the evolution of Catholic opinion after 1572 expressed itself in the development, on the one hand of the party of the League, on the other of the party of the Politiques. The word ' Politique ' was first applied to the party by its enemies, derisively, as signifying men who set their own ease before their duty to God and peace and quiet above religion. The Politiques, at first, seem to have agreed about nothing except that a continuance of civil war was intolerable. After the failure of the royal army before La Rochelle in 1573 and the formation of the Huguenot leagues in the south, it had become tolerably obvious that complete victory was no longer possible. The adoption of some system of practical toleration was the only way of peace and the only way, finally, of preventing a break-up of France. The Politiques may be defined as a group of Catholics who advocated toleration of the heretics for the sake of peace and national unity.

Horror at the devastation and ruin caused by the wars and the apparent hopelessness of the attempt to beat down the Huguenot resistance, account sufficiently for the appearance of such a party. If the figures given by Fromenteau in 1580 [2] even roughly expressed the ravages of the war, it is no wonder that it seemed to many that any compromise, however illogical or deplorable, would be justified. It may be noted that, as soon as the Politique party had come into

[1] Samuel i. viii. 11–18.
[2] *Le Secret des Finances de France . . . par N. Fromenteau.* The book contains a statistical account of the loss and devastation caused by the wars.

definite existence, the hope of crushing the Huguenot resistance by force became feebler than ever. Toleration of two religions in the kingdom might be but the lesser of two evils : it could not be shown to be so ruinous as continued war. Such sentiments and perceptions were expressed in pamphlet after pamphlet. As early as 1572, before the siege of La Rochelle had even been begun, Catholic writers suggested that toleration was the only possible road and advocated the summons of a States-General to arrange terms of peace. A pamphlet of 1574 sombrely depicted the wretchedness of all classes and appealed to the Huguenots to co-operate in a States-General for the salvation of France.[1] Alencon's manifesto of 1576 struck the same note. Nor was it only material devastation that aroused horror. La Noue expressed the horror that was felt by many at the demoralization caused by the wars. Civil war, he declared, has already engendered a million libertines and ' epicureans '. Religion itself is in danger of perishing. ' Ce sont nos guerres pour la religion qui nous ont fait oublier la religion. . . . Si la guerre civile n'est chassée, c'est folie de parler de restauration.'[2] Most of the argument on behalf of toleration tells the same tale. Nearly all of it was frankly utilitarian. Even if it were possible, it was argued, to ruin the heretics by force, every one else would be ruined in doing it.[3] The dream of unity in religion must perforce be abandoned : there is not a kingdom in Christendom that can keep itself in peace without tolerating two religions. Persecution, it was declared, is in any case useless : it does nothing but make atheists. ' Vous pouvez contraindre de faire, de dire, mais de croire il est impossible.'[4] Even La Noue, a Protestant but a true Politique, advocated toleration mainly on political and utilitarian grounds.[5] France, he argued in 1587, was being torn in pieces, in danger of splitting up into a multitude of petty principalities and republics. Toleration and the revival of monarchy were the only remedies possible.

Out of all this was arising a conviction, not merely that it was impossible to maintain unity in religion, but that, in any case, it

[1] *Avis et tres humbles remonstrances*, etc., 1574. Referred to by Weill, p. 135, op. cit.

[2] *Discours politiques et militaires*, 1587. Bodin had expressed the same view.

[3] *Exhortation et Remonstrance faite d'un commun accord par les François Catholiques et Pacifiques pour la Paix*, 1587. In Vol. II of *Mémoires de la Ligue*. But actually it seems to be Mornay's and composed in 1576.

[4] *Le Labyrinthe de la Ligue et les moyens de s'en retirer*, 1590. Quoted by Weill, p. 297, op. cit.

[5] Yet not entirely. ' Puisque chacun confesse,' he wrote, ' qu'il adore un même Dieu à avoue pour sauveur un même Jesus Christ ; puisque les Ecritures et fondements sont semblables, il doit y avoir telle fraternité entre eux, que, cessant toutes haines, cruautés et guerres, on vienne à quelquè reconciliation.' (*Discours politiques et militaires.*) Here we have an echo of Castellion or at least of L'Hôpital.

would really be useless to do so. The State could flourish even though it recognized two religions at once. The State, if not independent of religion, was independent of any one religion. This conception it was that came to be characteristic of the Politique party and was in the long run the most important of its political ideas. It was argued even, that there was little real difference between the two religions. In a dialogue of 1590 a Catholic and a Protestant are made to discover, with justifiable surprise, that their essential beliefs are the same.[1] Above all it was argued that to suppose that two religions necessarily produce disorder in the State is altogether a mistake. In a declaration issued in 1585 Henry of Navarre himself hit the mark as exactly as was usual with him. 'Pourvu que le fond de bonne conscience y soit,' he proclaimed, ' la diversité de religion n'empêche point qu'un bon prince ne puisse tirer bon service indifférement de ses sujets.'[2] La Noue pointed out that the existence in the same society of vicious and of virtuous persons tended to produce dissension, not less than the existence of two religions ; and yet that no one proposed to remedy this state of things by war.[3] The Politiques had begun to perceive that the ' unity ' which men spoke of as necessary to orderly society did, in fact, never exist at all. To sacrifice order for the sake of moral unity was to sacrifice what all needed to a chimera. ' Que chacun se-sonde au dedans,' wrote Montaigne, ' il trouvera que nos souhaits interieurs pour la pluspart, naissent et se nourrissent aux depens d'aultruy.'[4]

Added to all this was an increasing scepticism, which went with increasing disillusionment. Disillusionment and scepticism were essential elements in the mental constitution of the Politique party. If there were as yet little doubt of the validity of the foundations and essential elements of the Christian faith, there was a large and increasing amount of scepticism as to the claims of the Churches, above all as to their claim to an exclusive possession of saving truth. Along with this went impatience, increasingly contemptuous, of all religious political idealism. Increasingly men had come to doubt the validity of any attempt to fashion the State after the Scriptures or bring it into real union with any particular Church. What had come of all these endeavours but confusion and misery ? The sincerity even of the religious idealists was jeeringly impugned. It was but too evident that men followed their inclinations and professed the beliefs that were consistent with their desires. How many of those engaged on either side, asked Montaigne, have troubled to understand the position and arguments of their adversaries ? ' C'est un nombre, si

[1] *Le Pacifique*, 1590. Referred to by Weill, p. 297.
[2] *Declaration contre les calomnies.* In *Mémoires de la Ligue*, I, p. 66.
[3] *Discours politiques et militaires.*
[4] *Essais*, I, 21.

c'est nombre,' he added caustically, 'qui n'aurait pas grand moyen de nous troubler.'[1] That people like Catherine de Medicis or Louis de Gonzague[2] should have seen nothing but hypocrisy in religious politics is not surprising ; but many others of different type took the same view. Guy Coquille declared that religion was the merest pretext alike with the Huguenots and the League. More significantly, Pierre Pithou saw that there was in the League an element of genuine religious idealism and counted it as folly. ' Votre esperance envers. Dieu est bonne,' his Maheustre told his Manant, ' mais je vois des effets contraires a votre esperance.' What folly, in fact, to throw society into confusion for the sake of doubtful dogmas ! Here, again, it was Montaigne who best expressed the thought of the party.

' Si me semble,' he wrote, ' qu'il y a grand amour de soy et presomption, d'estimer ses opinions jusques là que, pour les establir, il faille renverser une paix publique et introduire tant de maux inevitables et une si horrible corruption de moeurs que les guerres civiles apportent et les mutations d'estat en choses de tel poiš, et les introduire en son pais propre. Est ce pas mal mesnagé d'avancer tant de vices certains et cogneus, pour combattre des erreurs contesteés et debattables ? '[3]

The Politiques were agreed that toleration was the only means of putting an end to civil war or preventing the break-up of France. But, whatever they felt, they knew that merely to say this was insufficient. They had to argue that persecution was in any case futile, that it was mere folly to wreck society for the sake of a unity that could never really exist, that two religions in a kingdom did not necessarily breed war. Practically they were agreed that governments, at least, should regard all controverted questions as in doubt. Taxed with putting their own security before the duty of maintaining true religion, they took refuge in the ambiguity of a common Christianity. With them, already, the word has begun to lose definition.

But as to what the constitution of the monarchy of France was or should be, the Politiques were not agreed, at least at first. In 1580, as earlier, several different views on this subject can be distinguished. There were the absolutists, who held that the King was bound by nothing but the obligation to respect the Salic Law and not to alienate domain. ' Si veut le roi, si veut la loi,' was their maxim ; and to them the King was responsible only to God. But there were still many who conceived the monarchy of France as Seyssel had conceived it, as limited, not specifically and yet absolutely by custom and tradition. The difficulties of maintaining this con-

[1] Ib., III, 8.
[2] Duke of Nevers and author of a *Traité des causes et des raisons de la prise des armes*, 1590. (Cimber et Danjou.) He maintained that neither religion nor patriotism counted with either side.
[3] *Essais*, ' De la coustume,' 1572.

ception had now become so great that it tended to be replaced by another. According to this newer view the King was sole sovereign and could not rightfully be forcibly resisted. Yet not only was he in some sense bound by ' natural ' and divine law, he was bound also by fundamental laws which extended further than merely to succession and domain. Above all, he could not impose direct taxation without a grant from Estates. Finally, there were those who, going a long step further, claimed for the Estates a share in sovereignty more or less definitely. All these different views were held among Catholics in general and among the Politiques in particular.

It seems indeed that so late as 1585, and perhaps later, most of the Politiques clung to the tradition of a monarchy limited by custom or some theory of a constitutional monarchy resting on the Estates of the realm. The attitude of the Estates of Blois in 1576 practically represented Politique opinion at least as much as that of the League.[1] In Du Haillan's *Histoire Générale*, Parlement and States-General appear as subordinate but essential parts of the constitution, not depending for existence on the will of the King. The historian Belleforest speaks of [2] the King's authority as ' non du tout absolue, ne de tant restreinte que le pourvoir lui soit ôté,' precisely as Seyssel had done. He declares also that King and Estates together form a ' perfect ' body, which would appear to imply some sort of inadequacy in the King alone. La Noue wrote that it was monstrous to say that the Prince may do just as he pleases, and that his magistrates and officials were bound to refuse to do injustice if ordered to do it.[3] According to Guy Coquille [4] edicts issued with the consent of the Estates were irrevocable without their consent and ordinances affecting the whole kingdom should always receive their approval. He, like Hotman, believed in the legendary constitution of old France and reproached Louis XI for destroying it. The *Miroir des Français* of 1581 was perhaps rather Politique than Leaguer.[5]

For every French Catholic, Politique or Leaguer, above all for every Catholic who believed in royal absolutism, the claims of the Pope constituted a difficulty, though this was hardly felt till 1585. The Politique party developed a pronounced Gallicanism, that was sharpened by the open conflict with the League.

In 1590 Avocat-Général Louis Servin published an answer to Bellar-

---

[1] Gentillet's *Anti-Machiavel* or *Discours sur les moyens de bien Gouverner*, published in 1576, contains an appeal to Alençon, to drive out foreign tyrants and re-establish the ancient constitution. This much too celebrated book was really an attack on the actual government of France and shows very little knowledge of Machiavelli.

[2] *Grandes Annales de France*, 1579.

[3] He might have derived this from Bodin.

[4] *Institution au droit français.*

[5] For the *Miroir*, see p. 345.

mine.[1] On this remarkable man, a friend of Hotman and a pupil of Ramus, a portion of his old master's spirit of combativeness had descended. His religious opinions were suspect and he was accused of saying that Protestants were in every way as good as Catholics. He was, at all events, an extreme ' Gallican '. The kingdom of Christ, he declared, is not at all of this world. The King holds authority direct from God and only God can judge him. His authority extends even to ecclesiastical causes and he can release from any excommunication. Heresy and consecration, he roundly declares, are alike irrelevancies. The King is King by hereditary succession and the grace of God. The Pope is no more than a chief among bishops and has no right to interfere with the King's action or in a question of succession in France. For all practical purposes, in fact, the Pope is ruled out altogether.[2]

Few of the Politiques perhaps would have gone so far as this : few, certainly, would have said as much. More typical was Guy Coquille, the most eminent of the jurists of the party. He laid down [3] that the Church was not a monarchy but an aristocracy of which the Pope was a mere suzerain.

All French clergy, he declared, owed obedience primarily to the King, and he denied that the liberties of the Gallican Church were in any sense privileges granted by the Pope. Apparently the liberties of the French Church consisted in an obligation to obey the King rather than the Pope. His language has the ambiguity of timidity ; but he was clear at least that no Papal action could determine succession to the throne in France. Pierre Pithou's famous book,[4] which appeared in 1594, was a declaration and a definition rather than an argument. Its main propositions were, first that the Pope has no kind of authority in temporal matters in France, and secondly that even in ' spiritual ' causes the Pope's authority is bounded by such canons and conciliar decrees as the French Crown chooses to recognize as valid. He was expressing what was, at that time, the attitude of the Politique party and of Henry IV himself. It was not, practically, different from that of the outspoken Servin.

It might be said that the attitude and policy of Pope Sixtus V forced the Politiques into Gallicanism. Catholics, but advocates of toleration and supporters of Henry of Navarre's claim to succession, they were bound to deny the validity of his claim to dictate to France.

---

[1] *Vindiciae secundum libertatem ecclesiae gallicanae.*

[2] Evidently the line is a fine one between the views of the extreme Gallicans and the view adopted by Henry VIII in England.

[3] *Traité des libertés de l'eglise de France.*

[4] *Les Libertés de l'Eglise gallicane.* The immense success of the book is significant. Edition after edition appeared, with added documents to support its contentions. In the seventeenth century it was referred to as authoritative even in royal edicts.

The more they became convinced that the only way of salvation for France lay in the recognition of a practically unlimited duty of obedience to a national sovereign, the more were they bound to adopt 'Gallican' opinions. Logic bound them as well as circumstance. They were asserting that it was not a duty for government to maintain true religion and stamp out by force what the Church called heresy. The more clearly they conceived the State as independent of any one form of religion and of an unlimited duty of obedience to a secular sovereign, the more were they logically bound to a Gallicanism as extreme as Servin's.

It may be said that the Politiques were inclined, at first, to maintain at once that the King was not an absolute sovereign, and yet that no justification for rebellion was possible. Of the truth of the latter proposition every year that passed after 1585 convinced them more profoundly. They found it increasingly difficult to maintain the former. For some years the disintegration of France continued. Between 1588 and 1593 France looked like breaking up, not into a Catholic kingdom in the north and a Protestant kingdom in the south, but rather into a multitude of petty principalities and republics. ' De degré en degré il ne se trouvera village en France qui ne se fasse souverain,' wrote a Huguenot in 1593.[1] It is not surprising that the tendency to see nothing but the need for order and restoration became overwhelmingly strong. Up to 1585 the divergence of views among the Politiques was considerable ; after that year there was steady convergence. Slowly, and not of course completely, the hope of defining limits to the King's authority was abandoned. What was wanted, it was felt, was not restriction but simply universal obedience to a directing will. Very soon after 1572, indeed, pamphleteers had begun to write extravagantly about the King's divine right. A writer of 1575,[2] contemplating the sovereignty of Kings, had worked himself up to the pitch of ecstatic nonsense. Kings, he declared, not only hold authority from God but themselves participate in divinity. Angels have them in special charge and God comforts and confirms them with signs and wonders. Behind this silliness was the growing sense that it was a question for France between royal absolutism and no government at all. What did it matter even though the King played the tyrant ? ' Better a hundred years of tyranny,' wrote the lawyer Le Jay, ' than a single day of sedition.'[3]

It was a matter of course that the Huguenots should join in the chorus. So soon as they saw a clear prospect of their champion succeeding to the throne of France, they began hastily to readjust

---

[1] *Quatre excellents discours sur l'état de la France*, 1593.

[2] D'Albon : *Traité de majesté royale.* Lyon, 1595. So also Forcadel : *De Gallorum imperio et philosophia.* Paris, 1580.

[3] *De la dignité des roys*, 1589.

their views. The sails were trimmed to the new wind and the *Vindiciae* thrown overboard. Soon after 1585 they had convinced themselves that nothing justifies rebellion, They congratulated Henry III on the Blois murder in the name of a right of summary justice granted by God to Kings. In 1585, Hotman of the *Franco-Gallia* published a book to prove that, strictly and simply by hereditary right, Henry of Navarre was heir to the crown of France and that no resistance to his claim could be justified.[1] Gentillet, the author of the *Anti-Machiavel*, made his apology that same year.[2] The Huguenots retorted on the League the accusation, made a few years before against themselves, of aiming at the establishment of a democracy and the destruction of noblesse.

Very soon they were declaring that royal authority, God given, had no conceivable limits. ' No violence, no cruelty, no tyranny, no. circumstance whatever,'· wrote a Huguenot, ' justifies a subject in rebellion.'[3] Never perhaps did a political party make so quick and complete a change of front. Yet it must not be said that all this was merely insincere. The actual condition of France between 1588 and 1593 was enough to convince even a Huguenot, and even a Leaguer, that rebellion was never justified. What is the use of talking about religion ? asks the Maheustre of Pithou's dialogue. What is the sense of saying that a good Catholic ought to join the League, when it is clear that no good can come of it ? The only government the League could conceivably give France would be a Spanish government. If the League were to triumph, France would be destroyed but not heresy. The Politiques are doing for religion all that can be done. The only hope for us all lies in submission to our natural King as the lieutenant of God. The Huguenots were coming honestly to the same conclusion.

§ 4. BLACKWOOD AND LE ROY

Reference has been made to various writings of the period from 1572 to 1594, but none of the more important royalist writers of those years have yet been dealt with. The most outstanding and important of these were Pierre de Belloy and, of course, Bodin. To them may be added the Gallicized Scot, Andrew Blackwood, the Italian Zampini and Louis Le Roy, ' royal professor ' in the University of Paris. Bodin wrote his *Republic* with remedial purpose in view of actual conditions. But his work as a whole does not belong merely to this period ; nor was the *Republic* itself a work of party politics. Bodin's work as a whole is so much that of a philosophic jurist detached from practical

---

[1] *De jure succession is regiae in regno Francorum leges aliquot ex probatis auctoribus collectae studio et opera,* 1588.

[2] *Apologie pour les chrétiens de France,* 1588.

[3] *Quatre excellents discours,* 1593.

politics and has an importance so far-reaching, that it must be separately considered. The first two parts of Blackwood's *De Vinculo Religionis* appeared in 1575 ; the third and last part not till 1611. His *Apologia pro Regibus*, written as an answer to Buchanan, was published in 1581. In the *De Vinculo* he expressed views that were not either those of the Politiques or those of the League. He argued against the toleration of Calvinism and believed only vaguely in the divine right of the King. He was an absolutist in the sense of Bodin, not in the sense of Belloy· or Barclay. He declared that, just because the Christian religion forbids resistance even to the most manifest tyranny, Christianity affords the only solid basis for settled government. The implication was clear. Peace and order depend on the recognition of an unlimited sovereignty in the State and no State can afford even to tolerate the assertion of a principle justifying in any case resistance to the sovereign. He went on to argue that Calvinism included a theory of a right of rebellion against impious or tyrannical Princes and that Calvinists were bound, by their conception of what the State should be, to strive for the establishment of what in effect was at once clerical and republican government. Calvinism, therefore, must needs be a source of disorder in all states not governed Calvinistically. It was radically incompatible with any state organization not based on its own principles. He was essentially right, though this Calvinism he spoke of was not quite that of Calvin and though what he said was, even in 1575, only partially true of the Huguenot party. Everywhere the fact to which he pointed was being more and more clearly perceived, though no one had yet stated it so distinctly.[1] He concluded that, not for the sake of religion but for the sake of order, Calvinism must be suppressed in France. But what was to happen if the King himself insisted on tolerating this disruptive force ? Blackwood's argument fortified the position of the League rather than that of the Politiques. It is a little surprising that the defenders of the League did not adopt it to their purposes. But what Blackwood had chiefly meant to insist upon, was the idea that any claim to a right of rebellion is incompatible with social order ; and in this he is at one with all the upholders of royal absolutism. To this idea he returned in his Apologia, which is little more than a reflection of Bodin's views on sovereignty.

Louis Le Roy [2] had published in 1568 a translation of Aristotle's

---

[1] Erastus, however, had come very near to stating it in his *Confirmatio*, not published till 1589. ' Sane Magistratus quem sibi subjecit Presbyterium, nihil aliud est quam servus Presbyterii.' *Confirmatio*, V, 1.

[2] He was appointed to a ' royal readership ' in Greek in the University of Paris in 1572 ; and seems to have been the first teacher of the University to lecture in French upon classical authors. He lectured in French on Demosthenes in 1567.

Politics, the preface to which crudely reflects something of Bodin's theory of climate, as he had sketched it in the *Methodus* of 1566. In 1570 he published an *Exhortation aux Français pour vivre en concorde et jouir du bien de la paix* ;[1] and in 1575 appeared the most significant of his political writings, under the title : *De l'excellence du Gouvernement Royale.* In 1579 he published the treatise, *De la Vicissitude ou Variété des Choses en l'Universe*, in which he again expatiated upon Bodin's theory of climate., He was to some extent a disciple and to some extent a precursor of Bodin.[2]

Le Roy, though he expressed himself only vaguely on the question of toleration, can be classed as a Politique more definitely than can Blackwood. He was a thoroughgoing monarchist though not exactly an absolutist. The really striking feature of his thought is the way his mind turned constantly to an idea of evolution in the past to explain actually present facts and anomalies.

Monarchy, he insisted, is the most natural form of government. It originated, not in any agreement or election, but simply in the ' natural ' monarchy of the head of a family. This notion was widely current in the sixteenth century, though it is not easy to say exactly what the notion was. Le Roy, like others, contented himself with the bare assertion. In any case, monarchy is declared to be ' natural ', because it resembles in form the only kind of government that arises inevitably. But it is natural, Le Roy asserted, for another reason also. He argued that men always find it easier to obey a single person, crowned and consecrated, than to obey any group or assemblage of men, however representative. He only weakened the force of this contention, by implying that a group or a ' people ' must needs be foolish or self-seeking. It is this naturalness of monarchy, Le Roy suggested, that explains why it is that monarchies have always been more common than republics. Further, just because monarchy is natural, it may be regarded as normally, practically the best form of government. But he admitted that it was not actually best for all times and in all places. In mountainous regions, he says, among rude and poverty-stricken people, democratic institutions tend to develop.[3] This fact, he characteristically argued, points of itself to the real inferiority of such institutions. Ideally, monarchy must be held to be always greatly superior to the ' état populaire '. Le Roy shared the usual contempt of the learned of his time for common folk in the mass and expressed it pointedly.

' Rien n'y a plus ignorant ne plus insolent qu'un populaire occupé en vils métiers et gains deshonnêtes, n'ayant appris bien ni honneur, qui se rue indis-

---

[1] This was reprinted in 1579.
[2] Like Bodin, he proclaimed the superiority of the modern to the ancient world.
[3] See Bodin, *République*, V, 1.

crètement sur les affaires. Leur principal but est la liberté et equalité, procurant soigneusement qu'aucun pour vertueuse qu'il soit, savant, vaillant ou habile, ne s'avance ou élève par dessus les autres : qui est au grand avantage des mauvais et inutiles.'

But there is nothing really distinctive about this passage except its ·vigour. The republicans of the sixteenth century took the same sort of view.

From these generalizations Le Roy turned to the consideration of the actual position in France. Only frantic folly, he declared, would desire to break down the superb structure of French monarchy. But any attempt to introduce sweeping changes into the form or character of government involves a danger of catastrophe. Every nation, he declared, has developed from crude and barbarous beginnings and hence retains traces of the clumsy and barbaric in its laws and institutions. Change, therefore, is always desirable and indeed unavoidable ; but every change is dangerous. Bad arrangements to which people are accustomed may work better and do less harm than new arrangements however excellent.[1] One is reminded of Montaigne's saying : ' Je suis desgouté de la nouvelleté, quelque visage qu'elle porte.'

Almost in the words of Seyssel Le Roy spoke of the French monarchy as neither ' totalement absolue ne trop astreinte '.[2] The Prince, he declared ambiguously, subjects himself to laws. But he will not hear of any positive or legal restraints. It may be, he wrote, that the Estates of France once shared sovereignty with the King. If they ever held such a position they have lost it : and this fact points to the conclusion that it was found best that they should not have it. The truth is, he asserted, that all such assemblies are incompetent to direct. Nothing is gained by gathering into council the ignorance of their individual members. The people of France, he concluded, will have the sense to retain its monarchy, and in obedience to its King will find liberty and peace, as it has done in the past.

§ 5. MATTEO ZAMPINI

In 1578 was published at Paris a book written in Italian under the title *Degli stati di Francia e della potenza*. It was written by a man named Zampini, an Italian protégé of Catherine de Medicis and was dedicated to her. Though it can have had little influence, it is a somewhat remarkable book. One can hardly say that it was the work of a ' Politique ' : yet if Bodin is to be regarded as a Politique,. Zampini was one also. How far the Italian was consciously reproducing the ideas of the *Republic* it is impossible to know.

---

[1] *De l'excellence du Gouvernement Royale*, 1575. The view expressed is precisely that of Bodin. See *Rep.*, IV, 2.
[2] *Exhortation aux Français*, 1579.

Organized society arose, Zampini asserted, from the instinct of self-preservation. The idea was old and seems to be the same as that more fully stated later by Mariana. Under the pressure of fear only small groups were at first formed ; but these found themselves still too weak for safety and a process of amalgamation of groups set in. So, gradually, the great national State or kingdom came into existence, the completed political society, self-sufficing and able to defend itself effectively.

Society is nothing but a mutual defence association and, at first, the fear that formed it was a fear of external enemies. But every individual member of that association has his own inclinations and point of view and, though all desire security, the desires of men in other respects are irreconcilable. It became necessary, therefore, for the sake of internal order, to develop government concerned with the repression of internal strife as well as with defence against external enemies. It was found, by experience, that the security of all was best maintained by obedience to a single will. Hence arose monarchy. Before the institution of monarchy authority, Zampini thought, would ' naturally ' have resided in some kind of Estates or representative body. This form of government disappeared by reason of its felt inadequacy and was replaced by the government of an hereditary monarch with unlimited authority. The change involved no sharing of sovereignty between the new monarch and the old assembly. Sovereignty, Zampini argued, cannot be either divided or limited. All limitation would involve division and division of authority can produce only disorder. The ' Estates ' abdicated their authority in favour of a King and henceforward the King need never summon them. Occasion might arise, he admitted, when an assembling of the Estates would even be imperative : but to summon them periodically would be inconsistent with the position of the monarch. Elective monarchy would have produced constant friction and tended to defeat the purposes for which the change was made. The conclusion is clear. Absolute and hereditary monarchy was evolved by a natural process from the same needs which first brought men into organized association.

The absolute monarchy of Zampini was not, however, quite ' absolute '. Certain fundamental understandings or laws were involved in its creation. The monarch could not, in the nature of things, be entrusted with power to ruin the society he was created to protect. It must have been understood that the King had no right to cede to others any portion of his dominions without a common consent signified by his Estates. Apparently it would also have been understood that he had no right to make war offensively, since this would bring society needlessly into danger. Finally, the King must not change his religion or the religion of his people. He is bound to maintain true religion and true religion is defined not by the King but by the Church. At this point, clearly, the argument becomes confused. By 'the Church' Zampini meant the Roman Church. This, apparently, had been divinely superimposed upon the evolved structure of the monarchy.

The original authority of the Estates, Zampini finally observed, was derived from the mere fact and from the cause of association. It was derived from the nature of man and his needs : it was inevitably recognized. But that which is 'natural', he argued, that which arises inevitably, is of God. Hence first the Estates and later the King possessed a real authority to command derived from God.

Zampini's King derived his authority from God only in the same sense as did the Prince in the *Vindiciae*. He was not a King by divine right in the sense of Belloy and Barclay. More important is the fact that he presented his argument in a form quasi-historical. In the latter part of the sixteenth century it was becoming increasingly common to endeavour to explain the nature of actual institutions by reference to evolution in the past. There was a tendency to represent them as having developed, as it were automatically, in response to needs. This way of thinking appears more or less distinctly in Buchanan, Louis Le Roy, Zampini, Bodin and Mariana. It may of course be said with truth that Zampini's argument is historical only in form. He gave to conclusions drawn simply from his conception of man and man's needs an historical form that was quite arbitrary. He does not argue from ascertained facts about the past, but makes dogmatic assertions as to what must have been. This is equally true of all this group of thinkers ; but the fact remains that they conceived of government, in any form, as a result of human experience and as developing by natural processes and inevitably. Almost always, in France as in England, the word 'natural' conveys this notion of necessity.

The Huguenot writers of this time were maintaining that government having been established by a popular will to definite ends, sovereignty must be held to be limited by the nature of those ends. They repeated over and over again the truism that magistracy exists for the sake of the governed, not for the sake of the magistrate, as though they had made a surprising discovery. Zampini was going much deeper. His sovereign, equally with theirs, was a creation of popular will to security. The Huguenots, hopelessly confused by their notion that the good of the people implied the establishment of Calvinistic religion, concluded for a right of rebellion against tyranny. On the side of the Politiques men were beginning to see tyranny as a mere accident. Zampini, it may be said, concluded that there could be no limit to the authority of the sovereign except such as was implied in the will of society to preserve itself and that rebellion against the constant will embodied in the sovereign could not be justified. Though not fully clear to himself, the thought of this obscure Italian was approximating to the later view of Hobbes.

§ 6. PIERRE DE BELLOY AND DIVINE RIGHT

Far more significant both at the moment and for the future than the speculations of Zampini and Louis Le Roy or, indeed, than the theory of the *Vindiciae*, were the writings of Pierre de Belloy. His *Apologie Catholique* was published in 1585 ; the more important *De l'autorité du roi* in 1587. Born about 1540, de Belloy had both studied and taught law in the great royalist school of the University of Toulouse. He was, I think, the first in France to expound with any fullness a theory that may conveniently be called, *par excellence*, the theory of the divine right of Kings.[1]

The *Apology* [2] was occasioned by the excommunication of Henry of Navarre in 1585 and its object was merely to show that his right of succession remained unaffected. A crown, argued Belloy, comes to a particular man by the providence of God. Law merely determines the line along which succession shall take place : the actual individual heir is of God's own creation. The right of God's chosen cannot be taken away by any human action, Papal or other. Consecration is not necessary to make of the true heir a true King and heresy is an irrelevance. It seems to be implied that if God did not mean that he should succeed, the heir would die from natural causes.[3] If the Pope could bar the succession of the natural heir he could depose an actual King. But Kings cannot be deprived of their kingdoms, ' parce qu'ils sont tenus immédiatement de la main de Dieu éternel, non des hommes '. The declaration appears here as a mere assertion at once dogmatic and ambiguous. In the *De l'autorité du roi* we find some explanation of what was meant.

On the title-page of this treatise [4] are the words : ' La terreur du Roi est comme le rugissement d'un lyonceau : celui qui le fait courroucer pêche contre son âme.' Below is added : ' Le Roi, séant

---

[1] Imprisoned, later, by the Leaguers, he was rewarded by Henry IV with the post of Avocat-Général at Toulouse.

[2] *Apologie catholique contre les libelles, déclarations, avis et consultations faites, écrites et publiées par les Ligués, pertabateurs du repos de la royaume de France.*

[3] So the matter was explained in a *Discours* by Claude de Morenne, a Parisian curé, in 1594. He explains that it is really God who selects the heir and ' pour cet effet ôte les uns hors de ce monde, aux autres qui ja y sont abrège les jours, à cette fin que celui qui lui plaît, eloigné qu'il en semblera être, vienne à jouir de cette Lieutenance, dont il veut l'honorer '. In *Mémoires de la Ligue*, VI, 31. This way of thinking was, of course, a very old one.

[4] *De l'autorité du roi et crimes de lèse-majesté qui se commettent par ligues, désignations de successeur et libelles écrits, contre la personne et dignité du prince,* 1587.

sur le siége de Justice, dissipe mal par son regard.' Together they form the text of what is something like a sermon. Immediately after the fall of man, declares de Belloy, God established government among men. He instituted the authority of the father or patriarch and the rights of primogeniture. Monarchy corresponds to this original arrangement. 'La principauté royale et monarchique a sa source de la paternelle oeconomie.' This alone would be quite inconclusive. What it is essential to grasp is the fact that real authority, a right to rule and demand obedience, could have been established only by God. All that the people could have given to a Prince is an uncertain amount of actual power. A Prince so created would have no authority except' so far as a purely voluntary submission was made to him. No obligation to obey could arise from or be created by any need or any act of men. But government can only rest on such an obligation. God, therefore, created what is needful. The question, that might be raised, as to whether God has conferred a real right to command on sovereigns other than monarchs did not interest Belloy and he did not touch on it. He simply remarked that monarchy is the only form of sovereignty that God definitely approved and instituted.

Authority, then, must be conceived as created and conferred by God. There can be no limit, de Belloy declared, to authority so created. Why this should be so he did not make very clear. He had, evidently, been influenced by Bodin, whose definition of the State he paraphrased and adopted. He made free use of the expression 'puissance souveraine' and in Bodin's sense. The recognition of such a power in the State was, he asserted, necessary : there must be a supreme will as the source of law. 'Le principal caractère du monarque,' he declared, almost in Bodin's very words, 'git en ce qu'il peut donner la loi à tous en général et à chacun en particulier, sans le consentement ni volonté d'autre quel qu'il soit.'

As God's lieutenant the King can be responsible only to God. 'A la seule Majesté appartient de commander, approuver ou reprouver tout ce que bon lui semblera.' The King is the very image of God, the very hand of Justice, ' ains est lui même la Justice,' for the measure of justice is his will. No distinction between the King and the Monarchy is of service. The Monarchy but makes the King's person sacred. Even in the Church the King, he asserts, is supreme so far at least as all its this-worldly aspects go. He quotes Optatus of Milevis.[1] It is the duty of the King to see to it that in his dominions the divine will is not defied and blasphemed ; and his authority must needs extend to all that concerns the maintenance of the faith. Rebellion for any cause must, he concludes, be rebellion against God. Man

[1] 'Non enim respublica est in Ecclesia sed Ecclesia in respublica est.' *De Schismate Donatistatum*, III, 3.

can have no right to rebel against an authority he could do nothing to create. It is not enough to be neutral as against the League : we shall all incur damnation if we do not actively oppose it.

None of the numerous writers of late sixteenth-century France who expressed the same views as de Belloy, succeeded in saying or in seeing all that they meant. It was better put, perhaps, by an anonymous pamphleteer of 1589 than by either Belloy or Barclay. ' La puissance première du Prince,' he wrote, ' vient immédiatement du peuple, mais après qu'il est fait roi, Dieu le confirme et lui donne l'autorité.' [1] Barclay's elaborations made the matter no clearer than it had been before. This is, perhaps, one reason why ' the theory of the divine right of Kings ' has been so little understood. Yet the nature of the thought is surely clear enough. The very root of the theory is the idea that authority to command, implying obligation to obey, cannot possibly be created by man. It is futile to say that man needs authority, for no obligation can be created out of need. My need may not be yours, nor is your need necessarily anything to me. My need to-day may not be my need to-morrow. The mere fact that authority is needed, even if it be regarded as justifying coercive action, creates no categorical imperative. Whether a community set up a King to satisfy its needs or decided to govern itself by majority vote, the case would be exactly the same. Every one, everywhere, under such circumstances, would always have a right to rebel. One man has no right to give orders to another and, this being so, it matters not in the least how many give the order. The right to rule must be a right to demand obedience in the name of God : it cannot be a right to demand it in the name of the people, for the people itself can have no right to demand. To say that the King derives his authority from the people is to say that government rests on force only and may always and at any time be rightfully overthrown by force. No peace or security can be based on such an understanding. Either there is a religious duty of obedience to the sovereign, which is a duty to God, or there is no duty in the case at all. If the King does not hold authority direct from God he holds no real authority.[2] ' Men being by nature equal,' declared a writer of 1589, ' it is not possible to persuade one to obey another, unless royal power be strengthened by a super-human authority which is divine.'

Up to a certain point, it must be observed, the theory is the same as that of the Huguenot writers of the years 1572–1579. Those writers confusedly declared that the King held his power and his office from the people and his right to command from God. De

---

[1] De la puissance des rois, 1589. Quoted by Weill, p. 252 n.
[2] Compare Wyclif : ' Non enim est jus humanum nisi de quanto fundatum fuerit in lege Dei divina.' De Officio Regis, ed. Wyclif Soc., p. 73.

Belloy and the absolutists would have none of this. When once the right to command has been given how can there be any longer a right to rebel ? The only possible answer was that the right to command had been given conditionally. The King is under contract with God. This, it was replied, can only mean that the King is responsible to God for the exercise of his authority. No one of course denied that that was so. But it cannot, it was asserted, mean that he is responsible to the people. What is the people that it should judge between God and the King God has chosen ? For God chooses the King even though he be hereditary. Again, who are the people who have the right to judge ? The absurd answer given by the Huguenots to this question put them out of court in the eyes of anyone who saw peace and order as the primary end of government. All France was coming to see it so in 1593. To say that anyone but God can judge the King is to destroy sovereignty and invite anarchy.

The sentiment dominant in France in 1593–4 was finely expressed in the oration attributed to M. d'Aulnay in the *Satyre Ménippée*.[1]

' Le roi que vous demandons,' he is made to say, ' est déjà fait par la nature, né au vrai parterre des fleurs de lys de France, jetton droit et verdoyant du tige de Saint Louis. Ceux qui parlent d'en faire un autre se trompent et ne scauraient en venir à bout : on peut faire des sceptres et des couronnes mais 'non pas un arbre ou un rameau vert ; il faut que nature le produise par espace de temps du suc et de la moelle de la terre. . . . On peut faire un jambe de bois, un bras de fer et un nez d'argent, mais non pas un tête ; aussi mous pouvons faire des maréchaux à la douzaine, des pairs, des admiraux et des secretaires et des conseillers d'état, mais de roi point : il faut que celui—là seul naisse de lui—même pour avoir vie et valeur.'

Edmund Burke, had he been a Frenchman of 1593, might have used these very words. The King whom all men are bound to obey must be born, not made ; for no man need obey a King of man's making. Grown on the soil of national tradition, chosen by God out of all potential heirs, Henry of Navarre alone could be King of France.

§ 7. WILLIAM BARCLAY

After 1594 assertions of popular sovereignty, of a joint sovereignty in King and Estates, of the elective character of monarchy, were still made, but with increasing infrequency. On the other hand, the assertion that the King holds a practically unlimited authority directly from God and that rebellion, if justified ever, is justified only in the most extreme cases imaginable, became more and more a confident commonplace. In spite of all discontents, France under Henry IV was enjoying an immense relief. Controversy, after 1594, turned more and more

---

[1] The first edition of this was published in 1593. The speech quoted was probably written by Pierre Pithou.

on the question of the relation between a Catholic King and the Papacy. The political literature of the last years of the century reveals nothing new or specially significant, until we come to the *De Regno* of Barclay. Even that is new only in form and in scale. It is a little strange that the conclusions to which France was coming at the end of the century should have been summarized and formulated by a Scot. But William Barclay, even more than Buchanan, had made himself French. Born in Scotland in 1546, he received education at the University of Aberdeen. But in 1573 he left his native country for ever. He studied law at Bourges and became professor in civil law, first at Port à Mousson and later at Angers, where he died in 1608. His *De Regno et Regali Potestate* was published in Paris in 1600.

Barclay seems to have set to work, conscientiously and laboriously, to sort out and summarize and arrange in a logical order all the arguments for absolute monarchy by divine right that he could find in the controversial literature of the last thirty years. He undertook, also, to refute in detail the assertions of Buchanan, ' Brutus ' and Boucher and, incidentally, those of Hotman. He seems to have been under the impression that in this way he would exhaust the subject. But he did not succeed in making anything clearer than it had been before. He tried hard to reach precision and definition, but he really got no further than his predecessors. He was a compiler and arranger rather than a thinker. He displays a feeble fondness for verbal syllogism, for the most part empty or question-begging, He devoted long chapters to the cases of Samuel and David and to St. Peter and St. Paul. He goes through all the hackneyed texts reproducing the hackneyed interpretations. Even his illustrations are drawn from the common stock-in-trade of the pamphleteers. His only claim to originality lies in his attempt to make an exhaustive survey. The general effect is one of conscientious dullness.

Barclay's most essential contention was the same as that of Belloy. Authority to command can only be derived from God : it cannot conceivably be derived from man. He explains, carefully, that even if a King be regularly elected, all that the electors do is to decide who shall hold an authority they could not themselves confer.[1] It follows, he argued, that, even in this case, the people cannot take away what they did not and could not give.

Sovereignty is requisite in human society and sovereignty, for that very reason, is constituted by God. But sovereignty, he lays it down, is incapable of limitation. The very essence of it consists in a power to make law for all and sundry : if this power do not exist there is no sovereignty. In every community such a power is needed. It cannot

---

[1] ' Eligendi regis facultatem a constituendi potestate longo plane intervallo distinguimus.' Ed. 1600, III, Chap. 3, p. 115.

be limited, for any positive limitation would involve division of the sovereignty and in fact destroy it. That way lies anarchy. Further, the sovereign law-maker must be held to be himself above or outside law. He must be *legibus solutus*, not so much because he can repeal any law as because he cannot be subject to another's jurisdiction.[1] There is none but God who can judge his doings.

Social order rests and can only rest on an obligation to obedience. As the authority constituted by God possesses an unlimited power to make law, so the obligation must also be unlimited. No wickedness or oppression on the part of the King can deprive him of authority or give to the subject a right to rebel.[2] A true 'tyrant' may indeed be resisted. But Barclay limits the application of the term 'tyrant' to such as thrust themselves by force into a throne to which they have no rightful claim. The legitimate monarch cannot, whatever he does, become a tyrant.[3] He particularly insists that no amount of religious persecution can ever justify forcible resistance, though it is true, he admits, that should the King command a positive transgression of divine law he must not be actually obeyed.[4]

He went, even, a little further. He admits that it is theoretically possible that a King might behave in such a manner as would give the community a right to collective, forcible resistance. If a King were to hand over his subjects to the dominion of a foreign Prince, he might fairly be taken as having abdicated all authority in the very act. In that case resistance to the foreign usurper would be lawful.[5] Barclay recognized no 'fundamental laws'; yet he comes near to saying that the King cannot change the line of succession. But, further, if a King were deliberately to set to work to wreck and destroy his kingdom, were to burn his capital like Nero or wantonly organize the massacre of his subjects, corporate resistance would be justified.[6] If the King be responsible only to God, it is not quite clear why this should be so. Barclay might have said that resistance would be justified by the sheer insanity of such conduct : or he might have said that such action on the part of a King is a self-contradiction equivalent to abdication. He said neither of these things. Very rashly he asserts that resistance in such a case is justified under the

---

[1] 'Neque enim cogi a seipso potest, neque ab alio, cum nullum in terris judicem vel superiorem habeat.' Ed. 1603, III, 16, p. 209. In all this he is following Bodin.

[2] 'Ego alium scio nullum quo rex ipso jure, ipsove facto regiam dignitatem perdat ; non enim si adulter, si homicida, si perjurus, si (quod damnosius et detestabilis est) haereticus fuerit ; nec si populum iniquis vectigalibus premat, vel in civitates quasdam severius et injustius animadvertens aratrum inducat.' Ed. 1600, III, 16, p. 214.

[3] See IV, p. 268, and VI, p. 483, ed. 1600.

[4] Ed. 1600, III, pp. 153, 154.

[5] Ib., III, Chap. 16.   [6] Ib., III, Chap. 8 and Chap. 16.

law of nature. It is not clear why the law of nature should operate only in so extreme a case. In effect, Barclay was saying that resistance is justified only when the King has lost all understanding of his own position and behaves like a mere lunatic.

There were gaps in the argument which Barclay did not attempt to fill. It was little to the purpose to say, as he said, that absolute monarchy had been instituted immediately by God and was the only form of sovereignty of which God is known to approve.[1] There remained an apparently unbridgeable gap between the asserted appointment of Saul as King of Israel and the accession in France of Henry IV. What was supposed to be the connection between these two events ? Still less use was it to say that monarchy is ideally the best and noblest form of government, comparable in its nature to the sovereignty of Adam and the patriarchs and even to that of God Himself and confirmed by the behaviour of bees and cranes. Admittedly, aristocracies and even democracies had in fact existed.[2] What reason was there for supposing that France was favoured ?

But though the statement is incomplete, there are implications and the argument may, I think, fairly be summarized as follows : We know, by the bitterest experience, that peace, order and security can be maintained only where a practically unlimited duty of obedience to a sovereign authority is recognized. In France such sovereignty might conceivably belong either to the King or to the Estates. It cannot conceivably belong to both. But in France, at least, the mere fact that the Estates can only meet when the King choses to summon them and must disperse at his pleasure, makes it impossible to attribute sovereignty to them. Barclay, attacking Hotman by name, tried to show that popular assemblies had never in France been understood to possess any authority not derived from the King.[3] In France, therefore, sovereignty either belongs to the King or it does not exist at all.

But sovereignty, a right to demand obedience as a duty to God, could only be created by God. What reason is there for supposing that upon the King of France such authority has been conferred ? It is a far cry from Saul to Henry IV ; but we know that sovereignty is needed by human society, we know that God wills the good of man and we know that God Himself established monarchy among the chosen people. The authority so created must have been intended to be perpetual since the need of it is perpetual. Here, in France for many centuries, we have had Kings holding a sole and uncontested supremacy, recognized and consecrated as God's lieutenants. It may be rash to assume that there is any real authority where there is no King : on this point Barclay gave no opinion. But we, in France,

[1] Ib., III, Chap. 2.   [2] Ib., Bk. II.
[3] Ib., IV, Chaps. 14–18.

are bound to believe that God confers upon our Kings the same authority He gave to Saul and David. If this be not so, then no authority remains on earth and God has deserted his people. All this, I think, was to Barclay so well understood that it did not need stating.

If Barclay was convinced that authority could not be created by any act or device of man but only by act of God, he was yet more profoundly convinced that only by recognizing that rebellion was practically never justified could men escape anarchy. To this thought and to the thought of the horrors of civil war, to which he devotes a whole chapter,[1] he constantly recurs. It might be said that he believed that authority could not be created by man because he felt sure that men would never obey a sovereign they thought they had created. The admission that any but the most extreme and unlikely circumstances could justify rebellion, seemed to him to be necessarily fatal to order. Buchanan's principles led, he declared, straight to anarchy : those of ' Brutus ' practically legalized rebellion by every factious noble or discontented town. On whatever principle rebellion might be held justified, neither argument nor occasion would be wanting. Government can only rest on the sense of a duty of obedience. Once that obligation is held to be limited by anything short of a specific divine law, it is practically destroyed. But who will believe in such unlimited obligation, who, even, can conceive it, unless the sovereign holds his claim to obedience direct from God ? If man believe that he has himself created sovereignty, he will not obey ; nor is there any good reason why he should, if he does not wish to do so. It is useless to talk of pacts and covenants. An inexplicit compact can bind no one ; an explicit pact could effect nothing but the destruction of authority.

To Barclay the existence of the Catholic Church and Papacy raised no serious difficulties. He would not admit that there was involved any limitation of the King's power or any insecurity in his position. His views as to the relation of Prince to Pope were fully expounded, in answer to Bellarmine, in his not quite finished *De Potestate Papae,* published only in 1609.[2] He admitted that a Pope could excommunicate a King, but denied absolutely that he could in any way affect the obligation of his subjects. His argument rested on the assumption that the distinction between temporal and spiritual things or purposes is clear and absolute. That being so, there is no ground for saying that the Church needs power to depose a King or to abrogate civil law, to be a *perfecta communitas* capable of realizing her spiritual ends. The end of civil power, he declared, is only a temporal

---

[1] Ed. 1600, Book IV, Chap. 21.

[2] *De Potestate Papae : An et quatenus in Reges et Principes seculares jus et imperium habeat.* An English translation appeared in 1611.

felicity and tranquillity.[1] It has no reference whatever to any spiritual end ; and there is therefore no reason why it should be in any degree subject to a spiritual authority. He argued that Bellarmine's view, just as much as that of the extreme Papalists, really made of the Pope temporal sovereign of the world. For if the Pope may depose a King on the ground that it is necessary to do so for the sake of his subjects' souls, then, since he must be the sole judge of the necessity, he becomes the real sovereign in all States. Barclay was denying, in effect, that any Christian commonwealth existed and what·exactly he conceived of as spiritual ends, it would be hard to say.

Barclay's views on this subject were substantially those of all French Gallicans and believers in the national absolutism. The Pope has no right to interfere in any way with secular jurisdiction. The clergy are subjects as other men are : their bodies and their goods and their legal status are all temporal things. All exemptions or privileges enjoyed by them are derived, not from the Pope or from canon law, but from the indulgent will of the Prince.

' I will speak therefore and I will speak a great word,' says Barclay, ' which peradventure either no man hitherto hath remembered or, if any have, he hath not at the least put in mind, as he ought, whom it concerned to know the same. And that is, that the Clergy thorough the whole world, . . . are not to this day in any manner or degree exempt and freed from the temporal authority of secular Princes . . . but are subject to them in no other manner than other citizens, in all things which belong to civil and temporal administration and jurisdiction : and that the same Princes have power of life and death over them, as well as over their other subjects.'

But he took immensely too much credit to himself for this assertion. He could have found it all in the *Defensor Pacis* of 1324.

From the simple belief that God commands obedience to constituted authority in society and prohibits absolutely forcible resistance and rebellion, there had been evolved, in controversy, a theory which may fairly be styled the theory of the divine right of Kings. The earlier and simpler doctrine, taught by Protestants and Catholics alike, had had no specific reference to monarchy and had been compatible with any view of the origin of political authority. Now it was asserted that monarchical sovereignty was alone natural and alone definitely approved and instituted by God. The earlier belief had left it easy to doubt whether God's prohibition of rebellion extended to all cases whatsoever. Now it was asserted that the right to demand obedience as a duty had been directly conferred by God upon particular persons and that, therefore, rebellion against God's agents must always be rebellion against God. It was asserted too, that in no other way

[1] *De Potestate Papae*, Chap. XIV.
[2] I quote the English translation of 1611 : Chap. XXXIII, p. 177. In the Latin of 1609, XXIV, p. 265 : ' Dicam ergo, et grande verbum proloquar,' etc.

could such a right have come into existence. It could not be created by any act or recognition of the populus nor could it be derived from natural law.

Even in France and at the end of the century no one had achieved a full and adequate presentation of the theory of the divine right of Kings. Yet enough had been said or implied to make it clear that the theory was neither incoherent nor absurd. The notion that it was one, the other or both, seems to be largely due to the inadequacy of its expositors. It received in the seventeenth century, clearer expression ; but it never, it seems to me, was quite competently presented. It has been misunderstood, by reason of the vagueness that attaches to it in the writings of most of its exponents and by consequent failure to apprehend its negative contentions.

Under ' natural law ', it was generally admitted, a man is bound to consider and to promote the interests of his fellows and certainly to do nothing injurious to the general welfare. He was bound therefore, for the sake of peace and order, to be obedient to the magistracy under which he lived. But it was impossible to derive from one's duty to one's neighbour an absolute prohibition ever to rebel against the Magistrate. If the Sovereign be impious, idolatrous or tyrannical, if he act in a manner destructive of that general welfare he exists to promote, natural law does not forbid, it may even be held to enjoin, rebellion. It matters not at all that the mass of his subjects may support the Sovereign's action : their folly or their wickedness can bind no one. Once I am convinced that the action of the Sovereign is detrimental to the whole community, I may see it as my duty to rebel. No outcry about the wickedness of disturbing public peace will then, to me, be relevant ; since there may, conceivably, be worse things than disturbance of public peace. It is not possible, on the basis of men's duty to each other, to constitute an authority against which rebellion is in no case justified. Nor can such an authority be created by any act of man. Under natural law, which is divine law, no man has the right to command another ; and no number of men can confer on anyone what not one of them possesses. The vote of a majority cannot of itself morally bind the minority ; the judgement of the people as a whole is nothing to me if I consider it mistaken. All obligation is to God and no human judgement can create for me an obligation that does not exist under natural law.

But it was just a conviction of the wrongfulness of rebellion in every really conceivable case that was held to be needed for the welfare of society. That conviction could not be based on mere assertions of the need of it. If there be any authority in human society against which rebellion is always rebellion against God, it must have been created by special act of God and vested in one who, literally, is God's lieutenant and responsible to God only.

So thought believers in the divine right of Kings at the end of the sixteenth century. Barclay's theory, the theory that begins to dominate France under Henry IV, left practically no room or ground for rebellion in any case likely ever to occur. Both in form and in content the theory was religious ; but neither in France nor anywhere else was there enough religion to support it. The actual basis of the French monarchy and of the belief in the theory of the divine right of Kings, was, and remained, utilitarian.

But it must be added that, extreme as was the view taken of the obligations of subjects, the theory did not claim for the Prince that he could create any right but right in law. Barclay's King was not, practically, bound to respect any sort of right ; but he could both act and judge wrongly. He could not, any more than the community itself, actually create obligation, for all obligation is derived from God and is to God. A theory of sovereignty in which law and right become one and in which no right exists except that of the Sovereign's creation, was held by no one in the sixteenth century. Such a view was impossible to anyone who held that right was divine. It was wholly incompatible with the theory of the divine right of Kings. Just so far as men came to believe in sovereignty to this extent, the right of the Sovereign lost its divinity. Historically it is those who lost faith in the divinity of right, and of Kings, who believed in the absolute right of the political sovereign.

CHAPTER VIII

JEAN BODIN

§ 1. HIS CAREER

JEAN BODIN, the most powerful of French and perhaps of all political thinkers of the century, was born at Angers in 1529 or in 1530. Of his family nothing is really known. His father is likely to have been a lawyer and it was asserted, much later, that his mother was a Spanish Jewess. In view of his knowledge of Hebrew, his acquaintance with Jewish writings and his profound respect for the Old Testament, it seems not improbable that this was so ; but the positive evidence amounts to nothing. In any case, the young Bodin was trained for the profession of the law. He studied first at the University of Angers and later in the great nursery of royalist lawyers at Toulouse. First as a student, then as a teacher in the University, he lived at Toulouse for about twelve years, though it is possible that for a short time he was at Geneva.[1] By 1553 he had completed his first literary effort : a translation into Latin verse of the long Greek poem about hunting, which an unknown person, called Oppian, had dedicated to the Emperor Caracalla.[2] This exercise not only shows the varied character of his studies, but to some extent exhibits the real bent of his mind. He avowed that he had chosen Oppian's very uninspired verses, because they dealt with matter of fact rather than vain imaginations. Other writings of his at Toulouse, under such titles as *De Decretis* and *De Imperio*, foreshadowed his later work. He ordered in his will that these early writings should be destroyed and they have, in fact, almost all disappeared.

It was probably ambition that took Bodin to Paris in 1560 or 1561, as it took so many others, even then. As a practical advocate, however, it is said that he was not successful : he disdained the necessary quibbling.[3] His ill success was probably exaggerated, but from the

---

[1] He shows particular knowledge of the Genevan constitution, and it seems that, for a time, his views were more or less Calvinistic.

[2] The *Cynegetica*. Bodin's translation was published, apparently, in 1555.

[3] See Baudrillart : *Jean Bodin et son temps*, p. 115 ; and R. Chauviré : *Jean Bodin* (1914), p. 30. The latter is by far the best study of Bodin known to me.

irst his bent must have been rather to the scientific study of jurisprudence than to practice at the Bar. In any case he found time for
much thinking and enormous reading. His first book of importance,
the *Methodus*, was published in 1566. Already his mind was busy
with fundamental problems of politics in general and the constitution
of France in particular. He was clearing the ground and laying
foundations for a great construction. He had been seeking a method
of approach ; and his method of studying history was to his mind a
method for the study of all questions concerning the State or any
state. It seems that he had already in mind the plan of a synthetic
philosophy of the universe, to be built up, stage by stage, in logical
sequences. The execution of that plan occupied the rest of his life.

Bodin was resolved, in 1566, to do all he could towards the reconstruction of France, but he did not yet see his way clearly. He turned,
for a time, to the study of economic conditions in France, convinced
already that these were fundamentally important. In 1568 was published his *Réponse au Paradoxe de Monsieur de Malestroict*. It has been
said that with this remarkable book Bodin founded political economy.[1]
It was perhaps the most original of all his contributions to the study
of society. In it he analysed with some success the causes of the
rise of prices that was afflicting western Europe, pointed out the disastrous consequences of depreciation of coinage, advocated freedom
of trade and suggested that the relations of States were largely determined by economic factors. No one, certainly, before him had seen
so clearly the nature, or the importance, of economic processes or had
dealt with them so definitely as a whole.[2]

The *Methodus* and the *Réponse* may both be considered as preliminary studies for the great work that appeared in 1576 : the *Six
Books of the Republic*. In one way or another Bodin had been at work
on it for the last ten years at least. It summed up and stated all
the results of his studies and meditations. On certain sides the book
is an amplification of what he had said in the *Methodus* ; while in the
last ' book ' he went again over much of the ground covered by the
Réponse. To the end of his life, with whatever additions, he continued
to repeat himself.

The importance of the *Republic* was immediately perceived by
Bodin's contemporaries. New editions appeared almost every year
down to 1583. In 1586 Bodin published a translation of the book
into Latin, made by himself and somewhat augmented. Before the
end of the century translations were published in Italian, Spanish

---

[1] ' Ou peu s'en faut,' writes Prof. Chauviré (p. 482).

[2] The *Réponse* was published in 1574 under the title : *Discours sur l'extrême
cherté qui est aujourdhuy en France* ; and in 1578 under yet another title : *Discours de Jean Bodin sur le rehaussement et diminution des monnoyes*. A Latin
translation appeared in 1591.

and German. The book was violently attacked and the edition of 1583 included Bodin's reply to the fiercest of the attacks upon him, under the title *Apologie de Rene Herpin pour la République de Jean Bodin.*[1]

It was a few months after the publication of the *Republic*, at the assembly of the Estates at Blois, that Bodin made his first and only important appearance in practical politics. It is important to notice that it was only after he had completed his ideal construction of the State that his personal connection with the politics and parties of the day became at all close. In 1571 Bodin had acquired a place of trust in the household of the Duke of Alençon, but his official connection with the Duke seems to have ceased before 1576 and can hardly be supposed to have compromised him seriously. His connection with Alençon was certainly not such as to injure him with Henry III, who showed him marked favour. After 1576 it may be said that, down to the time when he joined the League, he was a member and even a somewhat prominent member of the Politique party. But it is clear that the *Republic* was not written to serve the interests of any mere group. It was written to serve the interests of France. All parties found in the book both something to accept and make use of and something to reject and abhor. Bodin was not a detached thinker in the sense that he cared for truth and for nothing else at all. He earnestly desired to assist in the regeneration of his country. His mind was full of schemes for practical reform that he ardently wished to see realized. It was inevitable that in the long run he should connect himself more or less definitely with some political party. Yet at no time of his life can his point of view have been that of a mere partisan. He was more jurist than philosopher, perhaps ; but he was far more a philosopher than a party politician.

Bodin attended the assembly of Estates at Blois in 1576 as elected deputy for Vermandois. Of his conduct during the meetings he has himself left a detailed account.[2] The assembly was to a great extent dominated by the League, of which Henry III was at the moment trying to assume the leadership.[3] Bodin may be said to have led the opposition. He opposed the proposal to start a war against the Huguenots ; he upheld what he regarded as ancient rules of pro-

---

[1] The publication, at Lyon, of the *Six Livres de la République* was followed by new editions in 1577, 1578, 1579, 1580, 1582, 1583, and 1593. Bodin's Latin version appeared in 1586 and was reprinted in 1588 and in 1591. An Italian translation appeared in 1588 : a Spanish in 1590 and a German in 1592. The book was being expounded in England in 1581, but no English translation seems to have been made.

[2] *Recueil de tout ce qui s'est negotié en la compagnie du Tiers Estat de France, en l'assemblée générale des trois Estats.* Published 1577.

[3] He had declared himself its head : to the intense annoyance, of course, of the real leaders.

cedure involving the right of the Third Estate to refuse to be dictated
to by the other Orders ; and he asserted vigorously, against the King,
the inalienability of domain property. His whole attitude was in
a high degree disinterested and honourable. It is clear that he did
not regard Henry III as possessing that quite absolute sovereignty
which he had defined in the *Republic*. The success of his opposition
lost him the favour of the King.

It seems to have been in 1577 that he acquired a post in the magistracy of Laon ; but he did not take up permanent residence there
till later. After 1576 he attached himself more closely than ever to
Alençon. He went with the Duke to England in 1581 and to the
Netherlands in 1583. It was only after the Duke's death in 1584 that
he went into what, politically, was a retirement at Laon.

In 1588 the League became master at Laon and Bodin joined the
League. It is quite clear that he did not in any sense or degree
share the views of the Leaguers except, at most, as regards the incom-
petency of Henry III. If, as De Thou says, he denounced Henry III
as a traitor and a hypocrite, it may be that he did so sincerely.[1] But
it is clear that he hoped nothing from the League. He may, nevertheless, have believed for a time that the League would triumph ;
and he may have been seriously influenced by the consideration that
Henry III was, as he says, the sixty-third king of France since Faramond. It is yet more probable that he was influenced by the action
of the Parlement of Paris. But a reign of terror was established in
Laon and Bodin's place and property and even his life were threatened.
There is little need to search for other reasons for his unheroic but
very excusable conduct. In a strange letter written, apparently, to
justify his adherence to the League, he remarks naïvely that ' étant
dans une ville, il est necessaire d'être le plus fort ou du parti le plus
fort ou du tout ruiné '.[2] He repudiated the League in 1593, as soon,
that is, as he could safely do so. He died at Laon three years later,
in 1596.

In the *Methodus* Bodin had laid it down that knowledge of God,
without which there is no real knowledge, is best attained through the
study first of man and then of ' nature '.[3] With the *Republic* he had
completed his studies of man and of human society : he went on to
complete his programme. For the rest of his life he was building up
his synthetic philosophy. In 1580 appeared that strange and repulsive

---

[1] In the *Republic* he severely criticizes Henry III's policy in certain respects.
[2] *Lettre de Monsieur Bodin ou il traicte les occasions qui l'ont faict rendre
ligueur*, 1590. Weill denies the authenticity of this letter, but Prof. Chauviré
upholds it, and I humbly agree with him. It was published, probably, by the
enemies of Bodin. In it occurs the characteristic remark about Faramond
referred to above.
[3] In Chap. I of the *Methodus*.

book, the *Demonomanie des Sorciers*.¹ It was written to establish the fact of sorcery and witchcraft against the sceptics ² and to provide a practical manual of legal procedure for the use of magistrates. But it was written, also, because Bodin was profoundly convinced that man lives constantly under the influence of spiritual beings good and evil. Sorcery was a danger arising incidentally from man's constant relation to a world of spirits, and it was a very serious danger. There is nothing strange in the belief. The assumptions or conclusions, valid or not, which make such belief difficult or impossible in our days, were not present in the sixteenth century. The actual evidence was bewildering. What is repulsive and a little surprising in the book is what seems the evident injustice of the procedure advocated. Yet even for this a case could be made out.³

Bodin's plan was hardly much advanced by the *Demonomanie*. It was only in the last year of his life that he gave to the world his final conclusions about the universe, in a book far more astonishing than the *Demonomanie* : the *Universae naturae Theatrum*.⁴ Bodin had written the *Republic* with a profound sense of the mysterious character of human life : as he grew older the mystery of the universe seems more and more to have preoccupied him. But he was not content with not understanding. He desired to explain everything and apparently he believed it possible to do so. He has been called a mystic ; but he was not one of those who make a happy home in mystery and know that there is no explanation or feel that there is nothing to explain. His philosophy as a whole does not concern us here. It is an astonishing jumble. Critical acumen and extreme credulity went to the making of it ; logical method, the crudest speculation and the wildest guessing went hand in hand to its construction.

But Bodin left behind him unpublished writings, one of which is important for the understanding of his political thought. His *Paradoxon* was posthumously published in 1596.⁵ Like all the rest of his later books, with one exception, it has only a remote if any bearing on his political conceptions. The one exception is the *Heptaplomeres*,

¹ The book went through many editions up to 1604. A Latin version appeared in 1581 and an Italian version in 1587.

² There were many sceptics. Bodin had particularly in view the book of Jean Wier : *De praestigiis daemonum ac in cantationibus ac veneficiis*, 1564.

³ The *Demonomanie* has become almost unreadable. But there is some good thinking in it, though perhaps not much. It is an absurd book to us partly because, knowing what it is about, we have not patience to read it.

⁴ *Universae naturae Theatrum, in quo rerum omnium effectrices causae et fines contemplantur et continuae series quinque libris discutiuntur*. A French translation appeared in 1597.

⁵ *Paradoxon quod nec virtus ulla mediocritate nec summum hominis bonum in virtutis actione consistere possit*. A French version, made by Bodin himself, appeared in 1598.

published in its complete form only in 1857, after it had remained almost unknown for centuries.[1] This book, in which Bodin attacked the orthodox forms of Christianity, expounded true religion as he conceived it and concluded not merely in favour of religious toleration but for the utter futility of argument about religion, was probably written in 1593. It was perhaps the most original of all his writings. It is curious to consider that it may have been begun while he was still a member of the League.

§ 2. MIND AND WRITINGS

The study of Bodin's writings leaves on one's mind an impression best described, perhaps, as one of vastness. There is vast book-learning, vast confusion and a vast, all-embracing effort, ceaseless and prodigious, to arrange logically and to synthesize all human knowledge. Behind that effort lay, it seems, a conviction that once this done, a satisfactory account of the universe will have been given. Knowledge, Bodin seems to have conceived, must be complete to be knowledge at all : but at least the main lines of the structure of the universe can be made out. Yet at times he doubted the sufficiency of human knowledge and even the sufficiency of human reason. ' C'est faire injure a Dieu,' he wrote, ' de ne reconnaître pas la faiblesse de son cerveau.' [2] He was far too intelligent not to see mystery everywhere. He admitted that astrology was not yet advanced enough to enable us to be prophetic. He was aware that much remained to be discovered.[3] For all that, he was ready to dogmatize about the influence of the stars and of angelic and demonic intelligences.

By the time Bodin came to grips with his great task of expounding the nature of the ' République bien ordonnée ', his mind was stored with a vast and miscellaneous mass of information and ideas gathered from books. His reading must have been prodigious. He knew Hebrew and Greek and was in some degree acquainted with German and Italian. He knew the Talmud and the orations of Demosthenes and Plutarch. He knew the Roman historians and had drunk deeply of Cicero. He had some knowledge of the medieval scholastics, though he knew the jurists better. He knew something of the law and constitution of all European states. He seems to have made a particular study of the constitutions of Florence and of Venice and of the Swiss cantons. For England he relied chiefly on Polydore Vergil : and it is said that while in England with Alençon his curiosity about the English constitution led him to ask indiscreet questions.

[1] *Heptaplomeres colloquium de abditis sublimium rerum arcanis.* It was first printed, but in an imperfect form, in 1841.

[2] *Demonomanie.* Preface.

[3] ' Habet natura scientiarum thesauros innumerabiles, qui nullis aetatibus exhauviri possunt.' *Methodus,* ed. 1566, Vol. II, p. 360. One is reminded of Francis Bacon.

He knew the chronicles of France and had studied with profit the writings of Du Haillan and the registers of the Parlement of Paris. He knew the Old Testament line by line ; though his acquaintance with the New Testament seems to have been slighter. He had studied as best he could the strange jumble of the sciences of his time : astronomy and astrology, geography, physics and medicine and magic. He made, himself, experimental investigations. But the chief influences in his intellectual life seem to have been the Old Testament and Neoplatonic philosophy as interpreted by the Italian Platonists.

It is impossible to separate Bodin's political from his religious thought. The whole history of his mind was that of a development of views essentially religious. Yet it is difficult to say what his religion was at any time before he wrote the *Heptaplomeres*. In the sixteenth century he was described as a Jew in religion, as a Calvinist and as an atheist.[1] He was denounced as an atheist both before and after his death and seems narrowly to have escaped death in the massacre at Paris in 1572. There can be no doubt that his religious views underwent a series of changes in the course of his life.[2] He was brought up in Catholicism and no doubt remained for some time a Catholic. But if the letter to Jan Bautru des Matras be genuine, as seems to be hardly doubtful,[3] his views had become Calvinistic or at least ' Protestant ' by about 1562. There is equally no doubt that when he wrote the *Heptaplomeres*, Bodin was neither a Catholic nor a Calvinist nor a Christian of any sort at all : and it is certain also that his religion was not that of the Jews. In that astonishing book he subjected Catholicism and Calvinism and the central doctrines of Christianity and even Judaism, to destructive criticism to which he supplies, through the mouths of their representatives in the dialogue, only the feeblest answers. So feeble is the defence put up by Coronoeus the Catholic and Frederick the Lutheran and Curtius the Calvinist or Zwinglian, that Bodin seems to have overlooked or forgotten what they might have said. Feeblest of all is the defence of Coronoeus. He is represented as a learned, tolerant and amiable person ; but he has practically nothing to say except ' Credendum est Ecclesia '. Frederick and Curtius are allowed to smash his position : and Salomon the Jew attacks Christianity itself. But Salomon in his turn is thrown back on an ineffective defence by the attacks of Toralba the philosopher

[1] Jacques Gillot writing to Scaliger in 1607 says that he died like a dog, neither Jew, Christian nor Turk.

[2] ' De religione hominis certius nihil dici potest, quam secundum varios aetatis annos variam fuisse.' Diecman. *De naturalismo*, 1683. But he did not know the *Heptaplomeres*.

[3] This letter was published by Calomiès in his *Gallia Orientalis* in 1665. It is reprinted in the appendix to Prof. Chauviré's *Bodin*. See also the same work, pp. 142, 143.

and Octavius the Mohammedan. It is Toralba and not Salomon, evidently who represents the views of the author of the dialogue; while Senamus, the sceptical 'Epicurean', who finds truth in all religions and the truth in none, and remains unconvinced even by Toralba, represents at least a point of view with which Bodin sympathized. The religion of Bodin in 1593 included a belief in the permanence of man's soul and the freedom of his will, in a world of angels and demons in touch with man's world, and above all in God. The Old Testament stood alone in this religion as a sacred and revealing book. But even the Old Testament was not infallible. The New Testament had all but disappeared. Intermediary between man and God were no priests or churches but a host of spiritual intelligences. But every man must seek God in his own way and there is truth in all religions. The one thing intolerable is atheism, which makes nonsense of the universe.

How far did Bodin hold in 1576 the views he held in 1593 ? As early as the letter to Bautru he had given utterance to the very un-Calvinistic sentiment that differences on religion are of no account among friends. It is, I think, clear that when he wrote the *Republic* he was already neither Catholic nor Protestant. But whether he had yet reached the positive conclusions of the *Heptaplomeres* is doubtful and it seems improbable that he had gone so far.

But it is not the exact nature of Bodin's religious views that is important here. What is important in connection with his political conceptions is the man's intense religiousness. Unless this be realized it is impossible to understand the *Republic*. It is not merely a question of the religious quality of his mind, so plainly apparent in all his writings. ' Il n'y a rien de fortuit en ce monde,' he wrote : and this because all things are regulated by eternal laws proceeding from the will of God. The study of history and the study of the State as such were, to him, ways of approach to that knowledge of God which unifies all knowledge. He saw the State as one manifestation of God's will. In inevitable sequences and associations, in enduring conditions and institutions, even in successful enterprises, he saw a revelation of that will.

But Bodin was very far from being only a speculative philosopher. In the *Republic*, at least, he aspired above all to be practical. He wrote, avowedly, in view of the evils of the time. Since the Ship of State is labouring in a storm so violent, that captain and crew are worn out with toil, ' il faut bien que les passagers y pretent la main, qui aux voiles, qui aux cordages, qui à l'ancre, et ceux à qui la force manquera qu'ils donnent quelque bon avertissement '.[1] He set himself to deal with every question of the moment that seemed to him important. He wrote the *Republic* not only to expound

[1] Preface of the *Republic*.

the nature of political society and to state the laws that govern it, but also to lay down general rules of policy and to advocate a number of definite and circumstantial reforms in France. In reading the book one sometimes gets the impression that Bodin was a great statesman wasted.[1] He never makes any positive proposal of reform without trying to show in detail how it might practically be effected. He insists that statesman and theorist alike must think first of what is possible. It is absurd to struggle against the overpowering. It is useless merely to imagine a State such as we should like to see. What is wanted is understanding of things as they are, not dreams of what they might be. The political philosopher must study history and law and geography; but even that is not enough. He should have practical experience in affairs and administration. Bodin attributes the insufficiency of Aristotle partly to his lack of such experience. His own determination to be practical led him, sometimes, to confuse right with power. He even writes as though force could create what he calls sovereignty. But this is no mere confusion. To Bodin power lay, in the long run, with reason and with virtue : in the long run it expressed the will of God. The 'natural', that is the inevitable, is always the just, because the inevitable necessarily expresses that will.

The chief influences that went to the formation of Bodin's philosophy were those of the Old Testament and of Italian Platonism. How far was his political thought derived from earlier or from contemporary writers ? Bodin himself was fully conscious of great power and originality. No thinkers before himself had, he imagined, seen the State rightly. Aristotle had based his work altogether too narrowly : he had groped in darkness and found little. Plato and More had constructed ideal States without reference to history or circumstance ; [2] and such work is useless. Machiavelli, he seems to have thought, had committed the fundamental mistake of supposing that the State could exist without a moral basis and without religion. Quite definitely Bodin claimed to be an explorer and a discoverer in country almost unknown.

The search for literary sources of a man's thought leads commonly merely to fallacious conclusions. It might, for instance, be imagined that Bodin's theory of climate was suggested to him by Aristotle.[3] But Bodin's multifarious reading gave him an idea of the diversity of races and of climatic conditions : he had only to see a correlation.

---

[1] This is probably an illusion. As a statesman Bodin would probably have been no more effective than was L'Hôpital. · In any case why 'wasted' ? The use of the word calls for apology.

[2] 'Voulants batir de beaux discours en l'air sans fondement aucun.' *Rep.*, I, 6.

[3] Or why not by Pierre Dubois ?

It is possible that Aristotle's suggestion made him look for it, but as he has not himself told us that it was so, we, evidently, cannot know. Bodin says many things that were said by obscure pamphleteers of his time and many things that were said by practically everybody. Such facts afford no ground for any supposition of influence. There is a rather close correspondence, as Chauviré points out, between passages in the *Republic* and the speeches of L'Hôpital. The two agree rather strikingly as to the need of certain practical reforms. But the correspondence is not close enough to prove anything beyond a certain similarity between the two minds. Aristotle appears to have influenced the plan of arrangement of the earlier part of the *Republic*, so far as there is one. But for the rest Bodin took from Aristotle only those terms and categories that every one had taken. He regarded Aristotle as an adversary and frequently attacks him. Of contemporary writers I know none to whom Bodin was certainly and directly indebted except Du Haillan and Louis Le Roy and Machiavelli. From them he derived a number of facts, illustrations, historical theories and even phrases.[1] But he went to Du Haillan's book [2] for what he wanted, as to that of a specialist in the history of France. From Le Roy it may be that he derived more than information. Le Roy may have helped to convince him of the danger of innovation and the absurdity of popular government.

The debt of Bodin to Machiavelli was, perhaps, considerable, but in unimportant ways. He spoke contemptuously of the author of the *Prince* rummaging in all the corners of Italy for petty tricks of statecraft. Yet, in his own grave discourse, Princes are advised to have recourse on occasion to some of those very tricks. But the fact that Bodin may have got from Machiavelli suggestions as to how Princes should act under particular circumstances is of little significance. It was above all in writing of war that Bodin drew upon Machiavelli. Much that he says concerning the weakness of foreign mercenaries, the uselessness of fortresses, the illusion that money is the sinews of war, appears to be copied straight from Machiavelli and of course without any sort of acknowledgment. Bodin can have known nothing of war except from books : Machiavelli's views on the subject struck him as evidently just and he embodied them wholesale in the *Republic*. In doing so he was only doing what many other writers of his own time and earlier, from Seyssel onwards, had done. He may even have been copying from Seyssel rather than from Machiavelli. The views expressed by Machiavelli concerning the art of war are reproduced by a long series of sixteenth-century

---

[1] For the indebtedness of Bodin to Du Haillan and Le Roy see Chauviré: *Jean Bodin*, III, 4.

[2] *De l'Estat et succez des affaires de France*, 1580 ; but apparently first published as early as 1570.

writers who agree with the Italian about nothing else. Bodin, in fact, was one member of that series. His manner of regarding the State was totally unlike Machiavelli's and on the development of his substantive thought about it Machiavelli had no influence whatever. There was certainly no need for any Royalist lawyer of France to go to Florence for the idea of a national monarchy.

Bodin was a great thinker; yet nowadays no one reads him, even in France, except willing or unwilling students of the history of ideas or of sixteenth-century France. The fact that his *Republic* was concerned largely with problems of practical politics of his own time, is one reason for this neglect of him. The fact that he tries to answer fundamental questions which, though still unanswered, interest but few people except in times of social disturbance, is another. The fundamental questions concerning the end of organized society and the nature of political authority are the same for us as for him. But we do not feel that we have anything to learn from him about them. We think, perhaps, that they cannot be answered or, perhaps, that they have been answered. Yet Hooker is still read, and Calvin; and every one reads Montaigne. The neglect of Bodin seems to be mainly due to faults of arrangement and defects of style. He was apparently incapable of grouping his facts or arranging his argument in any reasonable order. The plan of the *Republic* is so confused that one wonders, in reading it, what he thought he was writing about. He could never keep to one point at a time. In the first three books of the *Republic* the arrangement, in which he seems to be guided by Aristotle, is tolerably orderly and logical : the rest is chaos. All the later books are miscellanies ; even the chapters tend to be miscellaneous. He goes back and forth and back again in the same chapter ; he turns from ideal considerations to actual France without seeming aware of the change of subject ; he discusses the means of guarding against revolution in one chapter and the question whether the property of condemned felons should go to the treasury in the next ; he repeats himself constantly and from book to book of the *Republic* ; he overwhelms the reader with illustrations that do not illustrate, with irrelevant references and with remarks on events of Roman and other history ; he interlards the discussion with disquisitions on astrology and the magic of numbers. It is as though he felt that every scrap of the information he had collected, bearing even remotely on any of his miscellaneous subjects of discussion, must be crammed into his book. His verbosity, his enormous prolixity, his utter lack of any sense of humour, reduce the reader to something like despair. Powerful and original thinker as he was, he was yet, in the highest degree, a bore.

All this might have been partially forgiven him if he had written well. Bodin's style has indeed its merits, negative and positive.

It has power and weight : generally too much weight but never too little. There is no affectation ; his pedantries and his verbosity are natural. His style has the merit of spontaneity and sincerity : he is always trying to say what he really means. Occasionally his earnestness makes him almost eloquent and occasionally he finds striking phrases or happy images. His style is undecorated and lacking in colour, but so is Calvin's. But it has deficiencies far graver. It lacks grace and balance and any kind of harmony : it is positively hard and arid. It lacks completely that quality of charm which, derivable in many ways, is as important to a writer as to a woman. The weightiest thought becomes in the long run negligible if there be not added to it the charm of personality or of art.[1]

§ 3. THE *METHODUS*

In the *Methodus* [2] Bodin may be said to have embodied the results of his preliminary reflections in preparation for his great task. By 1566 he had become convinced that in the study of history is to be found the key to the problems of practical politics. There are three very different branches of science that may, he says, be called history. There is divine history which deals with God and with God's dealings with man. There is natural history which deals with the things of the world of sense distinct from man. Finally, there is the history of man. But, though God is the beginning and end of all things, these things can only be rightly studied in reverse order. Knowledge of God is attained most surely through the study of man and of nature. But he pointed out that these studies cannot be entirely separated. Divine history connects through religion with human history and, through geography, human connects with natural history.

The understanding of human history must commence with and be based on knowledge of ourselves. Bodin is not very explicit on the point, but he had at least a glimpse of a notion that all historic change resolves itself ultimately into psychological change. From knowledge of the elements of human nature we may go on to the study of the family, the primary and ' natural ' form of human association. Lastly we must grapple with the history of civil and political society.

The chief use of the study of history is to subserve politics ; to help us to understand the meaning and the function of the State,

---

[1] Bodin expressed himself perhaps more clearly and exactly in Latin than in French. Yet his Latin style is, naturally, stiffer, more imitative and conventional. His most vivid and telling passages are, I think, in French. I shrink from attempting any comparison of styles in different languages, neither of which is my own ; but certainly, in important passages, the French version of the *Republic* should always be compared with the Latin.

[2] *Methodus ad facilem historiarum cognitionem*, 1566. Other editions followed in 1572, 1576, 1579 and 1583.

its needs and its structure, the causes of its prosperity or decline. The business of the historian is, above all, to explain the revolutions, the profound and radical changes, through which human societies pass. From a sufficiently wide study of history it should be possible to draw accurate conclusions as to the laws governing human society and to determine the best form of government and the best form of law under given conditions. The study of the history of human society must, Bodin thought, be primarily a study of systems of law. The character and manners of a people, the nature of their society and co-operation, the form of the government and the changes all these undergo are all written in the history of its law. Roman law, he asserted, is far too exclusively studied. It is not only a dead system ; it is but one of many dead systems. What is needed is a comparative study of all legal systems, with constant reference to that natural law, 'that essential justice which changes not with man's caprice but is fixed by a law eternal'.

But we must begin, so far as that is possible, with a study of those determining factors that derive not from man's will but from nature and are permanent or only with great effort alterable at all.[1] The 'theory of climate', expounded more fully in the *Republic,* is sketched in the *Methodus.* Geographical and climatic conditions must, Bodin declared, have played a great part in determining the character of peoples and so that of their law and institutions. To a great extent human history may, he asserted, be explained by reference to these permanent factors. But he was quite aware that it could not wholly be so explained. He pointed out that complete understanding of human history would involve knowledge not only of the origin of society but of the origin of man. Many factors remain unknown or not understood. It is certain, he thought, that there exists a mysterious correlation of human history with planetary movements and positions and with numerical and proportional relations. · These things still need much study. But, as things are, knowledge of the history of human societies is the only sure thread we have with which to guide ourselves in the labyrinth of politics.[2]

That human history showed progress Bodin asserted emphatically. He was impatiently contemptuous of talk about a golden age in the past. If the human race were degenerating we should long since have reached the lowest depths of degradation.[3] But, in fact, we have improved not only on primitive society but on that of the classic

---

[1] 'Quaeramus igitur illa quae non ab hominum institutis sed a natura ducuntur, quaeque stabilia sunt, nec unquam nisi magna vi aut diuturna disciplina mutantur.' *Meth.*, ed. 1566, V, pp. 91, 92.

[2] 'Qui sine ratione temporum historias intelligere se posse putant, perinde falluntur ut si labirinthi errores evadere sine duce velint, hi enim vagantur huc illuc, nec ullum erroris exitum reperire possunt.' *Meth.*, ed. 1566, VIII, p. 362.

[3] *Meth.*, VII, p. 356.

age. We are more moral than Rome and we have more knowledge. He cites the compass and America and the printing press. The art of printing alone is a greater discovery than any that was made by the peoples of antiquity. It was with these convictions and fortified further by his studies in economics, that Bodin came to the solution of the political problems of his time. He saw France disorganized by faction, increasingly disordered. On all sides irreconcilable views were being expressed of the nature of the French monarchy, of the nature of State authority and the duty of subjects. So it was that all the questions debated in France at the time received reasoned answers in the *Republic*. Bodin set himself to deal with every aspect of the problem. He dealt generally with questions of policy and method in relation to circumstance, he warned of actual and immediate dangers and suggested positive remedies and reforms. But he was aware that no argument from mere circumstance and immediate needs could satisfy in the long run or even at all. Most important of all was it that agreement should be reached on fundamentals, for so only could order be permanently established. The foundations of the ordered State must be dug deep. Formulæ had to be found of general application, by which all vexed questions of duty could be decided. What was, above all, wanted was an understanding of the nature of political authority. Bodin tried to show that the nature and extent of such authority was involved in the history, the structure and the end of political association. He strove to find some principle of order and unity, that should reconcile liberty and subjection, define political obligation and satisfy conscience and reason. Only on the recognition of such a principle could the well-ordered State be built. In his doctrine of sovereignty, he imagined, he had found what was needed.

§ 4. THE STATE AND ITS SOVEREIGNTY

The first chapter of Bodin's *Republic* is headed with the words : ' Quelle est la fin principale de la République bien ordonnée.' This, it must be observed, is not the same thing as asking simply the old, ambiguous question : ' What is the end of the State ? ' It is not very clear whether the definition that follows refers to the State absolutely or only to the State ' bien ordonnée '. Bodin confuses himself and his reader by frequently forgetting his own distinction. ' La République est un droit gouvernement de plusieurs ménages et de ce qui leur est commun avec puissance souveraine.' [1] ' Droit gouvernement ' is government ' suivant les lois de la nature ', recognizing and basing itself upon eternal principles of justice. There can be no well-ordered State that does not do so. Why the State

[1] *Republic*, I, 1. In the Latin version : ' Respublica est familiarum rerumque inter ipsas communium summa potestate ac ratione moderata multitudo.'

is to be conceived as a group of families or households, what ' puissance souveraine ' is and why it is required, these things have still to be explained. ·Characteristically Bodin starts with a definition of which the terms are not made clear, goes on at once to speak of the ' end ' of the State and then returns to explain his definition. Some alteration of his peculiar methods is desirable for the sake of clearness. The family is ' la vraie source et origine de toute République et membre principal d'icelle '.[1] Bodin repeats this assertion again and again. The ' mesnage ', consisting essentially of man, wife and children together with such things as are necessary for its maintenance, is ' une communauté naturelle '.[2] It is ' natural ' because it arises of necessity from the nature of man. It is not merely the primary but an inevitable form of human association. So much a matter of course is its existence that there is no need to consider men as simple individuals outside the family. The family must have come into existence with man and there never was a time when it did not exist. It does not necessarily or even rightly include slaves, for slavery, to Bodin, was both unjust and noxious. But it does involve property, since the family requires property to maintain its existence. Private property therefore or at least property attached to households, was to Bodin as primitive and natural as the family itself. This conception of the family is fundamental in his system.

The family, founded on the inevitable association of man and woman, involves, in the nature of things, not only children and property but rightful authority and government. ' Ménage est un droit gouvernement de plusieurs sujets sous l'obeissance d'un chef de famille et de ce qui lui est propre.'[3] Man, woman and child being what they are, the man must and ought to be the master. It is not a mere matter of force. Bodin might have said that because man has force he has authority and that this is natural and unavoidable. But to say so would have been to fall into fallacy ; since it is a question of right, not of mere power, and a question of will, not of mere force. Bodin asserts that it is not woman's physical weakness but her moral and intellectual inferiority that makes of her the natural subject of man. It is a primary law of nature, he declares, that reason should rule appetite. Man in relation to woman represents reason. To emancipate her can but be disastrous since to do so is to disregard unescapable facts that cannot be altered.[4] ' Naturally ', it appears, a man may not kill or sell his wife : she is not a slave. But he may enforce upon her complete obedience and may divorce her if he be

[1] *Rep.*, I, 2, ed. 1580, p. 10. [2] Ib., III, 7.
[3] Ib., I, 2. In the Latin : ' Familia est plurium sub unius ac ejusdem patrisfamilias imperium subditorum, earumque rerumque ipsius propriae sunt, recta moderatio.' Ed. 1591, p. 12.
[4] In his discussion of the Salic Law Bodin's language about women reminds one of Knox. See *Rep.*, VI, 5.

not satisfied.[1] Over his children a man's 'natural' authority is even greater : it extends in their case to life and death. 'Le pere est le vrai image du grand Dieu souverain.' [2] But again it is not the mere helplessness of children that creates this authority. It is rather the fact that they possess reason, as Aristotle says, only imperfectly and are incapable of judging for themselves, even as women are. It is not made very clear why the father should have power of life and death and the husband should not ; but apparently it is because children are conceived as owing existence to their father. Bodin was deeply convinced that much of the moral and of the political disorder of his own time was due to the changes of law which had reduced paternal authority and led to a general decay of family discipline. He wrote almost bitterly on the subject. The very ancient Romans had been, he thought, in the right. 'Il est besoin, en la République bien ordonnée,' he roundly declared, 'rendre aux pères la puissance de la vie et de la mort que la loi de Dieu et de nature leur donne.' [3] No State can be orderly or well-governed if its unit, the family, be not rightly constituted. 'Il est impossible que la République vaille rien si les familles, qui sont les piliers d'icelle, sont mal fondées.' [4]

It must be remembered that to Bodin the rightly constituted family involves a ' droit gouvernement '. A man who should own no duties to wife and children and should treat them as mere slaves would be a mere slave owner and not the head of a *ménage*. Bodin argued at length [5] that slavery is unjust and noxious. He would not allow that it was, strictly speaking, ' unnatural '. So ancient and enduring a fact, he thought, could hardly be called that, since nothing unnatural can last long. Slavery, like the family itself, arose immediately from the nature of human desires. Yet, in a sense, it was to him ' unnatural ' because unjust, in contradiction, that is, to that law of nature which shines on all like the sun. There is radical injustice, he declared, in a system under which wise men may be mastered by fools and good men by evil. He argued, too, that experience has shown that slavery is dangerous and harmful to society. Slavery, then, has no place in the rightly constituted *ménage*.

The family it might be said constitutes, according to Bodin, the first and ' natural ' form of the State. The authority of the head of the family is the only form of authority which is strictly ' natural '

[1] It has been pointed out by Prof. Chauviré that to give the husband an unlimited power of divorcing the wife would tend to destroy the family and so defeat Bodin's own purpose. But Bodin, I suppose, must have assumed that if marriage were rightly conceived and wives effectively made subject, any tendency to the abuse of the power of divorce would be checked by convention and public opinion.

[2] *Rep.*, I, 2.
[4] Ib., I, 4. Ib., p. 34.
[3] Ib., I, 4, ed. 1580, p. 32.
[5] Ib.., I, 4.

in that it develops inevitably. Nevertheless, under Bodin's definition the *ménage* is not a State. The State is an association of families recognizing ' puissance souveraine '. In the order of time the formation of civil societies preceded the formation of the State. Families grouped themselves about advantageous sites, were drawn into trade and into co-operation for defence and other common purposes, developed a common worship. Then followed union among these loose associations. In the process of amalgamation war and conquest played a large part. Bodin was not so much interested as logically he should have been in the question of how the State came to be formed. But two things were clear to him. The State is only fully formed when ' puissance souveraine ' is recognized and the family remains always the essential unit of the structure.

' Puissance souveraine ', essentially an unlimited power of making law for itself, is the mark of the fully-formed State ; but, obviously, it can only be an instrument. The State could not conceivably be formed for the sake of ' puissance souveraine '. What were the ends for which the State came into existence and for which ' puissance souveraine ' was recognized ? The family, it seems, existed only for the sake of primal needs and universal desires. Following Aristotle, Bodin seems to conceive of the State as distinguished from the *ménage* by its recognition of higher and larger ends. The end of the State, however, he emphatically declares, is not mere ' happiness '. Even the ' well ordered ' Republic may be poor and miserable. Nor can unity be rationally conceived as an end. It is due to the absurd conception of unity as an end in itself that men have advocated communism. Communism, to Bodin, is absolutely incompatible with a well-ordered State or even with any State at all. The idea of a levelling equality of goods and honours is merely absurd. Such a conception is contrary to nature : incompatible, that is, with the nature of man.[1] Upon the recognition of private property and the natural inequality of man the State rests absolutely. Take away private property and the family itself will disappear. ' En ôtant les mots Tien et Mien, on ruine les fondements de toutes Républiques.' [2]

The end of the State, according to Bodin, cannot be stated as anything less than the realization of all good for mind and body. In a sense the body must come first. A State that lacks means of subsistence will have no great care for moral or intellectual values. In a well-ordered State, government will concern itself first of all with justice, defence and economics.[3] All the same, it is the realization of ' virtue ', of moral and intellectual values, for ' virtue ' includes knowledge, that is the final, justifying end. ' Le premier et principal but de toute république doit etre la vertu.' [4]

[1] *Rep.*, VI, 4. See also *Methodus*, Chap. VI.   [2] Ib., VI, 4.
[3] Ib., I, 1.   [4] Ib., IV, 4, ed. 1580, p. 582.

But Bodin does not say that the State comes into existence through an increasingly clear recognition of its true end. He did not clearly see that recognition as a process in time past. Never anywhere does he give any clear and coherent account of how or why the loose early associations of families were transformed into States.

'Toute République,' he wrote, 'prend origine de la famille multipliant peu a peu, ou bien tout à coup s'établit d'une multitude ramassée ou d'une colonie tirée d'une autre République. . . . Or l'une et l'autre République s'établit par la violence des plus forts ou du consentement des uns qui assujettissent volontairement aux autres leur pleine et entière liberté, pour en être par eux disposé par puissance souveraine sans loi ou bien à certaines lois et conditions.' [1]

It is clear from this passage that he did not think that the State was always and everywhere established by force. Yet he certainly imagined that the State very commonly originated in some kind of conquest : monarchy, he seems to have thought, always did. He speaks of what he calls ' seigneurial ' monarchy, which was to him the earliest kind, as being rightfully established over a people whom conquest has rightfully made slaves.[2] But all his language on this subject is confused and inconclusive. If slavery be radically unjust how can conquest make people slaves rightfully ? Again, who is this conqueror and where does his force come from ? Is he already the head of a State, possessing ' puissance souveraine ' ? But in that case what happens at the conquest is not the creation of a new State but the extension of an old one ; and we are no nearer the origin of the State than before. Bodin could not have thought that the State was really created by mere ' force '. The human exercise of force can be nothing but an expression of will, and to say that the State is created by force is not so much an erroneous as a meaningless assertion. But Bodin was caught in the net of his own definition. All he meant was that, since wherever there is ' puissance souveraine ' there is a State, and since the recognition of ' puissance souveraine ' may be compelled by fear, States may be and have been established by force. Even so, he seems for the moment to have forgotten that by his own definition there is no State without ' droit gouvernement '.

It is clear, too, that when a State is, in this sense, established by conquest, the process involves no recognition of what Bodin describes as the ends of the State. The State may exist without any reference to its ends ! This, in fact, is precisely what Bodin did think. All that is necessary to constitute a State is the acceptance of ' puissance souveraine ', and the ' ends ' Bodin speaks of are not those of the

---

[1] *Rep.*, IV, 1, ed. 1580, pp. 503, 504. In the Latin version we read ' qui se libertatemque suam sub alterius imperium ac arbitrium sponte subjecerunt '. Ed. 1591, p. 580.
[2] Ib., II, 2.

State as such, but those of the 'République bien ordonnée'. Often Bodin loses sight of his own distinction ; but always it is there. All he really asserts concerning the ends of the State as such is that no lesser end than that which he describes can justify its existence to reason. The well-ordered State will be conscious of such ends : how far conscious is matter of degree only. In any case, Bodin affirmed emphatically tha⁺ the State cannot rationally be conceived as existing for merely material ends. Defence and material prosperity, even the administration of legal justice, are not of themselves sufficient to justify its existence. Man needs very much more. The fully developed State is one that endeavours to satisfy all the needs of man. Even though bare acceptance of 'puissance souveraine' will make a State of sorts, it will not make a well-ordered State. But the ends of the well-ordered State imply and necessitate that acceptance.

What, then, precisely is this 'puissance souveraine' and why is it necessarily recognized in the fully-developed State ? ' Il est ici besoin,' wrote Bodin very justly, ' de former la definition de souveraineté, parce qu'il n'y a jurisconsulte ni philosophe politique qui l'ait definé, jacoit que c'est le point principal et le plus nécessaire d'être entendu au traité de la République.' [1] He proceeds to give a formal definition : ' La souveraineté est la puissance absolue et perpetuelle d'une République.' [2] The definition, evidently, does not help us much. Bodin proceeds to expound his meaning at great length but with much confusion. He saw that 'puissance souveraine' must consist essentially in authority to make law. ' Le point principal de la majesté souveraine et puissance absolue,' he wrote, ' gît príncipalement a donner loi aux sujets en général sans leur consentement.' [3] He returns to and emphasizes this point again and again.[4] Yet he does not seem to have seen quite clearly that such power, if unlimited, includes all other conceivable powers. He went on, quite needlessly, to inform his readers that the Sovereign must possess right to make peace or war, to appoint magistrates, to decide all causes in the last resort and to grant pardons.[5] It would seem that he never quite clearly separated the conception of sovereignty from the idea of a group of legal prerogatives. All the same, he asserts quite distinctly that law is nothing else than the command of a sovereign. ' Loi est le commandement du souverain touchant tous les sujets en général ou de choses générales.' [6] Mere customary law can derive authority

[1] *Rep.*, I, 8, ed. 1580, p. 122.
[2] *Rep.*, I, 8. In the Latin : ' Majestas est summa in cives ac subditos legibusque soluta potestas.' Ed. 1591, p. 123.
[3] *Rep.*, I, 8, ed. 1580, p. 142.
[4] ' Hoc igitur primum sit ac praecipuum caput majestatis ; legem universis ac singulis civibus dare posse . . . sine superiorum aut aequalium aut inferiorum necessario consensu.' *Rep.*, I, 10, ed. 1591, p. 240.
[5] *Rep.*, I, 10.   [6] *Ib.*, I, 10, p. 126.

only from the Sovereign's sanction. It holds good only so long as it pleases the Sovereign to treat it as law.[1]

But Sovereignty involves more than a mere power to make law; for it is not the same thing as mere, actual power. A distinction has to be established. A legal dictatorship, absolute while it lasts but limited in time, would not be a sovereignty; it could be only the creation of a Sovereign. Sovereignty must be permanent: it can suffer no limitation in time, in function or in law.[2] For, rightly considered, sovereignty belongs rather to the State itself than to the Sovereign. It is 'la puissance absolue et perpetuelle d'une République', absolutely vested or realized in a Sovereign. It can be conferred, but it cannot be conferred on conditions. If ruling powers were conferred conditionally sovereignty would remain with those who conferred it.[3]

There are things, Bodin points out, that, just because he can always do anything, the Sovereign cannot do. He cannot bind his successor because, in the nature of the case, his successor cannot be bound. What is even more important to understand is that he cannot bind himself. He cannot, conceivably, limit his own powers. Essentially, it seems, sovereignty consists in a right always to do anything. Obviously such a right is incapable of limitation. Morally the sovereign ought to hold himself bound by any promises he makes, so far, at least, as consideration of the general welfare allows him to keep them. But that is a matter between himself and God. Legally he can never be bound even though he wish to be so. Willy-nilly he must remain always *legibus solutus*. It seemed strange to Bodin that anyone could conceive of the Sovereign Prince as bound by his own law; for that means simply by his own will, ' a thing by nature altogether impossible '.[4] A Sovereign may be mortal but sovereignty is indestructible.

Sovereignty to Bodin is a recognized and unlimited authority to make law. However it arose it is always and necessarily indivisible. For an unlimited authority to make law involves and includes all other powers and is not ideally separable. To talk of mixed sovereignties or partial sovereignties is to talk mere nonsense. The ' mixed state ' in this sense simply cannot exist. ' Il ne s'en est jamais trouvé et il ne se peut faire ni même imaginer, attendu que les marques de souveraineté sont indivisibles.'[5] Under a constitution in which division of sovereignty is attempted, ' il faudra toujours en venir

---

[1] *Rep.*, I, 10, p. 222.

[2] ' Majestas vero nec majore potestate, nec legibus ullis, nec tempore definitur.' Ed. 1591, p. 125.

[3] ' Summum imperium conditione aliqua vel lege datum, summum non est.' *Rep.*, I, 8, ed. 1591, p. 130.

[4] *Rep.*, VI, 4, p. 965.   [5] Ib., II, 1, p. 266.

aux armes jusqu'à ce que la souveraineté demeure a un prince ou a la moindre partie du peuple ou a tout le peuple '.[1] Sovereignty was conceived by Bodin independently of its form. In a monarchy it lies with one man, in an aristocracy it rests with some relatively small group, in a democracy with the numerical majority of the whole community. Quite distinctly Bodin defines democracy as the sovereignty of a numerical majority of the whole people.[2] Though it seemed clear to him that the sovereignty of a group must always be theoretical rather than real,[3] yet wherever sovereignty is regarded as existing, whether in a single person or a body of persons, there, theoretically at least, sovereignty and the State exist. In no other wise can the State exist at all.

It is a mistake to suppose that Bodin's conception of sovereignty was clear or complete. Often he seems to have been thinking of sovereignty as a mere legal fact. It seemed to him that the mere existence of law implied the existence of a sovereign in his sense. For law, he thought, must be conceived as command and command is an act of will and the expression of will must be single or there is no command, and once a sovereign will is recognized its action cannot logically be limited by law. Yet evidently this absolute law-making power which, apparently, belongs to the community and is actualized in some legal sovereign, cannot be a mere legal fact. It might as well be said that it is a mere legal fiction ; since, whatever law may say, no ruler can actually do anything he pleases. The question, to Bodin, was never really one of mere legal fact ; rather, it was always essentially a question of the obligation to obey. He seems to be asserting the existence in all ' republics ' of an unlimited authority to which all owe obedience as a duty. Whence is this authority derived and on what is it based ? Bodin gave no distinct answer to the question. Evidently this sovereignty of his rests always on recognition : he never suggests that he conceived of sovereignty as capable of existing unrecognized. He thought of this recognition now as creating the State, now as something simply highly desirable, now as connected with the conception of the true end of the State or even as necessary in view of that end. But he did not attempt to make it clear how this recognition originated or even why it is desirable. He speaks of sovereignty as being established, or appropriated, by force : but evidently a sovereignty that is either inherent or necessary, is not created by force in any sense, even though an actual sovereign may be. He speaks of it, also, as being conferred. ' Le peuple ou les seigneurs d'une République peuvent donner purement et simplement la puissance souveraine et perpetuelle à quelqu'un pour disposer des biens, des personnes et de tout l'Etat à son plaisir.' But this, seemingly, is a mere transference of legal

[1] *Rep.*, II, 1, p. 266.   [2] *Ib.*, II, 7.   [3] For this important point see p. 437.

sovereignty from one to another. At least the 'people' that gives must have possessed it.[1] Confusedly, Bodin seems to have thought that legal sovereignty must be the formal expression of a sovereignty inherent in the nature of human association and determined by its ends. If the end of political association be the realization of all possible good, if, therefore, the government should have power to control all relations, the recognition of a sovereignty unlimited in law seemed to him to be a necessity. Since the end of the State is an unlimited good, the State must itself possess sovereignty in[this absolute sense or contradict itself by admitting that its end is unattainable. It seemed to him to follow that in every State there must be a recognized legal sovereign with unlimited powers.

To say that Bodin thought of the recognition of sovereignty as the only radical remedy for the disorders of his own France, is true but is far from sufficient. To him it seemed that the conception of legally complete sovereignty at once explained and justified political society. It ensured order and unity, it defined the duty of the citizen, it answered all questions. Bodin argued that it had long existed and did still exist in fact and in law. But he was still more concerned to argue that it must exist. It must exist because it is implied in the very notion of man-made law and because it alone explained political society. How it had come into existence he hardly inquired. It was enough that actually men had everywhere set up political society and that in this, so it seemed to him, sovereignty in fact was logically involved. The long continuance of political society proved to him that its existence accorded with the will of God. Since it is the will of God that man should realize good in political society, the sovereign Prince may even be called God's vicar. 'Puisqu'il n'y a rien de plus grand en terre après Dieu que les princes souverains,' he wrote, ' et qu'ils sont etablis de lui comme ses lieutenants . . . qui méprise son prince souverain, il méprise Dieu duquel il est l'image.' [2] Bodin sometimes uses language that might have been used by Barclay, but it might equally have been used by Calvin. Barclay's Prince is sovereign by virtue of a special divine commission. Bodin believed in the divine right of Kings only in the sense in which almost every one of his time believed in it. God created all things ; but sovereignty and sovereigns were, to Bodin, created by no special act of God. Sovereignty was to him of man's creation : it arose from the nature of man and of human needs and aspirations. You can eliminate from Bodin's *Republic* all his references to God, and to Princes as the

[1] *Rep.*, I, 8, p. 128. 'Nam populus summum perpetuumque imperium in cives, ac vitae necisque potestatem, legibus omnibus solutum uni ex civibus tribuere potest.' Ed. 1591, p. 130. It is noteworthy that, here, both the 'République' and the 'seigneurs' of the French version disappear.
[2] Ib., I, 10, p. 211.

lieutenants of God, and the whole structure will stand unaltered. But if you eliminate God from the system of Barclay nothing whatever will remain. We are still far from having reached the end of the complexities and confusions of Bodin's theory of sovereignty. It appears, after all, that Bodin did not conceive of sovereignty as necessarily involving a strictly unlimited power, even in law. His Sovereign is, or at least may be, restrained in three different ways. He is, in a sense, bound always by natural law ; he may or may not be restrained by what Bodin, like all the French jurists of his time, calls ' fundamental ' laws or ' leges imperii ' ; he is bound always to respect the sanctity of property and of the family, which together form the foundations of the State.

' Mais quant aux lois divines et naturelles,' wrote Bodin in that eighth chapter of the first book of the *Republic* in which he commenced his exposition of sovereignty,[1] ' tous les princes de la terre y sont sujets et n'est pas en leur puissance d'y contrevenir, s'ils ne veulent être coupables de lèse-majeste divine. . . . Et par ainsi la puissance absolue des princes et seigneuries souveraines ne s'étend aucunement aux lois de Dieu et de nature.'[2] His declarations to this effect are emphatic and uncompromising. He makes, however, no attempt to define precisely in what ways natural or divine law limits the Sovereign's right of action, though he does mention murder and robbery as among the forbidden things. It is indeed clear that he views the obligation of the Sovereign to respect natural law as moral only and as involving no strictly legal obligation. There can be no lawful means of compelling the Sovereign to obey even divine law. It might seem therefore that if any question arises, it is a question for the Sovereign's own conscience alone. But this is not quite the case. It is not a matter for the conscience of the Sovereign only : the consciences of other people may be concerned. Bodin himself states the difficulty clearly and frankly. Since, he asks, no subject need obey an order which the subordinate magistrate who gives it has no right to give, even though such order be in itself just and reasonable, ' comment serait tenu le magistrat d'obéir ou d'executer les mandements du prince en choses injustes et deshonnêtes : caren ce cas le prince franchit et brise les bornes sacrées de la loi de Dieu et de nature ? '[3] The question was, obviously, a serious one, since

[1] *Rep.*, I, 8. Headed : ' De la souveraineté ' or ' De jure majestatis '.
[2] Ib., I, 8, p. 133.
[3] Ib., III, 4, p. 414. In the Latin the passage stands as follows : ' Quod si magistratu extra fines provinciae aut supra quam jure debeat imperanti, omnibus imperium recusare fas est, tametsi honestum sit illud quod jubetur ; quanto minus principi turpia et injusta praecipienti parebitur ? terminos enim ac fines imperii a natura ipsa positos movet ac suae jurisdictionis leges ab immortali Deo sacratas perrumpit.' Ed. 1591, p. 461.

the Sovereign can practically act only through agents, and Bodin discusses it seriously. He distinguishes clearly between an order from the Prince which merely contravenes the Prince's own law and an order which is inconsistent with the law of God. In the former case the Prince is merely acting inconsistently with his own standing orders. That is not the magistrate's business and the magistrate, his conscience unconcerned, is bound to obey. But what, for instance, if the Prince orders a slaughter of manifest innocents ? The principle uncompromisingly stated by Bodin is clear and simple. The magistrate must be quite sure of his ground ; but if he is quite certain that the order he has received is contrary to the law of nature, he is bound to disobey it. There is no question of any right of rebellion unless mere disobedience be rebellion. The unhappy official is not entitled, like the magistrate of the *Vindiciae*, to set about organizing armed revolt. He is bound to disobey and risk the consequences. Yet it is not clear how such a recalcitrant is to be punished. An order for his punishment would be manifestly unjust and contrary to natural law, and all his fellow magistrates and officials would be bound to ignore it. An order of the Sovereign seen by all to be unjust and iniquitous could not be carried into effect nor, practically, would punishment be possible, if all did their duty. There is no escape from this conclusion ; nor is there any ground for supposing that Bodin would have sought to escape it. No more than medieval believers in natural law could Bodin believe in a sovereignty strictly unlimited.

Sovereignty viewed in abstraction, divorced from all circumstance, is not, it seems, quite the same thing as actual sovereignty. An actual sovereign may be bound by ' leges imperii '. These are described by Bodin as laws ' qui concernent l'état du Royaume et de l'établissement d'icelui . . . annexées et unies avec la couronne '.[1] He speaks of them as those laws on which the sovereign power is itself based and founded. In the kingdom of France he recognizes only two such laws and they are those which were recognized as ' fundamental ' by all French jurists of his time : the Salic Law and the law prohibiting alienation of domain. ' Le domaine appartient a la République,' he declared. ' La République l'apporte au prince comme dot a son époux pour la tuition, défense et entrenement d'icelle et que les rois ne se peuvent approprier en sorte quelconque.'[2] Concerning the Salic Law he argued at length that it was for France indefeasible, binding absolutely on the monarch. Most of his argument on the subject is concerned with France merely and not with the

---

[1] *Rep.*, I, 8, p. 137. ' Quantum vero ad imperii leges attinet, cun sint cum ipsa majestate conjunctae, Principes nec eas abrogare nec iis derogare possunt.' Ed. 1591, p. 139.

[2] *Ib.*, VI, 2.

State as such. But it appears clearly that, in Bodin's view, fundamental laws, binding on the sovereign, may exist as part of the constitution of a monarchy. Even in law sovereignty need not be unconditioned : and Bodin evidently thought that it should not be. Yet he had declared elsewhere that sovereignty cannot be conferred on conditions. How did these 'leges imperii' originate? They cannot have originated in an act of the Sovereign, for the Sovereign can bind neither himself nor his successors.

Would Bodin have admitted that sovereignty in the fullest sense, sovereignty as he had described it detached from circumstance, did not actually exist in France ? I feel sure that he would have admitted no such thing. It would seem that he conceived of his 'leges imperii' as logically involved in the necessary conditions of actual sovereignty. If sovereignty be vested in an hereditary monarch there must be a law of succession ; and this law, whatever it may be, may be conceived as necessarily binding the monarch who owes his crown to it. Bodin's acceptance of the rule about domain as fundamental is more difficult to account for. Did he argue that if the King alienates his domain he deprives himself of the means of fulfilling his function ? Sovereignty exists for the sake of the State, for the sake, that is, of the attainment of the ends for which the State exists. The Sovereign, therefore, cannot be logically conceived as having a right to deprive himself of the means of action. Bodin does not exactly say these things : it seems as though he must have thought them. But what he says is that the domain belongs to the Republic. What, then, is the Republic apart from its sovereignty ? In all this there is, if not gross inconsistency, at least serious confusion.

The monarchy has been endowed with a domain and this endowment may be conceived as having originally been made out of the property of those who recognized the sovereign. It was implied from the start that the King must 'live of his own ', and since, if he had nothing of his own, he could not live, he must not alienate domain. Bodin does not put the matter quite like this [1] nor do I suppose that he would, in any case, have done so. Yet this way of putting it would seem to fit in with his view of the relation between the Sovereign and property. For Bodin declared quite distinctly that the Sovereign could, normally, take no man's property and no part of any man's property without obtaining, in some sense, his assent. We come, here, to what is practically by far the most important of the limitations of sovereignty according to Bodin. Sovereignty, it appears, does not necessarily include the right to levy direct taxation

---

[1] Yet he very nearly does do so. It is, he declares, 'à fin que les Princes ne fussent contraints de charger d'impôts leur sujets ou chercher les moyens de confisquer leurs biens,' that royal domain has always been regarded as inalienable. *Rep.*, VI, 2, p. 857.

without consent. In a 'seigneurial monarchy' the monarch may possess such a right : it does not exist in well-regulated States. It seems significant that this rather bewildering assertion is made by Bodin incidentally and that no great stress is laid on it. Yet it is not easy to be sure what this signifies. Much of Bodin's language on the subject is ambiguous in phrasing or in reference. When he denounces the arbitrary seizure of private property by the Prince as mere robbery and quotes Seneca with approval in the connection,[1] he is merely denouncing a breach of natural law. He is thinking not of taxation but of mere occasional confiscations. Yet at times he seems to be confusing such arbitrary confiscation of the property of individuals with actual taxation. In any case, in one passage at least, he seems to assert that a right to tax is not included in sovereignty. ' Il n'est en la puissance de prince du monde,' he wrote, ' de lever impôt a son plaisir sur le peuple, non plus que prendre les biens d'autrui ' ; and referred to the famous remark to that effect of Philippe de Commines.[2] Elsewhere he seems to imply that in France, except at least under extraordinary circumstances, direct taxation cannot be levied save under a grant from the Estates. ' S'il est besoin de lever deniers,' he writes, ' cela ne se peut faire que par les Etats du peuple, et de chaque province, ville ou communauté.'[3] If this does not mean that the Estates are entitled to refuse the grant asked for, it means nothing. In another passage he lays down that, if urgent need arises, the Prince will be justified in levying a tax without waiting for a grant. But this implies clearly that the right to tax property at will does not attach to sovereignty.

It is astonishing that Bodin should have made these assertions almost casually, almost without argument, without any attempt to reconcile them with, or exhibit their relation to, his theory of sovereignty. He makes them almost as though they were self-evident truths, needing no discussion.

In discussing the financial position and resources of the French monarchy Bodin dealt last of all with direct taxation.

' Le septième moyen,' he wrote, ' est sur les sujets, auquel il ne faut jamais venir si tous les autres moyens ne defaillent et que la necessité presse de pourvoir a la République, auquel cas, puisque la tuition et défense des particuliers dépend de la conservation du public, c'est bien raison que chacun s'emploie : alors les charges et impositions sur les sujets sont tres justes, car il n'y a rien plus juste que ce qui est nécessaire.'[4]

---

[1] ' Ad reges potestas omnium pertinet, ad singulos proprietas.' See *Rep.*, I, 8.
[2] ' Ego vero coeteris regibus non plus in eo genere quam regibus Anglorum licere puto ; cum nemo fit tam improbus tyrannus qui aliena bona diripere sibi fas esse putet, ut Philippus Cominius,' etc. Ed. 1591, I, 8, p. 96.
[3] *Rep.*, III, 7.
[4] Ib., VI, 2, p. 879.

He would seem, then, to have thought of direct taxation as a last resource, exceptional in its nature and justified only by dire necessity. Such taxation, under normal conditions, would be a mere arbitrary seizure of property, indistinguishable from brigandage, a manifest breach of the law of nature. Even when ' necessity ' was alleged to justify it, the necessity must be generally recognized and a formal assent given to the levy.

But such an interpretation of Bodin's words raises difficulties. It ignores the fact that Bodin knew better. In the very chapter just quoted from he pointed out that it would be absurd to advocate the suppression of the ' tailles ' or even their reduction to what they had amounted to under Louis XII. He knew and declared that the domain had been largely alienated already. He was aware of the extent of the Crown's debts. He held, quite justly, that enormous savings could be effected by making an end of waste and peculation. But he knew that the King could not possibly, in any case, ' live of his own '.

Did Bodin really mean that the political sovereign has no right, of his own mere will and judgement, to tax property for public purposes ? Or did he mean that, whatever may be the case in democracies, sovereign princes at least have no such right ? If he meant that, he was denying full sovereignty to any prince. It might be suggested that he really meant neither of these things. The importance of any such assertion must have been clear to him. If he really meant to assert either of these propositions, why did he not state it fully and give reasons ? He was emphatic in declaring that the confiscation of individual properties is mere robbery, unless justified under rules of law. But the larger, quite different and immensely more important proposition he lays no stress upon. When he said that no King on earth could tax his subjects without consent, can it be that he meant only that, by common consent, it has been established in custom, that in practice the King shall not do so ?

But Bodin's words and his references to the granting power of Estates will hardly bear this interpretation. It has been maintained, on the other hand, that in giving the ' Estates ' power freely to grant or refuse taxation, Bodin not merely took away with one hand the sovereignty he had given with the other, but handed it over to the Estates. It has been argued that his system really places sovereignty with the ' people ' and that he must have conceived the monarchy of France as a ' constitutional ' monarchy. His view of it, it is said, differed from that of Seyssel only because Bodin, lawyer and philosopher, must needs define what Seyssel had left vague. Sovereignty, on this view of his meaning, belongs really to the community itself. It is indivisible, perpetual and unconditioned, save by the law of nature. But the actual legal Sovereign is a delegate and does not possess absolute sovereignty, even though no one may either command or punish him.[1]

I do not think that this way of putting the matter expresses what was in Bodin's mind. Since, according to Bodin, sovereignty may be conferred by the people, it may indeed be argued that, on his own showing, sovereignty originally belonged to ' the people ', that is to a numerical majority of the community. In a democracy it remains with that majority. But, at least, Bodin makes it clear that when conferred it is conferred entire. Sovereignty may be conceived as ' the power of a State '; but Bodin thought of it always as power actualized in a legal Sovereign. Essentially it is a power of making law and what Bodin above all insists upon is that such power cannot logically be conceived as divided or as legally limited or conditioned. Nor is there a phrase in the *Republic* which suggests that he ever thought of the King in France as not possessing full sovereignty in his own sense. In discussing the position of the Estates in France he denies emphatically that the Estates have any share in sovereignty.[2]

We are forced, I think, to the conclusion that, to Bodin, the Prince has no right to levy taxes at his pleasure because a power of arbitrary taxation is somehow inconsistent with the purposes for which sovereignty exists or with the existence of the State itself. We must not misrepresent Bodin by representing his thought as clearer than it was; and that his thought on this subject was confused is not doubtful. But the root of his assertion seems to lie in his conception of the relation of the family and of property to the State. The family was to him the indispensable unit of political society and private property he associated absolutely with the family. Property was to him sacred for this if for no other reason. To say that the Sovereign is not bound to respect property is to say that he is not bound to respect the State itself, for the destruction of one would be the destruction of the other. The necessity, for the Prince, of obtaining a grant before levying direct taxes on property is not derived from any sort of ' sovereignty of the people ', but simply from the fact that to allow the Sovereign power to destroy the State is inconsistent with the ends for which sovereignty exists. Bodin must have known that lawyers had long been claiming an unlimited power of taxation for the King of France. To him, perhaps, that was just because they had never understood the real meaning and basis of sovereignty. Sovereignty must be conceived as absolute and legally unlimited in relation to the ends for which the State exists : it cannot rationally be so conceived except in reference to those ends. Bodin's admission that, in case of dire need and urgency, the Prince

---

[1] This is the view taken by A. Franck in *Reformateurs et Publicistes de l'Europe*, II.

[2] ' Si le Prince souverain est sujet aux Etats, il n'est ni Prince ni souverain.' *Rep.*, I, 8. Again and again he declares that the King is sole sovereign in France.

could rightfully levy taxation without waiting for consent, was logically quite accordant with this principle. Such a right involved no power to destroy. If this interpretation of Bodin's language be correct, then, in spite of his confessions, he cannot rightly be accused of radical inconsistency. The assertion that the legal Sovereign cannot tax without consent is no doubt inconsistent with the Hobbesian conception of sovereignty. But Bodin's conception is radically different from that of Hobbes. Between Hobbes and Bodin is no mere difference of degree, but rather a great gulf fixed.

To say that Bodin's main contribution to political thought was his conception of a sovereignty, absolute and unlimited, as logically involved in the conception of the State, is at once ambiguous and inaccurate. It is not true that Bodin conceived of sovereignty as an unlimited right. It may, perhaps, be said that he thought of it as legally limited only by such 'leges imperii' as were logically involved in the position assigned to an actual Sovereign. But certainly he did not conceive it as unconditioned or as involving a right to do anything. It existed only to subserve the ends for which the State existed ; and only in relation to those ends could it be conceived as existing at all. He thought of all political sovereignty as necessarily and absolutely limited by the law of nature, the measure of which was the common consciousness of right and wrong. Bodin saw no difficulty here : he refers always to this natural law as something that is clearly known to all men. A conception of sovereignty as actually creating right would have seemed to him an atheistic blasphemy. It is right, according to him, to obey the Sovereign in view of the ends for which sovereignty exists : but it is wrong to obey him if he command injustice. Nor is this all : for, to Bodin, the structure of the State implies, at least in all well-ordered States, the recognition of limitations to sovereign power. Three things to Bodin were essential in the structure of political society : sovereignty, the family and private property. And the last were first. The Sovereign could not rationally be conceived as having a right to destroy that which he existed to maintain and which alone justified his existence. To allow the Sovereign a right to tax property at pleasure seemed to Bodin to be inconsistent with the conception of the State. He was quite willing to allow that in case of emergency the Prince may levy taxes without consent and that it is for the Prince to judge when such emergency has arisen. But whatever practical difficulties might follow on this admission, it does not affect the principle. The Sovereign can no more tax at pleasure than he can bind himself. To do the one would destroy sovereignty ; to do the other might destroy the State. Bodin's theory of sovereignty is, first of all, one which, accepting the distinction between right and wrong as absolute and unchangeable, cannot admit the existence of any unlimited human right. It rests, furthermore, upon a conception of the structure of the State which involves limitation of any legal power. Confusedly Bodin saw that to conceive of sovereignty as a mere legal fact is to conceive of it as mere legal fiction.

It must, too, be pointed out that in the bare conception of an unlimited legal sovereignty there was nothing new. Actually the French civilians of the reign of Francis I had claimed for the French King a right less limited than was claimed by Bodin. It is true that they had hardly troubled to generalize their conception : they were thinking of France and its law and not of the State in general. But, long before, Pope Boniface VIII had claimed for the Pope a sovereignty more extensive and complete than any conceived by Bodin. Neither the conception of law as command nor the perception that there can only be one Sovereign in a State nor the idea that sovereignty consists essentially in right to make law were in any sense new. I am inclined to think that William of Occam and Wyclif were nearer to a conception of secular authority as absolutely unlimited than ever was Bodin. It may, indeed, be said that Bodin was the first to declare that the distinguishing mark of the State was its recognition of legal sovereignty. But this assertion does little more than illustrate Bodin's love of formal definition. It may be said that what Bodin did was to detach the notion of sovereignty from all circumstance and see it as legal theory logically necessary in all associations for other than specifically limited purposes. It may, perhaps, be said that in doing this, in detaching the idea of sovereignty from association with Emperor, Pope or King and attempting to define its nature apart from all circumstance, he was doing what had never quite been done before.

The originality of Bodin's theory of sovereignty consisted essentially, I think, at least in relation to his own age, in the fact that he did not connect it specifically and directly with the will of God. Sovereignty was not created, for him, by any special act of God. It was a creation of man in the only sense in which man can create. It came into existence because the ends and the nature of human co-operation logically require its existence. To Bodin sovereignty was created by need, as the school of Barclay, implicitly at least, denied was possible. Though Bodin himself never quite clearly saw what he was trying to prove, his *Republic* is, among other things, an attempt to show that political authority is derived from human nature and human need. Viewed as a complete whole his theory of sovereignty may certainly be fairly said to be original. But of the various elements that went to its construction the only one that is new is the conception of political society as absolutely and necessarily associated with the existence of the family and of private property and the conception of a consequent limitation of political authority.

This conclusion may be a little surprising in view of much that has been written about Bodin : but I do not see how it can be escaped. Some at least of the difficulties and ambiguities of Bodin's exposition of sovereignty disappear when we read his discussion of the different kinds of monarchical sovereïgnty. It appears that, after all, there may exist a sovereignty absolutely unlimited save by that law of nature which can never be abrogated. This is what Bodin càlls ' monarchie seigneuriale ' or ' dominatus '. The seigneurial monarch is regarded in law as sole proprietor of everything in his dominion : all property is his and he governs his subjects as slaves.[1] Bodin thought of this form of sovereignty as rightful but as primitive. It was, he says, that which was earliest established among men,[2] and he appears to think that, in Christendom at least, it exists no longer. But how could he conceive of such a monarchy as constituting a State, since, under such conditions, neither private property nor the family can have any assured existence, even if they exist at all ? The inconsistency is, I think, only verbal. Seigneurial monarchy corresponds to an incomplete recognition of the nature of society and its needs. We may say, perħaps, that Bodin saw ' seigneurial monarchy ' as the first step towards the formation of a true State.

It is clear at least that, to Bodin, a seigneurial monarchy does not constitute a ' républiçue bien ordonnée '. The monarchy of every well-ordered State is a ' monarchie royale, ou légitime ',[3] one in which the monarch is obedient to the laws of nature as are his subjects to him, ' laissant la liberté naturelle et la proprieté des biens à chacun '.[4] The form of the definition implies that it is only in this type of monarchy that the true ends of the State and its structure, and the consequent limitations of sovereign power, are definitely recognized.[5] Yet, having declared that the Sovereign Prince has no right to do this and that, Bodin will not formally admit that there is any right forcibly to resist his wrongful action. He justifies rebellion only against a ' tyrant '. But he distinguishes carefully between the true tyrant and the ' roi tyrannique '. The ' monarchie tyrannique ', into which seigneurial monarchy tends to degenerate, is not, strictly speaking, a tyranny. The tyrant proper is a mere usurper and pretender, who seizes power ' sans élection ni droit successif, ni sort, ni juste guerre, ni vocation spéciale de Dieu '.[6] Such a monster

---

[1] Rep., II, 2, p. 273.   [2] Ib.   [3] ' Monarchia regalis.'
[4] Rep., II, 3, p. 279. ' Rex est qui in summa potestate constitutus, naturae legibus non minus obsequentem se praebet quam sibi subditos quorum libertatem ac rerum dominia aeque ac sua tuetur, fore confidit.' Ed. 1591, p. 312.
[5] Bodin's ' Monarchia regalis ' corresponds to the ' Dominium Politicum et Regale ' of the English lawyer Fortescue ; his ' Dominatus ' is Fortescue's ' Dominium Regale '. While, however, Fortescue had regarded power to tax as derived from power to make law, Bodin separates the two completely.
[6] Ib., II, 5, p. 297.

in nature may always rightfully be resisted and slain. But in the case of the lawfully possessed monarch who behaves tyrannically, ' il n'appartient à pas un des sujets en particulier ni a tous en general d'attenter à l'honneur ni a la vie du Monarque, soit par voie de fait, soit par voie de justice, ores qu'il éut commis toutes les méchancetés, impietés et cruautés qu'on pourrait dire'.[1] For in no case can the subject logically be conceived as possessing any jurisdiction over the sovereign. Any sort of ambiguity is removed by the words that follow. Bodin goes on to say that it would be waste of time to answer the ' frivolous ' argumentation of those who deny what is so evident and maintain the proposition that subjects may justly take arms against a tyrannical Prince. It seems clear that to Bodin rebellion is never, in any case or sense, justified.

Bodin was, no doubt, in a logical difficulty. It was clear to him that subjects could have no jurisdiction in any case over their sovereign, since jurisdiction derives from sovereignty. But it is hard to reconcile his assertion of the absolute unrightfulness of rebellion with what he says about taxation and about fundamental law. Bodin believed at once that the Sovereign could not rightfully do certain things and that, if he did them, there was no remedy. Was he content to think that an attempt to tax unjustly could be defeated by universal passive resistance ? He was intensely aware of the dangers and disadvantages of hereditary absolute monarchy.[2] He must, too, have been aware that even though the recognition of sovereignty be necessary, recognition of a particular sovereign is not. A displacement of sovereignty would, as he puts it, destroy a State : in another sense it might save the State. Though he will not admit that rebellion is anything but pernicious, he admits that rebellion may possibly produce good results.[3] His mind seems to have wavered between the notion of legal sovereignty as complete and indivisible and the conception of sovereignty as necessarily limited by the nature and purposes of the State. No State, he was convinced, can be well-ordered in which the Sovereign does not recognize limits to his right. But, by 1576, he had become convinced that no claim to a right to maintain those limits by rebellion could be either logically justified or in practice anything but ruinous.

§ 5. THE CONSERVATION OF THE STATE

It is the recognition of undivided sovereignty that gives ideal unity to the State and such actual unity in co-operation as is possible. Bodin, accordingly, defines revolution as a displacement or transfer of sovereignty. The destruction of sovereign power would, of course, destroy the State altogether : a displacement of it ends one State and

---

[1] Ib., II, 5, p. 302.   [2] See *Rep.*, VI, 4, and p. 435.
[3] Ib., IV, 7, p. 634.

starts another. No change in law or custom or religion or even in space, is of itself anything but alteration.[1] But in his lengthy and elaborated discussion of the causes of revolution, Bodin, happily, does not adhere very closely to his definition. He was trying to discover all the factors that make for social disturbance and civil war, for the condition that Aristotle called ' stasis '. In the two chapters specially devoted to the subject he follows Aristotle closely and has apparently obtained many suggestions from Machiavelli. He was preoccupied with France, but he was, nevertheless, honestly trying to generalize from his knowledge of history.

Few things are more striking to a reader of the *Republic* than Bodin's profound sense of the perishable nature of all human arrangements. The tendency to revolution is always strong and is absolutely constant. Monarchies tend to become oligarchies, oligarchies to become democracies. Little by little the State reaches its highest point of power and prosperity, but this prosperous condition cannot last long. It is true that a State solidly founded and well regulated is not easily broken down. ' Et neantmoins il n'y a point de république qui par trait de temps ne souffre changement et qui ne vienne enfin à ruiner.'[2] He seems to see change as the one thing certain. It may partly be foreseen and provided against, it may be made gradual or turned to good ends, but, change being always certain, the end is sure.

Seditions and revolutions arise from man's incalculable will or the unaccountable acts of God. There is no such thing as chance, but there is something mysterious and inexplicable in the ruin of States. In that astonishing second chapter of the fourth book of the *Republic* Bodin tries to find suggestions of an explanation in the influence of planetary positions and in fortunate and unfortunate numerical coincidences. But no wisdom or prudence or human calculation can assure stability. Stability, in fact, does not exist in our world. Yet prudence and wisdom can do much. The causes of unrest and disturbance are to a great extent such as can be removed or mitigated by governmental action. It is on the action and policy of the Sovereign that such stability as is possible mainly depends.

The first condition of success is a comprehension of the nature of the particular State that is to be maintained and the particular disorders it suffers from. It is of little use to know what is, ideally, the best form of State; and indeed such knowledge may be altogether irrelevant. An effort to make of the State what you think it ought to be may well ruin it completely.[3] Violent remedies should be tried only in desperate cases. Rebellion may possibly produce good results, but only accidentally.

The policy to be adopted by different forms of State for self-

[1] *Rep.*, IV, 1.   [2] Ib., IV, 1, p. 539.   [3] Ib., IV, 3, p. 574.

preservation must always more or less differ. Bodin's perception that an aristocracy will tend to rule in one manner, a monarchy or democracy in another, was as clear as was, later, Montesquieu's. He saw, too, quite clearly that the form of the State, that is the mode in which its sovereignty is actualized, is independent of the form of its governmental system.[1] A sovereign Prince may organize a government aristocratic in personnel, may exalt and privilege a nobility, or, on the other hand, he may destroy nobility and rule through democratic machinery. Yet measures of self-preservation must always be related to the nature of the thing to be preserved. An arrangement good in a monarchy may be ruinous to a democracy.[2]

'La première et principale cause de sédition est l'inegalité.'[3] Bodin mentions inequality in possessions, monopolies of office by any class and exemptions from taxation, as alike dangerous and tending to produce sedition. Office should never be allowed to be hereditary : it is doubtful even whether it should ever be conferred for life, since in that case so few can hope to hold it.[4] The practice of selling office under the Crown is one of the most pernicious that can afflict a State. On this point Bodin wrote feelingly, as well he might. ' Il est bien certain que ceux là qui mettent en vente les états, offices et benefices, ils vendent aussi la chose la plus sacrée du monde qui est la justice. Ils vendent la république ; ils vendent le sang des sujets ; ils vendent les lois.'[5] But most dangerous of all are great inequalities of wealth. ' De toutes les causes des seditions et changements de Républiques, il n'y en a point de plus grande que les richesses excessives de peu de sujets et la pauvreté extrême de la plus-part.'[6] So impressed was Bodin with the danger of such a state of things that he devoted a whole chapter to its exposition. He argued at length against ' usury ', which in sixteenth-century language often signifies not merely the taking of interest on loans but every kind of ' profiteering ' ; and he did so mainly because he saw in it a source of this worst kind of inequality. In this connection, he suggested that what we call the Reformation was essentially due to the over-great wealth of the Church. ' L'inegalité si grande a peutêtre donné occasion des troubles et seditions advenues presqu'en toute l'Europe contre l'état ecclesiastique, ores qu'en apparence on faisait voile de religion ; car si cette occasion là n'y eût été, on en eût trouvé quelqu' autre.' On the other hand, it must be remembered that Bodin was profoundly impressed by the natural inequality of man.[7] Equality in legal qualification for office was to him a means of giving effective expression to that natural

[1] Ib., I, 10.   [2] Ib., IV, 3, p. 574.   [3] Ib., IV, 4, p. 583.
[4] Ib., IV, 4, p. 585.   The question is discussed at length.
[5] Ib., V, 4.   [6] Ib., V, 2, p. 702.
[7] So much impressed that he saw in the natural inequality of man a reason for declaring democracy ' unnatural '.

inequality. He saw a grave danger in great inequalities of possession ;
but he saw attempts absolutely to equalize possession as absurd and
ruinous.

If Bodin viewed inequality of some sort, inequalities needlessly
created by law and extreme inequalities of possession, as the principal
direct cause of ' sedition ', there was another upon which he laid
almost equal stress. He insists that attempts to change the law to
which people are accustomed are always dangerous. ' Il n'y a chose
plus difficile à traiter, ni plus douteuse à réussir, ni plus perilleux à
manier, que d'introduire nouvelles ordonnances.' [1] It is easy to enact
law but very difficult to enforce it. Law is obeyed largely from habit
and tradition. Men tend to dislike and despise all new-fangled
arrangements. A law may be ideally ' good ' : but it is worse than
useless if it be not obeyed. ' La loi, pour bonne qu'il soit, ne vaut rien
si elle porte un mépris de soi-même ' ; and ' la nouvauté en matière
de lois est toujours méprisée '.[2] Above all, dangerous is any new law
touching the organization of power in the State or what we call its
' constitution ' and Bodin calls simply ' l'état '. ' Tout changement
de lois qui touchent l'état est dangereux.'

Bodin was careful to point out that he was not saying that the
State must be the slave of its own law. Changes in law can no more
be avoided than change in anything else. ' Si on me dit que le changement de lois est souvent nécessaire, je dis que nécessité n'a point de
loi.' [3] He quotes the maxim : ' Salus populi suprema lex est,' conscious that it cuts both ways. What he wished to insist upon was
that all changes in law, necessary or not, are more or less dangerous, as
tending to bring law and so the Sovereign into contempt. Bodin, it
seems, fully recognized that, however absolute the Sovereign may
be in theory, he is very far, actually, from being able to do as he
pleases.[4]

Writing between 1572 and 1576 it must have seemed to Bodin that
religious dissensions might be the most terrible of all dangers to public
peace. Yet it is singular how small is the space devoted in the *Republic*
to discussion of the questions involved. On all sides in 1576 two
questions were being asked : Is it the duty of the magistrate to maintain true religion by force ? Have the adherents of the true religion
a right forcibly to resist persecution ? Bodin put neither of these
questions. His language on the whole subject is cautious to the point
of evasion. He answers the first only by implication and the second
only by a sweeping assertion that rebellion against the Sovereign is
for no cause justified.

The very atheists, Bodin declared, agree that religion is the main

[1] *Rep.*, IV, 3, p. 575. [2] *Ib.*, IV, 3, p. 574. [3] *Rep.*, IV, 3, p. 576.
[4] In all this, consciously or not, Bodin was repeating what Le Roy had said
already.

foundation of order in society. Reverence for the magistrate, obedience to law, the fear of wrongdoing, even mutual friendliness, all practically depend upon religion. So far Calvinists and Leaguers alike would have gone with him. But, to Bodin, it is not any particular form of religion, it is not even ' true ' religion that is needed. He remarks that he is not here considering the question as to which religion is the best : the question is not relevant. What is needed is that the form of religion established in any particular society should not, there, be questioned or denied. ' La religion étant recue d'un commun consentement il ne faut pas souffrir qu'elle soit mise en dispute, car toutes choses mises èn dispute sont aussi revoquées en doute . . . il faut bien prendre garde qu'une chose si sacrée ne soit méprisée ou revoquée en doute par disputes car de ce point-là dépend la ruine des Républiques.' [1] It is not, it is clearly implied, the duty of government to maintain true religion ; but it is the business of government, for the sake of public order, to suppress if possible all questioning and disputation concerning whatever religion is actually established.

But what if this has not been done or been done so ineffectively that the Sovereign finds himself confronted with a large and organized body of heretics ? Bodin argues that in that unhappy case the Prince should refrain from any attempt to establish unity by force, even though he himself has certain assurance which of the rival religions is the true one. By toleration and the persuasiveness of his own example he will be able both to avoid civil war and gradually to draw all his subjects into the right way. But ' plus la volonté des hommes est forcée, plus elle est revêche '. The appeal to force is likely to produce mere exasperation. Even if the Prince succeed in overcoming resistance and compelling conformity he will make not converts but atheists. ' Il adviendra que ceux qui sont frustrés de l'exercice de leur religion et dégoûtés des autres, deviendront du tout athéistes, comme nous voyons, et après avoir perdu la crainte divine, fouleront aux pieds et lois et magistrats.' That last state will be worse than the first. ' Tout ainsi que la plus forte tyrannie n'est pas si miserable que l'anarchie . . . aussi la plus forte superstition du monde n'est pas, à beaucoup pres, si detestable que l'athéisme.' [2]

It is clear that Bodin, in the *Republic*, is an advocate of toleration only in a very limited sense. He lays down nothing that can be called a principle of toleration. Unity in religion is highly desirable, he declares, but civil war is still worse than the loss of it. The establishment of conformity by force creates a danger greater than that it suppresses. On the other hand, so long as it can be done with safety, the suppression of all questioning concerning established religion

[1] For all this see the important passage, *Rep.*, IV, 7, pp. 652–655.
[2] *Rep.*, IV, 7, p. 655.

should be undertaken by government. At what exact point such suppression should cease and toleration begin is not clear : but it is impossible to infer from what he says that a government would be in any sense wrong in exterminating a helpless body of heretics. Bodin was an advocate of toleration only under special circumstances. He does not stand with Castellion and Acontius : he does not even quite go so far as L'Hôpital. His view seems to have been that of the ordinary ' Politique '. Acontius had seen in free disputation the only way of arriving at truth. But Bodin was not concerning himself with truth, he was concerned only with public order. He represents the whole question as one of mere expediency.

Was he suppressing his real opinions ? In the *Heptaplomeres* his standpoint is quite different. There, having demolished orthodox Christianity of all sorts, he comes to two conclusions. In the first place, argument about religion is futile : in the second, one religion is for practical purposes about as good as another, and there is no reason why men of different religions should not live together in peace. In the final passage of that work Bodin expressed his main practical conclusion. At the end of the long discussion the representatives of different religions embrace in charity and go each to his own quarters. ' And thereafter they lived together wondrously united, in piety and exemplary fashion, taking their meals and their studies in common. But never again did they talk of religion, each of them holding firmly and constantly to his own and persevering in it to the end in a manifest holiness of living.' [1]

If Bodin held these views in 1576 he certainly completely suppressed them. But it must be noticed that the view expressed in the *Heptaplomeres* is not actually inconsistent with that expressed in the *Republic*. In 1590 Bodin may have hoped that some day such tolerance as he imagined would become part of law and the general conduct of life. But he knew that, for the present, it was not so. That a few cultivated men, after long discussion of their differences, should agree to differ and find themselves able to live together in concord, proved nothing to the purpose. The discussion in the *Heptaplomeres* is concerned only with truth ; in the *Republic* it is a question of social order. In the *Heptaplomeres* men are arguing about religion in a world void of circumstance : their conclusions have only the remotest if any bearing on the circumstantial questions that governments must deal with. Even in the *Heptaplomeres* Bodin did not suggest any applications of those conclusions in the world of politics. It seems indeed that, in 1576, he thought that one religion would serve society as well as another. It did not follow that the Sovereign should not endeavour

---

[1] 'Deinceps mirabili concordia pietatem ac vitae integritatem communibus studiis ac convictu cohuerunt ; sed nullam postea de religionibus disputationem habuerunt, tametsi suam quisque religionem summa vitae sanctitate tueretur.'

to suppress all criticism of the religion established. Bodin asserts only that it is not a matter of obligation and that the cost must be counted. It must, too, be remembered that Bodin influenced opinion on the question only through the *Republic*.

§ 6. CLIMATE

Though Bodin's theory as to the effects of ' climate ' is an essential element in his thought, it may fitly enough be dealt with here. It was in connection with the problem of maintaining healthy life in the State that he himself expounded it in the *Republic*. Behind all policies and constitutions lie those fundamental facts which are permanent or hardly alterable. It is these that determine, within limits, the characters and potentialities of peoples and therefore their forms of government and law. It is these permanent factors that give a stability to human institutions in this world of continuous change. Failure to understand the limitations they impose may result in the ruin of the State.

According to Bodin the permanent differences that exist among the peoples of the earth are due to differences of ' climate '. He uses the word climate to include all those conditions of man's life which, practically permanent for any one area, yet vary from part to part of the earth's surface. It includes heat and cold, humidity and dryness, sun, rain and wind ; it includes topographical permanencies mountain and marsh and plain, proximity to or distance from the sea it includes the character of the soil and its products. It includes also, for Bodin, starry influences mysterious and diverse ; for different peoples live under different stars. Just as, he argued, we find on the earth a great variety of animal life and different types of creatures inhabiting different regions, so also we find the same among men.[1] Man differs from north to south and from east to west ; he is different on mountain and on plain ; he is different inland and on the coast. The coincidences are altogether too great to be matter of chance, even if there were such a thing as chance. These differences among men are permanent or only slightly alterable : the explanation of them must lie in the differences of the permanent conditions under which they live. When we look closely at the facts we find that the world can be divided into climatic zones, differentiated not only by climate but by the character of the peoples inhabiting them. These zones lie north and south, they follow the lines of latitude, though in each zone there is difference discernible also east and west, on the lines of longitude. ' Et qui plus est, en même climat, latitude et longitude, et sous même degré, on aperçoit la difference du lieu montueux à la plaine.' [2]

Looking closer yet, we find, according to Bodin, that the peoples

[1] *Rep.*, V, 1, p. 663.　　　　[2] *Ib.*, V, 1, p. 663.

of the northern zone are strong of body, energetic, turbulent and rest-less, and rather stupid : those of the southern zone are subtle and contemplative, inclined to philosophy and religion, relatively feeble in body, somewhat averse to action and unpractical. The peoples of the middle zone, which includes the Mediterranean region and France, possess, in less extreme degree, the good qualities of north and south. They are better balanced, more active and practical than the south-erners, more intellectual, less violently egotistic, more disciplined than the northerners. If from the north come the great armies and the great invasions, yet the people of the middle zone are ' more apt for war ',[1] since war demands intelligence and discipline rather than mere brute force and courage. Still greater is the superiority of the middle peoples in all the arts of government and it is by them that all the great empires have been established. The southerners have led the way in philosophy and mathematics and all occult knowledge ; but it is the middle peoples who have developed law and jurisprudence and ' political sciences '.[2] God has so arranged things that ' les peuples du Midi sont ordonnés pour la recherche des sciences les plus occultes, afin d'enseigner les autres peuples ; ceux du Septentrion au labeur et aux arts mécaniques ; et les peuples du milieu pour négocier, trafiquer, juger, haranguer, commander, établir les Républiques, composer lois et ordonnances pour les autres peuples.' [3]

All this was set forth by Bodin not so much as matter of interest in itself but because he regarded comprehension of these facts as necessary to the right conduct of government. The ' psychology ' of a people [4] has been determined by the permanent conditions of its life and can only very slowly and partially be altered. ' Il faut donc que le sage gouverneur d'un peuple sache bien l'humeur d'icelui et son naturel . . . car l'un des plus grands et peutêtre le principal fonde-ment des Républiques est d'accommoder l'état au naturel des citoyens et les édits et ordonnances à la nature des lieux, des personnes et du temps.' [5] This ' naturel ' has in fact determined, within limits not strictly definable but nevertheless absolute, both the form of govern-ment and the character of law ; and except within the limits imposed, these cannot be altered. It is necessary to know what can and what cannot be done. A good architect conforms his building to the material he finds on the spot.[6] Northern peoples must be governed mainly by force since, apparently, they understand nothing else : middle peoples must be governed with justice and southerners by

---

[1] *Rep.*, V, 1, p. 671.   [2] Ib., V, 1, pp. 571, 572.   [3] Ib., V, 1.
[4] Bodin does not, of course, use this absurd expression, but he is speaking of the thing.   [5] *Rep.*, V, 1.
[6] ' The character of the aggregate is determined by the character of the units.' Herbert Spencer's remark may be a truism but is certainly not a dis-covery.

religion. He who would govern Africans or Swedes as Italians or French are governed, ' il ruinerait bientôt leur état '.[1] Even the form of sovereignty tends to be determined by climate. In the south the tendency is to theocracy, but ' les peuples du Septentrion ou qui demeurent aux montagnes veulent les états populaires '.[2]

Bodin was anxious not to overstate the case. He remarked that in every country there are men of all sorts ; that everywhere there are some who seem more or less to have escaped climatic influences. But these exceptions are too few to do more than help to exhibit the rule. He was aware that change of circumstances may quickly produce some degree of alteration in the character of a people. He remarks that, as a result of civil war, the French ' sont bien fort altérés de leur naturel et devenus farouches ', while, in contrast, the turbulent English under the benign rule of Elizabeth ' sont bien fort apprivoisés '. On the other hand, Bodin asserted emphatically that change of abode will always produce in a people a corresponding change of character. If a people migrate from one region to another ' il ne sera pas si tôt changé que les plantes qui tirent le suc de la terre, mais il changera : comme on peut voir des Goths . . .'[3]

It may well be said that Bodin's exposition of his theory of climate is the most profound and original portion of his book. But it would be a bad mistake to think of it as though it were an isolated and unessential feature of his theory of the State. It is, in the highest degree, characteristic of his mode of thought. It was only his incapacity for arrangement that placed his exposition of it towards the end of the *Republic* : after reading the *Methodus* we should expect to find it at the beginning. But when at last we reach it, it becomes clear that for Bodin the study of human life in society begins with psychology and its determination. Human character, ' le naturel de l'homme ', differs in different parts of the world as a result of climatic influences ; and the main features of all man's political systems are ultimately expressions of a mentality that has been determined by ' climate '. Individuals may escape those influences, but the mass does not ; conscious effort or temporary circumstances may modify, but the main lines remain unalterable. There is no inconsistency between this view and Bodin's conception of the State as created by the recognition of sovereignty. The State, in his sense, does not exist everywhere. The north tends to democracy, the south to theocracy, the middle peoples to monarchy. Bodin agreed with Le Roy that these different peoples to monarchy.

[1] *Rep.*, V, 1.
[2] Ib., V, 1, p. 694. ' Certes a grande difficulté,' Le Roy had written in 1575, ' pourrait on jamais dresser république en pays disposé a la Monarchie et Monarchie là où les moeurs et conditions tendent a république. Le pays plein de montagnes, de rochers et de bois . . . auquel y a beaucoup de pauvres . . . est plus propre a Démocratie.' *De l'excellence du gouvernement royal*, 1575.
[3] Ib., V, 1, p. 698.

tendencies marked the superiority of the middle peoples. It is they only, it is implied, who have fully grasped the conception of the State, with all its implications. It is among them alone that the ' République bien ordonnée ' comes to birth.

In reading the great first chapter of the fifth book of the *Republic* we realize, if we had not realized before, how very far was the thought of Bodin from that of Calvinists or Leaguers or that of the divine-right school of Barclay. Even the form of religion may, it is suggested, be ultimately determined by climate. The ' Republic ', as Bodin defines it, is the highest form of human association ; but it is not for every one. There is, ideally, a best form of State ; but it is not actually the best everywhere. If a rude people wills democracy, it is absurd to say that for it monarchy is best : it is only best for a superior type of humanity. It may be a misfortune for the peoples of the north and of the south that they do not grasp the full meaning and value of the State and that the ' République bien ordonnée ' exists with difficulty, if at all, among them. But God has so arranged things that, inevitably, different forms of State and types of association develop among different peoples, as a result of the adjustments between man and climatic conditions. God shows no political preferences. ' All nature demands monarchy,' declared Bodin in the *Methodus* : but this nature is not ' le naturel des hommes '. As so often with Bodin, there is some confusion here but no real inconsistency. All Nature's analogues may point to monarchy ; but the northern peoples are too stupid to see it and the southerners do not care. Evidently no ruler can claim a special divine commission nor any human institution direct divine establishment. The value of all institutions is strictly relative and is ultimately determined by permanent local conditions. Though it is true that Bodin did not quite clearly perceive all the implications of his theory of climate, I do not think that he ever quite forgot them. The very worst of his failures was his failure to relate it to his conception of the origin of the State and its sovereignty. Yet all that he has to say about the well-ordered State is most fully intelligible when read in the light of the theory of climate. It is, I think, a fact that Bodin's thought was, actually, more like thought of the twentieth century than was ever that of Hobbes : a fact curious and challenging perhaps, but of no clear significance.

§ 7. THE BEST STATE

In the *Methodus* Bodin expressed wonder that in all the centuries no one had yet succeeded in determining what is the best form of State.[1] By the time he had reached the sixth book of the *Republic* he was ready with a demonstration. The question, for him, was

---

[1] ' Mirum videri debeat tot saeculis neminem adhuc constituisse, quis esset optimus civitatis status.' *Methodus*, ed. 1566, VI, p. 177.

simply whether sovereignty is best recognized in a monarch or in an aristocracy or in a mere majority. His answer was emphatic and unqualified. It must be remembered that he was not asserting that his answer applied to every kind of actual condition. On his own showing there exist climates and peoples unsuited to monarchy. But this merely means that such peoples are on a low plane. The absolutely best is not for every one. It must be remembered, too, that the monarchy which is, to Bodin, the best form of State is not any sort of monarchy but is the ' monarchie royale '. The ' dominatus ' was to him an inferior thing, though perhaps no worse than a democracy.

Bodin saw the whole question as one of expediency. Expediency considered in relation to circumstance may give different answers for different peoples ; but expediency considered with reference only to the highest ends of the State can give but one answer. It is important to notice that Bodin argued the question almost entirely on grounds of expediency. There was, for him, no question of monarchy being the only form of government approved by God. There was no ' ought ' in the matter. The question was what form of sovereignty answers most fully to all the needs and purposes for which the State should be conceived as existing. It is true that he, like Aristotle, argued as though it were mainly a question of stability merely. Yet he preferred monarchy above all because it seemed to him that only in a monarch could that sovereignty he thought of as necessary to well-ordered society be fully realized.

No writer of the sixteenth century stated so clearly and forcibly as Bodin the dangers and disadvantages of hereditary monarchical sovereignty. With every change of sovereign, he pointed out, there comes a dangerous breach of continuity. The new Prince brings with him a new policy, new favourites, new ministers, and is tempted to get himself talked about by upsetting the arrangements of his predecessor. Alliances become insecure and treaties are shaken. Again, the new Prince may be too young to realize the gravity of his position : worse still, he may be a minor. Most serious of all is the fact that so much depends on the character of the monarch.

' Si le Prince est subtil et méchant il établit une tyrannie ; s'il est cruel il fait une boucherie de la République ; ou bien un bourdeau s'il est paillard, ou l'un et l'autre ensemble : s'il est avare, il arrache le poil et la peau des sujets : s'il est prodigue, il suc le sang et la moelle, pour souler une douzaine de sangsues, qui seront autour de sa personne. Et fera pis encore, s'il est sot et ignorant.' [1]

This gives a poor prospect ; but there is yet worse behind, for Bodin avers that the possession of supreme power has of itself a deteriorating effect on character. ' La souveraineté a cela de malheur, que le plus souvent les sages deviennent fols, les vaillans deviennent poltrons, les bons deviennent méchants.' [2] It is no wonder, as he else-

[1] *Rep.*, VI, 4, p. 961.   [2] Ib., VI, 4, p. 961.

where remarked, that there are so few virtuous Princes. There are few virtuous men ; and even if a virtuous man becomes Prince, so demoralizing is power that ' c'est un miracle s'il continue en sa vertu '.[1] It might be supposed, from all this, that no form of sovereignty could well be worse than monarchy. But Bodin was, I think, deliberately over-emphasizing for the sake of argument.[2] He must have been aware that a Prince who turned his dominions into a slaughterhouse would be a very rare kind of madman. He was, certainly, aware of the instability of all human arrangements. ' Voilà les dangers de la monarchie, qui sont grands ; mais il y a bien plus de peril en l'état aristocratique et plus encore en l'état populaire.' [3] That, after all, was all he had to show.

Bodin admitted that, at first sight, the ' état populaire ' or democracy might well seem to be the best of all forms of State. The democratic State may be conceived as most of all consonant with the law of nature, in that it allows of no privilege or legal superiority and gives equal justice to all without respect of persons. Here all partake in sovereignty ; public affairs are the affairs of every one and none is subject but to law and the agent of the law. History, too, it might be said, shows that it is democracy that produces the greatest personalities.[4]

But Bodin proceeded to demolish this illusion. Conceived in ideal perfection the democratic State may be the best. Actually, men being what they are, no such State can exist. No democracy has ever realized [5] or can ever realize the dream of equality in goods or honours or power ; and if ever this dream were realized the result would be disaster. The radical fact is the inequality of men ; and the craving for equality expressed in democracy is a rebellion against nature. Nature, it is true, does not unequally distribute wealth or honours : she does not distribute them at all. Equality in power is always a fiction : whatever arrangements are made, only a few can govern. But the more completely an equality in power is realized, the worse will be the case. ' Les voix en toute assemblée sont comptées sans les peser ; et toujours le nombre des fous, des méchants et ignorants est mille fois plus grand que des gens de bien.' [6] So far from being consonant with the law of nature, ' l'état populaire est établi contre le cours et ordre de nature, laquelle donne le commandement aux plus sages '.[7] As to liberty, there is less real liberty in a democracy than

[1] *Rep.*, IV, 1.
[2] In other passages of the *Republic* Bodin seems to express a wonderful confidence in the beneficence of the monarch.
[3] *Rep.*, VI, 4, p. 961.   [4] Ib., VI, 4, pp. 937, 938.
[5] Ib., VI, 4, p. 939.   [6] Ib., VI, 4, p. 949.
[7] Ib., VI, 4, p. 950. ' Est autem popularis status ab universa natura plane discrepans.' Ed. 1591, p. 1100.

in any other form of State. For the liberty that is worth having does not consist in a fictitious share in political power but depends upon stability and order in the State. 'La vraie liberté populaire ne gît en autre chose sinon a jouir de ses biens en sureté et ne craindre qu'on fasse tout à l'honneur ni à la vie de soi, de sa femme ni de sa famille.'[1] In a democracy sovereignty is vested in a majority : and a majority is not only, at best, an ignorant, foolish and emotional mob, but shifts continually and alters from year to year. In such a State nothing can be looked for but a constant disorder.

Yet more summarily did Bodin dismiss the case for aristocracy. It may, he admitted, be fairly argued that government by the rich is best, because the rich, having most to lose, will be most of all careful of the general welfare. He alluded to Venice as a standing example of successful aristocracy of this type. But he would allow no more than that an aristocratic State is more likely to be stable and orderly than is a democracy. Venice stands alone on its peculiar circumstances. An aristocracy, he declared, is almost certain to be distressed and finally ruined by the feuds and jealousies of its members. The sovereignty, too, of a small group is open to the same objections as that of a large group. The able and virtuous members of an aristocracy will always be a minority and the majority that is dominant to-day will not be the sovereign to-morrow. He argued also that a degenerate aristocracy is a greater danger than a degenerate monarch. Monarchy has a greater power of recovery.

The experience of mankind, Bodin declared, has shown that hereditary monarchy gives the most stable and satisfactory form of State ; and mankind has learnt the lesson.

'Les peuples, ayant decouvert à vue d'oeil et par longue suité de siècles aperçu, que les monarchies étaient plus sures, plus utiles, plus durables que les Etats populaires et aristocraties, et, entre les monarchies, celles qui étaient fondées en droit successif du male le plus proche, ils ont reçu presque par tout le monde les monarchies successives.'

Bodin and Le Roy, both believers in progress, agreed that the prevalence of the monarchical State went far to prove its real superiority.

But Bodin's preference for monarchy seems to have rested above all on his sense that only in monarchy could the conception of sovereignty be completely realized. The essential feature of the State, which is sovereignty, he declared, cannot, strictly speaking, exist except in monarchy. Only in a single will can sovereignty actually exist. The sovereignty attributed to an aristocracy or to a whole people is necessarily fictitious. In an aristocracy or in a democratic State the majority may at any one moment be sovereign : but this majority is a shifting thing that may and does change from day

[1] Ib., VI, 4, p. 948. See ed. 1591, p. 1098.

to day. A majority of wills has neither definite form nor any constant substance. A group is always divided : it has, strictly speaking, no will at all. Compromise distorts its action and faction disorders it. A monarch alone can give real unity to society and establish definitely the distinction between sovereign and subject.[1]

Inconclusive, of course, all this is and was ; but Bodin himself seems to have felt no doubt. ' La Monarchie pure et absolue,' he wrote, ' est la plus sure République et sans comparaison la meilleure de toutes.'[2] A public-spirited Frenchman, unhampered by sectarian ideals and writing in 1576, was not likely to think otherwise. Though he argued the case for monarchy without reference to France, yet it was of France that he was always thinking. It was only natural that what was so clearly best for France at the moment should seem to him to be ideally best. His detachment from mere passing conditions was not great enough to allow of any conclusion less drastic.

§ 8. THE CONSTITUTION OF FRANCE

One must carefully endeavour to distinguish what Bodin had to say of the actual constitution of France from what he had to say concerning political society under all conditions. It is not always quite easy to do so, because Bodin himself does not always seem to know what he is writing about. His view of the actual constitution of France might be supposed to be completely irrelevant to an exposition of his theory of the State. But that is not actually quite the case. Bodin was never satisfied with mere practical suggestions or vith merely juristic reasoning. He sought always for principles. He sought to interpret the constitution of France by reference to the conclusions he had arrived at concerning all political societies. He endeavoured to justify practical recommendations by reference to principles derived from his theory of the State as such. In these ways he gives concrete illustrations of how he thought his principles applied ; and in so doing makes his meanings clearer.

Bodin saw France as potentially a well-ordered State of the best possible kind. The constitution of France, as he understood it, seemed to him, apparently, the best possible constitution. Unfortunately Frenchmen were not agreed on the subject. They disputed as to where sovereignty lay, nor had the mass of them grasped what was involved in sovereignty. Bodin wrote to enlighten his countrymen

---

[1] *Rep.*, VI, 4, pp. 961, 962. ' Majestas autem imperii praeterquam in uno principi vere ac proprie consistere nullo modo potest. Nam si duo pluresque principes fuerint, summum imperium nullius est : quia nec alter alteri imperare, nec parere tenetur, ac tametsi universis in aristocratia ac democratia majestas attribuitur, singulis non item ; nusquam tamen summum illud imperium subsistere videtur, nisi princeps aliquis exstiterit, qui universos ac singulos quasi membra corporis apta et colligata inter se unire possit.' Ed. 1591, p. 1111.

[2] Ib., VI, 4, p. 965.

on this point and to show that the constitution of France was that of a 'monarchie royale'.

The starting-point of his thought about the actual constitution of France was the safe assumption that France was a true 'State' and that, therefore, in France sovereignty must exist somewhere. An assertion that France was not a 'Republic' at all, within his definition, might have embarrassed him ; but no one was likely to make such an assertion and no one did make it. The application of his theory to the facts disposed at once of all claims of customary right as against the Sovereign. There are recognized fundamental laws of the constitution and there is the fundamental principle that the Sovereign cannot tax property at pleasure. But there is no rational basis for any limitation of sovereignty founded on mere custom or class or provincial privilege. Custom is binding only so far as it receives the Sovereign's sanction and all privilege is held of him at pleasure. The actual position is, thus, at once enormously simplified.

With the position and claims of the noblesse and of the Parlements Bodin dealt at length. With regard to the privileges of the nobles he advocated no drastic or immediate change. He thought it only natural and proper that, in choosing his agents, the King, other things being equal, should prefer a noble to one of lower rank. He wrote of the great houses of France as ' gros pilliers immuables ' of the State. It seems, indeed, that he regarded the position of the nobles in France as a safeguard against tyranny. But he made it quite clear that the whole position of the nobles, the very existence of noblesse, must be conceived as depending on the Sovereign's will. He remembered the great maxim enunciated so far back as the reign of Louis IX : ' Fief et justice n'ont rien de commun.' All jurisdiction belongs to the Sovereign and if a seigneur holds an hereditary jurisdiction this is only because it is the will of the Sovereign that it should be so. Hereditary office and jurisdictions and exemptions from taxation can all alike be abolished by an act of sovereignty. Bodin suggested, even, that with the establishment of the national army he strongly advocated, and the consequent disappearance of the need of maintaining a noblesse for military service, the time may come when this should be done.[1]

Bodin's attitude towards the Parlements of France was like his attitude towards the noblesse in being at once conservative and radical. What he had specially to deal with was the claim of the Parlements to a real share in sovereignty, through a power practically to veto royal edicts. On the question of this claim Bodin's views seem to have changed between 1566 and 1576. In the *Methodus* he inclined, at least, to the view that the claim was well-founded. The Parlements,

---

[1] For the whole of this discussion of noblesse see *Rep.*, V, 2 and III, 5, 6.

he says, approvingly, claim that they cannot be compelled to register.[1] But in the *Republic* he argued elaborately that no power absolutely to refuse edicts existed. The Parlements may present ' remonstrances ', they may ask the Sovereign to reconsider the matter, they may make recommendations ; but if the Sovereign positively orders registration, register they must. How far this change of view was due to a logical process and how far to a growing conviction of the need of absolutism in France it is, of course, impossible to say. But Bodin continued to see in the Parlements, in their powers recognized and unrecognized, in their tradition and prestige, a real barrier against tyranny, a real safeguard against the dangers inherent in monarchy. They too, like the great families, were to him pillars of the State. He refers, triumphantly, to the fact that the King has again and again yielded before the righteous protests of his chief magistrates.[2] Had he lived in happier times Bodin might have retained to the end his belief in the validity of the claims of the sovereign courts.

Essentially there remained only the question of where, in France, sovereignty actually lay. To Bodin it seemed so clear that it could not lie with the Estates or be in any sense shared by them, that little argument was needed. He was completely and rightly unimpressed by the historical argument of Hotman, to which he makes passing and contemptuous allusion. Sovereignty in France must, he concluded, lie solely with the King. His view of the function of Estates, national and provincial, was precisely similar to that of L'Hôpital and he insisted with equal emphasis on their value for good government. It is, he thinks, an excellent thing that the Sovereign must find it difficult to refuse demands presented by the Estates.[3] But he will not admit that there is any question of the King's right to do so. Even in asserting that the Sovereign cannot tax without consent of the Estates he formally denies to them any share in sovereignty.

As to the claims of the Pope, Bodin's language was that of the later Gallican writers and of the Politique party generally. On all questions connected with religion he shows caution and reserve. But it is clear that he recognized no claim of the Pope to arrest in any way the action of the Sovereign in France or interfere with the order of succession to the throne. The Salic Law was to him fundamental and he argued elaborately to prove its superiority to all other laws of succession.[4]

We are not here concerned with Bodin's specific proposals for reform in France. But his suggestions, when pieced together, make a striking picture. He had, it seems, a broken vision of the recon-

---

[1] ' Nec vero curiae superiores ullam habent legum rationem, nisi quas sua promulgatione comprobarint : nec se cogi posse aiunt.' *Meth.*, VI, p. 304. The view of the constitution of France expressed in the *Methodus* is much nearer Seyssel's than is that presented in the *Republic*.

[2] *Rep.*, IV, 4. [3] Ib., III, 7. [4] Ib., VI, 5.

structed France of a far future. In that dream of his the sovereignty of the King is more universally and profoundly recognized than ever it was under Louis XIV. The national government possesses a national standing army which at once gives France security and makes factious resistance to the Crown practically impossible. All waste and peculation have been eliminated more completely than ever Colbert succeeded in eliminating them. All forms of religious belief and worship are tolerated ; weights, measures and coinage have been unified and education is organized and controlled by the State, as under Napoleon I. It would seem also that hereditary office and juris-diction, class monopolies and exemptions, have at last disappeared. There are, it is true, what may be considered drawbacks. In that reformed France of Bodin's vision law will, perhaps, have revived the ancient power of the father in the family with merciless completeness. Alternatively, the State will have established the severest censorship of morals and of the Press and will have abolished the theatre altogether. It will certainly, too, pay particular attention to witchcraft. All these suggestions were made by Bodin more or less clearly, but to say that all this was ever at one time present to his mind would be saying far too much. From his scattered and hardly connected suggestions we can piece together a picture he never made himself.

§ 9. CONCLUSION

The temptation to end this chapter with some kind of summary should be resisted. It is, of course, possible to separate the essential structure of a complex system of thought from its mere details and accre-tions ; though in doing this there is serious danger of losing sight of the reality. But at least the thing presented must be a completely articulated skeleton or it will be quite worthless. Such a skeleton it is that I have tried to exhibit in this chapter which is, as written, probably only too summary. To isolate Bodin's theory of sovereignty or his theory of climate would be to present them in a form in which they did not exist in his mind. The result would be a mere distortion, representing the mind of the commentator rather than anything else.

But, a survey concluded, there remain always many things that may be and some that should be said on the elusive subject of Bodin's influence. The *Republic*, as has been seen, went through many editions in the sixteenth century and was translated into several languages. Alike in the sixteenth and in the seventeenth centuries it was not only widely read but seriously studied and commented upon. For more than a hundred years after its publication it must have been known to all serious students or thinkers on the subjects it deals with. In France its direct influence was greatest, I think, in the sixteenth century ; in England and elsewhere it was more potent in the seven-teenth. It must have made many and diverse suggestions to very many minds. In France it seems to have helped to determine the attitude of the Politique party and it furnished weapons of argument to the extreme royalists. The violence of the attacks made on ·it in France, especially by adherents of the League, by La Serre and Possevin, and by the author of the *De justa Reipublicae*, testify to a recognition of its importance. It was read and admired by Montaigne. In Italy Botero learned and took much from it. In the seventeenth century it was studied, apparently with profit, by Grotius and by Pufendorf, perhaps even by Spinoza. In the eighteenth century it passed, gradually, out of ken even of the learned : yet so late as 1756 there was published what purported to be a summary of the *Republic* and was actually a travesty of the first book.[1] A work so widely read must needs, one supposes, be influential. But it is always, save in special cases, impossible to disentangle such influence from the multitude of factors operating to produce opinion.

When Bodin is spoken of as making a contribution to political thought there seems, sometimes, to be an implication that this contribution was made to some body of truth concerning political society which is being slowly accumulated. The existence of that body of truth requires a demonstration at present rather evidently lacking. Similarly it has been said that Bodin's theory of sovereignty constituted an ' advance ' in thought. It may, I suppose, fairly be said that any way of conceiving political association that is at once coherent and in some degree new, constitutes an advance, wholly irrespective of its alleged truth or falsity. If this be not what is meant, the advance must presumably be towards something : and this something requires definition. But it may be that what is referred to as contribution is not the actual thought of the contributor, but suggestions his writings happened to convey to other minds. What a writer suggests may be something merely incidental and unimportant in the thought system of the writer, or even something that is not there at all.

Bodin's fate was that of all great thinkers : men took from him the suggestions they needed and ignored the rest. It was so with him even in an exaggerated degree, because of the incoherencies and confusions of his thought. Few ever try to master the complexes of another's thought ; to do so serves no practical purpose, unless of exposition or of refutation. So far as I can ascertain, Bodin made no converts to his system either in France or elsewhere. The writers he informed did not need to understand him. De Belloy and Barclay took from him the suggestion of the need, practical and logical, of a sovereignty absolute and unlimited, consisting essentially in a power to make law. They use almost his very phrases. But the conception thus isolated was not Bodin's. Doubtless Bodin's influence streng-

---

[1] *De la république, traité de Jean Bodin.* Paris, 1756. Attributed to Lescalopier de Nourar.

thened the dominant tendency in France towards the construction
of a system of absolute monarchy, ideally and in fact. This, it may
be said, is what he wished to do. There is just a doubt; but I think
it is true that he wished to see established in France something that
we may call absolute monarchy. But we are not concerned here
with Bodin's influence upon practical politics. He did something
to convince France of its need of absolute monarchy : the Huguenot
party did much more. But we are concerned to insist that Bodin's
absolute monarchy is very unlike Barclay's ; and that had it ever
been translated into act it would have been very unlike that of
Louis XIV.

In the seventeenth century Filmer made much use of Bodin and
perhaps learned something from him. But Filmer's view was completely unlike that of Bodin. Bodin probably assisted Hobbes to
reach conclusions totally irreconcilable with his own. Of all later
systems that of Montesquieu is perhaps nearest to Bodin's ; but the
amount of absolute connection between the mind of Montesquieu
and the writings of Bodin remains doubtful. Of sixteenth-century
writers the one whose views correspond most closely to those of Bodin
seems to me to be Louis Le Roy. He seems to have been about the
only writer of that century outside Italy to make anything of Bodin's
theory of climate.[1] But except in this respect he was hardly a disciple : he was rather, in a small way, a precursor. To a considerable
extent the arguments and the suggestions of the *Republic* became
commonplaces in the seventeenth century ; but this of itself proves
nothing. Bodin's thought, filtered through countless minds, flowed
in many channels through the seventeenth century, disintegrated,
distorted and finally lost in the process.

In modern times Bodin has been very variously interpreted.
Some have seen in him an asserter of the sovereignty of the people
and some a champion of monarchic absolutism. He was the latter
rather than the former ; but he was not exactly either. He conceived
of unlimited sovereignty ; but he did not think it should exist. He
has been praised for recommending this or that reform, and censured
for refusing to allow of any right of rebellion. Praise and blame alike
appear to me simply superfluous. No light is thrown on Bodin by
our censures or our commendations ; nothing is revealed except,
perhaps, our own opinions. Bodin's claim to special honour rests
primarily on the fact that he, almost alone among sixteenth-century
thinkers, made an honest effort to construct a comprehensive theory
of political society. All that we are rationally entitled to demand
of such a system of thought as his, is that it should be coherent and
intelligible and that it should not ignore or distort indisputable facts.

[1] See especially the section headed : ' De la variété des choses selon la difference des lieux ' in the first book of his treatise *De la Vicissitude*, 1579.

To demand that it should be in some sense ' true ' is, I fear, to make our own opinions the measure of its value. In such a connection there is nothing more presumptuous than praise, except condemnation. I have endeavoured to represent Bodin's thought as substantially coherent. He himself has made it difficult to do this : it must indeed be admitted that it is ultimately impossible. Reluctant as one should be to confess to finding incoherency in the thought system of so powerful and earnest a thinker, one is forced finally to the conclusion that in the structure of that system there exist not only confusions but incompatibilities. Repetition would be worse than useless ; but it remains to point out that much of Bodin's confusion and all his important inconsistencies connect with a radical flaw in the foundations of his great construction. That flaw consists, I think, in his failure definitely to connect his theory of sovereignty with his conception of the ends of the State and in his failure to adjust both to his own theory of climate. He has not accounted for the existence of what he calls sovereignty : he has not explained how it is that groups of families coalesce into a State by the recognition of it. He does not even say that sovereignty is created by recognition. He connects it definitely only with the conception of law as command. Even if his legal sovereignty be created by recognition, what recognition is it that precedes this one ? Bodin saw sovereignty as limited by a law of conscience and by the structure of society : is recognition of all this involved in the act that creates sovereignty ? In what sense is sovereignty the power of a State as distinguished from the power of a legal Sovereign ? How is it that domain belongs to the Republic and not to the Sovereign ? How is it that ' leges imperii ' come into existence ? Whence, after all, is the obligation to obey political authority derived ? For all his pains Bodin has answered the question so obscurely and so indirectly that we are not sure he has answered it at all. Vaguely we apprehend that sovereignty is somehow inherent in human association and that obligation to obey is derived from recognized ends. There is confusion and ambiguity at the starting-point. Bodin's theory of the State is a grand edifice in the very latest Gothic, built up on disjointed and rotten foundations. In consequence it tended from the first to disintegrate, crumble into ruin and disappear. But, after all, to say this is to say little. Omitting the word ' grand ', and the reference to Gothic, may not the same be said of all similar structures ?

PART IV

ITALY

CHAPTER I

PRELIMINARY

WHEN Charles VIII of France and his nobles and his men-at-arms entered Italy in 1494, they entered what was to them a world strange and new. Florence must have been a revelation to them. We know with what wonder and delight they beheld, there and elsewhere, the gardens and the palaces, the churches, and statuary of the day, and the vestiges of a remote antiquity. Hardly had they returned home before gardens in the Italian manner were being laid out at Amboise. In Florence they saw Brunelleschi's dome and the palaces of Michelozzi and Alberti and those gates of Ghiberti that Machiavelli described as worthy to be the gates of Heaven. They had finer things at home, palaces at least as superb and incomparable churches, but nothing that resembled these things. Still less had they at home anything like Ghirlandajo's frescoes or the altar-pieces of Botticelli or the sculpture of Donatello. It was a stranger world that they had entered than they at all realized. They saw pride of life, sumptuousness and luxury, they saw symmetry and completeness, a strange system of decoration, glowing colour and movement, new artistic effects produced by a technique that to them was new ; and they saw, perhaps, little more. Behind all that was a mental world unknown to them or but barely suspected ; a world of neo-paganism and of Neoplatonism, a world of scepticism and materialism, of mockeries more audacious than those they knew of and of enthusiasms to them still stranger. They had stepped into the flood-tide of the Renaissance and did not know where they were. All about them in that Italy of Laurentius Valla and Leonardo, of Luigi Pulci and Aretino, of Michelangelo and Marsilio Ficino, of the Sforza and the Malatesta, the traditional and conventional Christianity they knew of, lay in a ruin almost as complete as that of the monuments of old Rome. Theology had vanished from Italian universities ; law, medicine, the classics and a philosophy that owed nothing to the schoolmen, reigned in its stead. They had come into a world which put images of pagan poets and demi-gods on its churches and prized the bones of Livy above all the bones of the saints. It was a world of which the hero was the successful adventurer in art or in arms, in study or in politics. It was a world in which the purest devotion to art or to truth lived alongside the most brutal pursuit of wealth, pleasure and power ; a world in which refined æstheticism and love of learning was often wedded to an extreme of moral dullness.

Politically, too, Italy was unlike any other part of Europe. It was, for the most part, dominated by cities and by princely adventurers and mercantile princes. The numerous States into which it was divided were not only small in extent but extremely unstable. Hardly one of them can be said to have possessed any sort of solid basis, moral or material. Venice stood firm almost alone. Milan's effort to unite the Lombard plain had ended in failure ; Florence had never yet succeeded in really mastering the Tuscan country. Everywhere existed governments without supporting tradition or recognized moral authority. The military weakness of those governments was such as to leave all Italy an easy prey to the spoiler. It was with an odd mixture of arrogant brutality and contempt and ignorant wonder and admiration, that the French and Spaniards took possession of a world they did not understand.

Any political thought produced in this Italy was likely to be completely dissociated with any kind of Christianity and completely detached from the thought of medieval schoolmen. The Protestant Reformation had yet to come ; but Italy had already gone beyond. It is true that great changes were soon coming. Foreign domination was soon to be fastened on the country and with it came the almost complete extinction of Italy's republican traditions. The great Catholic revival of which Savonarola may be regarded as a crazy forerunner, was to give new directions to Italian thought. But however much the quality of Italian political thought was changed in the course of the sixteenth century it remained throughout remote from that of the rest of Europe. Italian thinkers, to the end of the century, concerned themselves little, or not at all, with the questions that disturbed men elsewhere.

CHAPTER II

MACHIAVELLI

§ 1. INTRODUCTORY

IN the porch of the sixteenth century stands the enigmatic figure of Niccolo Machiavelli, a figure that, for centuries to come, was sinister and a rock of offence. No writer, probably, has been so persistently used and abused or so little understood. From beginning to end of the sixteenth century rolled over him a chorus of denunciation, which continued through the seventeenth and eighteenth centuries. Echoes of it are heard even now. He found, it is true, defenders ; but for the most part these seem to have understood him as little as those who condemned. The misunderstanding of him was due partly to sheer ignorance of his writings. Few or none of those who, in the sixteenth century, denounced him, had read his works or had read any of them but the misleading *Principe*.[1] It was due, also, to ignorance of the conditions under which he wrote and to the fact that those conditions passed so rapidly away that, even in Italy, only a few years after his death, his writings, once so topical, had lost their bearing. But the failure to understand was due perhaps yet more to the man's own intellectual attitude and mode of dealing with things. For indeed that attitude of his was a challenge to sixteenth-century thought as a whole. What he implied shocked the men of his time outside Italy even more, perhaps, than what he said. People felt that he was, in their language, an atheist ; and that his method of approach to every sort of question and his whole system of values, involved a negation of all their assumptions and a denial of the validity of their way of thinking.

Niccolo Machiavelli was born in Florence in 1469, the year of the accession to power in the city of Lorenzo the Magnificent and the year of the marriage of Ferdinand of Aragon with Isabella of Castile. His family was of Tuscan nobility, not wealthy, but possessed of a competence. He seems to have held no office under the Medici,

---

[1] Osorio knew next to nothing : De Nobilitate Christiano (1552). Possevino (1592) and Ribadeneya (1595) appear to have known nothing at all. Gentillet's *Antimachiavel* (1576) is little better informed.

but on their temporary eclipse in 1494, he entered the service of the Republic. Rising rapidly in that service he became, in 1498, Secretary to the Council of the Ten which managed the foreign relations and the wars of Florence. This important position he held till 1512 ; and as a friend and intimate counsellor of Piero Soderini, his importance increased. During these years, while the crazily constituted Republic, torn by faction and beset by enemies, was drifting helplessly to ruin, Machiavelli was entrusted with a series of missions, diplomatic, administrative, even military. He saw much of administration, much of diplomacy, something of war, something of Germany and a good deal too much for his liking of France and the French.

Through all these years down to 1512, when his literary career commenced, Machiavelli's energies were evidently completely absorbed in business of State. He obtained a wide experience of political affairs and of how things were done administratively and diplomatically. He was not very highly educated in a wide sense. His serious training was that of the practical politician and man of affairs ; and a politician he remained to the end of his days, in office or out of office. His experience went far to determine his views about politics, but it did not and could not make of him a political philosopher.

It is likely that Machiavelli would never have written anything but despatches, reports and letters, but for the disaster that overwhelmed his political career on the restoration of the Medici in 1512. It was a fortunate accident that drove him to literature, though it did not seem so to him. Expelled from Florence, an exile and a politician out of place, he seems to have suffered for the rest of his life from a sense of wasted powers and lost opportunity. There can be little doubt that, throughout his political writings, he was animated by the hope of attracting such attention as would lead to his being again employed, at Florence or at Rome. The *Principe* was avowedly written in the hope that it would win for him the patronage of the Medici. A similar aim would seem to have been present in the composition of the *Discorsi*, of the *Art of War* and of the *Florentine History* which he dedicated to Pope Clement VII. Both the *Discourses* upon Livy and the *Principe* were commenced in 1513 and the latter was completed within that year. The *Art of War* was written in 1519–1520, and the *Florentine History* after 1522.[1]

It would, however, be very foolish to suppose that Machiavelli wrote merely to attract attention and obtain a post for himself. His desire to be employed politically must have been largely due to his sense of power and understanding and his conviction that, as adviser to some powerful Prince, he might forward the realiza-

[1] The *Libro della arte della guerra* was published in 1521, the *Istorie Fiorentine* in 1532. The *Discorsi sopra la Prima Deca de T. Livio* was not published till 1531 ; the *Principe* only in 1532. Machiavelli died in 1526.

tion of his dream of a free Italy. The same reasons and motives that made him desire a post made him write the *Discorsi* and the *Principe*. For even Machiavelli could not escape the idealism that besets us all. He desired above all things to find remedy for the chaotic confusion and distress of Italy, so great already in achievement, so immense in promise, and yet so helpless, so torn and disordered, so trampled on and oppressed by foreign ' Barbarians '. He desired to see his Florence once again free and glorious ; and glorious at least if she could not be free. He dreamed of seeing her take the lead in a liberation of Italy from the foreigner. He must have desired, even if he did not actually hope, to see Italy united politically.

When, in 1512, he was driven into exile, the form of his thought and the nature of his hopes must already have been fixed. That his practical experience before that year goes far to account for his judgement of human nature, for his intense preoccupation with war and the foundations of military strength, for his hatred of the foreigners who were making a prey and a battlefield of Italy, is sufficiently manifest. He had evidently been profoundly impressed by what he had seen during the discharge of his mission to Cæsar Borgia. Here was a man, who in a region that had been a chaos of tyranny and brigandage, was establishing order and security by the most ruthless methods, by accurate judgement and unfailing energy, by daring, treachery and murder. It was clear that only by such methods could he have succeeded. Scruples or hesitations or any failure of will would have ruined the work. Probably, too, his experience in France had given him the idea of a monarchy radically distinct in kind from the principalities of Italy. His experience during the war with Pisa had helped him to grasp the nature of military power and to see clearly the ruinous weakness of Italian military methods. Now, in his enforced retirement, he had leisure to think things out and to diagnose thoroughly the disease from which Italy suffered. He set himself to do so. He set himself, therefore, to find out what are the causes of the greatness and decline of States, what are the factors of political success, how a State may attain stability and, above all, what is needed in Italy to secure the expulsion of the barbarians.

Of Machiavelli's writings, by far the most important, for our present purpose, is the *Discorsi*. In this alone did he reveal his whole mind on the subject of the State and its life. The *Art of War* is but an expansion of one of its favourite themes. The *Florentine History* does little but confirm and illustrate the impression one derives from it. Least revealing of all is the *Principe*, a *livre de circonstance* that was only partially sincere. The fact that Machiavelli was known in the sixteenth century mainly through the *Principe* in no way affects this judgement. The fact, however, goes far to account for the gross misunderstanding of his mind that was general throughout the century.

Anyone who wishes to understand the political thought of Machiavelli must go first of all to the *Discorsi*. Yet, regarded as an exposition of political theory, the book is exceedingly unsatisfactory. It has, on the face of it, a rough plan. The first book was apparently designed to deal with the constitution of States and the factors that conduce to vigour, to public spirit, stability and expansion and to liberty or its contrary. The second book deals mainly with the methods of expanding dominion and hence contains a great deal about military matters. The third book was apparently planned to deal with the ·causes of revolution and of ruin and how these may be avoided. But this rough plan is so roughly adhered to that, looked at closely, the book appears as a disorderly medley of reflections on various, slightly connected, subjects. Often there is no apparent connection between the subject of a chapter and that of those preceding and following it. Often a chapter is unconnected with what appears to be the subject of the ' book ' it stands in.[1] Reflections on war are scattered about in the second and third books, as though, as new points occurred to the writer, they were set down at once without reference to what preceded or followed. Insertions made, almost at random, after the first draft of the book was completed, might account for much of this patchwork.[2]

Superficially considered, the *Discorsi* can hardly be said to have a subject. Nowhere is the purpose of the book definitely stated nor any effort made to show clearly the connection between the numerous topics discussed. But the matters discussed were those that Machiavelli regarded as practically the most important for Italians at the moment to consider. Almost all of them actually bear, directly or indirectly and in some degree, upon the question of what constitutes strength and weakness for States in peace and war, of what conduces to stability, and to dominance and what to disorder and ruin. Whether he is writing of the quality of man's will, or of the factors that make for success in war, or of the superiority of popular as against princely government, or of the relation between morals and political action, his topics are all intimately connected, however disjointed his chapters. Only occasionally did he slip into what looks like pure digression, as in the famous chapter in which he gave such excellent advice to

---

[1] In Book I, Chap. 19 is sandwiched between reflections on the Decemvirs ·and has no direct connection with the subject of the ' book '. Similarly there is no connection between I, 41, and I, 42 and 44. In Book III there is hardly any connection between the chapters from 21 to Chap. 49, where the book ends with absolute abruptness.

[2] Book I seems to have been written in 1513 and Book III to have been finished by 1516. But an event of 1521 is referred to in Book II. It is possible that the *Discorsi* was never really finished.

conspirators.[1] Yet even this was no mere digression. Always, whatever might be the subject under discussion, even if it were artillery, or the Decemvirs, Machiavelli was thinking of his own Italy. Conspiracy was not only a common feature of Italian politics ; it might well be the only means of restoring freedom to a city. Had Machiavelli frankly taken as his subject existing conditions in Italy and his own views and hopes in connection with them, we should have had a more coherent statement than actually we find. But he intended, apparently, to give his book a wider bearing.

§ 2. THE PREMISES

In his preface to the *Discorsi* Machiavelli announced that he had resolved to start upon a road hitherto untravelled by anyone.[2] What was it that he thought of himself as doing for the first time ? We hold antiquity, he says, in great reverence ; we study the law and the medicine of the ancients and their works of art ; and yet no one goes to them for instruction in the arts of government and war. This is not due so much to our wretched education or to our apathy about things political, as to our failure to understand what we read in history and to see its practical value. Not Athens but Rome was, to Machiavelli, the eminently successful State of antiquity. The experience of the Romans could not but be rich in suggestion, alike as to the causes of success and of failure. We must study Roman history and see what profit can be made of it for our own use. So he called his book *Discourses upon Livy*. Actually there is not very much of Livy in it, and it seems clear that it was from Italy and not from Livy or Polybius, Plutarch or Cicero, Aristotle or Xenophon, that Machiavelli derived his main conceptions and conclusions.

But his own explanation of his image was inadequate. The road he was taking was, at least for the world outside Italy, even stranger than he seems to have thought it. He insisted upon the need of studying history because, for him, the experience of himself and of others, past or present, was the only guide. He was proposing to concern himself only with things as they actually are. He was not troubled by any doubts as to what that may mean. Man is the very stuff of politics and man's nature may be judged of by his conduct. In thinking of the State he would think only of actual States, past or present. For a thousand years and more men had been thinking of politics theologically and juristically. Machiavelli will do neither. ' He takes the data of his own experience and checks the conclusions which he learns from them by reference to certain canons derived

---

[1] *Discorsi*, III, 6.

[2] ' Ho deliberato entrare per una via, la quale non essendo stato per ancora da alcuno pesta.'

from a study of history.'[1] That, in fact, is all he does. From knowledge of man as he is and always has been, from knowledge of the constitution of States as they are and have been, of their modes of action and good or evil fortunes, one can draw conclusions, valid and positive, as to the causes of political success and failure, as to the greatness and decline of States, as to the most efficient form of government, as to what makes for stability and what for disorder and ruin. What we need is positive knowledge of these things and this can only be arrived at by looking at things as they are, without fear or preconceptions. This is the only road to whatever we desire to attain. This is the new road of Machiavelli ; and certainly it had not been trodden for a long time, except by Italians. In Italy it did not seem strange. Machiavelli's ' realistic ' mode of thought was only an extreme illustration of a tendency visible in Italian thought since the days of the last Hohenstaufen Emperor.

Machiavelli was not a systematic thinker. He was a man of extremely acute perceptions and capable of subtle and searching analysis of the concrete. Failure to co-ordinate his observations is conspicuous throughout the *Discorsi* and the *Principe* and shows itself in the confusion of their structure. He seems to have paid little or no attention to the implications of what he said. Consequently, in spite of his lucidity of statement, he falls easily into inconsistency. The elusive quality of his writing, which accounts for a good deal of the disagreement about him, arises, I think, from the fact that, in spite of the sharpness of his vision of the actual, his thought was at bottom confused.

Fundamental in his thought would seem to be his notion of the origin and purport of the sense of good and evil in action and his conception of the quality of man's will. The two are intimately connected, in the sense that the latter is unintelligible till the former is understood. At some early stage of human history, he informs us, men, considering that the injuries they saw done to others might be done to themselves, protected themselves by the establishment of laws, with penalties for their infringement, and hence arose the recognition of justice.[2] From this establishment of government and legal justice ' was born the knowledge of what things are good and honourable in distinction to those that are evil and shameful '.[3] Generalized notions of right and wrong, in fact, developed from the

---

[1] L. A. Burd's great edition of the *Principe*, p. 172, note. My references are all to this edition.

[2] ' E pensando ancora che quelle medesime inguire potevano esser fatte a loro ; per fuggire simile male si riducivano a fare legge, ordinare punizioni a chi contrafacesse ; donde venne la cognizione della guistiza.' *Discorsi*, I, 2.

[3] ' Da questa nacque la cognizione delle cose oneste e buone, differenti dalle perniciose e ree.' Ib. But see the whole important passage.

effort to repress forms of activity, recognized as dangerous to himself by every individual. In course of time, it is true, men came to think of certain kinds of action as good or evil absolutely. But this, it is implied, is a delusion, due either to confusion of mind or to religious superstition. There is no absolute good. Goodness is simply that which subserves, on the average or in the long run, the interests of the mass of individuals. The terms good and evil have no transcendental reference; they refer to the community, considered as an association of individuals, and to nothing else. At bottom, apparently, they refer only to the universal desire for security. Such a view involves, of course, an absolute denial of the validity of the conception of natural law. For Machiavelli there was no *lex aeterna* and therefore no *lex naturalis*. He never even thought it worth while to refer to that conception. There was nothing new, it must be remarked, in his way of putting the matter. It was at least as old as the *Defensor Pacis*. Yet Machiavelli himself does not seem to have had a clear grasp of the implications of his own doctrine or even always to remember what he had said. From this primary assertion of his, his view of morals in politics can be derived quite simply. But that he himself understood it so, is by no means clear. As I hope to show, in discussing his political ethics, his language is not wholly consistent with that interpretation of his meaning.

If we take Machiavelli to mean that ' goodness ' in action signifies simply a tendency to promote the general welfare of the community, then we can give definite meaning to his oft-repeated assertion that men are radically bad. It is proved, he says, to demonstration, and all history confirms it, that in ordering a State, this must always be assumed.[1] Men will always show themselves wicked unless they are compelled to goodness.[2] The ligament of obligation is a thing which, men being the poor creatures they are, is broken upon every occasion for their own personal profit.[3] He means, apparently, that every man is always ready to act in a manner detrimental to the community if he sees any advantage to himself from doing 'so. Good is that which, in my own interest, I wish my neighbour to do; but my neighbour and I, in our own interest, are always ready to do evil. It would be difficult to give any other meaning than this to Machiavelli's declaration that all men are wicked. Man's will must be conceived as, at bottom, anti-social and anarchical: and it is this fact that constitutes the central problem of politics and the difficulty of actual government.

---

[1] *Discorsi*, I, 3. *Opere*, III, pp. 19, 20 (1813).
[2] *Principe*, Chap. 23.
[3] ' Perchè l'amore è tenuto da un vinculo di obbligo, il quale, per essere gli uomini tristi, da ogni occasione di propria utilità è sotto.' *Principe*, Chap. 17, p. 293.

Yet it cannot be said that Machiavelli held this view without qualifications ; which, indeed, he himself supplies. Evidently he did not think that man's will was wholly anarchical. Man, he thought, cares for nothing but himself ; he is a rascally, mean, greedy, sensual creature, more ready to forgive the murder of his father than the seizure of his property : gratitude for him is but the hope of benefits to come and what he calls his love is but love of himself.[1] But the selfish will is a will to order and security and all men, therefore, may see the general interest as their own. Man wills government and the State for his own profit and protection. He is, furthermore, a timid creature and a creature of habit. He dislikes what he is not used to and seeks the lines of least resistance. He tends to follow well-beaten tracks. It is a fact of great importance, practically, that it is generally easier and safer to conform than to rebel.

Too much stress has sometimes been laid upon Machiavelli's insistence on the predominance of the purely selfish will in man. He knew, even, that there were men, though certainly few, capable of labouring for the common benefit without regard to their personal interests. He even claimed to be one of them himself.[2] But what is, in this connection, of the greatest importance, is the fact that man's capacity for developing public spirit to a point at which mere personal interests are wholly subordinated, is implied everywhere in the *Discorsi*. It was on just such a development that, in Machiavelli's view, the stability and the strength of the State depended. It is his own fault that he has been misread. So convinced was he that the ferocious egotism and egregious lack of public spirit prevalent in his Italy, was the main general cause of the land's weakness and disorder, that he was led to lay disproportionate stress on the selfishness of man. None the less is it true that he actually measures the strength of a State mainly by the amount of public spirit developed within it. It was, he thought, just such a development that had constituted the strength and accounted for the success of the great Roman Republic. There is, as usual in the *Discorsi*, a failure to state the matter fully ; but there is, I think, no real inconsistency. Public spirit may be developed in a community and so long as it lasts, and in the measure of it, a State is likely to be strong and flourishing. On the other hand, he insists that it is unlikely to last long. Everything tends to corruption : nothing lasts except the radical selfishness of man.

That was in the beginning and shall be as long as man lasts. It is a supposition of the greatest importance in Machiavelli's thought that the quality of man's will never changes. It remains constant through all time ; it is, in fact, unalterable. It is true, Machiavelli admits, that in different parts of the world, the character of men to

---

[1] *Principe*, Chap. 17, p. 247.
[2] See Preface, I, (i). 'Spinto da quel naturale desiderio,' etc.

some extent differs. But he adds that men of the same region retain through all ages almost the same character.[1] It is mainly upon this supposition that he bases his opinion of the practical value of history in teaching by examples. Owing to the constant character of humanity man's history tends constantly to repeat itself, with mere circumstantial differences.

'The judicious are wont to say that he who would foresee what is to happen should look to what has happened : for all that is has its counterpart in time past. This is so because all happenings are brought about by the will of man, whose desires and dispositions remaining in all ages the same, it follows that like results are produced continually.'[2]

Not only does human history tend to repeat itself but all States tend to move as it were on a circular track. The suggestion of this cycle would seem to have come from Polybius, but to Machiavelli it appeared that it must actually be a fact. He conceived it as resulting from the unchanging nature of man and from the special quality of his will acting under changing conditions. Action and reaction alternate and out of prosperity comes decay and out of dissolution rebirth. Every human institution, like every individual, has inherent defects which must eventually destroy it. But new growth follows.[3] States normally commence as monarchies ; but monarchy becomes tyrannical and is overthrown by a combination of magnates, who form an oligarchy. All goes well so long as the oligarchs are animated by public spirit. But degeneration follows inevitably. The oligarchs in their turn are overthrown and a popular government is established. Then liberty passes into license and so into anarchy ; and the result of anarchy is a reversion to monarchy and the dreary round recommences. Machiavelli points out that the cycle is only rarely actually completed. At one of its moments of greatest weakness the State will probably be destroyed or conquered by aliens. Assuming this not to happen, it might hopelessly continue to infinity to turn on its circular course.[4] In any case, men remaining always the same poor creatures, no real progress is possible.

The finally inevitable ruin that awaits all States seems to be conceived by Machiavelli as partly the result of another peculiarity of human nature. The appetite of man is for ever insatiable. By nature he desires all things, but fate allows him little. Man is eternally desirous and eternally unsatisfied, raging at the present, extolling the past, hoping in the future.[5] No human community,

---

[1] 'Che gli uomini che nascono in uno provincia, osservano per tutti i tempi quasi quella medesima natura.' *Discorsi*, III, 43. Heading of chapter.
[2] *Discorsi*, III, 43.
[3] See *Florentine History*, Book V, opening passage.
[4] *Discorsi*, I, 2.   [5] Ib., II, Preface. *Op.*, pp. 178, 179.

no human government, any more than any single human being, is ever content with its position. Hence arises a constant effort after aggrandisement and domination which leads, sooner or later, to ruin. But this ruinous effort in unavoidable. It results partly from man's everlasting discontent and partly from the fact that conflict and war are necessary to the health of the body politic. War and fear are what give the State such vital unity as it has and counteract the anarchic tendency which is rooted in the nature of man's will. Peace is relaxing and disruptive : ' Damn braces, bless relaxes.' Under these circumstances, equilibrium is impossible, all human affairs being in perpetual motion and never remaining for an instant as they were. The movement of the State must needs be upward or downward.[1] Hence, though the better its laws and the more intelligent its ruler, the more stable will be the State, there is yet no possible escape from ultimate ruin.

§ 3. DISCORSI

In reading Machiavelli with intent to grasp his thought as a whole, we have constantly to make correlations that he did not distinctly make, to take note of implications about which he is silent and to give some degree of definition to what he has left indefinite. The result must, to some extent at least, be to give his thought a fullness and coherency which his writings afford no solid ground for supposing that it possessed. The whole process is fallacious and, if we adopt it, it is only by the greatest care that we can hope to avoid gross misrepresentation. What we actually find in the *Discorsi* is a large number of observations and reflections on many different topics of which the connection is not made clear. Yet there is no doubt that to Machiavelli all these topics and all these reflections, converged to what he regarded as a practical issue. We are bound to look for a unity which, however loosely articulated, must have been there. We cannot know for certain how much of what he left unexpressed was actually in his mind, but it is certain that he left much unexpressed. Machiavelli came to the consideration of the Italian States and policies of his own day with preconceptions derived partly from his own observation and experience and partly from his readings among classical authors. How much exactly they meant to him is doubtful. The consciousness of man's natural wickedness was indeed with him always. The unchangingness of man's nature was, in his eyes, important, because it afforded ground for the belief that it was possible to argue simply from the past to the present. He conceived morality as strictly utilitarian and as having an extremely restricted reference. But that conception he had not worked out. The fundamental question involved did not interest him : to him secondary questions

[1] *Discorsi*, I, 6.

and conclusions of some immediate practical bearing were vastly more important.

It is a little difficult to say what is the main subject of the *Discorsi*. But the mass of the miscellaneous reflections that make up the book seem to bear directly or indirectly on the question of what constitutes political strength and stability. It was because this was to him the main question to be considered that he turned to Roman History. For in the State of old Rome he saw the strongest and most stable of all States that had ever existed. His reflections on what he calls religion and on what he calls liberty, on the need of native armies, on the importance of strict and impartial administration of law and the maintenance of security for life and property, and on the importance of a large population, all bear directly on the question. So also do his reflections on the danger and difficulty attendant on the introduction of changes in law or in institutions, on the danger of arbitrary and tyrannical action or on the folly of trusting for defence to money or to fortresses. The question seems to have been in his mind throughout.

But just as the question is not distinctly stated, so no distinct answer is given. The stability of a State, its power for offence or defence, its power to repress faction and maintain security, depended, Machiavelli was well aware, on many unstable factors. Such as occur to him he discusses as they occur. But there seems to be one factor on which, directly or by implication, he lays stress constantly. More than on anything else, he seems to think the strength of a State for all purposes depends on the amount of public spirit it generates. He connects public spirit with religion and with ' liberty ' and, more definitely, with military strength. His insistence on the importance of administration without fear or favour, on adherence to law and on caution in making changes, on the necessity of securing and of respecting life and property, seems to arise from his perception that in these ways public spirit is fostered. Lack of public spirit appears to be the chief symptom of what he calls corruption. His virtù is indeed a highly inclusive term. It denotes energy, hardihood, boldness, unflinching will, even intelligence. Yet he seems sometimes to use the word as though it were almost equivalent to public spirit or patriotism ; and certainly to him that was an ingredient in the highest virtue.

But how is any degree of public spirit to be developed in a community composed of people who care nothing at all for public welfare apart from their own ? The answer, of course, is, first of all, that public welfare is not and cannot be apart from their own. They are all concerned in it. Recognition of this fact is involved in all co-operation. Yet the two things do not exactly coincide and where they do not, man is normally always ready to sacrifice the common good to his own. All the same, it is a fact that, under appropriate conditions, even a high degree of public spirit may exist, even such a degree as will lead to men being ready to give up their lives for their country. How does this happen and under what conditions? Machiavelli's answer to this question seems to be that there are two main factors concerned. The one he calls religion and the other he calls liberty.

It may seem strange that Machiavelli should have insisted strongly on the social and political value of religion, but in fact, even in the sixteenth century, few writers or none insisted on this more strongly. This insistence of his was quite unconnected with any sort of religiousness or interest in religion, as such, in himself. He was interested in religion only as a factor in society, he does not seem to have any conception of it as a mode of philosophy or as a mode of being. But as to its political importance his language is emphatic. 'As the observance of divine worship,' he says, ' is the cause of the greatness of a State, so the contempt of it is the cause of its ruin. For where the fear of God is wanting, either the State must needs be ruined or it must be maintained by the fear of some Prince, supplying the defect.' [1] But, he goes on to remark, the fear of a Prince is but a poor substitute for the fear of God and the State that is so sustained will not last long. Wherefore every State, principality or republic, needs above all else to hold fast to its religion and maintain in veneration uncorrupted the ceremonial of its cult.[2]

Religion, Machiavelli explains, keeps good men in the right way and puts bad men to open shame. Its doctrine of rewards and punishments, in this world or another, appeals definitely to the selfishness of men and induces conduct beneficial to the State.[3] He states his conviction that the lack of patriotism in Italy and its political apathy are largely due to lack of religion. The destruction of religiousness in Italy, he thought, had been the work of the Pope and of the clergy. It is the peoples who have the misfortune to live nearest to the head and centre of Christendom who have most completely lost religion. It is to the Church and its priests, he declared, that we Italians owe it that we have become wicked and irreligious.[4] It seems odd that

---

[1] ' E come la ossevanza del culto Divino è cagione della grandezza delle reppubliche, cosi il dispregio di quella è cagione della rovina di esse. Perchè dove manca il timore di Dio, conviene che o quel regnorovini, o che sia sostenuto dal timore d'un principe, che supplisca a difetti della Religione.' *Discorsi*, I, 11. *Op.*, III, p. 51. [2] *Discorsi*, I, 12.

[3] Pietro Pomponazzi, in his *De Immortalitate* of 1516, declared that the doctrine of reward and punishment in a future life had been patronized, if not actually invented, by rulers for governmental purposes, and that this fact accounts for the prevalence of belief in it. The same suggestion had been made, with an even wider reference, in the *Defensor Pacis* of 1324.

[4] *Discorsi*, I, 12.

it did not strike him that the irreligiousness of Popes and clergy might be due to the irreligiousness of Italy. But the contention is quite unimportant to his argument. Rulers, therefore, he concluded, should favour and augment everything that makes for belief in religion, even though they themselves believe it to be false : and all the more should they do so the wiser they are and the better acquainted with the facts of nature.[1] Machiavelli evidently considered it unlikely that rulers would themselves have any religious beliefs. He complains that it is taught by religious persons that princes must be simply obeyed and, if they act wickedly, must be left to the judgement of God. This, he remarks, merely encourages them in tyranny, since they have no fear of punishments which they neither see nor believe in.[2] He cites with approval several cases of fraudulent practising on popular superstition in the service of the State. Religion, it seems, was to him almost exactly equivalent to popular superstition.

But clearly not every religion, and clearly not the Papal religion, will serve the purpose. It is not by any means every form of popular superstition that is useful. Christianity glorifies men of humble disposition and contemplative rather than active life. It teaches men to return good for evil and calls upon them rather to endure than to do. Such teaching has enfeebled the world and left it a prey to the wicked.[3] Possible indeed it is, that had Christianity retained its original character, things might be very different from what they now are. But it has become something so much unlike what at first it was, that who so considers the foundations of the Church and its present condition might well believe, undoubtingly, that its ruin or its chastening is at hand.[4] What is needed is a religion after the fashion of old Rome : a religion that teaches that he who best serves the State best serves the gods.

The effectiveness of such a religion in producing that energetic service to the State which is so sorely needed, is manifest. It is not so obvious how what Machiavelli calls liberty also tends to generate public spirit. Yet it is clear enough that Machiavelli considered ' liberty ' as at once a symptom of public spirit and as tending to create it. Such difficulty as there is, arises from the difficulty of understanding what exactly he meant by liberty.

The ' liberty ' of which Machiavelli had so much to say is not easy

[1] ' E debbono tutte le cose che nascono in favore di quella, come che le giudicassero false, favorirle ed accrescerle ; e tanto piu, lo debbono fare, quanto piu prudenti sono, e quanto piu conoscitori delle cose naturali.' *Discorsi*, I, 12. *Op.*, III, p. 53.

[2] *Discorsi*, III, 1. *Op.*, III, p. 306.

[3] Ib., I, 12. So Guicciardini : ' Fu detto veramente che la troppa religione guasta il mondo, perche effeminina gli animi,' etc. *Ricordi Politici a Civili*, N. 254. *Opere Inedite*, 1857.

[4] Ib., *Op.*, III, p. 54.

to define from his own language about it. But it is certainly a complex. It seems to consist essentially not in any form or mode of government, but in security for life, honour and property under law.[1] He speaks of the benefits that all share under a ' free ' government, which consist ' in being able freely to enjoy without anxiety what is our own, without misgiving for the honour of our women and children or fear for oneself '.[2] In free countries men know that their children may rise to the highest positions. Such security, he remarks, tends to produce increasing wealth and a high birth-rate. But such benefits may be enjoyed as well under a monarchy as under ' free ' or republican government; and of this fact Machiavelli was aware. He wrote admiringly of the constitution of France, where the King is so bound by law and custom that his people enjoy perfect security.[3]

Such a monarchy, restrained by law and by general respect for law, is quite admirable and I see few signs that Machiavelli considered such a constitution inferior to that of a republic.[4] The antithesis to liberty, in his mind, was not monarchy simply, but such principality as existed in Italy; 'tyranny', which involved a power of purely arbitrary action and tended to identify law with the caprice of the Prince. Princes, he remarks, will always respect law, if they are wise, ' for men, when they are well governed, neither seek nor wish for any other liberty '.[5] There are, he says, a few men who desire a republic in order to obtain authority for themselves ; but the mass of men desire only to live securely. If the Prince provide for general security and enforce strictly and respect his own law, they will be well content.[6] The liberty that is an object of general desire is merely security under law.[7] When men find that they are well off, they ask no more.[8] ' It is but the name of liberty that men worship.'[9]

But there is a further freedom. Under the term liberty Machiavelli indubitably included a share in the direction of public affairs. Was it to him a question of degree ? Can we express his thought by saying that men may have as much liberty as they generally want without any voice in government, but that, with this, they have

---

[1] ' Men,' says Guicciardini, ' are not content with freedom and security but will not rest until they also govern.' Ricordi, 109. Op. Ined., 1857.
[2] ' La quale e di potere godere liberamente le cose sue senza alcuno sospetto, non dubitare dell'onore delle donne, di quel dei figliuoli, non temere di se.' Discorsi, I, 16. Op., III, p. 65.
[3] Discorsi, I, 16.
[4] But in I, 55 of the Discorsi he seems to suggest that it is a certain lack of public spirit in France that makes a republic there impossible.
[5] ' Perchè gli uomini, quando sono governati bene, non cercano nè vogliano altra liberta.' Discorsi, III, 5. Op., p. 314.
[6] Discorsi, I, 16.
[7] ' If one were certain,' says Guicciardini, ' that justice would be observed . . . there would be no need greatly to desire liberty.' Ricordi, 365.
[8] Principe, Chap. 27, p. 353.   [9] Florentine History, IV, I.

more ? The thought in his mind was, I think, rather that, whatever might be the case in France or elsewhere, in Italy even the liberty that is security was very unlikely to exist except under republican government. It will hardly exist under a Prince not exceptionally intelligent, and he remarks that of all the many Princes who have ever lived, few have been wise or good.[1]

When he declares that laws favourable to freedom in a republic, originate in conflict between the faction of the nobles and the faction of the populace,[2] he seems even to suggest that the more democratic the constitution the greater the liberty.

As to how liberty is connected with public spirit Machiavelli makes no explicit statement, though he quite evidently did connect the two things in the closest manner. Up to a certain point, indeed, the thought is clear enough. That liberty which is security under fixed law will endear the State to its citizens, because the State is giving them what they most of all want. The public spirit of its citizens will rest on the sure foundation of their own self-regard. But it is not so clear how possession of a share, necessarily for most people minute, in the management of public affairs, would conduce to the same result. Perhaps Machiavelli conceived this as creating a stimulating illusion : a sense that the acts of government are one's own or a hope that they some day will be. In any case, he seems to associate patriotism almost exclusively with republican liberty. It may exist under a Prince of exceptional ability ; but the case is too rare. On the other hand, in a republic it must exist, unless the State is on the point of collapse. A corrupt people, among whom there is no public spirit, cannot maintain liberty. For such a people there is no escape from servitude, their State can only be maintained at all ' by the fear of some Prince '. Such a people, unhappily, it seemed to Machiavelli that the Italians had become. Italy, he declared, is corrupt above all other countries.

In 1513 Italy was, and had for nearly twenty years been, oppressed by foreign domination and distracted by the wars of aliens within her borders. The entry of Charles VIII into Naples had heralded a struggle between France and Spain for dominance in the peninsula. In 1513 the Spaniards were at Naples, the Swiss in Lombardy and the French, in the background, were about to set on foot a new invasion. Machiavelli thought ill of princely government, but he hated far more the devastating and brutalizing foreigner. The immediate cause of this foreign oppression seemed to be the utter inadequacy of Italian military systems. The intensity of his desire to see the barbarians expelled from Italy caused him to give much thought to the question of what constitutes military strength. I think it may be said that he valued public spirit, above all because it seemed to him to be the

---

[1] *Discorsi*, I, 58.   [2] Ib., I, 4.

very essence of fighting power. The unreliability and general ineffi-
ciency of Italian mercenary armies had become glaringly obvious.
An effort to form a citizen army had begun at Florence in 1506 and
Machiavelli, though not, apparently, the originator of the scheme,
had been the chief agent. He became convinced, both from his own
experience and from that of the Romans of old, that the only good
army was an army drawn from the native soil. The use of mercenaries,
he declared, has brought Italy to servitude and derision.[1] In the
Discorsi, in the *Principe* and in the *Art of War* alike, he preaches
on this text continually. The *Art of War* is an essay on the methods
by which Italy may hope to deliver itself from the foreigner. Even
in the *Discorsi*, Machiavelli gave what might seem an altogether
disproportionate amount of space to the discussion of purely military
questions.[2]

Machiavelli's views upon problems of strategy and tactics, extraordinarily acute and interesting as they are, do not concern us here.
He did not miraculously foresee the enormous development of the
power of fire-arms that was coming and he seems to have underestimated
the effectiveness of even the artillery of his own time. Marignano might
have taught him a lesson on that point, but apparently did not. But
he grasped the essential principle of the necessity of the offensive,
though he seems hardly to have realized the difficulty of taking and
keeping it with such armies as actually existed. Equally striking
is his insistence that money is not the sinews of war. A Prince,
he declared, will always deceive himself as to his military strength
if he measure it in money.[3] He was convinced that the main strength
of an army must lie in its infantry and that fortresses were of little
use. For a Prince there is no fortress so strong as the affection of
his people. He did not deny that the possession of money was an
advantage. But he asserted that war is made not with gold but with
iron and that the sinews of war are good soldiers. He was quite
aware, also, that you do not make a good army merely by levying
troops within your own territory. If he had ever had any illusion
on that point, his experience at Florence would have destroyed it.
' Prince or Republic is much to be blamed if without an army
of its own.' [4] But the strength of an army consists essentially, Machiavelli maintained, in its attachment if not to the ' cause ', at least to
the State for which it fights. The reason why mercenary troops are
worthless is that they have no motive for fighting beyond their pay.
Public spirit and appropriate training are the things that constitute

---

[1] *Principe*, Chap. 12.
[2] Such questions occupy twelve chapters out of the forty-nine of Book III.
[3] *Discorsi*, II, 10.
[4] ' Quanto biasimo meriti quel principe e quella republica de manca d'armi
proprie.' *Discorsi*, I, 21. Chapter heading.

ιilitary power. In the *Art of War* he declared that all citizens, between ιhe ages of seventeen and forty, should be trained to arms.

In this way Machiavelli connects his hopes of the construction of native armies with his hopes of a revival of public spirit in Italy. Patriotism seemed to him to be alike the foundation of the internal order and stability of a State and of the fighting power of an army. He thought of a development of public spirit as leading naturally to the formation of such an army. A citizen army is a natural expression of patriotism.

The principal foundation of all States alike, he declared, are good laws and good arms ; and ' there cannot be good laws where there are not good arms and where there are good arms it follows that there are good laws '.[1] Good arms are the very own arms of the State and imply public spirit in its citizens and this in turn implies good laws. A State must have liberty, at least in some sense or degree, before it can have good arms. Sufficient liberty for the purpose may exist under a wise and popular Prince, who gives his subjects the liberty of security under law. It is far more likely, however, to exist in a republic. In any case, it is only men who have liberty and prize it, who make good soldiers.

There are people wholly unfit for liberty, for whom, indeed, liberty is impossible. But that the patriotic republic is the strongest and most stable of all possible States, Machiavelli asserted with emphasis. It is easy, he says, to see whence the love of liberty has sprung, since States have never increased in dominion or in wealth save while they lived in liberty.[2] In the *Principe* he advised the conqueror of a free city to destroy it utterly, since a people accustomed to freedom can never be reconciled to the loss of it.[3] Such States as are under popular government make rapidly great advances, far exceeding what is achieved under princes.[4] It is easy to see why the ancient world was so superior to ours, for then men lived in freedom and now in servitude.[5] The worst of the evils attendant on incapable government in a republic is a tendency to the establishment of tyranny ; while tyranny, if incapable, has at least the advantage that it may issue in freedom.[6] The arbitrary government of a Prince was, apparently, to Machiavelli the worst of all kinds of government. It is the

---

[1] *Principe*, Chap. 12. ' E perche non possono essere buone leggi dove non sano buone armi, e dove sono buone armi conviene che siano buone leggi,' etc. (p. 254).

[2] ' Perche si vede per esperienza le cittadi non aver mai amplicato, nè di dominio, nè di richezza, se non mentre sono state in liberta.' *Discorsi*, II, 2. *Op.*, p. 185.

[3] *Principe*, Chap. 5. Guicciardini was of opinion that the difficulty the Florentines found in extending their dominion over Tuscany, was due to the firm establishment of 'liberty' in the Tuscan cities. *Ricordi*, 353.

[4] *Discorsi*, I, 58.   [5] Ib., II, 2.   [6] Ib., I, 58. *Op.*, p. 170.

fitting government for a thoroughly corrupt people, but it is fit for nothing else. In the cycle in which States move it has inevitably its appointed place, and that place corresponds with the point of lowest degradation. Machiavelli argued elaborately and at length in the *Discorsi* to show that popular government is normally in most respects superior and in few inferior to that of a Prince. ' The mass is wiser and more constant than a prince,' [1] is the heading of his fifty-eighth chapter. It is true, he admits, that a people is fickle and inconstant, simply because that is what all men are. But this fickleness is greater, he declares, in the individual than it is in a multitude. It is true that Princes and People are alike ungrateful ; but Princes are the more so. A Prince will confer high office on infamous persons ; you will never persuade a People to do so. A Prince has rarely any respect for law ; a People loses respect for law only when utterly corrupt. The worst fault he finds in popular governments is that they are prone to rash courses, and more easily deceived than are Princes, by large hopes and brave promises. ' I affirm that a people is more prudent, more stable and of better judgement than a Prince. Not without reason is the voice of a people likened to the voice of God.' [2]

Throughout the sixteenth century Machiavelli was very generally regarded as a believer in the excellence of, and as a practical supporter of, the personal despotism of a Prince. This certainly erroneous notion was mainly due to the fact that the *Principe* was the only one of Machiavelli's writings that was then, and for long after, at all widely read. It is true that no one reading the *Principe*, or even the *Florentine History*, would suppose that Machiavelli was republican in sentiment and in theory, or that he regarded the arbitrary government of a Prince as the worst possible and as a mark of degeneracy in the people governed. But that he saw the State at its healthiest as a republic, the *Discorsi* makes quite clear. The *Principe* has to be interpreted by the light thrown by the *Discorsi*. The reverse process can lead to nothing but confusion. If we assume that, in the *Discorsi*, Machiavelli expressed, however fragmentarily, his real views, we can understand the *Principe* and see it as, at bottom, consistent with those views. If, on the other hand, we assume that certain apparent implications of the *Principe* represent Machiavelli's real opinions, then the *Discorsi* becomes unintelligible. It has been suggested that Machiavelli, radically and hopelessly insincere, was ready to argue on behalf of any views and that it is, in consequence, impossible to say

---

[1] ' La moltitudine è più savia e piu costante che un principe.' *Discorsi*, I, 58.

[2] ' Ma quanto alla prudenza ed alla stabilità, dico : come un popolo e più prudente, più stabile, e di miglior giudizio che un principe. E non senza cagione si assomiglia la voce d'un popolo a quella di Dio.' *Discorsi*, I, 58. *Op.*, p. 168.

what his opinions were or whether he had any. To this view of the case, anyhow improbable, the *Discorsi* makes a fatal objection. That in writing the *Principe* he should to some extent have suppressed his real opinions is, I take it, a matter of course. That he should have expressed such views as he did express in the *Discorsi*, unless he really held them, is not intelligible. We are bound to conclude that Machiavelli conceived of ' popular' government as a character of the healthiest, most vigorous and lasting type of State and of the arbitrary government of a Prince as a desperate remedy for corruption. This was not a sentiment merely but a deliberate judgement.

But we must beware of going too far. To speak of Machiavelli as a champion of democratic government, as Gentili spoke of him,[1] is nearer the truth than to speak of him as a supporter of despotism. But neither description really fits the elusive personage that was Niccolo. What he really cared about was the establishment of orderly government and general security. What he above all hoped, was to see Italy so strengthened that she should be able to rid herself of foreign domination. He had to deal with an Italy in which the restraints of religion, of respect for law, even the belief in moral obligation, seemed almost to have perished. He desired to show his countrymen the causes of the public misery, of the extreme instability of Italian governments, of the ruinous faction struggles and the helplessness before foreign invaders, from which the country suffered. It was not for any particular type of government but for a revival of public spirit that he contended.

§ 4. *IL PRINCIPE*

It has been said that the *Principe* is not an exhaustive treatise upon absolute government. That it most obviously is not : I am inclined to say that it is not any kind of a treatise on ' absolute ' government. There are no signs in Machiavelli's writings that he had any conception of legal or theoretic absolutism. A government, to Machiavelli, princely or popular, had power to do what it could do and no more. Far more important than law was, to him, the power to enforce it. He seems hardly to connect the idea of law with the idea of obligation. He was convinced of the difficulty of effecting changes in law and on this he lays stress both in the *Discorsi* and the *Principe*. But whether a ruler can or cannot make law was to him a question of fact simply. The amount of actual power possessed by a government seemed to him to depend little, if at all, on legal theory, to which he never refers. Nor does he make any distinction between power and right ; for of ' right ' he knew nothing. Nowhere

---

[1] 'Democratiae laudator et assertor acerrimus . . . tyrannidis summi inimicus.' *De Legationibus*, III, 9.

does he ever raise any question as to how far the rights of rulers extend. That question with which, all through the sixteenth century, men were above all to concern themselves, did not exist for him. Nowhere does he ever suggest that what is needed is the recognition of a positive right to demand obedience. I should imagine that such a recognition would have seemed to him impossible. I do not see, therefore, in what sense Machiavelli can be said to have conceived at all of absolutism. To his mind the difficulty was to discover how, in any way, States could be kept in order.

The *Principe* was written of a Prince for a Prince and for no one else ; it was certainly not written for the general public.[1] It is an essay on what makes for success in Italy from the point of view of a Prince. It is an endeavour to show what a Prince must understand, what he must do and be, and what he must not do, in order to consolidate and extend his dominion. It has reference throughout to Italian conditions of the moment. It is all but a piece of journalism dealing with current politics. It was written, too, in the hope that it would secure for its author the patronage of the Medici. Probably it was the very last of his writings by which Machiavelli would have wished to be judged.

As the object of the writer was to please as well as to edify, and as it was a Prince he had to please, he was bound to put things pleasantly and to suppress what would certainly be unwelcome. In many passages it might seem as though the Prince is being counselled to think only of himself and is being told that, as a Prince, he has a right to commit any abomination for mere personal gain. But careful reading even of the *Principe* will dissipate this impression ; while comparison with the *Discorsi* makes the supposition wholly untenable. We are told, practically in so many words, that a Prince, if he be wise and if he is to be successful, will consider nothing but his own interests. But in reading the *Principe* there is a good deal to read between the lines ; and it is to be found in the *Discorsi*. In a corrupt State the one thing to be hoped for is the success of the Prince. There is no other chance of stability or order. In such circumstances it is not possible to separate the interest of the Prince from the interests of his subjects. Their interests are his and his are theirs. Naturally, writing to a Prince, Machiavelli did not put it like this. But he did venture to point out to Giuliano and Lorenzo di Medici, and that with emphasis and reiteration, that a Prince cannot hope to be successful unless he regards the interests of his subjects as his own. The chief interest of a Prince is public welfare. ' It is above all things necessary that a Prince should retain the affection of his

---

[1] ' It is imperative,' neatly remarks Professor Hearnshaw, ' that those who read it should realize that they were not meant to do so.' *Social and Political Ideas of Renaissance and Reformation*, p. 108.

people, otherwise, in any crisis, he has no remedy.'[1] The only solid foundation for his position is a felt public need of him. A Prince ' should think out means whereby in all manner of times and occasions his subjects may have need of the State and of him and they will then ever be loyal '.[2] Whatever else he is and whatever he does, the Prince must see to it that he is in some sense popular. The enmity of a small group of nobles or rich men will be of little importance to a popular Prince, but to one not popular may easily be ruinous.

It is true that it is safer to be feared than to be loved. It is best of course to be both, though that is barely possible. If one must be wanting, it is best to be feared. You cannot rely on the love of your subjects because it is, really, nothing but love of themselves. You can rely upon fear just as long as you can keep it up. But though it is good to be feared, it is ruinous to be hated ; and the danger is that in trying to make yourself feared you may make yourself hated. But you will not be hated as long as you commit no outrage on property or women and do not kill people without plausible pretexts. What you have to remember is that your subjects will support you so long as they receive and expect benefit from you.[3]

In all this Machiavelli is but applying, in language adapted to a Medici, the principle stated in the *Discorsi*. The strength and stability of a State, and therefore of the Prince's position, depends finally on the public spirit or patriotism of its citizens. In a State governed by a Prince it is only loyalty to him that can supply the lack of public spirit among his corrupt people. All that the Prince has to do to secure their loyalty is to maintain security for life, honour and property. He cannot practically be strong or safe without a citizen army ; but even this will be useless if he has not the affection of his people.

' It is but natural that Princes should desire to extend their dominion.'[4] To say this was but to say feebly and incompletely what is much more fully stated in the *Discorsi*. There it is clearly laid down that a healthy State will always seek expansion. The necessity for that ceaseless effort to extend dominion which Machiavelli suggests to his Prince, derives partly from the perpetually unsatisfied soul of man and partly from the fact that States must always be either increasing or diminishing. ' Nature never suffers anything in this world to come to a stand.'[5] Security is impossible unless you

---

[1] *Principe*, Chap. 9, p. 240.

[2] ' E però un principe savio deve pensare un modo per il quale i suoi cittadini sempre ed in ogni modo e qualità di tempo abbiano bisogno dello Stato di lui, e sempre poi gli saranno fideli.' *Principe*, Chap. 9, p. 244.

[3] *Principe*, Chap. 17. [4] .Ib., Chap. 2.

[5] *Florentine History*, V, I.

are stronger than your neighbours and, to be securely stronger, you must dominate, if not conquer outright. It may be worth remarking that this conception of the necessary policy of neighbouring States is precisely analagous to Machiavelli's view of the necessity of the offensive in war. The idea is more emphasized in the *Principe* than in the *Discorsi*, because, in the *Principe*, Machiavelli was bent on suggesting to the Medici an attempt to unite Italy against the foreigner. But it is important, in this connection, that he was more or less aware of limits to possible expansion. Newly acquired territory is easily kept if its people be of the same country and language as your own, so long as they are not too much accustomed to liberty. But he insisted that it is very difficult to establish secure possession of a territory differing from one's own in language, custom and law.[1] He did not regard the difficulty as insurmountable absolutely ; but evidently it would become so if attempted on a very large scale. It seems to follow that expansion beyond a certain undetermined point is impossible. Community in language and custom is, it appears, the natural and solid basis for a State and there exist natural frontiers that can only be crossed with difficulty and danger.

In his chapter on Fortune,[2] Machiavelli shows that he was worried by the controversy over fixed fate and free will which troubled many minds in Italy in his time. He shows also that he did not really understand what the question was. He writes of Fortune almost as of an active and personal agent, as other men might have written of God. But she was to him a deity who could be conciliated, if never entirely won over. He was greatly impressed by the amount of the things that can neither be foreseen nor prevented nor controlled by the people they affect. Mere chance, he saw, had a great deal to say to the best-laid plans. Anyone, however able, may, like Cæsar Borgia, be ruined by accidents, by circumstances or events altogether beyond his control. Fortune, he thought, determines perhaps half of man's life. But on the whole, he concluded, men's hopes and projects are wrecked, not so much by adverse chance, as by failure to adapt themselves to changes of circumstance. The Prince who has grown great by audacity breaks down when circumstances imperatively demand caution ; he whose caution was his strength, fails when the moment absolutely requires audacity. If you cannot be both, he remarks, it is better to be audacious than to be merely prudent, for Fortune is a woman and to be kept under must be beaten and handled roughly.[3] Great as is the part played by accident in human affairs, the Prince who can accurately adjust his means to his ends and who pursues those ends with single-minded ruthlessness, is always likely to be successful. What is required for success is just two things :

---

[1] *Principe*, Chap. 2. [2] *Ib.*, Chap. 25.
[3] *Ib.*, Chap. 25, p. 365. Another case in which offensive strategy pays.

will and intelligence, a ruthless will and an intelligence that sees things
as they are. It may be pointed out that, assuming that success means
the achievement of a strictly limited and defined end, the proposition
is so undeniably true as hardly to be worth stating.

The *Principe* might, I think, be described as a particular application
to Italy of the principles laid down in the *Discorsi*. Italy must look
for liberation to the dominance of a successful Prince, because the
Italian is one of those corrupt peoples for whom a Prince is the only
possible, or at least the best possible, ruler. The principles on which
a Prince must work in order to be successful are those expounded or
implied in the *Discorsi*. In writing, in the *Discorsi*, about republics,
Machiavelli had insisted on the importance of religion and on the
desirability of giving all citizens a direct interest in the government
of the State, in order to the development of public spirit. When
he came to address a Prince it was a different matter. It is almost
hopeless to expect religion in a Prince and quite hopeless to make
him see the advantages of a democratic constitution. The Prince,
as a mere man, will care no more for public welfare in itself than other
men do. Appeal can only be made to his egotism, because, after all,
he is like other men. On the one hand, therefore, Machiavelli tries
to show him that the interests of his subjects are his own ; on the
other, he tells him that in the furtherance of his interests, the extension
or the consolidation of his dominions, he need have no scruples whatever. There was no real inconsistency. Nothing was suppressed
except an aspect or portion of the truth that was certain to be
offensive.

In the famous last chapter of the *Principe*, Machiavelli breaks
abruptly, with real eloquence, into a passionate appeal to the Medici
to raise the standard of Italy against the foreigner. Till that last
chapter is reached not a hint is given of any such issue. Yet it would
seem that it must have been the hope of this that in the main inspired
the writing of the book. Machiavelli seems to have felt little doubt
that the expulsion of the barbarians could actually be accomplished.
At the moment when he was writing the Medici held Florence and the
Papacy and there was a prospect of their coming shortly into possession
of Parma, Piacenza and Modena. So many conditions combined, he
declared, to favour the enterprise that no moment could be more
propitious.[1] Italy, he felt sure, was ready and eager to follow a
Prince who should give the signal : ' You see how she prays to God
daily to send someone to deliver her from the cruelty and insolence
of the barbarians. You see how fain and ready she is to follow the
banner if only it were set up.' [2] All that is wanted is a leader and a
native army. A Prince at the head of such an army would be recognized as a deliverer all over Italy.

[1] Ib., p. 367.   [2] Ib.

' I am not able to express with what love he would be welcomed in all the provinces that have suffered from this alien inundation, with what a thirst for vengeance, with what stubborn fidelity, with what devotion, with what tears. What gates would be closed against him ? Who would refuse him obedience ? What jealousy would oppose itself ? What Italian would deny him homage ? ' [1]

The sanguine optimism of it is strange. Of Giuliano or of Lorenzo di Medici, Machiavelli can surely have known little. But what exactly was he hoping for ? Did he believe that the Medici would be able not only to drive out the foreigner but to found a national Italian State ? There is no word in the *Principe* to suggest so much. He speaks only of the deliverance of Italy from the barbarians. For that a united effort would be needed ; but permanent union would not necessarily follow. It has been suggested that he hoped for no more than a return of the conditions existing before 1494. Even that was far too much to hope for. That Machiavelli did hope for an ultimate union of Italy there can, I think, be no serious doubt. He seems to have been convinced that there could be no safety or prosperity for Italy until she should become as united as France or Spain.[2] The first thing to be done was to secure independence : the rest might follow. But I am not, after all, concerned here with Machiavelli's hopes.

The *Principe* expresses no theory of government. Though it tends to leave an impression that Machiavelli considered despotism the most effective form of rule, there is really nothing in the book from which such a conclusion can logically be drawn. It can, at most, be inferred that he considered such government best for Italians in the year 1513. But even that is not clearly implied. All that is definitely implied is that a Prince who adopts the right policy and is intelligent and ruthlessly resolute, might well succeed in liberating Italy from the foreigner, if not in overcoming all opposition and uniting the whole country. That is a judgement that concerns the Italy of 1513, and nothing else in the world. It is a proposition in no way inconsistent with the views developed in the *Discorsi* : it is, rather, completely irrelevant to them. Or is there, indeed, an inconsistency ? If no State ever greatly flourished or extended its dominion except in liberty, how could Machiavelli hope for such great achievement by a Prince ? There is, perhaps, a slight degree of inconsistency here : the inconsistency of a man whom hope has made a little blind. Yet, after all, the possibilities of achievement under a Prince must be a matter of degree. And when we come to the last chapter of the *Principe*, we see that Machiavelli's hope was founded not so much

---

[1] *Principe*, p. 371.
[2] The first Book of the *Florentine History* makes it clear that Machiavelli saw Italy as having disastrously lost a unity that was in some sense natural.

on the personality of any Prince, as on his belief in the fervour of Italy's hatred of the foreigner and longing for deliverance.

There is, I am inclined to say, no political theory whatever in the *Principe*, or at least none that is not in the *Discorsi*. But for the fact that Machiavelli's view of political ethics, or of ethics in relation to politics, seems to be expressed in the *Principe* more fully than in the *Discorsi*, the book would have little value for the student of political philosophy. Even in that connection the *Principe* is a misleading book.

§ 5. ETHICS AND POLITICS

To· many people in the sixteenth century—people who, for the most part, knew little or even nothing about him—Machiavelli's name was anathema, because they supposed him to have been a supporter of despotism and even an apologist for the worst kinds of tyranny. To others his hard sayings about the Church and the Papacy and his implication that the claims of the Pope as the religious head of Christendom were not worth serious consideration, suggested satanic influence. This alone is sufficient to account for the hatred and the fear of him displayed by the Pope and the Jesuits. But what most of all shocked most people, and made him seem to some terrible and to some contemptible, was that he seemed to teach that reasons of State might justify every degree of treachery and brutality. To many he seemed to go further and to imply that the highest virtue was that quality which enabled a man, without fear or scruple, to deceive and to assassinate, whenever he could gain a desired end by so doing. He seemed to have taken evil for good and to ask admiration for the worst deeds of the worst men.

In later days also his name continued to be chiefly associated with his political ethics or his separation of ethics from politics, in whichever of the two ways it might be put. Denunciation of him as a teacher of political immorality has continued to the present day. But what his thought concerning ethics and politics really was, I find it by no means easy to discover. That he raised a very serious question is evident. How far he answered it, or what his answer was, it is not easy to say.

In the *Discorsi* Machiavelli seems to assert that 'goodness' in action is to be understood as its tendency to promote the welfare of the individuals of a community as a whole. · 'Badness', of course, will consist in the reverse tendency. Standing alone this proposition would convey very little, but Machiavelli makes it clear that 'welfare' consists essentially in security for person and property. Experience has led to generalizations as to conduct which are generally valid as between members of any community. But to apply those rules of conduct to strictly political action or relations is to misapprehend and make nonsense of them. For a governing person or body the essential principle remains valid, and just because it holds good always, the morality of politics cannot be that of private life. Murder and breach of faith among the members of a co-operative society strike at the security of all and are therefore ' bad '. But if murder or breach of faith can be made to promote the general welfare of that society, then, by definition, they become ' good '. A private citizen acts for himself only : a government acts for all. The application of the same principle must needs have different results in the two cases.

If this be what Machiavelli meant, then it is not true to say that he separated ethics from politics. That sounding cliché is, in any case, ambiguous. It would be more accurate to say that he separated political ethics from the ethics of social life, by applying the same principle to both. Exactly the same test makes an action bad in one connection and good in another ; and Machiavelli, by implication at least, denies that any other test is valid. Nor is the use of the word ' unmoral ' illuminating. To urge the doing of dishonourable things as a patriotic duty is certainly not unmoral, whatever else it may be. Can we characterize the doctrine as one that makes the end justify the means ? We may say so, if, in doing so, we distinguish. It is the actual effect of action which determines for Machiavelli the goodness or the badness of it : it is men's sentiments about it that are irrelevant. It is not the end, in the sense of the intention, that justifies ; what justifies is success in the promotion of public welfare. Machiavelli would not have regarded a miscalculated murder, however well-intentioned, as a truly virtuous action. Intelligence as well as will are needed, in his view, to make up virtue. Machiavelli was never in the least concerned with the moral quality of the ruler himself. He seems to have known nothing of personal goodness ; he saw goodness only in action. If that be so, he may, perhaps, be called unmoral ; and in that sense ' unmoral ' seems to signify the most hopeless kind of immorality.

Only ambiguously do we express the difference between the thought of Machiavelli and that of most men in the Middle Ages, or in the sixteenth century, when we say that he separated ethics from politics. We come much nearer to the difference in noting the complete absence from Machiavelli's mind of the conception of natural law. The belief that men's intuitions as to right and wrong are, in fact, intuitions of an absolute or of God's purpose in the universe, was at the root of the most characteristic thought of the Middle Ages and, in somewhat less degree, of that of the sixteenth century. Machiavelli must have met with this belief : there is no sign that he understood it. To him the words good and bad referred only to human welfare in a particular society. With a superficial consistency he argued that if massacre can be made to promote that welfare, massacre becomes virtuous.

It has frequently been said that the hero of the *Principe* is Cæsar Borgia, in spite of the fact that he appears prominently in only two chapters of the book. Machiavelli had, no doubt, been deeply impressed by what he saw of Cæsar and his work. Cæsar furnished him, as has been said, with just the example he needed. But Machiavelli proposed him ' as an example for the imitation of all such as by the favour of fortune or the help of other princes are got into the saddle '.[1] Quite definitely he is presented as a model for such adventurers as are conquering for themselves a principality rather than for Princes actually established and ruling. If the subject of the *Principe* were simply the new Prince engaged in founding a dominion, then certainly we might have said that Cæsar Borgia was its hero. As it is not so, the most we can rightly say is that, of all the Princes known to Machiavelli, Cæsar approached most nearly to his idea of what a Prince who has to found a new dominion should be and perhaps to his idea of the man needed to unite Italy against the foreigner. But, whether we call Cæsar the hero of the *Principe* or not, Machiavelli certainly had no doubt of the excellence of the work Cæsar had done. Cæsar, he remarks, was reckoned cruel. ' But that ruthlessness of his reduced the Romagna to order, united it and settled it in peace and loyalty.'[2] Where such excellent results follow, a little scandal matters nothing. If by honourable and merciful conduct you encourage rapine and anarchy, in no real sense are you honourable or merciful, since your conduct injures a whole universality.[3] It is not enough to say that, in looking at Cæsar Borgia, Machiavelli did not allow his vision to be disturbed by moral considerations. He says, or he distinctly implies, that Cæsar's treachery and ruthlessness were not evil but good.

But for all that, when we come to examine Machiavelli's declarations closely, we find, it seems to me, that his language is not quite consistent with any simple theory of his meaning. I get the impression that he himself did not know exactly what he wanted to say. Sometimes he seems merely to be saying, ' If this be the end, then these are the means and whether they are good or evil is irrelevant.' But at other times it would appear that his meaning is : ' Anything whatever that is to the advantage of the State and promotes its general well-being, may and should be done.' Sometimes again, and perhaps most often, he seems to be saying, ' To do this or that is wicked ; but, if you do not do it, you will be ruined.' Or perhaps it is : ' The business of a Prince is to make himself and his people secure against all possible enemies, and to do this he must often act

---

[1] *Principe*, Chap. 7.   [2] Ib., Chap. 17, p. 290.
[3] Ib. ' Perchè questa sogliono offendere una universalità intera.'

wickedly, because the world is so wicked that he cannot, otherwise, attain his end.' There are here, at least, three perfectly distinct propositions and between them Machiavelli fails clearly to distinguish. There is, consequently, a constant ambiguity. There are, even, passages that suggest that it is only in extreme cases that unjust and disgraceful courses of action are justified. ' When the safety of our country is absolutely at stake,' wrote Machiavelli in the *Discorsi*, ' there need be no question of what is just or unjust, merciful or cruel, praiseworthy or disgraceful ; but, all other considerations set aside, that course alone is to be taken which may save our country and maintain its liberty.' [1] So, also, in the *Principe*, he tells his Prince that he need never hesitate to incur a certain amount of infamy for wickedness without which the State could hardly be saved. ' For if he well consider all things, he may find that certain courses, in appearance virtuous, would be his ruin if pursued, and that others, in appearance evil, will if followed lead him to security and well-being.' [2] Did Machiavelli mean that it is only when complete ruin is threatened that anything whatever may be done to save ourselves ? It is an impossible interpretation, for the line could not be drawn. Yet it may be that, while he was certain that the saving or the founding of a State would justify any needful atrocity, he was clearer about that than about any other case.

But, most often, Machiavelli seems to be merely insisting that evil courses must, occasionally or frequently, be adopted, because the world is so wicked that success cannot otherwise be had. He was perfectly aware that a reputation for wickedness might be injurious and he warns his Prince accordingly ; adding that, if he be successful in maintaining his authority, his means to that end will always be found honourable and be approved by every one.[3] But he seems to think of treachery and murder as normally necessary weapons of all successful statecraft. He suggests a picture of a terrible world in which such doings are the only road to peace and security. Was that world merely Italian ? Machiavelli was writing and thinking of his actual Italy. He was very sure that in that Italy success depended partly on unscrupulous ruthlessness. Would he have admitted that outside Italy his generalization would not apply ? We cannot put it so : it could be only a matter of degree. Machiavelli's impression was no doubt derived from Italy, but it seems likely that he would have got the same impression anywhere else.

---

[1] ' La quel cosa merita d'esser notata ed osservata da qualunque cittadino si trova a consigliare la patria sua ; perchè dove si delibero al tutto della salute della patria, non vi debbe cadere alcuma considerazione nè di giusto nè d'ingiusto, nè di pietoso nè di crudele, nè di laudibile nè d'ignominioso, anzi posposto ogni altro rispetto seguire al tutto quel partito che gli salvi la vita e mantengali la libertà.' *Discorsi*, III, 41. *Op.*, p. 435.

[2] *Principe*, Chap. 15, p. 285.   [3] Ib., Chap. 18.

'The manner in which we live and that in which we ought to live are things so widely different, that he who leaves what is done to follow after that which should be done, learns rather how to ruin than to save himself.'[1] Was Machiavelli chiefly bent on pointing out that, however you feel about it, treachery and even massacre are or may be necessary to political success? But to what does such an assertion amount? If he were saying : 'This should not be done, but, since you will be ruined if you don't do it, therefore you should do it,' he would be talking sheer nonsense. I do not suspect him of that. He was saying, rather, that if you will political success, you must act consistently with your will and do what is necessary to your end and accept the consequences.

'There is no disgrace,' wrote Machiavelli, 'in not keeping promises that were imposed on you by force, and extorted promises that concern public interests will always without shame be broken when the power to enforce them is wanting.'[2] This is stated simply as a fact. The assertion that there is no disgrace refers only to the feelings of people in general, who, in similar circumstances, would themselves do the same. In the *Principe* he went further. Discussing the question how far a Prince is obliged by his promise, the point to notice, he says, is that though, in general, promises should be kept, a Prince should not keep his word when the keeping of it is to his hurt and the reasons for his promising have passed away.[3] They will, of course, have passed away when power to enforce the promise has failed or when the lie has had the hoped-for effects. 'This rule would not be good,' he adds, 'were all men good ; but since they are wicked and will not keep faith with you, you are not bound to keep it with them.'[4] The miserable excuse here given for breaking faith seems inconsistent with an assertion that to break faith to the advantage of the community you are governing is, simply, a virtuous action. But it is possible to understand the passage otherwise. Machiavelli may have meant that, if the keeping of a promise would have ill results for Prince and people, it cannot be a 'good' deed to keep it ; but that if all men always kept faith the case would be quite different, because, then, breach of faith would always do you more harm than good.

The results of examination of Machiavelli's text seem, so far, to be inconclusive. It is possible to explain his utterances by reference to a fundamental assertion concerning the criterion of good and evil.

[1] *Principe*, Chap. 15, p. 283.
[2] *Discorsi*, III, 42. *Op.*, p. 437.
[3] 'Non puo pertanto un signore prudente, nè debbe osservare la fede, quando tale osservanza gli torno contro, e che sono spente le cagioni che la fecero promettere.' *Principe*, Chap. 18, p. 303.
[4] 'E si gli uomini fussero tutti buoni, questo precetto non sarebbe buono ; ma perchè sono tristi e non l'osserverebbero a te, tu ancora non l'hai da osservare a loro.' *Principe*, Chap. 18, p. 303.

On this view the essence of his doctrine is that, when the welfare of a community is thereby promoted, any act whatever becomes strictly ' good '. He simply draws the conclusion that, for the sake of that public welfare, which is their concern, rulers should always be ready to do dishonourable things. But his language is not consistent with a supposition that his views were but a logical development of this principle. It was not really on his notion of the origin of man's sense of right and wrong that his conclusions were based.

It is possible, however, to effect a reconciliation among his loose utterances. It is clear enough that he says now one thing, now another ; but he was, all the same, I think, saying the same thing all the time. It is not a simple thing, but it is coherent. To be successful in politics, he asserts, you must be ever ready to deceive or to slaughter and in fact to commit any atrocity ; and whether you call the doing of such things good or bad, does not alter the fact that the doing of them may, and often does, conduce to the general welfare of a political society. It was, roughly speaking, on this principle that Italian politics had long been conducted. Machiavelli could have taught nothing, in this connection, to Gian Galeazzo Visconti. So far we have merely a judgement or a generalization concerning political activities in general. What is needed for political success is, first of all, clear perception of what and how things actually are, then accurate adjustment of means to ends and, finally, ruthless execution with complete absence of moral scruple. Why should success be desired at all on such terms ? That question had to be answered and Machiavelli supplies an answer. His answer is that men may desire wealth or honour or power, but that all men desire security of life and property. That security only the State can give and, to make the State secure, methods have to be adopted repugnant to normal sentiment and deeds to be done that are commonly regarded as evil. When he suggests that wicked actions become good when they benefit the community, he means that, if you must do these things to attain what every one desires, it is absurd to call them evil. There is no criterion of badness in action except its actual effects, and these must be judged of by reference to what is desired. So we come back to the essential proposition that ' good ' action is that which tends to the satisfaction of universal desires and that, apart from these desires of men, there is no good or evil. This, surely, is ethical doctrine ; and if so we can hardly say that Machiavelli separated ethics from politics. But, whether we say so or not, all this, taken together, seems to represent what Machiavelli's assertions amount to. The whole system stands or falls, not with its utilitarian ethics, but with the doctrine that political success must be measured in terms of security and power and with the validity of Machiavelli's judgement as to how alone these things can be attained.

It is an essential fact in this thought system that, to Machiavelli, the particular community in which a man lived was the only one with the welfare of which that man was concerned. Machiavelli thought of the State as a morally isolated thing. The 'good' he speaks of refers only indirectly, even, to the well-being of the community regarded as an undying entity. It is simply that which individual members all desire. Rational ethics can have no reference except to the interests of the individual. It was said, in the sixteenth century, that a man does not live merely within a particular community or State, but is a member of a far greater society, which is Christendom or which is, even, mankind. Good action must therefore, it might be inferred, be defined as that which tends to benefit not only fellow-citizens but humanity. Machiavelli's answer would, presumably, have been that, even within a particular State, the interest of the individual is far from coinciding exactly with that of society. Enlarge the conception of the community to include all mankind and the connection between the interests of the individual and of the community practically disappears. No amount of security in China or England will help me if, here in Italy, I am insecure.

With the question how far or in what sense Machiavelli's premises and conclusions were valid, I am not here concerned. I am concerned only with what he thought. Could a demonstrative answer be given to the question of how far he was right, it would, indeed, be a different case. The intrusion of mere personal opinion would be merely impertinent. But it seems undeniable that if Machiavelli were wrong he was very profoundly wrong. It seems clear, also, that his political immorality or unmorality or his conception of the ethics of politics, as we like to put it, was not, as Macaulay called it, a 'blemish' on his work. It is no accident or superficial character but of the very substance of his thought.

A few remarks and suggestions may be made here, even by one prepared to demonstrate nothing. It is, of course, true that Machiavelli did not admire or advocate murder as a fine art.˙ What he admired in Cæsar Borgia, or in that Castruccio Castracani of whom he made the hero of an historical romance, was a singleness of purpose and energy of will that might or might not issue in murder. It is not his judgement as to the means necessary to the attainment of security and power that should revolt us. What is revolting in Machiavelli is that he himself feels none. He speaks with, perhaps amused, approval of the habitual and successful mendacity of Pope Alexander VI. He feels nothing but admiration for the dastardly treachery and ruthless brutality of his Castruccio.

It is well, says Machiavelli, to appear to be merciful and honourable, humane, religious and sincere, and even to be all these, so long as your mind is so framed that you can, when need arises, change to the contrary.[1] Even to be so ! The words suggest that Machiavelli had not the faintest notion what being so must mean. He would have his Prince commit murder and feel like Lady Macbeth : ' A little water clears us of this deed.' He has no glimpse of the possibility that, later, the murderer may in despair be asking : ' Will these hands ne'er be clean ? ' The sense of the mysterious in good and evil, the sense of the poisonous nature of evil that Shakespeare felt so strongly, had no existence for his mind. He saw very clearly, but he did not see very much.

It might have suggested itself to Machiavelli that the futility of Italian political effort, measured by his own measure, might possibly be due to the fact that his principle had long been held to and acted on in Italy. But no such idea could have occurred to him. He saw no incompatibility between the means he suggests as necessary and the results he hoped for. It is certainly permissible to be astonished that he should have supposed that Italy could be liberated by such means or that any solid structure could so be built up. It must never be forgotten that Machiavelli referred all political action to public welfare. It is only the promotion of public welfare that justifies. It must be remembered, too, that what he desired above all things was to revive public spirit in Italy. If to him the State was an expression of the purely selfish will in man, yet its health and strength depended, for him, on a patriotic devotion that could not be merely self-regarding. He was in a way a moralist, but he was a moralist without any sense of the beauty of goodness or of the horror of evil. His judgement of human nature was, surely, profoundly at fault. May it not be said that he lacked understanding of just what he most of all needed to know ?

However unsatisfactory his answer to it, Machiavelli had raised a very serious and disturbing question. The mere raising of it was important. It was, in 1513, about as new as any question has been for a very long time. For most medieval thinkers it did not exist. It is true that in the later Middle Ages there had been a tendency to ask it, and a tendency, even, to answer it in Machiavellian fashion. The authors of the *Defensor Pacis* had given to the term natural law the same meaning that Machiavelli gave to ' goodness '. Pierre Dubois seems to have had no belief in ' right ' except in a sense strictly legal. In political practice, too, and especially in the politics of fourteenth- and fifteenth-century Italy, the question had constantly been raised by implication, but by implication only. It is probable that

---

[1] ' Anzi ardiro di dire questo, che avendole ed osservandole sempre sono damnoso, e parendo d'averle sono utili: come parere pietoso, fidele, umano, religioso, intiero, ed essere, ma stare in modo edificato con l'animo che, bisognando non essere, tu possa e sappia mutare il contrario.' *Principe*, Chap. 18, pp. 304, 305.

no question at all existed in the minds of the Visconti or the Borgia ; but the admiration aroused in Italy by their successful operations certainly challenged the old beliefs. But no one before Machiavelli had raised the question formally and explicitly. It must of course, by his time, have been in many minds. It was the same, for instance, for Guicciardini as for him. Fundamentally there was, indeed, nothing new about the question whether a State has any obligation to its neighbours or a government to an opposition, how far a governing body is bound by rules of conduct or whether it is bound at all. Fundamentally the question was the old problem of the nature of good and evil. Machiavelli himself did not see clearly that it was so ; and for that reason his answer had been a partial answer only. The mere raising of the question was more important than any answer he could give. But, in any case, whether Machiavelli had raised it or not, the question must have been asked before long. That it should be first explicitly raised in Italy was only what was to be expected.

§ 6. THE MACHIAVELLIAN STATE

It has been said that Machiavelli suggested a new conception of the State, or, at least, that he made suggestions that assisted others to form such a conception. It would be difficult to say what a reading of Machiavelli's writings might or might not suggest. What I am here concerned with is Machiavelli's conception of the State, or how far there was in his mind anything that can so be called. Whether he conceived at all of the State as such and in the abstract, seems dubious. If he ever asked himself the question, What is the State ? he certainly never answered it. He was really concerned only with the actual States of his day. He had, indeed, crude notions of how the State came into being and he had the idea that all institutions tend to corruption owing to inherent defects arising from the nature of man. He believed that out of corruption comes, or may come, new healthy growth, and that all States tend to move in a circle. He conceived the State as something very unstable, moving on a course that practically ended in ruin. There is, however, little connection between these conceptions and the body of his thought. He conceived of the State as necessary in the sense that only governmental organization could give security and peace. Because all men desire peaceful possession and the liberty that is freedom from the fear of other men, effective government was desirable in the highest degree. But, in the main, Machiavelli expressed ideas about the States of his own time rather than about the State.

If the besetting sin of medieval political thought was that it too much disregarded the actualities of the moment, the sin of Machiavelli lay in regarding nothing else. The typical medieval thinkers lost sight of how things were in considering how they should or might be ;

were so anxious to make clear the nature of political obligation that they ignored the lack of sanction for existing law ; so anxious to get clear the nature of law that they took no thought for the amendment of laws ; they were so anxious to relate the State to God's purpose that they forgot the purposes ot men.[1] They had a twofold excuse. In the first place, so chaotic was their political world, that they might well have thought it best to ignore it and busy themselves with laying the foundations of a world rational. In the second place, the State, in the twelfth or in the thirteenth century, was a barely visible thing ; or if there were an ideally visible State it was Christendom. Unfortunately, Christendom was not an actual State : it was a figment of pious and aspiring and optimistic imagination. But, by the end of the fifteenth century, in France, in Spain, in England, even in Italy, the State has become a plainly visible thing, obviously distinct, and attached to Christendom only by slender bonds of organization, overstrained and on the point of snapping. Men's thoughts turned to it as a matter of course. But Machiavelli, instead of building on the foundations the schoolmen had dug deep, ignored them altogether. Not only did he ask no fundamental questions, he implies that they are not worth asking.

Yet not asking implied, in his case, a philosophy of a sort. He was concerned, he fondly imagined, only with what really is. Man does actually desire security and is a creature of habit and of fear. Governments of all sorts do naturally seek stability and strive for domination and expansion. Machiavelli was utterly unconcerned with the justification of desire to reason. It is useless to ask whether men's desires are rational or are what they should be, because, whatever the answer may be, it will not alter anything. Man is what he always has been and always will be. The end of the State is that which rulers and peoples do actually propose to themselves. You may ask why men desire security or power ; and the only and sufficient answer is that man, a being wholly self-regarding and for ever unsatisfied, is made like that. Machiavelli had no glimpse of any purpose but the purposes of man ; was unconcerned with obligations, for he recognized none ; and saw no foundation for government but the achievement of the security all men desired.

Nevertheless, a conception of the State, meagre and incomplete, may be derived from the writings of Machiavelli. It can be derived, however, only from what is little more than description of the character of States of his own time. The Machiavellian State is, to begin with, in the completest sense, an entirely secular thing. Not only has it no vital relation to the Church or any church ; it has no relation to God or to any cosmic purpose. These things are eliminated from

---

[1] These statements are, I fear, gross exaggerations. The only excuse for them is that they do suggest the nature of a contrast that is real.

Machiavelli's system as unknown or unknowable or non-existent, or simply, perhaps, as irrelevant : one does not quite know which. The State needs religion, but any church within it should be its instrument.

Further, the State is conceived as so perfectly distinct an entity that it may be regarded as isolated. It is morally isolated because it has no obligations to anything outside itself. All its relations and connections are accidental.

No reason can be given for its existence, except that men necessarily will it to exist. Not that men care for the State ; men care only for themselves. But all men desire security in the possession of what they have, and it is only in and by means of the State that even a small measure of security can be obtained. The State is an organization of force for the maintenance of security of possession. But not only do all men desire this much, but all men are unsatisfied by the possessions they have. For this reason and because every State has neighbours, who are actual or potential enemies, every State aims and must aim at increasing its power. For power is the measure of security. The persistent effort to increase power may easily lead to ruin ; but final ruin is unavoidable. Every State tends to corruption. Necessarily it passes from revolution to revolution, and in the long run cannot escape destruction. But it may, for a time, develop an active public spirit ; and the best check upon men's evil and anarchic tendencies is religion. Governments, therefore, must foster any religion that will help them to keep order, and especially any religion that teaches service to the State as a supreme duty. But no relation of the State to the will of God is involved here. It matters not a tittle whether the religion of the State be ' true ' or not.

Governments must aim at popularity, and the government that gives the most complete security will be most popular. The strength of the State, other things being equal, depends upon its patriotism. It must have a regular army of its own citizens, for it can trust no others. The greater the amount of public spirit in the State the stronger that army will be. The best organization of government is that which gives all, or at least a large number of citizens, a share in it. Such an organization tends to promote public spirit. Popular governments, also, are on the whole more intelligent and less capricious than Princes. But only clear vision of things as they are, intelligent adjustment of means to ends and ruthless will to the public good, can long maintain any State against internal faction and external enemies. Other things equal, that State will be strongest that is most homogeneous. The strongest State of all will be that which includes the largest number of people, similar in language and usage and animated by patriotism. The ruin of such a State may be long in coming.

These appear to be the chief characters of the State as Machiavelli saw it. When we consider the picture we must, I think, perceive that it is, in the main, a descriptive commentary on the States of his own time and that it applies better to the Italian States than to others. It is a picture of Italian States and politics as they had long been, rather than of anything else. It is seen with extraordinary clearness and precision. And certainly there was much that was new in 1513, at least in literature, in this way of presenting the State. No writer, since the collapse of the Roman Empire, had so isolated the State or so clearly described it as a simply secular and earthly thing, unrelated to any divine revelation or to any other world, to any church or to any God.

May we say then, as has been said, that we find in Machiavelli's writings the conception of a national State ? About the term ' national State ' there is a certain ambiguity ; and, in seeking to answer this question, we are in danger of falling into barren disputation about the use of terms. That Machiavelli perceived the advantage to a government of having subjects similar in language, customs and habits of life, is quite clear. In the *Principe* he lays a good deal of stress on the difficulty of extending one's rule over peoples of alien speech and custom. There is, further, a strong suggestion, both in the *Discorsi* and in the *Principe*, that he saw in France and Spain States solidly founded on what we should call a racial basis and that he attributed their strength partly to that. In the last chapter of the *Principe* and in the first Part of the *Florentine History* there is a suggestion, still stronger, that he saw Italy as naturally a single State, wanting only a government and the expulsion of foreigners. In the *Discorsi* there is a fainter suggestion that a modern Italian republic might do what Rome had once done. He seems certainly to have seen Italy as a natural State that had lost its formal and actual unity. We may fairly say that he saw community of language and custom as forming the best basis for a State ; and so thinking he could not but see Italy as a State potentially. Again, his healthy State is one animated by strong public spirit and armed with an army of its very own.[1] It was evident enough that no high degree of public spirit and no strong citizen army was likely to exist in a State conglomerate of alien peoples. The conception of what we call racial unity as the surest foundation for a State was present to his mind ; but nowhere does he give it clear expression. It may fairly be said that he aspired to make Italy a national State. That, however, does not involve a conception of the national State. Machiavelli knew that Italy had once been brought into political union ; he believed that it might be done again ; he saw in such union the only security against foreign domination ; and he saw that there was sufficient similarity among the

[1] But we must not translate ' armi proprie ' by ' national troops '. This is to commit the unpardonable sin of reading into a text what is not there.

peoples of Italy to make a solid union possible. He went no further. The formation of a concept of the national State, as such, was foreign to his mode of thinking. It remains true that, from what he said or implied, that concept would easily be derived.

But Machiavelli's account of the State was, after all, much more than a description : it was a forecast. Machiavelli had perceived and defined many of the leading characteristics of the States not only of his own time but of those of the sixteenth century as a whole. We might go further and say, boldly, of the modern State, meaning by that of States ever since. He had perceived much of what, under the given conditions, needs must, if not exist, at least be desired and insisted on and striven after. He had described the Church as a dead-weight upon Italy, as a prime cause of its disunion and a hindrance to the development of the secular State. Many countries, in the time immediately coming, broke altogether with that Church, while even those that did not do so took measures to make themselves practically independent of the Pope. Even the Catholic States assumed, more and more, the merely secular character. He had suggested that any church within the State could and should be made an instrument of government. All through Lutheran Germany and in Sweden and England, at least, the attempt was made. He had emphasized the State's need of religion ; and throughout the century that need was acutely felt, even though it was generally insisted upon in a different sense. All through the century, again, the idea that the main business of government is to give security to person and property continually recurs. Machiavelli had laid it down that States inevitably aim at increasing power and at dominating their neighbours. The policy and action of sixteenth-century States confirmed his view. He had implied, at least, that neighbour States must always and steadily be regarded as potential if not actual enemies. The statesmen of the sixteenth century, to say the least, habitually thought as he would have had them think. The treacherous and ' Machiavellian ' quality of sixteenth-century diplomacy was a further confirmation of his perceptions. If the *Principe* were not actually the gospel of Thomas Cromwell or Catherine de Medici, Philip II or Henry IV, it was, at least, not difficult to believe that it was so. The actual relations of sixteenth-century States were much as Machiavelli had implied they must be. The effort to reach natural or racial boundaries hardly became very distinct till the next century ; and for long Machiavelli's warning of the difficulty of taking over the government of alien populations was largely disregarded. Acquiescence, at least in some measure, came later. But his insistence on the need of patriotism is echoed throughout the century by writers and by governments. So, equally, his insistence on the need of intelligence and of consistent will in the conduct of government, was repeated all through the century ; though it was often made an argument against the 'popular' government he had favoured.

Machiavelli's writings may be regarded as a forecast extraordinary in its accuracy. To a great extent he anticipated the needs that were most acutely felt for at least the next hundred years. The sixteenth-century State did imperatively need religion and did need a church it could control ; it did imperatively need public spirit also : and the connection between these things was real and close. It was, actually, rent by faction and at the same time pressed by external enemies. Its neighbours were, in fact, always dangerous. It needed, as never before, a strong hand and a clear intelligence at the helm. Machiavelli's perception of the needs of the growing States was, indeed, remarkably accurate as far as it went. Even the people who most fiercely denounced him often agreed with him far more than they knew. But it must be remembered that those needs were altogether independent of his forecast and would equally have been felt and appreciated if he had never made it. The accuracy of that forecast involves what may be called accurate political thinking. It can hardly be called a contribution to political thought. What Machiavelli did not in any measure forecast was the course and character of political thought in the century, except so far as that thought merely reflected needs obvious and pressing.

When we speak of Machiavelli as unmedieval we seem rather to be forgetting fourteenth- and fifteenth-century Italy and, indeed, more also. Yet there does seem to be truth in this saying, Machiavelli's thought, his mode of thinking, his whole outlook, were far more unmedieval than was the thought of the sixteenth century as a whole. His total disbelief in natural law in the ordinary medieval and sixteenth-century sense and his attitude to the Christian religion, alike isolate him. His interest in things as he thought they were, and in their immediate causation, and his practical insistence on a process of induction from them, were analogous to the new art and the new literature of the Renaissance. Just as Renaissance Italy had detached the statue from the great architectural background which gave it symbolic meaning and set it up on a pedestal to stand by itself as the expression of, or comment on, a mere visible thing, so Machiavelli detached the State from the Church, making it an organization of force for the attainment of merely earthly ends. Whether anything was gained, on the whole, in one case or the other, is a question that cannot be discussed here, but should not be rashly answered.

§ 7. THE METHOD

What was most new and original in the work of Machiavelli was, perhaps, his method, or his manner, of approaching problems of politics. That method had two aspects, positive and negative. Machiavelli made none of the assumptions that had been, and still were, usually made concerning divine revelation or the Church. He discarded completely the theory of natural law. This negative side of his procedure was perhaps that which was most startling to his contemporaries outside Italy, though in Italy it startled few. On the positive side, Machiavelli relied on undeniable experience and attempted to proceed as far as possible by induction from it and no farther. But he did not rely only on his own experience and on that of his contemporaries, he turned also to the past, and he has been especially lauded as having been the first for a very long time to make use of the historical method in dealing with political problems.

Written history, as distinct from documents on which it is based, is the result of an effort to ascertain the facts of the past and to relate them, and especially to relate them in terms of cause and effect. That endeavour inevitably involves an attempt to state conclusions in the form of ever wider generalizations. Approximately accurate generalizations concerning the life of humanity in the past are assumed to be theoretically possible, however difficult to reach. But, supposing that we were in possession of a great complex of such generalizations, analysed and tested to the utmost degree possible, what sort of inferences could be drawn from them? Evidently we could not extract from them any unvarying laws of sequence unless we postulated, like Machiavelli, an unchanging humanity. If we think of the history of man as a vast process of psychological change, the difficulty of drawing inferences of practical value will seem, to say the least, very great. Our generalizations, it would seem, could do nothing for us except guide us, to a slight extent, in our little opportunist dealings with what we call the present. Perhaps they might show us what was immediately possible or impossible to effect. Of what may be, in the long run, they could tell us little or nothing : of what should be, if anything should be, they could certainly tell us nothing at all. Nor could they give us any real reason for desiring one consummation rather than another. The study of history cannot teach values, though it may of course deepen our sense of and confirm our hold on what we have. Further, owing to the extreme complexity and multiplicity of the facts that have to be considered, interpretation in any sense is monstrously difficult and all inferences correspondingly doubtful. We can find in history anything we want to find, for all that man has said and felt and done is there.

I fear that all this may be counted as mere digression. Right or wrong, it has certainly little bearing on the use that Machiavelli actually made of history. For in fact, so far as I can see, he made

very little use of it. He started with the assertion that man, remaining
always the same mean and selfish creature, it is possible to infer from
what has been, what methods should be pursued now in respect of a
given object. 'Past things,' as Guicciardini wrote, 'throw light
on things to come, for the world was ever of the same sort and
all that which is and will be has been in other times and the old
things return with different names and colours.'[1] Inferences
of practical value nowadays may be drawn from the study of
Roman or other history and rulers may find in it valuable suggestions. Machiavelli can hardly be said to have claimed more
than this; and the claim was quite reasonable. It would have
been strange if some thinker of the Italian Renaissance had not
made it.

But how far were the principles or the conclusions of Machiavelli
derived from what he found in his classical and historical authors ?
I do not think that they were so derived to any extent that matters,
or even that they could have been. He came, he tells us, to the study
of politics after ' a long experience of modern affairs and a continual
study of the ancient '.[2] But his experience of things modern counted
for far more than his reading. His idea of the cycle in the life of
States was evidently suggested by Polybius. Though he connected
it with the conception of an unchanging humanity, he did not quite
know what to do with it. His belief in the thorough ' badness ' of
man, his sense of the instability of the State, his sense of the need of
public spirit, his view of the ethics of politics, were evidently derived
from his own Italian experience and from his own limitations. He
was, of course, much impressed by what he derived from his authorities
concerning Roman religion and republican organization, Roman
patriotism and military and political methods. All this confirmed
and fortified the impression he had already acquired. But who, in
reading the *Discorsi*, feels that Machiavelli's case is strengthened by
his citations from Livy ?

It is significant, rather than strange, that so critical and sceptical
a thinker as Machiavelli should have used his authorities so uncriti-
cally as he did use them. He went to Livy expecting what he would
find there, duly found what he wanted and asked no questions. It
is hardly relevant, in this connection, to point out that criticism of
historical tradition or critical examination of historical evidence was
little known of or understood at the time.[3] An approach to politics

---

[1] *Ricordi*, 336.

[2] ' Una lunga sperienza delle cose moderne ed una continua lezione delle
antiche.' *Principe*, Preface.

[3] Also it must be remembered that Florence produced in the first half of the
sixteenth century a remarkable group of historians, of whom Machiavelli himself was one.

through history logically involves such criticism. To fail to see that it does is really to fail to conceive what we call the historical method.

It may be remarked, also, that the validity of conclusions drawn as to things present from the past, must depend on the degree of similarity between conditions at one time and the other. Men may be always much the same, but their circumstances are not nor their ideas. Machiavelli made no attempt to compare the conditions of Roman Italy with those of the Italy of his own day. He made no account of differences of outlook, beliefs and ideas; he seems to have seen little in the world but selfish will to riches or power or mere security. He wrote as though he assumed that conditions generally in ancient and in modern Italy were alike for all practical purposes.[1] Such an assumption is inconsistent with any valid use of an historical method, if not with any use of one at all. Machiavelli was convinced that much might be learned from the ways and fortunes of the ancients, and he himself read the works of ancient historians and derived from them suggestions and illustrations and a comforting assurance. But to call this a use of historical method seems a little grandiloquent.

It is not an approach to politics through history that really distinguishes Machiavelli, but rather the use of inductive processes in place of the largely deductive reasoning that had been general earlier. Too much, however, may easily be made of this. It seems to me that perception played a much greater part in bringing about Machiavelli's conclusions than any sort of reasoning. We are all of us prone to generalize the impressions derived from our own little experience and put faith in these generalizations. In the *Discorsi*, Machiavelli frequently announces the widest generalizations without giving any reasons for his belief. Of his most fundamental beliefs is there one that can be said to have been arrived at by inductive reasoning? How did he derive his explanation of the sense of right and wrong in man? He saw that the kinds of action, or the qualities, denominated good, involved a tendency to promote general welfare : and he adopted straightway the delightfully simple seeming explanation of the moral sense that lay on the surface. A minimum of reasoning was concerned in the process.

Similarly, his belief in the radical selfishness of man was derived directly from his own experience of men, fortified to some extent by his reading, which added a fainter experience. It is a generalized impression but not a reasoned conclusion from anything. So also with his conception of fear and of use as dominant factors in human doings. His belief in a tendency to corruption and ruin inherent in all institutions might possibly have been arrived at

[1] Guicciardini comments on the fallacy in *Ricordi*, No. 110.

by inductive reasoning; but the process hardly appears in his writings. Reasoning, again, might have helped him to see patriotism as the health of a State and the strength of an army; but, with the object lesson of Italian States under his eyes, very little reasoning was required. The fact seems to be that Machiavelli was in no sense a systematic or methodical thinker. His sense that dishonesty paid in politics was only a general impression, though, in expounding it, he of course illustrated by examples. It is strange, even, how little thought he seems to have given to the moral question he raised. Hardly indeed does he seem to have seen what the question was.

Yet, after all, Machiavelli, in respect of his method of dealing with political problems, must be reckoned among the great pioneers. He had endeavoured to discover what are the permanent factors of strength and stability in the State and what form of government most conduces to health and vigour. He had endeavoured to show what makes for success in war and in diplomacy. In attempting to do all this by means of observation of and inferences from undisputed facts of the past and the existing, he was doing what had never been done before, since, at all events, the classical days of antiquity. By assuming a permanency of essential conditions he had, indeed, illegitimately avoided one of the greatest practical difficulties of the use of history. But, however partially and faultily, he had applied, if he had not invented, what was practically a new method of dealing with problems of politics. It is clear that his method possessed a high degree of validity in relation to such questions as he asked. And, in fact, it had a great future before it.

This method of his, however, was valid only in relation to secondary questions and only to a certain point. But to say this is not to criticize Machiavelli adversely. He had, as far as possible, limited the field of his inquiry to questions in respect of which his procedure was more or less adequate theoretically. Yet it was just the limitation of inquiry that his method involved that made his writings to a great extent useless for the sixteenth century. That his method was not, in that century, made more use of was due, I think, to the fact that men's minds were then occupied chiefly with questions in relation to which the Machiavellian method, however fortified and improved, would have been quite useless. It could throw no light on the things that men, then, most wanted to know.

§ 8. THE INFLUENCE OF MACHIAVELLI

In writing of the influence of Luther, I had occasion to remark upon the extremely difficult and elusive character of the question involved. Nothing, in fact, seems to me more difficult to trace, nothing harder to estimate, than the influence of any man on the thought of others. A man exerts influence on his fellows by example, by speech or by writing. Of these three, example and speech seem to be the more powerful agents. But the influence of example is moral rather than intellectual and the power of speech can act directly on few. Of all kinds of speech, public speaking is probably the least effective. Weakest of all these agencies is surely the written word. It has only the advantage of a relative permanence : in the long run it may reach many more people than can be reached in other ways. But how often do we find, in actual experience, that men's thought is seriously affected by the books they read ? Now and again the reading of a book, or even of a single sentence written, may mark a turning-point in the thought of a young man or woman ; and it is, no doubt, upon the young that writings act most powerfully. Yet it remains true that, in general, a man finds in a book what, consciously or unconsciously, he is looking for. He accepts its teaching so far as it fits with or clarifies his own thought or expresses his own secret tendency and desire. He rejects it so far as it does not conform. It is difficult to state the fact without overstating it. A writer may, of course, do much to clarify and define the thought of others ; he may bring order into what was chaotic and give the formless form. By providing answers to perplexing questions or simply by force of comfortably dogmatic assertion, he may confirm a wavering faith. He may show a man clearly what he wanted to see and could not see unaided. But all such influence is secondary. It will add force to a current, but not deflect its course. It defines, but it creates nothing. It may provide a channel for scattered waters to flow in ; but the direction of the flow is not altered.

Even more difficult than usual in such cases is it to trace the influence of Machiavelli upon the thought of the sixteenth century or even to make sure that he had any important influence. In this connection, indeed, it has to be remembered that a writer may exercise influence through mere misinterpretation. It is not necessarily what a writer says, it is what he is understood as saying, that influences others, though whether such influence can properly be styled his, is open to question. It must also, of course, be remembered that the mere coincidence of the thought of two men is not even evidence of influence by one or the other, unless it be very peculiar and exact. That So-and-so should say that government exists mainly to secure life and property or that religion is the salt that keeps society from corruption, is not evidence that the writer knew anything of Machiavelli. Some modern students have attributed to Machiavelli a great amount of influence on sixteenth-century thought. But a case can be made out for saying that he had no influence of any serious importance.[1]

He was very much talked of and written about. Botero says that in the various courts of kings and princes to which his business took him, he found every one talking about Reason of State and citing Machiavelli and Tacitus.[2] But the immense majority of sixteenth-century writers on political questions either ignore or repudiate him, if they do not denounce. His writings, for the most part, were actually little known. The *Principe*, indeed, went all over western Europe and was widely read in various languages.[3] The *Art of War* seems to have been fairly well known; the *Discorsi* and the *Florentine History* were known to few. Even in Italy Papal effort to suppress his writings was more effective than might be supposed would have been the case. The criticism and denunciation of Machiavelli in sixteenth-century writings is, for the most part, so ignorant, as to be hardly significant even of revolt against his actual doctrines. It was often not Machiavelli's teaching that was denounced, but a mere bogy. Such ignorance necessitates misunderstandings; but the positive misreading that is read into the imperfectly known writer comes from the reader's own mind. Courtiers and adventurers of all sorts, then as always, pushed their fortunes by any means and without any scruples; and such men may often have comforted themselves with the authority of Machiavelli, whose books they had not read. To speak of these people as influenced by Machiavelli would be ridiculous; but they were understood to be Machiavellians. The anti-Machiavellians attacked them rather than Machiavelli. It was from them perhaps, rather than from his writings, that he became a by-word for knavery, hypocrisy and godlessness.

It should be needless to point out that the facts, if they be facts, that Machiavelli influenced Catherine de Medici or that Charles V and Thomas Cromwell and Henry of Navarre set store by the Prince or that Henry III of France habitually carried a copy about with him, are perfectly insignificant to the historian of political thought. Catherine may have found in the *Principe* comforting confirmation of her natural way of seeing things and even hints and suggestions that she judged practically valuable. Henry IV may well have chuckled appreciatively over certain passages and Henry III been

---

[1] Victor Weille : *Machiavel en France,* written with the object of tracing his influence rather gives one the impression that he had none of importance. The same, I think, is true of the studies of Dr. J. W. Horrocks of his influence in Tudor England. See also article by L. A. Weissberger in *Political Science Quarterly,* Dec., 1927.

[2] *Della Ragion di Stato,* 1589. Dedicatory letter.

[3] The *Principe* was first printed at Rome in 1532 and new editions rapidly followed. A French translation appeared in 1553 and a Latin version in 1560. I know of no translations into English or German before the seventeenth century.

tickled by the fancy that he was something like Cæsar Borgia. But even if, which is very unlikely, the action of these personages were actually affected by their reading of the *Principe*, the fact would have a bearing on the history of political activity, but little or none on the history of political thought. At the very most it would mean that practical maxims for the conduct of their affairs were gleaned by these rulers from the *Principe*. It might be added that, if Catherine and her son were disciples of Machiavelli, they were very unworthy disciples. They had not even understood the *Principe*.

The opinions expressed by Machiavelli about war and armies seem to have influenced a good many people, especially in France; and especially, it seems, people who had had no experience of war. Many writers repeat much of what he had said about the uselessness of mercenary troops and the superiority of citizen armies, and the folly of trusting to fortresses or money. Occasionally they did so critically, more often, apparently, in simple faith. Only to a very slight extent can this be reckoned as influence on political thought. Many writers, also, pick up in passing from Machiavelli stray scraps of wisdom or maxims of practical value, while the structure of their thought remains quite unaffected. This, so far as it goes, is evidence that he did not seriously influence them.

The main currents of thought and subjects of controversy in the sixteenth century lay outside Machiavelli's range. The century was concerned above all with two questions : the question of the relation of the State to the Church and to true religion and the question of the relation of subject to ruler, which included the question whether constituted authority might ever righteously be forcibly resisted. On these two main questions and the subsidiary questions arising out of them, the great mass of political controversy turned. And on these subjects Machiavelli had really nothing to say that was not negative. What he actually said simply shocked people. For, if he said anything relevant, he said that the State was not concerned at all with ' true ' religion, that the religion the State needed was something different from traditional Christianity, that there was no divine sanction for authority and no duty of obedience, but only a tendency to obey arising from fear and habit and intelligent selfishness. He said, in fact, that there was no question of ' right ' at all.

None of the greater thinkers of the century show any definite and serious trace of Machiavelli's influence. Bodin alluded to him with contempt and though he took hints from him and embodied in his *Republic* much of what he had said about war, this affected in no way the character of his thought. Calvin and Hooker might be almost unaware of Machiavelli's existence. Huguenots and Leaguers in France, Puritans and supporters of royal supremacy in England, could find nothing to help them in his writings. Their way of seeing

things and their sense of the problems that were to be solved were
so unlike his, that they could think of him only as the spirit that
denies. In the great controversy over toleration, no one dreamed
of arguing the question from Machiavelli's point of view. The opportunist argument of French Politiques might have been adopted by
him, but certainly owned nothing to him. Machiavelli had regarded
the State as morally isolated, and had seemed implicitly to deny the
existence of obligation between States. No sixteenth-century thinkers,
save in Italy, agreed with him. The thinkers of the century were
working out a theory of international obligation. Considering all
these things one is tempted to say that on the serious political thought
of the sixteenth century, Machiavelli had no influence whatever.

But, obviously, his influence must not be looked for in these
directions. His writings did not influence thought on the main controversial questions of the period and could not possibly have done
so. Those questions, in themselves, denied the validity of his point
of view.

But his writings may have done something to impress people with
the conception of the State as completely secular and independent and
with the conception of a State based on natural or racial affinities.
Yet it does not seem possible that he can have done much in these
directions. The thinkers of the sixteenth century did not, as a rule,
regard the State as completely secular. Even those who regarded
supreme power as secular did not detach it from the Church. The
King, to be supreme, must be Head of the Church. Wholly dissimilar
to the Tudor conception of royal supremacy was Machiavelli's notion
of a religion fostered and controlled by the State for merely earthly
ends. The conception, again, of a natural or racial basis for the
State is none too clear in Machiavelli ; and so far as it occurs distinctly
in sixteenth-century thought, I know of nothing to indicate that anyone derived it from him. Again, Machiavelli may have done a good
deal to strengthen the perennial tendency to believe that hoped-for
good may be reached through evil. But that view had little currency
in sixteenth-century thought as expressed in writing. The influence
of any writer who may be supposed to have had influence is, I
believe, habitually exaggerated. It seems fairly safe to say that in no
case has there been more exaggeration than in that of Machiavelli.

But we cannot rightly leave it at that. The abuse bestowed on
Machiavelli throughout the century has a serious significance. It
betokened mental disturbance and fear. Ignorant and foolish as
it mostly was, those who denounced him had good reason for their
fears. He was denounced as anti-Christian, atheistic, immoral, as
an advocate of Turkish despotism and an apologist for every crime.
He was not exactly any of these things ; but that does not matter.
The denunciation of him was occasioned partly by misapprehensions,

partly by association of him with things and people with whom he had no real connection and partly by what he said. But it was occasioned still more by his intellectual attitude and manner. For, by implication at least, he denied the assumptions on which thought was mainly proceeding. He implied that the questions which most of all disturbed men's minds need not and should not be asked at all.

His denials and the questions he raised could not be put aside. His method of reasoning was a challenge to existing authority ; [1] and it was just in that challenge that lay his value for sixteenth-century thought. Had he really been seen as the contemptibly perverse being his enemies tried to make out that he was, men would quickly have ceased to read or to denounce him. They did not do so ; and controversy goes on about him into the next century and beyond. Throughout the century there was growing a sceptical attitude in relation to the claims of churches. The development of political thought frankly utilitarian is marked towards the close of the century in the writings of the French Politiques, in Mariana and in England. The tendency to rely simply on verifiable and indisputable or undisputed facts for the solution of problems of politics and to refuse to face such problems as could not so be approached, was evidently strengthening. How much of all that was due to the influence of Machiavelli's writings, it is evidently quite impossible to know. But it may well be that he was no inconsiderable factor in these developments. As the process went on, so did he slowly come to his own. There are signs that his influence was more real at the end of the century than it had ever been. Living at the close of the century we find writers who were more clearly and definitely influenced by Machiavelli than any we can find earlier. In England, Raleigh and Bacon are conspicuous examples ; [2] in France, Politique writings more doubtfully tell the same tale. The *Politics* [3] of that very unoriginal writer, Justus Lipsius, timidly repeats a good deal of what Machiavelli had said. Gentili's attitude towards him betokens some understanding and a new respect.

Machiavelli's writings form a part of those Renaissance influences which, all through the sixteenth century, made for freedom in thought and the practical toleration of adverse opinion. It is at least in some small degree due to him that political thought assumed, more and more, a practical, common-sense and opportunist character, and turned away from questions it could not answer. It might be said that it was in some degree due to him that governments ceased to be urged to do impossible things. He had at least some share in releasing men from assumptions imposed by churches and by States. It was not his conclusions that

---

[1] L. A. Burd in *Cambridge Modern History*, I, Chap. 6, p. 213.

[2] Raleigh's writings and Bacon's relevant writings belong to the seventeenth century, which is the inadequate reason why they are not dealt with in this book.

[3] Published 1589.

were suggestive or stimulating, but the methods by which he reached them. It is not a question of the validity of his denials or assertions or even of his method of reasoning. He stood, in the long run, for the principle that there is no question that must not be asked nor assumption that must be made.

CHAPTER III

GUICCIARDINI

COMPARISON between the views of Machiavelli and the expressed opinions of his younger contemporary, Francesco Guicciardini, is instructive.[1] It at least illustrates the fact that Machiavelli's outlook was by no means exceptional in the Italy of his time. Of all the critics of Machiavelli in the first half of the sixteenth century, Guicciardini, diplomatist, administrator, states-man and historian, was at once the best equipped and by far the most able. All the more illuminating is his criticism because his outlook was so like that of Machiavelli. Cynical in the extreme, greedy of power, honours and money, scheming and unscrupulous, he might have served as a model to Machiavelli, had he been a Prince instead of a minister of princes. ' Three things,' he wrote, ' I should like to see before I die ; but I fear that even if I live long, I shall not see one of them : a well-established republican life in our city, Italy freed from the barbarians and the world freed from the rascally priests.' [2] But, for the greater part of his active life, he served the Papacy which he detested, and the Medicean ' tyrants ' of Florence. As expressive of his outlook on politics he has left us only fragments and indications. These fragments, however, are fairly explicit and these indications are clear so far as they go. There is the early *Discorsi Politici*, written during his embassy in Spain, the disserta-tion on Machiavelli's *Discorsi*, the *Dialogo del Reggimento di Firenze* and the illuminating *Ricordi Politici e Civili*, a note-book collection of observations, of which many of the later repeat the earlier. There is also the *Istoria Fiorentina* and the great *Istoria d'Italia*, in both which Guicciardini's way of seeing men and institutions is clearly indicated.[3] It may perhaps be regretted that he did not give us a regular treatise on politics. He had all the intellectual detachment and analytic power necessary. He might have left something which would have diminished the reputation of Machiavelli both for good and

---

[1] Guicciardini was born in 1482 and died in 1540.

[2] *Ricordi Politici e Civili*, 236.

[3] None of these writings was published in the sixteenth century, or indeed the nineteenth, except the *Istoria d'Italia*.

for evil. Yet it seems that had he written such a treatise, he would have had little to offer but criticism of other men's views.

It is perhaps a little difficult to say whether the points of agreement or the points of difference between Guicciardini and Machiavelli are the more important. Guicciardini's criticism of Machiavelli's work is, in the main, a criticism of his method of attacking political problems. It rests on a scepticism of the reliability of any conclusions based on experience of affairs or knowledge of political events of the past. Guicciardini, indeed, agreed with Machiavelli that man does not change except superficially and that events repeat themselves. The faces of men change, he says, and the outward semblance of things, yet the same things come round again nor does any event occur which has not occurred already.[1] But, though he agreed so far, he found fault with Machiavelli for arguing from Roman experience and declared he drew conclusions far too absolutely. He denies, in fact, that any reliable conclusions as to what should now be done and what is best now, can be drawn from past experience. He denies that it is possible to extract from man's experience any sort of valid rule of action or law of movement. 'It is a great error,' he wrote, ' to speak of the affairs of this world absolutely or without discrimination and so to say by rule, for almost every rule has qualifications and exceptions, owing to the variety of circumstance.' [2]

He was far more deeply impressed than was Machiavelli by the differences that accompany all circumstantial similarities. Not only so, but he was sceptical as to whether we really ever know or understand the past at all. It is not surprising, he declared, that we know very little about past events, for, even in a single city, we do not know what happens from day to day.[3] It seemed to him that successful political action depended on minute adjustments and that no general rules were likely to be of use in any given case. No two occasions are sufficiently alike to allow of the application of any general principle to both ; and all general principles of action are therefore invalid. Every case must be judged of as it arises from day to day, as he says,[4] with little or no reference to what may have occurred earlier in some somewhat similar case. It makes, of course, no absolute difference whether the ' history ' on which you base your conclusions is that of the old Roman Republic or that of the day before yesterday, whether the experience you rely on is your very own or that of Agathocles of Syracuse. Everything you can think of is past or future : the present is past before you can think of it. The wider your generaliza-

---

[1] *Ricordi*, 110. See also No. 336, quoted on p. 486, and No. 76.
[2] Ib., 6. ' E grande errore parlare della cose del mondo indistintamente e assolutamente, e, perdire cosi per regola, perche quasi tutte hanno distinzione ed eccezione per la varietà delle circumstanze.'
[3] Ib., 141.   [4] Ib., 114.

tion the more useless it will be. Everybody, Guicciardini points out, agrees that the rule of a single person is the best of all governments when it is good and the worst when it is bad. But what nobody tells us, he adds, is whether government by a single person or few or many is actually most desirable.

As criticism of Machiavelli's method all this seems to be fallacious and superficial. Guicciardini could see trees very distinctly, but apparently could not see a wood. He writes as though Machiavelli had asserted that by applying generalizations based on past experience you could say exactly what should be done under given circumstances. But only incidentally, if at all, did Machiavelli say anything of the kind. He had been trying to discover the permanent in a world of perpetual motion. To say that, because circumstances are never exactly the same, you cannot come to any conclusions as to what factors, permanently and under all circumstances, make for strength or stability or success in the life of States, would be absurd. Did Guicciardini mean that there were no such permanent factors ? That, on his own admissions, could not possibly be true. But he did not mean that. All he says is that no two calls for political action are so much alike that the same rule will apply to both. That assertion, true or false, is mainly irrelevant. It touches only the fringes of Machiavelli's thought. Guicciardini was criticizing not Machiavelli's method but unintelligent application of it.

To Guicciardini, apparently, Machiavelli was an optimistic dreamer. He agreed with him that the expulsion of foreigners from Italy was highly desirable, he completely disagreed with the assertion made in the *Principe* that the moment and opportunity had arrived. He agreed, too, that the power and policy of the Papacy had been the chief agent in keeping Italy disunited. But he denied that Italy's disunion was a misfortune. But for the Church, he says, Italy would probably have become a monarchy, but whether this would have been a good or a bad thing for the country is at least very doubtful. Italy, he says, has perhaps suffered at different times more than she would have done if united. But, on the other hand, the establishment of a central government in one city would have depressed all others, and Italy would certainly not have developed so many flourishing cities as actually she has done. For this reason, he concludes, union would have been rather a misfortune than otherwise.[1] This view of the matter seems to be quite as reasonable as that of Machiavelli.

Guicciardini seems to have shared the preference expressed by Machiavelli for a republican form of government, at least for his native Florence. He would no doubt have refused to generalize that preference. In his *Dialogo* on the government of Florence he criticized

[1] *Considerationi intorno ai Discorsi di Machiavelli. Opere Inedite*, p. 28.

severely the management of the Medici, asserted that democratic government had proved itself at least as incapable and oppressive and that government by the aristocracy would be worst of all. What Florence needed, according to him, was a ' governo misto ', something after the fashion of that of Venice. He certainly had not Machiavelli's belief in the superiority of popular government and he repeatedly expresses contempt for the populace. ' Who speaks of the people speaks of a mad monster full of errors and confusions.' [1] The populace, he says, knows as much of the motives and even of the acts of its government as it does of what is happening in India.[2] Its determinations are a matter of chance rather than of reason.[3] Yet he favours republican ' liberty ' as the best safeguard against oppression. In Florence at least, he declared, the people should be allowed to elect officials and put a veto on proposed legislation.[4] Republican ' liberty ' he apparently regarded as serving no purpose but that of preventing tyrannical action. These judgements seem to differ rather widely from those of Machiavelli, but the difference is not really great and certainly there is no difference of principle. Machiavelli had more belief in the intelligence and justice of popular government ; and he hoped more from it than Guicciardini was able to hope from anything. But they appear to have agreed that there is little real desire for any ' liberty ' save that which is security. Men care, says Guicciardini, far more for their own power and personal prominence than they do for freedom ; and often the tyrant slayer is a would-be tyrant. He remarks that he has often noticed that the name of liberty serves rather as a pretext or a cloak to ambition than expresses a real desire natural to man. What is natural to man is desire for superiority and domination.[5]

Guicciardini's judgement of human nature seems to me to have been even more cynical than that of Machiavelli. It is true that in the *Ricordi* he declared, emphatically and more than once, that men are naturally inclined to the good and even that whoso is without this inclination is a monstrosity.[6] It is not, however, very clear what he meant. Though he declared that ' men are all by nature more inclined to good than to evil ', his writings show that he saw, in the political world at least, very few signs of that natural inclination. He advises you never to do a good turn to anyone, at the expense of a third person, because the injury will be remembered and the benefit forgot.[7] Montaigne noted ' que parmi tant d'âmes et d'effects qu'il juge, de tant de mouvemens et conseils, il n'en rapporte jamais un seul a la vertu, religion et conscience . . . et de toutes les actions

---

[1] *Ricordi*, 140. [2] Ib., 141.
[3] Ib., 378. [4] *Considerationi. Op. Ined.*, p. 13.
[5] *Reggimento di Firenze. Op. Ined.*, p. 51.
[6] *Ricordi*, 134, 135, 225. [7] Ib., 25.

pour belles par apparence qu'elles soient d'elles mêmes, il en rejette la cause a quelque occasion vicieux ou a quelque proufit . . . et peult estre advenu,' added this coolest and sanest of observers, ' qu'il ayt estimé d'aultruy selon soy.'[1]

If we examine the opinions expressed by Guicciardini as to moral obligation, we shall, I think, find that the term ' unmoral ' applies to him far better than to Machiavelli. Machiavelli was a moralist by intelligence with little moral sense. It seems to have been a question for him whether immoral action could be justified under the conditions of political activity. He tried to escape from the difficulty by suggesting that all action that produces a generally beneficial affect is strictly and positively moral. His justification of treachery and crime in politics is fully consistent with this view, even though his language be not so always. But to Guicciardini there seems to have been no question. Where he apparently differs from Machiavelli is in thinking that treachery and crime only pays occasionally either in private or in public life. But he held, at least as assuredly as Machiavelli, that such conduct justifies itself by success ;[2] and that without referring success to public welfare. He does not appear to have considered the matter worth arguing about. He remarks that frankness and sincerity are generally applauded and dissimulation condemned, but that the former is most useful to other people and the latter to oneself. Therefore, ' I should commend such as are ordinarily frank and sincere and use dissimulation only on occasions of much importance which rarely occur. In this way a man acquires a reputation for frankness and honesty and enjoys the approval that attends such qualities, while he will be able in matters of real importance to deceive all the more effectively.'[2] These remarks are made with no special reference to political life. Machiavelli had said that it was well for a Prince to be reputed truthful and honourable so long as he was ready to lie and cheat on occasion. He had never suggested that the same principle held good for all men under all circumstances.

As a matter of course Guicciardini's principle applied to political life. Here, also, he thought that treachery rarely pays ; and here he differed, or thought he differed, from Machiavelli, to whom, he says, drastic and violent measures always appeal. More cautious, less eager and hopeful than Machiavelli, he was sceptical of the value of such means except in extraordinary cases. It is easy, he says, to terrorize, but it is rarely expedient.[3] He agreed with Machiavelli that a man who restored order in a chaotic city by means of treachery and cruelty, would be praiseworthy. 'But it is very undesirable,' he remarked, ' that one should be brought to this, not only because it may lead to the establishment of tyranny, but also because evil

[1] *Essais*, II, 10. [2] *Ricordi*, 104. [3] Ib., 341.

means corrupt good intentions.' [1] This last remark seems to show intellectual perception of a moral fact to which Machiavelli's eagerness made him partially blind.

Guicciardini appears, in fact, as more Machiavellian than ever was Machiavelli. The phrase, perhaps, means little ; but in any case, I think that the agreement between these two great Italians is substantial and fundamental and that their differences are relatively unimportant. The colder and more cautious temperament of Guicciardini and his more detached attitude enabled him to see some things more clearly than did Machiavelli. He was able to see that there was little or no chance of driving the foreigner out of Italy. He was able, too, to see than an earlier political union of the country might have depressed or extinguished the vivid and splendidly productive life of the Italian cities. This does not mean that he did not see that the rule of foreigners and petty despots might have similar results. Very few men can have had so little capacity for deceiving themselves.

Guicciardini's judgements differ, one might say, from those of Machiavelli in degree rather than in kind. The thought of both was concerned with the actual and to a great extent with the immediately actual. Both eschewed all ultimate questions. Both relied for conclusions wholly on observation and experience. Though Guicciardini criticized Machiavelli's method, it was nevertheless his own. Both believed that man has been, and is, what he always will be. Both saw the State as a wholly secular thing. In the mind of neither of them was there any conception corresponding to the term ' natural law '. Neither seems to have had any sense of or belief in real obligation and both had to conceive the State without it. Naturally both saw the State as normally extremely unstable. Machiavelli, indeed, had a theory of the origin and meaning of morality, but it was not a theory of obligation. Guicciardini had, apparently, no ethics at all. To him moral rules of conduct were simply more or less convenient conventions, more useful to others than to oneself.

Most important of all is it, in establishing the relation of these two thinkers to the main stream of sixteenth-century thought, to note the negative aspects of their way of thinking. Neither of them saw the Church except as a temporal power in Italy, or as an organization of hypocrisy and superstition. Before the Reformation, or quite independently of it, they had gone, in a sense, much further than the Reformers. Both were sceptical not only of the truth of Christian revelation but of the social or political value of Christianity. Both had to solve their problems without any data supplied by the Scriptures or the Church. Machiavelli turned from the Bible to Livy and Polybius ; Guicciardini seems to have stood as much alone as any man can. Neither could see any ends for the State but mere security or

[1] *Considerazioni. Op. Ined.*, p. 22.

mere power or a fictitious glory. They were ignorant and contemptuous of medieval philosophy and had broken with Christian tradition. Such emancipation may be honourable to them ; it may, or it may not, mark a step in intellectual progress ; but it would certainly seem that it disabled them from finding any basis for obligation and, one might say, any basis for the State.

The two men thought habitually in the same way and about the same things ; and neither the way nor the things were those of the thought of the sixteenth century. When one passes from Machiavelli or Guicciardini to contemporary France or Germany or England, one enters a different world. Even in Italy, long before the end of the century, thought had assumed directions and a quality quite different from that of Machiavelli. The attitude of these two was one that belonged more to Italy in the fifteenth than to any country in the sixteenth century. That it was reproduced in one way or another, with increasing frequency, in later centuries is a fact the significance of which cannot as yet be fully determined.

CHAPTER IV

LATER ITALIAN THOUGHT

§ 1. ITALY AFTER MACHIAVELLI

AFTER Machiavelli's death in 1526, Italian speculative activity, to the end of the century, turned mainly on philosophical and religious questions. Except indirectly, through jurisprudence and to some extent in connection with the development of theories of international law, Italian thought, for the greater part of the century, was little concerned with politics. In Pierino Belli [1] Italy produced one of the most distinguished of the precursors of Gentili and of Grotius ; and Gentili himself was, of course, an Italian. It is true that Italians played a leading part in developing that form of Catholic political theory which is especially associated with the name of Roberto Bellarmino. But that theory was rather Jesuit than specifically Italian and arose out of the great European controversies between Catholic Papists and Catholic nationalists and between Catholics and Protestants generally. The fact that it was to some extent specially associated with Italy is one sign how far Italy travelled in the sixteenth century from the thought of Machiavelli. But, if we put aside the Jurists and the Papalist theorists, there appear to be only two Italian writers on politics of any marked distinction later than 1540. Both of these, Paolo Paruta and Giovanni Botero, belong to the closing years of the century. Paolo Sarpi and the controversy in which he was engaged belonged to the early years of the next century.

Machiavelli's influence on the thought of his own land in his own century seems to have been almost negligible. To a considerable extent this was due to the fact that the Pope and the Church, and especially the Jesuits, did their utmost, officially and otherwise, to suppress his writings and blast his reputation and make of his name a thing of fear and horror to the faithful. In the Index of 1559 it was ordered that no one should print or copy, buy or sell, or keep any of the works of Machiavelli ; [2] and the Council of Trent confirmed the judgement.

---

[1] His *De Re Militari et de Bello* was published at Venice in 1563.

[2] The same honour was accorded to Erasmus.

The Papacy associated the free-thinking scepticism prevalent in Italy with the Protestantism to the north ; and the earlier popularity, or notoriety, of Machiavelli's writings caused him to be singled out for attack. But mere Papal prohibitions would probably have had little effect of themselves. Vastly more important was the great revival of Catholicism under a reformed Papacy, that took place in Italy as elsewhere. Nothing is more striking in the history of the sixteenth century than the increase of the spiritual influence of the Church in Italy.

It must be remembered, too, that the problems which most of all interested Machiavelli, ceased to be practical problems soon after his death, if not earlier. By 1540, at latest, expulsion of the foreigner could no longer be seen as possible and very doubtfully even as desirable. The gradual abandonment of the French attempt to establish dominion in Italy established the dominion of Spain. Machiavelli had been acutely interested in the new Prince, getting himself into the saddle or trying to consolidate a new dominion. But the overwhelming power of Spain put an end to such adventures. Under Charles V Italy was settling down and frontiers becoming fixed. The domination of the foreigner, after all, gave Italy that peace and security Machiavelli had desired. The tendency of political thinking in Italy was, consequently, towards the acceptance of absolute monarchy as the safest and most comfortable form of government.

Republican tradition hardly survived that peace, save in the highly aristocratic republics of Venice and Genoa. No other part of western Europe accepted monarchic absolutism so easily and quietly as did Italy. There had been, of course, a long period of preparation. In the petty principalities and oligarchic republics into which Italy was now fixedly resolved, no serious friction of political opinion showed itself. Italian thought turned in every direction rather than to politics. There may have been in this silence some of that despair of political speculation which marked the world of Hellenic thought after Alexander the Great.

§ 2. PAOLO PARUTA

In traversing country in which most of the tracks lead to quagmires and which is always thorny, and in places desolatingly arid, it is pleasant to meet with a person like Paolo Paruta. A Venetian subject who passed most of his life of high content in Venice, he links ideally with the earlier Italian Platonists and with such men as Cardinal Pole and in hardly any way with Machiavelli. For many years he lived in a studious retirement, but the publication of his *Della perfezione della vita politica*, in 1579, brought him into local prominence.[1] He became official historian to the Republic and served it with dis-

---

[1] A French translation appeared in 1583 and a translation into English, by Henry Cary, in 1657.

tinction on embassies. He gathered round him a circle of friends, interested like himself in literature and philosophy ; and his *Perfezione* may fairly be taken as giving an idea of the discussions that took place in his own house. It is written in the curious form of a conversation among actual and named persons, all of whom Paruta personally knew.

In lengthy and leisurely fashion they discuss the question whether the active life of politics is worthy of a wise man. It was a question that had long been a favourite topic in such circles.[1] The views of Paruta himself are expressed in the name of Suriano. He asserts that man has no higher end to pursue than the service of his country. ' He who would live well must think not only of himself but of the city also.' [2] It is objected that the special temptations of political life are too great to take risks with ; that in politics there is too much of unavoidable compromise to satisfy any philosopher and too much disappointment and failure to make the life worth while. We, it is declared, are citizens of the world ; and that we belong to one particular State or country is a mere legalized convention. The individual carries within him all the authority he needs for his own doings and must never allow himself to be enslaved by society. Man's end is spiritual and cannot be attained in the service of material interests.

To this Paruta replies that a man may lead a peaceful and harmonious life, neither desiring nor despising honours, in the thick of political strife. Man is not all spirit, and to take account of body also is more in accord with our nature than an attempt to live a life of pure contemplation. Body, it is pointed out, has much to say in spiritual affairs and will not be denied. It has always been noted that there exists a correspondence between the character of men and the climatic conditions under which they live. The qualities that distinguish people of different nations seem almost inseparable from these conditions.[3]

The supreme end of life is to live virtuously. But, for virtuous living, convenience and amenities of life are needed ; and the State therefore is necessary to one as to the other.[4] Man cannot live virtuously without possessions and without friends ; [5] and for both these good things he is dependent on civil society. The individual, therefore, needs the State absolutely. Again, to pursue virtue it is not enough to see it and to will it : it must become active and without government and ordered living it cannot do so. The proper function of the State is the liberation of men for the higher life, and it is only in and through the State that we possess those things which make the life of virtue possible. External benefits, derived to man through the State, are

---

[1] One is reminded of Pole's remarks at the beginning of the Starkey Dialogue.
[2] *Perfezione*, ed. 1579, p. 8.　　　　　[3] Ib., p. 40.
[4] Ib., p. 47.　　　　　[5] Ib., p. 57.

to the wise man what the viol is to the musician or marble to the sculptor.[1] It is suggested, on the other side, that, even though all this be so, it should at least be admitted that the end of political activity should be a life of study and contemplation. Paruta will not admit it. He regarded activity directed to high ends as always in itself finer than contemplation or than ever imperfect knowledge.

'Only too great,' Paruta concludes, 'is the obligation under which we lie to our country: a society not gathered accidentally or for a brief time, as is a ship's company, but founded on nature itself, confirmed by our own will, at all times needed and at all times dear: nor, in the perils of our city do we stand to lose, as in a ship, a few poor goods, but rather all our dearest possessions, our very truth and summum bonum of virtue.' [2]

It is a man's bounden duty to do what he can for the welfare of the society in which he lives. After all this the friends proceed to a discussion of the qualities of the perfectly virtuous politician. The perfect politician, they conclude, must have knowledge of the past and of the elusive present and a vision of the future. He should study history. He must, of course, be intensely public-spirited, absolutely just and perfectly self-controlled.

Paruta's *Discorsi Politici* appeared in 1599, the year after his death. It does not add very much of interest. It deals largely with Roman history and Venetian constitutional arrangements. Venice, he thought, had maintained her liberty and independence by means of her admirable constitution. But the chief interest of this work lies in the expression it gives to Paruta's views as to the worthiness of different forms of government. Forms of government, he points out, necessarily vary with place and circumstance and the nature of the people concerned. He was quite free from any notion that God prefers one form to another, or that any form of government was divinely established. Monarchy, he says in the *Perfezione*, is a moral, not a religious institution.[3] The constitution that is most stable and that is most efficient in the work of liberating its citizens for the life of virtue, is a mixed constitution in which an aristocratic element predominates. It was, he thought, the over-great strength of the democratic element in the constitution that ruined the Roman Republic. Rome ended in tyranny, 'which is born of the popular State'. It is always an aristocracy and not the 'people' that cares for liberty; where the people rules liberty quickly vanishes. To this intellectual aristocrat it seemed quite clear that popular government was the least stable and the most inefficient possible. Equality of political rights, he declared, is fatal to good government. He remarked that among all the various kinds of 'popular' State 'that may be esteemed the worst in which artisans do most abound'.

Comparing Venice with Carthage, Paruta remarks that no purely maritime power has ever established a lasting empire. But the loss of the Venetian over-sea dominion gave him no concern. States, he says, should seek peaceful development within natural limits only and there is always injustice involved in conquest. ' The true end of the State is the virtuous life of its citizens and not the greatness of dominion.' [1] The effort to extend dominion implies a wrong spirit in the citizens and such aggressiveness tends to produce internal strife. The greatness of a State is the greatness of its citizens.[2] Only once does Paruta refer to Machiavelli ; and then it is to express a hope that his works will remain for ever in oblivion. He reflects, it is evident, at once a scepticism of the value of the State and a conception of its value, alike wholly alien to the thought of Machiavelli. But it may be worth while to point out that, in one respect, his view resembled that of the great Florentine. It is characteristic of him that he seems to have known little of and cared less for the Roman or any other Church. As Machiavelli turned to Livy, Paruta turned to Plato. His conception of the function of the State as the liberation of men for the higher life of virtue is, it is true, radically similar to the conception of Aquinas. Yet this State of his is wholly secular. It has no necessary relation to any Church. There is, indeed, no suggestion in Paruta that the Church can do anything worth speaking of for the life of virtue. But all through the sixteenth century Italian thinkers seem to have seen the State as purely secular. Even the Papalists, I think, did so, though they claimed powers for the Pope in relation to it. To suppose, however, that this was due in any appreciable degree to the influence of Machiavelli would be gratuitously absurd.

There is another and completely negative respect in which Paruta resembles Machiavelli. He stood as much apart as his predecessor from the main currents of thought and subjects of controversy in the sixteenth century. No question of the relation of State to Church or of the rights or duties of subjects in relation to rulers, troubled his Platonic serenity. In this, also, he was characteristically Italian. It is, I think, just the fact that for Italy these questions were not practical or vitally stirring that accounts for the relative absence of political thought and controversy in Italy.

§ 3. BOTERO

Very unlike the rather dilettante Paruta, with his preoccupation with the ideal of the wise and virtuous man, his belief in aristocratic government and his conviction that the moral end of the State involves obligation to serve it, was Giovanni Botero. Born at Bène in Piedmont and hence sometimes called Benisius, Botero took orders, became

---

[1] *Discorsi*, p. 18.   [2] Ib., p. 25.

the friend and the private secretary of Cardinal Borromeo, served on embassies for the Duke of Savoy and became tutor to his children. He was a conscientious student and took his work very seriously. His most famous book, *Della Ragion di Stato*, was published in 1589 and became widely known.[1] But some of his shorter treatises are also of some importance. Particularly characteristic and distinctive is the *Delle Cause de la Grandezza delle Citta*, published in 1596.

Botero's opinions coincided in several particular respects with those of Machiavelli, whom he described as an empty writer. What he says about the Florentine does not leave the impression that he understood him. Whether his thought was influenced by what he read of Machiavelli's writings it is not possible to say. More important, in any case, is the fact that his mode of thinking was similar to Machiavelli's in an essential respect. His mind was wholly occupied with the question of how things actually are and how they actually move. His *Ragion di Stato* consists almost entirely of what he took to be simply statements of verifiable fact. However dubious his assertions, that is what he intended them to be. There was, he thought, a great deal to explain in connection with this thing, the State : and he seems to have thought it was all rather easily explained. He asked no question about the ultimate nature of political authority ; the questions for him were how it actually arose, how it is maintained and what is the most efficient form of it. He was as unconcerned as Paruta with the main questions that agitated the minds of thinkers outside Italy. Though he believed religion to be a political factor of the greatest importance, he considered it only as it subserved the purposes of government. Though he could not think of the Church as Machiavelli had done and speaks of it as a divinely established monarchy, he does not seem to have attributed to it any specific authority except in relation to questions of strictly Christian doctrine. He asked no questions about its relation to the State. It is perhaps worth notice that he argues at length that dishonesty in politics does not even pay. Whether or no he were influenced by Machiavelli, he seems certainly to have been influenced by Bodin. His theory of climate, at least, looks as if it were derived directly from the French writer. But what above all distinguishes Botero is his assertion of the fundamental importance of economic factors in society. The suggestion of that may also have come from Bodin.

The earliest form of government, Botero opined, was monarchy ; and the important thing to notice is, he says, that it was established by popular consent for the common good and security.[2] It was not, he specifically declared, instituted by any special act of God. The

---

[1] It was translated into Latin, French, Spanish and German. A French translation appeared in 1599.

[2] *Ragion*, ed. 1589, pp. 16, 17.

only monarchy directly established by God is that of the Church. Nor has God prescribed or recommended to men any particular form of government and any form of government in the world may be the right one.[1]

What is right at any particular time and place depends on circumstances and the nature of the people concerned. That being so, it is, he pointed out, difficult to decide what form of government is above all preferable. But he does not really seem to have seen any difficulty. He had no doubt whatever that monarchy pure and simple, the sole sovereignty of an hereditary person, was the best of all forms of government. The reasons he gives for this belief are, for the most part, at once wholly unoriginal and quite fantastic. God is a monarch and has established monarchy in the Church ; all light comes from the sun and the unity of a whole goes with a multitude of parts.[2] It is a little odd to find this kind of thing in the mind of a thinker usually so positive and rationalistic. More pertinently he pointed out, as others had done and were doing, that monarchy has tended to displace all other forms of government. It has established itself even among the rough and violent peoples of the north who are naturally averse to it. He adduced also the commonplace contention that speed in action is most likely to be had in a monarchy.

The well-being of the State, however, Botero declared, depends less on the form of its government than on the obedience of the subject.[3] Most important of all factors in maintaining obedience is justice. To make every one secure in respect of his property and other rights in law, is the only means of establishing peace and harmony in society.[4] Judicial administration should be uniform, alike for all without favour or corruption and should also be speedy. Botero descanted at length on the lamentable failure actually visible in these respects everywhere.[5] Almost equally important is it that the ruler should understand his people. Nothing is more necessary than this for good government.[6] In this connection, Botero remarked, the effects of climatic conditions on character have to be considered. Important also is it that the government should concern itself with the needs of the poor, and should promote education and the arts.[7] Botero was as sure as was Machiavelli that a government must be popular to be strong and stable.

Like Machiavelli also, Botero held that the strength and stability

---

[1] *Discorso dell' Excellenza della Monarchia.* Printed along with Botero's *Della Relationi Universali* in 1612, p. 81.

[2] Some might say, Botero ingeniously remarks, that God being a Trinity of Persons, His government is an aristocracy rather than a monarchy. But the works of God, he rejoins, are a product of His unity.

[3] *Ragion*, p. 18. [4] Ib., p. 22. [5] Ib., p. 39.
[6] Ib., p. 50. [7] Ib., p. 42.

of a State depended, perhaps most of all, upon religion. Unless his subjects be religious, Botero declared, no Prince, however just and prudent, can be really secure. All those who have founded new States have found it necessary either to revive an old religion or introduce a new one.[1] All religions alike, he seems to have imagined, teach service to the State as a duty, and for this reason all alike have social value. But none, he argued, more effectively subserves the cause of order than does Christianity. For the Christian religion subjects to the Prince not only the bodies and goods of the subjects, but even their souls and consciences ; it binds not only their hands but their thoughts and affections ; it enjoins them to obey dissolute as well as temperate Princes, and to suffer all things that the peace be not broken. There is no act that frees the subject from his duty of obedience unless one contrary to the laws of nature or of God ; and even in such cases everything is to be endured rather than an open breach.[2]

Botero was an ecclesiastic and presumably a believer. But he did not himself argue the duty of submission from the Scriptures or teachings of the Church. He committed himself only to the statement that Christianity, so teaching, subserves the purposes of the State at least as well as any other religion. It is not unlikely that he was here thinking of Machiavelli's assertion that this was just what Christianity had failed to do.

Botero fully adopted Bodin's theory that the character of a people's mentality is determined by permanent ' climatic ' conditions. He connected it with his assertion that any form of government may be appropriate in a particular place more definitely than did Bodin himself. He has the distinction of being the only writer of the century who grasped at all fully the significance of the theory. His own exposition of it, however, is by no means so full or so clear as Bodin's. He seems to take the theory as one fully established and generally accepted, as indeed did Paruta. He repeats a good deal of what Bodin had said and adds very little. But, so far was he from being shocked by it, that he did add something to Bodin's suggestion that even the form of religion may be ultimately determined by climate. The heresies, he remarked, that have originated among the subtle and philosophically inclined, though unpractical, peoples of the south, have been highly speculative and concerned with the most difficult questions of Christian theology, relating to the Trinity and the nature of Christ. Those, on the other hand, originating among the rude and energetic, undisciplined and rather stupid northern peoples, have been correspondingly gross and simple, turning on mere questions of practice, such as clerical celibacy and the authority of the Pope. Did he mean definitely to suggest that Protestantism was really a

[1] Ib., p. 93.   [2] Ib., p. 94.

product of the stupefying effects of a northern climate ? But the suggestion cuts both ways.

It was especially in his essay on the greatness of cities that Botero developed his view of the importance of economics. In the *Ragion di Stato* he tells us that governmental authority originated in deliberate action, taken mainly for the sake of defence and justice. In the *Grandezza* he explains that social life developed, presumably earlier, under economic pressures. He adopted the view, that had already become a commonplace, that, in the very earliest days of humanity, men lived like the beasts. But men came to see how much would be gained if they formed themselves into a society for the sharing of all they produced.[1] Quite evidently he was not thinking of any communistic sharing. The sharing he speaks of was by way of trade and barter.

He explains that a city or a large town, the grandezza of which is measured by population and wealth, is a centre to which people gather for the sake of security, ease and plenty. The growth of such a place is not and cannot be brought about by any governmental action, nor can force either create or sustain it.[2] A strong internal authority is indeed necessary to its existence for the sake of order, while the maintenance of order promotes the growth of the city by making it attractive. Nevertheless, the real cause of the development of cities is simply the opportunities they offer for profitable production and dealing. It is what Botero calls their nutritive virtue that makes them great. The essential factors are a site suitable for trading and good transport facilities. Justice depends on the strength of the government ; but the strength of the government is largely dependent on plenty. The wealth of a Prince depends on the possessions of his subjects : ' their goods and their traffic ; the fruits of the earth and of industry, exports and imports and means of transport from one place or country to another '.[3] The Prince, therefore, should introduce every sort of craft and manufacture. Peace in the city depends partly on justice and partly on plenty. But plenty depends not only on soil and roads and water-ways and minerals, but on the amount of labour available. Botero insists that labour, not capital, is the essential factor in the production of wealth.[4] It follows that idleness is a curse to the community. The idle, he says, are those who live on the labour of others. The concentration of wealth in a few hands he also declares to be an evil, on the ground that it acts as a check upon the increase of population.[5]

It is evident that Botero was to some extent conscious that the views he expresses as to the development of cities would for the

---

[1] *Grandezza*, I, Chap. 2, ed. 1596, p. 6.
[2] Ib., Chaps. 2 and 3.　　　　[3] *Ragion*, pp. 30, 31.
[4] *Grandezza*, 1596, p. 43.　　　　[5] Ib., Chap. 7.

most part apply also to communities or States of any size. He was certainly writing of city States as well as of mere cities and his pre-occupation with economics is as marked in the *Ragion di Stato* as in the *Grandezza*, though his conclusions are not there made so clear. In one place, at least, in the *Grandezza*, he widens his outlook to include the whole State. Explaining that no amount of violence will con-strain men to stay in unprofitable cities, he adds that the same holds good of States and that dominions acquired by sheer violence cannot long be mantained.

Thinking thus so largely in terms of economics, Botéro could not but see war as a sheer evil. It was to him, as things stood, an evil unescapable and therefore to be studied. He repeated the ancient commonplace that defensive war is alone justifiable ; but he left the epithet undefined and therefore almost meaningless. On the question of what constitutes military strength he followed Machiavelli very closely, emphatically agreeing with him that men and not money are the sinews of war and that men fight best when they love their cause or their country. But his consideration of war led him finally to what was perhaps the most striking of his conclusions. War, he thought, was unavoidable only because the world is divided into a number of States. Monarchy is the best form of government ; the mischief is that there are so many monarchies. Princes, he remarked, are without affections ; they have, properly speaking, neither friends nor enemies. Each is guided by consideration of his own interests alone. That being so, they are all compelled, for safety's sake, to prepare for war and to make it ; to hoard treasure and overtax their subjects. What is really needed is a universal monarchy. Under a single monarch the world would become a common fatherland and home, and man would attain happiness. It would then, he adds, be possible to enforce the use of a universal language and a universal coinage, to the great profit and comfort of every one. The Monarch of the world would have no need of armies and therefore the whole scale of taxation could be lowered. Nor would there then be need to provide against dearth and famine, for a bad harvest in one part of the world could be made up for by the good crops of another, as now it is not. The striking passage in which he indulges in these speculations forms the conclusion of his treatise on the Excellence of Monarchy. It was an old dream with a somewhat new meaning. What is perhaps new in Botero's dream of a World-State is the implied conception that there existed already in economic facts and in the world's desire for peace and plenty, a real basis for such developments.

CONCLUSION

I AM told that, in this concluding chapter, I ought to summarize
the results of my explorations in the political thought of the
sixteenth century. It would certainly be well to do so, were it
not for the fact that this whole book is but a summary and a summary
summary and incomplete at that. It is with deep misgivings that
I attempt still further to condense.

People in the sixteenth century, when they thought politically,
were above all preoccupied with the problem of establishing and
maintaining order. Just because order was the thing most needed
it was a century of efforts to create and to centralize administrative
arrangements for its enforcement. In England solid success was
achieved : in France there was failure so pronounced that the country
all but broke in pieces. In Spain the success was, it seems, both
illusory and disastrous. In Germany, as a whole, the effort produced
disintegration ; but that disintegration was due to the success of
the effort to establish new centres of order and strong government.
The Italian settlement, largely brought about by the wisdom and
moderation of Charles V in victory, stereotyped a series of petty
despotisms and oligarchies, but at least put an end to chronic internal
warfare.

Intentness on a practical need acutely felt involves of itself no
kind of political theory. But, under the actual circumstances, recognition of the need of order, and policies of centralization, involved
preoccupation with certain questions incident and relevant to the
practical problem. It was very manifest that what above all was
needed was a profound recognition of the duty of obedience to duly
constituted political authority. The question how such authority is
derived, on what rests the obligation to obey and how far and in what
sense it is limited, was, above all else, the question of the century.

It was answered in various ways ; but the assumptions habitually
made as to natural law and as to the absolutely imperative nature
of Scriptural commands and directions, limited the possibilities of
answer. Study of the Scriptures led, indeed, to quite different conclusions. Yet certain points remained fixed. One must in any case
obey God's commands whatever the political sovereign might say ;
and there was a general persuasion that one ought to disobey commands

clean contrary to natural law. The relation, in fact, between sovereign and subject, or between the State and its members, could not be considered in isolation. Involved in it was the relation of man, and therefore of the State, to Divine Will. That was primary. Man transcended the State and his duty to it could be secondary only. Sixteenth-century theories of sovereignty were, for the most part, fundamentally as theocratic as those of the Middle Ages.

That government represents the will of God, Who wills the good of man and therefore his peace, and that obedience to constituted authority is, therefore, normally a duty to God, this no one in the century openly denied. In the earlier years of the century there appears a very general tendency to believe that, though Divine law might make passive resistance obligatory, yet active resistance was always wrong. How far this tendency was due to an acuteness of the sense of the need of order that grew, gradually, less insistently sharp, it is not possible accurately to say.

This doctrine of non-resistance was not a theory of the divine right of Kings or necessarily a theory of right at all. It was, indeed, generally put as depending on God's commands in the Scriptures. But it was often put on grounds of mere expediency. Resistance leads to disorder, perhaps to civil war, and this is the greatest of evils. The doctrine had no specific reference to Kings but applied to all magistrates and was insisted upon as much at Geneva as at Paris. It was held by people of all kinds of religious opinions and by people of none to speak of. Different lines of thought seemed for a time to be converging to the same conclusion. But the convergence was illusory and even the appearance of it did not last long.

The whole question was complicated and confused by the development of a number of religious sects or parties all claiming sole possession of ' true religion '. It was further complicated by the claims of churches, Catholic or Calvinistic, to control or to limit the action of secular authorities. The Reformation forced men to consider under more or less new forms, the old question of the relation of State to Church. That was, of course, really involved in the ultimate question of the right relation of the State to God. The Protestant could escape it, logically, no more than the Catholic ; and, practically, even less. It was a cause of friction and disorder, or the menace of disorder, throughout the century.

The struggle between religious parties, or between governments and religious dissidents, was the chief factor in breaking down, here and there and more or less completely, the belief in the wickedness of overt resistance to authority. Bodies of people who felt themselves wronged or oppressed and who, for whatever reasons, had come to feel themselves in a position to resist effectively, could not long continue to hold such doctrine. Under the appropriate conditions it was a matter of course that a right and even a duty of rebellion should be asserted, now by Protestants, now by Catholics. It seems that the first body of people to make that assertion were the militant Anabaptists. Partly because they grossly miscalculated their power to rebel effectively, they have not received their fair share of whatever credit may attach to the making of it.

Once that assertion was made there was no escape from the questions logically involved in it. What, then, is the basis of governmental authority and how is it derived ? What are the limits of political obligation ? Under what circumstances does God's command to obey give place to a permission, or become a command, to rebel ? Implied was the question : does there really exist anywhere a right to demand obedience as a duty to God ?

In answer to these questions there developed, roughly speaking, two schools of thought. One asserted that real authority can exist only under a special Divine grant. God must immediately confer it, since men, even though they can give coercive power and define function, cannot create obligation. This doctrine was held not only by those who believed in an almost unlimited and indefeasible right given by God to a divinely chosen King. It was held also by some who claimed a right of rebellion when God's lieutenant exceeded his granted authority or became a rebel against the Giver. It might well be a duty to God to depose his unfaithful viceroy.

On the other hand, it was maintained that a real right to command may be and is created by man out of his own need of it ; God being concerned only in that he created the need and sanctions the means. You may put it, like Bodin, that authority to demand obedience as a duty is logically involved in the ends for which organized society exists ; or, like Hooker, you may say that every potential community has a right to make law for itself. In either case you deny the need for any special divine creation. Man is potentially possessed of all he needs : he needs authority and can, therefore, create it. But it must be observed that Divine sanction is conceived as being as necessary in this case as is Divine grant in the other.

That two main schools of thought arose also on the question of the right relation of State and Church has already been sufficiently insisted upon. One subordinated all secular government to the control of an ecclesiastical organization ; the other, indentifying Church and State, placed the Church in the hands of the secular sovereign. Much of sixteenth-century thought about the State was, it may be remarked, religious rather than strictly political : concerned, that is, mainly with the function of government in relation to another world than this. After all, the political thought of a religious man must needs be religious. But on this question, as on the other great question of the century, the dividing line between the two schools of thought does not coincide with that between Protestant and Catholic.

Perhaps the main lines of sixteenth-century political thought may fairly be thus roughly summarized. But the summary is very rough and it leaves out not only all of Italy but much else. In the sixteenth century we find those who see in the recognition of an all but unbounded duty of obedience to the political sovereign the only hope of salvation ; and those also who ignore or despise the State or who deny and denounce it. Again, while there is much that is religious in the thought of the century, there is also much that is not religious at all and at most pays lip service to religion. And throughout the century there was going on a development of points of view simply opportunist or utilitarian and more or less sceptical of current and traditional beliefs.

In the shifting sands of positive political theory no foundation can be laid for an assertion of progress, if by progress we mean advance in the discovery of truth. Will it be said that no one nowadays supposes that truth concerning the State can be other than relative ? But if it be said : ' There exists in society a right to require my obedience as a duty, but, if I am commanded to deny my faith and betray myself and say I believe what I do not believe, then I have a right to rebel,' there is no reason why this should not be true under all circumstances, so long as meaning is given to the word ' right '. If, indeed, we deny that the word right has any but a legal or conventional meaning, then the whole proposition becomes meaningless. In that case, we have answered the question as to the basis of real authority and of political obligation by denying that such things exist.

I have heard it said that the important thing about a political theory is that it should ' work '. Any theory that ' works ' is true for its time. But in what sense does any theory work ? If a man's activities are really determined by his theory, as may be the case, then, indeed, the theory may be said to be working. But that his activities determine his theory would seem to be the commoner case. The theory is an afterthought, a by-product, an apology, even a pretext. When we say that a theory works, do we mean more than that it plausibly justifies some actual arrangement or the attitude of some dominant group ? In that sense many contradictory theories may be working in different places at the same moment. But, indeed, in that sense all or almost all theories work in some degree and none, surely, quite satisfactorily. There never was a dominant theory or a dominant group unchallenged. In that sense, I suppose, Calvin was right, here and there, for a time ; and Barclay was right for France at the end of the century. It would be hard to say who was right in England. It would also, I think, be hard to say what theory it is that works so well in the modern world. In this sense, anyhow, there can hardly be any question of 'progress'.

Does the political thought of the sixteenth century exhibit tendencies which have ever since persisted and may yet work themselves out to some logical fulfilment? But of course it does: it exhibits many such tendencies; it exhibits them everywhere through all its phases. Particular stress has been laid on one of them: a tendency towards a democratic conception of the State. That tendency has, I think, existed always, along with others. But, granted that it has since been persistent and increasing, I suggest that its increasing force is simply a necessary result of changes social and economic. And how much longer will it persist? I suggest that of how men will think in the future we know absolutely nothing.

Yet prophecy is an amusing game, though he is but a foolish prophet who believes in his own prophecy. Modern political thought is evidently at least as diverse and as full of contradictions as was that of the sixteenth century. It seems also to be a good deal vaguer; but that impression may easily be an illusion. But in one respect there seems to be a difference that is really profound. It might be said that we have latterly succeeded in solving the problem of the relation of the State to a Divine Will and purpose in the world, by the simple process of eliminating one of its terms. Yet it is not, of course, true that we have done this: it is only some of us who have done it. But it seems possible that it is the tendency in sixteenth-century thought towards scepticism, not only of the claims of Churches or of traditional Christianity but of all religious idealism, that has above all persisted and grown and become dominant in the modern world. That tendency pointed forwards to a scepticism not only of the government of the world by an ultimate and supreme Will and Intelligence, but to a scepticism of all values. It may be that this is the direction in which modern thought, as a whole, is moving. If that be so, faith in democracy will fade as completely as faith in the divine right of Kings. But that is little: that is in any case probably to be expected. It may be that as man advances in phenomenal knowledge he loses belief in values and even in the possibility of knowing. May we look forward to a time when man will be able to do what he will and have no rational motive for doing anything? Then he will have achieved his sword of sharpness and his cap of invisibility, his magic carpet and Aladdin's lamp and find no reason for using them. For complete scepticism must needs destroy the basis of even the crudest utilitarianism. It may be that, in the long run, even desire will fail.

But I am not suggesting that anything like this is likely to happen. I think that of the future we know nothing at all.

Preface to the Bibliography

'The main purpose of these notes is to provide a list of the more important writings of the sixteenth century expressive or illustrative of political thought. There exists, of course, a great amount of many sorts of literature which expresses such thought incidentally or by implication only. The phraseology, too, of statutes, edicts, proclamations, even of State papers and of course of private letters, is often significant and indicative. But all this material is so scattered and fragmentary, that no catalogue of it is practically possible. It is not easy to draw a line; but a line has to be drawn. I have mentioned a few works containing collections of documents that I have found useful.

With all its limitations my list of sources of information on the political thinking of the century is very far from complete. It includes only such writings as I have myself been able to make some use of; and for various reasons it does not include all of them.'

So wrote J. W. Allen in the first edition of this book. His list of primary sources reflected the concern of his book—mainly with political treatises and tracts, less with the political ideas and ideologies expressed in other ways such as official documents and the symbolism inherent in ceremony. Despite its limitations the book remains valuable for what it is. At his best Allen takes account of the situation in which a book was written and the purposes for which it was written in explaining its political doctrine. He is aware that a man's views may change; he is often sensitive to nuance and to complexity: he knows that even formal treatises may contain inconsistencies; he recognizes that sixteenth-century theorists may hold views which we find incompatible and that they may lack concepts which we have. Thus he attempts to unravel Luther's views about politics; he points out that Calvin and his followers (among others) saw no inconsistency in advocating that they should be permitted to worship in their manner but that others should not; he concludes that Bodin's views are incapable of being rendered consistent; he notes that Machiavelli had no clear, new conception of 'the State'.

Allen's commentaries are scholarly and careful, but they are not bland—he is more capable of curtly dismissing thinkers as confused,

517

overrated or even violent, rhetorical and worthless than of failing to tell us what he thinks of them. But it is not only for its commentaries that the book remains valuable. Providing an extensive survey of prominent thinkers and noticeable controversies, it is essential as an introductory guide to the literature of the period and useful as a work of reference.

Of course Allen's book has weaknesses. After an initial section on Protestantism the remaining sections were devoted to England, France and Italy respectively. As a result Calvinism exists both as an international movement and as an influence within England and France, but Jesuit political thought is subsumed under France. Another anomaly is that the discussion of Machiavelli appears only after that of the anti-Machiavels.

Recent work has revealed aspects of sixteenth-century thought of which Allen was ignorant or which he neglected or undervalued. Our views of the period have been affected by studies of, for example, Florentine 'civic humanism', millenarianism, the symbolism of royal ceremony, legal humanism in France, the organization of Calvinism in Geneva and its missionary apparatus, the political activities of Tudor commonwealthsmen. Savonarola is more important and more interesting than Allen supposed; so is Thomas Munzer. Some subjects seem simply to have slipped through Allen's net: here I would include the absence of a discussion of Erasmus (perhaps Allen thought him insufficiently political). Although Allen discusses Mariana and Suarez he omits Vitoria and de Soto. Little has yet appeared in English on another subject Allen skipped, namely the literature of the revolt of the Netherlands. (Books on most of these matters have now been included in the bibliography.)

With its flaws and its virtues Allen's text remains as he wrote it. My task has been to revise the bibliography. It still does not pretend to be a complete bibliography of sixteenth-century political thought. The first section of the bibliography, primary sources, is based on Allen's list, but it has been completely reorganized. Allen's divisions, which followed the organization of the book, have been eliminated and the list arranged in alphabetical order.[1] I have attempted to check every entry; these have been corrected where necessary. Above all I have sought modern editions, recent reprints of original editions and especially modern, available English translations. I have added very few titles to Allen's list of primary works.

---

[1] This suggestion I owe to Dr. H. M. Höpfl, for whose help I am grateful.

The list of secondary works is mainly a new list.   A few older works, having become 'classics', have been retained but none has been retained simply because it was in the bibliography of a previous edition—in any case Allen's original secondary list contained only ten titles.   Although this list is now much longer it is by no means complete.   Firstly, it is a list of books, none of the many worthwhile articles has been included. Secondly, with a few exceptions, it is a list of books in English. Thirdly, it is a list selected for those who wish to pursue some subject further than Allen takes them.   I hope they enjoy the chase.

M. M. Goldsmith
May 1977

Bibliography

I. PRIMARY WORKS

ANON. and PSEUDON. *A briefe and plaine declaration, concerning the desires of all those faithfull Ministers . . . or A learned discourse of Ecclesiasticall Government*, London, 1584.

A necessary doctrine and erudition for any Christen man (King Henry's Book), 1543; see *Formularies of Faith*, ed. Charles Lloyd, Oxford, 1825, 1856.

A petition directed to her most excellent majesty, 1589(?).

De vera differentia . . .; see Fox.

Dialogue d'Archon et de Politie, 1576.

Dialogue entre le Maheustre et le Manant, 1593.

Eusebius Philadelphe Cosmopolite, *Le Reveille-Matin des François*, Edinburgh, 1573-4.

Réponse sur la question à savoir s'il est loisible au peuple . . . de resister par armes, 1576.

Satyre Ménippée, Paris, 1593-95, by P. Le Roy, J. Gillot, J. Passerat, N. Rapin, F. Chrestien, P. Pithou; ed. Paul Demey, Dublin, 1911.

Stephanus Junius Brutus, *Vindiciae contra tyrannos*; see Mornay.

ACONTIUS, JACOBUS. *Strategemata Satanae*, Basle, 1565; ed. G. Koehler, Monaci, 1927.

Satan's Stratagems, trans. W. T. Curtis, intro. C. D. O'Malley, San Francisco, 1940.

AINSWORTH, HENRY. *A true confession of the faith*, 1596, in W. Walker (ed.), *Creeds and Platforms of Congregationalism*, London, 1893.

ALLEN, WILLIAM CARDINAL. *An apologie and true declaration of the institution and endevours of the two English colleges*, Rome and Rheims, 1581.

A true, sincere and modest defence of English Catholiques, 1584; rep. London, 1914; and in William Cecil, *The Execution of Justice in England*, ed. R. M. Kingdon, Ithaca, N.Y., 1965.

BACON, FRANCIS. *An advertisement touching the controversies of the Church of England*, 1589.

Works, ed. J. Spedding, R. L. Ellis and D. D. Heath, 14 vols, London, 1858-1901; rep. Bad Cannstatt, 1963.

BAGSHAW, CHRISTOPHER. *A true relation of the faction begun at Wisbich*, 1601; see T. G. Law, *A historical sketch of the conflicts between Jesuits and Seculars*, London, 1889.

BANCROFT, RICHARD. *A sermon preached at Paules Crosse*, 1588; University Microfilms, 1954.

A survey of the pretended Holy Discipline, 1593.

Daungerous positions and proceedings, 1593; rep. Farnborough, 1968.

Tracts, ed. Albert Peel, Cambridge, 1953.

BARAUD, NICHOLAS. *Dialogue*, 1593.

BARCLAY, WILLIAM. *De potestate papae*, 1609.

De regno et regnali potestate, 1600.

BARNES, ROBERT. *Supplication unto the most gracious prince, King Henry VIII; Mens constitutions bind not the conscience*, in *The Whole Works of William Tyndale, John Frith and Doctor Barnes*, 1573; see *Reformation Essays of Dr. Robert Barnes*, ed. N. S. Tjernagel, London, 1963.

BARROW, HENRY. *A briefe discourse of the false church*, 1590.

The Platform, 1590; see *Writings of Henry Barrow, 1587-90*, ed. L. H. Carlson, London, 1962.

BEKINSAU, JOHN. *De supremo et absoluto regis imperio*, 1546; see M. Goldast, *Monarchia S. Romani Imperii*, vol. I, Hanoviae, 1611.

BELLARMINO, ROBERTO. *Disputationes de controversiis christianae fidei*: vol. I, *De summo pontifice*, 1586; *Opera Ommia*, rep. Frankfurt, 1965.

Responsio ad praecipua capita apologia . . . pro successione Henrici Navarreri, published under the name Franciscus Romulus, 1587.

Tractatus de potestate summi pontificis in rebus temporalibus, 1610; see *Scritti politici*, ed. Carlo Giacon, Bologna, 1950.

BELLOY, PIERRE DE. *Apologie Catholique*, 1585.

De l'autorité du roi, 1587.

BEZA, THEODORE. *Du droit des magistrats*, 1574 (French); 1576 (Latin); ed. Robert M. Kingdon, Geneva, 1970; see Julian H. Franklin, trans. and ed., *Constitutionalism and Resistance in the Sixteenth Century*, New York, 1969.

Concerning the rights of rulers over their subjects, trans. H. L. Gonin, intro. A. A. Van Schelden, ed. A. Murray, Cape Town, 1956.

De Haereticis, 1554(?); 1560 (French).

BILSON, THOMAS. *The perpetual gouernement of Christes Church*, 1593; ed. Revd Robert Eden, Oxford, 1842.

The true difference between Christian subiection and vnchristian rebellion, 1585.

BLACKWOOD, ADAM. *Apologia pro regibus*, 1581 (i.e. *Adversus Georgi Buchanani dialogum*, etc.).

De vinculo religionis, 1575, 1611.

BODIN, JEAN. *Oeuvres philosophiques*, ed. Pierre Mesnard, Paris, 1951.

Heptaplomeres (Suerini Megaloburgiensium), 1857; rep. Hildesheim and New York, 1970.

Colloquium of the seven about secrets of the sublime, trans. Marion Leathers Daniels, Princeton, 1975.

Les six livres de la république, 1576 (French), 1586 (Latin).

The six bookes of a commonweale, trans. Richard Knolles, London, 1606; ed. K. D. McRae, rep. Cambridge, Mass., 1962.

Six Books of the Commonwealth, abridged and trans. M. J. Tooley, Oxford, 1955.

Lettre . . . où il traicte les occasions qui l'ont faict rendre ligueur, 1590.

Methodus ad facilem historiarum cognitionem, 1556; *Method for the Easy Comprehension of History*, trans. Beatrice Reynolds, New York, 1945.

Réponse au paradoxe de M. de Malesdroict, 1568.

BOTERO, GIOVANNI. *Delle cause de Grandezza della citte*, 1596.

Della ragion di stato, 1589.

The reason of state, trans. P. J. and D. P. Waley, and *The greatness of cities*, trans. Robert Paterson, London, 1956.

Discorsi dell'excellenza della monarchia, 1612.

BOUCHER, JEAN. *De justa abdicatione Henrici tertii*, 1589.

Sermons de la simulée conversion . . . de Henri de Bourbon, 1594.

BRIDGES, JOHN. *A defence of the gouernement established . . .*, 1587.

The supremacie of Christian princes, 1573.

BRINKELOW, HENRY. *The complaint of Roderyck Mors*, 1542 (1548?); ed. J. Meadows Cowper, London: E.E.T.S., 1874.

BROWNE, ROBERT. *Writings*, 1582–89; see *Writings of Robert Harrison and Robert Browne*, London, 1953.

BUCER, MARTIN. *De regno Christi*, 1557; see *Opera omnia*, Paris, 1955; trans. William Pauck with Paul Larkin in *Melancthon and Bucer*, Library of Christian Classics, vol. 19, London, 1969.

BUCHANAN, GEORGE. *De jure regni apud scotos*, 1579.

The powers of the crown in Scotland, Austin, Texas, 1949.

The art and science of government among the Scots, ed. D. H. MacNeill, n.p., 1964.

BUDÉ, GUILLAUME. *Tesmoinage de tempe, ou enseignemens et exhortemens pour l'institution d'un prince*, 1547; see C. Bontems, L. P. Raybaud and J.-P. Brancourt, *Le prince dans la France des xvie et xviie siècles*, Paris, 1965.

CALVIN, JEAN. *Institutio*, 1536, 1539–41, 1559–60.

Institution of the Christian Religion, 1536, trans. F. L. Battles, Pittsburgh, 1969.

Institutes of the Christian Religion, ed. J. T. McNeill, trans. F. L. Battles, 2 vols, London, 1961.

Opera Selecta, ed. P. Barth, W. Neisel, D. Scheuner, 5 vols, Munich, 1926–52.

Oeuvres complètes, Paris, 1936.

Commentary on Seneca's De Clementia, ed. F. L. Battles and A. M. Hugo, Leiden, 1969.

Theological Treatises, trans. Revd J. K. S. Reid, London, 1954.

Tracts and Treatises on the Reformation of the Church, trans. Henry Beveridge, notes and intro. by F. Torrance, 3 vols, Edinburgh and London, 1958.

Defensio orthodoxae fidei or *Declaration pour mantenir la vraye foi*, 1554.

Lettres Françaises, ed. J. Bonnet, 2 vols, Paris, 1854.

Letters trans. from J. Bonnet by D. Constable, 4 vols, Edinburgh and Philadelphia, 1855–7.

Prelectiones in librum prophetiarium Danielis, 1561; trans. Thomas Myers, 2 vols, London, 1852–3.

On God and Political Duty, ed. J. T. McNeill, Indianapolis and New York, 1956.

Selections, ed. J. Dillenberger, Garden City, N.Y., 1971.

CARRERIUS, ALEXANDER.   *De potestate romani pontificis*, 1599.

CARTWRIGHT, THOMAS.   *A directory of church government*, 1644; in D. Neal, *A History of the Puritans*, London, 1848.

Cartwrightiana, ed. A. Peel and L. H. Carlson, London, 1951.

A full and plaine declaration of ecclesiastical discipline, 1574; an English version of Trevers' *Explicatio*.

A replye to an answere, 1573.

The second replie, 1575.

The rest of the second replie, 1577.

CASTELLION, SEBASTIEN.   Preface to Latin Bible, 1551.

De Haereticis an sint persequendi or *Traité des hérétiques*, 1554.

Concerning Heretics, trans. R. H. Bainton, New York, 1935.

Contra libellum Calvini, 1612 (written 1554).

Conseil à la France desolée, 1562, ed. M. F. Valkhoff, Geneva, 1967.

CECIL, WILLIAM, LORD BURGHLEY.   *The Execution of Justice in England*, London, 1583; ed. Robert M. Kingdon, Ithaca, N.Y., 1965.

CELSI, MINO.   *In haereticis coercendis quatenus progredi liceat*, 1577; republished as *De haereticis capitale supplicio non afficiendis*, 1584.

CHEKE, SIR JOHN.   *The hurt of sedicion howe greveous it is to a Communewelth* (or *The True Subject to the Rebel*), 1549; rep. Menston, Yorks., 1971.

CRAIG, SIR THOMAS.   *The right of succession to the Kingdom of England*, London, 1703; trans. by James Gatherer of lost original, ded. 1603.

CRANMER, THOMAS.   *Works*, ed. Rev. John Edmund Cox, 2 vols, London: Parker Society, 1844–6.

CROWLEY, ROBERT.   *Select Works*, ed. J. M. Cowper, London: E.E.T.S., 1872; reissued 1905.

DANEAU, LAMBERT.   *Politices Christianae, ethices Christianae*, 1577.

DU MOULIN, CHARLES.   *Traicte de l'origine, progres et excellence du royaume et monarchie des Francois et coronne de France*, 1561.

DU TILLET, JEAN.   *Memoires et recherches*, 1578.

ELYOT, SIR THOMAS.   *The boke named the Governour*, 1531; ed. H. H. S. Croft, 2 vols, London, 1880; ed. S. E. Lehmberg, London and New York, 1962.

FERRAULT, JEAN.   *Jura regni Franciae*, 1515.

FIELD, JOHN and THOMAS WILCOX.   *The first admonition to Parliament*, 1571; *The second admonition*, 1572; in *Puritan Manifestoes*, ed. W. H. Frere and C. E. Douglas, London, 1954.

FISH, SIMON. *A supplicaeyon for the Beggers*, 1529.
Supplication of the poore Commons, London, 1546; ed. F. J. Furnival, London: E.E.T.S., 1871; also ed. E. Arber, English Scholar's Library, no. 4, London, 1878.

FORREST, WILLIAM. *Pleasant poesie* in *England in the reign of King Henry the Eighth, Part I: Starkey's Life and Letters*, ed. S. J. Herrtage, London: E.E.T.S., 1878.

FORTESCUE, SIR JOHN. *The governance of England*, ed. C. Plummer, Oxford, 1885.
De laudibus legis Angliae, 1537; ed. and trans. S. B. Chrimes, Cambridge, 1942.
De natura legis naturae, London, 1864.

FOX, EDWARD. *De vera differentia regiae potestatis et ecclesiasticae*, 1538; English, 1548.

FULKE, WILLIAM. *Works*, ed. C. H. Hartshorne, London: Parker Society, 1843.

GARDINER, STEPHEN. *De vera obedientia*, 1535; Eng. trans., 1553; rep. Leeds, 1966.
Obedience in Church and State: Three political tracts, ed. and trans. Pierre Janelle, Cambridge, 1930.

GENTILLET, INNOCENT. *Anti-Machiavel*, 1571 (Latin); 1576 (French); ed. C. Edward Rathé, Geneva, 1968).
De jure successionis, 1588.
Apologie ou defense pour les Chrestiens de France qui sont de la Religion Evangelique ou reformée . . . au Roy de Navarre, 1578; 1588 (Latin).

GILBY, ANTHONY. *An admonition to England and Scotland*, in *The Works of John Knox*, ed. D. Laing, 6 vols, Edinburgh, 1844–64.

GIRARD, BERNARD, SEIGNEUR DE HAILLAN. *De l'estat et succez des affaires de France*, Paris, 1570; or *De la fortune et vertu de la France*, Paris, 1571.
L'histoire de France, Paris, 1576.

GOODMAN, CHRISTOPHER. *How superior powers ought to be obeyed*, Geneva, 1558; rep. with a bibliographical note by C. H. McIlwain, New York, 1931.

GOUSTÉ, CLAUDE. *Traicté de la puissance et autorité des rois*, Paris, 1561.

GRASSAILLE, CHARLES DE (or DEGRASSALIUS). *Regalium Franciae*, Lugduni, 1538.

GRIMAUDET, FRANCOIS. *Les opuscules politiques*, Paris, 1580.

GUICCARDINI, FRANCESCO. *Dialogo e Discoursi del Reggimento di Firenze*, ed. Roberto Palmarocchi, Bari, 1932.
Opere inedite, Firenze, 1857–67.
Opere, Bari, 1929.
Ricordi, ed. Raffaele Spongano, Firenze, 1951.
Maxims and Reflections, trans. Mario Domandi, intro. Nicolai Rubenstein, New York, 1965.
Selected writings, ed. Cecil Grayson, trans. Margaret Grayson, London, 1965.

Il dialogo, 'Del reggimento di Firenze', ed. L. Scarano, E. Giornale, *Storico della letteratura Italiana*, vol. 145, 1968.

History of Italy and *History of Florence*, ed. J. R. Hale, New York, 1964.

HAYWARD, SIR JOHN. *An answer to the first part of a certaine Conference*, London, 1603; rep. Amsterdam and Norwood, N.J., 1975.

HERMINJARD, A. L. *Correspondance des Réformateurs dans les pays de langue française*, 9 vols, Paris, 1866–97.

HOMILIES, i.e., *Certain sermons or homilies appointed to be read in the Churches*, esp. 'An exhortion concerning good order', 1547; 'Against disobedience and willful rebellion', 1571.

HOOKER, RICHARD. *Of the Laws of Ecclesiastical Polity*, 1597; rep. Menston, Yorks., 1969.

A learned discourse of justification, Oxford, 1612.

Works, ed. W. Speed Hill, Cambridge, Mass., 1976–; see also *Works*, Oxford, 1888.

HOOPER, JOHN. *Later writings*, London: Parker Society, 1843.

L'HÔPITAL, MICHEL DE. *Oeuvres complètes*, ed. P. J. S. Duféy, 8 vols, Paris, 1824–6.

HOTMAN, F. *Francogallia*, 1573; French, 1574; ed. Ralph Giesey, trans. J. H. M. Salmon, Cambridge, 1972.

HURAULT, MICHEL. *Excellent et libre discours sur l'estat present de la France*, Paris, 1588.

JAMES VI AND I. *Political Works*, ed. C. H. McIlwain, Cambridge, Mass., 1918, rep. 1948.

Workes, London, 1616.

KNOX, JOHN. *Works*, ed. D. Laing, 6 vols, Edinburgh, 1846–64, esp. the *Appellation* and the *Letter to the Commonalty*, 1558.

KOSSMAN, E. H. and A. F. MELLINK. *Texts concerning the Revolt of the Netherlands*, Cambridge, 1974.

LA BOËTIE, ETIENNE. *Discours de la servitude volontaire*, 1576; intro. Hem Day, Brussels, 1954.

Anti-Dictator, trans. H. Kurz, New York, 1942.

LA NOUE, FRANÇOIS DE. *Discours politiques et militaires*, Basle, 1587; ed. F. E. Sutcliffe, Geneva, 1967.

LATIMER, HUGH. *Works*, ed. Rev. George Elwes Corrie, 2 vols, London: Parker Society, 1844–45; see *Selected Sermons*, ed. A. G. Chester, Charlottesville: for the Folger Library by University of Virginia Press, 1968.

LE ROY, LOUIS. *De la vicissitude*, Paris, 1576.

De l'excellence de Gouvernment Royale, Paris, 1575.

Exhortation aux François, Paris, 1570.

LEVER, THOMAS. *Sermons*, 1550; ed. E. Arber, English Reprints, no. 25, London, 1869, rep. 1895.

LUTHER, M. *Werke*, ed. J. F. C. Knaake *et al.*, Weimar, 1883–.

Briefwechsel, ed. C. A. H. Burchhardt, Leipsig, 1866.

Briefwechsel, ed. E. L. Enders, 19 vols, Frankfurt am Main, 1884–1932.

An den Christlichen Adel deutscher Nation, 1520, Weimar VI.

Bericht an einen guten Freund, 1528, Weimar XXVI.

De Captivitate Babylonica Ecclesiae, 1520, Weimar V.

De Libertate Christiani, 1519, Weimar VII.

Ermahnung zum Frieden auf die zwölf Artikel der Bauerschaft, 1525, Weimar XVIII.

Ob Kriegsleute auch in seligem Stande sein könnten, 1526.

Verantwortung, 1533, Weimar XXXVIII.

Von Kaufshandlung und Wucher, 1524, Weimar XV.

Von Weltlicher Obrigkeit, 1523, Weimar XI.

Wider die himmlischen Propheten, 1525, Weimar XVIII.

Wider die räuberischen und mörderischen Rotten der Bauern, 1525, Weimar XVIII.

ENGLISH TRANSLATIONS

Works, ed. J. Pelikan and H. T. Lehmann, St Louis and Philadelphia, 1955–.

Reformation Writings, trans. and ed. B. L. Woolf, 2 vols, London, 1952.

Selections, ed. John Dillenberger, New York, 1961.

Three Treatises: Letter to the Christian Nobility; The Babylonian Captivity of the Church; On Christian Liberty, intro. and trans. C. M. Jacobs *et al.* Philadelphia, 1947.

MACHIAVELLI, NICCOLO. *Tutte le opere*, ed. F. Flora and C. Cordie, Rome, 1949.

Tutte le opere, ed. Mazzoni and Casella, Florence, 1928.

Opere, ed. S. Bertelli, Milan, 1960.

Opere, ed. Mario Bonfantini, Milan and Naples, 1954.

Lettere, ed. F. Gaeta, Milan, 1961.

The Letters of Machiavelli: A selection, trans. A. Gilbert, New York, 1961.

The Chief Works and others, trans. Allan Gilbert, 3 vols, Durham, N.C., 1965.

Discorsi, Rome, 1531; *Discourses*, trans. with an introduction and notes by Leslie J. Walker, 2 vols, London, 1950; rev. and rep., 1975.

Istorie Fiorentine, Rome, 1532; *History of Florence*, intro. Felix Gilbert, New York, 1960.

Libro della arte dello guerra, Firenze, 1521; *The Art of War*, trans. Ellis Farnesworth, rev. with intro. by Neal Wood, Indianapolis, 1965.

Il principe, Rome, 1532; ed. L. Arthur Burd, Oxford, 1891.

The Prince and the Discourses, ed. M. Lerner, New York, 1940, 1950.

The Prince, trans. George Bull, Harmondsworth, Middlesex, 1961.

MAGDEBURG. *Bekentnis Unterricht und vermanung der Pfarrhern und Prediger der Christlichen Kirchen zu Magdeburgk*, April 13, 1550.

MARIANA, JUAN DE. *De rege et regis institutione*, 1589.

MELANCHTHON, P. *De expressa politicae potestatis institutione*, in *Corpus reformatorum*, ed. C. G. Breitschneider, XVI.

De officio principum, Breitschneider, II.

Disputationes de rebus politicis, Breitschneider, XII.

Moralis Philosophiae epitomes, Breitschneider, XVI.

MERBURG, CHARLES. *A briefe discourse of royall monarchie*, London, 1581.

MOLINA, LUIS. *De jure et justitia*, Conchae, 1593–1600.

MORE, SIR THOMAS. *Works*, 1557. Besides *Utopia*, see the *Dialogue concerning Hereseyes* and the *Apology*.

Works of St. Thomas More, esp. vol. 4, *Utopia*, ed. E. Surtz, S. J. and J. H. Hexter, New Haven and London, 1965.

MORNAY, PHILLIPE DU PLESSIS. *Vindiciae contra tyrannos*, 1579 (Latin); 1584 (French).

A defence of liberty against tyrants, ed. H. J. Laski, London, 1924; rep. Gloucester, Mass., 1963, and in J. H. Franklin, ed., *Constitutionalism and Resistance in the Sixteenth Century*, New York, 1969.

ORLEANS, LOUIS D'. *Apologie ou défense des Catholiques unis*, 1586.

Advertisement des Catholiques Anglois aux Francois Catholiques, 1586.

PARKER, MATTHEW. *Correspondence*, London: Parker Society, 1853.

PARSONS, ROBERT (alias DOLEMAN). *A conference about the next succession to the Crowne of England*, 1594.

PARUTA, PAOLO. *Della perfettione della vita politica*, Venice, 1579.

Discorsi politici, Venice, 1599.

Opere politiche, ed. C. Monzani, 2 vols, Florence, 1852.

PASQUIER, E. *Exhortation aux Princes*, 1561.

Recherches de la France, Paris, 1560.

Écrits politiques, ed. D. Thickett, Geneva, 1966.

PENRY, JOHN. *Writings*, esp. *A Treatise wherein is manifestly proved, that Reformation and those that sincerely favour the same are unjustly charged to be enemies* . . . and *Petition to the Queen*, Edinburgh(?), 1590.

PITHOU, PIERRE. *Les libertez de l'Eglise Gallicanae*, 1594.

POLE, REGINALD CARDINAL. *Pro Ecclesiasticae Unitatis Defensione*, Rome, c. 1537.

Defense de l'Unité de l'Église, ed. and trans. N. M. Egretier, Paris, 1967.

Defense of the Unity of the Church, ed. and trans. J. G. Dwyer, Westminster, Md., 1965.

PONET, JOHN. *A short treatise of politicke power*, London, 1556; rep. Menston, Yorks., 1970; also in W. S. Hudson, *John Ponet, 1516?–1556, Advocate of Limited Monarchy*, Chicago, 1942.

REYNOLDS, WILLIAM. *De justa republicae Christianae*, 1590.

ROTHMANN, BERNARD. *Von tydliker und irdischer Gewalt*. Appears to exist only in MS at Munster. I have had to trust to Jochinus, *Geschichte der Reformation zu Munster* (J.W.A.).

SALAMONIUS, MARIUS. *De principatu*, Rome, 1544; ed. M. d'Addio, Milan, 1955.

SANDERS, NICHOLAS. *De visibili monarchia ecclesiae*, Lovanii, 1571.

SANDYS, SIR EDWIN. *A relation of the state of religion*, 1605; rep. 1629 as *Europae speculum*, London, 1605; Hagae-Comitis, 1629.

SERVIN, LOUIS. *Vindiciae secundae libertatem ecclesiae Gallicanae*, Turoni, 1590.

SEYSSEL, CLAUDE DE. *Le grant monarchie de France*, 1518.
    La monarchie de France et deux autres fragments politiques, ed. Jacques
    Poujol, Paris, 1961.
SMITH, HENRY. *The magistrates scripture*, London, 1591.
SMITH, SIR THOMAS. *De republica Anglorum*, 1583; rep. Menston, Yorks.,
    1970; ed. L. Alston, Cambridge, 1906.
SPIFAME, RAOUL. *Dicaearchia*, 1556(?).
ST GERMAN, CHRISTOPHER. *An answere to a letter*, London, 1535.
    Dialogus de fundamentis Legum Angliae et de conscientia, London, 1604.
    Treatise concernynge the division betwene the spirytualtie and temporaltie,
    London, 1530; ed. Arthur Irving Taft, London: E.E.T.S., 1930.
STARKEY, THOMAS. *Dialogue between Cardinal Pole and Thomas Lupset*,
    written 1536–38; ed. Kathleen M. Burton, London: E.E.T.S., 1948.
THOMAS, WILLIAM. *Works*, London, 1774.
TRAVERS, WALTER. *Ecclesiasticae disciplinae et Anglicanae Ecclesiae . . .
    explicatio*, London, 1574; also *A full and plaine declaration of
    Ecclesiasticall Discipline*, London, 1574.
TYNDALE, WILLIAM. *The obedience of a Christen man*, Marlborow in Hesse,
    1528; London: Parker Society, 1848.
UDALL, JOHN. *A demonstration of the trueth of that discipline which Christe
    hath prescribed, etc.*, London, 1588; ed. E. Arber, London, 1880.
WENTWORTH, PETER. *A pithe exhortation to Her Majesty for establishing her
    successors to the Crowne whereunto is added A discourse . . . of the true and
    lawful successor to Her Majesty*, London, 1598.
WHITGIFT, JOHN. *Works*, esp. *Defense of the Answer*, 1574; London: Parker
    Society, 1851.
WILSON, THOMAS. *A discourse upon usury*, London, 1572; ed. R. H.
    Tawney, London, 1925.
ZAMPINI, MATTEO. *De gli stati de Francia et de lor possanza*, Paris, 1578.
ZWINGLI, HULDREICH. *Von gottlicher und menschlicher Gerechtigkeit*, Zurich,
    1523; in *Corpus reformatorum*, LXXXIX.
    Sämtliche Werke, Berlin, 1905–.

II. SECONDARY WORKS

ANGLO, S. *Machiavelli: A Dissection*, London, 1969.
BAINTON, R. H. *The Reformation of the Sixteenth Century*, London, 1953,
    1965.
BARON, H. *The Crisis of the Early Italian Renaissance*, Princeton, 1955;
    rep. 1966.
BAUMER, F. LE V. *The Early Tudor Theory of Kinship*, New Haven, 1940.
BURCKHARDT, J. *The Civilization of the Renaissance in Italy*, London,
    1965.
BUTTERFIELD, H. *The Statecraft of Machiavelli*, London, 1955.
CARLYLE, R. W. and A. J. CARLYLE. *Medieval Political Theory in the West*,
    vol. VI, Edinburgh, 1936.

CHABOD, F. *Machiavelli and the Renaissance*, London, 1958.

CHURCH, W. F. *Constitutional Thought in Sixteenth-Century France*, Cambridge, Mass., 1941; rep. New York, 1969.

COHN, N. *The Pursuit of the Millennium*, New York, 1961.

COLLINSON, P. *The Elizabethan Puritan Movement*, London, 1967.

CRANZ, F. E. *An Essay on the Development of Luther's Thought on Justice, Law and Society*, Cambridge, Mass., 1959.

DAVIES, E. T. *The Political Ideas of Richard Hooker*, London, 1946.

DE CAPRARIIS, V. *Propaganda e Pensiero Politico*, vol. I, Naples, 1959.

D'ENTREVES, A. P. *The Medieval Contribution to Political Thought*, Oxford, 1939.

DENZER, H. (ed.). *Jean Bodin*, Munich, 1973.

DICKENS, A. G. *Reformation and Society in Sixteenth-Century Europe*, London, 1966.

The German Nation and Martin Luther, London, 1974.

FERGUSON, A. B. *The Articulate Citizen and the English Renaissance*, Durham, N.C., 1965.

FIGGIS, J. N. *Studies of Political Thought from Gerson to Grotius, 1414–1625*, Cambridge, 1916; rep. 1956; rep. New York, 1960.

The Divine Right of Kings, Cambridge, 1922; rep. New York, 1965.

FRANKLIN, J. H. *Jean Bodin and the Rise of Absolutist Theory*, Cambridge, 1973.

Jean Bodin and the Sixteenth-Century Revolution in the Methodology of Law and History, New York, 1963.

GARIN, EUGENIO. *Italian Humanism: Philosophy and Civic Life in the Renaissance*, Oxford, 1965.

GIERKE, OTTO VON. *Natural Law and the Theory of Society*, 2 vols; Cambridge, 1934; rep. in 1 vol., 1950.

GILBERT, A. H. *Machiavelli's Prince and its Forerunners*, Durham, N.C., 1938.

GILBERT, F. *Machiavelli and Guicciardini: Politics and History in Sixteenth-Century Florence*, Princeton, 1965.

GOUGH, J. W. *The Social Contract: A Critical Study of Its Development*, 2nd ed.; Oxford, 1967.

GREENLEAF, W. H. *Order, Empiricism and Politics: Two Traditions of English Political Thought, 1500–1700*, London, 1964.

HALE, J. R. *Machiavelli and Renaissance Italy*, London, 1961.

HAMILTON, BERNICE. *Political Thought in Sixteenth-Century Spain*, Oxford, 1963.

HANSON, D. W. *From Kingdom to Commonwealth: the Development of Civic Consciousness in English Political Thought*, Cambridge, Mass., 1970.

HAY, DENIS. *The Italian Renaissance in its Historical Background*, Cambridge, 1961.

HEXTER, J. H. *The Vision of Politics on the Eve of the Reformation*, New York and London, 1973.

More's Utopia, Princeton, 1952; rep. New York, 1965.

KANTOROWICZ, E.   *The King's Two Bodies*, Princeton, 1957.

KING, P. T.   *The Ideology of Order*, London, 1974.

LAGARDE, G. DE.   *Recherches sur l'Esprit politique de la Reforme*, Douai, 1926.

LEWY, G.   *Constitutionalism and Statecraft during the Golden Age of Spain: A Study of the Political Philosophy of Juan de Mariana, S. J.*, Geneva, 1960.

MCCONICA, J. K.   *English Humanists and Reformation Politics under Henry VIII and Edward VI*, Oxford, 1965.

MCNEILL, J. T.   *The History and Character of Calvinism*, Oxford, 1954, 1967.

MATTINGLY, G.   *Renaissance Diplomacy*, London, 1955, 1963.

MEINECKE, F.   *Machiavellism*, London, 1957, 1962.

MESNARD, F.   *L'Essor de la Philosophie Politique au XVIe Siecle*, Paris, 1951.

MUNZ, P.   *The Place of Hooker in the History of Thought*, London, 1952.

MURRAY, R. H.   *The Political Consequences of the Reformation*, London, 1926.

POCOCK, J. G. A.   *The Machiavellian Moment*, Princeton, 1975.

RAAB, F.   *The English Face of Machiavelli: A Changing Interpretation*, London and Toronto, 1964.

REYNOLDS, B.   *Proponents of Limited Monarchy in Sixteenth-Century France*, New York, 1931.

SABINE, G. H.   *A History of Political Theory*, New York, 1961; London, 1964.

SALMON, J. H. M.   *The French Religious Wars in English Political Thought*, Oxford, 1959.

Society in Crisis: France in the Sixteenth Century, London, 1975.

TAWNEY, R. H.   *Religion and the Rise of Capitalism*, London, 1922; rep. 1967.

TROELTSCH, E.   *The Social Teaching of the Christian Churches*, 2 vols, New York, 1931.

WALZER, M.   *The Revolution of the Saints*, London, 1965.

WEBER, M.   *The Protestant Ethic and the Spirit of Capitalism*, London, 1965.

WEINSTEIN, D.   *Savonarola and Florence: Prophecy and Patriotism in the Renaissance*, Princeton, 1970.

WHITFIELD, J. H.   *Machiavelli*, Oxford, 1947.

Discourses on Machiavelli, Cambridge, 1969.

WILLIAMS, G.H.   *The Radical Reformation*, Philadelphia, 1962.

WOLIN, S. S.   *Politics and Vision*, Boston, 1960; London, 1961.

ZEEFELD, W. G.   *Foundations of Tudor Policy*, Cambridge, Mass., 1948; London, 1969.

INDEX